EU Tax Law and Policy in the 21st Century

EUCOTAX Series on European Taxation

VOLUME 55

Introduction

EUCOTAX (European Universities Cooperating on Taxes) is a network of tax institutes currently consisting of eleven universities: WU (Vienna University of Economics and Business) in Austria, Katholieke Universiteit Leuven in Belgium, Corvinus University of Budapest, Hungary, Université Paris-I Panthéon-Sorbonne in France, Universität Osnabrück in Germany, Libera, Università Internazionale di Studi Sociali in Rome (and Università degli Studi di Bologna for the research part), in Italy, Fiscaal Instituut Tilburg at Tilburg University in the Netherlands, Universidad de Barcelona in Spain, Uppsala University in Sweden, Queen Mary and Westfield College at the University of London in the United Kingdom, and Georgetown University in Washington DC, United States of America. The network aims at initiating and coordinating both comparative education in taxation, through the organization of activities such as winter courses and guest lectures, and comparative research in the field, by means of joint research projects, international conferences and exchange of researchers between various countries.

Contents/Subjects

The EUCOTAX series covers a wide range of topics in European tax law. For example tax treaties, EC case law, tax planning, exchange of information and VAT. The series is well-known for its high-quality research and practical solutions.

Objective

The series aims to provide insights on new developments in European taxation.

Readership

Practitioners and academics dealing with European tax law.

Frequency of Publication

2-3 new volumes published each year.

The titles published in this series are listed at the end of this volume.

EU Tax Law and Policy in the 21st Century

Edited by

Werner Haslehner
Georg Kofler
Alexander Rust

Wolters Kluwer

Published by:
Kluwer Law International B.V.
PO Box 316
2400 AH Alphen aan den Rijn
The Netherlands
Website: www.wolterskluwerlr.com

Sold and distributed in North, Central and South America by:
Wolters Kluwer Legal & Regulatory U.S.
7201 McKinney Circle
Frederick, MD 21704
United States of America
Email: customer.service@wolterskluwer.com

Sold and distributed in all other countries by:
Quadrant
Rockwood House
Haywards Heath
West Sussex
RH16 3DH
United Kingdom
Email: international-customerservice@wolterskluwer.com

ISBN 978-90-411-8815-1

e-Book: ISBN 978-90-411-8816-8
web-PDF: ISBN 978-90-411-8817-5

Editors

Werner Haslehner is Professor of Law at the Faculty of Law, Economics and Finance at the University of Luxembourg, where he holds the ATOZ Chair for European and International Taxation, and Director of its LL.M. Programme in EU and International Tax Law. He joined the Faculty as Associate Professor in 2013, previously holding full-time academic positions in Austria at JKU Linz and in the UK at the London School of Economics and Political Sciences (LSE), and was appointed Full Professor in 2015. His research interests cover all aspects of international taxation, including the impact of EU law, and tax policy.

Georg Kofler is Professor of Law and Head of the Institute for Fiscal Law, Tax Law and Tax Policy at Johannes Kepler University of Linz Law School. He previously worked with the International Department of the Austrian Federal Ministry of Finance, as Acting Assistant Professor at New York University, and as Assistant Professor at the University of Linz. An active member of several professional organizations, he serves as the chairman of the ECJ Task Force of the *Confédération Fiscale Européenne* (CFE). His research focuses on international and European direct tax law and all aspects of Austrian tax law.

Alexander Rust is Professor of Tax Law at the Institute for Austrian and International Tax Law of WU (Vienna University of Economics and Business). He previously worked as Professor of Tax Law and Director of the Master Programme in European and International Tax Law at the University of Luxembourg, as Acting Assistant Professor at New York University and as assistant at the University of Munich. He is a member of the editorial board of Intertax and Internationale Steuer-Rundschau as well as Co-Editor of *Klaus Vogel on Double Taxation Conventions*. His main research interests are tax treaty law, EU tax law, and tax policy.

Contributors

Andreas Bartosch, a German attorney-at-law, is a partner at LUTZ | ABEL, Brussels, where he practises in the area of European competition law, particularly European State-aid control. He is also the chairman of the *European State Aid Law Institute*, the only think-tank exclusively dedicated to EU State-aid control, which he co-founded in 2002.

Gianluigi Bizioli is Professor of Tax Law and International and EU Tax Law at the University of Bergamo (Department of Law). He is also *Of Counsel* at Ludovici Piccone & Partners in Milan. He can be contacted at gianluigi.bizioli@unibg.it.

Fatima Chaouche is research assistant and doctoral candidate in tax law at the University of Luxembourg.

Rita de la Feria is the Chair of Tax Law at the University of Leeds, an International Research Fellow at Oxford University, and a Visiting Professor at the University of Lisbon.

Clemens Fuest, Professor Dr Dr hc, is the President of the IFO Institute – Leibniz Institute for Economic Research at the University of Munich.

Eric C.C.M Kemmeren, Professor Dr, is Professor of international tax law and international taxation at the Fiscal Institute Tilburg of Tilburg University, The Netherlands. He is also a member of the board of the European Tax College, deputy justice of the Arnhem Court of Appeals (Tax Division), and of counsel to Ernst & Young Belastingadviseurs LLP, Rotterdam, The Netherlands.

Katarina Köszeghy, Ph. D., Attaché, Luxembourg Ministry of Finance.

Michael Lang, Univ.-Prof. Dr DDr hc, is Head of the Institute for Austrian and International Tax Law of WU (Vienna University of Economics and Business) and Academic Director of both the LLM programme in International Tax Law and of the doctoral programme in International Business Taxation (DIBT) of this university.

Pierpaolo Rossi-Maccanico, LL.M. International Tax NYU 2002, Attorney at law, European Commission, Legal Service.

Pierre M. Sabbadini is a Brussels-based lawyer specialized in competition and State-aid law.

Serge Schroeder, Judge, Administrative Court of Luxembourg and Guest Lecturer at the University of Luxembourg.

Daniel S. Smit, Professor in Taxation at the Fiscal Institute Tilburg, Tilburg University, the Netherlands; Senior Manager Tax at EY, Amsterdam, the Netherlands.

Edoardo Traversa, Professor of Tax Law, Catholic University of Louvain, guest professor at KU Leuven and Vienna University of Business and Economics; *Of Counsel*, Liedekerke Law Firm, Brussels.

Michael Tumpel, Professor of Tax Law at Johannes Kepler University Linz.

Piergiorgio Valente, President of the *Confédération Fiscale Européenne* (CFE); Valente Associati GEB Partners, Link Campus University (Rome).

Frans Vanistendael, Professor Emeritus KU Leuven (Belgium).

Alexander Zeiler, LL.M. is a research associate at the Christian Doppler Laboratory for "Savings Taxation in a Globalised World" established at the Institute for Austrian and International Tax Law at WU (Vienna University of Economics and Business).

Summary of Contents

Table of Contents

Chapter 2

Equality and Non-discrimination in European Tax Law

Alexander Rust 51

Part II

State Aid and Tax Law 67

Chapter 3

A Proposed Framework to Review Tax Rulings under State-Aid Rules

Pierpaolo Rossi-Maccanico 69

Preface and Acknowledgements

This book constitutes the latest volume in a series of publications by the University of Luxembourg's ATOZ Chair for European and International Taxation, which are based on annual conferences on current issues of international and European tax law and were previously published in a separate Series called '*International Tax Conferences of the University of Luxembourg*'. These conferences bring together leading tax experts from various areas of tax practice, academia, and governmental entities to facilitate high-level discussions that are both topical and that foster dialogue among the different actors.

This book is the result of two conferences held in 2015 and 2016, respectively, on 'Primary Law Limits to European Taxation' and 'EU Tax Policy in the 21st Century' and combine a unique perspective on both the law and the policy of European taxation at this time. The authors finalized their chapters over the course of several months following each conference, updating them in early 2017 to incorporate relevant points and additional information generated since the discussion at the conference, as well as addressing more recent developments in legislation and the case law. As this was particularly burdensome for those contributors who participated in the first of the two conferences, we are especially grateful to them for their continued commitment to complete their particular chapters in a timely manner. Although such a book necessarily provides a snapshot of the current state of affairs in a constantly evolving context, the analysis provided by the authors allows it to remain relevant as the law develops further over the years to come.

We would further like to express our sincere gratitude towards the moderators of each section at the conference, whose insightful perspectives significantly added to the intellectual debate both during and after the conference. In that regard, special thanks go to the First Advocate General of the Court of Justice, Melchior Wathelet, who participated in our conference in 2015, and the President of the EFTA Court, Carl Baudenbacher, who did so in 2016.

The editors are also very thankful for the cooperation with the ECJ Task Force of the *Confédération Fiscale Européenne*, as many of the contributors to this volume form part of that working group. We also wish to thank Keith O'Donnell, managing partner at ATOZ and Chairman of the ATOZ Foundation, which generously sponsors the ATOZ

Chair for European and International Taxation and its activities, including the establishment of this conference series.

We further owe thanks to our publisher Kluwer and, especially, Simon Bellamy, for their professional and kind assistance through the publication process and for assuring the timely publication of this book. We are, finally, sincerely grateful for the assistance of Suzanne M. Larsen, who edited the chapters contained in this book.

Werner Haslehner
Georg Kofler
Alexander Rust

PART I Fundamental Freedoms and Tax Law

CHAPTER 1

The CJEU and the Internal Market Concept in Direct Taxation

Eric C.C.M. Kemmeren

§1.01 INTRODUCTION

From the ever-growing body of case law of the Court of Justice of the European Union (CJEU),[1] it is clear that primary European law sets limits to Member States' domestic tax law and tax treaty law.[2] In this context, the Treaty on the European Union (TEU) and especially the fundamental freedoms included in the Treaty on the Functioning of the European Union (TFEU), restrict the Member States' competence to make, interpret, and apply their direct tax laws and tax treaties. The role of the CJEU as highest interpreter of EU law is an essential element in the organization of the European Union (EU).[3]

One of the aims of the EU is to establish an internal market.[4]

> The internal market shall comprise an area without internal frontiers in which the free movement of goods, persons, services and capital is ensured in accordance with the provisions of the Treaties.[5]

---

1. For purposes of this chapter, the abbreviation 'CJEU' or 'the Court' will also be used for its predecessor-in-interest, the European Court of Justice, for which the abbreviation 'ECJ' was used.
2. *See, e.g.*, the growing number of books entitled *ECJ-Recent Developments in Direct Taxation* (typically followed by the relevant year), edited by Michael Lang, Pasquale Pistone, Josef Schuch, Clause Staringer, and Allen Storck, all of which form a part of the Series on International Tax Law (Ser. Int'l Tax L.) published by Linde Verlag under ISBN 9783709406830.
3. *See, e.g.*, Arts 19 & 267 TFEU.
4. Art. 3(3) TEU.
5. Art. 26(2) TFEU.

The research question of this chapter is, therefore:

> What is and what should be the role of the CJEU in establishing the EU's internal market in direct tax matters?

In this context, the author will analyse existing jurisprudence, identify recent trends and investigate potential future developments in selected areas. It is obvious that, in the context of this chapter, a selection must be made. It is not possible to comprehensively cover the field of direct taxation. It is simply too extensive. Therefore, the author will discuss three of the main issues in the field of direct taxation. They potentially have a great impact on the establishment of the internal market. Furthermore, for at least two of the areas, the CJEU has developed an extensive body of case law. The three selected issues are: (1) personal and family circumstances, (2) tax treaty override, and (3) exit and final settlement taxes.[6]

In order to be able to deliver a reasoned answer to the research question, a benchmark will be first developed.[7] This benchmark will be used to assess the Court's case law and as a basis on which to make suggestions for improvement, if necessary. After having developed the benchmark, the author will discuss, in more detail, the role of the CJEU in relation to the internal market in the context of direct taxation. Subsequently, the author will discuss the role of the CJEU in the context of developing the internal market with respect to the three issues mentioned above. With respect to personal and family circumstances, the author will discuss the *Schumacker*[8] doctrine. With respect to tax treaty override, the author will address the pre- and post-Lisbon era. Finally, with respect to exit and settlement taxes, the author will review developments from *De Lasteyrie*[9] to *Commission v Portugal 2016*.[10] The author will end with some main conclusions and recommendations.

---

6. Other important issues that will not be discussed in this chapter include neutralization, cross-border losses, tax avoidance, relief from international juridical double taxation, relief from international economic double taxation, outbound dividend taxation, outbound real estate income taxation, and transfer pricing. These issues may be subject to further research.
7. This benchmark has been developed, in part, on the basis of: Eric C.C.M. Kemmeren, *Principle of Origin in Tax Conventions, A Rethinking of Models* 21–45, 177–181 (Eric C.C.Kemmeren/Pijnenburg vormgevers•uitgevers, 2001) (also available at https://pure.uvt.nl/portal/files/439888/87428.pdf) [hereinafter 'Kemmeren Dissertation']; Eric C.C.M. Kemmeren, *The Internal Market Approach Should Prevail over the Single Country Approach, in A Vision on Taxes Within and Beyond European Borders, Festschrift in Honor of Prof. Dr. Frans Vanistendael* 557–560 (Luc Hinnekens & Philippe Hinnekens eds., 2008) [hereinafter 'Kemmeren in Hinnekens']; Eric C.C.M. Kemmeren & Daniël S. Smit, *Taxation of EU-Non-Resident Companies under the CCCTB system: Analysis and Suggestions for Improvement, in Corporate Income Taxation in Europe, The Common Consolidated Corporate Tax Base (CCCTB) and Third Countries* 51–59 (Michael Lang et al. eds., 2013) [hereinafter 'Kemmeren & Smit']; Eric C.C.M. Kemmeren, *The Netherlands: What Are the Right Comparators under Article 63 TFEU When Assessing a Dividend Withholding Tax Refund Claim? Cases C-10/14 (*Miljoen*), C-14/14 (X), and C-17/14 (*Société Générale*)* [hereinafter 'Kemmeren in Lang/Linde 2014'], *in ECJ-Recent Developments in Direct Taxation 2014* 121 (vol. 91, Ser. Int'l Tax L., Michael Lang et al. eds., 2015) [hereinafter 'Lang/Linde 2014'].
8. *Schumacker*, C-279/93, Judgment, EU:C:1995:31.
9. *De Lasteyrie du Saillant*, C-9/02, Judgment, EU:C:2004:138 [hereinafter '*De Lasteyrie*'].
10. *Commission* v *Portugal*, C-503/14, Judgment, EU:C:2016:979 [hereinafter '*Commission* v *Portugal 2016*'].

§1.02 BENCHMARK: ESTABLISHING AN INTERNAL MARKET

[A] Internal Market Is of Essential Importance

Like the former EC Treaty, the TEU and TFEU contain broadly phrased declarations of the EU's objectives.[11] Two of the most important means to reach these mixed, and sometimes contradictory, objectives[12] are the establishment of an internal market and an economic and monetary union (EMU).[13]

The internal market is characterized by the abolition, as between the Member States, of internal frontiers to the free movement of goods, persons, services, and capital.[14] An internal market requires, *inter alia*: a common commercial policy; a system ensuring that competition in the internal market is not distorted; and an approximation of the Member States' laws to the extent necessary for the functioning of the internal market.[15] For operations within the EU, it is essential that the internal market be analogous in nature to the domestic market in a single state.[16]

It follows from the CJEU's case law that the internal market is not just a means, but that it must be considered an end, that is, an aim or objective in and of itself:

> Again, it is to be borne in mind that in 1986 the Single European Act added to the EEC Treaty Article 8a (then Article 7a of the EC Treaty, and now, after amendment, Article 14 EC), which set as an *aim the establishment of an internal market* before 31 December 1992.[17]

It should be emphasized, however, that a genuine internal market still does not exist.[18] At best, we are heading towards an internal market. This situation is evidenced, for

11. Arts 2–6 TEU and Arts 3–6, 8, 119–120 TFEU.
12. *E.g.*, Paul Beaumont & Gordon Moir, *European Communities (Amendment) Act 1993 with the Treaty of Rome (as amended)* s32, s32-37, s32-38 (1994); and Kamiel Mortelmans, *The Common Market, the Internal Market and the Single Market, What's in a Market?* 35 Common Mkt. L. Rev. 101, 118–119 (1998).
13. *E.g.*, Ben J.M. Terra & Peter J. Wattel, *European Tax Law* 3–4 (5th ed., 2012); and Paul J.G. Kapteyn & Pieter VerLoren van Themaat, *The Law of the European Union and the European Communities* 115–137 (2008). The term 'internal market' and the old term 'common market' were considered to be synonyms. *See, e.g., France* v *Commission*, C-41/93, Judgment, EU:C:1994:196; and Kapteyn & van Themaat, *supra*, at 127–128. The term 'single market', also frequently used by the CJEU and others, is considered to be synonymous with both terms. *See, e.g.*, Mortelmans, *supra* n. 12, at 107; Kemmeren Dissertation, *supra* n. 7, at 118–121; and Luc Hinnekens & Johan Meeusen, *Fiscaal Recht in de Europese Unie: Een schets van het institutionele kader, in* Bruno Peeters, *Europees Belastingrecht* 33–34 (2005).
14. Art. 26(2) TFEU.
15. Arts 114–116, 119–121 TFEU.
16. *E.g., Polydor*, C-270/80, Judgment, EU:C:1982:43; and *Gaston Schul I*, C-15/81, Judgment, EU:C:1982:135.
17. *Carbonati Apuani*, C-72/03, Judgment, EU:C:2004:506, para. 23 (emphasis added); *see also, e.g., Alevioz*, C-392/05, Judgment, EU:C:2007:251, para. 39.
18. *See also* Mortelmans, *supra* n. 11, at 101–136; Eric C.C.M. Kemmeren, *Source of Income in Globalizing Economies: Overview of the Issues and a Plea for an Origin-Based Approach* 60 Bull. Int'l Tax'n 430, 441–442 (2006); Sociaal en Cultureel Planbureau and Centraal Planbureau, *Marktplaats Europa, Vijftig jaar publieke opinie en marktintegratie in de Europese Unie*, Europese Verkenning 5, 75–78, 126 (SCP/CP 2007) [hereinafter 'Planbureau']; and Kemmeren & Smit, *supra* n. 7, at 51–59.

example, by the fact that all twenty-eight Member States still have their own system of direct taxation, including tax treaties. The concept of the market is reflected in the basic principle of 'an open market economy with free competition' mentioned in Articles 119 and 120 TFEU, on which the policy concerning the EMU, as well as the Member States' and EU's, economic policies must be based. An 'open market economy' means a market economy characterized by a liberal commercial policy.

With the establishment of the EU, a solid contribution has been made to a rather peaceful Europe since World War II. Looking at history, we may conclude that a peaceful era in Europe has never lasted as long as it has now. Prosperity in Europe has increased over the decades and the introduction and enlargement of the European Union has certainly played an important role in this respect. In this process, the introduction and development of the internal market has been, and remains, a very important element. The level of integration of the national economies of the Member States has increased over the years. As a consequence, the level of national prosperity of Member States depends largely on the integration of its economy with the economies of other Member States (economic integration).[19] Therefore, Member States can no longer afford to make war with each other, because that would jeopardize their level of prosperity. Thus, the establishment of the European Union and its enlargement, including an internal market, is one of the best guarantees for a peaceful and prosperous Europe. The importance of the internal market was also underlined by the European Council in the context of the European Union's treaty reform process. It was one of the results from the very difficult political debate on the European Constitution. At that time, the Council declared: 'Further strengthening the four freedoms of the internal market (free movement of goods, persons, services and capital) and improving its functioning remain of paramount importance for growth, competitiveness and employment.'[20]

The conclusion must be that the establishment of an internal market is still one of the most important objectives of the EU.

[B] Establishing the Internal Market Requires Tax Neutrality

Economic openness is vital for creating jobs and growth in all Member States and for their international competitiveness. Protectionism raises prices for consumers and business, and limits choice. Economic openness is also the basis on which the internal market must be established, because it must be established in accordance with the principle of an open market economy with free competition favouring an efficient

19. *Compare* Planbureau, *supra* n. 18, at 7, 9–10, 39–40, 49–57, 68–71, 75–78, 94–95, 105–116, 126; Michael Dauderstädt, *Increasing Europe's Prosperity*, IPG 1/2007 28 (http://www.fes.de/ipg/inhalt_d/pdf/04_A_Dauderstaedt_GB.pdf); Harry Anastasiou, *The European Union as a Peace-Building System: Deconstructing Nationalism in the Era of Globalization*, 12 J. Int'l Peace Stud. 31; Mario Monti, *A New Strategy for the Single Market, Report to the President of the European Commission*, 9 May 2010, (http://ec.europa.eu/internal_market/strategy/docs/monti_report_final_10_05_2010_en.pdf); and Kristin Archick, *The European Union: Questions and Answers* 7-5700, RS21372 1 (Cong. Res. Service 2016) (https://www.fas.org/sgp/crs/row/RS21372.pdf).
20. Brussels European Council 21/22 June 2007, *Presidency Conclusions*, 11177/07, 23 June 2007, 8.

allocation of resources.[21] Tax systems in the EU should contribute to optimizing the allocation of two production factors, labour and capital, in order to improve the overall welfare or, maybe even more widely, the overall wellbeing of the European Union.[22]

In respect to economic openness, tax neutrality should prevail; that is, taxation should not influence an efficient allocation of the production factors (capital and labour) or, at least, should do so as little as possible.[23] The concept of efficiency is based on the assumption that productivity will be highest when the production factors are distributed by a market mechanism without governmental interference or, at least, with as little interference as possible. A given economic arrangement is efficient if there can be no rearrangement that will leave someone better off without worsening the position of others.[24] Economic considerations, not tax motives, should determine the behaviour of economic operators.[25] Complete neutrality is probably not possible, but,

---

21. Arts 119(1) & 120 TFEU.
22. As far as elements of the internal market have been extended to third states, such as Switzerland in connection with the free movement of persons through the Agreement between the European Community and its Member States, of the one part, and the Swiss Confederation, of the other, on the free movement of persons, (OJ L 114, 30/04/2002 6–72) [hereinafter, the 'EC/Swiss Free Movement Agreement'], the same is true in respect of the area of the EU and that third state, to the extent that the internal market has, in substance, been extended to this area by means of specific arrangements.
23. *See also* Hugh J. Ault, *Colloquium on Corporate Income Tax: Corporate Integration, Tax Treaties and the Division of the International Tax Base: Principles and Practices*, 47 Tax L. Rev. 565, 572 (1992); Gary Clyde Hufbauer & Joanna M. van Rooij, *U.S. Taxation of International Income, Blueprint for Reform* 50 (992); Albert J. Rädler & Jens Blumenberg, *Harmonization of Corporate Income Tax Systems within the European Community, in Report of the Committee of Independent Experts on Company Taxation Annex 10A* 439, 441 (1992); Stephen G. Utz, *Taxation Panel: Tax Harmonization and Coordination in Europe and America*, 9 Conn. J. of Int'l L. 767, 785 (1994); Sijbren Cnossen, *Om de toekomst van de vennootschapsbelasting in de Europese Unie*, 1996/6203 Weekblad voor Fiscaal Recht 872, 876, 889–90; and Sijbren Cnossen, *Tax Policy in the European Union, a Review of Issues and Options*, Valedictory Address 3 (2001).
24. *See e.g.*, Richard A. Musgrave & Peggy B. Musgrave, *Public Finance in Theory and Practice* 60 (1989).
25. *See* Otto Gandenberger, *Die EinfluB der Einkommen- und Korperschaftsteuer auf die internationalen Wirtschaftstrome, in Grundfragen des Intemationalen Steuerrechts* 36–37 (Klaus Vogel ed., 1985); Richard Doernberg, *International Taxation in a Nutshell* 3–6 (1999); and US Congressional Joint Committee on Taxation, *JCT Reports on International Taxation*, 19 Tax Notes Int'l 69, 92 (1999). *Contra*, D. Juch, *Internationaal fiscaal (verdragen)recht* 1999/3 MBB 115, 116 (1999). In light of reports on harmful tax competition, it appears that a number of states pursue a policy that deviates from the concept of tax neutrality (*see e.g.*, OECD, *Harmful Tax Competition, An Emerging Global Issue* (1998); Code of Conduct Group to ECOFIN Council on 29 Nov. 1999, *Code of Conduct (Business Taxation)*, SN4901/99 (1999); and OECD/G20 Base Erosion and Profit Shifting, *Countering Harmful Tax Practices More Effectively, Taking into Account Transparency and Substance, Action 5–2015 Final Report* (2015). It is also clear that taxation affects the decision-making process in the context of making investments; but the extent of the impact is heavily debate. *See, e.g.*, OECD/G20 Base Erosion and Profit Shifting Project, *BEPS Project Explanatory Statement: 2015 Final Reports* 4 (2016):

    > Although measuring the scope of BEPS proves challenging, the findings of the work performed since 2013 confirm the potential magnitude of the issue, with estimates indicating that the global corporate income tax (CIT) revenue losses could be between 4% to 10% of global CIT revenues, i.e., USD 100 to 240 billion annually.

    See also Commission Staff Working Document Accompanying the Document Communication from the Commission to the European Parliament and the Council: Anti-Tax Avoidance

from an efficiency perspective, the highest possible level of neutrality should be pursued.[26] Taxation should contribute to a level playing field. Other values, like equity, may justify a deviation from the efficiency rule in specific situations.

In scholarly literature, various approaches to international tax neutrality can be identified. Traditionally, the focus was either on an optimal allocation of savings (under capital import neutrality), an optimal allocation of production (under capital export neutrality), or an optimal allocation of ownership (under capital ownership neutrality).[27] In the author's opinion, international tax neutrality implies that the relationship between taxes (burdens) and public goods (benefits) should not be disturbed to the disadvantage of transnational investment. This is because the effect of taxes cannot be isolated from the overall effects of all other state-induced transaction and production costs and benefits.[28] Under this condition, fair competition between foreign and domestic persons who carry on the same, genuine economic activities under the same market conditions and who use the same public goods to the same extent in the same state is promoted. Taxation on the basis of residence is incompatible with such an approach to neutrality, as no state can ensure that foreign activities carried out by its residents are subject to the same transaction and other state-induced costs and benefits. Therefore, in the author's view, international tax neutrality is also in line with capital and labour import neutrality (CLIN), which is defined as follows: labour and capital funds originating in various states should compete on equal terms in the labour and capital markets of a state, irrespective of the place of residence of the worker or the investor.[29] CLIN is generally regarded as fostering competitiveness,[30] but the author believes that it also fosters efficiency.

Capital and labour export neutrality (CLEN) is defined as: an income recipient should pay the same total (domestic plus foreign) tax, irrespective of whether he derives a given amount of labour or investment income from foreign or from domestic sources. Some argued in favour of CLEN, saying that, if a perfect capital market is presupposed, a tax system based on CLEN would not disturb competition in the state

---

Package: Next Steps Towards Delivering Effective Taxation and Greater Tax Transparency in the EU {COM(2016) 23 final} SWD(2016) 6 final, 5–7 (referring, *inter alia*, to 'a recent study commissioned by the European Parliamentary Research Service finds that the revenue loss from profit shifting within the EU amounts to about EUR 50–70 billion, equivalent to 17–23 per cent of corporate income tax (CIT) revenue in 2013' (footnote omitted)).

26. *Compare also, e.g.*, Klaus Vogel, *Taxation of Cross-Border Income, Harmonization, and Tax Neutrality under European Community Law, An Institutional Approach* 27–28 (1994); and Johan Brands, *Comment: Trade-Off between Subsidiarity and Neutrality, in* Vogel, *supra*, 38.
27. *See, e.g.*, OECD, *Taxing Profits in a Global Economy* 39 (1991) (concerning capital import neutrality (CIN) and capital export neutrality (CEN); and Mihir A. Desai & James Hines, *Evaluating International Tax Reform*, 56 Nat'l Tax J. 487, 487–502 (2003) (concerning capital ownership neutrality (CON)).
28. *See, e.g.*, Vogel, *supra* n. 26, at 26.
29. The author adds another neutrality factor, labour, to the regular definitions of CIN and CEN because he believes that, as explained below, labour is the origin of all income. Therefore, labour cannot be ignored in neutrality definitions, although the concepts have traditionally been defined only in terms of capital neutrality.
30. *Compare, e.g.*, David L. Forst, *The U.S. International Tax Treatment of Partnerships: A Policy-Based Approach*, 14 Berk. J. Int'l Law 239, 242 (1996).

in which an investment is made.[31] As long as the investment is profitable, a competing enterprise that is taxed more heavily in its residence state would always be able to compensate its reduced supply of after-tax capital by financing through external funds.[32] By contrast, the author thinks that taxation based on the universality principle creates a non-neutral and, therefore, inefficient system due to the differences in the residence-state taxation of the competitors in the relevant market. Residents of high(er)-tax states will be deterred from investing or working in low(er)-tax states because the residents of the low(er)-tax states who have a higher after-tax return will have a competitive advantage.[33] In this respect, it should be emphasized that the level of taxation and the level of public goods and services, like infrastructure, are often correlative.[34] Allocating tax jurisdiction based on the principle of territoriality should, therefore, be favoured. It enables enterprises to compete on a level playing field with their foreign competitors.[35] 'Business competes with business, not owners with owners.'[36] The same applies, *mutatis mutandis*, to workers: workers compete with workers. In such a case, economic decisions would not be distorted by differences in taxation because all competitors are, presumably, subject to the same tax treatment. A tax system based on the principle of territoriality would contribute to an efficient allocation of the production factors worldwide.[37]

In the author's view, capital ownership neutrality (CON) is not particularly helpful in the context of establishing tax neutrality, because business competes with business; owners do not compete with other owners.

Since CLIN fosters not only competitiveness but also efficiency, it best satisfies the development of the internal market, which is based on the idea of an open market economy with free competition, favouring an efficient allocation of resources.[38]

31. *See* OECD, *Taxing Profits in a Global Economy, Domestic and International Issues*, 39–40 (1991).
32. *Compare, e.g., ibid.*
33. *See, e.g.*, Gandenberger, *supra* n. 25, at 42; Ault, *supra* n. 23, at 572; Hufbauer & van Rooij, *supra* n. 23, at 57–61; Klaus Vogel, *Worldwide vs. Source Taxation of Income: A Review and Re-Evaluation of Arguments (Part I)*, Nos. 8/9 Intertax 222 (1988); Cnossen, Valedictory Address, *supra* n. 23, at 872; and Stanley I. Langbein, *The Future of Capital Export Neutrality: A Comment on Robert Peroni's Path to Progressive Reform of the U.S. International Tax Rules*, 51 U. Miami L. Rev. 1019 (1997).
34. *See, e.g.*, Gandenberger, *supra* n. 25, at 44; and Daniël S. Smit, *EU Freedoms, Non-EU Countries and Company Taxation* 76–101 (EUCOTAX Ser., 2012).
35. *See, e.g.*, Paul Vlaanderen, *Why Exempt Foreign Business Profits*, 22 Tax Notes Int'l 1095, 1098–1100 (2002); and Smit, *supra* n. 34, at 76–101.
36. *See, e.g.*, Michael J. Graetz & Michael M. O'Hear, *The 'Original Intent' of U.S. International Taxation*, 46 Duke L. J. 1021, 1037 (1997), citing Thomas S. Adams, *Fundamental Problems of Federal Income Taxation*, 35 Q. J. Econ. 527, 542 (1921).
37. *See* Kemmeren Dissertation, *supra* n. 7, at 74–77; and Smit, *supra* n. 34, at 76–101.
38. For a more detailed discussion, see Eric C.C.M. Kemmeren, *Source of Income in Globalizing Economies: Overview of the Issues and a Plea for an Origin-Based Approach*, 60 B.I.T. 430, 438–443 (2006).

[C] Ability-to-Pay Principle

A person's wealth gives him/her the ability to pay taxes.[39] Therefore, in the author's view, the ability-to-pay principle should play an important role when designing a comprehensive tax system in modern societies, including (the internal market of) the EU.[40] It should be noted that this principle is not only relevant in the context of income taxes. The ability-to-pay principle implies that persons in similar economic positions should be treated equally (horizontal equality) and that persons in dissimilar economic positions should be treated differently according to the degree of dissimilarity (vertical equality).[41] The 'ability-to-pay-time line', as the author calls it here, in fact offers four moments to tax a person's wealth:

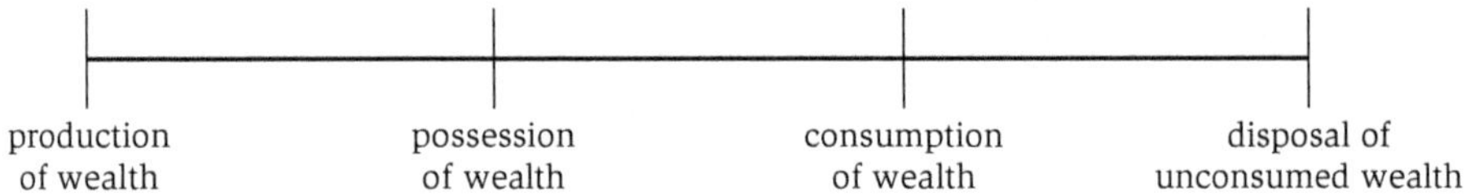

It could be argued that more or fewer moments of taxation can be determined. Nonetheless, these four moments are often part of a state's tax system. For the purposes of this chapter, it is especially relevant that both the production of wealth and the disposal of non-consumed wealth are often taxed. Whereas a person disposes of his non-consumed wealth because of his death or because of a gift, one may hold that another person acquires wealth, which acquisition could be considered as the production of wealth on his ability-to-pay time line. Therefore, either an inheritance/gift tax or an income tax may cover a taxpayer's ability to pay. If both taxes cover this situation, they should be attuned to each other in order to be justified in a comprehensive system of taxation of wealth.[42]

39. Other terms used as synonyms for the ability-to-pay principle include 'economic faculty' and 'faculty' (*see, e.g.*, Gijsbert Weijer Jan Bruins et al., *Report on Double Taxation: Submitted to the Financial Committee by Professors Bruins, Einaudi, Seligman and Sir Josiah Stamp* 18, (Document E.F.S. 73 F.19, 1923) [hereinafter the '1923 League of Nations Report']; Peter Essers & Arie Rijkers, in *General Report* [hereinafter 'Essers & Rijkers'], *in The Notion of Income from Capital* vol. 1, 290-291 (Essers & Rijkers eds., EATLP Int'l Tax Ser., 2005) [hereinafter 'Vol. 1 EATPL'], suggest not trying to define or explain the ability-to-pay principle. They believe that all that can be done is to try to shape the principle into a real and convincing tax system in a certain environment. A common understanding of a practical ability-to-pay principle on an international level is not likely to be developed.
40. *Compare, e.g.*, Joachim Lang, *The Influence of Tax Principles on the Taxation of Income from Capital* in Vol. 1 EATPL, *supra* n. 39, at 8–13; and Essers & Rijkers *in* Vol. 1 EATPL, *supra* n. 39, at 281–293.
41. *Compare, e.g.*, Nancy H. Kaufman, *Fairness and the Taxation of International Income*, 29 L. & Pol'y Int'l Bus. 145, 164-166 (1998); and Sijbren Cnossen & A. Lans Bovenberg, *Vermogensrendementsheffing: Vondst of Miskleun?* 2000/6369 Weekblad Fiscaal Recht 8 (2000).
42. *Compare, e.g.*, Claudio Sacchetto and Laura Castaldi, *Relationship between Personal Income Tax on Income from Capital and Other Taxes on Income from Capital (Corporate Income Tax, Wealth Tax, Inheritance and Gift Tax and Real-Estate Tax) in* Vol. 1 EATPL, *supra* n. 39, at 77–83, and Essers & Rijkers *in* Vol. 1 EATPL, *supra* n. 39, at 299–300.

The ability-to-pay principle also justifies a consumption tax, because consumers benefit from public expenses providing a proper environment, which renders the consumption of wealth possible or agreeable.[43] The consumption side of the ability-to-pay principle occurs at a later moment on the ability-to-pay time line than the production of the ability to pay. Therefore, in the author's opinion, a proper and comprehensive system of taxing wealth based upon the ability-to-pay principle should, especially in an international context, not only entail taxation of the production of wealth, but also taxation of the consumption of wealth.[44]

After wealth has been produced, it becomes a person's property and remains his property, as long as it is not consumed or disposed of.[45]

In a comprehensive tax system, the taxes on the production, possession, consumption, and disposal of wealth, respectively, need to be attuned to each other, because the individual's ability to pay, as a whole, should only be taxed once.[46]

Therefore, the author believes that the ability-to-pay principle is an essential element for establishing an internal market and, thus, for answering the research questions of what is and what should be the role of the CJEU in establishing the EU's internal market in direct tax matters.

[D] Origin-Based Taxation

In the author's view, international tax neutrality, CLIN, and the ability-to-pay principle imply adherence to a system of origin-state-based taxation.[47] That is to say, income, including capital gains, should only be taxed in the state in which that income was generated. This is because the public facilities or benefits provided by that state contributed to the operation of the income-producing activities (the direct-benefit principle). In substance, the direct-benefit principle is part of the ability-to-pay

43. *See, e.g.*, 1923 League of Nations Report, *supra* n. 39, at 18; and Heiko Meyer, *Die Vermeidung internationaler Doppel- und Mindestbesteuerung auf der* Grundlage *des Ursprungsprinzips*, Dissertation PhD Thesis, 33–36 (Georg-August-Universität 1970) [hereinafter 'Meyer Dissertation'].

44. If taxes are levied at these four moments in a taxpayer's ability-to-pay time line, the tax system spreads that taxpayer's obligation to contribute to public expenses based on that taxpayer's ability to pay over his or her entire ability-to-pay time line. In theory, at least in a fully autarkic community, it would also be possible to tax a person's ability to pay only at one moment. Nevertheless, the author believes that a more open economy needs more moments of taxation, in order to attain a desirable allocation of tax jurisdiction between states connected with such an open economy. For example, a person's wealth might be produced in State A, after which it might be transferred and kept for a while in State B, and finally be consumed in State C. Allocation of taxation to all three states is justified, but needs to be balanced. *Compare* Daniel Gutmann, *Relationship between Personal Income Tax on Income from Capital and Other Taxes on Income from Capital (Corporate Income Tax, Wealth Tax, Inheritance and Gift Tax and Real Estate Tax: – A Response in* Vol. 1 EATPL, *supra* n. 39, at 97–98.

45. *See* Essers & Rijkers *in* Vol. 1 EATPL, *supra* n. 39, at 297–299.

46. *See* J. Lang *in* Vol. 1 EATPL, *supra* n. 40, at 17–18; and Essers & Rijkers *in* Vol. 1 EATPL, *supra* n. 39, at 294–295.

47. Elaborated in Vogel, *supra* n. 26; and Kemmeren Dissertation, *supra* n. 7, at 35–55, 69–83, and 110–115.

principle.[48] The state in which the income was created contributes to the person's wealth, which gives him the ability to pay taxes.[49] Therefore, an origin-based allocation of tax jurisdiction is in line with the ability-to-pay principle.

The subsequent question that must be asked is how one should determine the state in which the income originated. In other words: in which state was the value added? The author thinks that only individuals can create income; things, by themselves, cannot. The intellectual element is the key component for the production of income. Through the action of an individual, with or without using a device (i.e., a capital component), value may be added to things. The author believes that, in many cases, the person of the recipient will also be the originator of the income. However, it is also possible that they will not coincide. If the income received is produced, to a substantial extent, through activities of an independent person (i.e., he is the person who adds the intellectual element) and the benefits from such activities do not inure to this independent person, but are passed on to another person (i.e., the income recipient), then the income does not originate with the recipient but with that independent person (i.e., the originator). The author thinks that the independent person from whom such income is passed on to the income recipient, can in substance be put on a par economically with a person dependent on the income recipient, for instance an employee.[50]

An origin-based taxation system justifies taxation of income by a state if the income is created within the territory of that state (i.e., the cause of the income occurs within the territory of that state), because that state makes the yield or the acquisition of wealth possible. Whereas the causal relationship between production of income and the territory of a state is predominant under the principle of origin,[51] it is of minor or no importance under the principle of source. Therefore, the principle of origin and the principle of source are not necessarily identical.[52] If the income is not generated in a state but, nevertheless, physically appears to be from that state, tax jurisdiction may be allocated to that state on the basis of the principle of source, but not on the principle of origin.[53] Furthermore, it should be noted that an activity of a person who only hops in and out of a state, but still produces income in that state, generally lacks a sufficient nexus – that is, a sufficient economic relationship – with that state to justify taxation.[54]

48. *See* 1923 League of Nations Report, *supra* n. 39, at 18, 22; *compare*, Kaufman, *supra* n. 41, at 158 (1998), who asserts that the benefit theory and the ability-to-pay theory are competing theories. She connects, however, the ability to pay with a redistribution of goods in society.
49. In this context, profit making must be interpreted in such a way that it also includes the situation in which losses are incurred.
50. For a more detailed discussion, see Kemmeren Dissertation, *supra* n. 7, at 37–40.
51. *Compare also, e.g.*, Jan A.G. van der Geld, *De herziene deelnemingsvrijstelling* 68 (1990).
52. *Dissenting, e.g.*, Meyer Dissertation, *supra* n. 43, at 29.
53. Therefore, the author is not convinced that the principle of source, as used generally, serves as a justification for a tax on income, including capital gains, as the income may be produced in a state other than the one in which the person from whom the income has been received. For a more extensive discussion, see Kemmeren Dissertation, *supra* n. 7, at 33–35.
54. This view seems to be confirmed by, *e.g.*, the OC (2008), Art. 7, Preliminary remarks, para. 1: 'The permanent establishment criterion is commonly used in international double taxation conventions to determine whether a particular kind of income shall or shall not be taxed in the country from which it *originates*' (emphasis added).

For the allocation of tax jurisdiction on income from activities, a substantial relationship between the activity and the state concerned is required. That sufficient relationship should be found to exist if a substantial income-producing activity is exercised in the state concerned. An income-producing activity is considered to be substantial if such an activity forms an essential and significant part of the activity as a whole.[55]

In respect of direct taxation, the author believes that, the CJEU's case law, in the context of the freedom of establishment, provides practical guidelines for further developing the concept of substantial income-producing activity. From that case law, one can infer that 'establishment' is, essentially, an economic concept and implies a genuine economic link with the territory of a Member State through the exercise of a genuine economic activity.[56] The notion of economic activity under EU law can be characterized as an activity, not being of a purely marginal or ancillary nature, which is usually carried out on a continuing basis by a private undertaking in a market with a business or commercial purpose, particularly the desire to maximize returns from invested capital.[57] A company can carry on a genuine economic activity directly. However, a company that, owning controlling shareholdings in another company, actually exercises that control by involving itself, directly or indirectly, in the management thereof must be regarded as taking part in the economic activity carried on by the controlled undertaking.[58]

It follows that a clear relationship exists between the benchmark of international tax neutrality, on the one hand, and the prerequisite of a genuine economic link under the freedom of establishment, on the other. International tax neutrality implies that income should be taxed only in the state to which that income can be linked economically: the state of origin.

[1] Origin-Based Taxation of Income and Personal and Family Circumstances[59]

The location of the income-producing activities should be co-decisive for determining which state should consider a person's personal allowances, reliefs, reductions, or tax credits. In substance, such a person is passing on a part of his income produced in the state involved without benefiting from it. The income is not considered to increase a

55. For a more extensive discussion, see Kemmeren Dissertation, *supra* n. 7, at 35–45.
56. *E.g.*, *Daily Mail*, C-81/87, AG Opinion, EU:C:1988:286, paras 3, 5.
57. *See, e.g.*, *Lehtonen and Castors Braine*, C-176/96, Judgment, EU:C:2000:201, paras 42–44; *Pavlov and Others*, Joined Cases C-180/98 to C-184/98, EU:C:2000:428, para. 75; and *EDM*, C-77/01, AG Opinion, EU:C:2002:483, paras 44–46. For a more extensive discussion, see Daniël S. Smit, *Freedom of investment between EU and non-EU Member States and its impact on corporate income tax systems within the European Union*, Dissertation PhD Thesis, 46 et seq. (Tilburg Center, Center for Economic Research, 2011) [hereinafter 'Smit Dissertation'].
58. *See Cassa di Risparmio di Firenze*, C-222/04, Judgment, EU:C:2006:8, paras 109–110.
59. For a more extensive discussion, see Kemmeren Dissertation, *supra* n. 7, at 469–484; and Eric C.C.M. Kemmeren, *The Netherlands I: Personal Circumstances of a Non-Resident Taxpayer with income from the Netherlands and Switzerland (Case C-283/15 (X))* [hereinafter 'Kemmeren in Lang/Linde 2015'], *in ECJ-Recent Developments in Direct Taxation 2015* 121 (vol. 100, Ser. Int'l Tax L., Michael Lang et al. eds., 2016) [hereinafter 'Lang/Linde 2015'].

person's ability to pay. If, in such a case, the income received is passed on to another person (e.g., as alimony) and that other person should be considered the recipient of the income passed on. Therefore, personal allowances, reliefs, reductions, and tax credits should be taken into account in the state of origin, if necessary, on a pro rata basis, if more than one state of origin is involved, to prevent them from being utilized more than once.[60] Both the numerator and the denominator of the fraction representing how much of the total income has been created in the state of origin should be calculated according to the tax laws of the state of origin.

If, in one of the states involved, the taxpayer is in a loss position, for example, business profits of −100, the minus sign should not be considered, because personal circumstances do not relate to a specific item of income, but should be taken into account in a state in which substantial income-producing economic activity is or was carried out. Whether such activity results in positive or negative income is not relevant for the allocation of personal allowances, reliefs, reductions, or tax credits. Moreover, under such a system, each state of origin applies its own system of taking into account personal and family circumstances. Whether it is done through personal allowances, reliefs, deductions, tax credits, or a lower general tax rate with neither specific deductions nor tax credits, is of no concern. The principle of sovereignty is, therefore, satisfied in an optimal way. Furthermore, distortions are not likely to arise in the state of origin, since that state will treat all income substantially produced in its territory in the same manner.

In this way, not only will the ability-to-pay principle be satisfied on a structural basis, but the principles of sovereignty, subsidiarity, international tax neutrality, and CLIN will also be satisfied.[61]

An origin-based system is not only justified, equitable, neutral, and consistent with the EU's internal market, but it can also be implemented feasibly. A person who wants to utilize his personal circumstances for tax purposes may be asked to provide the necessary information and cooperation in this respect. In order to consider such circumstances, a state may require the necessary information be provided with the tax return. Technologies, like the Internet and intranets, make it possible for tax administrations to exchange the necessary information more easily than used to be the case.

60. *Compare* Georg Schanz, *Zur Frage der Steuerpflicht, in Finanz-Archive. Zeitschrift für das gesamte Finanzwesen* 1, 10–11 (Georg Schanz ed., 1892); Horst-Walter Endriss, *Wohnsitz- oder Ursprungsprinzip?* 73–74 (1967); Eric C.C.M. Kemmeren, *Persoonlijke verminderingen op grond van non-discriminatie in belastingverdragen*, 1993/6044 Weekblad Fiscaal Recht 227 (1993); Kees van Raad, *Comment: The Meaning of Nondiscrimination, in Taxation of Cross-border Income, Harmonization, and Tax Neutrality under European Community Law, An Institutional Approach* 43, 45 (Klaus Vogel ed., 1994); Peter J. Wattel, *Progressive Taxation of Non-Residents and Intra-EC Allocation of Personal Allowances: Why* Schumacker, Asscher, Gilly *and* Gschwind *Do Not Suffice*, 40 Eur. Tax'n 210 (2000); John F. Avery Jones, *A Comment on 'Progressive Taxation of Non-Residents and Intra-EC Allocation of Personal Tax Allowances'*, 40 Eur. Tax'n 375 (2000); Daniël S. Smit, *Pending Case C-14/09,* Kieback*: Pro rata Application of the* Schumacker/Renneberg-*Doctrine, in* Lang/Linde 2014, *supra* n. 7, at 169–82; and Hannelore M.L. Niesten, *Persoonlijke belastingvoordelen*, 2015/1292 Weekblad Fiscaal Recht (2015). For objections, see Manuel Pires, *International Juridical Double Taxation of Income* 159–160 (1989).

61. An origin-based allocation of personal allowances, relief, deductions, and tax credits is not only essential under the exemption method, but also under a tax credit system.

Such exchanges of information could be made dependent on the person's consent (e.g., by ticking a box on the tax return). If such consent is not given, no personal allowances, reliefs, reductions, or tax credits would need to be granted.

[2] Origin-Based Taxation of Employment Income[62]

The origin of income from employment is rather easy to determine: it is the individual, human activity of the employee. Therefore, under an origin-based system, tax jurisdiction on income from private employment should be assigned to the state in which the employee's substantial employment activities occur. If an employee does not exercise substantial employment activities in a state other than the state in and from which he usually exercises his employment activity, he can hardly be considered a competitor on the labour market of that other state. The state of origin is, then, the state in and from which an individual usually exercises or has exercised his employment activity (State U), unless he substantially exercises his employment activity in the other contracting state (State S). If he incidentally works in a third state (State T) and those incidental activities are functionally connected with the substantial activities in State S, the income should be assigned to State S. If they are not connected with those activities, they are (deemed to be) functionally connected with the activities in State U, in which case State U has tax jurisdiction over that income. If the incidental activities are connected with both State U and State S activities, the income is assigned, on a pro rata basis, depending on the functional connection. If the employee does not usually exercise his employment activity in and from one contracting state or does not satisfy the requirement of substantial employment activities in any of the tax jurisdictions, the income is attributed to the state in which the incidental activities are or were exercised. An employee carries out or has carried out a substantial employment activity in the other contracting state if that employment activity forms or has formed an essential and significant part of the employment activity as a whole.[63] Expenses that are incurred for the purposes of substantial employment activities should be attributed to the substantial employment activity concerned and should be deductible regardless of where they were incurred.

62. For a more detailed explanation, see Kemmeren Dissertation, *supra* n. 7, at 389-402.
63. If it is considered desirable to define the term 'substantial' more precisely, it could be done by reference to the proportionate share of the employment activities in the other state, the nature of the activities performed, and the relative contributions made to the employment activities carried out in both states. For practical reasons, the introduction of safe harbours could be considered. If, for example, a minimum period of human activities is considered to be a desirable threshold with regard to entrepreneurial activities (*see* s §1.02[D][3], *infra*), a minimum period with respect to employment activities should be attuned to it, unless the nature of the activities indicates otherwise. In this way, a coherent system of allocation of tax jurisdiction can be created. Assessing whether an employee carries out or has carried out a substantial employment activity in a contracting state must be done on a stand-alone basis (i.e., the standing of the employer is not relevant).

[3] Origin-Based Taxation of Business Income[64]

In an origin-based system, tax jurisdiction with respect to business profits is allocated to the contracting state in which a person's enterprise carries on or has carried on its substantial entrepreneurial activities. As a consequence, all income, whether it has arisen in the contracting state in which the entrepreneurial activity is carried on, in the other contracting state or in a third state, is taxable only in the state of the substantial entrepreneurial activity, unless another income allocation rule of the relevant tax treaty derogates from this rule. A substantial entrepreneurial activity is present if the relevant entrepreneurial activity in a state forms an essential and significant part of the entrepreneurial activity of the enterprise as a whole. It is sufficient that an individual pursues substantial activities for an enterprise in the state concerned: an enterprise carries on or has carried on a substantial entrepreneurial activity in the other contracting state if that activity, carried on by individuals attributable to the enterprise, in itself forms or has formed an essential and significant part of the activity of the enterprise as a whole ('a branch'). A distinction between business activities and independent personal services is not necessary.

This is also in line with the EU fundamental freedom of establishment. As a rule, services or activities cannot be performed at any place other than where the individual performing them is physically present. The decisive factor is where that person works and not where the results of his work are exploited. If an enterprise of a person carries out substantial entrepreneurial activities not only in one contracting state, but also in the other contracting state, the income must be allocated to both states as far as it is produced in the respective states. Attribution of income to each part of the enterprise must be neutral. Expenses which are incurred for the purposes of entrepreneurial activities should be attributed to the substantial entrepreneurial activity concerned and should be deductible regardless of where they were incurred.

Based on the principle of origin, tax jurisdiction with respect to dividends and capital gains on shares must be assigned to the state in which the profits were produced, which is not necessarily the state in which the paying company is resident. The allocation of tax jurisdiction with respect to a company's profits, the dividends paid on its shares, and the capital gains on its shares is harmonized in order to avoid both international juridical and economic double taxation. The shareholder's state should refrain from taxing the company's profits, the capital gains on its shares and the dividends received by the shareholder. It should be noted, however, that the suggested allocation rules do not compel this state to apply an income exemption system as a method to eliminate double taxation. The suggested allocation rules can also be applied under a system based on capital export neutrality.

If the company carries on its enterprise in its state of residence, the state of origin and state of residence coincide. If the enterprise also carries on substantial business

64. For a more extensive discussion, see Kemmeren Dissertation, *supra* n. 7, at 322–351; and Eric C.C.M. Kemmeren, *Netherlands: Taxation of Notional Amount (Box 3) Rather than Paid Dividend: No Tax Treaty Override, in Tax Treaty Case Law around the Globe 2015* 141 (Michael Lang et al. eds., 2016).

activities in the other contracting state (a branch), the state of residence and the state of origin do not coincide. In this case, a branch profits tax must play a role to ensure that the assignment of tax jurisdiction with respect to profits is neutral regarding the legal form in which the business activities are carried on (i.e., it does not matter whether a subsidiary pays out its profits to its shareholder or a branch transfers its profits to its head office). The same goes for capital gains. The systems are harmonized in order to avoid both international juridical and economic double taxation irrespective of whether the substantial entrepreneurial activities are carried on directly by a sole proprietor, through a branch, or through a company.

To sum up, tax jurisdiction with respect to business profits should be allocated to the contracting state in which a person's enterprise carries on its substantial entrepreneurial activities (a branch). Tax jurisdiction with respect to dividends and capital gains on shares should be assigned to the state in which the profits were produced. If dividends are taxed, a branch profits tax must also play a role when profits are transferred from a branch to a head office. The origin-based system allocates a greater share of tax jurisdiction on business profits, transfer of profits, and capital gains on shares, to capital importing countries.

[E] Interim Conclusion

In conclusion, international tax neutrality and CLIN imply that income should be taxed only in the state to which it can be economically linked. Therefore, creating a level playing field, international tax neutrality, CLIN, satisfying the ability-to-pay principle, and establishing an origin-based allocation of tax jurisdiction on income, all go hand in hand and all five of these factors contribute to the development of the internal market of the European Union.

§1.03 THE ROLE OF THE CJEU IN RELATION TO THE INTERNAL MARKET

The CJEU plays, in the organization of the EU, a vital role in developing the internal market.[65] As discussed above, the concept of 'the internal market' is reflected in the basic principle of an open market economy with free competition favouring an efficient allocation of resources. In this context, it is essential that the CJEU's decisions contribute to improving tax neutrality (i.e., that they contribute to a level playing field). Its decisions should contribute to optimizing the allocation of the production factors, labour and capital, in order to improve overall welfare of, or perhaps more broadly, overall wellbeing within, the European Union. As far as elements of the internal market have been extended to third states, like to Switzerland for the free movement of

65. *See* Kapteyn & van Themaat, *supra* n. 13, at 237–243; Koen Lenaerts and Piet van Nuffel, *European Union Law* 524–534 (2011); Kemmeren *in* Hinnekens, *supra* n. 7, at 560–564; and Terra & Wattel, *supra* n. 13, at 37–39.

persons,[66] the same is true with respect of the territory of the European Union and that third state, to the extent that the internal market has, in substance, been extended to it by means of specific arrangements. The concept of economic efficiency is based on the assumption that productivity will be highest when production factors are distributed through a market mechanism without public interference or, at least, with as little interference as possible.

As held as well, complete neutrality is probably not possible but, from an efficiency perspective, the highest possible level of neutrality should be pursued. Other values, like equity, may justify a deviation from these rules in specific situations. Therefore, the CJEU's decisions may also deviate from creating a level playing field in order to further develop the internal market if other values require to do so. This methodological approach is reflected by the Court's rule-of-reason case law,[67] in which it permits discriminations and restrictions because of imperative requirements in the general interest. However, measures that may justify such deviations should be suitable for securing the attainment of the objective which it pursues (appropriateness) and should not go beyond what is necessary in order to attain that objective (proportionality).

The tasks of the CJEU are set out in Article 19(1) and 19(3) TEU:

> 1. The *Court of Justice of the European Union* shall include the Court of Justice, the General Court and specialised courts. It shall *ensure* that in the *interpretation and application of the Treaties the law is observed.*
>
> ...
>
> 3. The *Court of Justice of the European Union* shall, in accordance with the Treaties:
>
> (a) rule on actions brought by a Member State, an institution or a natural or legal person;
> (b) give *preliminary rulings*, at the request of courts or tribunals of the Member States, *on the interpretation of Union law* or the validity of acts adopted by the institutions;
> (c) rule in other cases provided for in the Treaties.[68]

It is further discussed in Article 267 TFEU, which states, in relevant part:

> The *Court of Justice of the European Union* shall have jurisdiction to give preliminary rulings concerning:
>
> (a) the *interpretation of the Treaties*;

66. The EC/Swiss Free Movement Agreement, *supra* n. 22.
67. *See, e.g.*, *De Lasteyrie*, C-9/02; *N*, C-470/04, Judgment, EU:C:2006:525; *National Grid Indus*, C-371/10, Judgment, EU:C:2011:785; *Commission* v *Spain*, C-269/09, Judgment, EU:C:2012:439; *Commission* v *Portugal*, C-38/10, Judgment, EU:C:2012:521 [hereinafter *Commission* v *Portugal 2012*]; *DI. VI. Finanziaria di Diego della Valle & C.*, C-380/11, Judgment, EU:C:2012:552; *Commission* v *Netherlands*, C-301/11, Judgment, EU:C:2013:47; *Commission* v *Spain*, C-64/11, Judgment, EU:C:2013:264; *Commission* v *Denmark*, C-261/11, Judgment, EU:C:2013:480; *DMC*, C-164/12, Judgment, EU:C:2014:20; *Verder LabTec*, C-657/13, Judgment, EU:C:2015:331; and *Commission* v *Portugal 2016*, C-503/14.
68. Art. 19(1) & (3) TEU (emphasis added).

(b) the *validity and interpretation of acts* of the institutions, bodies, offices or agencies of the Union.[69]

As a consequence, the CJEU is able to promote uniformity in the interpretation of Union law in the legal practice of the Member States. Therefore, it can make a real contribution to the legal protection of individuals against acts of those Member States that infringe Union law.[70]

In this context, the CJEU must play a key role in realizing an internal market within the European Union. As argued above, the establishment of an internal market is one of the main aims of the European Union. If a Member State produces legislation that endangers the realization of the internal market, the CJEU has no other option than protecting the individuals concerned against such legislation. Therefore, the internal market should be and is a key standard on which the Court can build its case law. This is also true in respect of tax legislation. The author refers, as an example, to the CJEU's 2007 decision in *Commission v Belgium*,[71] which addressed Belgian tax legislation that provided for: less favourable treatment of contributions to occupational pension schemes paid to insurance undertakings established abroad; taxation in Belgium of capital and surrender values paid to beneficiaries who had transferred their residence abroad; tax conventions preventing double taxation; and a requirement that a representative must reside in Belgium. The CJEU explicitly put the issues in the context of the internal market, using its synonym the 'single market':

> *With reference to* the *single market* and *in order* to *permit the achievement of its objectives*, Article 49 EC precludes the application of any national rules which have the effect of making the provision of services between Member States more difficult than the provision of services purely within one Member State (citation omitted; emphasis added).[72]

The author believes that many of the CJEU's preliminary rulings concerning the interpretation of the fundamental freedoms can be better understood if we take into account that one of the main tasks of the Court is to ensure (or at least to contribute to) the aim of realizing an internal market.[73] So, even if the Court does not explicitly refer to the internal market in its ruling, it must be borne in mind that the rationale of the Court's judgment on one of the fundamental freedoms is, most likely, its attempt to aid in the realization of the internal market. Therefore, neither the Member States nor taxpayers should complain when they lose a case, if the Court's judgment is based on this rationale, taking into account at the same time the constraints originating from the existence of twenty-eight different tax jurisdictions within the Union. The Court is only fulfilling the role for which it was established. Furthermore, the author would like to emphasize that the European Union's treaty reform process resulting in the Treaty of

69. Art. 267 TFEU (emphasis added).
70. *See also* Kapteyn & van Themaat, *supra* n. 13, at 237–243.
71. *Commission* v *Belgium*, C-522/04, Judgment, EU:C:2007:405.
72. *Ibid.* para. 37.
73. *See also, e.g.*, Axel Cordewener, *The Prohibitions of Discrimination and Restriction within the Framework of the Fully Integrated Internal Market*, *in EU Freedoms and Taxation* vol. 2, 5 (EATLP Int'l Tax Ser., 2006).

Lisbon did not change the position of the CJEU. Substantively, the 2007 Conference regarding that process only underscored the primacy of EU law and recalled the existing case law of the CJEU.[74]

Therefore, the establishment of the internal market is one of the most important aims of the European Union. It is one of the fundamentals of European law. Part of the CJEU's role is to protect the realization of the internal market, subject to the constraints of the existence of twenty-eight different tax jurisdictions within the Union. In this context, the author believes that the Court should apply an internal-market approach rather than a single-country approach, which means that, for this assessment, the CJEU should not only take into account the domestic tax law of a Member State and secondary EU law (such as directives), but also any double tax convention that the relevant Member State has concluded with the other (Member) State, *as well as* the domestic tax law of that other state. Under a single-country approach, the domestic tax law of that other state is ignored. So, even without assessing the actual Court's case law, the general European law framework implies that the Court should apply an internal-market, and not a single-country, approach. A single-country approach is inconsistent with the aim of realizing an internal market since, for operations within the European Union, it is essential that the internal market be analogous in nature to the domestic market of a single state.[75] Therefore, the Court should not only take into account the domestic tax law of the relevant Member State, but also any double tax convention which that state has concluded with another (Member) State and the domestic tax law of that other state.

If the result is that, on balance, a transnational situation is not treated worse than a purely domestic situation, the different treatment of domestic and transnational situations under the domestic tax law of a Member State does not constitute an infringement of the fundamental freedoms of the TFEU.[76] The author believes that this is a sound approach, because, on balance, the exercise of the fundamental freedoms by an individual or company is not restricted in such a situation.[77] The functioning of the internal market at the highest level possible at that moment, considering the current constraints, is not hindered by such different treatment if the tax burden, on balance, does not differ. It is, rather, immaterial to an individual or company whether their taxes are paid in Member State A, in Member State B, or a part in both Members State A and B or according to what fraction, at least, from a substantive law perspective. From an administrative-burden perspective, there is, of course, a difference and there it does matter whether a taxpayer has to comply with and apply one tax system or two or

74. *See* Declaration 17 concerning primacy, annexed to the Final Act of the Intergovernmental Conference which adopted the Treaty of Lisbon, signed on 13 Dec. 2007, OJ 2010/C 83/01.

75. *See Polydor*, C-270/80 and *Gaston Schul I*, C-15/81.

76. *See, e.g., De Groot*, C-385/00, Judgment, EU:C:2002:750.

77. *See* Eric C.C.M. Kemmeren, *Marks & Spencer: Balanceren op Grenzeloze Verliesverrekening*, 2006/6660 Weekblad Fiscaal Recht 211, 215–216, 219–221; and Peter J. Wattel, *Eénjurisdictionele of overalltoepassing van EG-verboden op bronheffingen*, 2006/6680 Weekblad Fiscaal Recht 847. *Compare* Michael Lang, *The Marks & Spencer Case, The Open Issues Following the ECJ's Final Word*, 46 Eur. Tax'n 54, 57 (2006); Cordewener, *supra* n. 71, 23–25; and Dennis Weber, *In Search of a (New) Equilibrium between Tax Sovereignty and the Freedom of Movement within the EC* 33–48 (2006).

more. However, that is a logical and inherent consequence of accepting the existence of twenty-eight different domestic-tax systems.

A recent example of this internal-market approach can be found in the *Société Générale* case.[78] One of the questions asked was whether a discriminatory Dutch dividend-withholding tax could be neutralized by a French direct-tax credit included in the 1974 Netherlands-France Treaty.[79] The Court answered this question in the affirmative:

> 80 In that regard, it must be recalled that the Court has held that in order to attain the objective of *neutralisation*, the application of the method of deduction should enable the tax on dividends levied by the Member State from which the dividends are paid to be deducted in its entirety from the tax due in the Member State of residence of the taxpayer receiving those dividends in such a way that, if those dividends are ultimately taxed more heavily than the dividends paid to taxpayers residing in the Member State from which those dividends are paid, *that heavier tax burden may no longer be attributed to that Member State, but to the State of residence of the recipient taxpayer* which exercised its power to impose taxes (see, to that effect, judgment in Commission v Spain, C 487/08, EU:C:2010:310, paragraph 60).
>
> ...
>
> 85 With regard to the situation at issue in Case C 17/14, arising from the application of the Franco-Netherlands Convention, it is apparent from the documents before the Court that *the restriction alleged* was entirely *neutralised* by the fact that, in France, the tax on dividends for the tax years 2000 to 2007 inclusive were offset in full (emphasis added).[80]

The internal-market approach should not only be applied within the EU, but also in relation to third countries to the extent that the internal market has, in substance, been extended to such third countries by the TFEU or by means of specific arrangements.[81]

To sum up, one of the main tasks of the CJEU is ensuring, or at least contributing to, the aim of realizing an internal market within the European Union and, as the case may be, in relation to any third countries included in all or part of that internal market. The Court is a protector of the internal market in direct tax matters. As a consequence, the Court's decisions should be built (more) on creating a level playing field, ensuring international tax neutrality, adhering to CLIN, satisfying the ability-to-pay principle, and establishing an origin-based allocation of tax jurisdiction.

78. *Miljoen*, Joined Cases C-10/14, C-14/14, & C-17/14, Judgment, EU:C:2015:608.
79. Convention between the Republic of France and the Kingdom of the Netherlands for the Avoidance of Double Taxation and the Prevention of Fiscal Evasion with Respect to Taxes on Income and on Capital, 16 Mar, 1973, effective as of 1 Jan. 1974, Treaties IBFD ['1974 Netherlands-France Treaty'].
80. For more detailed discussions of this case, see Kemmeren in Lang/Linde 2014, *supra* n. 7, at 152–167; Jasper Korving, Miljoen, X *and* Société Générale*: The Final Curtain of the Dividend Withholding Tax Saga?*, 24 EC Tax Rev. 281 (2015); and Karin Spindler-Simader, *Dividend Withholding Taxes after* Miljoen, X *and* Société Générale, 25 EC Tax Rev. 70 (2016).
81. *See* Art. 63 TFEU and the EC/Swiss Free Movement Agreement, *supra* n. 22.

§1.04 PERSONAL AND FAMILY CIRCUMSTANCES: THE *SCHUMACKER* DOCTRINE

Since the *Schumacker* case[82] was decided, a substantial body of CJEU case law has developed around the question of whether the state of source, rather than the taxpayer's state of residence should take into account the taxpayer's personal and family circumstances. The feeling that it is a never-ending story comes up.[83]

[A] Discrimination of Non-residents and Personal and Family Circumstances

It is settled case law that residents and non-residents are, as a general rule, non-comparable. The CJEU has held that the situations between them differ objectively from the point of view both of the source of their income and of their personal ability to pay tax or their personal and family circumstances.[84] The income received in the territory of a state by a non-resident is, in most cases, only a part of his total income, which is concentrated in his state of residence. Furthermore, a non-resident's personal ability to pay tax, determined by reference to his aggregate income and his personal and family circumstances, is assumed to be more easily assessed at the place where his personal and financial interests are centred, which is typically the place where he has his usual abode. As a rule, the taxpayer's state of residence must take into account the taxpayer's personal and family circumstances, which is in line with the OECD Model Tax Convention.[85]

However, the Court decided that the situations of residents and non-residents can be, by exception, comparable. In this context, it is important to identify the purpose and content of the national provisions, especially the rules concerning taking into account personal and family circumstances. If a person does not have significant taxable annual income in the Member State of residence *and* earns the major part of his taxable annual income from an activity in another Member State, the situations of residents and non-residents are comparable. The reason is that in such situations, the Member State of residence is not in a position to grant tax advantages connected to its resident's personal and family circumstances.[86] In this respect, the CJEU recently reiterated in its 2017 judgment in the *X* case:

---

82. *Schumacker*, C-279/93.
83. Rather recently, the CJEU has provided further guidance in *X*, C-283/15, Judgment, EU:C:2017:102 [hereinafter '*X 2017*, C-283/15']. For a more detailed discussion of this case, see Kemmeren, *supra* n. 58. This section of this chapter is based, in part, on that paper.
84. *See Schumacker*, C-279/93, para. 34; *De Groot*, C-385/00, para. 90; *Wallentin*, C-169/03, Judgment, EU:C:2004:403, para. 14; *Schempp*, C-403/03, Judgment, EU:C:2005:446, paras 27–35; *Kieback*, C-9/14, Judgment, EU:C:2015:406, para. 23; *Hirvonen*, C-632/13, Judgment, EU:C:2015:765, para. 31; *X 2017*, C-283/15, paras 30–31.
85. *See* Art. 24(3) OECD Model Tax Convention on Income and Capital (2014) and OECD Commentary (2014) on: Art. 18, para. 1, Arts 23A and B, paras 41–42, and Art. 24, paras 8, 36.
86. *See Schumacker*, C-279/93, paras 36–38; *De Groot*, C-385/00, para. 89; *Wallentin*, C-169/03, paras 17–18; *Kieback*, C-9/14, paras 24–35; *Hirvonen*, C-632/13, para. 31; and *X 2017*, C-283/15, paras 32–38.

> 33 One such case is where a non-resident taxpayer receives *no significant income in the Member State where he resides* and *obtains the major part of his taxable income from an activity performed in another Member State*, and *consequently the Member State of residence* is *not* in a position to grant him the benefits that result from taking into account *his personal and family circumstances*.
>
> 34 In such a case, discrimination arises from the fact that the personal and family circumstances of a non-resident who receives the major part of his income and almost all his family income in a Member State other than that of his residence are taken into account *neither in the Member State of residence nor in the Member State of employment*.[87]

According to the Court, residents and non-residents are not comparable by:

> *the mere fact* that a non-resident may have received, within the Member State where his activity is performed, income on conditions more or less similar to those of the residents of that State ...
>
> 38 It is *additionally* necessary, in order to establish that such situations are *objectively comparable*, that, due to that non-resident's receiving the major part of his income outside the Member State of residence, the *Member State of residence* is *not in a position to grant him the advantages which accrue from taking into account his aggregate income and his personal and family circumstances*.[88]

This means that the starting-point remains that the Member State of residence is primarily responsible for account being taken of the personal and family circumstances of its residents. If in that Member State sufficient taxable income is earned for doing so, the situation of this taxpayer in the Member State where the activity is performed, is *not* comparable to the situation of a resident of that State. However, strongly encouraged by the opinion of Advocate General Wathelet,[89] the Court refined its *Schumacker* case law by accepting that, if the taxable income in the Member State of residence is insufficient to take into account the personal and family circumstances, the situation of a non-resident taxpayer in the Member State of activity *is* comparable to that of a resident of that Member State:

> 39 Where the non-resident receives, within a Member State where he performs some of his activities, 60% of his total global income, it cannot be inferred that, *for that reason alone*, the Member State where he is resident will not be in a position to take account of his aggregate income and his personal and family circumstances. It would be *otherwise only* if it were established that the person concerned received, *within the Member State where he was resident*, either *no income* or *income of so modest an amount* that *that State* would *not be able to grant him the advantages that would accrue from account being taken of his aggregate income and his personal and family circumstances*.[90]

In this context, it does not matter that the non-resident taxpayer receives a remainder of his income in the year concerned within a State – a Member State or a third State –

87. *X 2017*, C-283/15, paras 33–34.
88. *Ibid.* paras 37–38 (emphasis added, citations omitted).
89. *See X 2017*, C-283/15, AG Opinion, EU:C:2016:638.
90. *X 2017*, C-283/15, para. 39 (emphasis added); *see also, e.g.*, Kemmeren, *supra* n. 58.

other than the Member State of activity and the concerned and the Member State of residence:

> 42 ... What remains the *decisive criterion* is whether it is *impossible* for a *Member State* to take into account, *for the calculation of tax*, the personal and family circumstances of a taxpayer *in the absence of sufficient taxable income*, although such circumstances can *otherwise* be taken into account *when there is sufficient income.*[91]

[B] Criteria to Establish the Obligation of the State of Activity to Take into Account Personal and Family Circumstances

To assess whether discrimination of a non-resident taxpayer is present, the author believes that, based on the *Schumacker* case law, the following criteria must be taken into account:

(1) The taxpayer's personal circumstances are not taken into account in either of the relevant Member States.[92]
(2) Due to the taxpayer's receiving *part of his income* from one or more (Member) States of activity, the (Member) State of residence is not in a position to grant the advantages that follow from taking into account the taxpayer's:
   (a) aggregate annual income, and
   (b) his personal and family circumstances.
(3) Not only must the taxpayer's annual income be taken into account, but also *his annual family income.*
(4) The taxpayer must make available to the competent national authorities all necessary information regarding his global income.
(5) In the case of simultaneous activities in several countries *after a change of residence*, the Member State of activity is not in a better position than his new state of residence to assess his personal and family circumstances.
(6) A Member State from which, during only a part of the taxable year, a part (but not the major part) of his annual income is received is not bound to grant the same advantages as granted to residents.

91. *X 2017*, C-283/15, para. 42 (emphasis added, citations omitted) and para. 51:

> There can be no other interpretation in a situation such as that at issue in the main proceedings, with respect to a Member State within which a self-employed person residing in another Member State has performed part of his activities, while carrying out the remainder of his activities *within a third State, even if the latter is not a Member State, but a non-Member State* (emphasis added, citation omitted).

See also, e.g., Kemmeren, *supra* n. 58.

92. *See Schumacker*, C-279/93, para. 38; *De Groot*, C-385/00, para. 89; *Wallentin*, C-169/03, para. 17; *Ettwein*, C-425/11, Judgment, EU:C:2013:121, paras 46–49; *Kieback*, C-9/14, paras 24–36; and, *X 2017*, C-283/15, paras 32–34.

If criteria 1–4 are met, discrimination against the non-resident taxpayer is present. However, if criteria *5 and* 6 are also met, then no discrimination arises, according to the CJEU. The author emphasizes that the CJEU has only decided that a state of activity is not obliged to grant a non-resident taxpayer any tax benefits connected with his personal and family circumstances if he has left both his state of residence and that state of activity, and further that, as a consequence thereof, only a part of his taxable annual income, not being the major part, is taxed in that state of activity during a part of that taxable year. However, if a non-resident has not left either his state of residence or his state of activity, it follows from the Court's recent decision in *X*, C-283/15 [hereinafter '*X 2017*'] that the state of source is obliged to grant to a non-resident taxpayer tax benefits connected with his personal and family circumstances if the non-resident has earned the major part of his income in the state of source and earned no significant income in the state of residence with the result that the personal and family circumstances are not taken into account in either state based on domestic and tax treaty rules.

Prior to the *X 2017* decision, the open issues before the Court were, amongst others:

(1) What is the function of the criterion that a non-resident taxpayer must have obtained the major part or almost all of his taxable income from an activity performed in another Member State; and
(2) How must the words 'major part'[93] and 'almost all'[94] be interpreted?

The author believes that *X 2017* makes clear that the criterion of having obtained the 'major part' or 'almost all' of the non-resident's taxable income from an activity performed in another Member State does not mean that this income must satisfy a certain threshold if it is otherwise impossible for the taxpayer's Member State of residence to take into account his personal and family circumstances in the absence of sufficient taxable income in that State. In that case, any income taxable income in other (Member) States of activity is sufficient:

> 48 In the situation where a self-employed person receives his taxable income within a number of Member States, other than that where he is resident, that reconciliation[95] can be achieved only by permitting him to submit a claim for his

93. *Hirvonen*, C-632/13, para. 34.
94. *Kieback*, C-9/14, para. 26.
95. The words 'that reconciliation' refer to *X 2017*, C-283/15, para 47:

> 47 It follows, in particular, that the freedom of the Member States, in the absence of unifying or harmonising measures adopted under EU law, *to allocate among themselves their powers to impose taxes*, in particular to avoid the accumulation of tax advantages, *must be reconciled* with *the necessity that taxpayers of the Member States concerned are assured that, ultimately, all their personal and family circumstances will be duly taken into account, irrespective of how the Member States concerned have allocated that obligation amongst themselves*. Were *such reconciliation* not to take place, the freedom of Member States to allocate the power to impose taxes among themselves would be liable to create inequality of treatment of the taxpayers concerned which, since that

> right to deduct 'negative income' to each Member State of activity where that type of tax advantage is granted, *in proportion to the share of his income received within each such Member State*, it being his responsibility to provide to the competent national authorities all the information on his global income needed by them to determine that proportion.[96]

The *X 2017* decision, best serves the internal market, the ability-to-pay principle, CLIN, and the principle of origin.

Moreover, the Court's decision in *X 2017* is in line with its *De Groot*[97] decision, in which the Court decided that several Member States of employment could release the state of residence from the obligation to take the taxpayer's personal and family circumstances into account, which is only possible if it is not necessary for the taxpayer's aggregate annual income to reach a minimum threshold of 90% earned in a Member State other than his Member State of residence. Therefore, the idea that the phrase 'a major part' of the income must be interpreted as a 90% threshold, as such, should not be deemed to have been adopted, despite the fact the Court in *Gschwind* specifically used that threshold.[98] However, it should be noted that the German system at issue in *Gschwind* did not just apply that threshold to grant tax benefits; it also used a certain ceiling, in absolute terms, if the 90% threshold was not met. The Court permitted both conditions in combination with each other, but against the background in which the possibility for account to be taken of the taxpayer's personal and family circumstances in the state of residence was maintained. If the 90% threshold were, indeed, a hard criterion on its own, a taxpayer's personal and family circumstances might not always taken into account. Such a result would be inconsistent with the ability-to-pay principle, the direct-benefit principle, the open-market economy with free competition, the efficient allocation of production factors, tax neutrality, the establishment of a level playing field, international tax neutrality, CLIN, and origin-based taxation. Such a condition would hamper the development of the internal market. Therefore, the refinement given by the Court in its decision in *X 2017* matches perfectly with its role as a protector of the establishment of the internal market.

In this context, the author is rather critical of the Court's decision in *Kieback*,[99] particularly with respect to criteria 5 and 6, that it developed in that case.[100] In 2005, Mr. Kieback left for the United States to reside and work there. Until 31 March 2005, he lived in Germany and worked as an employee in the Netherlands. In Germany, he possessed an owner-occupied house. This dwelling was financed with a mortgage loan on which he paid interest. Mr. Kieback claimed a deduction of negative income from his owner-occupied house, based on the Court's *Renneberg* decision, in which the

---

inequality would not be the result of disparities between the provisions of national tax law, would be incompatible with freedom of establishment (emphasis added, citations omitted).

96. *Ibid.* para 48 (emphasis added).
97. *De Groot*, C-385/00, paras 100, 102.
98. *Gschwind*, C-391/97, Judgment, EU:C:1999:409, para. 32.
99. *Kieback*, C-9/14. For a more detailed discussion of the pending case, see Smit, *supra* n. 53, at 169–182.
100. *Kieback*, C-9/14, paras 32–36.

deduction was qualified as a deduction based on personal and family circumstances.[101] He claimed to be entitled to deduct this negative income from his income from employment in the Netherlands. If Mr. Kieback had been a Dutch resident, he would have been entitled to fully deduct this amount from his employment income during the period from 1 January until 31 March 2005.[102] Since, he was a non-resident taxpayer of the Netherlands during this period and had received the major part of his income for 2005 in the United States, the Dutch tax authorities determined that he was not entitled to deduct in the Netherlands the negative income from his German owner-occupied home.[103] The CJEU decided that refusing to grant this deduction was consistent with the free movement of workers. The author is concerned that the CJEU overlooked the fact that the tax liability in the United States only started on 1 April 2005. In general, a state does not take into account any income, positive or negative, that is received in the period before tax liability commences. As a consequence, it is more than likely that Mr. Kieback was not able to take into account, in the United States, the negative income from his home in Germany received during the period 1 January 2005 to 31 March 2005. As a consequence of the CJEU's decision, Mr. Kieback's negative income could not be taken into account in any of the states involved: not in the United States (no tax jurisdiction during the period concerned), not in Germany (no income), and not in the Netherlands (non-resident status).

But, that result is now inconsistent with the CJEU's most recent decision in *X 2017*. Assuming that the mortgage interest deduction is indeed a deduction based on personal and family circumstances,[104] the lack of such a deduction for Mr. Kieback in the Netherlands was also inconsistent with establishing the internal market, an open-market economy with free competition, an efficient allocation of production factors, tax neutrality, a level playing field, international tax neutrality, CLIN, the ability-to-pay principle, the direct benefit principle, and origin-based taxation. In light of, *inter alia*, the CJEU's decision in *X 2017*, the author believes that the *Kieback* result should be reconsidered.

[C] How to Take Personal and Family Circumstances into Account

Assuming that not taking into account the personal and family circumstances of a non-resident taxpayer constitutes discrimination, the next question to be answered is: How are personal and family circumstances to be taken into account?

As noted above, the *X 2017* Court decided that Member States must permit a non-resident taxpayer:

101. *Renneberg*, C-527/06, Judgment, EU:C:2008:566.
102. *See* Art. 3.1 Wet inkomstenbelasting 2001 (author translation and hereinafter: Personal Income Tax Act or PITA 2001).
103. *See* Arts 7.2–7.4 PITA 2001.
104. The author does not agree with this qualification. Eric C.C.M. Kemmeren, *Renneberg Endangers the Double Tax Convention System or Can a Second Round Bring Recovery?*, 18 EC Tax Rev. 4 (2009).

> to submit a claim for his right to deduct 'negative income' to each Member State of activity where that type of tax advantage is granted, *in proportion to the share of his income received within each such Member State*, it being his responsibility to provide to the competent national authorities all the information on his global income needed by them to determine that proportion.[105]

The author believes that this pro-rata-parte approach is perfectly in line with the benchmark. This approach contributes to the development of the internal market. It best satisfies an open market economy with free competition, an efficient allocation of production factors, tax neutrality, a level playing field, international tax neutrality, CLIN, the ability-to-pay principle, the direct benefit principle, and origin-based taxation.

Therefore, any state in which a part of the taxpayer's aggregate annual income is earned, should *not* take into account the full amount of that taxpayer's negative income. If the full amount were to be allowed as a deduction, a substantial risk of double deduction (or a double dip) would exist. Such a double dip would infringe on an open market economy with free competition, an efficient allocation of production factors, tax neutrality, a level playing field, international tax neutrality, CLIN, the ability-to-pay principle, the direct benefit principle, and origin-based taxation. As a result, a double dip would hamper the development of the internal market. Both in *De Groot* and in *X 2017*, the Court explicitly dealt with this issue.[106] It is sufficient if the state of activity takes into account the taxpayer's personal and family circumstances based on its domestic tax law. The Court's approach – that is, that a taxpayer's personal and family circumstances must be taken into account within the EU once, but only once – contributes to the establishment of the internal market.

The obligation to take into account a taxpayer's personal and family circumstances should *not* fall on only one of the states concerned in which taxable income is earned. All of the relevant states contribute to the taxpayer's ability to pay taxes; in each of those states, the taxpayer benefits from the state's infrastructure to create his wealth. The taxpayer competes in all of those states in an open market. Therefore, free competition, an efficient allocation of production factors, tax neutrality, a level playing field, international tax neutrality, CLIN, and origin-based taxation require that all relevant states take into account the taxpayer's personal and family circumstances, not just one of them. This approach also fits into the Court's pro-rata-parte approach as applied in its decision in *X 2017*

For the same reasons, each of the relevant states in which any of the non-resident taxpayer's taxable income is earned should take a part of the taxpayer's personal and family circumstances into account, if the domestic tax system does so for a resident taxpayer. If his circumstances are taken into account by means of a deduction from his taxable income, the personal allowances must be taken into account in proportion to the aggregate annual income earned in each state of origin/source. Both the numerator and the denominator of the fraction, representing how much of the total income has been created in each state of origin/source, should be calculated according to the tax

105. *X 2017*, C-283/15, para 48.
106. *De Groot*, C-385/00, paras 100–102; and *X 2017*, C-283/15, para 47.

laws of the state in which the particular part of the taxpayer's income has been earned. This issue, however, was not addressed in *X 2017*. The state in which the taxpayer's income-generating activity was actually performed is not the decisive factor; rather, the decisive factor is which state has the power to tax the income earned.[107] Only states that *can and may* tax the income of a taxpayer under their domestic tax laws respectively tax treaties can grant tax advantages connected with the non-resident taxpayer's personal and family circumstances. If a state cannot or may not tax his income, it simply cannot not take into account the taxpayer's personal and family circumstances for tax purposes.

Under the pro-rata-part system, each state of source/origin applies its own system of taking into account personal and family circumstances. Whether this is done through a personal allowance, a relief, a deduction, a tax credit, or a general lower tax rate with neither specific deductions nor tax credits, does not matter. Therefore, the principle of sovereignty is also satisfied in an optimal way.[108]

[D] Interim Conclusion

In conclusion, the author believes that the Court's case law with respect to a taxpayer's personal and family circumstances generally contributes to the establishment of the internal market. Therefore, to date, the CJEU has generally fulfilled, to a large extent, its role as a protector of the EU's internal market in the field of direct taxation, with the exception of its decision in the *Kieback* case. Unfortunately, as developed so far, the Court's case law leaves open a risk that, in cases like *Kieback*, a taxpayer's personal circumstances will not always be fully taken into account.

§1.05 TAX TREATY OVERRIDE: PRE- AND POST-LISBON

Union loyalty, as laid down in Article 4(3) TEU, requires Member States to facilitate the achievement of the Union's tasks and refrain from any measure that could jeopardize the attainment of the Union's objectives.[109] In this context, the author believes that tax treaty override must be considered inconsistent with Union loyalty.

In, for example, the *Gilly* case, the CJEU regarded the prevention of double taxation as a Community (now, in current EU law language: Union) objective: 'the *abolition of double taxation* within the Community is … included among the *objectives of the Treaty*'[110] based on Article 220 EEC Treaty (subsequently, Article 293 EC Treaty), which provided, so far as relevant here, that: 'Member States shall, so far as is

107. *X 2017*, C-283/15, para 45.
108. *Ibid.* paras 47–48.
109. This section is based, in part, on Kemmeren in Lang/Linde 2014, *supra* n. 7, at 155–158, and Eric C.C.M. Kemmeren, *Double Tax Conventions on Income and Capital and the EU: Past, Present and Future*, 21 EC Tax Rev. 157, 171–172.
110. *Gilly*, C-336/96, Judgment, EU:C:1998:221, para. 16 (emphasis added); *see Saint-Gobain NZ*, C-307/97, Judgment, EU:C:1999:438, para. 56; *De Groot*, C-385/00, paras 99–102; *Amurta*, C-379/05, Judgment, EU:C:2007:655, para. 17; and *Columbus Container Services*, C-298/05, Judgment, EU:C:2007:754, paras 27, 45, 51.

necessary, enter into negotiations with each other with a view to securing for the benefit of their nationals: ... the *abolition of double taxation* within the Community'.[111] Article 293 EC Treaty, however, was repealed as from 1 December 2009 by the Lisbon Treaty.[112]

It is not immediately clear what the impact is of that deletion.[113] However, the author believes that the repeal of Article 293 EC Treaty does not mean that the abolition of double taxation is no longer a Union goal, since double taxation is harmful to the establishment of the internal market.[114] Support for this believe can be found in the *Kerckhaert and Morres*[115] and *Columbus Container Services*[116] decisions, in which the CJEU found that: 'conventions preventing double taxation ... are designed to eliminate or mitigate the negative effects on the functioning of the internal market resulting from the coexistence of national tax systems.'[117]

From, *inter alia*, the *Gilly* case, it could be understood that Article 293 EC Treaty merely prevented direct effect.[118] Thus, it could be argued that, in the absence of a relevant tax treaty, the provision only contained an explicit restriction on the possibility of individuals directly claiming, before the national courts, the realization of one of the objectives of the EC Treaty: the abolition of double taxation. The CJEU could not disregard this restriction since it was part of the legislative system under European law at that time. It had to take into account that in the absence of a European legislative instrument or a tax treaty, Member States were not obliged to eliminate double taxation. However, it is also clear that the abolition of double taxation was, and still is, part of the objectives of European law, as evidenced by the CJEU's case law discussed above. Since the restriction on direct effect was taken away by repealing Article 293 EC Treaty, it could be strongly argued that it is consistent with both the aim of realizing an internal market and the CJEU's case law, which remains relevant in this context, that abolition of double taxation could be applied more widely under the TEU and TFEU than under either the EEC Treaty or the EC Treaty.[119]

In this context, the author asserts that tax treaty override must be considered inconsistent with Union loyalty. From the *Bouanich* case, we learned that the relevant tax treaty 'must be taken into account' in the interpretation of Union law.[120] This could

111. Art. 220 EEC Treaty (emphasis added).
112. Treaty of Lisbon amending the Treaty on European Union and the Treaty establishing the European Community, Brussels, 13 Dec. 2007, (OR. fr) CIG 14/07 (Treaty of Lisbon), OJ 17 Dec. 2007, 2007/C 360/1.
113. *See, e.g.*, Terra & Wattel, *supra* n. 12, at 20–22; and AG Wattel, 25 Apr. 2013, no. 12/04717, *BNB* 2014/66, pt. 7.6.
114. Eric C.C.M. Kemmeren, *After Repeal of Art. 293 EC Treaty under the Lisbon Treaty: the EU Objective of Eliminating Double Taxation Can Be Applied More Widely*, 17 EC Tax Rev. 156–158, *see also* Terra & Wattel, *supra* n. 13, at 20–22.
115. *Kerckhaert and Morres*, C-513/04, Judgment, EU:C:2006:713.
116. *Columbus Container Services*, C-298/05.
117. *Kerckhaert and Morres*, C-513/04, para. 21; *Columbus Container Services*, C-298/05, para. 44; *see also* Kemmeren Dissertation, *supra* n. 7, at 117–131.
118. *Gilly*, C-336/96, para. 16.
119. Compare L. Hinnekens, *The Uneasy and Fate of Article 293 Second Indent EC*, 37 Intertax 602 (2009), and AG Wattel, 9 Jan. 2013, no. 12/02502, *BNB* 2014/65, point 8.5.
120. *See Bouanich*, C-265/04, Judgment, EU:C:2006:51, para. 51.

only be done adequately if the Member State concerned was obliged to apply the tax treaty (i.e., to fulfil its obligations under the relevant tax treaty). Thus, any non-application of a tax treaty should be regarded as inconsistent with the fundamental freedoms, including the free movement of capital. The fulfilment of tax treaty obligations by Member States, with the result that double taxation would be removed, or at least mitigated, would benefit the functioning of the internal market. It would also contribute to creating a more level playing field among the Member States and to satisfying the ability-to-pay principle to a greater extent.[121] However, it is also clear that not accepting tax treaty override is not an issue that is causally connected with the benchmark in all respects. Therefore, whether not accepting tax treaty override contributes to the application of EU law, in the context of tax treaties based on the benchmark, depends on the facts and circumstances of the case at hand.

Due to Article 293 EC Treaty, the author believes that the CJEU had to pass up an opportunity to contribute to the establishment of the internal market in its *Damseaux*[122] and *Levy-Sebbag*[123] decisions, because the Court refused to alleviate international, juridical double taxation in those two cases.[124] In the *Damseaux* case, a dividend withholding tax was levied by France on a dividend distributed by Total to Mr. Damseaux, a resident of Belgium. Belgium did not allow to credit the French dividend withholding tax as a consequence of changed Belgian domestic legislation after that the French-Belgian tax treaty was concluded. It could be disputed whether this was a case of tax treaty override. In any case, the result of the application of the tax treaty in *Damseaux* case was international juridical double taxation. In its prior *Kerckhaert and Morres* and *Columbus Container Services* judgments, the Court itself ruled that tax treaties were put in place to prevent double taxation and that double taxation had negative effects on the functioning of the internal market.[125] From the perspective of protecting the fundamental freedoms, the Court should have alleviated the international, juridical double taxation suffered by Mr. Damseaux based on his exercise of the fundamental freedoms, but the Court was constrained by Article 293 EC Treaty. Without that constraint, the Court could have easily linked its reasoning up with international tax practice. In other cases, it had done exactly that, often referring to OECD practices.[126] It had even accepted, referring to OECD practices, tax-treaty allocation rules based on nationality without the need to justify them,[127] whereas, normally, a distinction made on the basis of nationality constitutes a direct discrimination that needs to be justified by a rule of reason.

121. For a more extensive discussion, see Kemmeren, *Non-Application of DTCs: Inconsistent with Community and EEA Loyalty, in The EU and Third Countries: Direct Taxation* 57 (vol. 17, EUCOTAX Ser. Eur. Tax'n, Michael Lang & Pasquale Pistone eds., 2007).
122. *Damseaux*, C-128/08, Judgment, EU:C:2009:471.
123. *Levy-Sebbag*, C-540/10, Judgment, EU:C:2011:145.
124. *See* Carla de Pietro, *Tax Treaty Override* 191-207 (vol. 40, EUCOTAX Ser. Eur. Tax'n, 2014).
125. *Kerckhaert and Morres*, C-513/04, para. 21; and *Columbus Container Services*, C-298/05, para. 44.
126. *Gilly*, C-336/96; *Test Claimants in the Thin Cap Group Litigation*, C-524/04, Judgment, EU:C:2007:161 [hereinafter, '*Thin Cap GL*']; and *SGI*, C-311/08, Judgment, EU:C:2010:26.
127. *Gilly*, C-336/96.

In the *Damseaux* case, typical international tax practice would have led to an ordinary tax credit provided by Belgium, which practice is found in Article 23A(2) and Article 23B OECD Model. Furthermore, requiring such an ordinary tax credit based on EU law, whether or not the case was a case of treaty override, would have been far more consistent with the Court's case law, which had recognized that the avoidance of double taxation is a Union aim, that income may be taxed in the state where the income has been created,[128] that tax treaties have been designed to eliminate or mitigate double taxation, and that the typical OECD practice is relevant as a standard for EU law purposes. However, it could not do so. In the *Damseaux* case, it did not give priority to the state of source.[129] Rather, it ruled:

> 33 ... that Community law, *in its current state* and in a situation such as that at issue in the main proceedings, does *not* lay down any *general criteria for the attribution* of areas of competence between the Member States in relation to the elimination of double taxation within the Community.
>
> 34. ... the fact that both the Member State in which the dividends are paid and the Member State in which the shareholder resides are liable to tax those dividends does *not* mean that *the Member State of residence* is obliged, *under Community law*, to prevent the disadvantages which could arise from the exercise of competence thus attributed by the two Member States.[130]

The conclusion seems to be that, in the pre-Lisbon era, the result of the *Damseaux* and *Levy-Sebbag* cases was that, to a large extent, the Union aim of preventing international juridical double taxation was an empty shell. In an earlier, 2015 *X* case,[131] the Dutch Supreme Court also (implicitly) raised the issue of tax treaty override.[132] However, the CJEU did not address the issue at all. It should be noted that the 2015 *X* case was also a pre-Lisbon case. Therefore, if the Court would have addressed the question, the answer would have been, without doubt, in line with its *Damseaux* and *Levy-Sebbag* decisions.

It is clear that the *Damseaux* and *Levy-Sebbag* rulings are inconsistent with the benchmark of establishing an internal market. They do not advance a level playing field, international tax neutrality, CLIN, the ability-to-pay principle, or an origin-based allocation of tax jurisdiction.

In the post-Lisbon era, the author believes that the CJEU has a great opportunity to adapt its case law on tax treaty override to the new legal framework under the Lisbon Treaty. As from 1 December 2009, it is no longer constrained by a provision similar to Article 293 EC Treaty. Based on Union loyalty (Article 4(3) TEU) in conjunction with the fundamental freedoms, the Court can now be a better protector of the establishment of the internal market than it could prior to 1 December 2009.

In conclusion, tax treaty override must be considered inconsistent with Union loyalty in conjunction with the fundamental freedoms. Non-application of a tax treaty

128. *Thin Cap GL*, C-524/04, paras 88–89.
129. *Damseaux*, C-128/08, para. 32.
130. *Ibid.* paras 33–34 (emphasis added, citations omitted).
131. *Miljoen*, Joined Cases C-10/14, C-14/14 & C-17/14.
132. *See* HR 20 Dec. 2013, no. 12/04717 (*X*), published in, *inter alia*, BNB 2014/66, para. 4.1.3 (prelim. question 3).

is inconsistent with the functioning of the internal market. Whether not accepting tax treaty override contributes to the application of tax treaties based on the benchmark depends on the facts and circumstances of the case at hand. Whereas, the CJEU was constrained from removing tax treaty override by Article 293 EC Treaty, such a constraint does no longer exist as from 1 December 2009. Therefore, now, the Court is in a better position to play its role as a protector of the internal market. In the context of tax treaty override, it had not yet reached primary law limits.

§1.06 EXIT/FINAL SETTLEMENT TAXES: FROM *DE LASTEYRIE* TO *COMMISSION V PORTUGAL 2016*

[A] Introduction

The third and final main issue to be discussed is exit/final settlement taxes.[133] In this field as well, the Court has developed a substantial body of case law.[134] It started with *De Lasteyrie*,[135] which addressed an exit tax levied on an individual who was a substantial shareholder who migrated from France to Belgium and the latest one, *Commission v Portugal 2016*,[136] which dealt with an exit tax on individuals who migrated from Portugal to another Member State after a share-for-share merger and a final settlement tax on a transfer in return for shares of an enterprise of a sole proprietor to a company resident in another Member State of the EU or EEA than Portugal. The context of this chapter does not allow the author to address all possible issues in respect of exit/final settlement taxes; he must limit the discussion to the most important main issues. Furthermore, as the focus of this chapter is on the role of the CJEU, the author will also not discuss the recently adopted Article 5 of the Anti-Tax Avoidance Directive, which includes a minimal rule on exit taxation.[137]

133. This section is based, in part, on: Eric C.C.M. Kemmeren, *Pending Cases Filed by Dutch Courts I: The Van Dijk and Bujura Cases, in ECJ Recent Developments in Direct Taxation* 219 (vol. 16, EUCOTAX Ser. Eur. Tax'n, Michael Lang, Josef Schuch, & Claus Staringer eds., Kluwer Law International, 2006); Eric C.C.M. Kemmeren, *The Netherlands: Pending Cases Filed by the Netherlands Courts: The National Grid Indus (C-371/10) and Feyenoord (C-498/10 (X)) Cases, in ECJ-Recent Developments in Direct Taxation 2010* 157–176 (vol. 67, Ser. Int'l Tax L., Michael Lang, et al. eds., 2011) [hereinafter, 'Kemmeren in Lang/Linde 2010']; and Eric C.C.M. Kemmeren, *The Netherlands: Infringement Procedure on Exit Taxes on Business (C-301/11), in ECJ-Recent Developments in Direct Taxation 2012* 83 (vol. 77, Ser. Int'l Tax Law, Michael Lang et al. eds., 2013) [hereinafter, 'Kemmeren in Lang/Linde 2012').

134. *E.g., De Lasteyrie*, C-9/02; *N*, C-470/04; *National Grid Indus*, C-371/10; *Commission* v *Spain*, C-269/09; *Commission* v *Portugal 2012*, C-38/10; *DI. VI.*, C-380/11; *Commission* v *Netherlands*, C-301/11; *Commission* v *Spain*, C-64/11; *Commission* v *Denmark*, C-261/11; *DMC*, C-164/12; *Verder LabTec*, C-657/13; and *Commission* v *Portugal 2016*, C-503/14.

135. *De Lasteyrie*, C-9/02.

136. *Commission* v *Portugal 2016*, C-503/14. At the time of finalizing this chapter, it was the latest case on exit/final settlement taxes, but it should not come as a surprise if new cases are added to the already-long list of cases.

137. *See* Art. 5, Council Directive (EU) 2016/1164 of 12 July 2016 Laying Down Rules Against Tax Avoidance Practices that Directly Affect the Functioning of the Internal Market (OJ L 193, 19/07/2016 1–14).

The term 'exit tax' is often used as a synonym for 'final settlement taxes'. If a distinction can be made, exit taxes seem to be more related to emigration of persons and final settlement taxes seem to be more related to a transfer of assets of persons. What they have in common is that unrealized capital gains are taxed at the moment of emigration of the person involved or of a transfer of the asset concerned, although in neither case is a capital gain actually realized. Therefore, in this chapter, both taxes are discussed together and the terms are used interchangeably.

[B] The *De Lasteyrie* and *N* Cases: Wide Application of the Internal Market Concept

In both *De Lasteyrie* and *N*, the exit taxes concerned were imposed on substantial shareholders who transferred their residence outside their initial state of residence, France and the Netherlands, respectively. Both were granted only a non-automatic and conditional deferral of payment. Under the Dutch system, a decrease in value was not taken into account. These regimes were not found to be consistent with EU law, more precisely with the freedom of establishment. If the taxpayers concerned would have moved within their state of residence within France or the Netherlands, respectively), they would have only been taxed on increases in value only when, and to the extent that, they were actually realized. The French system required immediate payment of the tax due if, *inter alia*, no guarantee was set up and no agent was nominated. Furthermore, the taxpayer was required to make a declaration. The CJEU explicitly decided that 'guarantees *in themselves* constitute a restrictive effect, in that they deprive the taxpayer of the enjoyment of the assets given as a guarantee' (emphasis added).[138] As held by the Court in the *N* case:

> the Community legislature has already taken harmonisation measures, *which essentially pursue the same goal*. In particular, Council Directive 77/799/EEC ... allows a Member State to request from the competent authorities of another Member State all the information enabling it to ascertain the correct amount of income tax.
>
> Moreover, Council Directive 76/308/EEC ... provides that a Member State may request the assistance of another Member State in the recovery of debts relating to certain taxes, including those on income and capital (emphasis added).[139]

Therefore, the condition for a deferral (i.e., requiring a guarantee) was decided not to be proportional.

This was also decided with respect to the rule that Dutch exit tax system did not take into account decreases in value after emigration:

> Finally, in order to be regarded in this context as proportionate to the objective pursued, such a system for recovering tax on the income from securities would have to take *full account of reductions in value* capable of arising *after the transfer*

138. *De Lasteyrie*, C-9/02, para. 47.
139. *N*, C-470/04, paras 52–53.

> *of residence* by the taxpayer concerned, *unless such reductions* have already been taken into account *in the host Member State* (emphasis added).[140]

In both rulings, the Court takes on its role as protector of the internal market in direct tax matters. Its decisions contribute to creating a level playing field between shareholders and satisfying the ability-to-pay principle, because emigrants are treated (more) like resident substantial shareholders, who are not taxed at all when they move their residence within the relevant countries. The decisions do not really contribute to international tax neutrality and CLIN or establishing an origin-based allocation of tax jurisdiction, but the Court is not accountable for this. Exit taxes are the result of a residence-based tax system. The Court has to live, at least to a large extent, with this policy choice by the Member States' legislatures. Given that starting point, the Court reduced the impact of the residence principle in these decisions and, therefore, they should be welcomed. They really contribute to the establishment of the internal market and, therefore, satisfy the benchmark to a large extent.

[C] The *National Grid Indus* Case: Ambivalent Application of the Internal Market Concept

However, in respect of exit taxes, the Court became in general more reluctant over the last years in creating a level playing field and satisfying the ability-to-pay principle. The first example thereof is the *National Grid Indus* case.[141] A corporation established under Dutch business law, National Grid Indus BV (the BV), moved its place of effective management to the United Kingdom. The Netherlands applied the incorporation system under business law, so the BV did not cease to exist, but continued its life in the United Kingdom. As a consequence, the Court decided that BV could invoke the freedom of establishment.[142] Under Dutch domestic corporate tax law, the BV continued to be a resident taxpayer, because it was still a corporation under Dutch business law. However, because of the fact that its place of effective management was transferred to the United Kingdom, the BV was a dual resident for tax treaty purposes and because of the treaty's tiebreaker rule, the BV was determined to be only a resident of the United Kingdom for tax treaty purposes. As a result, the Netherlands was no longer entitled to tax the BV, since no permanent establishment remained in the Netherlands. As a consequence, the Dutch exit tax for corporations was applied. In respect of the unrealized profits, an exit tax was levied. The only asset of the BV was a group loan receivable denominated in pounds sterling. In substance, the exit tax was only levied on a currency result triggered by a rise in value of the pound sterling against the Dutch guilder. A tax assessment, including an amount of interest on the overdue

140. *Ibid.* para. 54.
141. *National Grid Indus*, C-371/10.
142. For an extensive discussion of access to the freedom of establishment, see Frank P.G. Pötgens, et al., *The Compatibility of Exit Tax Legislation Applicable to Corporate Taxpayers in France, Germany, Italy, The Netherlands, Portugal, Spain and The United Kingdom with the EU Freedom of Establishment-Parts1-3*, 44 Intertax 40-62, 163-179, 247-265; and Terra & Wattel, *supra* n. 13, at 962-965.

exit tax that was not recovery interest[143] was handed down. The Dutch tax system did not provide for a deferral of payment for either the exit tax or the interest on the overdue tax. It did not take into account a decrease in value after emigration, either. The Court decided that the Dutch exit tax on business was inconsistent with the freedom of establishment.

[1] Option to Defer Payment Until Realization

The *National Grid Indus* decision includes at least two sticks and two carrots. Let us start with the first carrot. The Court decided that the taxpayer must be given the option of either paying the exit tax and the interest on overdue tax immediately or deferring the payment of both until realization of the accrued value:

> 68 … it must be stated that *recovery of the tax debt* at the time of the *actual realisation* in the host Member State of the asset in respect of which a capital gain was established by the authorities of the Member State of origin on the occasion of the transfer of a company's place of effective management to the host Member State *may avoid the cash-flow problems* which could be produced by the immediate recovery of the tax due on unrealised capital gains.
>
> …
>
> 71 It thus cannot be ruled out that the administrative burden that would be entailed by the annual return suggested by the Commission, which would necessarily relate to every asset in respect of which a capital gain was established at the time of the transfer of the place of effective management of the company concerned, would give rise as such, *for that company*, to a hindrance to freedom of establishment that would not necessarily be any less harmful to that freedom than the immediate recovery of the tax debt corresponding to the capital gain.
>
> …
>
> 73 In those circumstances, national legislation *offering a company* transferring its place of effective management to another Member State *the choice* between, first, immediate payment of the amount of tax, which creates a disadvantage for that company in terms of cash flow but frees it from subsequent administrative burdens, and, secondly, *deferred payment* of the amount of tax, possibly together with interest in accordance with the applicable national legislation, which necessarily involves an administrative burden for the company in connection with tracing the transferred assets, would constitute a measure which, while being appropriate for ensuring the balanced allocation of powers of taxation between the Member States, would be less harmful to freedom of establishment than the measure at issue in the main proceedings. If a company were to consider that the administrative burden in connection with deferred recovery was excessive, it could opt for immediate payment of the tax (emphasis added).[144]

143. At this time, the author will refrain from discussing that the *National Grid Indus* case and subsequent case law (e.g., *DMC*, C-164/12, para. 61), do not allow the tax authority to charge recovery interest in the context of a deferral of payment of the exit tax and the interest on the overdue exit tax. For a more detailed discussion, see Kemmeren in Lang/Linde 2012, *supra* n. 133, at 206–210; and Pötgens, *supra* n. 142, Part 2, para. 6.3.3.
144. *National Grid Indus*, C-371/10, paras 68, 71, 73. *See also Commission* v *Portugal 2012*, C-38/10, paras 31–34; and *Commission* v *Portugal 2016*, C-503/14, paras 58–59, 87–88, 90.

Also in this context, the Court takes up its role as protector of the internal market. Its decision contributes to creating a level playing field and satisfying the ability-to-pay principle, because taxpayers are offered the opportunity to pay taxes upon realization of the capital gains similar to what is the system for resident taxpayers. As a result of the option, they can pay taxes at the same moment as their domestic competitors. The option contributes to the establishment of the internal market and therefore satisfies partly the benchmark.

[2] Permitting the Condition of a Bank Guarantee

However, the Court also introduced two sticks, which are a deviation from its decisions in the *De Lasteyrie* and *N* cases. The first stick is that it permitted a bank guarantee, where such a condition was explicitly found to be inconsistent with EU law in the *De Lasteyrie* case. It is remarkable that the Court did not even addressed that case in the *National Grid Indus* case. It held that the condition of a bank guarantee was permitted because 'account should ... be taken of the risk of non-recovery of the tax, which increases with the passage of time.'[145]

The Court did not take into account, as it did in the *De Lasteyrie* case, that the Union legislature had already taken harmonization measures, which essentially pursued the same goal: Council Directive 77/799/EEC (now 2011/16/EU) and Council Directive 76/308/EEC (now 2010/24/EU). The latter provides specifically for assistance in the recovery of debts relating to income taxes. As acknowledged in the *De Lasteyrie* case, a bank guarantee requirement, in itself, constitutes a restrictive effect, in that it deprives the taxpayer of the enjoyment of the assets given as the guarantee. This is not different for entities. Such an effect will not arise if Member States are not allowed to reduce the risk of non-recovery of the tax by including, in their national legislation applicable to deferred payments of tax debts, measures such as the provision of a bank guarantee, but to instead demand that they cooperate with each other, based on the directives mentioned that pursue the same goals as the Court has itself recognized. Therefore, its case law is not consistent.[146] In the *National Grid Indus* case, by permitting a bank guarantee, the Court has stepped back from its role as protector of the establishment of the internal market without good reason. Permitting a bank guarantee does not contribute to creating a level playing field or to satisfying the ability-to-pay principle, because emigrating taxpayers face additional expenses that resident taxpayers who only move within their state of residence do not face. Therefore, domestic competitors have an advantage over their competitors who make use of their freedom of establishment. According to the author, the only conclusion that can be drawn is that permitting a bank guarantee as part of an exit tax system does not contribute to establishing the internal market and therefore does not satisfy the benchmark at all.

145. *National Grid Indus*, C-371/10, para. 74.
146. *See* Terra & Wattel, *supra* n. 13, at 966, 970.

[3] Not Taking into Account Currency Rate Losses After Emigration in State of Departure

The same is true for the second stick, although this one is, according to the author, really of minor importance compared to the first one. Contrary to what was decided in the *N* case, the Court decided, in *National Grid Indus*, that the state of departure was not obliged to take into account the decreases in value after the emigration of the company.[147] The Court makes a distinction between emigrating private individuals holding a substantial interest in a company and emigrating companies.[148] In the case of emigrating private individuals, an exit tax is disproportionate if the state of departure does not take into account decreases in the value of the substantial interest after emigration, unless the new state of residence takes them into account. An exit tax on companies is, according to the Court, not disproportionate if the state of departure does not do so, irrespective of whether the new state of residence takes any decrease into account. At least, that is the result in the *National Grid Indus* case. The loan receivable was denominated in pounds sterling. In the UK, it is likely that the company had to report in pounds sterling and not in Dutch guilders.[149] If that was the case, any decrease in value because of the exchange rate risk could not be taken into account the United Kingdom, simply because it would never arise there. Other decreases in value (e.g., because of the fact that the full principal amount would not be repaid) could be reflected in the United Kingdom. The Court acknowledged these consequences as well,[150] but, according to the author, its decision missed the effect in respect of the exchange rate risk as consequence of the emigration. In respect of this risk, the BV was in the same position as a private individual shareholder, for whom the decrease in value would not be taken into account in the new state of residence. Therefore, the author believes that in respect of the potential decrease in value of the pound sterling against the Dutch guilder, the decision made in the *N* case should have been equally applied in the *National Grid Indus* case: the Netherlands should have been obligated to 'take full account of reductions in value capable of arising after the transfer of residence by the taxpayer concerned, unless such reductions have already been taken into account in the host Member State.'[151]

Then, too, the case of a subsequent emigration out of the United Kingdom to another EU/EEA Member State would be covered. To the extent that the new host state took the decrease in value of the pound sterling against the Dutch guilder into account, the Netherlands would be relieved of its obligation. In such a case, no double dip could arise, as the Court assumed. The Court could have even extended the exclusion to any state, including a third country. The Court's case law would, then, not only be consistent, but also coherent. That approach would also better fit the Court's role as a protector of the internal market. It would contribute to creating a level playing field and

147. *National Grid Indus*, C-371/10, paras 54–64.
148. *See, e.g.*, Pötgens, *supra* n. 142, Part 2, para. 6.3.1.
149. If the company could report in the United Kingdom in Dutch guilders as functional currency, the currency rate result could be reflected in the UK.
150. *See National Grid Indus*, C-371/10, para. 55.
151. *N*, C-470/04, para. 54.

satisfying the ability-to-pay principle, because emigrating companies would be treated (more) like resident companies who would only be taxed on realized currency results and who could never benefit from a double dip when they move their residence within the country concerned. However, even this approach would not really contribute to international tax neutrality or CLIN or establishing an origin-based allocation of tax jurisdiction, but as held before, the Court is not accountable for this, because exit taxes are the result of a residence-based tax system.

The Court attempted to justify the different treatment of private individuals and companies as follows:

> 57 The *assets* of a company are assigned directly to economic activities that are intended to *produce a profit*. Moreover, the extent of a company's taxable profits is partly *influenced by the valuation of its assets* in the balance sheet, in so far as depreciation reduces the basis of taxation.
>
> 58 Since, in a situation such as that at issue in the main proceedings, the profits of a company which transfers its place of effective management are, after the transfer, taxed exclusively in the host Member State, *in accordance with the principle of fiscal territoriality linked to a temporal component, it is also for that Member State*, in view of the above-mentioned connection between a company's assets and its taxable profits, and hence for reasons relating to the symmetry between the right to *tax* profits and the possibility of deducting losses, *to take account in its tax system* of *fluctuations in the value* of the assets of that company *which occur after the date* on which the Member State of origin loses all fiscal connection with the company.
>
> 59 In those circumstances, *the Member State of origin*, contrary to the Commission's submissions, *is not obliged to take account of any exchange rate losses that may occur after the transfer by National Grid Indus of its place of effective management to the United Kingdom* until the satisfaction or assignment of the claim held by that company. The tax due on the unrealised capital gains is determined at the time when the Member State of origin's power to tax the company ceases to exist, in the present case at the time of the transfer of the company's place of management. The taking into account by the Member State of origin either of an exchange rate gain or of an exchange rate loss occurring after the transfer of the place of effective management could not only call into question the balanced allocation of powers of taxation between the Member States but also lead to double taxation or *double deduction of losses*. That would in particular be the case if a company possessing a claim such as that at issue in the main proceedings, expressed in sterling, transferred its place of management from a Member State whose currency is the euro to another Member State in the euro zone.[152]

The residence-based compartmentalization for taxing a company's profits, as expressed by the Court in paragraphs 57 and 58, satisfies the benchmark to a certain extent. The Court's arguments are also, to a large extent, in line with the OECD's current BEPS approach: taxing profits where the value is added.[153] As held, though, in respect of exchange rate losses, the Court missed the train.

152. *National Grid Indus*, C-371/10, paras 57–59 (emphasis added).
153. *See* OECD, *BEPS Project Explanatory Statement*, *supra* n. 25, at 4.

[4] Obligation to Provide a Step-Up in Basis by the Host State

On the other hand, the author believes that the *National Grid Indus* Court also provided a second, essential carrot in the context of an exit/final settlement tax: the host state – in this case, the new state of residence, the United Kingdom – must give a step-up in basis in respect of the assets and liabilities over which it gets tax jurisdiction after immigration of the company into the United Kingdom.[154] This obligation follows from the freedom of establishment, more specifically, from the 'principle of fiscal territoriality linked to a temporal component'. In this way, potential double taxation is avoided when the domestic tax laws of the host state do not provide for such a step-up. The author believes that the Court has formulated, in paragraph 58, an obligation for the host state, rather than an option: 'it *is* also for that Member State … *to take account* in its tax system of *fluctuations in the value* of the assets of that company *which occur after the date* on which the Member State of origin loses all fiscal connection with the company'.[155]

The obligation to a step-up contributes to creating a level playing field and international tax neutrality, and satisfying the ability-to-pay principle, because it avoids double taxation. Competitors that do not transfer their place of effective management do not face double taxation, either. Therefore, the introduction of this obligation matches with the Court's role as protector of the internal market.

[D] *Commission v Denmark, DMC, Verder LabTec, and Commission v Portugal 2016*: More Ambivalent Application of the Internal Market Concept

[1] Deferral of Payment Until Realization Is Required No Longer Required

In these cases, the most important issue is that Court restricts the option granted to taxpayers in the Nation Grid Indus case to choose for direct payment of the exit tax and overdue interest on the exit tax or to defer the payment of both until actual realization of the capital gains. The latter option brought the position of an emigrating company close to the position of a competitor who did not emigrate. They paid the (corporate) income tax at the same time: upon realization of the capital gains. This Court took its role as protector of the internal market. Its decision contributed to creating a level playing field and international tax neutrality, and satisfying the ability-to-pay principle. The option to pay the amounts due upon realization contributed to the establishment of the internal market and satisfied the benchmark to a large extent.

154. *Compare, e.g.*, Terra & Wattel, *supra* n. 13, at 966, 970; and Pötgens, *supra* n. 142, Part 2, para. 6.2. Both read the step-up in basis as a recommendation to host Member States, not as an obligation.
155. *National Grid Indus*, C-371/10, para. 58 (emphasis added); *compare also Commission* v *Portugal 2016*, C-503/14, para. 57.

However, in *Commission v Denmark*,[156] *DMC*,[157] *Verder LabTec*,[158] and *Commission v Portugal 2016*[159] the Court permits Member States to collect taxes on accrued value of transferred assets not only upon actual realization of the capital gains, but also already before actual realization. The first signal was given by the Court in its decision in *Commission v Denmark*.[160] The Court did not specify a term, but it held that a system of payment later than upon transfer of the assets concerned but before realization of the capital gains is in any case restricting the freedom of establishment less than a system of direct payment upon transfer of the assets:

> 37 *En effet, les États membres étant en droit d'imposer les plus-values qui ont été générées alors que les actifs en cause se trouvaient sur leur territoire ont le pouvoir de prévoir, pour cette imposition, un fait générateur autre que la cession effective, afin de garantir l'imposition des actifs qui ne sont pas destinés à être cédés, et moins attentatoire à la liberté d'établissement que le prélèvement au moment du transfert.*[161]

The Court did not explain its reasoning for this restriction of the scope of the option provided to taxpayers in its *National Grid Indus* decision.

This generally worded restriction was fleshed out in the subsequent *DMC* and *Verder LabTec* cases. In the *Verder LabTec* case, the Court permitted a system of paying in ten annual instalments.[162] This decision did not come as a surprise, because in its *DMC* decision, it already permitted a more restrictive system: a system of paying in five annual instalments.[163] In the *DMC* case, the Court accepted this system with the following motivation:

> 62 In the light of the fact that *the risk of non-recovery* increases with the passing of time, the ability to spread payment of the tax owing before the capital gains are actually realised over a *period of five years* constitutes a satisfactory and *proportionate* measure for the attainment of the objective of preserving the balanced allocation of the power to impose taxes between Member States.[164]

In *Commission v Portugal 2016*, the Court seems to return to the more general wording of its *Commission v Denmark* decision:

> 59 In that regard, the Court has found that national legislation offering a company which transfers its place of effective management to another Member State the choice between, first, immediate payment of the tax and, second, *deferred payment* of that tax, possibly together with interest *in accordance with the applicable national legislation*, would constitute a measure less harmful to freedom of establishment than the immediate recovery of that tax.

156. *Commission* v *Denmark*, C-261/11.
157. *DMC*, C-164/12.
158. *Verder LabTec*, C-657/13.
159. *Commission* v *Portugal 2016*, C-503/14.
160. *Commission* v *Denmark*, C-261/11, paras 36–37.
161. *Ibid.* para 37.
162. *Verder LabTec*, C-657/13, paras 48–52.
163. *DMC*, C-164/12, paras 59–64.
164. *Ibid.* para. 59 (emphasis added); *see Verder LabTec*, C-657/13, paras 50–52.

Is the term of five years as mentioned in the *DMC* case not a minimum term? Is any term of deferred payment included in national legislation proportional as long as it does not come close to immediate payment?[165] In any case, the decision in *Commission v Portugal 2016* does not indicate that the Court is willing to depart from its *Commission v Denmark*, *DMC* and *Verder LabTec* decisions and to return to its *National Grid Indus* decision in respect of the deferral of payment (i.e., deferral of payment until realization).

The risk of non-recovery was also the basis for permitting a bank guarantee in the *National Grid Indus* and *Commission v Portugal 2016* cases. However, in respect of the recovery of taxes, the Court had already found, in the *De Lasteyrie* case, that the Union legislature had already taken harmonization measures that, essentially, pursue the same goal as a bank guarantee through Council Directive 77/799/EEC (now 2011/16/EU) and Council Directive 76/308/EEC (now 2010/24/EU). The latter specifically provides for assistance in the recovery of debts relating to income taxes. As in respect of permitting a bank guarantee in *National Grid Indus* and *Commission v Portugal 2016*, the Court did not take into account its *De Lasteyrie* decision in either its *DMC* or *Verder LabTec* decisions when restricting the scope of the deferral of payment from the moment of actual realization of the capital gain to a system of five (or more) annual instalments. As held by the Court in *De Lasteyrie*, the goal of the directives is ensure that taxes due are paid. Therefore, the EU developed specific mechanisms to reduce the risk that taxes are not paid. Consequently, the author believes that it cannot really be justified that, next to this specific EU law, it is necessary for the Court to accept more restrictive mechanisms than those directives.[166] Therefore, the author believes that Court did not take up its role of protector of the establishment of the internal market. Its decisions did not contribute to creating a level playing field and international tax neutrality, or satisfying the ability-to-pay principle. Domestic competitors have an advantage over their competitors who make use of their freedom of establishment. They pay tax later than the ones who make use of the freedom. Therefore, similar to permitting a bank guarantee in the context of exit taxes, permitting a system of paying an exit tax and overdue interest on exit taxes over ten, five or, perhaps, even fewer annual instalments does not contribute to the establishment of the internal market and does not satisfy the benchmark.

[2] Zigzag Course with Respect to a Bank Guarantee Requirement

In the *DMC* case, the Court restricted its *National Grid Indus* decision to permit a bank guarantee. As consequence, it reversed, to a certain extent, its wrong track and came

165. *Compare also, e.g.*, Reinout Kok, *Exit Taxes for Companies in the European Union after National Grid Indus*, 21 EC Tax Rev. 203; and Olga Sendetska, *ECJ Case Law on Corporate Exit Taxation: From National Grid Indus to DMC: What Is the Current State of Law?*, 23 EC Tax Rev. 230–237.
166. For another opinion, see Terra & Wattel, *supra* n. 13, at 965–966, 970–971 (they believe it is very difficult, if not impossible, to trace the (remainders of the) relevant latencies that existed upon emigration or to establish when realization arises). However, the author believes that these issues are not really problems if residence-based compartmentalization, as developed by the author, is applied. Kemmeren in Lang/Linde 2010, *supra* n. 133, at 171–174.

closer again to its decisions in the *De Lasteyrie* and *N* cases.[167] Unlike the *National Grid Indus* case, the *DMC* decision explicitly referred to both decisions.[168] However, the author regrets that the Court did not completely return to its decision in those cases, because not allowing a bank guarantee in the context of exit tax cases contributes to the establishment of the internal market. The risk of non-recovery of the exit taxes (and any interest on overdue exit taxes) is sufficiently covered by Council Directives 2011/16/EU and 2010/24/EU. Nevertheless, by reversing, to a certain extent, its *National Grid Indus* decision, the author welcomes this part of the *DMC* decision. He hoped that that the Court would take the final step, by returning completely to its decisions on bank guarantees in the *De Lasteyrie* and *N* cases. However, as we learn from the *Commission v Portugal 2016* decision, the Court did unfortunately the opposite.

Whereas in the *National Grid Indus* case, the Court unconditionally permitted a bank guarantee as part of an exit tax system, in the *DMC* case, it set a condition. Unlike the *National Grid Indus* case, it now explained why requesting a guarantee may be appropriate in the context of exit taxes. It started by acknowledging, again, that guarantees in themselves constitute a restrictive effect. Then it continued as follows:

> 67 Therefore, such a requirement cannot, as a matter of principle, be imposed without *prior assessment of the risk of non-recovery.*
>
> 68 In particular, in the main proceedings, it is necessary to assess that risk, *inter alia,* in the light of the fact that, first, the unrealised gains, which are subject to the contested tax, *relate solely to one form of assets,* namely shares held by only two companies *with their registered office in Austria* and, second, that those shares are held in a capital company *with its registered office in Germany.*
>
> 69 Consequently, the answer to the second question is that the national legislation of a Member State which provides for the immediate taxation of unrealised capital gains generated in its territory does not go beyond what is necessary to attain the objective of the preservation of the balanced allocation of the power to impose taxes between Member States, provided that, where the taxable person elects for deferred payment, the requirement to provide a *bank guarantee* is imposed on the basis of the *actual risk* of non-recovery of the tax.[169]

The conclusion to be drawn from *DMC* had seemed to be that the Court *only* permitted the provision of a (bank) guarantee if an *actual risk* of non-recovery of the exit tax (and interest on overdue exit tax) existed.[170] However, the Court did not explain, at least not explicitly, whether or to what extent Council Directives 2011/16/EU and 2010/24/EU are insufficient to remove an actual risk of non-recovery. It only referred, as examples, to the facts of the case at hand: one form of asset held by certain persons (i.e., shares held by two Austrian companies). Further, it found that the shares were held in a company with its registered office in Germany, which was also the state that levied the final settlement tax. Furthermore, if we assume that the Court found the Directives to be insufficient means of ensuring recovery of the taxes, the

167. *See, e.g.*, Pötgens, *supra* n. 142, Part 2, para. 6.3.2.
168. *DMC*, C-164/12, para. 66.
169. *Ibid.* paras 67–69 (emphasis added).
170. *See, e.g.*, Pötgens, *supra* n. 142, Part 2, para. 6.3.2.

author believes that Court should have explained why that was the case. The Member States have agreed on the Directives in the context of establishing the internal market. In this context, they have agreed to assist each other to recover direct taxes. Union loyalty requires that the Member States cooperate with each other in order to recover taxes.[171] Non-recovery of direct taxes jeopardizes the level playing field, since if taxes due are not recovered from one part of the competitors on a market, they will have an advantage that tax-paying competitors do not have. Consequently, the non-paying competitors can offer their products at a lower price than the tax-paying competitors. Such a situation is adverse to the establishment of the internal market.

By bypassing Council Directives 2011/16/EU and 2010/24/EU, by permitting a bank guarantee that is more restrictive than the Directives, one could believe that the Court was acting more like a supplementary legislature to the Council by restricting the development of the internal market more than the European legislature does, than as a judge who should protect the establishment of the internal market.

On the other hand, the *DMC* decision also offers a path for the Court to completely return to its earlier decisions in *De Lasteyrie* and *N*. In *Commission v Portugal 2016*, it did not argue that, in respect of assessing whether there is an actual risk of non-recovery of the exit tax (and interest on overdue exit tax), a national court must also take into account both Directives. On the contrary, in the context of the deferred payment, the Court accepted a bank guarantee without any condition. With respect to such a bank guarantee, the Court only referred to its *National Grid Indus* decision; it did not refer at all to its *De Lasteyrie*, *N*, or *DMC* decisions. As a consequence, the Court did not explain why those decisions were not relevant in *Commission v Portugal 2016*:

> 59 ... Moreover, the Court held that it is *permissible for the Member State* to take account of the risk of non-recovery of the tax, which increases with the passage of time, in *its national legislation* applicable to deferred payment of tax liabilities, by measures such as *the provision of a bank guarantee* (see, to that effect, judgment of 29 November 2011, *National Grid Indus*, C-371/10, EU:C:2011:785, paragraph 74).
>
> 60 ... to opt between, on the one hand, the immediate payment of the amount of the tax on capital gains resulting from an exchange of shares and, on the other hand, the deferred payment of that amount, ... *accompanied by a bank guarantee* (see, *par* [*sic*] *analogy*, judgment of 29 November 2011, *National Grid Indus*, C-371/10, EU:C:2011:785, paragraphs 73 and 74).[172]

A bank guarantee was unacceptable in both *De Lasteyrie* and *N* with respect to individuals/shareholders. The scope of the then-unexplained acceptance of such a bank guarantee in *National Grid Indus* was subsequently restricted by the Court's decision in *DMC*. The conclusion must be that the Court has followed an as-yet-unexplained zigzag course with respect to bank guarantees: its initial non-acceptance when applied to individuals (*De Lasteyrie* and *N*), followed by its unconditional acceptance with regard to businesses (*National Grid Indus*), then followed by its

171. *See* Art. 4(3) TEU: 'The Member States shall facilitate the achievement of the Union's tasks and refrain from any measure which could jeopardize the attainment of the Union's objectives.'
172. *Commission* v *Portugal 2016*, C-503/14. paras 59–60 (emphasis added).

conditional acceptance in respect of businesses (*DMC*), and as a provisional climax unconditional acceptance with regard to both individuals and businesses (*Commission v Portugal 2016*).

The author would urge the Court to return to its decisions in the *De Lasteyrie* and *N* cases, because they best fit its role as a of protector of the establishment of the internal market. Moving back toward that case law would contribute to the realization of two important EU principles: the creation of a level playing field and the execution of the ability-to-pay principle. Competitors who make use of their freedom of establishment would no longer face additional expenses because of a bank guarantee compared to domestically operating competitors who do not have to provide for a bank guarantee. Effectively not permitting a bank guarantee in the context of exit taxes would contribute to the establishment of the internal market and will partly satisfy the benchmark.

[3] Inconsistencies in Respect of Capital Losses After Emigration

Another surprise was found in *Commission v Portugal 2016*. Again, referring only to its *National Grid Indus* decision, the CJEU held that capital losses incurred after emigration do not have to be taken into account by the former Member State of residence, irrespective of whether the new Member State of residence takes such capital losses into account after immigration,[173] specifically:

> 55 Moreover, in so far as the Commission questions the legitimacy of the objective of ensuring a balanced allocation of the power to impose taxes between Member States with regard to the exit taxation of *natural persons'* unrealised capital gains on the ground that any *capital losses realised after the transfer of residence* to another Member State *cannot be deducted* by them *in that other Member State, suffice it* to recall that the Court has already held that *a possible omission* by the *host* Member State to take account of *decreases in value* does *not* impose any obligation on the Member State *of origin* to *revalue*, at the time of the *definitive disposal* of the new shares, a *tax debt* which was definitively determined at the time when the taxable person, because of the transfer of its residence, ceased to be subject to tax in the Member State of origin (see, *by analogy*, judgment of 29 November 2011, *National Grid Indus*, C-371/10, EU:C:2011:785, paragraph 61).
>
> 56 Accordingly, there is *no objective reason for distinguishing*, for the purposes of the justification deriving from the objective of ensuring a balanced distribution of the power to impose taxes between Member States, *between the exit taxation of natural persons and that of legal persons in respect of unrealised capital gains.*[174]

However, in the *N* case, the Court decided quite differently:

> 54 Finally, in order to be regarded in this context as *proportionate* to the objective pursued, such a system for recovering tax on the income from securities *would have to take full account of reductions in value* capable of arising *after the transfer*

173. *Ibid.* paras 53–57.
174. *Ibid.* paras 55–56 (emphasis added).

> *of residence* by the taxpayer concerned, *unless* such reductions have already been taken into account in the *host* Member State.[175]

The Court's 2006 decision in *N* was not addressed - at all - in *Commission v Portugal 2016*; thus, the Court did not explain why it came to a decision that contradicted its earlier decision. The *N* case dealt with a natural person who had moved his residence from the Netherlands to the United Kingdom. One of the reasons why the Court found the Dutch exit tax incompatible with EU law (i.e., it was found disproportional) was that the Netherlands did not take account of any capital losses suffered by the taxpayer after emigration, in the event that the United Kingdom did not take such losses into account. As the Court argued at that time, in such a situation, the Netherlands had to take account of the whole capital loss:

> 37 ...In that event, tax on income would have been calculated on the basis of the increase in value actually achieved at the time of the disposal, which could have been less, or even non-existent.[176]

Such taxation is consistent with the ability-to-pay principle, which is part of the benchmark and would contribute to the establishment of the internal market. The Court, however, did not explicitly refer to these principles to explain why a proportionate exit tax must take into account capital losses after emigration by the former Member State of residence if the host Member State did not do so, but the author believes that they provide an appropriate basis for the Court's decision.

The fact that the Court decided differently in the *National Grid Indus* case, holding that decreases in value after emigration did not have to be taken into account by the former Member State of residence, can be explained by the fact that *National Grid Indus* dealt with a business that emigrated from the Netherlands to the United Kingdom, and not with the emigration of a private individual as in the *N* case.[177] Since the *National Grid Indus* case dealt with business profits or capital gains enjoyed by a business, the idea is that, normally, capital gains and losses are part of taxable business income, whereas with respect to natural persons, it is less obvious that capital gains form part of their taxable income. For example, a number a countries do not levy a capital gains tax on natural persons who do not carry on a business. The Court's reasoning clearly made a distinction between exit taxes concerning businesses and exit taxes levied on private individuals:[178]

> 54 It should be recalled that in *N*, which related to national legislation under which a *private individual* was subject, at the time of the transfer of his residence for tax purposes to another Member State, to tax on the unrealised capital gains relating to a substantial shareholding he had in a company, the Court held that, *in order to be regarded as proportionate* to the objective of ensuring a balanced allocation of powers of taxation between the Member States, a system of tax must take full account of decreases in value that may arise after the transfer of residence

175. *N*, C-470/04, paras 37, 54–55 (emphasis added).
176. *Ibid.* para. 37.
177. *National Grid Indus*, C-371/10, paras 19–20, 54–64, 86.
178. *See also*, *e.g.*, Terra & Wattel, *supra* n. 13, at 969–970; and Kemmeren in Lang/Linde 2012, *supra* n. 133, at 204–206.

> by the taxpayer concerned, unless those decreases have already been taken into account in the host Member State (*N*, paragraph 54).
>
> ...
>
> 56 However, *in contrast to the position in* N, the failure of the Member State of origin to take into account, in the dispute in the main proceedings in the present case, decreases in value that occur after the transfer of a company's place of effective management cannot be regarded as *disproportionate* to the objective pursued by the national legislation at issue in those proceedings.
>
> 57 The assets of a company are assigned directly to economic activities that are intended to produce a profit. Moreover, the extent of a *company's taxable profits* is partly *influenced by the valuation of its assets* in the balance sheet, in so far as depreciation reduces the basis of taxation.
>
> 58 Since, in a situation such as that at issue in the main proceedings, the profits of a company which transfers its place of effective management are, after the transfer, taxed exclusively in the host Member State, in accordance with the principle of fiscal territoriality linked to a temporal component, *it is also for that Member State,* in view of the above-mentioned connection between a company's assets and its taxable profits, and hence for reasons relating to the symmetry between the right to tax profits and the possibility of deducting losses, to take account in its tax system of fluctuations in the value of the assets of that company *which occur after the date* on which the Member State of origin loses all fiscal connection with the company.[179]

Therefore, the author finds the reasoning in the Court's *Commission v Portugal 2016* decision hard to understand, because it held that the conclusion to be drawn from its *National Grid Indus* decision was that: 'there is no objective reason for distinguishing ... between the exit taxation of natural persons and that of legal persons in respect of unrealised capital gains'.[180]

This Court's reasoning is not only inconsistent with *National Grid Indus*, but also with its decision in the *N* case, thus, the author believes that Court should have confirmed its decision in *N*, in which it decided that a proportionate exit tax requires taking account of capital losses after emigration by the former Member State of residence if the host Member State did not do so.[181] The author does not share the Court's concerns regarding the risk of taxpayers' double dipping as the Court seemed to fear in *National Grid Indus*.[182] If a capital loss can be taken into account in the host Member State, the former Member State of residence would not be obliged to take that loss into account. In such a situation, the loss would only be taken into account once, thereby depriving the taxpayer of any chance at double dipping. As already noted above, the approach the Court took in the *N* case remains in line with the ability-to-pay principle, which the author firmly believes is equally relevant with respect to entities and which is part of the benchmark.[183] As a result, confirming the approach taken in

179. *National Grid Indus*, C-371/10, paras 54–59 (emphasis added).
180. *Commission* v *Portugal 2016*, C-503/14, para 56.
181. For a different opinion, see, e.g., Terra & Wattel, *supra* n. 13, at 970, who fully agree with the Court.
182. *National Grid Indus*, C-371/10, para. 59.
183. A person's wealth gives him/her the ability to pay taxes. An entity is also a person.

the *N* case would contribute to the establishment of the internal market, rather than stifle it. With regret, the author must conclude that the Court's spate of inconsistent case law does the latter. Therefore, the author calls upon the Court to return to the sound approach it took in its *N* decision.

[E] Interim Conclusion

To sum up, in the context of exit/final settlement taxes, the Court appears ambivalent about its role as a protector of the establishment of the internal market. On the one hand, the Court has, at least in certain cases, protected the development of the internal market by preventing restrictive conditions, such as the immediate payment of exit taxes and by obliging Member States to offer emigrating taxpayers the ability to pay exit taxes upon realization of accrued capital gains. It also held that tax payment deferral must be granted automatically and, at least initially, unconditionally (e.g., without a bank guarantee). Furthermore – again, at least initially – it determined that a decrease in value after emigration must be taken into account by the state of departure if such decrease is not taken into account by the host state. Finally, it obliged host states to provide a step-up in basis, at least in the context of business taxation. On the other hand, however, the Court has developed, over the last several years, a line of cases that limits the breadth of its earlier starting points: it has permitted Member States to adopt systems for paying exit taxes (with interest on overdue exit taxes) in first ten, then five annual instalments, but it might accept even fewer instalments. It has also permitted Member States to require bank guarantees (at one time, only in cases of an actual risk of non-recovery, but then later, once again unconditionally). Furthermore, the Court has limited the Member States' obligation to take account of decreases in value after emigration, first in the context of business taxation (even in cases in which the host state does not take them into account), and then expanded that limitation to exit taxation of natural persons. These restrictions on the starting points do not contribute to the establishment of the internal market and these changes wrought by this line of case law does not facilitate an open market economy with free competition, an efficient allocation of production factors, a level playing field, international tax neutrality, and the application of the ability-to-pay and direct-benefit principles. Thus, the author firmly believes that the Court should reconsider the altered path it is on and give itself opportunities to return to its earlier, and better road, which, in turn, will allow it to better fulfil its role as a protector of the establishment of the internal market.

§1.07 CONCLUSIONS

The research question of this chapter has been: What is, and what should be, the role of the CJEU in establishing the EU's internal market in direct tax matters? Considering the above, the author believes that, in answering this question, the following main conclusions can be drawn:

(1) International tax neutrality and CLIN imply that income should be taxed only in the state to which it can be economically linked. Creating a level playing field, international tax neutrality, CLIN, satisfying the ability-to-pay principle, and establishing an origin-based allocation of tax jurisdiction on income go hand in hand and all five of these factors contribute to the development of the internal market of the European Union.

(2) One of the main tasks of the CJEU is ensuring, or at least contributing to, the aim of realizing an internal market within the European Union and, as the case may be, in relation with third countries. The Court is a protector of the establishment of the internal market in direct tax matters. As a consequence, the Court's decisions should be built (more) on creating a level playing field, international tax neutrality, CLIN, satisfying the ability-to-pay principle, and establishing an origin-based allocation of tax jurisdiction.

(3) In general, the Court's case law in respect of personal and family circumstances contributes to the establishment of the internal market. In general, and up to now, the CJEU has fulfilled, to a large extent, its role as a protector of the EU's internal market in this field of direct taxation; its *Kieback* decision was an exception. The Court's latest refinement in its line of cases provides that personal and family circumstances must be taken into account in proportion to the aggregate annual income earned in each state of source/origin in the relevant tax year. Under such a system, each state of source/origin applies its own system of taking into account personal and family circumstances. Whether this is done through personal allowances, reliefs, deductions, tax credits, or a general lower tax rate without specific deductions or tax credits, it does not matter. The principle of sovereignty is also satisfied in an optimal way. The refinement is also in line with the ability-to-pay principle, the direct-benefit principle, an open market economy with free competition, an efficient allocation of production factors, tax neutrality, a level playing field, international tax neutrality, CLIN, and origin-based taxation.

(4) Tax treaty override must be considered inconsistent with Union loyalty in conjunction with the fundamental freedoms. The non-application of a tax treaty is inconsistent with the functioning of the internal market. Whether not accepting tax treaty override contributes to the application of tax treaties based on the benchmark depends on the facts and circumstances of the case at hand. Whereas, the CJEU was constrained from removing tax treaty override by Article 293 EC Treaty, such a constraint does no longer exist as from 1 December 2009. Therefore, now, the Court is in a better position to play its role as a protector of the establishment of the internal market.

(5) In the context of exit/final settlement taxes, the Court appears ambivalent about its role as a protector of the establishment of the internal market. On the one hand, the Court has, at least in certain cases, protected the development of the internal market by preventing restrictive conditions, such as the immediate payment of exit taxes and by obliging Member States to offer emigrating taxpayers the ability to pay exit taxes upon realization of accrued

capital gains. It also held that tax payment deferral must be granted automatically and, at least initially, unconditionally (e.g., without a bank guarantee). Furthermore - again, at least initially - it determined that a decrease in value after emigration must be taken into account by the state of departure if such decrease is not taken into account by the host state. Finally, it obliged host states to provide a step-up in basis, at least in the context of business taxation. On the other hand, however, the Court has developed, over the last several years, a line of cases that limits the breadth of its earlier starting points: it has permitted Member States to adopt systems for paying exit taxes (with interest on overdue exit taxes) in first ten, then five annual instalments, but it might accept even fewer instalments. It has also permitted Member States to require bank guarantees (at one time, only in cases of an actual risk of non-recovery, but then later, once again unconditionally). Furthermore, the Court has limited the Member States' obligation to take account of decreases in value after emigration, first in the context of business taxation (even in cases in which the host state does not take them into account), and then expanded that limitation to exit taxation of natural persons. These restrictions on the starting points do not contribute to the establishment of the internal market and these changes wrought by this line of case law does not facilitate an open market economy with free competition, an efficient allocation of production factors, a level playing field, international tax neutrality, and the application of the ability-to-pay and direct-benefit principles. Thus, the author firmly believes that the Court should reconsider the altered path it is on and give itself opportunities to return to its earlier, and better road, which, in turn, will allow it to better fulfil its role as a protector of the establishment of the internal market.

(6) In the context of personal and family circumstances, the Court is close to reaching the limits of EU primary law. Yet, with respect to tax treaty override, there is still room for further refinement. In the context of exit taxes/final settlement taxes, the Court has recognized some primary law limits that do not contribute to the development of the internal market and, therefore, should be reconsidered. Rather, the Court should strengthen its case law by better applying the internal market concept, taking into account the existence of twenty-eight (soon-to-be twenty-seven) tax jurisdictions. In this way, the Court has the opportunity to strengthen its role as a protector of the establishment of the internal market.

CHAPTER 2

Equality and Non-discrimination in European Tax Law

Alexander Rust

§2.01 INTRODUCTION

This chapter will analyse the differences and commonalities of the principles of equality and the non-discrimination principles in international and European tax law.[1] It focuses on constitutional principles of equality, on non-discrimination provisions in Double Tax Conventions (DTCs) and foremost on the non-discrimination provisions in the Treaty of the Functioning of the European Union (TFEU) and the principles of equality in the Charter of Fundamental Rights of the European Union (the Charter).

Non-discrimination provisions prohibit a more burdensome taxation. They do not prevent a state from granting a more favourable treatment to taxpayers. By contrast, the principle of equality requires an equal treatment of similar situations. It prevents both a more favourable and a more burdensome treatment. Traditionally, a vertical comparison is made: for inbound situations, the tax burden of the foreigner (non-resident) is compared with the tax burden of a national (resident) of the taxing state. For outbound situations, the tax burden of a resident taxpayer when investing in another state is compared with the tax burden of the same resident taxpayer when investing in the home country.

However, it is also possible to make a horizontal comparison and compare the tax burden of two foreigners of different nationality (two non-residents established in different countries) or outbound investments in two different countries. Most-favoured nation provisions take this horizontal perspective. They require a state to treat nationals (residents) of another state at least as well as nationals (residents) of a third

1. *See already* Alexander Rust, *Gleichbehandlungsgebote und Diskriminierungsverbote im Internationalen Steuerrecht, in Internationales Steuerrecht* 71 (Markus Achatz ed., 2013).

state. If the national of the third state is entitled to fewer tax privileges than a national of the taxing state, the protection granted by most-favoured nation treatment stays behind the protection granted by non-discrimination provisions. If, however, the national of the third state is entitled to a treatment comparable to the national of the taxing state, then most-favoured nation treatment has the same effect as non-discrimination or equal treatment. In case the national of the third state is entitled to even better treatment than the national, then most-favoured nation treatment exceeds the protection granted by equal treatment.[2]

In general, states tend to discriminate against cross-border investments. They refuse to grant certain tax benefits if the taxpayer invests abroad while granting these benefits if the taxpayer invests at home. The reason for this disincentive is that domestic investments create jobs and increase domestic tax revenue while foreign investments might lead to fewer jobs at home and no additional tax revenue.[3] Foreign nationals (residents) very often have to suffer discriminations, as they are not entitled to vote and tax benefits are reserved to the electorate. Another explanation for the more burdensome treatment of non-residents is that the taxing state assumes that non-residents already benefit from similar advantages in their respective residence states and that it is undesirable to grant these benefits twice.

Non-discrimination and equal treatment provisions do not necessarily lead to harmonization of the national tax systems. Each state is still competent to draft and implement its own tax policy. Each state may decide to levy a high or a low effective tax rate. Non-discrimination and equal treatment provisions only prevent a country from levying higher taxes on cross-border situations. Conversely, full harmonization of all national tax systems would not automatically mean that all discriminations disappear.

Non-discrimination and equal treatment provisions may apply simultaneously in several states. However, they are directed at each state individually. The states individually – not both states together – have to respect their non-discrimination and equal treatment obligation. The taxation in the other state might only be relevant for the question of whether the taxpayer – who is also taxed in the other state – is situated in a similar situation or, alternatively, whether a more or less burdensome treatment might be justified by the tax treatment in the other state.

§2.02 NON-DISCRIMINATION CLAUSES IN TAX TREATIES

Non-discrimination provisions can be found in Article 24 OECD MC. In contrast to most provisions in tax treaties, they not only apply to taxes mentioned in Article 2 OECD MC

2. Axel Cordewener, *Europäische Grundfreiheiten und nationales Steuerrecht* 836 (2002), regards national treatment as the maximum entitlement a most-favoured nation provision can convey in the EU context. Otherwise, an already existing distortion of competition would be intensified, which would run contrary to the goal of having an open market economy with free competition as is contained in Art. 119(1) TFEU.
3. For the question whether foreign direct investments substitute domestic investments or whether foreign and domestic investments are complementary, see Daniel Shaviro, *Fixing U.S. International Taxation* 148 & references cited therein (2014).

but to all taxes of every kind and description.[4] The different paragraphs of Article 24 apply to completely different situations and lack an overarching concept. Van Raad labelled these non-discrimination clauses as an 'incoherent collection of fairly narrow clauses'. The paragraphs have a different history. While the nationality non-discrimination provision of Article 24(1) OECD dates back to the beginning of the nineteenth century, where similar provisions were included in friendship, commerce, and navigation treaties, the deductibility non-discrimination provision of Article 24(4) OECD MC was only inserted into the OECD MC in 1977.

Article 24(1) OECD MC prohibits discriminations based on foreign nationality. Paragraph 2 extends this protection to stateless persons. In practice, both provisions are not very relevant as most countries levy taxes based on residence of the taxpayer or on the basis that the income is earned within the territory of the state. The nationality of the taxpayer does not play a major role in taxation.[5] Article 24(3) OECD MC prevents a Contracting State from taxing a permanent establishment of a non-resident enterprise in a more burdensome way than it taxes domestic enterprises. Article 24(4) OECD MC requires a Contracting State to allow a deduction for payments made to enterprises of the other Contracting State in the same way as it allows a deduction for payments made to domestic enterprises. According to Article 24(5) OECD MC, an enterprise may not be discriminated just because it is controlled by residents of the other Contracting State.

The tax-treaty non-discrimination provisions only cover a small fraction of possible discriminations. They only address the host state and do not prevent the residence state from discriminating against outbound investments. Even with regard to inbound investments, they only apply to business income in the sense of Article 7. Inbound situations that fall within the ambit of other distributive rules may be subject to discriminations without violating the non-discrimination provisions.[6] The OECD[7] suggested extending the ambit of the non-discrimination provisions to also cover other activities, but no work has been done in this direction to change Article 24. The author proposes to introduce a non-discrimination provision similar to Article 24(3) whenever the source state may tax the income without any restriction. Such non-discrimination provision should apply to income covered by Article 6 (income from immovable property), Article 16 (directors' fees), Article 17 (entertainers and sportspersons), and Article 19 (government service). On the contrary, the introduction of non-discrimination provisions does not seem to be advisable if the tax treaty restricts taxation in the source state.

With regard to Articles 10 and 11, the OECD MC allows taxation on a gross basis and caps the maximum tax rate. Non-discrimination provisions would allow the deduction of income-related expenses and, therefore, would not be consistent with the

4. *See* Art. 24(6) OECD MC.
5. However, in the US, nationals are subject to worldwide taxation. Many EU countries grant advantages based on EU citizenship.
6. Art. 24(3)–(5) OECD MC only apply to enterprises of a Contracting State. The permanent establishment non-discrimination provision will also apply to business activities that fall within the ambit of Arts 6 and 17.
7. OECD, *Application and Interpretation of Article 24 (Non-Discrimination), Public Discussion Draft* (3 May 2007) http://www.oecd.org/tax/treaties/38516170.pdf.

intention of Articles 10 and 11. Concerning outbound investments, there might be good (economic) reasons to incentivize domestic investments. Here, the author would be prudent as well, suggesting the introduction of non-discrimination provisions.

Article 24 OECD MC only prevents overt, direct discrimination. Hidden or indirect forms of discrimination are not prohibited by Article 24, even if – in most instances – the less advantageous treatment burdens the person protected by Article 24.[8] By contrast, the non-discrimination provisions of the TFEU are interpreted in a broader way to cover hidden and indirect forms of discriminations as well.

The OECD non-discrimination provisions have an absolute character.[9] Contracting States may not derogate therefrom. A distinction based on any one of the forbidden criteria is prohibited and automatically violates the non-discrimination article. Such different treatment cannot be justified by legitimate reasons. Although the public discussion draft of 2007 considered the introduction of a concept of justification, that idea should not be followed, at least as long as no world tax court exists to resolve potential disputes. Allowing a justification would mean that courts would have to balance the objective achieved by the discrimination against the disadvantages suffered by the taxpayer therefrom, which is, of course, a value judgment and different courts would, almost inevitably, come to different conclusions about the legitimacy of such justifications. The chances of reaching a common interpretation would be made far more difficult. The tax treatment in the other Contracting State (e.g., the ability to credit the taxes in the residence state) is to be disregarded as well. For purposes of applying Article 24 OECD MC, it does not make any difference if the discriminatory tax burden is, or could be, compensated in the other Contracting State, even if the ultimate tax consequences do not cause the taxpayer to suffer a combined, higher over-tax burden in the two Contracting States. By contrast, EU law permits tax discrimination by one Member State if it is neutralized through a bilaterally agreed compensation in the other Member State.[10]

If a domestic tax provision violates the tax treaty's non-discrimination provision, it has to be disregarded.[11] Instead of such discriminatory provisions, the more advantageous domestic rules laid down for the taxing state's own nationals or residents, as the case may be, become applicable.[12] In a tax treaty context, the taxpayer benefits from the better of the two rules. If the domestic rule for non-residents is more beneficial than the rule for residents there is no discrimination. If the domestic rule for non-residents is more burdensome then the tax treaty's non-discrimination provision applies and the taxpayer can rely on the more beneficial rule for resident taxpayers. By contrast, in constitutional law a violation of the principle of equality does not

8. *See* Alexander Rust, *Art. 24, Non-Discrimination, in* 2 *Klaus Vogel on Double Taxation Conventions* 1657, 1684, m.no. 5 (Ekkehart Reimer & Alexander Rust eds., 4th ed., 2015).
9. *Ibid.* at 1683, m.no. 4.
10. *See Amurta*, C-379/05, Judgment, EU:C:2007:655; *see also* Georg W. Kofler, *Tax Treaty 'Neutralization' of Source State Discrimination under the EU Fundamental Freedoms?*, 65 Bull. Int'l Tax'n 684 (2011).
11. This, of course, depends on whether the constitutional law of the affected Contracting State allows a treaty override.
12. *See* German Bundesfinanzhof of 22 Apr. 1998, I R 54/96, IStR 1998, 504.

automatically lead to the application of the more beneficial rule to the taxpayer. The violation of the principle of equality can be healed by extending the more burdensome treatment to resident taxpayers, by extending the more beneficial treatment to non-resident taxpayers or by enacting another rule that treats residents and non-residents in the same way. The decision how to remediate the violation of the constitutional principle of equality should be taken by the legislator and not by the judge in the particular case. This is required by the constitutional principle of separation of powers.

The legal consequences of the application of the tax-treaty non-discrimination provisions are national treatment (Articles 24(1) and (2)) or treatment similar to residents (Articles 24(3)-(5)). Article 24 OECD MC does not offer most-favoured nation treatment. About 20% of all tax treaties, however, contain a most-favoured nation clause.[13] Most-favoured nation clauses mainly concern the material scope of a treaty (Article 2), the permanent establishment definition (Article 5 OECD MC), the deductibility of costs within the framework of the business profits article (Article 7 OECD MC), the maximum tax rate especially with regard to dividends, interest and royalty payments (Articles 10-12 OECD MC), the method article (Article 23 OECD MC), non-discrimination provisions (Article 24 OECD MC), arbitration (Article 25 OECD MC) and even exchange of information (Article 26 OECD MC) and mutual assistance for the collection of tax revenue (Article 27 OECD MC).[14]

Most-favoured nation clauses generally apply to advantages granted in tax treaties with third countries, however, they may also concern advantages granted in the domestic law of a Contracting State. Some most-favoured nation clauses apply to both Contracting States, the scope of other most-favoured nation clauses is limited to one of the two Contracting States. Sometimes the clauses have direct effect; sometimes they oblige the Contracting States to renegotiate if a certain tax treaty with a third country is concluded. Most-favoured nation clauses in tax treaties add an additional layer of complexity: in case a most-favoured nation clause is included in a tax treaty, the taxpayer and the tax administration will have to analyse all tax treaties concluded by the other Contracting State, which very often only exist in foreign languages.[15] The OECD does not advocate including a most-favoured nation clause in a tax treaty.[16]

13. *See* Ines Hofbauer, *Das Prinzip der Meistbegünstigung im grenzüberschreitenden Ertragsteuerrecht* 192 (2005).
14. For a detailed description of the different types of most-favoured nation provisions, see *ibid.* at 131 et seq.
15. With regard to a potential conflict of most-favoured nation clauses with the rule of law principle, see Alexander Rust, *Meistbegünstigungklausln in den Doppelbesteuerungsabkommen, in Meistbegünstigung im Steuerrecht der EU-Staaten* 77, 82 (Axel Cordewener, Stefan Enchelmaier & Clemens Philipp Schindler eds., 2006); and Ines Hofbauer, *Das Meistbegünstigungsprinzip in den deutschen und österreichischen Doppelbesteuerungsabkommen*, 19 IStR 667, 672 (2004).
16. *See* the OECD Model Commentary 1977 on Art. 24 para. 55.

§2.03 NON-DISCRIMINATION CLAUSES IN THE TFEU AND PRINCIPLES OF EQUALITY IN THE EU'S CHARTER OF FUNDAMENTAL RIGHTS

The fundamental freedoms of the TFEU have had a much more important effect on national tax law than the tax-treaty non-discrimination provisions and the principles of equal treatment enshrined in the national constitutions. These fundamental freedoms – the free movement of goods contained in Article 28 et seq., the free movement of workers contained in Article 45, the freedom of establishment contained in Article 49 et seq., the freedom to provide services contained in Article 56 et seq., and the free movement of capital contained in Article 63 et seq. – primarily prohibit discriminations of foreign persons (goods, services and capital) in comparison to domestic persons (goods, services and capital). They mainly address the host state and give the foreigner the right to national treatment.

While the free movement of goods and the free movement of capital in Articles 35 and 63 explicitly address the home state as well and prohibit outbound restrictions as well the Court of Justice made it clear early on that outbound restrictions are also prohibited by the other fundamental freedoms. The Court stated, in its *Daily Mail* judgment,[17] that:

> [e]ven though those provisions are directed mainly to ensuring that foreign nationals and companies are treated in the host Member State in the same way as nationals of that State, they also prohibit the Member State of origin from hindering the establishment in another Member State of one of its nationals or of a company incorporated under its legislation which comes within the definition contained in Article [54]. ...[T]he rights guaranteed by Articles [45] et seq. would be rendered meaningless if the Member State of origin could prohibit undertakings from leaving in order to establish themselves in another Member State.

Although worded as nationality non-discrimination provisions, the Court of Justice also extended the scope of the fundamental freedoms to cover discriminations based on residence if residence serves as a proxy for nationality.[18] As a result, hidden or indirect forms of discriminations are also prohibited. It is now settled case law[19] of the Court that:

> rules regarding equal treatment forbid not only overt discrimination by reason of nationality but also all covert forms of discrimination which, by the application of other criteria of differentiation, lead in fact to the same result. It is true that the rules at issue in the main proceedings apply irrespective of the nationality of the

17. *Daily Mail*, C-81/87, Judgment, EU:C:1988:456, para. 16; *see also Imperial Chemical Industries (ICI)*, C-264/96, Judgment, EU:C:1998:370, para. 21 et seq.; *Cadbury Schweppes*, C-196/04, Judgment, EU:C:2006:544, para. 42; *Columbus Container Services*, C-298/05, Judgment, EU:C:2007:754, para. 33.
18. *See Sotgiu*, C-152/73, Judgment, EU:C:1974:13, para. 11. For the concept of hidden or indirect discrimination, see Cordewener, *supra* n. 3, at 118 et seq.
19. *See e.g., Schumacker*, C-279/93, Judgment, EU:C:1995:31, para. 26 et seq. For the first tax case, see *Biehl*, C-175/88, Judgment, EU:C:1990:186, para. 13.

> taxpayer concerned. However, national rules of that kind, under which a distinction is drawn on the basis of residence in that non-residents are denied certain benefits which are, conversely, granted to persons residing within national territory, are liable to operate mainly to the detriment of nationals of other Member States. Non-residents are in the majority of cases foreigners. In those circumstances, tax benefits granted only to residents of a Member State may constitute indirect discrimination by reason of nationality.

In contrast to the tax-treaty non-discrimination provisions, restrictions of the fundamental freedoms can be justified. A different treatment of non-resident taxpayers in comparison to resident taxpayers is only prohibited if the different rules are applied to comparable situations and if the different treatment cannot be justified by imperative requirements in the general interest. The domestic tax measures must be appropriate to achieve this goal and they must be proportionate which means that they must not go beyond what is necessary to achieve that goal.

While the written grounds of justification are exhaustive, the extension of the material scope to hidden and indirect forms of discriminations made it necessary to extend the list of grounds of justification as well. As judge-made law, the so-called unwritten imperative requirements in the general interest[20] were introduced to allow Member State to make reasonable distinctions in their domestic law. These unwritten grounds of justification also apply to distinctions between resident and non-resident taxpayers.

Later on, the Court of Justice even went one step further and extended the scope of the fundamental freedoms to apply to indirect and covert forms of discrimination if they are no longer a proxy for nationality. It allowed taxpayers who were nationals of a Member State to go against their own Member State if they had made use of the fundamental freedoms. In the *Asscher* judgment, the Court of Justice held that:

> [i]t is settled law that, although the provisions of the Treaty relating to freedom of establishment cannot be applied to situations which are purely internal to a Member State, Article [49] nevertheless cannot be interpreted in such a way as to exclude a given Member State's own nationals from the benefit of Community law where by reason of their conduct they are, with regard to their Member State of origin, in a situation which may be regarded as equivalent to that of any other person enjoying the rights and liberties guaranteed by the Treaty.[21]

In such cases, the discrimination is clearly not based on nationality, as nationals of the taxing state suffer the disadvantage. In these constellations, the non-discrimination provisions of the fundamental freedoms have a similar effect as the principle of equality. They ensure that similarly situated taxpayers are treated in a comparable way.

20. With respect to the free movement of goods, see the early case commonly known as '*Cassis de Dijon*': *Rewe/Bundesmonopolverwaltung für Branntwein*, C-120/78, Judgment, EU:C:1979:42, para 8. For a general application of the 'rule of reason', see *Gebhard*, C-55/94, Judgment, EU:C:1995:411, para 37.
21. *Asscher*, C-107/94, Judgment, EU:C:1996:251.

§2.04 MOST-FAVOURED NATION TREATMENT

The classical test, when applying fundamental freedoms in the tax area, is to analyse whether a non-resident is discriminated in relation to a resident taxpayer (inbound situation). For outbound situations, the tax treatment of a resident of a Member State when investing in the other Member State is compared with the tax treatment when investing in the same Member State. As a foreigner is compared to a domestic person or a foreign investment is compared to a domestic investment, this perspective is labelled as 'vertical comparison'. A different treatment can also occur between two foreigners or two foreign investments. Member State A might tax a resident of Member State B in a more burdensome way than it taxes a resident of Member State C. Alternatively, Member State A might tax its resident investing in Member State B in a more burdensome way than the same resident investing in Member State C. This form of comparison is named 'horizontal comparison'. The legal consequences of the horizontal approach would no longer be national treatment, but instead would be most-favoured nation treatment. One foreigner would be entitled to the same favourable treatment as the other foreigner. Likewise, the benefits granted to an investment in Member State B would have to be extended to an investment in Member State C.

For a long time, a dispute smouldered over whether the fundamental freedoms only allow a vertical comparison or whether they also permit a horizontal comparison. Some parts of the TFEU speak in favour of a horizontal comparison. For instance, according to Article 45(3)(c) TFEU, the free movement of workers entails the right to stay in a Member State for the purpose of employment in accordance with the provisions governing the employment of nationals of that State. Article 49 TFEU states that the freedom of establishment shall include the right to take up and pursue activities... under the conditions laid down for its own nationals by the law of the country where such establishment is effected. However, Article 45(2) TFEU more generally speaks about the abolition of any discrimination based on nationality. This same broad wording is used in Article 18, the general anti-discrimination provision. If any discrimination based on nationality is prohibited then the distinction between two foreigners needs to be justified as well.

On rare occasions, the Court of Justice applied a horizontal comparison approach. In the *Schumacker* judgment, the Court – when obliging Germany to allow a deduction for certain personal expenses of a Belgian frontier worker – also took a look at the situation of a Dutch frontier worker who was entitled to the deduction of certain personal expenses by virtue of the tax treaty between Germany and the Netherlands.[22] However, this horizontal approach only served to rebut the arguments brought forward by the German government that it cannot ascertain the income that non-residents working in its territory receive in their residence state.[23] By pointing to the situation of Dutch frontier workers, the Court showed that the German arguments were not well founded, as in relation to the Netherlands, Germany was able to calculate the foreign income. The starting point of the analysis in *Schumacker* was a vertical comparison.

22. *See Schumacker*, C-279/93, para. 45.
23. *See* Cordewener, *supra* n. 3, at 501 et seq.

In the *Avoir Fiscal* case, the Court also allowed a comparison between a French branch and a French subsidiary.[24] While French subsidiaries of foreign insurance companies were entitled to an *avoir fiscal* (an indirect tax credit), France denied such credit to local branches of foreign insurance companies. However, in the judgment, the Court did not deal with the question of whether investments in two legal forms have to be treated in the same way. It just pointed out that the discrimination of French branches of foreign companies in relation to French companies cannot be justified by the fact that foreign investors can avoid the discrimination by choosing a subsidiary, instead of a branch, as they must be at liberty to choose between the two legal forms.[25] In the end, the *Avoir Fiscal* judgment was about vertical comparison.

In *Cadbury Schweppes*, the Court of Justice not only compared a UK company having a subsidiary established in a low tax country with a UK company having a UK subsidiary but also with a UK company having a subsidiary in a high tax country.[26] However, it did not follow up on that point, as the vertical comparison was sufficient to show the discriminatory nature of the UK CFC rules.

In the *D* case, the Court for the first time applied a horizontal comparison on a stand-alone basis and not only as a side argument of a vertical comparison.[27] It was asked whether the free movement of capital required the Netherlands to extend an allowance it granted to Belgian residents to German residents. Here, the Court had to compare the situation of one non-resident with the situation of another non-resident. As the tax allowance was contained in a tax treaty between Belgium and the Netherlands, the Court found that the situation between the Belgian resident as not comparable with the situation of a German resident. The Court held that:

24. *See Commission* v *France ('Avoir Fiscal')*, C-270/83, Judgment, EU:C:1986:37, para. 11.
25. *See ibid.* para. 22:

> Furthermore, the fact that insurance companies whose registered office is situated in another Member State are at liberty to establish themselves by setting up a subsidiary in order to have the benefit of the tax credit cannot justify different treatment. The second sentence of the first paragraph of Article 52 [now Art. 49 TFEU] expressly leaves traders free to choose the appropriate legal form in which to pursue their activities in another Member State and that freedom of choice must not be limited by discriminatory tax provisions.

See also Cordewener, *supra* n. 3, at 400 et seq.

26. *Cadbury Schweppes*, C-196/04, para. 44:

> Where the resident company has incorporated a CFC in a Member State in which it is subject to a lower level of taxation within the meaning of the legislation on CFCs, the profits made by such a controlled company are, pursuant to that legislation, attributed to the resident company, which is taxed on those profits. Where, on the other hand, the controlled company has been incorporated and taxed in the United Kingdom or in a State in which it is not subject to a lower level of taxation within the meaning of that legislation, the latter is not applicable and, under the United Kingdom legislation on corporation tax, the resident company is not, in such circumstances, taxed on the profits of the controlled company.

27. *D*, C-376/03, Judgment, EU:C:2005:424, para. 44 et seq. The Court first decided that D, a resident of Germany who only held 10% of his assets in the Netherlands was not in a situation similar to that of a resident of the Netherlands. The Court then compared two non-residents: D, a resident of Germany, to a fictitious resident of Belgium.

> [t]he fact that th[e] reciprocal rights and obligations [contained in Article 25(3) DTC Belgium/Netherlands] apply only to persons resident in one of the two Contracting Member States is an inherent consequence of bilateral double taxation conventions. It follows that a taxable person resident in Belgium is not in the same situation as a taxable person resident outside Belgium so far as concerns wealth tax on immovable property situated in the Netherlands. A rule such as that laid down in Article 25(3) of the Belgium-Netherlands Convention cannot be regarded as a benefit separable from the remainder of the Convention, but is an integral part thereof and contributes to its overall balance.[28]

This decision has been criticized, as it declared provisions contained in a tax treaty to be immune from any scrutiny.[29] By including tax privileges in tax treaties, Member States could avoid their obligations imposed by the fundamental freedoms. Its legal form should not be decisive for the question whether a provision violates the fundamental freedoms or not. In the author's view, the Court of Justice should have made a distinction between tax treaty provisions that allocate taxing rights between the two Contracting States and a tax treaty provisions that concern the exercise of the taxing rights so allocated. While the allocation of taxing rights does not conflict with the fundamental freedoms, the exercise of the taxing rights has to be in line with the fundamental freedoms. As Article 25(3) DTC Belgium/Netherlands addressed the exercise of the taxing rights, the Court should have accepted the comparability of Belgian and German non-residents.

In the *Sopora* judgment, the Court of Justice finally applied a purely horizontal comparison and held that two different non-resident taxpayers can be in a comparable situation.[30] The decisive part of the judgment reads:

> Secondly, having regard to the wording of Article 45(2) TFEU, which seeks to abolish all discrimination based on nationality 'between workers of the Member States', read in the light of Article 26 TFEU, the view must be taken that that freedom also prohibits discrimination between non-resident workers if such discrimination leads to nationals of certain Member States being unduly favoured in comparison with others.[31]

The groundwork for this statement had already been laid by AG Kokott in her opinion.[32] She clearly advocated in favour of a horizontal comparison by stating:

> I am of the view that freedom of movement for workers prohibits in principle not only adverse unequal treatment of non-residents vis-à-vis residents, but also differentiation between non-residents of different Member States.[33]

28. *Ibid.* para. 61 et seq.
29. *See* Michael Lang, *The Decision of the European Court of Justice in the D Case – Is the Engine of Tax Harmonisation Sputtering?*, 8/2005 SWI 365, 370 (2005).
30. *Sopora*, C-512/13, Judgment, EU:C:2015:108. *See also* Eric C.C.M. Kemmeren, Sopora*: A Welcome Landmark Decision on Horizontal Comparison*, 24 EC Tax Rev. 178; Michael Lang, *Totgesagte leben länger: Horizontale Vergleichbarkeit und die Verwirklichung des Binnenmarkts*, 3/2016 SWI 118 (2016); Gerard Meussen, *Horizontal Discrimination and EU Law: The* Sopora *Case*, 54 Eur. Tax'n 322 (2014).
31. *Sopora*, C-512/13, para. 25.
32. *Sopora*, C-512/13, AG Opinion, EU:C:2014:2375.
33. *Ibid.* para. 27.

She based her arguments on Article 26(2) TFEU, according to which the internal market is to comprise an area without internal frontiers. A distinction between workers based on their State of origin erects new borders, even if no foreign worker is placed in a position that is inferior to that of national workers. A tax advantage granted to workers from only certain Member States worsens the conditions of competition for workers from other Member States. A true internal market can only be achieved if all workers from all EU Member States are treated alike.[34] AG Mengozzi, in his opinion in *Columbus Container,* had already argued that a Member State could not choose the other Member State in which its domestic companies may establish subsidiaries without infringing the rules of the Treaty. Moreover, unequal treatment of investments in different Members would entail 'the risk of fragmentation of the Common Market'.[35]

At the end of the day, the Court of Justice decided, in *Sopora,* that administrative simplification could justify the unequal treatment of different non-residents under certain conditions,[36] but, due to the *Sopora* judgment, it is now clear that the fundamental freedoms prohibit not only vertical discriminations, but also horizontal discriminations.[37] The judgment dealing with an inbound situation can also be transferred to outbound situations.[38] An investment of a resident of Member State A in Member State B is comparable with an investment by same person in Member State C.

A horizontal comparison changes the nature of non-discrimination provisions. In general, non-discrimination means that worse treatment is prohibited, but that more favourable treatment is still allowed. With a horizontal comparison, the non-discrimination obligation turns into an equal treatment obligation: a national of Member State A can demand of Member State B that he not to be treated in a more burdensome way than a national of Member State C. This would still allow a more favourable treatment. However, as the national of Member State C is also protected against more burdensome treatment in relation to a national of Member State A, at the end of the day, nationals of Member State A and nationals of Member State B must be treated in exactly the same way. If the vertical comparison is combined with the horizontal comparison, the nationals of Member States A and C are entitled, in Member State B, to treatment that is at least as good as the treatment of nationals of Member

34. *Ibid.* para. 29.
35. *Columbus Container Services*, C-298/05, AG Opinion, EU:C:2007:197, para. 117.
36. The *Sopora* Court, in its judgment at para. 35, held that administrative simplification would no longer justify benefits granted to certain expatriates if the flat-rate rule were drafted in a way to systematically give rise to a net overcompensation in respect of the extraterritorial expenses actually incurred. Gerard Meussen, *supra* n. 32, already demonstrated that the Dutch 30% rule systematically led to overcompensation. The Dutch rule treated 30% of the gross income from employment as extraterritorial costs and, as a consequence, as tax exempt. For high-income earners, such fictitious costs were much higher than the costs actually incurred for commuting and renting a second apartment.
37. While the *Sopora* judgment only concerned the free movement of workers, there are good arguments to extend its effects to all fundamental freedoms, especially as the horizontal-comparison approach was based on Art. 26 TFEU, which covers all freedoms; *see CFE-Opinion Statement ECJ-TF 3/2015 on the Decision of the European Court of Justice in* C.G. Sopora *(Case C-512/13) on 'Horizontal Discrimination'*, 56 Eur. Tax'n 94, 97 (2016); Lang, *supra* n. 32, at 132).
38. *Cadbury Schweppes*, C-196/04, AG Opinion, EU:C:2006:278, para. 77 et seq.; *Columbus Container Services*, C-298/05, AG Opinion, para. 113 et seq.; *see also* Lang, *supra* n. 32, at 132.

State B and that does not make a distinction between nationals of Member States A and C. This, however, is not yet the end of the story. Reverse discrimination has still to come into play, as well.

Reverse discrimination - in French, *discrimination à rebours* - occurs if a Member State treats a cross-border situation more favourably than a purely internal situation.[39] In general, Member State do not have any interest in discriminating against their own citizens, but reverse discrimination might, for instance, arise if EU law harmonizes certain cross-border movements and the Member States do not adapt their internal law accordingly. Another situation in which reverse discrimination can arise is when the Court of Justice finds a national provision to be in violation of the fundamental freedoms. As a consequence, the national provision has to be applied in cross-border situations, but remains applicable in purely domestic situations.[40] Countries may also simply favour foreigners and foreign investments over domestic investments in order to attract additional funds from outside.[41]

The scope of the fundamental freedoms is restricted. They only apply to cross-border movements, which means that the fundamental freedoms can only protect against discrimination if a particular situation entails a cross-border element. Conversely, the fundamental freedoms do not interfere with Member State's legislation on domestic issues. In its *Saunders* judgment, the Court of Justice held that:

> the provisions of the Treaty on freedom of movement for workers cannot therefore be applied to situations which are wholly internal to a Member State, in other

39. *See* Andreas Lach, *Umgekehrte Diskriminierungen im Gemeinschaftsrecht* 9 (2008).
40. Rudolf Streinz, *Art. 4 EUV, in EUV / AEUV*, para. 37 (Rudolf Streinz ed., 2d ed. 2012); *see also IN.CO.GE* 90, C-10/97, Judgment, EU:C:1998:498, para. 21:

> It cannot therefore, contrary to the Commission's contention, be inferred from the judgment in *Simmenthal* that the incompatibility with Community law of a subsequently adopted rule of national law has the effect of rendering that rule of national law non-existent. Faced with such a situation, the national court is, however, obliged to disapply that rule.

For instance, in *3 Glocken and Others*, 407/85, Judgment, EU:C:1988:401, para. 25, the Court made it clear that:

> it is the extension of the law on pasta products to imported products which is at issue, and that Community law does not require the legislature to repeal the law as far as pasta producers established on Italian territory are concerned.

41. In *Aubertin et al.*, Joined Cases C-29/94 through 35/94, Judgment, EU:C:1995:39, the Court had to decide whether a Member State could require a person wishing to operate a hairdressing salon to have a diploma while foreigners were exempt from this requirement under certain conditions. In its judgment, the Court held, in para. 13, that:

> Community law ... must be interpreted as not precluding national rules which require that nationals of that Member State hold a diploma in order to operate a hairdressing salon, while permitting hairdressers who are nationals of other Member States to operate a hairdressing salon without holding such a diploma and without being obliged to entrust its operation to a manager holding that diploma.

words, where there is no factor connecting them to any of the situations envisaged by Community law.[42]

Discrimination against its own nationals can, of course, violate the domestic constitutional principle of equal treatment. For instance, the French Constitutional Court, in its *Metro Holding* judgment, decided that reverse discrimination violated the principle of equal treatment.[43] In the *Metro Holding* case, French legislation provided that the participation exemption for dividends only applied if the shares granted voting rights to the shareholder. As this requirement was contrary to the Parent-Subsidiary Directive, the provision was no longer applied with regard to subsidiaries resident in other EU countries; but it remained in force with regard to dividends received by domestic subsidiaries. The French Constitutional Court held that the principle of equality did not prohibit France from distinguishing between EU and domestic situations, if the situations were different or if different treatment was justified by requirements in the general interest provided that the difference in treatment had a close connection with the purpose of the law. As the purpose of the law was to encourage the shareholder to participate in the management of the subsidiary, there was no justification to distinguish between domestic and EU subsidiaries with regard thereto. As a consequence, the less favourable treatment of domestic dividends, in comparison to EU dividends, was contrary to the constitutional principle of equality. The EU fundamental freedoms could not be invoked in the *Metro Holding* case, as the facts concerned a purely domestic situation.

However, as soon as a national of a Member State crosses the border and makes use of his or her fundamental freedoms, EU law protects said person against discrimination. He or she must not be discriminated against, either in relation to nationals who stayed in the Member State of origin, or in relation to other EU nationals who are treated better. As a result, reverse discrimination is no longer allowed, because the EU national has crossed the border and the situation is no longer purely internal.

The Charter contains a general principle of equality in Article 20, stating that 'everybody is equal before the law' and a prohibition of discrimination contained in Article 21(2). The protection granted by Article 21(2) of the Charter is identical to the protection granted by Article 18 TFEU.[44] According to Article 51(1) of the Charter, Member States are bound by the rights and principles of the Charter when they implement EU law. In the *Åkerberg Fransson* case, the Court of Justice held that fundamental rights are always applicable when situations are governed by EU law, but

42. *Saunders*, 175/78, Judgment, EU:C:1979:88, para. 11; *see also already Knoors*, 115/78, Judgment, EU:C:1979:31, para. 24; it has since become settled case law, *see e.g.*, *Iorio*, 298/84, Judgment, EU:C:1986:33; and *Van Hilten-van der Heijden*, C-513/03, Judgment, EU:C:2006:131.
43. French *Conseil Constitutionnel* of 3 Feb. 2016, n° 2015-520, Société Metro Holding France S.A. *See also* Alexandre Maitrot de la Motte, *L'extension des régimes fiscaux européens aux situations originellement exclues de leur champ : vers l'élimination des discriminations européennes par le principe constitutionnel d'égalité correlative?*, 37 Revue de droit fiscal 28 (2016); Emmanuel Raingeard de la Blétière & Frédéric Durand, *Affaire* Metro Holding*: le principe constitutionnel d'égalité devant l'impôt aux secours de la jurisprudence* Leur Bloem, 18–19 Revue de droit fiscal 26 (2016).
44. *See* Rudolf Streinz, *Art. 22 GR-Charta, in EUV/AEVU* para. 8 (Rudolf Streinz ed., 2d ed. 2012).

not outside such situations.[45] A Member State, therefore, has to comply with the fundamental rights guaranteed by the Charter when national legislation falls within the scope of EU law.[46] It can be argued that the Charter applies whenever a situation is covered by the fundamental freedoms or, in other words, in all cross-border situations.[47]

This conclusion could have far-reaching consequences. By invoking the fundamental rights enshrined in the Charter, a taxpayer could go against all cases of reverse discrimination in cross-border situations. To date, however, the jurisprudence of the Court of Justice does not seem to go that far. In its *Bukovansky* judgment, the ECJ refused to extend the preferential treatment Germany voluntarily granted to Swiss nationals to German nationals residing in Switzerland.[48] In *Bukovansky*, a German national moved from Germany to Switzerland. After his change of residence, he continued to work in Germany and was taxed in Germany as a non-resident. The tax treaty between Germany and Switzerland contained a special provision for frontier workers that reduced taxation in the source state to a maximum rate of 4.5%.[49] This provision would have been beneficial for Mr Bukovansky, as the tax level in Switzerland was lower than in Germany. However, he was not entitled to the benefits of this provision, as he was a German, not a Swiss, national. Had he been a Swiss national, the beneficial provision would have applied to him.[50] As a consequence, Germany was

45. *Åkerberg Fransson*, C-617/10, Judgment, EU:C:2013:105, para. 19.
46. *Ibid.* para. 21.
47. For a more detailed discussion, see Werner Haslehner, Ch. 8, *infra*, in this volume.
48. *Bukovansky*, C-241/14, Judgment, EU:C:2015:766. *See also* Alexander Rust, *Germany: Cases C-479/14 (*Hünnenbeck*), C-123/15 (*Feilen*), and C-522/14 (*Sparkasse Allgäu*) – Inheritance Taxes, Exchange of Information and Bank Secrecy, in ECJ-Recent Developments in Direct Taxation*, 61 (Michael Lang et al. eds., 2015); Franz Wassermeyer, *Steuerrecht: Verhältnis des Freizügigkeitsabkommen der EU und der Schweiz zum DBA zwischen Deutschland und der Schweiz*, 3/2016 EuZW 108 (2016).
49. *See* Art. 15A(1) DTC Germany-Switzerland:

> Notwithstanding the provisions of Article 15, salaries, wages and similar remuneration derived by a frontier worker in respect of an employment may be taxed in the Contracting State of which he is a resident. As compensation, the Contracting State in which the employment is exercised may withhold a tax at source in respect of such remuneration. Such tax shall not exceed 4.5% of the gross amount of the remuneration if proof of the residence is supplied through an official certificate of the competent authorities of the Contracting State of which the taxpayer is a resident. The provisions of paragraph 4 of Article 4 shall not be affected.

50. *See* Art. 4(4) DTC Germany-Switzerland:

> With respect to an individual who is resident in Switzerland and does not have the Swiss nationality, and who has been unlimitedly liable to tax in the Federal Republic of Germany for a period of at least five years in total, the Federal Republic of Germany may tax the income derived from the Federal Republic of Germany, and the property located in the Federal Republic of Germany, for the year in which the unlimited tax liability ended for the last time, and the five subsequent years, notwithstanding any provisions to the contrary in the Convention. The right to tax these income or property items in Switzerland in accordance with the provisions of this Convention remains intact.
>
> However, the Federal Republic of Germany shall, in analogical application of the German legislation with respect to the crediting of foreign taxes, allow as a credit the Swiss tax imposed on these income or property items, in accordance with the

entitled to tax the income from employment exercised in Germany without any restriction. The Court of Justice argued that Germany did not violate the non-discrimination provisions contained in the free movement of persons agreement it had concluded with Switzerland. Rather, it held that Mr Bukovansky was not discriminated against when compared to other German nationals living in Germany. According to the ECJ, his change of residence to Switzerland did not lead to a more burdensome treatment by Germany.[51] In addition, the Court stated that:

> [i]n the present case, it should be noted that the difference in treatment that Mr Bukovansky claims to have suffered results from the allocation of fiscal sovereignty between the parties to the agreement concerned and follows from the disparities existing between the tax schemes of those parties. However, as noted in paragraphs 37 and 38 of the present judgment, the choice by those parties, with a view to allocating fiscal sovereignty between them, of different connecting factors is not such as to constitute prohibited discrimination.[52]

The Court was, therefore, of the opinion that the distributive rules of tax treaties may distinguish between nationals of different states. This clearly is a pragmatic solution, as many tax treaties use nationality as a connecting factor to allocate fiscal sovereignty between the Contracting States.[53] However, in the author's opinion, it should not have mattered whether the discrimination is contained in the domestic tax law of a Member State or in a tax treaty concluded by a Member State. The legal form of the provision should be irrelevant.[54]

If one follows the *Sopora* judgment, horizontal discrimination is prohibited by EU law, as well. Mr Bukovansky could have invoked the principle of equality contained in the Charter, as the requirement of a cross-border movement was fulfilled and, therefore, he could have asserted that Germany had to implement EU law as the German-Swiss free movement of persons agreement forms an integral part of Union law.[55] Finally, he could have asserted that taxing Swiss nationals at a flat rate of 4.5% while taxing German nationals at a much-higher, progressive rate, constitutes reverse discrimination. It seems to be, at the very least, doubtful that nationality should serve as the connecting factor for the allocation of taxing rights within the EU or with regard to Switzerland.

---

provisions of this Convention, against that part of the German tax (with an exception for the trade tax) which is levied under this provision from these income or property items, in so far as it exceeds the German tax which may be levied according to Articles 6 to 22.

The provisions of this paragraph shall not apply if the individual has become a resident of Switzerland for the purpose of the exercise of a bona fide employment there by an employer, in which the employee has neither directly nor indirectly through participation, or in any other form, an economic interest other than his employment.

51. *Bukovansky*, C-241/14, para. 46.
52. *Ibid.* para. 45.
53. *See* Arts 4(2)(c) & 19 OECD MC.
54. *See also Saint-Gobain ZN*, C-307/97, Judgment, EU:C:1999:438.
55. *See Haegemann*, 181/73, Judgment, EU:C:1974:41, para. 5, regarding the Athens agreement.

§2.05 CONCLUSIONS

Both tax treaties and EU law contain non-discrimination provisions. While treaties only prohibit overt/direct forms of discrimination, EU law also protects against hidden and indirect forms of discriminations. This very broad scope of the fundamental freedoms makes the application of grounds of justification necessary. By contrast, the tax-treaty non-discrimination provisions do not allow any form of justification. EU law has further developed to protect also against horizontal discrimination. Member State A may not treat nationals of Member State B worse than nationals of Member State C. However, EU law cannot protect against reverse discrimination if no cross-border movement is involved. In these situations, EU law does not apply and taxpayers can only rely on the principle of equality contained in the national constitution. EU law does not prevent a Member State from treating foreigners better than its own citizens, if those citizens have never made use of their fundamental freedoms.

It is still disputed whether a reverse discrimination is prohibited by EU law if citizens of a Member State have crossed borders and pursue economic activities in their home state. In *Åkerberg Fransson*, the Court of Justice seems to interpret the scope of the Charter of fundamental rights in a very broad way and apply the Charter when a situation is covered by the fundamental freedoms. If a cross-border movement is sufficient to make the Charter applicable taxpayers could rely on the principle of equality contained in its Article 20 and the prohibition of discrimination contained in its Article 21(2) to ask for benefits granted to nationals of other Member States. As a consequence, all distinctions based on nationality would be prohibited unless they could be justified by imperative reasons in the general interest. This would mean that distinctions in tax treaties that are based on nationality – as for instance contained in Article 4(2)(c) or in Article 19 OECD MC – would no longer be allowed in relation to other EU Member States. The Court of Justice has not yet gone so far. In *Bukovansky*, the Court held that the allocation of taxing rights based on nationality is not prohibited by EU law. The Court, however, did not deal with the Charter. As the jurisprudence on the application of the Charter is still evolving, reverse discrimination might be prohibited in the future, due to Articles 20 and 21(2) of the Charter. It will be interesting to see whether the Court of Justice will deviate from its *Bukovansky* reasoning in the coming years.

PART II State Aid and Tax Law

CHAPTER 3

A Proposed Framework to Review Tax Rulings under State-Aid Rules

Pierpaolo Rossi-Maccanico[*]

§3.01 INTRODUCTION

In an early article after the start of State-aid proceedings relating to tax rulings,[1] I defended the idea of a more prominent role for the application of State aid rules in reviewing European Union (EU) Member States' tax measures that provide multinational enterprises (MNEs) with the ability to adopt aggressive forms of tax planning involving tax Base Erosion and Profit-Shifting (BEPS).[2] That article took note of the Commission's recent investigations into individual tax rulings granted to MNEs[3] and its

* The views expressed are solely those of the writer and may not in any circumstances be regarded as stating the official position of the Institution.

1. Pierpaolo Rossi-Maccanico, *Fiscal State Aids, Tax Base Erosion and Profit Shifting*, 24 EC Tax Rev. 63 (2015).

2. Tax planning involving aggressive forms of BEPS can be described as the use of legitimate planning strategies by MNEs to reduce or fully eliminate taxation in one or more tax jurisdictions in which these MNEs set up their operations by exploiting gaps or inconsistent interpretations (mismatches) by different national tax administrations based on internal tax law or tax conventions intended to eliminate double taxation (DTCs), by making double use of the same tax advantage intended to eliminate double taxation either in the form of double tax deductions, double exclusions from taxation, or a combination of exclusions and deductions in two or more such jurisdictions (tax arbitrage).

3. Amongst the most prominent investigations, it is worth mentioning that, on 11 June 2014, the Commission opened proceedings with respect to: (a) the individual rulings issued by the Irish tax authorities on the calculation of the taxable profit allocated to the Irish branches of Apple Sales International and of Apple Operations Europe (aid No SA-38373); (b) the individual ruling issued by the Dutch tax authorities on the calculation of the taxable basis in the Netherlands for manufacturing activities of Starbucks Manufacturing EMEA BV (aid No SA-38374); and (c) the individual ruling issued by the Luxembourgish tax authorities on the calculation of the taxable basis in Luxembourg for the financing activities of Fiat Finance and Trade - FFT (aid No SA-38375). On 21 Oct. 2015, the Commission decided that both Luxembourg and the Netherlands

innovative focus on single rulings as the object of review, and proposed an innovative framework for ensuring consistency and legal certainty in the application of State aid rules to individual rulings. In this chapter, I am proposing an innovative procedural framework for State aid review of tax rulings with a view to providing the needed legal certainty in this area of EU law.

An individual ruling, including an advance pricing agreement (APAs), are decisions granted to an MNE by the competent tax administration of a given State that provides legal certainty as to the determination of the income of that MNE to be taxed in that State. Against that background, the APA is an ahead-of-time tax assessment of future transactions or operations to be carried out by the MNE in the tax jurisdiction in which the APA is sought. APAs define an acceptable determination of the taxable income by a competent tax administration.

APAs may also provide favourable tax planning opportunities, consisting of specific lower taxation than the one applicable for local taxable entities not operating across borders, and, accordingly, can be identified as State aid where the resulting tax advantage goes beyond the elimination of international double taxation or, in any event, is not justified by the nature of the tax system of a given Member State granting the APA. Such opportunities include arbitrage and the creation of mismatches between what is considered taxable income for the MNEs by the different international tax jurisdictions concerned and, accordingly, can be identified as State aid if analysed from that perspective.

In practice, APAs are often released by the tax authorities to specify which method is preferred in determining the arm's length price of controlled transactions and which acceptable result the use of that method yields. If the agreed method is respected by the taxpayer, the APA reverses on the administration the burden to prove that the taxable income is understated. Should the latter want to correct the taxable base of an entity within the MNE, it has to prove evasion of tax.

It follows from this that State aid review may conclude that the favourable tax treatment resulting from an APA is State aid only if it is proven that the determination made by the competent tax authority is not justified under the nature or logic of the tax scheme, because it goes beyond what relief from international double taxation would possibly allow. The mere finding that income is understated is not sufficient to prove the presence of State aid in the absence of a verification of whether the logic and scheme of the system was, in fact, followed by the administration. Only in that case, can the APA system of a Member State be qualified as covert State aid.

had granted State aid in the form of individual tax rulings in favour of FFT and Starbucks and ordered recovery of the tax advantages granted. On 30 Aug. 2016, the Commission decided that Ireland had granted undue tax rulings to Apple and ordered the recovery of the resulting tax benefits.

§3.02 APAS AND STATE AID

With its *Forum 187* judgment of 2006,[4] relating to the tax-ruling system for Coordination Centres in Belgium (BCCs), the European Court of Justice (ECJ) concluded that the Commission had been correct in deciding that Belgian rules governing the advance determination of taxable income of BCCs in Belgium, applicable for a number of future years, provided State aid to the concerned entities taxable in Belgium and to the MNE to which such entities were part. In that judgment, the Court stressed the importance of assessing the justification of the method underlying the ruling system before concluding that a tax measure was a selective State aid. At Paragraphs 122–126 of the *Forum 187* judgment, the Court specifically pointed to the lack of consistency of the method of assessment of the taxable income in a BCC ruling as proof of selectivity. The Court concluded that the BCC rulings system was not justified, as a general tax regime, by the nature or general scheme of the tax system of which it formed part, and only after that assessment it concluded that the Commission had correctly established the selective nature of that general scheme.

That judgment shows that, when assessing a tax advantage, the Court adopts a rule of reason, by which the presence of a favourable tax system does not, *per se*, mean that this constitutes State aid. It must first be proven that the advantage is not justified by the logic or scheme of the tax system and only then that the tax system qualifies as State aid. It follows that a tax regime, such as one that uses APAs, cannot be deemed selective by its nature, just because it allows tax arbitrage, but that it is critical to investigate the possible justification of the tax preference by the logic of the tax system before concluding that the preference is State aid.

This is an indispensable guarantee that the Court recognizes to protect national tax prerogatives from State aid control and allows it to distinguish between State aid and legitimate (general) tax measures, similarly to what the Court has already done to justify tax restrictions on fundamental freedoms.[5] The *Forum 187* judgment is the perfect illustration of a classic conundrum of selectivity in tax matters. To address the jurisdictional issue of selectivity in reviewing tax measures under State aid rules, it is essential that one follows a coherent and consistent application of that case law; this can only happen if – the justification by the logic or scheme of the company tax system – is investigated and, once and for all, clarified as a notion under EU law that is dependent however from the assessment of the national tax system under its own standards, as it was many times suggested in the past.[6]

Going back to assessing APAs from a State aid viewpoint, it is true that APAs confer rights on individual taxpayers (the entities within an MNE) to use a given transfer-pricing methodology and to determine their taxable revenues deriving from a set of cross-border transactions over a fixed period of time. Under the logic of the

4. *See Belgium* v *Commission ('Forum 187')*, Joined Cases C-182/03 and C-217/03, Judgment, EU:C:2006:416, para. 95.
5. *See* Richard Lyal, *Compatibility of National Tax Measures with EU Law: The Role of the European Commission in Tax Litigation before the European Court of Justice*, 24 EC Tax Rev. 5, 7 (2015).
6. *See* Pierpaolo Rossi-Maccanico, *State Aid Review of Business Tax Measures – Proposals for State Aid Control of Direct Business Tax Measures*, 6 EStAL 16 (2007).

scheme, such methods of determination do not necessarily correspond to commercial reality. On the contrary, APAs are intended to differ from the business accounts of the entities operating under the same control because these are not reliable for tax purposes since they are internal to same multinational economic unit. Because of this tax logic and although different from the business accounts entered by the entities of a multinational economic unit, APAs are, nonetheless, deemed appropriate by the tax administration. They are not revocable unless avoidance of the applicable conditions or fraud is proven by the tax authority. An APA may cover one or more transactions, or even the total yearly taxable income, of an establishment of a given MNE for one or more years.

APAs may, accordingly, give rise to double non-taxation. APAs are generally national since no cross-border APA proceedings are in place between distinct tax jurisdictions. For this reason, APAs give a taxable entity of an MNE in a given jurisdiction an opportunity to plan ahead the income to declare as taxable in another jurisdiction, which may be beneficial in minimizing the overall taxes payable by the MNE. Such an advantage may give rise to State aid if it can be proven that selective tax relief has been granted. However, APAs are not State aid as such. Even if favourable or effectively beneficial to an MNE, they are selective only if unjustified under the nature of the tax system in question.

Against this background, everyone understands that the issue in applying State aid review to APAs is one of preventing the tax authority from abusing its discretion in granting a ruling. In that regard, one should bear in mind that discretionary practices play an important role in the assessment of whether a State measure is selective. For example, the ECJ has found that a general system of granting State assistance to enterprises in financial difficulties under objective conditions can be regarded as selective when an authority enjoys a certain degree of latitude in giving 'its financial assistance having regard to a number of considerations such as, in particular, the choice of the beneficiaries, the amount of the financial assistance and the conditions under which it is provided'.[7] It follows that if a general State treatment of undertakings is made on a discretionary basis, the measure is presumed to be selective, as also confirmed by the Commission in its 1998 Fiscal Aid Notice.[8]

The fact is that, as explained above, the power of the tax authority to take transactions at their real (arm's length) value and to disregard the value that the taxpayer has declared in its accounts, is a power that is necessitated by the aim of preventing tax avoidance and implies the use of discretion on the part of the tax administration in its task of administering the rules of the system. It follows that any presumption of selectivity is rebutted if proof is provided that the tax administration has acted within the limits of its ordinary discretion and with the aim of apportioning income under the arm's length standard. It also follows that State aid exists only if it is proven that a tax authority has gone beyond the appropriate management of the tax scheme. A violation of the due-process standard in the exercise of administrative discretion cannot be assumed, rather it must be proven in order to reach the conclusion

7. *See France* v *Commission*, C-241/94, Judgment, EU:C:1996:353, para. 23.
8. 1998 Fiscal Aid Notice, paras 21 and 22.

that State aid is present. One should stress the difference of this assessment as opposed to proving any other tax reductions. In the case of rulings, the reference for 'normal' taxation is not the one resulting from the nominal tax rate applied to the commercial income reported in the accounts of the taxpayer, but is rather the one that the administration would have normally accepted if it had followed the required process in determining the arm's length standard to apportion its share of the taxable income.

§3.03 TARGETING INDIVIDUAL RULINGS: PROCEDURAL IMPLICATIONS

What was described above is a systemic problem for tax administrations granting APAs and it arguably risks remaining unresolved if addressed one single ruling at a time via State aid review. From the above-mentioned State aid investigations regarding individual rulings granted by Ireland, Luxembourg, and the Netherlands,[9] one may think that the Commission is taking issue with the end result of the particular rulings, rather than the methodologies followed, by challenging the individual rulings and individual tax assessments in lieu of addressing general schemes as it did in the BCC case. In other words, the Commission may appear to be singling out examples of understatements of the taxable income and, therefore, focusing on tax evasion rather than investigating the logic of the scheme and, accordingly, this may lead to the incorrect result of leaving national practice unaddressed.

It also follows that a great deal of uncertainty is generated because each and every ruling can give rise to State aid because every individual tax ruling constitutes preferential taxation as opposed to taxation that would result from the general application of ordinary tax rules for domestic businesses. Moreover, with the wisdom of hindsight any ex-post re-examination of a tax ruling can lead to a different result than the one made *ex ante* by the tax administration. The Commission's reassurances that it 'does not call into question the granting of tax rulings by the tax administrations of the Member States' because it 'recognises the importance of advance rulings as a tool to provide legal certainty to taxpayers ... [p]rovided they do not grant a selective advantage to specific economic operators' do not seem too reassuring, nor does the Commission give certainty in light of its ominous commitment to focus 'on cases where there is a manifest breach of the arm's length principle',[10] since it is not clear what a constitutes a 'manifest breach'.

To date, these statements still stand, as does the Commission's practice to investigate single rulings on a case-by-case basis. The delimiting lines between daily tax-practice by national tax administrations and discretionary treatment of undertakings leading to possible State aid are blurred. On the one hand, the challenges brought by the Commission against single tax assessments could rightfully make national tax authorities aware of their obligations to correctly comply with State-aid rules and will contribute to bringing more fairness and equality of conditions to the determination of

9. *See supra*, n. 3.
10. These are excerpts from DG Competition's Working Paper of 3 June 2016 - Background to the High Level Forum on State Aid presented to the Member States representatives.

the tax liabilities of MNEs. On the other hand, should such challenges confirm that individual determinations of taxable income are biased in favour of the MNEs, the Commission would have no other option but to conclude they are State aid unlawfully granted and, therefore, must be recovered.

The Commission would then be under an obligation to order the concerned Member State to retrospectively recover the tax benefit granted in violation of EU rules on *ex ante* notification of State aid, plus interest, covering a period of up to ten years.[11]

Contributing to uncertainty is also the difficulty in determining the exact amount of the fiscal aid to recover. In so far as the calculation of the amount of aid to be recovered may call for consideration of tax regimes in which the basis of assessment, rates, and rules governing recovery are fixed directly by the relevant domestic legislation, the Commission is merely entitled to make a general statement that the recipient is obliged to repay the aid in question and to leave it up to the national authorities to calculate the exact amount of aid to be recovered.[12] The Commission is not obliged to determine the exact amount of aid to be recovered; it is merely required to indicate that the tax situation must be restored to that which would have prevailed if taxation had been imposed without the ruling, which calls for the recovery from the beneficiaries of the difference between theoretical standard tax, which may not necessarily take into account the incidence of foreign double taxation, and the tax effectively paid as a result of the ruling at issue.[13]

§3.04 A PROPOSED SOLUTION

The above uncertainties carry important procedural consequences. Since, under State aid rules, a national tax authority cannot autonomously decide whether a measure is State aid or not, at least not without a proper review by the Commission,[14] they may feel compelled to notify the Commission of all the individual rulings that they have already granted. If they do, they may want to suspend their application until cleared by the Commission.

Moreover, any interested individual undertaking or association of undertakings that look at the on-going Commission's probes into tax rulings could feel wronged by their competitors and lodge complaints before the Commission about the regularity of the rulings granted. The Commission would then be required in these cases to examine the complaints and if it is unable to exclude that individual rulings could be State aid, it must open in-depth proceedings to review them.

11. *See* Art. 14 of Council Regulation (EC) No. 659/1999 of 22 Mar. 1999.
12. *See Spain* v *Commission*, C-480/98, Judgment, EU:C:2000:559, para. 26.
13. *See Associazione italiana del risparmio gestito and Fineco Asset Management v Commission*, T-445/05, Judgment, EU:T:2009:50, para. 201.
14. The risk in omitting the pre-notification system in State-aid analysis of tax measures is in the possibility of a ruling being found by the Commission to be State aid. Moreover the same national courts may, by virtue of Art. 108(3) TFEU and its direct applicability, order the national tax administrations to suspend and recover without delay tax benefits that are deemed unlawfully granted under State-aid rules, because offered without prior authorization from the Commission, and without prejudice to the subsequent investigation that the Commission has to carry out, to ascertain their ultimate compatibility with State-aid rules.

Finally, any business that could prove to be affected by a ruling granted to a competitor could feel entitled to contest it before the competent national courts. A national court asked to rule on the matter should draw all the necessary and appropriate conclusions from the fact that a possible State aid was granted without respecting the stand-still clause of Article 108(3) TFEU, and possibly suspend, or even order the withdrawal of a ruling, pending the Commission's examination of its compatibility with State aid rules.

Alternatively, the national administrations might serve the Commission with mass notifications of individual ruling requests received for advance clearance by the Commission, a scenario that should be avoided. Again, the Commission would have to carry out an analysis of each and every one of the rulings notified with a view to determining its particular nature and possibly testing its concrete effects.[15]

The inability of tax authorities to provide certainty about the rulings sought by MNEs would eventually cause the ruling system to be discontinued, given the possible negative consequences deriving from the retrospective effects of any State-aid review.

To avoid such consequences, the Commission will likely be under pressure to adopt guidelines to limit the likely wave of Member State notifications of tax rulings and to define those cases in which the Member States are relieved of the obligation to notify to the Commission, which should then avoid taking a State aid decision on each ruling request. However, adopting guidelines has, so far, proven to be elusive. Back in 1998, the Commission committed itself to review its Fiscal Aid Notice, but has yet to take that step, choosing instead to adopt a generic notice on the notion of State aid without, however, giving specific guidance to taxpayers on what to notify.[16] The fact is that the value of a Commission notice on the notion of fiscal aid is necessarily limited, because it is not possible, not even for the Commission, to restrict the boundaries of State aid. In this respect, nothing leads to a conclusion that guidelines are going to be adopted to help distinguish whether individual rulings should be notified or not as potential State aid.

Guidelines are not legislation and may, at most, bind the Commission. Guidelines are, accordingly, insufficient to provide the needed certainty to national authorities faced with their obligations resulting directly from EU law.

If one was to draw a conclusion from the Commission's proceedings reviewing individual rulings, it would be to suggest a new framework under which individual tax rulings could be subject to *ex ante* review by the Commission, instead of waiting for single episodes to be brought to the attention of the Commission. This seems necessary with a view to bringing legal certainty to an area of State-aid control that is arguably problematic because of the overlap between national exclusive competence in taxation and the Commission's prerogatives in applying State-aid rules.

As already indicated, a solution based on the issuance of Commission guidelines is ineffective. Instead of leaving it to the Member States to decide whether or not to

15. Since the responsibility for State-aid clearance rests on the EU executive, the Commission would have the ultimate word on the compatibility of any rulings granted in the EU.
16. *See* Commission Notice on the notion of State aid as referred to in Article 107(1) of the Treaty on the Functioning of the European Union, OJ C262 of 19/7/2016, 1.

notify individual tax rulings, one could imagine the Commission adopting binding general rules specifying under which conditions it is appropriate for the competent tax administrations to notify their planned assessments to the Commission and providing a framework for preventing possible future infringements of State-aid rules. I suggest that such rules take the form of Commission directives in accordance with Article 106(3) TFEU.

Under Article 106(3) TFEU, the Commission is competent to adopt such rules in the form of directives, when it has to define rules to ensure the correct application of competition rules with respect to public undertakings or private undertakings to which the State grants special or exclusive rights.

To illustrate, Article 106 TFEU, provides:

> 1. In the case of *public undertakings* and *undertakings to which Member States grant special or exclusive rights*, Member States shall neither enact nor maintain in force any measure contrary to the rules contained in the Treaties, in particular to those rules provided for in Article 18 and Articles 101 to 109.
> 2. ...
> 3. *The Commission shall ensure the application of the provisions of this Article and shall, where necessary, address appropriate directives or decisions to Member States* (emphasis added).

Article 106 TFEU does not define the notion of public undertakings, but it is clear that these are the private businesses that are controlled by the State or in which the State participates. Similarly, Article 106 TFEU does not define the concept of undertakings to which Member States grant special or exclusive rights. The scope of the latter concept is less clear than it seems. Secondary EU law has defined the concept of exclusive or special rights as those rights deriving from authorizations granted by a competent authority of a Member State by law, regulation, or administrative action, having as their result the reservation, for one or more entities of the exploitation, of a given activity. Under this definition, the stress is on the reservation of an activity being the object of the special or exclusive right granted. However, this, arguably cannot be the meaning of 'special rights', as otherwise this would be a mere repetition of the 'exclusive rights' expression, which was the reading developed, for example, in the framework of the current Utilities Directive.[17]

While MNEs are clearly not public undertakings or undertakings that carry out, under exclusivity, specific activities on the basis of a right conferred by the State, they are undertakings that benefit from special rights, in the sense that, unlike other undertakings under the same tax system, their taxable income is determined under the specific transfer pricing authority of the tax administration, under specific guidelines and regulatory schemes that may include the grant of individual rulings intended to provide legal certainty to taxpayers in controlled situations.

17. Directive 2004/17/EC of the European Parliament and of the Council coordinating the procurement procedures of entities operating in the water, energy, transport and postal services sectors [2004] OJ L 134/11.

The grant of rulings under the transfer pricing guidelines confers special procedural rights exclusively reserved to MNEs because of the intra-group and cross-border aspects of their operations. As the individual-ruling proceedings indicate, the tax-rulings framework is a beneficial procedural scheme that allows MNEs to reverse the burden of proof incumbent on them back onto the tax administration and shelters them from tax corrections. MNEs are indisputably benefiting from special rights. It follows that an MNE receiving an individual agreement establishing its taxable income on the basis of the preferred method of assessment accepted by the tax administration could, therefore, be considered an undertaking to which the Member State grants special rights within the meaning of Article 106(1) TFEU.

Against this backdrop, Article 106(3) TFEU entrusts the Commission with the power to address not only decisions, but also directives to the Member States, although its power is limited to only 'where necessary'. This power gives rise to sensitive problems of a legal and, particularly, a policy nature. Thus, under Article 106(3) TFEU, the Commission enjoys a specific and autonomous rule-making power, although subject to strict limits.[18] Two are the possible functions of directives under Article 106(3) TFEU: the specification of existing obligations under the Treaty and the creation of additional obligations that should, however, be accessory to the fulfilment of such obligations. While the former means that the obligations under the Treaty can be specified, the latter means a directive under Article 106(3) TFEU may impose upon Member States additional obligations to the extent that they are intended to facilitate the Commission's task of ensuring Article 106(1) TFEU is respected.

The aim of the two recognized functions of directives promulgated under Article 106(3) TFEU is to specify the obligations (existing or new) that Member States have to follow when dealing with their State-owned undertakings or when granting special or exclusive rights to private undertakings with the aim of facilitating the application of the applicable competition rules, including preventing possible infringements of State-aid rules under Articles 107 and 108 TFEU. In other words, as opposed to adopting decisions to find infringements and imposing the appropriate remedies contemplated by the same Article 106(3) TFEU, the function of these directives is to provide general rules for the future,[19] to specify obligations, and to possibly prevent future infringements. The directives issued pursuant to Article 106(3) TFEU may operate in two ways: first, by creating the necessary mechanisms to enable the Commission to detect infringements in the event that they occur; and, secondly, by specifying the meaning and scope of the obligations that already exist under Article 106(1) TFEU and/or the exception under Article 106(2) TFEU. In both cases, legal certainty is increased and the risk of unintentional infringements is reduced.

An example of the first aim being dealt with is the so-called Transparency Directive,[20] while examples of the second type of provisions, where the Commission

18. *See* Michel Kerf, *The Policy of the Commission of the E.E.C. Toward National Monopolies – An Analysis of the Measures Adopted on the Basis of Article 90(3) of the E.E.C. Treaty*, 17 World Competition 73, 106 (1993).
19. *See France* v *Commission*, C-202/88, Judgment, EU:C:1991:120, para. 17.
20. Commission Directive (EEC) 80/723 concerning the transparency of financial relations between Member States and their public undertakings [1980] OJ L195/35. This Directive has been

has exercised its power to adopt directives pursuant to Article 106(3) TFEU, are the various directives regarding the liberalization of the telecommunications sector.[21]

A tax-rulings directive under Article 106(3) TFEU could fill the gap in the general framework for Member States' competent authorities to grant tax rulings to MNEs in compliance with State-aid rules. This would not bring any prejudice to the discretion that the tax authorities necessarily enjoy in exercising their power to take transactions at their arm's length value. The directive would identify and set the conditions under which Member States are obliged to notify the Commission of their individual rulings because they are susceptible of constituting State aid, as opposed to the cases where they need not notify such rulings. In particular, the directive would contain detailed procedural rules to examine and grant individual rulings, specifying, for example, what information is to be provided to the competent authorities and what attention should be paid to facts and circumstances, to ensure compliance with the arm's length standard.

Most importantly, the directive would relieve Member States from the obligation to notify, under State aid rules, the tax rulings that are granted in compliance with certain standards. The waiver would restore legal certainty to the ruling practices without prejudice to the possibility for the Commission to investigate single rulings or ruling schemes and to possibly discontinue them because found to effectively not comply with State-aid rules. In this case, a prohibition decision by the Commission would only take future effect, without need to recover the tax benefits eventually found to be aid and already granted.

§3.05 CONCLUSION

A possible directive under Article 106(3) TFEU would greatly differ from a legislative proposal to improve cross-border cooperation among Member States in terms of an exchange of information on their cross-border tax rulings, as provided by amendments to Directive 2011/16/EU on administrative cooperation in the field of taxation introducing an automatic exchange of information between tax authorities relating to cross-border rulings and advance pricing agreements.[22] While the latter directive is based on Article 115 TFEU under the special legislative procedure requiring unanimity between Member States and is limited to creating the conditions for an automatic exchange of information between the tax authorities of the Member States, excluding

modified by the following directives: (a) Commission Directive (EEC) 85/413 [1985] OJ L229/20; (b) Commission Directive (EEC) 93/84 [1993] OJ L254/16; (c) Commission Directive (EC) 2000/52 [2000] OJ L193/75; and (d) Commission Directive (EC) 2005/81 [2005] OJ L312/47.

21. *See* Commission Directive 2002/77/EC of 16 Sep. 2002 on competition in the markets for electronic communications networks and services [2002] OJ L 249/21.

22. *See* Council Directive of 8 Dec. 2015 amending Directive 2011/16/EU as regards mandatory automatic exchange of information in the field of taxation.

the Commission, with a view to achieving transparency about the rulings issues,[23] the former would be the Commission's own directive to be adopted under the specific conditions set out in Article 106(3) TFEU.

The proposed directive could refer to the transfer pricing guidelines accepted by most EU Members tax systems, including various alternatives to the mere research of 'comparables' for arm's length standard purposes, including, besides the comparable uncontrolled-price method (CUP) and amongst other methods available, the following:

- For sales of tangible property, a resale-price method and a cost-plus method can be applied.
- For transfers of intangible property, a comparable uncontrolled-transaction method (CUT) can be applied.
- For both sales of tangible property or transfers of intangible property where one of the parties in the controlled transactions uses valuable non-routine intangibles, a comparable-profits method (CPM) can be used.
- For transfers of tangible and intangible property where all the parties of the controlled transactions use valuable non-routine intangibles, a profit-split method can be used.

Essentially, the above-mentioned methodologies would all be deemed to be valid if tax authorities rely on an all-facts-and-circumstances analysis to grant their APAs. If the taxpayer respects an agreed method, the effect of the APA is essentially that of reversing the burden of proof if the administration wants to correct the tax base of a taxable entity within an MNE, as it would do with any other non-controlled taxpayer. In this case, the APA would not need to be notified to the Commission for State-aid clearance.

On the other hand, if none of the recommended methodologies is respected or if the tax authorities intentionally ignore facts and circumstances that would otherwise be significant to establish the taxable income of certain activities or arrangements, the resulting APA, although not prohibited, would need to be notified to the Commission, for prior State-aid assessment. The proposed directive will be for the Member States to transpose, which would enjoy flexibility and discretion in deciding how to implement the common framework or to set up a tax-ruling system, while leaving intact the national prerogatives in deciding, on the basis of all the facts and circumstances of the particular case, individual assessments.

The Commission's prerogative to bring State-aid proceedings against individual rulings would not be limited or altered in any way by such a proposed directive, as it would only specify the conditions under which individual tax rulings are to be granted without need of prior notification. This is without prejudice to the notion of State aid as applicable to measures relating to business taxation. Indeed, since Article 106(3) TFEU entrusts the Commission with the task of ensuring that Member States fulfil their obligations under Article 106(1) TFEU, the two instruments contemplated by Article

23. Because it is limited to providing transparency, the proposed Directive leaves open the identification of the rulings to be considered prone to create tax avoidance, and of the possible remedies to this situation.

106(3) TFEU are to be considered as alternatives. The role of decisions taken on the basis of Article 106(3) TFEU would remain that of eliminating infringements of Article 107 TFEU.

It follows that any such directive would be without prejudice to possible proceedings that the Commission could pursue under Articles 107 and 108 TFEU. Unlike Article 108(2) decisions, the role of Article 106(3) directives is preventive, not decisional. Not only can such directives provide general rules determining the obligations that Member States (rather than individual remedies concerning one Member State and an individual case) are to follow when granting special rights to private undertakings, but also they may provide framework rules and additional or accessory obligations intended to facilitate the Member States' observance of State-aid rules and allow the Commission to take State-aid decisions within the framework of Articles 107 and 108 TFEU, as contemplated by Article 106(1).

If the Commission intends to be assertive in tackling fiscal aids in the form of national tax-ruling practices, a specific procedural framework is not only appropriate, but also required to restore legal certainty for both the Member States' administrators and taxpayers. In those circumstances, State-aid proceedings relating to specific tax assessments under Articles 107 and 108 TFEU demand clear boundaries and can no longer be left to the self-discipline of national tax administrators or to episodic Commission interventions.

CHAPTER 4

Fiscal Aid: Recent Trends and Relationship to Fundamental Freedoms

Andreas Bartosch

§4.01 THE ISSUE

The guarantee of the fundamental freedoms, on the one hand, and State-aid review, on the other, both of which are firmly embedded in the Treaty on the Functioning of the European Union (TFEU), form two different regimes designed to control domestic measures taken by Member States of the European Union (EU). Despite the fact that they each focus on different sorts of infringements, they are often intimately intertwined. This interconnection is most apparent in Member States' fiscal measures. This chapter looks at the development of this interconnection, as reflected in the jurisprudence of the EU Courts and the European Commission's decisional practices.

§4.02 THE GENERAL RULES

[A] When Must Fundamental Freedom Compatibility Be Checked in a State-Aid Investigation?

The general prohibition on State aid, as laid down by Article 107(1) TFEU, provides that:

> Save as otherwise provided in the Treaties, any aid granted by a Member State or through State resources in any form whatsoever which distorts or threatens to distort competition by favouring certain undertakings or the production of certain goods shall, in so far as it affects trade between Member States, be incompatible with the internal market.

Articles 107(2) and (3), as well as Article 106(2), TFEU contemplate a number of derogations from the general prohibition. In a State-aid investigation, guided by Article 108 TFEU in conjunction with the so-called Procedural Regulation in State-aid matters,[1] the Commission enjoys a monopolistic competence to decide on the compatibility of a given measure with the internal market, perusing the flexibilities provided by the aforementioned primary-law provisions, as interpreted by numerous secondary law instruments developed on that basis.

Therefore, any State-aid investigation, regardless of whether the instrument used by the Member State is of a fiscal or non-fiscal nature, is conducted in two steps:

- first, the Commission determines whether the measure at issue fulfils all five of the necessary conditions of an 'aid' under Article 107(1)TFEU,[2] and
- second, when an aid within the meaning of Article 107(1) TFEU has been detected, the Commission must then determine whether such aid may be declared compatible with the internal market under one of the exceptions provided by the Treaty, which are found in Articles 106(2), 107(2) and (3), and 93 TFEU.

In such a State-aid investigation, the Commission might also be required, in certain circumstances, to verify if the measure complies with the Treaty's rules on fundamental freedoms. If the Commission determines that there is no aid within the meaning of Article 107(1) TFEU, the Commission is not otherwise obliged to investigate potential breaches of other provisions of the Treaty, including rules on the fundamental freedoms within the framework of its State-aid investigation. The Court of Justice of the European Union (CJEU) held that:

> In this regard, the Court would observe that it is not disputed that if the Commission reaches the conclusion that a measure does not constitute aid within the meaning of Treaty [Article 107 TFEU], it cannot have recourse to the procedure under [Article 108 TFEU] in order to decide that another provision of the Treaty, such as [Article 49 TFEU], has been infringed.[3]

If, however, the Commission determines that all five elements of an 'aid' under Article 107(1) TFEU have been fulfilled, the Commission must investigate, within the procedure laid down in Article 108 TFEU, whether such aid is compatible with EU law. In this framework, any potential infringement of other provisions of the Treaty, including provisions regarding fundamental freedoms, must be investigated. Again, the CJEU puts this as follows:

1. Council Regulation 2015/1588 of 13 July 2015 on the application of Articles 107 and 108 of the Treaty on the Functioning of the European Union to certain categories of horizontal State aid (codification), O.J. 2015 L 248/1.
2. The five-prong test requires: (1) an economic advantage that is (2) selective (i.e., favours certain undertakings or the production of certain goods) and such selective advantage (3) stems from State resources, (4) distorts competition, and (5) has an effect on trade between the Member States.
3. *Germany* v *Commission*, C-156/98, Judgment, EU:C:2000:467, para. 76.

> As the Court has consistently held, it is clear from the general scheme of the Treaty that the *procedure under [Article 108 TFEU] must never produce a result which is contrary to the specific provisions of the Treaty*. State aid, certain conditions of which contravene other provisions of the Treaty, cannot therefore be declared by the Commission to be compatible with the common market (see, to that effect, Case 73/79 *Commission v Italy* [1980] ECR 1533, paragraph 11, and Case C-225/91 *Matra v Commission* [1993] ECR I-3203, paragraph 41) (emphasis added).[4]

[B] Which Measures Must Be Checked?

The first, crucial question that needs to be answered in this context is exactly which forms of measures must be checked via this two-step State-aid investigation. In this regard, the CJEU developed its so-called rule of hypothecation. Literally, it held:

> For a tax, or part of a tax, to be regarded as forming an integral part of an aid measure, it must be hypothecated to the aid measure under the relevant national rules, in the sense that the revenue from the tax is necessarily allocated for the financing of the aid. In the event of such hypothecation, the revenue from the tax has a direct impact on the amount of the aid and, consequently, on the assessment of the compatibility of the aid with the common market (see, to that effect, Case 47/69 *France v Commission* [1970] ECR 487, paragraphs 17, 20 and 21). The Court thus held that, where there is such a link between the aid measure and its financing, the notification of the aid provided for in [Article 108(3) TFEU] must also cover the method of financing, so that the Commission may consider it on the basis of all the facts. If this requirement is not satisfied, it is possible that the Commission may declare that an aid measure is compatible when, if the Commission had been aware of its method of financing, it could not have been so declared.[5]

The consequence of this is that, when it comes to defining which measures must be checked for potential infringement of fundamental freedom rules, both the measure granting the selective advantage and the way such measure is financed must be looked at. If such financing is provided by way of a tax that is necessarily allocated to such measure, both the measure itself and the tax it is financed by are to be scrutinized for any potential infringement of the fundamental freedom rules, which can result in a somewhat surprising result.

It may turn out that the measure granting the selective advantage is qualified as an aid, but is regarded as compatible with the internal market on the basis of one of the derogations provided by the TFEU. Nevertheless, if the way it is financed infringes one of the fundamental freedoms, the measure (including its mode of financing) cannot be declared compatible with EU law.

4. *Ibid.* para. 78.
5. *SWNB*, C-174/02, Judgment, EU:C:2005:11, para. 26.

[C] Exceptions

The general rule that can be derived from the above-mentioned is that the procedure under Article 108 TFEU must never produce a result that is contrary to other provisions of the Treaty.[6] However, there are certain exceptions.

[1] On the Relationship Between State Aid and Freedom of Trade

Given the expansion of infringement of the freedom of trade laid down in Articles 34 and 35 TFEU, the CJEU, by its *Dassonville* decision,[7] limited the conditions of such infringement by an aid measure, otherwise compatible with EU law. It held:

> Similarly the fact that a system of aids provided by the State or by means of State resources may, simply because it benefits certain national undertakings or products, hinder, at least indirectly, the importation of similar or competing products coming from other Member States is not in itself sufficient to put an aid as such on the same footing as a measure having an effect equivalent to a quantitative restriction within the meaning of Article 30.[8]

[2] On the Relationship Between State Aid and Discriminatory Taxation

One feature of many parafiscal-aid schemes is the imposition of a levy on both domestic products and products imported into a given Member State, whilst the monies generated by the levy are used to benefit only domestic producers thereof. The CJEU regards such levies to run counter to Article 110 TFEU, leading to an incompatibility with EU law.[9]

Whilst the doctrine of hypothecation demands that the Commission investigate both the parafiscal levy and the way such levy is financed, when that method of financing forms an integral part of the levy itself,[10] it is irrelevant whether there is a competitive relationship between those paying the levy and those benefitting from it.[11]

[D] The Question of Defining the Material Standard

That said, the crucial materiality question remains: whether and, if yes, to what extent, the criteria for examining a *fiscal* measure under State aid remain the same, when looking at whether such a fiscal measure confers a selective advantage, on the one hand, and when assessing a potential infringement of a fundamental freedom under the Treaty, on the other hand.

6. *Matra* v *Commission*, C-225/91, Judgment, EU:C:1993:239, para. 41.
7. *Dassonville*, C-8/74, Judgment, EU:C:1974:82.
8. *Iannelli* v *Meroni*, C-74/76, Judgment, EU:C:1977:51, para. 10.
9. Consistent jurisprudence: *e.g.*, *France* v *Commission*, C-47/69, Judgment, EU:C:1970:60.
10. *Pearle and Others*, C-345/02, Judgment, EU:C:2004:448, para. 29.
11. *Regie Networks*, C-333/07, Judgment, EU:C:2008:764, para. 93 et seq.

[E] The Criterion of Material Selectivity

The most vital question that needs to be answered, when assessing the State-aid character of a fiscal measure, is whether it is selective, meaning that the measure under review favours certain undertakings or the production of certain goods.[12]

The concept of selectivity consists of two components. The first component is a geographical one - meaning, in essence, that a measure is selective if undertakings in a specific part of the entire territory of a Member State are treated differently (i.e., more favourably than in the rest of this territory). The second component looks at all other forms of unequal treatment of undertakings by the intervention of the Member State. Whilst the notion of territorial or geographic selectivity has been largely resolved by the EU Courts' jurisprudence,[13] the concept of *material* selectivity is still far from clear.

According to the classic test for judging material selectivity that the CJEU established in *Adria-Wien Pipeline*,[14] any assessment of this criterion is to be performed in three successive steps:

- The first step is to define the reference system, by examining whether and to what extent the measure under review results in unequal treatment - that is, the extent to which different undertakings or economic sectors being treated differently - within the Member State.
- The second step is to ascertain whether such unequal treatment occurs with respect to different undertakings or groups of undertakings that are, in light of the objective(s) pursued by the measure under review, in a comparable factual and legal situation, leading to more favourable treatment for some.
- The third and final step is to determine whether such 'favourable treatment may be justified by the nature or general purposes of the system of which it is a part, in particular where a tax regime results directly from the basic or guiding principles of the national tax system'.[15]

In performing this three-step test, it is of the utmost importance to keep in mind that the reference system within which such material selectivity must be ascertained is limited to the territory of the Member State granting the advantage. Thus, it is not permissible to compare a given national measure to other measures adopted by other EU Member States. In other words, the concept of material selectivity refers to unequal treatment of different undertakings or groups of undertakings by one and the same Member State, not to differences in such treatment between different Member States.[16]

12. As AG Kokott rightly opined in the *Finanzamt Linz* case, all the other requirements of Art. 107(1) TFEU are typically fulfilled. *Finanzamt Linz*, C-66/14, AG Opinion, EU:C:2015:242.
13. *See Portugal* v *Commission* ('*Azores*'), C-88/03, Judgment, EU:C:2006:511; *UGT Rioja*, Joined Cases C-428 to C-434/06, Judgment, EU:C:2008:488; as well as *Banco Comercial dos Açores* v *Commission*, T-75/03, Judgment, EU:T:2009:322.
14. *Adria-Wien Pipeline and Wietersdorfer & Peggauer Zementwerke*, C-143/99, Judgment, EU:C:2001:598.
15. *Paint Graphos and Others*, Joined Cases C-78/08 to C-80/08, Judgment, EU:C:2011:550, paras 65 & 69.
16. *See Salzgitter I*, T-308/00, Judgment, EU:T:2004:199, para. 81.

[F] The Material Standards

In this context, it is highly illustrative to quote Advocate General (AG) Kokott's opinion in *Finanzamt Linz*:

> I have pointed out before, in *Presidente del Consiglio dei Ministri*, that, on account of the criteria for examining selectivity which have been l The case, referred to the CJEU by the Austrian *Verwaltungsgerichtshof*, concerned in essence a fiscal system, by which the book value of foreign participations of Austrian companies could not be written-down, whereas this possibility was granted in case of domestic participations, thereby reducing the taxable base for corporation tax. The *Finanzamt Linz* had refused to recognise the amortizations claimed by the plaintiffs on the ground that these were possible only in the case of shareholdings in Austrian corporations, whereas they were claimed for shareholdings in Slovakian ones. (Footnotes omitted.)[17]

The *Finanzamt Linz* case,[18] referred to the CJEU by the Austrian *Verwaltungsgerichtshof*, essentially concerned a fiscal system in which Austrian companies could write down the book value of their shareholdings in domestic corporations and thereby reduce their taxable base. However, they could not so for their holdings in foreign entities. The *Finanzamt Linz* had refused to recognize amortizations claimed by the plaintiffs for their shareholdings in Slovakian entities on the ground that such amortization was only possible for shareholdings in Austrian corporations; the plaintiffs appealed that decision.

In essence, the CJEU was asked to answer two questions. First, did the *Finanzamt Linz*'s refusal to recognize the amortizations for foreign shareholding amount to an infringement of the right of establishment as laid down by Article 49 TFEU? And, second, did the differentiation between domestic and foreign shareholdings amount to an illegal State aid within the meaning of Article 107(1) TFEU?

[1] The Admissibility of the State-Aid Question

AG Kokott opined that the question of whether the Austrian measure constituted illegal aid within the meaning of Article 107(1) TFEU depended on whether allowing goodwill to be amortized only in relation to domestic shareholdings amounted to an infringement of the fundamental freedoms of the Treaty, more specifically Article 49 TFEU in

---

> In the present case, when a 'normal' tax burden within the meaning of the aforementioned case-law is being determined, comparison of the tax rules applicable in all of the Member States, or even some of them, would inevitably distort the aim and functioning of the provisions on the monitoring of State aid. In the absence of Community-level harmonization of the tax provisions of the Member States, such an approach would in effect compare different factual and legal situations arising from legislative and regulatory disparities between the Member States.

17. *Finanzamt Linz*, C-66/14, AG Opinion, para. 103.
18. *Finanzamt Linz*, C-66/14, Judgment, EU:C:2015:661.

conjunction with Article 54 TFEU. She reasoned that if there was such an infringement, the likely remedy would be to expand the right to amortize good will to foreign shareholdings. However, in that context, the remedy could potentially cause an expansion of an illegal State aid, which would be an unacceptable result. Thus, she opined, that, when such an infringement was present, the question must arise as to whether the potential remedy would have to be refused, because the underlying measure also constituted illegal State aid, such that any expanded application of such underlying measure would simply expand the group of persons subject to recapture of that illegal State aid.[19] The court rejected AG Kokott's reasoning - correctly so, in my view - arguing that, even if the measure would amount to a selective State aid, it would only give the one who had been refused such aid a claim to receive it, too.[20]

[2] Should the Same Material Standards Apply?

In my view, AG Kokott's general argument in favour of applying the same material standards to assessing both a fundamental freedom infringement and an illegal State-aid prohibition is somewhat confusing in light of her own findings.

First, AG Kokott limits, understandably so, her argument to cases 'where aid may be selective because it favours domestic situations over foreign ones'.[21] But, this is self-evident; if it were otherwise, no issue of an infringement of the fundamental freedoms could occur.

However, it becomes somewhat more difficult to understand her logic, when comparing it to her simultaneous opinion that the measure under review was an infringement of Article 49 TFEU in conjunction with Article 54 TFEU, but not from any of the three different angles she looked at:

- first, only legal persons taxed pursuant to the Corporate Tax Act 1988 were eligible for goodwill amortization, whereas natural persons, taxed in accordance with the Austrian Law on Income Tax, were not;
- second, the amortization of goodwill favoured companies subject to group taxation over companies that did not benefit from group taxation; and
- third, the limitation of goodwill amortization to domestic shareholdings and not foreign shareholdings.

Apart from the obvious lack of internal logic, it seems difficult to reconcile her approach with the way the criterion of material selectivity must be assessed. As pointed out above, material selectivity essentially boils down to whether two or more groups of undertakings are treated differently. Whether or not they are, in fact, treated differently depends on whether or not they are, in light of the aim pursued by the measure under

19. *Finanzamt Linz*, C-66/14, AG Opinion, paras 27-32,
20. Constant jurisprudence: *Banks*, C-390/98, Judgment, EU:C:2001:456, para. 80; *Air Liquide Industries Belgium*, Joined Cases C-393/04 and C-41/05, Judgment, EU:C:2006:403, para. 43.
21. *Finanzamt Linz*, C-66/14, AG Opinion, para. 103.

(State-aid) review, in a legally and factually comparable situation. Moreover, the measure must not be justifiable in light of the internal logic of the reference system to which it belongs. It is hard to imagine that Member States' measures, potentially caught by Article 107(1) TFEU, and reference systems follow the logic of the Treaty´s fundamental freedoms.

Finally, there is no reason to apply the same material standards to both assessments, because the jurisprudence of the EU courts expressly sees both sets of rules as a condition *sine qua non* for declaring a measure compatible with the internal market. In contrast to the EU rules for the protection of the environment, the General Court expressly highlighted the importance of the fundamental freedoms:

> After all, if aid for the protection of the environment can be declared compatible with the internal market under Article 107(3)(b) or (c) TFEU, aid which has harmful effects on the environment does not, by that fact alone, adversely affect the establishment of the internal market. Although it must be integrated into the definition and implementation of EU policies, particularly those which have the aim of establishing the internal market (Article 11 TFEU; see also judgment of 13 September 2005 in *Commission* v *Council*, C-176/03, ECR, EU:C:2005:542, paragraph 42), protection of the environment does not constitute, per se, one of the components of that internal market, defined as an area without internal frontiers in which the free movement of goods, persons, services and capital is ensured (Article 26(2) TFEU).[22]

This demonstrates that there is even no need to harmonize the criteria for assessing whether a measure is materially selective and whether it constitutes an infringement of one of the fundamental freedoms. Moreover, this is, quite evidently so, because, even if different standards were applied, a finding that a measure is not an aid, as it is not materially selective, would not thereby make it compatible with the law of the fundamental freedoms. Such a finding of non-selectivity would simply, and only, mean that the assessment of an infringement of the fundamental freedoms could not be undertaken in the framework of a procedure under Article 108 TFEU.

§4.03 THE OUTLOOK

The reflections set forth in this chapter highlight that, despite the fact that both set of rules – that is to say, the ones applicable to State-aid issues and the ones applicable to fundamental freedom issues – must be adhered to in order to declare a fiscal measure compatible with the internal market. They serve completely different purposes. Whilst EU jurisprudence firmly demands that the fundamental freedom rules be respected (i.e., meaning that no authorization for a State-aid measure may be granted if it contravenes the former), it is wrong to seek to harmonize the material standards to be applied when it comes to subjecting fiscal measures to both a State-aid investigation and scrutiny under the Treaty´s rules on fundamental freedoms. The main issue for

22. *Castelnou Energia*, T-57/11, Judgment, EU:T:2014:1021, para. 189.

assessing fiscal measure under Article 107(1) TFEU is the criterion of material selectively. In this opaque exercise, the aims pursued by a Member State's fiscal measure and the internal logic of the fiscal measure's reference system are the key parameters. They are, by definition, different from the aims pursued by the Treaty's fundamental freedoms, which is why both sets of rules have to be respected jointly, but without being harmonized.

CHAPTER 5

Discretionary Power of Tax Authorities as a State Aid Problem

Michael Lang & Alexander Zeiler[*]

§5.01 DISCRETION AS A LEGAL PHENOMENON

In this chapter, different aspects of tax authorities' discretionary power are examined in light of European Union (EU) State aid law. The first part will approach discretion from a general legal perspective and describe its role in a legal system. Based on these findings, the case law of the European Court of Justice (ECJ) regarding Member State provisions granting tax authorities a margin of discretion in their decision-making will be analysed in order to determine when such provisions may be considered State aid. Afterwards, the assessment of selectivity in the context of individual administrative decisions will be discussed. Finally, the chapter will examine the compatibility of tax rulings with State aid law.

Discretion is a phenomenon practically inherent in every legal order. Usually, positive law is created through the dynamic process of gradual concretization within a hierarchal structure of norms.[1] When enacting the law a competent organ always has to interpret a relatively abstract rule in order to reach a more concrete decision. During that process of gradual concretization, that organ is bound by a higher set of norms that establish the framework in which it has to come to its own decision. Within that leeway, contemplated by the higher norm, it is free to decide according to its own values.[2] Therefore, the application of the law is always a dualism of applying a higher norm, which binds the decision to a certain extent, and of creating new law within the

* Financial support from the Austrian Federal Ministry of Science, Research and Economy and the National Foundation for Research, Technology and Development is gratefully acknowledged.

1. Hans Kelsen, *Reine Rechtslehre* 228 et seq. (2d ed., 1960).
2. *Ibid.* at 351.

latitude provided by that higher norm.[3] If, for example, the legislator passes a new law, it has, on the one hand, a margin of discretion to enact a new statute according to the results reached in the political process, but, on the other hand, it is constrained by formal or material requirements stipulated in the constitution, such as fundamental rights. The same is true for authorities having the competence to flesh out a general law in the form of more detailed, abstract rules. Within the framework prescribed by the higher-ranked law, authorities are able to create new law and, therefore, can concretize the general law according to its own assessment of the relevant circumstances. Finally, the situation is not different where authorities have to decide a particular case. By making an individual decision based on general, abstract norms, authorities are bound by these rules; but, depending on their scope, they have more or less room to manoeuvre in order to come to a final decision. Therefore, the character of a legal decision at each level of the legal hierarchy is not different from a qualitative perspective. The competent authorities applying a higher norm are always bound, to a certain extent, by that higher rule, but, at the same time, they have a certain leeway in their decision-making, which they have to fill with their own values. The only difference between the various levels of law-making is the concrete degree of latitude enjoyed by the respective organ in its actual decision-making. In either case, the legislator or the authorities have discretion with respect to the manner of creating a lower norm or making a legal decision. Whereas the general legislator is just bound by the constitution and, therefore, has relatively far-reaching discretionary power to create new law, the authorities' leeway in applying more specific rules may be relatively minor.[4]

Consequently, the discretionary power of authorities cannot be considered the mere result of the indefinite nature of legal language or even as an arbitrary effect of the law. Rather, it is a phenomenon inherent in a system of positive law caused by the need to provide a relatively abstract norm in order to reach a relatively concrete decision.[5] There will always remain a certain amount of room to manoeuvre, as an abstract rule governing a more concrete decision can, by nature, only regulate certain elements of a decision, but must leave other aspects open for the assessment of the authorities in a specific situation.[6] Even if a very detailed tax rule does not seem to leave any room for interpretation and consequently reduces the tax authorities' discretion to nearly zero, they can, at least, still decide which tax returns handed in they want to deal first with and, thereby, influence which taxpayers eventually have to pay their taxes earlier when compared to others.[7] In the end, a general abstract rule, regardless of its level of detail, can never determine all of the relevant circumstances of a real situation.

3. Adolf Merkl, *Allgemeines Verwaltungsrecht* 142 (1969).
4. Kelsen, *supra* n. 1, at 351.
5. Merkl, *supra* n. 2, at 144.
6. *Ibid.* at 141.
7. *Cf.* Kelsen, *supra* n. 1, at 347.

§5.02 GENERAL RULES AND DISCRETION

Due to the systematic structure of positive law, every legal act is only partly governed by a higher set of rules and, eventually, there always remains an undetermined sphere for the authorities' decision. With respect to administrative decisions in a specific situation, the authorities' freedom depends on the degree of determination contemplated by the applicable law. In some cases, the authorities may, according to the wording of a provision, have extensive latitude, whereas in another situation, the law precisely prescribes administrative conduct and leaves the authorities with little room to manoeuvre.

However, the concrete meaning of a legal provision cannot be derived only from the abstract wording of a rule. Rather, the interpretation of the wording can be the beginning of the process of determining a provision's concrete scope. Just because a rule is explicitly designed as a discretionary provision or uses vague legal concepts to govern administrative conduct, does not automatically lead to the result that, in a specific case, more than one solution is correct. Even if a provision - from an abstract point of view - gives the authorities wide leeway, it cannot be assumed that they generally enjoy that wide margin of discretion in every situation. Frequently, rules are deliberately drafted in a broad manner, so that the law can be applied to a wide range of different cases or new developments not explicitly foreseen by the legislator.[8] Nevertheless, in a specific case, that does not mean that various legal interpretations are feasible, as a legal provision must always be exercised within the context of the law of which it forms a part. The fact that a rule - when considered in the abstract - seems to have a wide scope according to the letter of the law, does not mean that there always remains a broad range of possible outcomes.

For that reason, it is necessary to analyse a legal provision using all methods of interpretation. In that regard, the historic development of the law and assessments originally made by the legislator may provide indications as to how the law should be understood. Moreover, the purpose of the law must be taken into account and the meaning of a rule must be examined within its legal context, which means that all legal provisions, regardless of their level of detail, must be analysed from a teleological and systematic point of view. Most of the time, the scope of a provision that, at first glance, provides a wide margin of discretion will narrow down considerably in the course of the interpretation process.[9] Finally, there will often remain only one or, at least, just a few possible solutions concerning the particular case at hand. As a result, the authorities, in the majority of the cases, will not be free to decide the case in their unfettered discretion, but rather constrained by the purpose of the provision and the legal context in which the applicable rule is embedded. Of course, in the case of an explicit discretionary grant or vague legal concepts, the range of possible outcomes may be broader when compared to more detailed provisions.

8. Bruno Peeters, *European Supervision on the Use of Vague and Undetermined Concepts in Tax Laws*, 22 EC Tax Rev. 112 (2013).
9. Wolfgang Gassner, *Ermessen im Steuerrecht - Referate und Diskussionsbeiträge* 51 (1970).

Having shown, from a general legal perspective, that discretion is a general legal phenomenon inherent in the legal system, but its actual scope depends on the particular level of law being applied in the context of a certain case, such discretionary power will now be examined in light of Article 107(1) TFEU. As the prerequisites for State aid (i.e., aid granted through State resources distorts the internal market) are fulfilled in most tax cases, the following analysis just focuses on the criterion of a selective advantage conferred on certain undertakings.

The first ECJ judgment dealing with authorities' discretionary power from a State aid perspective was delivered in a French case: *Kimberly Clark*.[10] Under certain conditions, French labour law obliged undertakings laying off staff to draw up a social plan in order to reduce redundancies and to facilitate re-employment of those employees whose redundancy could not be avoided. In that regard, undertakings could negotiate agreements with the *Fonds National de l'Emploi* (FNE), which provided programs promoting alternatives to redundancy or training measures to improve redundant employees' chances in the labour market, which were, within defined limits, financed by the State.[11] The FNE, as the competent authority, enjoyed a rather wide margin of discretion to determine the concrete conditions of such agreements.[12] Kimberly Clark, a cellulose manufacturer that had to lay off staff in the course of a business restructuring program, concluded various agreements with the FNE. In a State aid procedure, the Commission classified the financial contribution made to Kimberly Clark's social plan as prohibited State aid, but at the same time declared the measure as compatible with the internal market. Nevertheless, France appealed that decision, arguing, *inter alia*, that the whole mechanism that served as basis for the contribution did not constitute State aid, as it was a general measure open to all undertakings.[13]

In its decision, the ECJ first acknowledged that FNE intervention was neither restricted to certain categories of undertakings nor limited by sector or territory.[14] However, the Court held that:

> the FNE enjoys a degree of latitude which enables it to adjust its financial assistance having regard to a number of considerations such as, in particular, the choice of beneficiaries, the amount of the financial assistance and the conditions under which it is provided.[15]

Consequently, the measure was considered as being 'liable to place certain undertakings in a more favourable situation than others and thus ... meet[s] the conditions for the classification as [State] aid'.[16] Thus, the broad leeway granted to the FNE, potentially allowing it to treat certain undertakings beneficially, was sufficient to qualify the whole system as selective State aid.

10. *France* v *Commission* [hereinafter '*Kimberly Clark*'], C-241/94, Judgment, EU:C:1996:353.
11. *Cf. Kimberly Clark*, C-241/94, AG Opinion, EU:C:1996:195, para. 6 et seq.
12. *Cf. ibid.* para. 31.
13. *Cf. ibid.* para. 25.
14. *Kimberly Clark*, C-241/94, para. 22.
15. *Ibid.* para. 23.
16. *Ibid.* para. 24.

In two Italian cases, *Ecotrade*[17] and *Piaggio*,[18] the ECJ reviewed a law conferring discretionary power on the Minister of Industry to put insolvent industrial undertakings under extraordinary administration, thereby granting them special protection from the ordinary rules of insolvency. In order to fall under the scheme, insolvent companies had to have at least 300 employees and their debts to publicly-controlled bodies had to exceed a certain level.[19] Consequently, the special regime was only applicable to large undertakings. Its rules included various derogations from the regular insolvency procedures, *inter alia*, granting undertakings under such administration a special suspension of tax and other public debts.[20] In both cases, the Court held that:

> having regard to the class of undertakings covered by the legislation in issue and the scope of the discretion enjoyed by the minister ... that legislation meets the condition that it should relate to a specific undertaking, which is one of the defining features of State aid.[21]

From the Court's statement, it is not entirely clear whether the discretionary power together with the specific requirement restricting the scope of the law to 'large industrial undertakings in difficulties'[22] caused the classification as State aid or if the discretionary power of the authorities, itself, would also have been enough to lead to that result. In his opinion regarding the *Ecotrade* case, Advocate General (AG) Fennelly located selectivity in the scheme at two levels. According to the AG, either the limited scope of the law restricting the special administration procedure or the discretionary power of the authorities would have separately led to the qualification of the measure as State aid.[23] Referring to *Kimberly Clark*, he opined:

> Even if this discretion were not exercised, as it is in fact exercised, in respect of an already limited class of companies, it would leave a degree of latitude to the minister concerned which would be liable to place certain undertakings in a more favourable situation than others.[24]

Consequently, the discretionary power would have been sufficient to classify the measure as State aid. As the Court also quoted its prior *Kimberly Clark* decision, it is also likely that in the absence of quantitative criteria, the measure would have been selective due to the wide discretionary margin granted to the Minister of Industry.[25]

17. *Ecotrade*, C-200/97, Judgment, EU:C:1998:579.
18. *Piaggio*, C-295/97, Judgment, EU:C:1999:313.
19. *Ecotrade*, C-200/97, AG Opinion, EU:C:1998:378, para. 2.
20. *Cf. Piaggio*, C-295/97, para. 12 et seq.
21. *Ecotrade*, C-200/97, para. 40; *Piaggio*, C-295/97, para. 39.
22. *Piaggio*, C-295/97, para. 37.
23. *Ecotrade*, C-200/97, AG Opinion, EU:C:1998:378, para. 26.
24. *Ibid.* para. 28.
25. *Ecotrade*, C-200/97, para. 40.

In *Territorio Historico*,[26] the General Court[27] had to deal with State aid granted to Demesa, a refrigerator manufacturer, for establishing a plant in the Basque region. In addition to other grants stipulated in an agreement between Demesa and the Basque authorities, the undertaking received a tax credit provided in the general tax law.[28] In that regard the Basque tax law provided for a 45% tax credit for the cost of investment as long as the investment exceeded a certain minimum amount. In its underlying decision, the Commission had argued that the tax credit was selective due to the discretionary power of the authorities to determine the actual parameters of the tax credit and the minimum investment requirement stipulated in the law.[29] Regarding the authorities' latitude, the Court decided, with reference to *Kimberly Clark*, that by granting the tax authorities discretionary power, the provisions 'concerning the tax credit are liable to place certain undertakings in a more favourable situation than other.'[30] Thus, the discretionary power in applying the tax credit was sufficient to find the provision selective. In that regard, the Court rejected the applicants' argument that the authorities actually had no discretionary power and had to apply the tax credit uniformly and automatically to every undertaking satisfying the requirements prescribed by the law.[31] Instead, the Court found that the Basque authorities had wide latitude in fixing the amount of the allowable investment and could lay down the specific conditions for the tax credit in each case.[32] Interestingly, the Court did not even consider it important that, according to the Spanish constitution, the authorities could not apply the law in an arbitrary manner and were effectively obliged to grant the tax credit to every undertaking that fulfilled the requirement prescribed by the law.[33] In that context, the Court stated that it was not necessary for the tax authorities to have exercised their discretionary power in an arbitrary way; rather, it was sufficient that they could vary the amount used to calculate the tax benefit.[34] So, following the statements by the Court, the mere possibility that the tax authorities could put undertakings in a favourable position seems to be sufficient to find a provision selective, regardless of whether, in a particular case, a specific advantage was granted to an undertaking when compared to others falling within the scope of the law. Moreover, the Court confirmed the Commission's view that the minimum investment requirement, which limited the scope of the tax credit to large investments, was selective too. Therefore, the Basque provision was selective both because the authorities had a considerable margin of discretion in applying the tax credit and it included

26. *Territorio Historico de Álva*, Joined Cases T-127/99, T-129/99 and T-148/99, GC Judgment, EU:T:2002:59, para. 11.
27. The term 'General Court' used herein ('GC' in footnotes) refers either to the Court of First Instance or the General Court, as the case may be.
28. *Territorio Historico de Álva*, Joined Cases T-127/99, T-129/99 and T-148/99, para. 18.
29. *Ibid.* para. 145.
30. *Ibid.* para. 151.
31. *Ibid.* para. 148.
32. *Ibid.* para. 150.
33. Malte Strüber, *Steuerliche Beihilfen: Eine kritische Analyse der Anwendung des Beihilfeverbots im Bereich der direkten Steuern* 200 (2006).
34. *Territorio Historico de Álva*, Joined Cases T-127/99, T-129/99 and T-148/99, para. 154.

a minimum investment requirement restricting the scope of the tax credit to large investors.

In the Belgian *Maribel I* case,[35] which dealt with the reduction of social security contributions for certain economic sectors employing manual workers, the authorities' margin of discretion in decision-making did not lead to a finding of selectivity. In that case, the law only governed the general principles of the scheme, but the actual scope of the measure was regulated by Royal decrees. Here, the Court decided that the measure at stake could not be declared State aid just because the authorities had discretionary power regarding the application of specific social charge reductions, as the general principle prescribed by the law were further detailed in legally binding Royal Decrees that left the authorities no latitude in their eventual decision-making.[36] Nevertheless, in the end, the Belgian Maribel scheme was determined to be selective, since the advantages were just granted in specific economic sectors.[37]

Lastly, the recent *P Oy* case,[38] concerning a Finnish loss deduction system, is of particular interest. The ECJ had to review a provision giving authorities latitude in granting taxpayers an exemption from a general prohibition of loss deduction in the case of a change in ownership in a company.[39] According to the Finnish provision, the tax authorities could, for special reasons in which it was necessary for the continuation of the activities of the company, authorize the deduction of losses.[40] In that case, the Court held that this discretionary provision could not generally be considered selective, as long as the authorities' scope of decision-making was limited by objective criteria related to the tax system 'such as the objective of avoiding trade in losses.'[41] Nevertheless, the latitude provided by the provision could be qualified as selective if criteria unrelated to the tax system, such as the maintaining of employment, could be taken into account by the tax authorities.[42] In that case, the Court explicitly referred to the possible administrative conduct under that provision, stating that the discretion granted to the authorities should not be regarded as selective if the authorities could only exercise their discretionary power in line with objectives inherent in the tax system and could not grant favourable treatment due to external parameters. Ultimately, the ECJ did not rule on the issue, due to its lack of information about the concrete scope of the discretionary provision under review.[43]

The ECJ's case law tends to find provisions conferring a wide margin of discretionary power on authorities to be selective, since they enable authorities to put certain undertakings in a more favourable position than others. This tendency is understandable, as Member States could otherwise implement legal provisions that create an impression of being general in nature, but that, in practice, just serve as a

35. *Belgium* v *Commission ('Maribel I')*, C-75/97, Judgment, EU:C:1999:311, para. 12.
36. *Ibid.* para. 27.
37. *Ibid.* para. 32 et seq.
38. *P Oy*, C-6/12, Judgment, EU:C:2013:525.
39. *Ibid.* para. 16.
40. *Ibid.* para. 6.
41. *Ibid.* para. 26.
42. *Ibid.* para. 30.
43. *Ibid.* para. 31.

legal basis for the administration to grant a selective advantage.[44] However, if one generalizes the statements made by the Courts, the outcome could be excessive, as then every provision that grants leeway to authorities would have to be qualified as State aid, since there would always be a possibility that an advantage could be granted to certain undertakings.[45]

As previously shown, discretion is a general phenomenon in every legal system. Therefore, provisions giving authorities broader latitude have to be interpreted – through more detailed rules, for example – in the context of the law and the specific circumstances of a case. Most of the time, the authorities' discretionary margin – which, from an abstract perspective, might seem to be relatively broad – narrows down considerably and often does not leave much room to manoeuver to the authorities, as the law, as a whole, substantially predetermines the exercise of such discretionary power.[46] It would lead to odd results if every vague legal concept was qualified as selective just because, in the abstract, it confers a certain leeway on the authorities, potentially enabling them to put certain undertakings in a favourable position. For that reason, it cannot, in general, be derived from the case law that every provision conferring such leeway on the authorities in their decision-making automatically infringes Article 107(1) TFEU. In that context, the ECJ developed a more differentiated approach in *P Oy*,[47] by holding that discretionary power is not to be regarded as selective, if the authorities' leeway is limited by criteria related to objectives inherent in the tax regime.[48] In that case the Court explicitly accepted a certain discretionary margin in the authorities' decision-making, if the discretionary power is restricted to objectives inherent in the legal system. Therefore, it is no problem under State aid law, if a provision grants authorities a certain leeway in their decision-making, as long as that latitude stays within the systemic framework of the respective tax law. On the contrary, if a provision provides authorities with sufficient discretion to enable them to

44. Michael Lang, *Die Auswirkungen des gemeinschaftsrechtlichen Beihilferechts auf das Steuerrecht* 48 (2009).
45. Franz Philipp Sutter, *Das EG-Beihilfenverbot und sein Durchführungsverbot in Steuersachen* 62 (2005).
46. *Cf.* Lang, *supra* n. 44, at 48.
47. *P Oy*, C-6/12.
48. It will be quite difficult to determine the objectives inherent in a tax system. But, regarding this judgment, the Court seems to focus on technical mechanisms, which are necessary for the proper functioning of a tax system. In the case at hand, an exemption from the general loss deduction prohibition in the case of a change in ownership of a company was at stake. Here, the Court seems to allow for a grant of discretionary power to tax authorities in so far as it is in line with the general goal of the loss deduction prohibition, namely to prevent loss trading. So, if authorities only have the power to evaluate a case under the premise of preventing loss trading, it should not be considered selective. This could, for example, be the case if a company having a considerable amount of loss carry-forwards is acquired by an investor who wants to pursue the business already conducted by the company. Whereas, in a case where, after the acquisition the original business activity is terminated and the company is now used to run another business, the situation would be different if the company could keep the losses due to the mere fact that it employs about the same number of staff. In such a situation, the leeway of the authority may be classified as selective, as here the approval would be given for the objective of maintaining employment and not just because of considerations of preventing loss trading.

treat undertakings favourably based on criteria unrelated to the law, such as maintenance of employment, it must be considered selective.[49] This position is perfectly in line with the ECJ's general case law regarding selectivity, where the Court rejects justifications for selective measures for external goals (e.g., environmental protection).[50]

Taking all that into account, only provisions with an indefinite scope, not giving guidance to the tax authorities and, thus, enabling them to put certain undertakings in favourable situations for reasons unrelated to the tax system, should be classified as State aid. Here, the recent cases *SIAT*[51] and *Itelcar*,[52] which finally introduce the concept of legal certainty as a fundamental principle of EU tax law,[53] have to be mentioned.[54] If a general, non-selective provision is '*clear, precise and predictable*'[55] regarding its effects and, therefore, suits the principle of legal certainty set out by the Court, it will not be considered State aid under Article 107(1) TFEU.[56] Because, under such a rule, the authorities' margin of discretion is sufficiently predetermined that no room for substantially different treatment in comparable situations is left. In that context, selectivity should only be assumed if authorities have room to confer a selective advantage on a specific taxpayer in the course of their administrative conduct.[57]

§5.03 INDIVIDUAL DECISIONS AND DISCRETION

The question is, now, under which circumstances administrative conduct must be qualified as State aid. The main issue in that regard is how to determine the selectivity of an administrative practice based on a general, non-selective rule. Unfortunately, in tax law, this is often not straightforward; due to a lack of case law, the ECJ has not yet developed specific guidelines for the review of individual acts as it has in other fields (such as, for instance, the private investor test for a capital contribution by a State in a certain undertaking[58]). Only in the case of a waiver or deferral of existing tax claims, has the ECJ offered a rather clear standard, adjusting the private investor test to a so-called private creditor test.[59] Accordingly, tax authorities are obliged to act like a creditor under market conditions: they must charge a certain amount of interest for

49. *P Oy*, C-6/12, para. 27.
50. *Cf. British Aggregates* v *Commission*, C-487/06 P, Judgment, EU:C:2008:757, para. 92.
51. *SIAT*, C-318/10, Judgment, EU:C:2012:415.
52. *Itelcar*, C-282/12, Judgment, EU:C:2013:629.
53. *Cf. Gebroedes van Es*, C-143/93, Judgment, EU:C:1996:45, para. 27.
54. *SIAT*, C-318/10, paras 58–59; *Itelcar*, C-282/12, para. 44.
55. *SIAT*, C-318/10, para. 58 (emphasis added).
56. For a general remark on vague and undetermined legal concepts, see Bruno Peeters, *European Supervision on the Use of Vague and Undetermined Concepts in Tax Laws*, 22 EC Tax Rev. 112 (2013).
57. *See* §5.03, *infra*, for a detailed discussion regarding the assessment administrative practice conferring a selective advantage on a certain taxpayer.
58. Helmuth Cremer, *Article 107, paragraph 11, in EUV/AEUV: Das Verfassungsrecht der Europäischen Union mit Europäischer Grundrechtecharta* (Christian Calliess and Matthias Ruffert eds., 4th ed. 2011).
59. *DMT*, C-256/97, Judgment, EU:C:1999:332, para. 25.

outstanding debts and, if the debtor is not able to settle the amount and the future prospect for the business is negative, they must initiate insolvency procedures.[60] Moreover, settled Commission practice makes clear that the persistent non-collection of outstanding tax claims is State aid under Article 107(1) TFEU.[61]

The State aid assessment, however, becomes more difficult regarding an allegedly selective calculation of the actual tax burden. In that respect, various questions arise from the evaluation of Member States' presumably beneficial administrative practices. First of all, cases in which the authorities exceed their predetermined margin of discretion, leading to a lower tax burden for specific undertakings when compared to similar situations where the law is correctly applied, should be considered. Such an administrative practice obviously treats taxpayers in comparable legal and factual situations differently. Therefore, the beneficial administrative conduct through misapplication of the law should be qualified as prohibited State aid. The current Commission practice also seems to tend toward that direction. In its notice concerning the application of State aid rules regarding business taxation, the Commission stated that an administrative practice 'that departs from the general tax rule to the benefit of individual undertakings in principle leads to a presumption of State aid and must be analysed in detail.'[62] In a published draft notice regarding the interpretation of Article 107(1) TFEU, the Commission got even more explicit by saying that it will consider settlements between tax authorities and certain taxpayers 'contrary to the applicable tax provision' that result in a lower tax burden to be a selective advantage.[63]

Such a position, however, could probably raise criticism, as it could be argued that it introduces an external review mechanism for domestic decisions beside the regular, domestic chain of appeal. But, from an effect-based State aid perspective, where every form of aid granted through State resources is prohibited, it has to be kept in mind that neither the authorities granting a benefit through an unlawful decision nor the favourably-treated undertaking would likely appeal the unlawful decision. Therefore, it would contradict the fundamental goal of State aid law, if a beneficial treatment generated by disregarding national law could not be investigated, only due to the argument, that in such a procedure, questions of domestic law would have to be examined.

In that regard, too, a situation is conceivable where the law is generally ignored and all relevant taxpayers are treated favourably by breaking the law. This could, for instance, be the case if an administrative circular indicates the common non-application of a burdensome provision and, as a result, all undertakings that would normally fall under the provision benefit from that illegal practice. Due to the general

60. Commission Decision 2003/283/EC of 27 Nov. 2002, *Refractarios Especiales*, OJ L 108/21 (2003).
61. Commission Decision 1999/509/EC of 14 Oct. 1998, *Magefesa*, OJ L 198/15 (1999); Commission Decision 2002/935/EC of 14 May 2002, *Empresas Álvarez*, OJ L 329/1 (2002), para. 51 et seq.
62. Commission Notice on the Application of State Aid Rules to Measures of Direct Business Taxation, OJ L 23/14 (1998) [hereinafter 'State Aid Direct Business Taxation Notice'], para. 22.
63. Draft Commission Notice on the Notion of State Aid Pursuant to Article 107(1) TFEU, http://ec.europa.eu/competition/consultations/2014_state_aid_notion/draft_guidance_en.pdf, para. 173 (accessed 23 Mar. 2017) [hereinafter 'Draft Notion of State Aid Notice'].

nature of the measure, such administrative conduct could not be seen as selective, as all taxpayers receive privileged treatment vis-à-vis the relevant provision.

However, it could be argued that, by assessing the selectivity of such a measure, not only must the actual treatment of taxpayers regarding the specific provision be evaluated, but also the unlawful administrative practice must be compared to the situation of other taxpayers who are covered under other rules and are treated in line with the law. Following that view, the general misapplication of the law in favour of all relevant taxpayers would lead to State aid. But, it must be emphasized that the other tax rules, which are applied correctly, have a different scope and do not lead to the same legal effects as the misapplied norm. Moreover, EU law is generally neutral regarding the legal quality of domestic provisions: the national legislator cannot defend a certain norm based on the argument that a law was enacted by subordinate local authorities. Therefore, from an EU law perspective, it should also not make a difference if certain rules are enacted by the legislator in the form of a general law or by an administrative regulation.[64] The degree of abstraction between a general law and a regulation is not different in principle. From an effect-based point of view, it remains at least doubtful that a beneficial-but-general administrative circular should be treated differently in comparison to a regulation.[65] In the end, if the view that a general misapplication of law should not be seen as State aid is accepted, an odd situation would remain: the more persistently a national law is broken, the greater the chance that there is no violation of State aid rules.

If a legal provision leaves the authorities a certain leeway in their decision making, then it can be assumed that every decision staying within the framework contemplated by the law is in line with State aid law. In that respect, the personal intention of the authorities is irrelevant; for State aid purposes, only the effect of a certain measure is relevant.[66] Consequently, if the tax authorities deliberately interpret the law in favour of a certain taxpayer, but stay within the discretion established by the applicable law, no selective advantage is conferred on the taxpayer, since the non-selective rule is applied correctly. Actually, if a certain provision really would enable the authorities to treat taxpayers in comparable situations substantially differently, such a rule might itself contain a selective element.

In that context, it should be pointed out that the latitude of the authorities can change over time, even if a specific legal provision remains unchanged. By nature, law is a living organism and can be subject to changes. The meaning of a law may evolve, for instance, due to supreme court decisions to which authorities are bound. If a court's judgment now holds a certain legal interpretation previously used by the authorities does not comport with the law the authorities' ability to exercise its discretion is thereby reduced and their prior decisions following that wrong line of reasoning have

64. In that context, the term 'regulation' meant an abstract, legally binding administrative act.

65. *Cf.* Michael Lang, *Die gesetzwidrige Begünstigung von Steuerpflichtigen als gemeinschaftsrechtswidrige Beihilfe in Ertragsteuern in Wissenschaft und Praxis, in Festschrift Doralt* 242 (Reinhold Beiser et al. eds, 2007).

66. *Cf. British Aggregates* v *Commission*, C-487/06 P, para. 85; *see also* Lang, *supra*, n. 44, at 23; for a critical view, see Wolfgang Schön, *Taxation and State Aid Law in the European Union*, 36 Common Mkt L. Rev. 23 (1999).

to be considered incorrect in light of the new case law. A decision must remain compatible with State aid law during its whole period of its application. Here, the question arises if earlier decisions according to which taxes are still to be paid, but which cannot be contested due to procedural rules, must also be revised because of EU State aid law. State aid law could, therefore, lead to the consequence that a Member State's domestic procedural laws would have to incorporate rules allowing for an amendment of such final administrative decisions.

A problem could also arises in jurisdictions where supreme court decisions do not generally have a legally binding effect for the authorities and are just relevant for the individual case before the court. For that reason, the authorities principally could deviate from the court's assessment and decide a case based on a different legal interpretation in order to 'provoke' another judgment. This gives the court the opportunity to review its prior decision and possibly change its legal opinion. If a favourable deviation from the case law would be automatically considered as State aid an important tool for reviewing legal decisions could possibly be removed in certain jurisdictions.

Moreover, State aid law could lead to the consequence that tax authorities are, to a certain extent, bound by their own decisions. Even if authorities have a certain amount of room to manoeuver in applying the law, any deviation from a prior assessment should be based on a proper justification. For that reason, if the authorities have interpreted the law in a certain way in one year, it should not be possible for them to change the assessment for the benefit of a taxpayer in the following year without sound reasons. The same would be true if authorities have to make decisions regarding different taxpayers. In comparable situations, the tax authorities should not be able to come to substantially different conclusions. Otherwise, prohibited State aid could be assumed with regard to the favoured company. Since State aid law is principally neutral regarding domestic competence rules, one could even argue for a legally binding effect of administrative decisions of different branches of the tax administration. If, for example, Tax Authority A has decided a case following a specific line of argumentation, Tax Authority B, responsible for another region, should not deviate from the view previously taken by Tax Authority A.

However, having regard to the ECJ case law concerning regional selectivity, a more differentiated evaluation may be appropriate to assess the possible, legally binding effect of administrative decisions in order to determine the selectivity of favourable administrative conduct.[67] Following the requirements developed by AG Geelhoed[68] and subsequently applied by the ECJ, a favourable tax measure only applicable in a specific region should not be regarded as selective, if a regional authority enacts the measure is sufficiently autonomous.[69] According to the ECJ's case law, the autonomy of regional authorities is sufficient and a favourable tax measure

67. *Portugal* v *Commission*, C-88/03, Judgment, EU:C:2006:511; *UGT Rioja*, Joined Cases C-428 to 434/06, Judgment, EU:C:2008:488, para. 51.
68. *Portugal* v *Commission*, C-88/03, AG Opinion, EU:C:2005:618, para. 54.
69. *Cf.* Michael Lang, *Beschlussrechtsabgaben der Gemeinden als regional selektive Beihilfen in Theorie und Praxis des Wirtschaftsrechts, in FS H. Rene Laurer* 521 (Clemens Jabloner et al. eds, 2009).

will not, therefore, raise an issue under Article 107(1) TFEU, if it is institutionally, procedurally and economically autonomous from a central government.[70] The condition of institutional autonomy requires that the local authority – from a constitutional point of view – has a political and administrative status separate from that of the central government.[71] Hence, the local body must be formally separated from the central organization. Moreover, under the requirement of procedural autonomy, the central government must not be able to directly intervene as regards the content of a certain tax measure, which means that the local authority can exercise its powers regardless of the conduct of the central authority.[72] But, in that context, it does not harm the autonomy of a local authority if it has to comply with certain conditions set out centrally, such as restrictions on a constitutional level.[73] This is even true if an act of the local authority can be reviewed by a national court, as long as the jurisdiction of the court is limited to deciding about compliance with constitutional requirements. Moreover, a conciliation or coordination mechanism in order to avoid conflicts between the local and central authorities does not, itself, lead to the consequence that the local authority is not considered as procedurally autonomous. In essence, to meet the requirement of procedural autonomy, the local body has to have the competence to adopt tax measures independently without direct interference from the central government on its actual content.[74] Finally, the local authority has to bear the financial consequences of its tax rules, in order to be qualified as economically autonomous. Consequently, any decrease in the tax income may not be offset or subsidized by the central body. However, financial transfers between a State's entities can have various reasons. According to AG Kokott, two requirements must be fulfilled to establish a connection between local tax legislation and a financial transfer:

> First of all, the level of the local tax revenue must be included as a parameter in determining any financial transfer. Secondly, a reduction in tax revenue must also lead to a corresponding compensatory adjustment in the transfer of funds between the State levels.[75]

In *UGT Rioja*, the ECJ looked for a causal relationship between a tax measure adopted by the local authority and the financial compensation from the central level.[76] As an individual favourable administrative decision and financial transfers between the central and local authority will hardly be related directly, an assessment whether there is a binding effect of administrative decisions between different local tax authorities should just focus on the requirements of institutional and procedural autonomy.

By applying the conditions as set out by the ECJ, a favourable decision deviating from the prior practice of another branch of the tax authorities should not be qualified

70. *Portugal* v *Commission*, C-88/03, para. 67; *UGT Rioja*, Joined Cases C-428 to 434/06, para. 51.
71. *Portugal* v *Commission* C-88/03, para. 67.
72. *Ibid.* para. 68.
73. *UGT Rioja*, Joined Cases C-428 to 434/06, AG Opinion, EU:C:2008:262, para. 88 et seq.
74. *UGT Rioja*, C-428 to 434/06, para. 107; *cf. UGT Rioja*, C-428 to 434/06, AG Opinion, para. 97.
75. *UGT Rioja*, C-428 to 434/06, AG Opinion, para. 110.
76. *UGT Rioja*, C-428 to 434/06, para. 129.

as selective, if the local authority is, first of all, formally separate from any central organization and, therefore, has its own constitutional, political, and administrative status. Moreover, another constitutionally separate body must not have the ability to directly intervene in the authority's decision-making process. Hence, if the central government can directly instruct a local authority on how it has to proceed in a specific matter, the local authority will not be found to be sufficiently autonomous. However, if there is no possibility for intervention and the local administrative body is constitutionally and politically separate from the central organization, autonomy can be assumed and the administrative decisions of other tax authorities will not have a binding effect on the local authority. In such case, differing decisions of different tax authorities in different regions of a Member State are acceptable under State aid rules.

§5.04 TAX RULINGS

Tax rulings, although recently drawing scrutiny from the Commission, are useful instruments to enhance the predictability of administrative decisions. In general, rulings can considerably contribute to legal certainty, as complex questions arising in practice are resolved in advance and, consequently, subsequent tax disputes are avoided. A ruling mechanism enables authorities to assess a certain case prior to its actual realization and binds them to a certain legal evaluation with regard to that specific situation. Therefore, the taxpayer has, in advance, information about the way the authorities will actually apply the law and can already take account of the authorities' assessments when planning its business activities. Often, rulings can compensate for some of the uncertainties described above and can provide more certainty.

Some jurisdictions explicitly provide a formal ruling procedure, others do not. Under State aid law, it should be irrelevant in which form a ruling is rendered to a taxpayer. It does not make any difference whether such an interpretation is provided to the taxpayer in an informal procedure, maybe just protected by good faith, or in a formal ruling mechanism resulting in a legally binding act. The only relevant question under Article 107(1) TFEU is whether some undertakings are treated more favourably than others in comparable legal and factual situations. So, if an administrative decision stays within the discretionary margin prescribed by the law, it cannot be assumed that a selective advantage was granted to a taxpayer. Of course, an informal decision-making process may give rise to suspicions about whether the authorities stay within their room to manoeuvre.[77] Therefore, at least in complex cases where the margin in decision-making for the tax authorities is rather broad, it might be useful to implement a formal ruling procedure consisting of clear requirements in order to achieve a proper assessment of difficult legal questions.

The fact that tax rulings are not published should not raise any issues under State aid law, as normal tax assessments are also not usually published in most of the countries. The situation would only be different if one assumes a competitor's right to

77. State Aid Direct Business Taxation Notice, *supra* n. 62, para. 22.

obtain information regarding the tax situation in order to initiate competitor claims based on State aid law.[78] However, this would then be an issue of general importance and would affect other administrative decisions, too.

In order to avoid an infringement of State aid law, a tax ruling procedure should not, itself, be selective. Consequently, the advantage of legal certainty should be available for all undertakings in comparable legal and factual situations.[79] As long as enterprises that are in comparable situations have access to the ruling regime, there should not be any State aid issue.

In conclusion, rulings can only raise problems under State aid law if a selective tax advantage is conferred on a certain undertaking. This could be the case when the law is misapplied or that authorities acting within their margin of discretion treat taxpayers in comparable situations substantially differently.[80] But, as shown above, this is not an issue particularly limited to rulings, as usual tax assessments conducted in such a manner would also be qualified as illegal State aid.

§5.05 CONCLUSION

As shown at the beginning, discretionary power of tax authorities is a general phenomenon inherent in the structure of a legal system. Depending on the actual scope of a legal provision, authorities have a certain leeway in their decision-making that they have to fill with their own values. But, the letter of the law is just the starting point for any attempt to determine the actual leeway the authorities enjoy in a specific case. To interpret the rule, teleological and systemic arguments have to be considered, as a rule only can be interpreted within the systemic framework of which it forms a part. In most cases, an allegedly wide latitude will narrow down considerably due to a thorough analysis of the concrete meaning of a legal provision. Therefore, even in the context of a discretionary provision or vague legal concepts, the authorities will not be free to decide a case in their unfettered discretion.

The ECJ already had to rule several times on provisions conferring discretionary power to authorities. The Court has qualified provisions granting a wide margin of discretion to the authorities, potentially enabling them to put certain undertakings in a favourable situation, as selective.[81] This qualification prevents Member States from implementing legal provisions that create the impression of being of general in nature, while in practice just serve as a legal basis for the administration to grant selective advantages.[82] However, if one would generalize the statements by the Courts, the outcome could be excessive, as then every provision that grants leeway to the authorities would have to be qualified as State aid, since there would always be a possibility that an advantage could be granted to certain undertakings. Taking into account that discretion is inherent in every legal decision, a legal provision that is not

78. *Cf.* Lang, *supra* n. 44, at 105 et seq.
79. Draft Notion of State Aid Notice, *supra* n. 63, para. 177.
80. *Cf.* Raymond Luja, *EU State Aid Rules and Their Limits*, 76 Tax Notes Int'l, 353, 354 (2014).
81. *Kimberly Clark*, C-241/94, para. 23.
82. Lang, *supra*, n. 44, at 48.

selective, but grants a certain leeway to the authorities, should not generally be qualified as prohibited State aid. In its *P Oy* decision,[83] the Court held that a discretionary provision should not be regarded as selective as long as the degree of latitude is limited to criteria related to the respective tax regime. Therefore, as long as the authorities' leeway under a certain provision stays within the systemic framework of the respective tax law, no issues should be raised under State aid law. However, a rule granting authorities broad discretion (e.g., allowing them to also treat undertakings beneficially based on criteria unrelated to tax law) must be considered as selective.

Individual administrative decisions based on general provisions should be regarded as selective if the law is misapplied in favour of certain taxpayers. In such situations, taxpayers clearly receive an advantage compared to situations where the law is enforced correctly. Only when the law is principally disregarded and all taxpayers receive favourable treatment regarding a specific provision, can administrative conduct be considered in line with State aid law. However, when assessing the selectivity of such a measure, one could argue for an extensive comparability assessment, by generally comparing the unlawful application of the law to the situation of taxpayer treated in accordance with the law.

Administrative practices staying within the framework predetermined by the law may be considered in line with State aid law. Usually, under a general rule clearly defining the administrative conduct, no substantially favourable treatment of certain taxpayers should be possible. Moreover, it has to be taken into account that the authorities' leeway can narrow in the course of the time, particularly due to changes in case law. Regarding tax rulings, the situation is not different. As long as rulings apply the law properly and do not confer a selective advantage by lowering the tax burden of a certain undertaking, they should not raise any State aid issues. However, ruling procedures only available for certain groups of undertakings might infringe State aid laws, as only these particular undertakings could obtain the benefit of enhanced legal certainty conferred by a ruling determining administrative conduct in advance.

83. *P Oy*, C-6/12, para. 26.

CHAPTER 6

State-Aid Policy and the Fight Against Harmful Tax Competition in the Internal Market: Tax Policy in Disguise?

Edoardo Traversa & Pierre M. Sabbadini

§6.01 INTRODUCTION

From the early days of European integration, Member States have been very reluctant to transfer powers to the European Union (EU) level in the area of taxation, in particular corporate and income taxes, which remain within their exclusive competence. Unlike Member States, EU institutions are, therefore, unable to introduce their own taxes or to determine their own tax policy, aiming to strike the right balance between budgetary, redistributive, economic, social, and environmental aims. The Court of Justice of the European Union (hereinafter, collectively, with its predecessor-in-interest the European Court of Justice, 'the Court' or 'the CJEU') has consistently stated that the powers retained by the Member States, must nevertheless be exercised consistently with EU law.[1] Those limits set by EU law on the Member States' taxing powers are essentially motivated by the objective of achieving the Internal Market and include (i) the prohibition of fiscal State aid, (ii) the freedom of movement and the principle of non-discrimination and (iii) the competence conferred by the Treaty to the Council to adopt secondary legislation aiming at the harmonization or the approximation of national tax laws.

In the area of State aid, the European Commission – subject to review by the CJEU – is free to determine its own policy and does not depend on the Council for its

1. *Commission* v *France ('Avoir Fiscal')*, Joined Cases C-6/69 and C-11/69, Judgment, EU:C:1969:68 [hereinafter '*Avoir Fiscal*, C-6/69'], para. 17; *Schumacker*, C-279/93, Judgment, EU:C:1994:391.

implementation, as is the case for the adoption of secondary tax legislation.[2] However, although the Court clarified, very early, that the concept of State aid could potentially encompass tax measures,[3] it took a long time before the Commission started to use its powers to monitor Members States' tax rules, and even longer to consolidate its practice and develop a 'fiscal State-aid policy'. Some authors tend to explain the Commission's reserve by the inherently sovereign nature of tax measures, which implement national economic, financial, and social policies and address market failures.[4]

The first wave in the Commission's momentum occurred at the end of the 1990s. While the Member States had endorsed the Code of Conduct in the area of business taxation, the Commission adopted its Notice on the Application of State Aid Rules to Measures Relating to Direct Business Taxation (the 'State-Aid Business Tax Notice').[5] It then launched several investigations against favourable tax measures adopted by Member States, mostly in order to attract foreign investment, many of them ending with a negative decision. A second wave started a few years ago and is still ongoing. The Commission started investigating individual tax rulings obtained by multinational companies, mostly concerning the application of double taxation conventions and transfer pricing rules. This chapter explores, whether – as it has been sometimes argued – the Commission is currently using its powers in the area of State aid as an instrument for carrying out not only a fiscal State-aid policy, but a genuine tax policy through State aid control, as an alternative to traditional harmonization and coordination via secondary law instruments, which the Commission is unable to get through the Council due to the unanimity rule and the opposition of the Member States.

§6.02 ACT I: THE 1997 MONTI PACKAGE COMMUNICATION AND THE STATE-AID BUSINESS TAX NOTICE

This section provides a description of the European approach to tax measures via State aid rules and notably important milestones such as the Communication to the Council and Parliament that included 'a package to tackle harmful tax competition',[6] also called the 'Monti Package' named after Commissioner Mario Monti (the '1997 Monti Package Communication') and the State-Aid Business Tax Notice.

In 1996, the Commission launched an initiative to comprehensively review the taxation policy of the EU, with an objective of better achieving the internal market, but

2. On these issues, see also Edoardo Traversa & Alessandra Flamini, *Fighting Harmful Tax Competition through EU States Aid Law: Will the Hardening of Soft Law Suffice?*, 2015 Eur. St. Aid L. Q. 323, 325 (2015).
3. *De gezamenlijke Steenkolenmijnen in Limburg*, 30/59, Judgment, EU:C:1961:2; *Italy* v *Commission*, C-173/73, Judgment, EU:C:1974:71; *Banco Exterior de España* v *Ayuntamiento de Valencia*, C-387/92, Judgment, EU:C:1994:100.
4. Claire Micheau, *Droit des Aides d'État et des Subventions en Fiscalité* 47 (2013).
5. Commission Notice on the Application of the State Aid Rules to Measures Relating to Direct Business Taxation, OJ C 384/3 (1998) [hereinafter, the 'State-Aid Business Tax Notice'].
6. *Ibid.* at 564.

also of stabilizing national fiscal systems and easing the tax burden on employment to stimulate growth and employment.[7]

The Commission justified the need for coordination, notably, by the fact that, while tax competition was generally to be welcomed because of its benefits for citizens (consumers) and its downward pressure on government spending, it also jeopardized efforts of Member States to reduce their budget deficits and to comply with other EU commitments contained in the Maastricht criteria[8] and in the Stability and Growth Pact.[9] The Commission wished to emphasize the link between national tax policies and European objectives in the context of the single/internal market and the European Monetary Union. Eliminating regulatory barriers made differences between tax systems more visible and reinforced the influence of national taxation policy choices on strategic decisions by economic actors (e.g., on allocation of capital and investment).

The Commission acknowledged in the 1997 Monti Package Communication[10] that, between 1981 and 1995, an increase in the tax burden on labour of seven percentage points of the implicit tax rate had occurred,[11] while for other factors of production (including capital, self-employed labour, energy and natural resources) had been subject in the same period to a decreasing rate of more than ten percentage points of the implicit tax rate.[12] The representation of the combination of, on the one hand, the increase of taxation on employed labour and, on the other hand, the decrease of taxation on self-employment and capital was named the 'Monti Cross' because of its graphic resemblance.[13] In addition, the Commission noted that another important factor of job creation: small- and medium-sized enterprises ('SMEs') were penalized in comparison to larger companies that had better access to benefits resulting from tax differentials and tax competition.[14] The Commission elaborated on this shift by explaining that the high rate of mobility of certain tax bases could have forced Member States to impose a lower tax rate than desired and to compensate it with increased

7. European Commission, Taxation in the European Union: Discussion Paper for the Informal Meeting of ECOFIN Ministers, SEC(96) 487 (1996); and Taxation in the European Union: Report on the Development of Tax Systems (Second Report of the Monti Group), COM(96) 546 (1996).
8. The so-called 'Maastricht Criteria' are named after the Treaty on European Union (TEU) signed in Maastricht on 7 Feb. 1992 which provided that, under Art. 121(1), four criteria (regarding price stability, government finances, exchange rates and long-term interest rates) must be met for Member States to participate in the third stage of Economic and Monetary Union.
9. The Stability and Growth Pact is a set of rules designed to ensure that EU Member States pursue sound public finances and coordinate their fiscal policies. The current legal bases are Arts. 121, 126 and 136 of the Treaty on the Functioning of the European Union ('TFEU') as well as Protocol 12 of the Treaty on the Excessive Deficit Procedure.
10. Communication from the Commission to the Council: Towards Tax Coordination in the European Union - A Package to Tackle Harmful Tax Competition in the European Union, COM(97) 495 (1997) [hereinafter the '1997 Monti Package Communication'], para. 4.
11. The implicit tax rate is the result of the division of tax revenues by the appropriate base. *See also*, Carlo Pinto, *Tax Competition and EU Law* 437 (2003).
12. Furthermore, the Commission noted that within the labour factor, the tax burden was shifting to the least skilled and less mobile category, while the highly-skilled employees were increasingly mobile and responsive to tax differentials.
13. Pinto, *supra* n. 11, at 35–37.
14. Communication from the Commission to the Council: Towards Tax Coordination in the European Union - A Package to Tackle Harmful Tax Competition in the European Union, COM(97) 495 (1997) [hereinafter the '1997 Monti Package Communication'], para. 4.

taxation on other, less-mobile bases. The Commission concluded that there was a need to reverse this trend, which had proved to have a negative effect on the level of employment and growth in Europe.

Based on the foregoing, the Commission outlined in the 1997 Monti Package Communication possible components of a package to tackle harmful tax competition, including the adoption of: (i) a code of conduct for business taxation in parallel with a Commission communication on fiscal state aids, (ii) measures to eliminate distortions of the taxation of capital income, (iii) measures to eliminate withholding taxes on cross-border interest and royalty payments between companies, and (iv) measures designed to eliminate significant distortions in the area of indirect taxation.

After a debate with Member States and stakeholders, the Commission published the '1997 Monti Package Communication'). The Commission stated that the Monti Package offered a real prospect of agreement between the Member States, provided that the spirit of compromise it had witnessed over the months of negotiation was maintained.[15] The objective of the final version of the Monti Package proposed by the Commission was to implement a new European tax strategy based on (i) a code of conduct for business taxation, (ii) a European solution in the area of taxation of income from savings, and (iii) measures to eliminate withholding taxes on cross-border interest and royalty payments between companies.[16]

On 1 December 1997, a code of conduct for business taxation ('Code of Conduct') was incorporated in a Council resolution to secure the commitment of Member States to respect the principles of fair competition by undertaking to roll back existing measures that constituted harmful taxation and to refrain from introducing similar tax measures in the future.[17] The Code of Conduct targeted tax measures originating from legislative, regulatory, and administrative action that had, or may have had, a significant impact on the location of businesses in the EU. The criteria established by the Code of Conduct for identifying potentially harmful measures included: (i) an effective level of taxation that is significantly lower than the general level of taxation in the country concerned; (ii) tax benefits reserved for non-residents; (iii) tax incentives for activities that are isolated from the domestic economy and, therefore, have no impact on the national tax base; (iv) granting of tax advantages even in the absence of any real economic activity; (v) the basis of profit determination for companies in a multinational group departs from internationally accepted rules, in particular those approved by the OECD; and (vi) lack of transparency.

To ensure the effective implantation of the Code of Conduct commitments, a monitoring mechanism was established in the form of the so-called Primarolo Group,[18] which was entrusted with the task of reviewing domestic tax systems and identifying tax measures that might fall within the scope of the Code of Conduct: its task was to

15. *Ibid.* at 564, para. 6.
16. *Ibid.* at 564, para. 8.
17. Conclusions of the ECOFIN Council Meeting of 1 Dec. 1997 Concerning Taxation Policy – Resolution of the Council and the Representatives of the Governments of the Member States, Meeting within the Council of 1 Dec. 1997 on a Code of Conduct for Business Taxation - Taxation of Saving, OJ C 2/01 (1998) [hereinafter, the '1997 Code of Conduct Resolution'].
18. The group was named after its chairman, UK Paymaster General, Dawn Primarolo.

report, with the technical assistance of the Commission, to the Council. In its report issued in November 1999, the Primarolo Group identified sixty-six tax measures displaying harmful features.[19] Member States then revised or replaced those sixty-six measures, sometimes subject to a 'grand-fathering' clause under which beneficiaries of certain regimes benefited from a transition period. Thereafter, the Primarolo Group continued its work; for example, it reviewed the tax systems of the Members States that joined the EU in 2004.

Along with these EU efforts to tackle harmful taxation, parallel discussions were conducted under the auspices of the OECD to address certain special tax regimes (i.e., harmful tax practices in the form of tax havens and harmful preferential tax regimes). Harmful tax competition had been identified as one of the consequences of the globalization of the twentieth century,[20] as the OECD Committee on Fiscal Affairs acknowledged in its 1998 Report entitled 'Harmful Tax Competition: An Emerging Global Issue'.[21] The 1998 OECD Report provided a list of the harmful effects of preferential tax measures, such as:

> distorting financial and, indirectly, real investment flows; undermining the integrity and fairness of tax structures; discouraging compliance by all taxpayers; re-shaping the desired level and mix of taxes and public spending; causing undesired shifts of part of the tax burden to less mobile tax bases, such as labour, property and consumption; and increasing the administrative costs and compliance burdens on tax authorities and taxpayers.[22]

The 1998 OECD Report further emphasized the link between the potentially harmful nature of a tax measure and its impact on the international allocation of taxable profits: 'If the spillover effects of particular tax practices are so substantial that they are concluded to be poaching other countries' tax bases, such practices would be doubtlessly labelled "harmful tax competition"'. Subsequently, a Forum on Harmful Tax Practices received a mandate from the OECD to monitor the situation and the implementation of the recommendations issued.

In its 1997 Monti-Package Communication,[23] the Commission had also indicated that many Member States had urged the Commission to re-examine its policy in the field of fiscal State aid to match its commitment to the political agreement of the Member States to the Code of Conduct. The Commission agreed that, on the one hand, it would review existing aid and, if necessary, propose that Member States make amendments or abolish aid. On the other hand, to make its enforcement policy as transparent as possible, thereby ensuring that its decisions would be predictable and equal treatment would be guaranteed, the Commission agreed to present a communication clarifying its policy on the application of the state-aid rules to fiscal measures in light of developments in the Single Market.

19. The geographic allocation of those measures was the following: forty in EU Member States, three in Gibraltar, and twenty-three in dependent or associated territories.
20. Carlo Pinto, *EU and OECD to Fight Harmful Tax Competition: Has the Right Path been Undertaken?*, 26 Intertax 386, 390 (1998).
21. OECD, *Harmful Tax Competition: An Emerging Global Issue* (1998).
22. *Ibid.* at 16.
23. The 1997 Monti Package Communication, *supra* n. 14, para. 17.

In relation to its commitment regarding fiscal State aid accompanying its endorsement of the Monti Package and the Code of Conduct, in particular, the Commission stated in its November 1997 Communication,[24] that it had already begun its review of certain cases and was continuing to reflect on these issues in order to come forward with an indication of its position as a basis for the normal consultations with Member States on guidelines in the area of State aid in parallel with the implementation of the Package.[25]

Following the Council's adoption of the 1997 Code of Conduct Resolution, the Commission published its State-Aid Business Tax Notice,[26] in which the Commission contemplated the application of State aid rules in relation to the objective of tackling harmful tax competition as a complement to the Code of Conduct.[27] Regarding the relationship between State aid enforcement and the Code of Conduct, the State-Aid Business Tax Notice provided that the qualification of a tax measure as harmful under the Code of Conduct would not affect its possible qualification as State aid. However, the assessment of the compatibility of fiscal aid with the Internal Market must be made, according to the Commission, by taking into account, *inter alia*, the effects of aid that are brought to light in the application of the Code of Conduct.[28]

The State-Aid Business Tax Notice also framed the intervention of the Commission in the context of the completion of the single/internal market and the economic and monetary union by highlighting that 'account must also be taken, in the common interest, of the major repercussions which some aid granted through tax systems may have on the revenue of other Member States.'[29] In other words, the harmful effects of tax competition between Member States must be taken into account in the monitoring of fiscal State-aid measures. The State-Aid Business Tax Notice further indicated that, although it was published for guidance purposes and was not exhaustive,[30] the Commission intended to ensure that its decisions would be transparent and predictable and that its rules would be applied consistently and with a guarantee equality of treatment among Member States.[31] Finally, the Commission indicated that it intended to (re)examine, case by case on the basis of the State-Aid Business Tax Notice, existing tax arrangements in the Member States.[32]

The primary objective of the State-Aid Business Tax Notice was to clarify whether a tax measure could be qualified as State aid.[33] It is interesting to note that while the State-Aid Business Tax Notice focused on the application of State-aid rules, which by nature could only be applied to selective domestic measures, the Commission also

24. Communication from the Commission to the Council and the European Parliament – A package to tackle harmful tax competition in the European Union, 5 Nov. 1997, COM(97) 564 FINAL, p.
25. The 1997 Monti Package Communication, *supra* n. 14, para. 13.
26. The State-Aid Business Tax Notice, *supra* n. 5.
27. *Ibid.* para. 1.
28. *Ibid.* para. 30.
29. The State-Aid Business Tax Notice, *supra* n. 5, para. 3.
30. *Ibid.* para. 37.
31. *Ibid.* para. 4.
32. *Ibid.* para. 4.
33. *Ibid.* para. 2.

referred to other types of EU actions that could be taken against general measures impeding the functioning of the internal market, such as unanimously adopted harmonization directives or Council directives adopted by a qualified majority aimed to tackle disparities between planned or existing general provisions in Member States' domestic tax law that might distort competition and, thus, create distortions.[34]

The Commission began by reiterating that it does not actually matter that a measure be of a tax nature to qualify as State aid, if it meets the constituting conditions of an aid measure under Article 107 TFEU (ex-Article 92 TEC[35]). Building on the case law of the Court of Justice, the Commission then described the four cumulative conditions for a measure benefitting a recipient firm carrying on an economic activity to be found to be State aid within the meaning of Article 107 TFEU [ex-Article 92 TEC] considering the nature of tax measures.[36]

First, the tax measures must constitute an advantage that relieves the recipients thereof of tax charges or expenses the recipients would otherwise bear. The advantage can be provided in various ways, including: (i) a reduction in the tax base (such as special deductions, special or accelerated depreciation arrangements, or the entering of reserves on the balance sheet); (ii) a total or partial reduction in the amount of tax, such as exemption or a tax credit; or (iii) deferment, cancellation, or even special rescheduling of tax debt.[37]

Second, such advantage must be granted by the State through State resources. Provision 'by the State' can be achieved through tax provisions of a legislative, regulatory, or administrative nature, as well as through the practices of the tax authorities. As far as tax measures are concerned, a loss of tax revenue is equivalent to consumption of State resources in the form of a fiscal expenditure. It also applies to aid granted by regional and local bodies in the Member States.[38]

Third, the measure must affect competition and trade between Member States, which requires that the recipient firm carries on an economic activity involving trade between Member States. It is sufficient if the measure strengthens the firm's position compared with that of other firms that are competitors in intra-Community trade.[39]

Fourth, the measure must be selective based on its focus, so that it favours: certain undertakings or 'the production of certain goods',[40] by favouring: a specific sector or an entire section of the economy (e.g., manufacturing); national products that are exported;[41] all the sectors that are subject to international competition;[42] certain

34. *Ibid.* paras 6–7.
35. References to articles of the TEU in the State-Aid Business Tax Notice (*supra* n. 5) are references to the 1992 Maastricht Treaty on European Union (OJ C 191/1 (1992)), as the Treaty of Amsterdam only entered into force on 1 May 1999.
36. The State-Aid Business Tax Notice, *supra* n. 5, paras 8–12.
37. *Ibid.* para. 9.
38. *Ibid.* para. 10.
39. *Ibid.* para. 11.
40. *Ibid.* para. 18.
41. *Avoir Fiscal*, C-6/69.
42. Commission Decision, 4 Dec. 1996 Concerning Aid Granted by Belgium under the Maribel bis/ter Scheme, OJ L 95/25 (1996); and *Belgium* v *Commission*, C-75/97, Judgment, EU:C:1999:311.

types of undertakings (e.g., public undertakings[43]); or undertakings performing certain functions (e.g., intra-group, production, intermediation, or coordination).[44] A measure can also be selective because of its design: selectivity, thus, can be the result of an exception to tax provisions of a legislative, regulatory, or administrative nature or of a discretionary practice of the tax authorities.

On discretionary administrative practice, the Commission, based on the *Kimberly Clark Sopalin* case,[45] underlined that selectivity can arise where a general measure is individually applied not merely based on objective criteria but also by way of a discretionary power. For example, the Commission took the view that there is a presumption of State aid if the tax administration enjoys the discretionary freedom to set, firm-by-firm or sector-by-sector, different depreciation periods or valuation methods, or to handle fiscal debts on a case-by-case basis with an objective different from the objective of optimizing the recovery of tax debts from the enterprise concerned. The Commission went even further, indicating that unless administrative rulings merely contain an interpretation of general rules, there is a presumption of aid warranting a detailed analysis for every decision of the administration that departs therefrom. According to the Commission, that presumption is reinforced by the 'opaque' nature of the decisions and the breadth of discretion enjoyed by tax authorities.[46] The Commission concluded that such a presumption 'does not make Member States any less able to provide their taxpayers with legal certainty and predictability on the application of general tax rules.'[47]

The Commission nuanced its stance on selectivity by explaining that Member States may first justify measures of a differential nature (i) when their economic rationale makes them necessary to the functioning and effectiveness of the Member State's tax system[48] or (ii) when they are based on the existence of objective differences between taxpayers.[49] Examples relating to the first category of justifications include: the progressive nature of an income-tax scale explained by redistributive purposes or the similar logic underlying certain specific provisions on the taxation of SMEs;[50] national calculation of asset depreciation and stock valuation methods; and arrangements for fiscal debt collection inherent in its national tax system.

According to the Commission, justifications based on the 'inherent' nature of objectives or the 'logic' of the tax system are limited to collecting revenue to finance State expenditure and having each firm pay tax only once, so that taxes paid in the State in which the firm is resident for tax purposes should be taken into account. Non-budgetary objectives (e.g., those of social, economic or regional nature) assigned to a tax scheme are, however, unlikely to justify selectivity. The Commission underscores

43. The State-Aid Business Tax Notice, *supra* n. 5, para. 19.
44. *Ibid.* para. 20.
45. *France* v *Commission*, C-241/94, Judgment, EU:C:1996:353.
46. The State-Aid Business Tax Notice, *supra* n. 5, para. 22.
47. *Ibid.*
48. Commission Decision 96/369/EC of 13 Mar. 1996 Concerning Fiscal Aid Given to German Airlines in the Form of a Depreciation Facility, OJ L 146/42 (1996).
49. The State-Aid Business Tax Notice, *supra* n. 5, para. 24.
50. *Ibid.* para. 27.

that more favourable treatment of non-resident companies compared to resident ones, or the grant of tax benefits to head offices or to firms providing certain services (for example, financial services) within a group, cannot be easily justified.

Regarding the second category of justification, which are those based on the existence of objective differences between taxpayers, the Commission accepts that foundations or associations – as non-profit undertakings – are specifically exempt from the national tax(es) on profits if they cannot in reality earn any profits or that cooperatives distributing all of their profits to their members are not taxed at the level of the cooperative, provided that tax is actually levied at the level of their members.

From a procedural point of view, the Commission reminds us that, subject to review by European courts, procedural requirements applicable to new State aid include (i) the obligation to notify proposed State-aid measures to the Commission and (ii) a stand-still obligation (i.e., not to put any proposed State-aid measures into effect until the Commission has approved them). A breach of those requirements implies an obligation to recover the amount, with interest, corresponding to the difference between the tax actually paid and the amount that should have been paid if the generally applicable rule had been applied, by the recipients, except where that would be contrary to a general principle of Community (now Union) law, such as legitimate expectations derived from the Commission's behaviour. Regarding existing State aid, the Commission pledges to keep under constant review all existing systems of aid in the form of tax measures and to require Member States to submit to the Commission annual reports on their existing State-aid systems, including an estimate of the any lost budgetary revenue.[51]

§6.03 ACT II: STATE-AID ENFORCEMENT FOLLOWING THE ADOPTION THE 1997 CODE OF CONDUCT AND OF THE STATE-AID BUSINESS TAX NOTICE

After the adoption of the Code of Conduct in 1997 and the issuance of the State-Aid Business Tax Notice in 1998, there were very few State-aid cases involving tax measures,[52] and little progress was made in the implementation of the package against harmful tax competition. Therefore, in 2000, after pointing out that it was 'disappointing that almost four years after the informal ECOFIN Council in Verona ... considerable uncertainty still surrounds the implementation of that package in spite of the determination shown by most Members States and by the Commission', Commissioner Monti instructed the Commission's Competition Department 'to examine all the relevant cases of fiscal state aids in business taxation', referring to the State-Aid Business Tax

51. *Ibid.* paras 34–36.
52. *See* Report on the Implementation of the Commission Notice on the Application of State Aid Rules to Measures Relating to Direct Business Taxation, paras 4 et seq. (C(2004)434) (2004) [hereinafter the 'Report on Implementing the State-Aid Business Tax Notice'].

Notice.[53] In July 2001, the Commission launched an investigation into fifteen regimes that had been listed among the sixty-six measures identified by the Primarolo Group as potentially harmful on the basis on the criteria laid down in the Code of Conduct.[54]

Four of those regimes had been previously vetted by the Commission under Article 107 TFEU, such as the Belgian Coordination Centres scheme. Under that regime, adopted in 1982, Belgium applied a special tax regime for approved coordination centres. This regime was scrutinized by the Commission in 1984 and, after a series of amendments, it was declared to be in-line with State-aid Treaty provisions.[55] In 1999, the Primarolo Group included it in the list of Member States' potentially harmful measures. The OECD did the same, by inserting the measure in its list of potentially harmful preferential regimes.[56] The Commission closed its reassessment of the measure in 2003, after concluding that it was incompatibility with State-aid provisions.[57]

The relevance of this Commission Decision in assessing the evolution in State-aid policy between 2001 and today is twofold. First, by referring to one of the OECD transfer pricing standards[58] (the cost-plus method[59])[60] as an appropriate guide for the assessment of transfer-pricing arrangements in intra-group transactions as a reflection of market conditions, it clearly indicates that domestic transfer-pricing practices can constitute State aid. Second, in its decision, the Commission stressed 'the parallels between the work of the code of conduct group and the Community's policy on State aid, both of which are aimed at eliminating those measures that distort or threaten to distort competition in the common market', and the relationship between the adoption of the Code of Conduct and the new orientation of State-aid control following the

53. European Commission Press Release, 23 Feb. 2000: 'Statement by Commissioner Monti Concerning the Control of Fiscal State Aids', http://europa.eu/rapid/press-release_IP-00-182_en.htm (last visited 10 Jan. 2017).
54. European Commission Press Release, 11 July 2001: 'Commission Launches Large Scale State Aid Investigation into Business Taxation Schemes', http://europa.eu/rapid/press-release_IP-01-982_en.htm (last visited 10 Jan. 2017).
55. For the background, see *Forum 187* v *Commission*, T-276/02, Order, EU:T:2003:151, para. 8 et seq.
56. *See* OECD, Progress Report in Identifying and Eliminating Harmful Tax Practices (2000).
57. Commission Decision, 17 Feb. 2003 on the Aid Scheme Implemented by Belgium for Coordination Centres Established in Belgium, OJ L 282/25 (2003) [hereinafter, the 'Belgium Coordination Centres Decision'].
58. The OECD work on transfer pricing was first addressed in a 1979 Report and followed by the publication Transfer Pricing Guidelines for Multinational Enterprises and Tax Administrations. *See* OECD, *Transfer Pricing and Multinational Enterprises* (1979); subsequently the OECD issued its *Transfer Pricing Guidelines for Multinational Enterprises and Tax Administrations* (1995), which were substantially revised in 2001 and again in 2010 [hereinafter, collectively, the 'OECD TP Guidelines']. *See also* a similar approach in Commission Decision, 2 Sep. 2002 on the Aid Scheme Implemented by Germany for Control and Coordination Centres, paras 22–28, OJ L 177/17 (2002); Commission Decision, 16 Oct. 2002 on the Aid Scheme C 50/2001 (Ex NN 47/2000) – Finance Companies – Implemented by Luxembourg, paras 43–44, OJ L 153/40 (2002).
59. The so-called cost-plus method consists of taking the costs incurred by the supplier of goods/services in a transaction between associated companies and then adding to those costs a cost-plus mark-up to obtain an appropriate profit in the light of the functions performed, assets used, risks assumed, and market conditions. *See* the OECD TP Guidelines, *supra* n. 58, and later updates.
60. The Belgium Coordination Centres Decision, *supra* n. 57, para. 95.

State-Aid Business Tax Notice.[61] The Commission had however clearly stated in the State-Aid Business Tax Notice that the review of domestic tax measures under State-aid rules had to be carried out independently from the Primarolo Group's conclusions,[62] which was later confirmed by the Court of Justice.[63]

The Commission had indicated, in its State-Aid Business Tax Notice, that it would conduct a review of its application two years after its publication. However, the Commission acknowledged that, since there were relatively few tax aid cases before 2001, it preferred to wait until February 2004 to produce a report (hereinafter, the 'Report on Implementing the State-Aid Business Tax Notice') on a larger set of cases.[64] The Report on Implementing the State-Aid Business Tax Notice was not designed to provide a list of all tax aid cases handled by the Commission, but provided an insight into how the principles enshrined in the State-Aid Business Tax Notice had been applied.[65]

Moreover, in the Report on Implementing State-Aid Business Tax Notice, the Commission, quoting the General Court,[66] emphasized that the State-Aid Business Tax Notice did not actually constitute a change in the State-aid approach in tax matters, but merely reflected a clarification, mostly based on the development of the Court's case law.[67] It also stressed that the concept of aid is an objective one, to be applied on the basis of principles falling outside the scope of the Commission's discretion, and reaffirmed the constitutive criteria of the notion of aid.[68] Then, the Commission provided, for each criterion, examples drawn from its decision practice and summarized its findings.

With respect to the existence of an advantage, the Commission stated that, to determine whether a tax scheme derogation from the normal system constitutes State aid, 'it must be established whether the resulting tax burden is lower than that which would have resulted from application of the relevant Member State's normal taxation method'.[69] The Commission noted that an advantage could take many forms (e.g., a reduction in the tax base or in the amount of tax, an exemption from property tax or a withholding tax, or a partial exemption from an annual flat-rate tax.[70] Referring to the

61. The State-Aid Business Tax Notice, *supra* n. 5, paras 1, 4, 5.
62. *Ibid.* para. 33.
63. *Belgium* v *Commission*, C-182/03, Judgment, EU:C:2006:89, para. 151: 'The conclusions of the Council ... could in no event bind the Commission in the exercise of its own powers, which are conferred on it by the Treaty in State aid matters'.
64. The Report on Implementing the State-Aid Business Tax Notice, *supra* n. 52, para. 4.
65. *Ibid.*
66. *Diputación Foral de Guipúzcoa e.a.* v *Commission*, Joined Cases T-269/99, T-271/99 and T-272/99, Judgment, EU:T:2002:258, para. 79.
67. The Report on Implementing the State-Aid Business Tax Notice', *supra* n. 52, para. 3.
68. It is interesting to note that affecting trade within the EU is presented in the Report on Implementing the State-Aid Business Tax Notice as the third criterion, while in the 2003 landmark *Altmark* case, the Court analysed the cumulative conditions to establish the presence of State aid in a different order. *See Altmark Trans et Regierungspräsidium Magdeburg*, C-280/00, Judgment, EU:C:2003:415, para. 75.
69. The Report on Implementing the State-Aid Business Tax Notice', *supra* n. 52, para. 16, box 1.
70. *Ibid.* paras 14–15.

Belgian coordination centres and *US sales corporations*[71] cases, the Commission also stressed that State aid could result from the selective application of alternative methods of computation of the corporate tax base, such as the use of a particular transfer-pricing method (in that case, the cost-plus method). While the Commission acknowledged that such methods are not, as such, caught under the prohibition of State aid, an advantage could still arise from its application if 'the economic reality of the transactions' is not properly considered (e.g., the exclusion of certain expenditures of the tax base or use of arbitrary levels of profit margins, etc.).[72] The Report on Implementing the State-Aid Business Tax Notice also addressed cases concerning measures intended to avoid international double taxation, particularly, the switch from the credit to the exemption method for foreign income in certain circumstances (repatriation for investment intended to create or safeguard employment).[73]

As to 'selectivity', the Commission distinguished between material selectivity and geographic selectivity. For material selectivity, the Commission emphasized that, next to situations where a measure is restricted to a certain economic sector or type of company, there are also situations where eligibility criteria, in practice, restrict the potential number of recipients (e.g., if the benefit of a measure requires a given economic strength that, in practice, is only available to large multinational groups of companies).[74] The Commission also elaborated on the ability to justify a measure of a differential nature by the nature or general scheme of the system, which would only apply if the measure is linked to intrinsic features of the system concerned, as the Commission acknowledged in two cases dealing with (i) a tax exemption for agricultural land, when compared to the standard land tax, justified by the specific role of land in agricultural production and (ii) a transaction –consisting of the mere transformation of public undertakings with special status into joint stock companies – being exempted from transfer taxes typically applicable to the creation of a new economic entity, based on the principle of tax neutrality.[75]

The Report on Implementing State-Aid Business Tax Notice also provided a list of justifications that were not accepted by the Commission, such as the need to make certain companies more competitive.[76] The Commission also indicated cases where it found the measures to be compatible State aid, although it acknowledged that it was not the purpose of either the Report on Implementing the State-Aid Business Tax Notice or the State-Aid Business Tax Notice.[77] Furthermore, the Commission recalled that the EU principle of the protection of legitimate expectations, which could bar the Commission from ordering recovery of unlawful State aid, should be applied restrictively according to the CJEU's case law.[78]

71. For examples, see the Report on Implementing the State-Aid Business Tax Notice, *supra* n. 52, para. 13.
72. The Report on Implementing the State-Aid Business Tax Notice, *supra* n. 52, paras 10–13.
73. *Ibid.* para. 16.
74. *Ibid.* paras 25–33.
75. *Ibid.* paras 34–37. *See* Cases N20/2000 (Netherlands) and N53/99 (Denmark) available on the website of DG Competition.
76. The Report on Implementing the State-Aid Business Tax Notice, *supra* n. 52, paras 39–42.
77. *Ibid.* paras 42–50.
78. *Ibid.* paras 57–63.

§6.04 ACT III: FROM HARMFUL TAX COMPETITION TO AGGRESSIVE TAX PLANNING – STATE-AID POLICY AND RULINGS IN THE BEPS ERA

[A] The Stage: The ECJ *Gibraltar* Case and the Media Leaks

The recent evolution of State-aid control as a tool in the fight against harmful tax competition has to be understood in the light of the extremely plastic nature of the State-aid concept, which leaves the Commission and the Court broad powers of interpretation as to its ultimate meaning and extent.[79] Over the last decade, the Commission has extended the concept of 'selectivity' of fiscal measures far beyond what some might have expected, despite the notion of harmful tax measures developed in the Code of Conduct.[80] A turning point was the adoption, in 2004, of the Commission's decision in the *Gibraltar* case.[81] After having been targeted by the Primarolo Group, Gibraltar redesigned its corporate tax system, instituting three general, and apparently independent, business taxes (i.e., a payroll tax, a business property occupation tax, and a – very modest – business registration fee). The Commission challenged the reform under State-aid rules, finding that it would result in a tax-free regime for offshore companies, who would be, de facto, exempt from corporate taxation[82] due to their small physical presence, in terms of employees and properties, in Gibraltar.

Because the measure was designed to apply, in principle, to almost all Gibraltar companies, it did not fit within the classic assessment used to identify a selective advantage, which was acknowledged by both the General Court, who annulled the Commission's decision on the grounds that it failed to identify a derogation from the common or 'normal' tax regime,[83] and the Advocate General of the Court of Justice on appeal, who expressed doubts regarding the extension of the reach of State-aid control: 'harmful institutional or tax competition between Member States clearly does not fall within the mechanism for controlling State aid established by the Treaty',[84] therefore 'if the tax system is of a general character, it falls outside the application of Article [107 TFEU]'.[85]

---

79. Francesco Nanetti & Giovanni Mameli, *The Creeping Normative Role of the EC Commission in the Twin-Track Struggle Against State Aids and Harmful Tax Competition*, 11 EC Tax Rev. 185, 188 (2002).
80. Leigh Hancher, Tom Ottervanger & Piet Jan Slot, *EC State Aids* s.10 (5th ed., 2016).
81. European Commission, Commission Decision, 30 Mar. 2004 on the Aid Scheme which the United Kingdom is Planning to Implement as Regards the Government of Gibraltar Corporation Tax Reform, OJ L 85/1 (2004).
82. *See* Alexandre Saydé, *Abuse of EU Law and Regulation of the Internal Market* 336 (2014).
83. *Government of Gibraltar* v *Commission*, Joined Cases T-211/04 and T-215/04, Judgment, EU:T:2008:595, para. 145 [hereinafter 'GC *Gibraltar* Judgment'].
84. *Commission and Spain* v *Government of Gibraltar and UK*, Joined Cases C-106/09 P and C-107/09 P, AG Opinion, EU:C:2011:215, para. 134 [hereinafter 'CJEU *Gibraltar* AG Opinion'].
85. *Ibid.* para. 140.

However, the Court of Justice ruled that the measure constituted selective aid because 'its very application resulted in a different tax burden for different undertakings'[86] and deemed it to be incompatible with State-aid rules. The Court used, as the reference framework, a corporate tax system, of which those three taxes were an integral part and whose aim was to tax all corporations.[87] The Court's *Gibraltar* judgment has been criticized on the grounds that the Court substituted its own logic or rationale for the one used by Gibraltar's government to determine the personal and material scope of Gibraltar's domestic tax system,[88] which was exactly what the Advocate General had warned against.[89] In any event, the case laid the foundations for subsequent evolutions of the notion of State aid towards becoming the ultimate weapon against (harmful) tax competition.

A different opportunity to further develop State-aid control was given by the wave of revelations concerning strategic international tax-planning by multinational groups of companies, which triggered (negative) reactions from, first, the public, various interest groups, and the media and, then, from governments at the global level,[90] which movement lead to the OECD BEPS Action Plan[91] and its implementation through several EU directives and recommendations.[92] It also drew the attention of the Commission on specific types of tax deals, the details of which were made public during hearings in the UK's House of Commons (2012) and the US Senate (2013),[93] as well as through information revealed by journalists, particularly the LuxLeaks investigation by the International Consortium of Investigative Journalists.

86. *Commission and Spain* v *Government of Gibraltar and UK* Joined Cases C-106/09 P and C-107/09 P, Judgment, EU:C:2011:732, para. 93 [hereinafter 'CJEU *Gibraltar* Judgment'].
87. CJEU *Gibraltar* Judgment, para. 101. *See* Edoardo Traversa, *State Aid and Taxation: Can an Anti-Avoidance Provision Be Selective?*, 13 EStAL 518, 521 (2014).
88. John Temple Lang, The Gibraltar State Aid and Taxation Judgment –A 'Methodological Revolution'?, 11 EStAL 805, 810 (2012).
89. CJEU *Gibraltar* AG Opinion, para. 202.
90. *See* the Declaration of the G20 Leaders in Los Cabos, 19 June 2012, http://www.g20.utoronto.ca/2012/2012-0619-loscabos.pdf (last visited 23 Mar. 2017). For a comment, see Edoardo Traversa & Alessandra Flamini, *The Impact of BEPS on the Fight Against Harmful Tax Practices: Risks ... and Opportunities for the EU*, 2015 Brit. Tax Rev. 396 (2015).
91. *See* OECD, *Action Plan on Base Erosion and Profit Shifting* (2013) available at http://dx.doi.org/10.1787/9789264202719-enat (last visited 24 Mar. 2016).
92. *See, e.g.*, Communication from the Commission to the European Parliament and the Council of 28 Jan. 2016 - Anti-Avoidance Tax Package: Next Steps Towards Delivering Effective Taxation and Greater Tax Transparency in the EU, COM/2016/023; Council Directive 2016/1164 laying down rules against tax avoidance practices that directly affect the functioning of the internal market, OJ L 193/1 (2016).
93. Johannes Laitenberger, Dir. Gen. of DG COMP, ICF St. Gallen (20 May 2016), http://ec.europa.eu/competition/speeches/text/sp2016_06_en.pdf (last visited 28 June 2016). *See, e.g.*, Minutes of Evidence, Oral Examination of Witnesses in HC 716, UK Public Account Committee Meeting 12 Nov. 2012 (representatives of Starbucks, Amazon, & Google), http://www.publications.parliament.uk/pa/cm201213/cmselect/cmpubacc/716/121112.htm (last visited 28 June 2016); Offshore Profit Shifting and the U.S. Tax Code - Part 2 (Apple Inc.): Hearings Before US Permanent S. Subcomm. on Investigations, 113th Cong. (21 May 2013) (testimony of Apple, Inc.), http://www.hsgac.senate.gov/subcommittees/investigations/hearings/offshore-profit-shifting-and-the-us-tax-code_-part-2 (last visited 24 Mar. 2016).

The reaction of the Commission was prompt and resolute. It publicly responded by announcing, on the one hand, the start of work related to the fight against base erosion and the transfer of profits (BEPS) through increased transparency and tax harmonization[94] and, on the other hand, by confirming that such now-public information was going to feed the work of DG Competition. In 2013, Belgium, Cyprus, Ireland, Luxembourg, Malta, the Netherlands and the United Kingdom received information requests from the Commission concerning schemes or specific tax rulings. Tension between Luxembourg and the European Commission followed, during which the former refused to provide the requested information and lodged an appeal against two injunctions before the General Court[95] before eventually withdrawing those appeals and agreeing to submit the requested information. Between June and October 2014, the Commission successively decided to open State-aid examination procedures against Ireland, the Netherlands, and Luxembourg to analyse – in detail – certain tax rulings awarded to Apple, Amazon, Starbucks, and Fiat Finance companies on the basis of State-aid rules.[96] The Commission also decided to extend its requests for information to all Member States to obtain the names of companies that had benefited from tax rulings between 2010 and 2013.

In 2015 and 2016, the Commission opened a review procedure against Luxembourg for tax rulings granted to McDonald's and GDF Suez (Engie) companies and against Belgium for its excess-profit tax-ruling aid scheme.[97] The Commission has, to date, issued final decisions in the cases against the Netherlands (Starbucks), Ireland (Apple), Luxembourg (Fiat Finance), and Belgium (excess profits),[98] concluding that tax incentives granted by the public authorities in each of these cases constituted State aid that was incompatible and had to be recovered from the beneficiaries.

94. *See* European Commission, *The Anti-Tax Avoidance Package – Questions and Answers*, http://europa.eu/rapid/press-release_MEMO-16-160_fr.htm (last visited 23 Dec. 2016).
95. *Luxembourg* v *Commission*, T-258/84, Order, EU:T:2015:22.
96. Case SA.38373, *Ireland – Alleged Aid to Apple*, Commission Decision to Initiate Investigation Procedure, 11 June 2014, C(2014) 3606 final; Case SA.38375, *Luxembourg – Alleged Aid to FFT*, Commission Decision to Initiate Investigation Procedure, 11 June 2014, C(2014) 3627 final; Case SA.38374, *Netherlands – Alleged Aid to Starbucks*, Commission Decision to Initiate Investigation Procedure, 11 June 2014, C(2014) 3626 final; Case SA.38944, *Luxembourg – Alleged Aid to Amazon*, Commission Decision to Initiate Investigation Procedure, 7 Oct. 2014, C(2014) 7156 final.
97. Case SA.37667, *Belgium – Excess Profit Tax Ruling System*, Commission Decision to Initiate Investigation Procedure, 3 Feb. 2015, C(2015) 563 (final); Case SA.38945, *Luxembourg – Alleged Aid to McDonald's*, Commission Decision to Initiate Investigation Procedure, 3 Dec. 2015, C(2015) 8343 final; Case SA.44888, *Luxembourg – Possible State Aid in Favour of GDF Suez*, Commission Decision to Initiate Investigation Procedure, 19 Sep. 2016, C(2016) 5612 final.
98. Case SA.38374, *Netherlands – Implemented State Aid to Starbucks*, Commission Decision Finding State Aid, 21 Oct. 2015, C(2015) 7143 final; Case SA.38373, *Ireland – Implemented State Aid to Apple*, Commission Decision Finding State Aid, 30 Aug. 2016, C(2016) 5605 final; Case SA.38375, *Luxembourg – Granted State Aid to Fiat*, Commission Decision Finding State Aid, 21 Oct. 2015, C(2015) 7152 final; Case SA.37667, *Belgium – Implemented an Excess Profit Exemption State Aid Scheme*, Commission Decision Finding State Aid, 11 Jan. 2016, C(2015) 9837 final.

[B] The Commission's 'New' Approach: An Overview of Ongoing Cases

As indicated above, the Commission opened formal State-aid investigations against Ireland, Belgium, the Netherlands, and Luxembourg regarding tax measures benefitting Apple, Amazon, Starbucks, Fiat Finance, McDonald's, GDF Suez (Engie) and several undertakings based on Belgium's excess profit tax scheme.[99]

Regarding Ireland, the Commission concluded, in August 2016, that certain Irish subsidiaries of the Apple group had received illegal and incompatible State aid through tax rulings and sought recovery thereof. The Commission decided that the effect of the rulings was to determine, in advance, the percentage of the net profit to be allocated to the Irish subsidiaries of Apple, so that the level of taxation applied to them was inferior to the amount that, according to the Commission, they should have paid under the ordinary Irish tax rules. Those rulings had been granted in a context, in which the particular subsidiaries were not considered resident anywhere because of a discrepancy between the Irish and US tax rules.

According to Irish tax laws applicable at the time, a company incorporated under Irish law was in principle considered a tax resident in Ireland, even if managed and controlled outside of Ireland. However, under the "relevant companies" exception – which applied to Apple's two subsidiaries ASI an AOE, a company incorporated in Ireland with a trading activity in Ireland but ultimately controlled by a resident of a EU Member State or tax treaty country (such as the US) was not considered as Irish resident if managed an controlled from outside Ireland. In addition, there was no requirement that the companies had a tax residence in another tax jurisdiction.

From a US point of view, since ASI and AOE's activities, including their head offices, lacked any physical presence and employees, they did not have a taxable presence in the US (or in any other jurisdiction), which made them "stateless" from a tax perspective.[100]

The Commission did not directly address this issue but nevertheless concluded that the Irish rulings resulted in incompatible State aid based on a presumption of selectivity[101]. According to the Commission, the attribution of profits to the Irish branches of these stateless subsidiaries in the rulings granted to Apple resulted in a reduction of the tax burden that should have been normally borne under market conditions by Apple's subsidiaries. This amounted to a derogation from the reference framework constituted by ordinary Irish tax rules applicable to resident companies. The Commission relied on the case-law of the Court of Justice in the Belgian coordination centres cases[102] to find that a method of profit allocation had to be based

99. Investigation of State Aid SA.38944 – Luxembourg/FFT, *supra* n. 96; Investigation of State Aid SA.38945 – Luxembourg/McDonald's, *supra* n. 97; Investigation of State Aid SA.44888 – Luxembourg/GDF Suez, *supra* n. 97. *See* the status board on DG COMP's website regarding on-going cases regarding tax rulings, http://ec.europa.eu/competition/state_aid/tax_rulings/index_en.html (last visited 16 Feb. 2017).

100. Ireland – Implemented State Aid to Apple, Commission Decision Finding State Aid, 30 Aug. 2016, C(2016) 5605 final, paras 48–52.

101. *Belgium* v *Commission*, C-270/15 P, Judgment, EU:C:2016:489, para. 49.

102. *Belgium* v *Commission*, Joined Cases C-182/03 and C-217/03, Judgment, EU:C:2006:416.

on the 'arm's length' principle and added that it is not bound by the relevant OECD TP Guidelines, even though they generally constitute a useful source of information.[103]

Regarding the Netherlands, the Commission scrutinized an advance transfer-pricing agreement ('APA') concluded between the Dutch tax authorities and Starbucks Manufacturing EMEA BV ('SMBV'), concerning, *inter alia*, the deductibility of SMBV's payment of a specific level of royalties to a related entity, resulting in a reduction in the tax base of SMBV. The Commission concluded that there had been illegal and incompatible State aid requiring recovery because it identified a derogation from the reference system of ordinary Dutch tax rules that could not been justified. The derogation arose from the fact that the valuation methodology chosen in the transfer pricing report in support of the APA was inadequate and did not reflect normal market conditions. According to the Commission, if the arm's length principle would have been properly applied, no royalties should have been paid at all (or the deductible amount of the royalty payments should have been equal to zero). The Commission also compared Starbucks' situation to that of a company that did not outsource its coffee-roasting function to third parties, but to a group company designated as a toll manufacturer that did not pay any royalty for the use of the intellectual property or the know-how used in the roasting process.

Regarding Luxembourg, the Commission investigated a tax ruling granted by the tax authorities to an entity providing financing and treasury services to the Fiat Chrysler group of companies (Fiat Finance and Trade Ltd. S.A. or 'FFT'), which ruling accepted a valuation method allowing a profit distribution favourable to the Fiat Chrysler group of companies. The Commission identified a derogation from the reference system of ordinary Luxembourg tax rules in the form of an inadequate choice of method-of-assessment and of other indicators (e.g., risks incurred by FFT and rate of return on capital) intended only to create a situation that reduced the tax burden on the Fiat Chrysler group. The Commission also compared the indicators used to support the ruling, particularly the reference for the estimated level of remuneration of capital, to indicators observed in the market, to come to the conclusion that the accepted indicators did not result in a reliable approximation of a market-based outcome. The Commission ultimately concluded there was a need to recover illegal and incompatible State aid.

Another pending investigation by the Commission relates to a 2003 tax ruling granted by Luxembourg in favour of Amazon EU S.à.r.l., (a Luxembourg-based subsidiary of the US parent company Amazon.com, Inc., NYSE publicly traded corporation incorporated in the State of Washington), that records the largest part of Amazon's European profits. The ruling allows it to pay a tax-deductible royalty to another Luxembourg-based Amazon limited liability partnership (Lux SCS) that is not subject to corporate taxation in Luxembourg. The Commission has taken the preliminary view that the amount of the royalty, which ultimately allows Amazon EU S.à.r.l. to lower its taxable profits every year, might not reflect market conditions and, thus, constitutes illegal and incompatible State aid.

103. OECD, Transfer Pricing Guidelines for Multinational Enterprises and Tax Administrations 2010 408 (2010); *see also* OECD, Model Tax Convention on Income and on Capital 2014 (2015).

As for Belgium, the Commission analysed an alleged State aid scheme based on an arm's length provision modelled after Article 9 of the OECD Model Treaty. In 2004, Belgium introduced Article 185§2 Belgian Income Taxation Code (BITC), making it possible for multinational enterprises to obtain an advance ruling on profit allocation and/or on the arm's length character of pricing arrangements in the framework of cross-border related-party relationships. It also permits downward adjustments to the taxable income tax base of Belgian companies, on assumption that it would entail an excess profit (i.e., the amount of profit that exceeds the profit that would have been realized by the Belgian company under arm's length conditions and that result from group synergies). The Commission deemed the excess-profit tax-ruling scheme to be illegal under EU State-aid rules, pointing to inconsistencies in the choice of transfer pricing methodologies made by the Belgian tax authority (e.g., the fact that exempted profit did not have to be included in the tax base of an associated foreign-group entity in another tax jurisdiction, nor did that profit have to be effectively taxed by that other jurisdiction); it further contested the Belgian tax authority's assertion that the scheme was an application of the arm's length principle.

[C] The Incorporation of the 'New' Approach in the 2016 Commission Communication on the Notion of Aid

In 2012, the Commission launched its State Aid Modernisation initiative ('SAM'), which was intended to provide legal certainty and cut red tape for public authorities and companies, as well as to help the Commission focus resources on enforcing State-aid rules in cases with the biggest impact on the Single Market. SAM updated all major State-aid guidelines and simplified the rules, so that unproblematic State aid measures could be implemented without prior Commission scrutiny. Thereafter, in mid-2016, the Commission issued its Notice on the Notion of State Aid[104] (the 'NofSA Notice') as the final piece of its SAM initiative: the NofSA Notice replaced the State-Aid Business Tax Notice, discussed above.[105]

Although any attempt to comment on the NofSA Notice would exceed the scope of this chapter, it is worth noting that its Section 5.2.3 on the condition of selectivity, addresses the issue of discretionary administrative practices[106] and states that if general measures apply, *prima facie*, to all undertakings, but are otherwise limited by the discretionary power of the public administration (i.e., if meeting the given criteria does not automatically result in an entitlement to the measure), the exercise of such discretion is deemed selective.

Further, Section 5.2.3. deals with how it will assess the material selectivity of measures mitigating the normal charges of undertakings, that is to say, when Member States adopt broader measures applicable to all undertakings fulfilling certain criteria that mitigate the charges that those undertakings would normally have to bear (e.g.,

104. European Commission, *Commission Notice on the Notion of State Aid as Referred to in Art. 107(1) TFEU*, OJ C 262/1 (2016), particularly s. 5 [hereinafter, the 'NofSA Notice'].
105. *Ibid.* para. 239.
106. *Ibid.* s. 5.2.3, para. 123–125.

tax or social security exemptions for undertakings fulfilling certain criteria): it explains that such measures will be subject to a three-step analysis.[107]

In addition, Section 5.4 of the NofSA Notice addresses specific issues concerning tax measures (cooperatives,[108] undertakings for collective investment,[109] tax amnesties,[110] tax rulings and settlements,[111] depreciation and amortization rules,[112] regimes that fix basis for specific activities,[113] anti-abuse rules,[114] excise duties[115]) and highlights that, while Member States are free to spread the tax burden as they see fit across the various factors of production, they must exercise that competence in accordance with Union law.[116]

On the specific issue of administrative tax rulings, the NofSA Notice acknowledged that, for reasons of legal certainty, many national tax authorities provide prior administrative rulings on how specific transactions will be treated fiscally, particularly how 'arm's-length profits' will be set for related-party transactions. The Commission emphasized that such administrative ruling practices are best if they are transparent and the rulings made public and, indeed, that the grant of a tax ruling must, in all cases, respect the State-aid rules.

In this regard, the Commission specifically indicated that tax rulings confer a selective advantage on their addressees, particularly when the administration applies a 'more favourable' tax treatment when compared to other taxpayers in a similar factual and legal situation, for example, by accepting a transfer-pricing arrangement that is not at arm's length because (i) the methodology endorsed by the ruling produces an outcome that departs from a reliable approximation of a market-based outcome or (ii) the ruling allows its addressee to use alternative, more-indirect methods for calculating its taxable profits (e.g., the use of fixed margins for a cost-plus or resale-minus method for determining an appropriate transfer pricing) when more direct methods are available.

The Commission defined the arm's length principle as the way to establish whether the taxable profit on the corporate income of a company that is part of a group has been determined on the basis of a methodology that produces a reliable approximation of a market-based outcome. The Commission indicated that, independently of whether or in what form a Member State has incorporated it into its national legal system, the arm's length principle applies to national tax rules and binds the Member States, such that and it necessarily forms part of the Commission's assessment of tax measures granted to group companies, particularly in the form of transfer-pricing rulings.

107. *Ibid.* s. 5.2.3.3, para. 138–141.
108. *Ibid.* s. 5.4.1.
109. *Ibid.* s. 5.4.2.
110. *Ibid.* s. 5.4.3.
111. *Ibid.* s. 5.4.4.
112. *Ibid.* s. 5.4.5.
113. *Ibid.* s. 5.4.6.
114. *Ibid.* s. 5.4.7.
115. *Ibid.* s. 5.4.8.
116. *See Glaxo Wellcome*, C-182/08, Judgement, EU:C:2009:559, para. 34, and the case-law cited therein.

On the question of how to apply the arm's length principle, the Commission stated that it may, but is not obliged to, look at OECD guidance, particularly the 'OECD Transfer Pricing Guidelines for Multinational Enterprises and Tax Administrations'. The Commission recognized that those guidelines do not deal with matters of State aid as such, but that they materialize the international consensus on transfer pricing and provide useful guidance to tax administrations and multinational enterprises on how to ensure that a particular transfer-pricing methodology produces an outcome in line with market conditions.

Therefore, the Commission took the view that if a transfer-pricing arrangement complies with the guidance provided by said OECD Transfer Pricing Guidelines, including its guidance on the choice of the most appropriate transfer-pricing method to lead to a reliable approximation of a market based outcome, a tax ruling endorsing that arrangement is unlikely to give rise to State aid.

In addition to the NofSA Notice, in the framework of the High Level Forum on State-Aid Modernisation held in Brussels on 3 June 2016, the Commission published a six-page Working Paper on State Aid and Tax Rulings (the '2016 Working Paper'), which contained a summary of the its preliminary review of more than one thousand tax rulings, notably those endorsing transfer-pricing arrangements and the 'Lux Leaks' rulings.[117] In that 2016 Working Paper, the Commission noted that recourse to

the arm's length principle to determine whether a fiscal measure prescribing a method to establish the taxable profit of a company forming part of an integrated group gives rise to a selective advantage for the purposes of Article 107(1) TFEU was endorsed by the CJEU in its 2006

Forum 187

decision.[118]

The Commission added that it will focus on cases where there is a manifest breach of the arm's length principle.[119]

§6.05 A CRITICAL APPRAISAL OF THE COMMISSION'S RECENT APPROACH

The Commission's recent investigations seem to indicate that its focus has shifted from preferential tax regimes whose selectivity clearly results from criteria contained in the tax legislation of Member States (e.g., size, nature of the activity, and prior authorization) to administrative decisions on the application of (more-or-less) general rules or principles whose effects are to validate complex, international tax-planning schemes set up by multinational groups of companies that ultimately result in a very low level of overall taxation.

117. DG Competition–Internal Working Paper–Background to the High Level Forum on State Aid of 3 June 2016 available at http://ec.europa.eu/competition/state_aid/legislation/working_paper_tax_rulings.pdf, (last visited 10 Feb. 2017) [hereinafter, the '2016 Working Paper'].
118. *Belgium* v *Commission*, Joined cases C-182/03 and C-217/03.
119. The 2016 Working Paper, *supra* n. 117, para. 23.

The first question that comes to mind when discussing this shift is: "To what extent should the fight against tax avoidance and the promotion of fair tax competition between EU Member States influence the nature and scope of State-aid control?" The doctrine has already been extensively debated: the rationale for State-aid control focused on the harmful nature of a measure that encourages tax competition among Member States, rather than on its discriminatory (i.e., selective) character compared to other undertakings in the same Member State. That approach is generally illustrated by the declarations of EU Commissioners who refer to 'fair tax competition' as 'essential for the integrity of the Single Market, for the fiscal sustainability of our Member States, and for a level-playing field between our businesses'[120] or who suggest that negative decisions, such as the Commission decision in the Apple case, are 'a good thing because illegal state aid harms competition'.[121] According to this view, tackling (harmful) tax competition appears to be not only a (desirable) side-effect of State-aid control, but also its main driver. The most critical opponents of the Commission's approach argue that it embodies a concept of primacy of the political over the law and an affirmation of a new - and as-yet-absent from the Treaty - objective of State-aid control, which almost results in a real *coup d'état.*[122] Other authors take a critical-but-less-radical view, arguing that, while limitations on the power of Member States to attract companies via harmful fiscal measures may derive from the prohibition of State aid, it may constitute its underlying objective. They add, however, that State-aid control is not suitable for tackling harmful tax competition: first, because of the wording of Article 107 TFEU and, second, due to the case-by-case nature of State-aid control, which is limited to the territory of one Member State and does not take into account other Member States' practices.[123] Some authors have also raised the argument

120. European Commission Press Release, 11 June 2014 'State aid: Commission Investigates Transfer Pricing Arrangements on Corporate Taxation of Apple (Ireland) Starbucks (Netherlands) and Fiat Finance and Trade (Luxembourg)', available at http://europa.eu/rapid/press-release_IP-14-663_en.htm (last visited 8 Jan. 2017).
121. *See* Commissioner Vestager's statement concerning the Apple decision, 30 Aug. 2016, Statement/16/2926:

> Today's decision shows that we can act when a Member State gives illegal state aid to a company. This is a good thing since illegal state aid harms competition. Looking ahead, the ultimate goal should of course be that all companies, big or small, pay tax where they generate their profits. Enforcement of EU state aid rules alone cannot achieve this - that's why we need a change in corporate philosophies and the right legislation to address loopholes and ensure transparency.

122. For a detailed commentary on the doctrinal debate, see Antonio Carlos do Santos, *L'Union Européenne et la Régulation de la Concurrence Fiscal* 432 et seq. (2009); *see also*, more recently, N. Kroes, *Why EU State Aid is not the Right Tool to Fight Tax Avoidance*, The Guardian, 1 Sep. 2016.
123. *See also* Reymond Luja, *EU State Aid Rules and Their Limits*, 76 Tax Notes Int'l 353, 354 (2014): 'One cannot expect an EU member state to compensate for hybrid situations and foreign check-the-box regulations by giving up its own legal standards unilaterally'. *See also* Massimo Merola, *The Rebus of Selectivity in Fiscal Aid: A Nonconformist View on and Beyond Case Law*, 39 World Competition 533 (2016).

that harmful tax competition falls within the scope of the State-aid provisions because a harmful tax measure always constitutes fiscal State aid based on the criteria contained in the Code of Conduct.[124] However, this view seems to run counter to the statement contained in paragraph 30 of the 1998 Commission Notice, which reads: 'the qualification of a tax measure as harmful under the code of conduct does not affect its possible qualification as a State aid'.

The second range of issues raised by the Commission's 'new' approach is of a legal nature and concerns its compatibility with the wording of Article 107 TFEU. The decisions of the Commission concerning Apple (SA.38373),[125] Fiat Finance (SA.38375),[126] Belgian excess profits scheme (SA.37667),[127] and Starbucks (SA.38374)[128] have all been challenged before the General Court division of the CJEU.[129]

The first ground raised against the Commission's decisions is the lack of selectivity inherent in the nature of the rulings and the Commission's error in its identification of the reference framework. Secondly, the challengers criticize the Commission's use of the arm's length principle to assess a hypothetical advantage in favour of multinational companies, even challenging the existence of such a arm's length principle in EU law. Some of the challengers also disagree with the European Commission's analysis, as it rejected the methodological choices made by the taxing authorities and the relevant group of companies to simulate market conditions for setting prices in certain transactions. Finally, some challengers assert that the Commission has infringed on the principle of legitimate expectations because the approach developed in the Commission's decisions constitutes a departure from the OECD TP Guidelines, which the Commission had accepted in previous decisions.

Even though it will be up to the General Court – and, probably, the Court of Justice – to have the final say, it is already possible to comment on each of those three issues. First, because the existence of State aid has to be assessed based on its effects, the fact that the Commission targets measures that implement general principles of international tax law, such as transfer-pricing rules, cannot be used as a valid argument against its negative decisions on appeal. The same can be said for the fact that only certain companies or countries appear to be the object of State-aid scrutiny: such investigations always concern individual measures and the fact that, even from a tax-competition perspective, a coordinated removal of measures having similar effects

124. Ben J. Kiekebled, *Harmful Tax Competition in the European Union. Code of Conduct, Countermeasures and EU Law* 83 (2004).
125. This decision is currently subject to an appeal registered with the General Court as T-778/16 (*Ireland v Commission*).
126. This decision is currently subject to an appeal registered with the General Court as T-759/15 (*Fiat Chrysler Finance Europe* v *Commission*) and T-755/15 (*Luxembourg* v *Commission*).
127. Decision on SA.37667 Excess profit tax ruling system in Belgium, *supra* n. 98.
128. This decision is currently subject to an appeal registered with the General Court as T-760/15 (*Netherlands v Commission*) and T-636/16 (*Starbucks and Starbucks Manufacturing Emea* v *Commission*).
129. This section is based on information available on 26 Jan. 2017 on the CJEU's website.

in all Member States should be preferred, that cannot, in and of itself, prevent the Commission from acting, whenever possible, on a case-by-case basis. However, such investigations must take into account that tax sovereignty remains with the Member States and, therefore, the Member States remain free to deviate from international (OECD) standards or to even decide not to implement them at all, but such a Member State's tax policy choice should not influence the Commission's assessment of the existence of State aid.

Secondly, and in connection with the first issue, the question to be addressed is whether the arm's length principle can be found to have been naturally derived from Article 107 TFEU – that is to say, can it be found to be a particular expression of the general principle of non-discrimination, one that has been tailored to be an application of the Market-Economy Investor Principle ('MEIP'). If so, it remains to be seen what flexibility the Member States have in transposing that principle into their respective national laws[130] and what role, if any, is to be given to the OECD TP Guidelines. A fundamental preliminary issue to be addressed is whether multinational corporations and standalone companies are to be considered comparable in the application of transfer-pricing rules, which by their very nature are only applicable in a cross-border context between companies belonging to the same group.

In its *Belgian Coordination Centres* decision, the Commission acknowledged the relevance of transfer-pricing methods for the purpose of assessing certain measures regarding State-aid rules. The Commission recently went a step further, providing a comprehensive and extensive analysis of the methods used and accepted in the assessment of tax rulings in the framework of State-aid enforcement. For example, in its decision opening a formal investigation into an alleged illegal State aid given by Luxembourg to Amazon,[131] the Commission focused its evaluation notably on the effective use of one of the OECD-recommended methods. However, those methods were, in fact, just recommended, but the Commission seems to believe that departing from them is unacceptable without appropriate underlying reasons.[132] Similarly, the Commission indicated that it is ready to denounce any wrong choice of an OECD method instead of another (more-common) one without a proper justification[133] or even any incorrect application of the standard methods,[134] which it indicated would be considered enough to establish the selective character of the measure and, eventually, the State-aid nature of the practice. However, although OECD standards are non-binding rules that were not adopted through democratic procedures, the Commission seemed to rely on OECD standards and to request that Member States fully conform to them. One could claim that the Commission turned the political compromise concretized in the OECD standards at a given point in time into EU indirect (i.e., via

130. It is important to note that, in the area of transfer pricing, Member States adopted Convention 90/436/CEE on the elimination of double taxation in connection with the adjustment of profits of associated enterprises, OJ L225/10 (1990). It is, therefore, a sensitive area when the Commission intervenes using other instruments, such as State-aid control.
131. Investigation of State Aid SA.38944 – Luxembourg/Amazon, *supra* n. 96.
132. *Ibid.* paras 64–65.
133. *Ibid.* para. 77.
134. *Ibid.* para. 68.

enforcement of individual cases) harmonization of Member States domestic tax provisions or their obligations deriving from international law, thereby affecting the exercise of their tax sovereignty. It seems, however, that this view does not exactly reflect the Commission's position, which, in its NofSA Notice appears to consider the OECD TP Guidelines as a 'safe harbour' by stating that:

> If a transfer pricing arrangement complies with the guidance provided by the OECD Transfer Pricing Guidelines, including the guidance on the choice of the most appropriate method and leading to a reliable approximation of a market based outcome, a tax ruling endorsing that arrangement is unlikely to give rise to State aid.'[135]

Thirdly, as to the criticism relating to the absence of relevant precedents on which to ground the Commission's recent approach, it is worth recalling the decisions of the Court of Justice, first, in *Gibraltar*,[136] where the Court departed from its usual formal criterion of the three-step test to attack a policy designed to be selective and, then, more recently in *Santander*,[137] where the Court indicated that:

> a measure ... may be regarded as selective if it benefits undertakings carrying out cross-border transactions, in particular investment transactions, and is to the disadvantage of other undertakings which, while in a comparable factual and legal situation, in the light of the objective pursued by the tax system concerned, carry out other transactions of the same kind within the national territory.[138]

Those two cases seem to establish a rather direct link between the nature of a measure as State aid and its impact on cross-border (tax) competition, to the extent that it results in putting undertakings operating in an international context in a more favourable situation than those operating in a purely domestic context.

Another question to be asked is whether – assuming that the Court accepts the Commission's approach – it does not introduce an element of novelty that, compared to previous practice,[139] could impact the recovery of State aid. As mentioned above, the recent Commission decision regarding tax rulings seems to show a shift in the enforcement of State-aid rules from selective, preferential tax-regimes that are clearly implemented in the tax legislation of Member States to administrative rulings on transfer pricing in the framework of tax-planning schemes set up by multinational groups of companies. One can wonder whether that shift also entails an evolution in the legal assessment of the notion of State aid by the Commission, which could not be foreseen when those rulings were granted. Moreover, for the future, applying an approach based on the way a general standard or rule is applied (or misapplied) in a

135. NofSA Notice, *supra* n. 104, para. 173.
136. *Gibraltar*, C-106/09 P.
137. *Commission* v *World Duty Free Group*, Joined Cases C-20/15 P and C-21/15 P, Judgment, EU:C:2016:981, annulling the GC's judgments in *Autogrill España* v *Commission*, T-219/10, EU:T:2014:939 and *Banco Santander and Santusa* v *Commission*, T-399/11, EU:T:2014:938.
138. *Commission v World Duty Free Group*, Joined Cases C-20/15 P and C-21/15 P, para. 119.
139. For the opposite view (i.e., there is nothing novel or unconventional in deployment of State-aid control in the manner adopted by the Commission in the recent cases involving tax rulings), see Richard Lyal, *Transfer Pricing Rules and State Aid*, 38 Fordham Int'l L.J. 1017 (2015).

single specific case in order to assess a differentiation among companies (i.e., the specific company subject to the ruling and other companies) may entail great uncertainty. Such reasoning could lead one to conclude that State aid exists in any situation where the Commission may identify any wrong application of tax rules by tax administrations, which is inevitable in complex matters such as an intercompany allocation of cross-border profits, even without any intention to confer an advantage on the relevant taxpayer.

Fourthly, the Commission's strategy raises questions of a political nature, concerning not only the relationship between EU institutions and the Member States, but also third countries. Indeed, the selection of companies that were suspected of having benefitted from State aid in the form of favourable tax treatment triggered a strong political reaction in the United States. Although the investigations were technically opened against Member States and not against individual companies or group of companies, the typically American-based companies were the ones to face the negative consequences of recovery of State aid. Political reactions included that of US Treasury Secretary J. Lew, who formally expressed concerns about the issue of retroactivity, in letter and a white paper[140] addressed to President Juncker and Commissioner Vestager last February, in which he urged the EU Commission to reconsider its approach. In essence, Secretary Lew outlined four types of concerns, namely (i) the retroactive application of a new and expansive application of State-aid rules, (ii) the disproportionate selection of a number of US companies (three out of four closed investigations) among the beneficiaries of the tax practices under scrutiny, (iii) the lack of a legal basis on which to tax income of US multinational companies and (iv) the consequences of this policy on foreign direct investment and the rights of the US in tax treaties concluded only with EU Member States and not the European Union. Secretary Lew acknowledged that a serious problem exists, under the U.S. tax system, whereby income is only taxed upon repatriation and many US firms choose to defer tax liabilities by keeping income overseas in low-tax jurisdictions. To solve this issue, he mentioned the considerable efforts made in the framework of the OECD/G20 and the business-tax reforms prepared by the Obama administration to improve the repatriation of revenues of US companies to the US.

Competition Commissioner Vestager replied on behalf of the Commission that the EU was making full use of the tools at its disposal to drive the reform agenda against tax avoidance, namely its (i) legislative action (i.e., its March 2015 Tax Transparency Package and its January 2016 Anti-Tax Avoidance Package) and (ii) continued enforcement of EU State-aid rules intended to protect fair competition in the EU's Single

140. Letter of US Secretary of the Treasury Jacob J. Lew to Jean-Claude Junker, President of the EU Commission (11 Feb. 2016), https://www.treasury.gov/resource-center/tax-policy/treaties/Documents/Letter-State-Aid-Investigations.pdf (last visited 24 Mar. 2017) and U.S. Department of the Treasury White Paper: The European Commission's Recent State Aid Investigations of Transfer Pricing Rulings (24 Aug. 2016), https://www.treasury.gov/resource-center/tax-policy/treaties/Documents/White-Paper-State-Aid.pdf last (last visited 24 Mar. 2017).

Market.[141] US legal scholars also commented on the approach of the Commission: Prof. Greenberg even suggested that the US Treasury should apply Section 981 of the US Tax Code against EU companies,[142] which allows, in situations where US corporations are subject to discriminatory tax treatment in a country, the US to double its income tax rates on foreign citizens and corporations.

Fifth, State-aid control is brought to a transnational dimension when the issue does not lie in national rules, but on their practical application to transnational transactions. A potential outcome may be counterproductive with respect to the political objective of avoiding double taxation. For example, in the Starbucks case, the fact that the Commission contested the Netherlands' acceptance of an overestimation of the royalties that the Dutch company should have paid to the UK company;[143] if the Commission's determination is confirmed, it would imply that the overestimated amount paid to the UK company should be included in the tax base of the Dutch company. Nevertheless, the enforcement of a recovery decision would theoretically lead to double taxation since the group already paid that sum in the form of IP-related income in the UK. One could also imagine a situation of misallocation of taxable items, whereby the recovery of the unlevied tax by one Member State should then correspond to the restitution of the unduly levied tax by the other Member State involved in the transnational transaction. However, this is not a result that the Commission can enforce, as it only has the power to impose the restitution of illegal State aid to the State having given it; it has no power to adjust the tax paid by the group to any other State. Although the Commission declared, after the Apple decision, that it would take into account any subsequent transfer-pricing adjustment by a Member State or even by a third country, in assessing the amount of the illegal State aid to be recovered by Ireland, that does not seem satisfactory in terms of legal certainty.[144]

141. Letter of EU Commissioner Vestager to Secretary Lew of the US Department of the Treasury (29 Feb. 2016), http://static.politico.com/cf/ba/b7725d194d84a1df018c28160048/margrethe-vestager-letter-to-secty-lew-on-eu-tax-investigations.pdf, (last visited 24 Mar. 2017).
142. *See, notably*, Itai Grinberg, *A Constructive U.S. Counter to EU State Aid Cases*, 2016 Tax Notes Int'l 167.
143. Investigation of State Aid SA.38374 - Netherlands/Starbucks, *supra* n. 98, paras 115–123.
144. According to the Commission:

> The amount of unpaid taxes to be recovered by the Irish authorities would be reduced if other countries were to require Apple to pay more taxes on the profits recorded by Apple Sales International and Apple Operations Europe for this period. This could be the case if they consider, in view of the information revealed through the Commission's investigation, that Apple's commercial risks, sales and other activities should have been recorded in their jurisdictions. This is because the taxable profits of Apple Sales International in Ireland would be reduced if profits were recorded and taxed in other countries instead of being recorded in Ireland ... The amount of unpaid taxes to be recovered by the Irish authorities would also be reduced if the US authorities were to require Apple to pay larger amounts of money to their US parent company for this period to finance research and development efforts. These are conducted by Apple in the US on behalf of Apple Sales International and Apple Operations Europe, for which the two companies already make annual payments.

§6.06 CONCLUSION: SAFEGUARDING A EUROPEAN COMMON INTEREST OR THE COMMISSION'S ATTEMPT TO SAVE MEMBER STATES FROM THEIR OWN TAX AMBITIONS

As highlighted by different elements published by the Commission, the choice and complexity of a group of companies' corporate tax structures, which take advantage of loopholes and mismatches caused by the absence of international coordination among domestic tax systems, clearly appear to be motivated by attempts to reduce the overall corporate tax paid by the group. These schemes result in highly significant overall loss in tax revenues in the countries concerned. Member States' tax administrations (through individual advance tax rulings) or their specific tax regimes favour such international tax-planning schemes and, thus, actively promote – through 'harmful tax practices' – what the OECD has called 'base erosion and profit shifting' or BEPS.[145] Such exercises of Member States' taxing powers could jeopardize the Single Market and result in calls to strengthen the tools for tax harmonization and the fight against harmful tax competition in the European Union.

The Commission's recent wave of investigations into domestic-text tax rulings cannot be isolated from this context. However, it remains to be seen whether State-aid control is the most-suitable instrument to address those issues. From a legal perspective, there is, at the moment, considerable uncertainty as regards the approach adopted by the Commission through its various negative decisions adopted so far, in particular as regards the status of the arm's length principle in EU State-aid law. However, the evolution of the CJEU's case-law on fiscal State aid seems to support the Commission's current practice, which can be seen as natural (and certainly not surprising) in the light of the contextually international evolution from the approach adopted in the 1990s, when intra-EU tax competition concerns fuelled the first wave of State-aid infringement procedures against preferential tax regimes.

Nevertheless, the case-by-case dimension of State-aid enforcement, as well as the recovery obligation associated with negative decisions, creates a feeling of unfairness for some undertakings and the Member States concerned by the rulings (which, on the other hand, appear unfair to many). Although it is always risky to attempt to rewrite history, we can guess that those decisions, ultimately, might not have been required if the Member States had made greater efforts to coordinate their corporate tax systems, as they finally did with Directive 2016/1164, which addresses tax avoidance and other exchange-of-information instruments.[146] In that sense, the Commission, by using its powers in the area of State aid, has sent a powerful signal to the Member States that it

145. Press Release (30 Aug. 2016), IP/16/2923, para. 4, http://europa.eu/rapid/press-release_IP-16-2923_fr.htm (last visited 24 Mar. 2017). OECD, *Action Plan on Base Erosion and Profit Shifting* (2013).

146. *See* Council Directive 2016/1164 laying down rules against tax avoidance practices that directly affect the functioning of the internal market, OJ L 193/1 (2016). *See also* Violeta Ruiz Almendral, *Tax Avoidance, the 'Balanced Allocation of Taxing Powers' and the Arm's Length Standard: an Odd Threesome in Need of Clarification, in Allocating Taxing Powers within the European Union* 131, 145 et seq. (Isabelle Richelle, Wolfgang Schon & Edoardo Traversa eds., 2013).

is not acceptable to redirect and channel investments in favour of a single national economy to the detriment of other EU Member States and that the Internal market's objective is not the promotion of international tax competition. The future will tell if fiscal State-aid policy will have contributed to a renewal of European tax-policy.

PART III Fundamental Rights and Tax Law

CHAPTER 7

An Enhanced Relationship Between Taxpayers and Tax Authorities: A Taxpayer Charter of Rights and the European Taxpayers' Code

Piergiorgio Valente

§7.01 BASIC PRINCIPLES OF TAXPAYER RIGHTS

Base erosion and profit shifting or BEPS issues show that there is a real need for a reshaping/rethinking of tax principles as well as an enhanced relationship between taxpayers and tax authorities.[1] This relationship should be based on mutual trust and cooperation and should be regulated by a clear definition of the rights[2] and duties of both taxpayers and tax authorities.[3]

1. *See* Organisation for Economic Co-operation and Development (OECD), *Addressing Base Erosion and Profit Shifting* (Feb. 2013) and OECD, *Action Plan on Base Erosion and Profit Shifting* (July 2013).
2. *See* Opinion Statement FC 11/2014 and PAC 2/2014, *The European Tax Advisers' Priorities in EU Policy: Goals for the Next 5 Years Ahead*, May 2014 (available at http://www.komitetpodatkowy.pl/pobierz/94.html):

> Taxpayer rights are not granted by the state but [*sic*] derived from human and fundamental rights. A balanced approach to taxpayer rights and obligations is a prerequisite for an increase in mutual trust of taxpayers, tax advisers and tax administrations. While some tax administrations have shown openness towards a relationship of mutual trust in which both advisers and administration help a taxpayer comply with the law, a change of mindset is still needed in other member states. This endeavour will only be worthwhile if the result is not a mere political statement of intent but [*sic*] has legal force and can be invoked by citizens and businesses.

   See also, Taxpayers Australia, *The Taxpayers' Guide 2013–2014* (2013).
3. *See* James Alm, *Measuring, Explaining and Controlling Tax Evasion: Lessons from Theory, Experiment, and Field Studies*,19 Int'l Tax & Pub. Fin. 54 (2012); James Androni, Brian Erard & Jonathan Feinstein, *Tax Compliance*, 36 J. Econ. Literature 818 (1988); Bruno S. Frey & Benno

It is expected that BEPS proposals may engender compliance burdens, both at the level of the private sector and the government, mainly due to the significant volume of BEPS measures, but also by reason of the various complex aspects of the recommendations themselves. A potential increase in disputes is of great concern to all taxpayers. Tax offices may experience serious problems in making proper use of the potentially voluminous additional information and in dealing effectively with the foreseeable increase in requests for tax information exchange between/among countries.

Thus, cooperative compliance would help to significantly decrease the compliance burden on most taxpayers while releasing the tax administration's resources and making them available for more constructive and value-creating activities. The endorsement of the OECD's 'enhanced relationship' principle (or cooperative compliance framework) would lead to an increase of voluntary compliance and early disclosure, reducing the 'appetite' to exploit BEPS opportunities, as well as litigation, while contributing to more effective tax collection.

As such, with the implementation of BEPS measures, having an instrument that:

- ensures that taxpayer rights and obligations are safeguarded,
- facilitates compliance by taxpayers by stimulating cooperation, trust, and confidence towards tax administrations,
- ensures greater fiscal transparency in respect of such rights and obligations, and
- encourages a service-oriented approach,

is, therefore, essential within the new international framework.

A fundamental principle should be that the taxpayer can expect the tax authorities to treat the taxpayer fairly and reasonably.[4] They should also make fair and equitable decisions in compliance with the law and resolve the taxpayer's concerns and complaints as fairly and as quickly as possible. Fair and equitable decisions should be guaranteed, assuming all relevant facts and circumstances are taken into account.[5]

Torgler, *Tax morale and conditional cooperation*, 37 J. Comp. Econ. 139 (2007); Erich Kirchler, *The Economic Psychology of Tax Behaviour* (2007); and Colin C. Williams, *Confronting the Shadow Economy: Evaluating Tax Compliance and Behaviour Policies* (2014).

4. For this purpose, tax authorities should behave with integrity and honesty, and act impartially. What induces compliance with tax law has been subjected to extensive research. The traditional view in economic models of taxpayer behaviour has not proven consistent with empirical evidence. A host of other factors, such as social values, public morality, and people's perception about the fairness of the system, also matter in shaping attitudes towards tax laws. *See* Michael W. Spicer & Lee A. Becker, *Fiscal Inequality and Tax Evasion: An Experimental Approach*, 33 Nat'l Tax J. 171 (1980).
5. *See* IRS, *The Taxpayer Bill of Rights*, Rev'd 2014 (available at http://www.irs.gov/pub/irs-pdf/p1.pdf):

   > 10. The Right to a Fair and Just Tax System:
   >
   > Taxpayers have the right to expect the tax system to consider facts and circumstances that might affect their underlying liabilities, ability to pay, or ability to provide information timely. Taxpayers have the right to receive assistance from the Taxpayer Advocate Service if they are experiencing financial difficulty or if the IRS has not resolved their tax issues properly and timely through its normal channels.

The taxpayer should be treated as being honest in tax affairs (unless otherwise established). The tax authorities should presume that the information provided by the taxpayer is complete and accurate.[6]

The taxpayer should expect to be provided with professional service and any assistance that might be necessary for it to understand and meet its tax obligations.[7] The taxpayer can easily comply with tax obligations, if the tax authorities:

- develop services, publications, and other information tools that meet the taxpayer's needs;
- use plain and clear language in publications and when communicating with the taxpayer; and
- provide reasonable access to enquiry services.[8]

Facilitating compliance involves such elements as improving services to taxpayers by providing them with clear instructions, understandable forms, and assistance

---

The same right exists under *The Canadian Taxpayer Bill of Rights* (available at http://www.cra-arc.gc.ca/E/pub/tg/rc17/rc17-e.html#_Ref191278812):

> You can expect we will treat you courteously and with consideration at all times, including when we ask for information or arrange interviews and audits. Integrity, professionalism, respect, and co-operation are our core values and reflect our commitment to giving you the best possible service. You can also expect us to listen to you and to take your circumstances into account, which is part of the process of making impartial decisions according to the law. We will then explain our decision and inform you about your rights and obligations regarding that decision.

6. *See* European Commission, *Risk Management Guide for Tax Administrations*, Version 1.02, 7 (European Commission's Taxation and Customs Union Directorate General 2006):

> The primary goal of the tax authorities is to collect the taxes payable in accordance with the law in such a manner that will sustain confidence in the tax system. Some taxpayers, due to ignorance, carelessness or deliberate actions as well as weaknesses in a tax administration, fail to meet their obligations. Therefore, tax administrations should have in place strategies and structures to ensure that non-compliance with tax law is kept to the minimum possible.
>
> ...
>
> Compliance essentially relates to the extent to which a taxpayer meets its obligations. Risk management looks at risks that affect compliance to fulfil the obligations such as registering, filing, reporting, and remitting of tax.

(available at http://ec.europa.eu/taxation_customs/resources/documents/taxation/tax_cooperation/gen_overview/risk_management_guide_for_tax_administrations_en.pdf). Certainly, there is a difference between errors/discrepancies and deliberate actions. If the taxpayer makes a mistake, it should always be granted the opportunity to provide an explanation and a correction.

7. On this subject, see also Valerie A. Braithwaite, *Defiance in Taxation and Governance: Resisting and Dismissing Authority in a Democracy* (2009); British House of Commons, Public Administration Select Committee, *From Citizen's Charter to Public Service Guarantees: Entitlements to Public Services*, Twelfth Report of Session 2007–08 (2008) (available at http://www.publications.parliament.uk/pa/cm200708/cmselect/cmpubadm/411/411.pdf); Victor Ayeni, *Empowering the Customer: The Citizen in Public Sector Reform* (Commonwealth Secretariat 2001).
8. Moreover, it is expected that tax authorities will accept that the taxpayer might choose to be represented by a person of its choice and seek advice about tax affairs (e.g., preparing tax returns and activity statements) and tax obligations.

and information as necessary.[9] Monitoring compliance requires information systems as well as appropriate procedures to detect non-compliance. Improving compliance requires a mix of both of these measures and additional measures to deter non-compliance, such as the effective application of penalties.[10]

The taxpayer's right to privacy is a major issue.[11] To this purpose, tax authorities should keep any information held about the taxpayer confidential, in compliance with law.[12] That information should be kept confidential, but, in some circumstances, the law should allow disclosure to others for specific purposes.[13] Generally, tax laws

---

9. *See* IRS, *The Taxpayer Bill of Rights, supra* n. 5:

> 1.The Right to Be Informed
>
> Taxpayers have the right to know what they need to do to comply with the tax laws. They are entitled to clear explanations of the laws and IRS procedures in all tax forms, instructions, publications, notices, and correspondence. They have the right to be informed of IRS decisions about their tax accounts and to receive clear explanations of the outcomes
>
> A similar right exists under the Canadian Taxpayer Bill of Rights, *supra* n. 5 ('You can expect us to provide you with complete, accurate, and timely information in plain language that explains the laws and policies that apply to *your situation*' (emphasis added)).

10. As a rule, successful strategies require an appropriate mix of all these approaches.
11. On this subject, see also Chris Evans, Judith Freedman & Richard E. Krever, *The Delicate Balance: Tax, Discretion and the Rule of Law* (2011); Georg Kofler, Miguel Poiares Maduro & Pasquale Pistone, *Human Rights and Taxation in Europe and the World* (2011).
12. Information about the taxpayer may be collected by the tax authorities directly from the taxpayer or from other relevant parties.
13. *See* IRS, *The Taxpayer Bill of Rights, supra* n. 5:

> 7. The Right to Privacy
>
> Taxpayers have the right to expect that any IRS inquiry, examination, or enforcement action will comply with the law and be no more intrusive than necessary, and will respect all due process rights, including search and seizure protections and will provide, where applicable, a collection due process hearing.
>
> 8. The Right to Confidentiality
>
> Taxpayers have the right to expect that any information they provide to the IRS will not be disclosed unless authorized by the taxpayer or by law. Taxpayers have the right to expect appropriate action will be taken against employees, return preparers, and others who wrongfully use or disclose taxpayer return information.

The same right exists under *The Canadian Taxpayer Bill of Rights, supra* n. 5:

> Under this right, you can expect us to protect and manage the confidentiality of your personal and financial information in accordance with the laws we administer, such as the Income Tax Act, the Excise Tax Act, the Excise Act, 2001, and the Privacy Act.
>
> Only employees who need your information to administer programs and legislation have access to your information.
>
> We also take other steps to protect your information and make sure it is kept confidential. For example, we follow government-wide and internal policies on the security of information and privacy. We also regularly review our internal processes to make sure your information is safe'.

should set forth secrecy provisions on the use and disclosure of information concerning taxpayers.[14]

As far as the right to information is concerned, the tax authorities should give the taxpayer access to:

- documents held in accordance with the law; and
- documents used in making decisions, such as public rulings, tax procedures, and guidelines.[15]

The right to information includes the taxpayer's right to obtain advice and information it can rely on. The tax authorities should be expected to provide advice and information that:

- allows the taxpayer to fully understand how tax laws apply,
- makes the taxpayer aware of his/her rights and entitlements, and
- helps the taxpayer understand and meet his/her tax obligations.

Advice and information should be given on how the law applies to the taxpayer's particular circumstances; information about how the law applies generally should be published.

Taxpayers need to be provided with a clear and exhaustive explanation of the decisions made, except under certain limited circumstances, such as when:

- releasing information about one taxpayer's decision would breach the right to privacy of another taxpayer;
- the tax authorities suspect fraud, since the release of information could be prejudicial to ongoing investigations.

The taxpayer should also have the right to a review of any such decisions.[16] When making a decision about the taxpayer's tax affairs, the tax authorities should

14. Tax officers can only look at, record, discuss, or disclose information about the taxpayer when it is a necessary part of their job or where the law specifies that they must do so. Taxpayer information may be disclosed if necessary:

    - to check taxpayer's eligibility for government benefits;
    - for law enforcement purposes; or
    - for statistics collection purposes.

15. The tax authorities may refuse to disclose documents to the taxpayer if disclosure could reasonably be expected to be prejudicial to an investigation or an inspection or any other activity carried out in accordance with law.
16. *See* IRS, *The Taxpayer Bill of Rights*, *supra* n. 5:

    > 4. The Right to Challenge the IRS's Position and Be Heard
    >
    > Taxpayers have the right to raise objections and provide additional documentation in response to formal IRS actions or proposed actions, to expect that the IRS will consider their timely objections and documentation promptly and fairly, and to receive a response if the IRS does not agree with their position.

explain how the taxpayer may obtain such a review and if any time limits apply.[17] Moreover, the tax authorities should be expected to:

- recognize the taxpayer's right to make a complaint. When dealing with complaints, the tax authorities should be expected to take an objective, impartial, and balanced approach;[18]
- administer the tax system in order to reduce the taxpayer's compliance costs. With the goal of dealing with the taxpayer in a straightforward and convenient manner, the tax authorities should provide the former with a clear explanation of how:
  - to meet tax obligations;[19] and
  - to comply with the law by reducing the workload, time, and effort involved.[20]

Accountability is a key issue. The tax authorities should be accountable for what they do and apply quality-assurance processes to the decisions they make.[21] If an issue cannot be quickly settled, the taxpayer should be kept updated as to the progress of the matter.[22]

Tax authorities are responsible for decisions that affect taxpayers, often having a direct impact on their financial position. In general, there is a significant imbalance of power between the tax authorities and most taxpayers, especially individuals and small businesses. Disputes between the tax authorities and taxpayers are typically resolved before courts and tribunals. However, that is often a costly and time-consuming process, despite improvements, such as the implementation of alternative dispute resolution mechanisms.

---

17. In case of several review options, the tax authorities should provide the taxpayer with a clear explanation of the differences among them. The best review option will normally depend on the taxpayer's situation.
18. In accordance with principles of natural justice and procedural fairness. Any such review should analyse the issues that led to the complaint, since those issues could be linked to weaknesses and/or loopholes in applicable policies.
19. *See* IRS, *The Taxpayer Bill of Rights, supra* n. 5:

    > 6. The Right to Finality
    >
    > Taxpayers have the right to know the maximum amount of time they have to challenge the IRS's position as well as the maximum amount of time the IRS has to audit a particular tax year or collect a tax debt. Taxpayers have the right to know when the IRS has finished an audit.

20. Services that fit with the systems the taxpayer uses should also be rendered. To this purpose, the tax authorities need to:

    - consult regularly with the taxpayers' community; and
    - involve the taxpayers' community in identifying the products supplied and services rendered.

21. When making a decision about the taxpayer's tax affairs, the tax authorities should also inform the taxpayer about its rights and obligations in relation thereto.
22. All reasonable steps need to be taken in order to lead to a resolution. Results of the actions taken and details of the issues dealt with should be made available to the taxpayer community.

Tax authorities should be independent in the administration of tax law, which independence is founded on strong and deeply rooted equity and integrity principles. Although independent, tax authorities still perform a critical governmental function, which means that effective monitoring and scrutiny are essential.

Public confidence in the tax authorities is particularly important in any self-assessment system. Such a system relies mostly on voluntary compliance, which is more likely to be attained when taxpayers have confidence that the tax authorities are administering the law fairly and efficiently.[23]

§7.02 BASIC PRINCIPLES OF TAXPAYER OBLIGATIONS

The relationship between tax authorities and taxpayers also involves some taxpayer obligations. The tax authorities should expect the taxpayer to:

- be truthful, by providing complete and accurate information regarding:
  - tax returns and other statements;
  - facts and circumstances when seeking tax advice or requesting a ruling (questions should be answered comprehensively, accurately, and honestly);
- keep complete records that allow the taxpayer to prepare accurate tax returns and other statements; and
- take reasonable care in providing complete and accurate information, as well as in preparing tax returns and other documents.[24]

Taxes have to be paid by the due date. The tax authorities could allow the taxpayer a further delay to remit payment when the taxpayer can provide proof as to the existence of genuine hardship if obliged to pay by the due date.[25]

Finally, the tax authorities should expect the taxpayer to be cooperative. If the tax system is based on taxpayers voluntarily complying with tax laws in a cooperative

23. *See Australia's Future Tax System: Final Report, Part 2: Detailed analysis, Chapter G1, Subpart G1-2, 'An Open and Accountable Tax Administration'*, available at http://taxreview.treasury.gov.au/content/FinalReport.aspx?doc=html/publications/Papers/Final_Report_Part_2/chapter_g1-2.htm (last visited 19 Jan. 2017):

> Principles: The tax authority should be independent in its administration of the tax laws. However, the independence of the tax authority, together with its considerable responsibilities and powers, means that it should have extensive and clear accountabilities, to help ensure that it administers the system fairly and efficiently.

24. Tax returns and other required documents or information should be filed by the taxpayer by the due date. In case of difficulties, and based on the taxpayer's circumstances, the taxpayer may be granted a further delay. Tax returns or activity statements should be filed on a timely basis even if the taxpayer cannot pay the amount owed. Penalties can apply if the taxpayer does not file on time.
25. When collecting taxes, the tax authorities should use the options, and carry out the actions, available under the law. Actions are expected to be fair and reasonable, although prompt and decisive. The tax authorities should take into consideration the taxpayer's own circumstances and act consistently with applicable guidelines.

    On this subject, see also Michael Lang, *Procedural Rules in Tax Law in the Context of European Union and Domestic Law* (2010).

manner, the tax authorities should be able manage the tax system at a relatively low cost, thereby reducing any unnecessary intrusion into the taxpayer's affairs.[26] The tax authorities should work with the taxpayer cooperatively, providing it with help to voluntarily meet its tax obligations.[27]

§7.03 MODEL TAXPAYER CHARTER: INTRODUCTION

The proposal - at the international level - for a Model Taxpayer Charter, was jointly submitted by the Asia-Oceania Tax Consultants' Association (AOTCA),[28] by the *Confédération Fiscale Européenne* (CFE),[29] and by the Society of Trust and Estate Practitioners (STEP),[30] with the purpose of designing a legislative model that might be adopted by the single States to regulate taxpayers' rights and duties vis-à-vis the Revenue Office.[31]

---

26. *See* European Commission, *Risk Management Guide for Tax Administrations, supra* n. 6, at 17:

    If the objective is to increase voluntary compliance [*sic*] such assumptions or principles could be:

    - as first priority [sic] address taxpayer future behaviour, to identify and correct historical errors are not equally important;
    - an assumption that the taxpayer is honest as long as nothing else is proven;
    - that there is not [*sic*] justification to use extreme measure[s] against one or a few taxpayers in order to influence behaviour of others;
    - to detect small errors early than to detect big errors late;
    - carried out in a way that shows respect and understanding for the situation of the taxpayer.

27. The tax authorities should be able to take firm action against uncooperative or obstructive taxpayers.
28. The AOTCA, established in 1992, represents well over 330,000 tax professionals operating in Asia in Oceania.
29. The CFE represents 26 professional organizations that are present in 21 European Countries, to which over 200,000 tax consultants refer. The CFE spearheaded the idea of creating a Model Taxpayer Charter in 2008, which was the central theme of the CFE Forum in the same year.
30. STEP is a worldwide organization of consultants in the area of planning and management of transfers of inheritance property, with special focus on tax issues. STEP aims to promote information connected to issues involved in their own operating context and to foster the growth of their own Members' professional competencies. STEP counts 20,000 Members located in 95 Countries, belonging to various professional categories (lawyers, professional tax consultants, trustees, and other kinds of professionals).
31. Ian Hayes (*A Model Taxpayer's Charter – Why?*, CFE News, 53 Eur. Tax'n 522 (2013)) wonders as to the reasons why each State should have its own Taxpayer Charter. Hayes finds motivations based on economic, social, ethical, and political aspects, particularly, from an economic perspective. Hayes observes how MNEs have rooted their presence at the global level:

    taking full advantage of existing tax law and practice in each country in which they operate ... Their ventures have been crafted to use the good offices of countries with favorable tax regimes and they have done so complying fully with the rules and regulations contained in the Double Tax Agreements of the countries within which they operate ... If as a result the tax taken in any jurisdiction looks disproportionate to revenues generated there, if criticism is due, it must be leveled at those who set policy, the politicians. Their failure is both national and international. As we move forward to create a global fiscal framework, taxpayers and tax authorities need to know the generally accepted and acceptable parameters within which they operate. A Model Taxpayer Charter which sets down those rights and responsibilities is a solid place to start.

There has been growing awareness in the past few years with regard to the fact that cooperation between Revenue Offices and taxpayers, and voluntary disclosure by these latter play a most fundamental role in strategic plans adopted in the fight against tax evasion and tax fraud.

On the one hand, Revenue Offices should be willing to implement, vis-à-vis taxpayers, an approach based on service, to complement a control-based philosophy. On the other hand, taxpayers should be motivated to greater transparency by submitting voluntary disclosure of information and self-compliance. Lastly, National Governments should guarantee taxpayers fair and transparent tax rules, based on the introduction and application of tax rules that are clear and simple.

The drafting of the Model Taxpayer Charter took place after an overall examination of the various taxpayers' Charters existing in other States that participated in the Survey, for the purpose of attaining a proposal that would have the consensus among all forty-one participating States.[32]

The final version of the Model Taxpayer Charter (consisting of thirty-seven articles) was submitted on 13 November 2015.[33] An innovative aspect of the final version was a list of Fundamental Principles entitled 'The Ten Commandments', which included ten fundamental rights and duties of both taxpayers and Revenue Offices.

The Model Taxpayer Charter has a subjective application scope that is rather broad-based, given that it is not only applicable to all taxpayers and Revenue Offices of all States, but also to the States themselves and to all of their various administrative offices and structures vested with taxing authority, as well as to taxpayers' own tax consultants.

The Model Taxpayer Charter's provisions are applicable to each single tax and payment, of any nature whatsoever, which may essentially be (deemed or) likened to a tax, with the aim to:

- define taxpayers' rights, as far as taxes imposed by the State;
- codify taxpayers' obligations/responsibilities vis-à-vis the State as provided by national laws.

Any amendment that might somehow weaken or prejudice taxpayers' rights acknowledged by national laws or Courts, or in any case, by any national practice of the States, is to be excluded.

See also Piergorgio Valente, Ian Hayes & Dick Barmentlo, *Il Model Taxpayer Charter – Statuto dei Diritti e dei Doveri del Contribuente, Cooperazione con il Fisco tra Tax Governance e Tax Compliance*, No. 36/2013 *Il Fisco* 5570; and Piergorgio Valente, Ian Hayes & Dick Barmentlo, *Il Model Taxpayer Charter: Statuto dei Diritti del Contribuente tra Tax Governance e Tax Compliance, in* Piergiogio Valente, *Elusione Fiscale Internazionale* 3437 (2014).

32. States participating in the Survey were forty-one as follows: Australia, Austria, Belgium, Bulgaria, Canada, China, Croatia, Finland, France, Germany, Japan, Greece, Hong Kong, India, Indonesia, Ireland, Israel, Italy, Latvia, Luxembourg, Mexico, Malaysia, Malta, Mongolia, New Zealand, The Netherlands, Poland, Portugal, the United Kingdom, the Czech Republic, Singapore, South Africa, South Korea, the Slovak Republic, Romania, Russia, Slovenia, Spain, the United States, Switzerland, and Vietnam.

33. Authors of the Model Taxpayer Charter, as well as the Report, are Michael Cadesky (STEP), Ian Hayes (CFE), and David Russell (AOTCA).

States' sovereignty to levy tax pursuant to the rights granted to them by their national laws, and to administer such taxes according to national legislation, is entirely safeguarded.

§7.04 TAX AUTHORITIES-TAXPAYER RELATIONS IN THE MODEL TAXPAYER CHARTER

In the drafting process of the Model Taxpayer Charter, a number of general principles – deemed absolutely fundamental and unalienable – were provided. The said principles are generally accepted by the vast majority of the various national legislations on a worldwide basis. First, there is a presumption of honesty and 'truthfulness' of behaviours adopted by taxpayers, until otherwise proven. Just as significant is the law abuse prohibition in the sense that taxpayers must not resort to the Charter to somehow create obstacles to or delays in the Revenue Office's actions and/or procedures when applying national tax provisions.

Any taxpayer is answerable to the extent of his payment obligations pursuant to national laws, even if the lack of due knowledge of tax laws does neither justify the non-application of tax, nor the non-payment of taxes due, nor the non-application of related penalties. Other key principles, set forth with the aim to attain a balance by means of the proper balancing between mutual rights and duties,[34] are:

- non-discrimination principle in the application of taxes;
- recognized exemption from interests and penalties (in specific cases and especially where the taxpayer may substantiate his/her own good faith), of the extension of the term(s) for preparing the relevant tax declarations and for any related causes to justify any exceptions to such terms; and
- tax laws should neither penalize a given industrial sector, nor any occupational sector without just cause.

Application of the most general principle of certainty of the law is the non-retroactivity of tax provisions, unless the retroactive application of the rule works to the taxpayer's advantage.

Further to the principle of non-retroactivity, the rule was endorsed in connection with a 'reasonable and fair transition period' between the previous regime and the one

34. On this issue, Ian Hayes remarked that important inspirational sources for crafting the Model were the UN Declaration on Human Rights and the declarations of rights of countries such as France, the United Kingdom and the Unites States:

> What we did not note in the book but which I do here is that those declarations are general precepts that have their origin in political struggle and which result in the citizen as taxpayer establishing his/her right to be taxed only with consent. We think it is a fundamental precept that taxation raised without consent, either overt or tacit, lacks the balance necessary to achieve political harmony and thereby general prosperity for the good of all. A taxpayer's charter, enacted as of right is one way to help secure such a balance.

Hayes, *supra* n. 31, at 523.

amending the effects thereof (both in terms of amendments to the taxation previously in force and in terms of the introduction of a new tax[35]).

There is a cross-border phenomenon known as double taxation - generally quite detrimental to taxpayers - which has been amply treated and regulated under the OECD Double Tax Treaty Model. Such phenomenon derives, as a rule, by the simultaneous taxation by both the source State and the State of residence on a given income category. In order to curb or eliminate double taxation, States grant taxpayers a tax credit, namely a mechanism to exempt income from their taxation.[36]

The Model Taxpayer Charter expressed itself in the same sense, suggesting the adoption of one of the two mechanisms to curb or eliminate any double taxation that might be applied to the taxpayer.[37]

A significant context for relationships between the Revenue Office and the taxpayer pertains to the fight against tax avoidance and evasion. The Model Taxpayer Charter favours the introduction of countering rules to the above-mentioned phenomena, while simultaneously restricting their effective applicability in order to prevent the Tax Authorities from challenging economic transactions/operations every time there is a tax advantage. In other words, it attempts to prevent benefits being derived from a tax advantage or even the benefits obtained by making a choice between possible, alternative economic-structures, being deemed to be an 'avoidance case'; therefore, the interpretation of avoidance phenomena by Revenue Offices is limited to cases in which an economic structure, clearly organized by artificial means to achieve a tax saving,[38] has been identified and ascertained.

The Model Taxpayer Charter makes a distinction between tax evasion - which derives from a dishonest and criminal behaviour vis-à-vis the State - and tax savings that might be achieved through 'aggressive tax planning'[39] schemes that, if at all, will be relevant for avoidance purposes.

35. The first release of the Survey disclosed that only five States have a general principle of non-retroactivity of tax laws, whereas in nineteen States non-retroactivity is only guaranteed in certain cases. Conversely, ten States have declared that a general non-retroactivity provision is not allowed due to constitutional restrictions. In that respect, *see* Michael Cadesky, Ian Hayes & David Russell, *Towards Greater Fairness in Taxation, A Model Taxpayer Charter, Preliminary Report* 137-138 (2013).
36. On the issue, see Cadesky, Hayes & Russell, *supra* n. 35, at 225-226 (shows that the Survey revealed that almost all States surveyed use a tax credit or exemption mechanism to reduce or eliminate double taxation; furthermore, it should be noted that the main regulatory source for mechanisms against double taxation is represented by international tax conventions).
37. Model Taxpayer Charter, Art. 19 ('Legislation shall provide for relief of double taxation, through an exemption or tax credit mechanism or as may be suitable in the circumstances').
38. On the issue, see Cadesky, Hayes & Russell, *supra* n. 35, at 176 (authors maintain that a clear distinction must be made between tax mitigation and artificial tax avoidance: only the latter should be countered by national legislations).
39. Tax planning schemes pursued by MNEs have grown particularly aggressive in the last few years. Such MNEs are generally known to transfer taxable profits to States with low tax regimes, by implementing transactions that appear to be formally lawful, but which are - nonetheless - in conflict with the purpose of the related rule. The OECD, the European Commission, and the International Community have firmly resolved to introduce and implement all necessary measures to forestall the erosion of taxable bases and any losses of tax revenue for States.

One of the fundamental rights of taxpayers is the right to a defence. Such right has the purpose of allowing the taxpayer to challenge a tax assessment notice before the competent authorities. Moreover, each State should be organized with regard to administrative procedures related to internal/domestic appeals.

It is necessary that Revenue Offices also further and motivate the taxpayers' tax compliance, recognizing to the latter the right to request assistance in order to draw up a complete and accurate filing of the tax return.[40]

Lastly, an aspect that plays in the taxpayer's favour is that the Model Taxpayer Charter acknowledges and safeguards the confidentiality of information. Such a right is particularly significant, given the sensitive nature and importance of data and information in the hands of the Revenue Offices, since the dissemination of such data/information might significantly damage the taxpayer, whether as an individual or corporation: think, for example, in the case of companies, how such information might be used by competitors to engage in speculative activities that might harm the taxpayer.[41]

The Model Taxpayer Charter, proposed by the AOTCA, the CFE, and STEP as a preliminary version of a Model Taxpayer Charter on a worldwide basis, has the main objective of ensuring greater fairness in relations between taxpayers and Revenue Offices in various countries and of regulating taxpayers' rights and duties vis-à-vis the Tax Authorities.

In representing the frame of reference for all States involved, the key elements are fairness, the purpose of which is to achieve an ever-greater tax compliance by taxpayers, and transparency, which requires the adoption and enforcement of clear and simple tax rules.

In relations between taxpayers and Revenue Offices, the principles of transparency and fairness may be exclusively guaranteed, if each State shall adopt its own taxpayer's Charter in line with the contents provided by the proposed Model Taxpayer Charter.[42]

40. The Survey addressing the matter of tax assistance and support to the interpretation of tax rules by the Tax Authorities were clearly indicative of the fact that most States provide tax assistance on a regular basis, by answering taxpayers' questions and also providing assistance for the proper interpretation of tax laws. On the issue, see Cadesky, Hayes & Russell, *supra* n. 35, at 113.
41. Data acquired disclosed that States do not disseminate, for any reason whatsoever, any information on the taxpayer's activities or other sensitive data; moreover, in most States, the right to privacy is guaranteed under national laws. In addition, in most States, the Officer who liaises personally with the taxpayer may not be engaged in audits or inspections being carried out vis-à-vis the same taxpayer. On the issue, cf. Cadesky, Hayes & Russell, *supra* n. 35, at 127; and Valente, Hayes & Barmentlo, *supra* n. 31.
42. All States that took part in the Survey deem that the Taxpayer Charter is a suitable tool to protect the taxpayers' rights and, as such, should be extended to all taxes and not only to income tax. *Cf.* Cadesky, Hayes & Russell, *supra* n. 35, at 151; Valente, Hayes & Barmentlo, *supra* n. 31.

§7.05 THE EUROPEAN TAXPAYERS' CODE

In 2012, the European Commission drew up an Action Plan (hereinafter, the 2012 Action Plan)[43] to pursue the primary objective of providing an effective response - at the EU level - to tax evasion and avoidance practices. Within that kind of scenario, therefore, the Member States' implementation and enforcement of measures aimed at protecting the tax base and tax revenue should remain a top priority.[44]

The Recommendation on the theme of tax good governance, published within the context of the 2012 Action Plan, finds concrete application in a strong and clear position against tax havens, which requires every single Member State to identify and draw up special, national blacklists. Specific measures should, moreover, lead third countries to apply EU good-governance provisions (first and foremost, transparency and fair competition, as well as counter-measures against tax regimes deemed harmful).

The development of relationships between Tax Authorities and taxpayers, based on transparency and fair competition, cannot leave aside the definition of clear-cut and certain rules, which ought to be codified within a 'European Taxpayers' Code' context and the spirit of the 'social responsibility of enterprises'.[45]

One of the initiatives launched by the 2012 Action Plan establishes - always with the aim to enhance taxpayers' tax compliance - the introduction of a European Taxpayer's Code. Such a tool, mainly patterned after 'best administrative practices' of Member States, should contain principles and regulations focused on enhancing cooperation, trust, and reliability between Revenue Offices and Taxpayers, so as to guarantee more transparency on rights and obligations of Taxpayers, while fostering a structural service-driven approach.

In response to a public consultation, launched in 2013 by the European Commission in order to acquire information to define rights and duties to be governed under the European Taxpayer's Code, the CFE submitted its own Opinion Statement.[46] According to the CFE, the advantages linked to the introduction of a European Taxpayer's Code involve:

43. Communication from the Commission to the European Parliament and the Council, An Action Plan to Strengthen the Fight Against Tax Fraud and Tax Evasion, COM(2012) 722 (hereinafter the '2012 Action Plan'), para. 17.
44. *Ibid.* The Commission maintained that interventions must, first and foremost, be introduced at the national level. The two Recommendations included in the 2012 Action Plan encourage Member States to implement, promptly and in a coordinated manner, any and all steps that shall be deemed necessary.
45. *Ibid.* The Commission pointed out that a more effective tax collection generally occurs through the best possible relations between taxpayers and tax authorities, greater transparency of tax rules/regulations, reduction of risks of errors/discrepancies with consequences that are potentially serious for taxpayers, and encouragement for compliance with tax obligations.
46. CFE Professional Affairs Committee, *Opinion Statement of the CFE on the European Commission's public consultation on 'A European Taxpayer's Code'* (CFE, May 2013).

- fundamental freedoms and a broader access to the internal market;[47]
- presence of a global benchmark;[48] and
- equitable treatment.[49]

On the occasion of the presentation of the Model Taxpayer Charter's final version by the CFE, AOTCA and STEP, the European Commission was requested to keep faith with its expressed intention to submit a proposal for the introduction of a European Taxpayer's Code, in the hope that both EU institutions and Member States could develop a document that guarantees the right balance in relations between Tax Authorities and Taxpayers.

In structuring its proposal for a European Taxpayer's Code, the European Commission considered choosing either a binding Directive (i.e., a Directive proposal) or a non-binding measure, so-called soft law,[50] represented, for example, by a code of conduct. Within the EU, such latter instrument was resorted to in relation to transfer pricing (with a Code of Conduct on documentary requirements and with a Code of Conduct for the implementation of the Arbitration Convention) and harmful tax practices (with the Code of Conduct on taxation of EU enterprises). A soft law measure may also be a recommendation, which has no binding effect.[51]

47. 'Fundamental freedoms and access to the internal market: Although EU Member states are governed by the rule of law and (tax) legislations of different countries share many common principles, the prospect of becoming subject to a different tax system if moving or conducting business with another country is a source of uncertainty and therefore a disincentive for cross-border activity, especially for citizens and small businesses. A Taxpayers' Code could help reduce this uncertainty. *Ibid.* s. 2.
48. 'A[n] EU Taxpayer's Code could become a benchmark also for non-European countries and, apart from helping them to improve their tax collection, help foster the rule of law in countries where this principle is not or less established.' *Ibid.*
49. 'Non-discrimination is already a principle of EU law, regardless of any Taxpayer's Code. We do not expect a Taxpayer´s Code to lead to full harmonisation of taxpayer rights and obligations but hope that it can contribute to a certain degree of approximation of laws.' *Ibid.*
50. The concept originates in national legislation from the 1970s, as an alternative instrument to international treaties, which was resorted to – for a number of reasons – whenever the interested parties did not wish to have or might not have recourse to the same. It refers to a rather variegated range of legislative phenomena that go from self-regulatory Codes adopted by the single enterprises, or other organizations, to deontological Codes or similar documents adopted by professional or trade associations; from certain Deeds of international laws to the collection of a series of principles and rules that originated spontaneously, developed by national or international organizations, whether governmental or not, although their regulations may be subsequently incorporated into a Treaty. The body of rules created by the Trade Community for international trade requirements may well fall under the category of soft law and the same applies to the so-called *lex mercatoria*. These rules originate from a different source, mainly derived from practice (in particular, such practice that may be inferred from the resolutions of some important International Arbitration Chambers), the nature of which is, moreover, rather controverted to the point that their existence is refuted.
51. Recommendations represent one of the tools that is most frequently used by the Commission for the purpose of influencing the behaviours of the Member States to which they are addressed. In fact, with their adoption, these latter are prompted to adopt (legislative or administrative) implementation measures for the purpose of steering their own legislation towards the purposes contained in the recommendations themselves. Their end is indicated in the alternative between the realization of a (closed) coordination and harmonization. This led eminent experts and case-law to maintain that quite frequently recommendations represent 'an instrument quite similar to the directive, except that in principle it does not have binding force.' The reasons for

Soft law measures are counter-posed to traditional EU-normative tools (among which we find regulations and Directives - so-called hard law), issued in accordance with some set procedures by subjects vested with the necessary authority, who produce norms with binding effects vis-à-vis the intended/interested parties.

Therefore, a hard-law measure (e.g., a directive), providing a European Taxpayers' Code would need to be implemented within the system of every single Member State. On the other hand, the definition of a European Taxpayers' Code, by means of a soft-law tool, would not have any binding effect on Member States, who - speaking frankly - might just disregard its provisions.

On 24 November 2016, the European Commission released its *Guidelines for a Model for a European Taxpayers' Code*[52] with the aim of consolidating a set of common principles underlying the relationships between taxpayers and the tax administrations of the Member States. The Model Code Guidelines, as such, are a soft-law instrument that is not binding on the Member States: they simply propose a model set of principles that the Member States are free to adapt to their own specific legal system and culture.[53]

The Model Code Guidelines are divided into two main parts: the first part includes nine general principles that have been observed to underpin - or should

---

which harmonization is pursued by means of recommendations, rather than through Directives, are essentially of two kinds. They are linked, in one way, to the entire framework in which such measures are comprised: in some sectors, or rather, at some given times, it might be convenient to move towards a gradual harmonization, with respect to which a recommendation merely represents an initial step. In some other way, there are contingent circumstances or matters in which Member States do not wish to adopt binding measures in view of their being too stringent for fear that there might be some conflicts with the principles of proportionality and subsidiarity. The desire of Member States not to be bound by Directive causes soft law (in this case, through recommendations) to function as a 'permanent para-law', given that the same may remain for a long time as the sole (and wished-for) normative in that sector and, therefore, not exercising any less influence on Member States' behaviour. The only difference from Directives, in this case, is that the legal/judicial remedies are lacking in case of non-compliance by Member States. *See* Francis Snyder, *Soft law and Institutional Practice in the European Community, in The Construction of Europe: Essays in Honour of Emile Noël* 197 (Stephan Martin ed., 1994); Daniel Thürer, *The Role of Soft law in the Actual Process of European Integration, in L'avenir du libre-échange en Europe: vers un Espace économique européen,* 132 (Olivier Jacot-Guillarmod & Pierre Pescatore eds., 1990); and Linda Senden, *Soft Law in European Community Law* 133 et seq. (2004).

52. European Commission, Directorate-General Taxation and Customs Union, *Guidelines for a Model for a European Taxpayers' Code* (2016) [hereinafter, the 'Model Code Guidelines'] available at: https://ec.europa.eu/taxation_customs/business/tax-cooperation-control/guidelines-model-european-taxpayers-code_en.

53. *Ibid.* at 4:

> This European Taxpayer's Code contains guidelines that aim to ensure a balance between the rights and obligations of both taxpayers and tax administrations. It is based on the main general principles and best practices in Member States deemed useful for enhancing cooperation, trust and confidence between tax administrations and taxpayers, ensuring greater transparency on the rights and obligations of both, and encouraging a more service oriented approach of tax administrations. It encourages tax administrations and European taxpayers to adopt and apply all these principles and practices, including new developments and further ideas. As a consequence, this code is not mandatory but should be considered as a model to follow, to which Member States could add or adapt elements to meet national needs or context.

underpin – the entire network of relationships between taxpayers and tax administrations. It also includes some more-specific principles, particularly arising out of three identified areas of taxpayer/tax administration interaction. The second part goes beyond the scope of a mere taxpayers' code, *stricto sensu,* by also outlining tax-related 'best practices' that have already been implemented in some Member States and that could be deemed useful in addressing deficiencies identified in the legal systems of other Member States.

The general principles included in the Model Code Guidelines are the following: (i) lawfulness and legal certainty, (ii) non-discrimination and taxpayer equality, (iii) the presumption of honesty, (iv) courtesy and consideration, (v) respect of law, (vi) impartiality and independence, (vii) fiscal secrecy and data protection, (viii) privacy, and (ix) representation. These principles incorporate, in essence, the fundamental civil rights and obligations of taxpayers (citizens) in the context of their relationships with tax administrations, who represent the Member State. According to the Model Code Guidelines, such principles constitute common standards within the EU Member States.

With regard to the specific principles included in the Model Code Guidelines, they are presented as relevant to three particular core areas of interaction between taxpayers and tax administrations, each specifying in detail the respective rights and obligations:

- cooperation between tax administrations and taxpayers, which is essential to establish lawfulness and legal certainty within the tax system and to boost tax compliance;[54]
- procedures (e.g., tax declarations, tax assessments, audits, payment and debt collection, voluntary disclosures, and imposition of sanctions);[55] and
- efficient dispute resolution,[56] the importance of which is highlighted in other recent initiatives of the European Commission, such as the proposal for amendment of the Arbitration Convention included in the 2016 Corporate Tax Reform Package.[57]

Apart from generally established principles, the Model Code Guidelines also incorporate 'best practices' that promote tax compliance within the EU. Thus, the

54. The Model Code Guidelines identify the elements necessary to build desirable cooperative relationships: (i) availability of up-to-date, accurate as well as clear information and guidance, including interpretations, for taxpayers, (ii) customer-type, service-oriented approach of tax authorities to taxpayers, (iii) establishment of key service standards (i.e., indicators allowing measurement of the administration's performance) and (iv) enhancement of legal certainty through issuance of advance rulings, where available and applicable.
55. The core standards identified as desirable to be instilled into tax procedures are (i) mutual transparency (i.e., on the side of taxpayers as well as on that of tax administrations) and (ii) service-oriented approach.
56. With respect to dispute resolution, the Model Code Guidelines make reference to (i) internal appeal procedures, (ii) Court or Tribunal review and (iii) a right of challenge. The most important principle is that taxpayers must have the right to challenge the decisions of tax administrations before independent authorities.
57. European Commission, Taxation and Customs Union, *Corporate Tax Reform Package*, Oct. 2016, available at: https://ec.europa.eu/taxation_customs/business/company-tax/corporate-tax-reform-package_en_en

Model Code Guidelines seek to share know-how among Member States on practices already tested in some of them, which could inspire other Member States to remedy their own deficiencies.

Amongst the best practices included in the Model Code Guidelines, one proposal refers to the use of electronic administration and online services (i.e., the exploitation of technology in the best interests of taxation). A second best practice refers to the identification and adoption of innovative voluntary-compliance incentives. Last, but not the least, a third best practice - transparency - demonstrates that it could be increased through a public naming-and-shaming of non-compliant taxpayers, coupled with tax administrations issuing regular reports on their activities.

By virtue of the Model Code Guidelines, the Commission pursues the following long-term goals: (a) improving transparency and clarity as far as taxpayers' rights and obligations are concerned; (b) fostering certainty and efficiency in the interactions between taxpayers and tax administrations; (c) improving compliance and minimizing the risk of disputes; and (d) setting benchmarks among the different tax systems of Member States. The Model Code Guidelines invite and encourage all Member States to align their legislation to the general standards set forth therein and draw further inspiration from the best practices used to tackle deficiencies in their tax system.

CHAPTER 8

Taxation at the Crossroads of Fundamental Rights and Fundamental Freedoms in the EU

Werner Haslehner

§8.01 INTRODUCTION

After nearly thirty years of dormancy with respect to direct taxation matters, the EU fundamental freedoms have been gradually accepted as a major determinant of the Member States' freedom to impose to taxes. Today, the power of the freedoms to limit the Member States' competence in this area of law is accepted without question. At the same time, EU fundamental rights have, to date, played almost no role at all with respect to tax matters, let alone direct tax matters, although they were already recognized as constituent elements of primary EU law by the Court of Justice of the European Union (the Court or the CJEU) in the 1960s. This dichotomy is remarkable, not least because it is difficult to neatly disentangle fundamental freedoms from fundamental rights, as the former may well be seen as a subset of the latter. This contribution explores the doctrinal underpinnings of their existing similarities and differences as well as the interaction of both, in order to offer an explanation for the seemingly contradictory perception of both fundamental bases of primary EU law.

In so doing, it will address the following questions: What is the relationship between fundamental rights and fundamental freedoms? To what extent do they limit or reinforce each other? Why has the CJEU not brought EU fundamental rights to bear in its jurisprudence on direct taxation thus far? Can or should the CJEU be more active in this respect?

Thus, this contribution, first, briefly recounts the development of EU fundamental rights and fundamental freedoms and the doctrinal underpinnings of this development as a basis to analyse the scope of both components of primary law and their relationship to one another. Second, it analyses the similarities and relevant differences between fundamental rights and fundamental freedoms and suggests an answer to the question of the extent to which the fundamental freedoms can or should be considered to be fundamental rights. Finally, it assesses the application of fundamental rights in direct tax cases by looking at the clues the CJEU has left in the very little case law available with implications for this question.

§8.02 PRINCIPLES AND DEVELOPMENT OF FUNDAMENTAL RIGHTS AND FUNDAMENTAL FREEDOMS

[A] The Fundamental Freedoms and Their Development in the Court's Case Law

The fundamental freedoms form the core of the economic constitution of the EU, as defined in its general objectives,[1] and are thus essential to its character as a political entity whose central policy, for most of its existence, has been the establishment of an Internal Market.[2] They have been instrumental in the development of EU law, forming the basis of the cases in which the CJEU announced the doctrines of primacy[3] and direct effect,[4] including for areas of exclusive Member States' competence[5] (such as direct taxation),[6] and elaborated on the principle of non-discrimination,[7] the prohibition of non-discriminatory restrictions[8] and attendant principle of mutual recognition,[9] as well as the principle of effectiveness. Although the EU Treaties do not contain the term 'fundamental freedoms',[10] it is nonetheless justified to use it to refer to the collection of freedoms guaranteed by Articles 34, 39, 45, 49, and 63 TFEU. Not only has the CJEU frequently used that terminology since the late 1990s, but it has also crucially developed the scope of protection offered by all freedoms in remarkable lockstep, leading to significant methodological convergence among them.[11]

1. *See* Art. 3(2) & (3) TEU, referring to the 'free movement of persons' in an area without internal frontiers (para. 2) and to the establishment of the Internal Market (para. 3).
2. Damian Chalmers, Gareth Davies & Giorgio Monti, *European Union Law* 675 (2d ed., 2010); Kamiel Mortelmans, *The Common Market, the Internal Market and the Single Market: What's in a Market?* 35 Common Mkt. L. Rev. 101 (1998).
3. *Costa* v *ENEL*, C-6/64, Judgment, EU:C:1964:66.
4. *Van Gend en Loos*, C-26/62, Judgment, EU:C:1963:1.
5. *E.g.*, *Factortame II*, C-221/89, Judgment, EU:C:1991:320, para. 13; and *Commission* v *UK*, C-246/89, Judgment, EU:C:1991:375, para. 12.
6. *E.g.*, *Schumacker*, C-279/93, Judgment, EU:C:1995:31, para. 21.
7. *E.g.*, *Asscher*, C-107/94, Judgment, EU:C:1996:251, holding that an individual can invoke nationality-based discrimination against his state of origin; *Sopora*, C-512/13, Judgment, EU:C:2015:108, holding that the freedom of workers prohibits also horizontal discrimination between two different non-resident taxpayers who are in comparable circumstances.
8. *Dassonville*, C-8/74, Judgment, EU:C:1974:82, para. 6; *Säger*, Judgment, C-76/90, EU:C:1991:331, para. 12; *Bosman*, Judgment, C-415/93, EU:C:1993:463, para. 96; *Gebhard*, C-55/94, Judgment, EU:C:1994:411, para. 37.
9. *Rewe/Bundesmonopolverwaltung für Branntwein* ('*Cassis de Dijon*'), C-120/78, Judgment, EU:C:1979:42.
10. *See* Thomas Kingreen, *Fundamental Freedoms, in Principles of European Constitutional Law* 515 (Armin von Bogdandy & Jürgen Bast eds., 2009 [hereinafter, 'Bogdandy/Bast 2009']).
11. *Ibid.* at 517.

In tandem with their ever-expanding scope, the fundamental freedoms have also been – by far – the most relevant influence of primary EU law on direct taxation in the Member States, even though not all elements of the CJEU's jurisprudence from other areas has been fully incorporated into the context of tax law; notably, the CJEU eschews the notion that a Member State's tax law comes within the scope of application of the freedoms merely by virtue of a necessarily restrictive effect on cross-border economic activity, even if it has an equal impact on domestic and foreign operators.[12] Instead, the CJEU focuses on the search for differential treatment of cross-border situations when compared to purely internal situations using a discrimination-based analysis.[13] Such restraint concerning the application of the fundamental freedoms to tax law is fundamentally justified by the balance of competences established in the EU's constitutional framework, which protects the Member States' fiscal sovereignty. In the words of AG Kokott:

> The levying of any tax hinders economic activity or makes it less attractive. If, however, a tax is capable of calling for review in the light of the fundamental freedoms of EU law even in cases where it is neither overtly nor covertly discriminatory and is as such levied on all EU citizens in the same way, then even the decision by a Member State to levy a tax in a particular situation and any increases in that tax would fall within the scope of EU law. This would effectively disregard the fiscal sovereignty which the Member States continue to exercise under the existing division of powers within the European Union. A tax that is levied without any discrimination at all cannot therefore, in principle, give rise to a restriction of a fundamental freedom.[14]

Nonetheless, direct tax law serves as a prime example of the immersive duty of Member States to exercise their competences consistently with the fundamental freedoms.[15]

Over the course of the last thirty years of CJEU case law on fundamental freedoms and direct taxation, the CJEU has shown great creativity in its endeavour to balance the respect for Member States' competence and national interests with the need to remove obstacles created by their tax systems to further integration of their businesses in the Internal Market. Important, early milestones in this development have been: the decision in *Commission v France* (commonly known as *'Avoir Fiscal'*), which first established an awareness of the potential impact of fundamental freedoms on direct taxation;[16] the judgment in *Biehl*, in which the CJEU pronounced the general equivalence of different treatment based on residence and nationality for purposes of

12. *Mobistar and Belgacom Mobile*, Joined Cases C-544/03 and C-545/03, Judgment, EU:C:2005:518, paras 30–33.
13. *Cf. X*, C-498/10, AG Opinion, EU:C:2011:870, paras 28–29; *X*, C-686/13, AG Opinion, EU:C:2015:31, paras 38–40.
14. *X*, C-686/13, AG Opinion, para. 40.
15. *See* Verica Trstenjak & Erwin Beysen, *The Growing Overlap of Fundamental Freedoms and Fundamental Rights in the Case Law of the CJEU*, 3 Eur. L. Rev. 293, 297 (2013).
16. *Commission* v *France ('Avoir Fiscal')*, C-270/83, Judgment, EU:C:1986:37. For an extended review of that decision and its continued impact on EU tax law, see Werner Haslehner, *'Avoir Fiscal' and Its Legacy after Thirty Years of Direct Tax Jurisprudence of the Court of Justice*, 44 Intertax 374 (2016).

reviewing tax legislation;[17] the distinction drawn with respect to comparability of resident and non-resident taxpayers depending on the relevant tax measures' scope and purpose in *Schumacker* and *Gerritse*;[18] and the creation of separate grounds of justification for substantively discriminatory direct tax measures over the course of two decades,[19] notably the principle of coherence,[20] the prevention of tax avoidance,[21] the effectiveness of fiscal supervision,[22] and the balanced allocation of taxing power.[23] In its more recent jurisprudence, the CJEU appears to retreat further and further from its earlier, seemingly 'pro-taxpayer' approach, which really should rather be seen as 'pro-Internal Market', especially with respect to the taxation of companies, for example, with respect to loss relief and exit taxation.[24]

[B] Fundamental Rights as General Principles of EU Law

In the three initial Community treaties, which formed the predecessors of the EU and have now been replaced by the EU Treaties (i.e., the TEU and TFEU), there was no reference to fundamental rights. It did not seem necessary to protect fundamental rights in a treaty setting up a community with enumerated competences in a mainly

17. *Biehl*, C-175/88, Judgment, EU:C:1990:186, para. 14; following the more general pronouncement of that equivalence, *see Sotgiu*, C-152/73, Judgment, EU:C:1974:13, paras 11–12.
18. Compare the approach in *Schumacker*, C-279/93, with the approach in *Gerritse*, C-234/01, Judgment, EU:C:2003:340. For a detailed discussion of both cases and their importance for the Court's case law, see Edoardo Traversa, *Objective Ability to Pay: The* Gerritse *Case, in Landmark Decisions of the ECJ in Direct Taxation* 1 (Werner Haslehner, Georg Kofler & Alexander Rust eds., 2015); and Alfredo García-Prats, *Subjective Ability to Pay:* Schumacker, *in Landmark Decisions of the ECJ in Direct Taxation* 21 (Werner Haslehner, Georg Kofler & Alexander Rust eds., 2015).
19. For an in-depth review of the development of the Court's case law in this respect, see Axel Cordewener, Georg Kofler & Servaas Van Thiel, *The Clash between European Freedoms and National Direct Tax Law: Public Interest Defences available to the Member States*, 46 Common Mkt L. Rev. 1951, 1953 (2009).
20. *Bachmann*, C-203/90, Judgment, EU:C:1992:35, paras 21–28; *Commission* v *Belgium*, C-300/90, Judgment, EU:C:1992:37, paras 14–21; *Manninen*, C-319/02, Judgment, EU:C:2004:484, para. 42; *Papillon*, C-418/07, Judgment, EU:C:2008:659, para. 43 et seq.; *Krankenheim Ruhesitz am Wannsee*, C-157/07, Judgment, EU:C:2008:588, para. 43 et seq.; and *K*, C-322/11, Judgment, EU:C:2013:716, para. 65 *et seq*.
21. *ICI*, C-264/96, Judgment, EU:C:1998:370, para. 26; *X and Y*, C-436/00, Judgment, EU:C:2002:704, para. 60 et seq.; *Lankhorst-Hohorst*, C-324/00, Judgment, EU:C:2002:749, para. 37; *Cadbury Schweppes*, C-196/04, Judgment, EU:C:2006:544, para. 51; *Test Claimants in the Thin Cap Group Litigation*, C-524/04, Judgment, EU:C:2007:161, para. 72; and *SGI*, C-311/08, Judgment, EU:C:2010:26, para. 65.
22. *Futura Participations and Singer*, C-290/95, Judgment, EU:C:1997:239, para. 31; *A*, C-101/05, Judgment, EU:C:2007:804, para. 55; *SIAT*, C-318/10, Judgment, EU:C:2012:415, para. 36.
23. *E.g.*, *Marks & Spencer*, C-446/03, Judgment, EU:C:2005:763, paras 43–46; *X Holding*, C-337/08, Judgment, EU:C:2010:89, para. 33; and *K*, C-322/11, para. 50–55.
24. The CJEU already significantly limited the need to provide relief for foreign losses under the '*Marks & Spencer* exception' in *Commission* v *UK*, C-172/13, Judgment, EU:C:2015:50; it went even further, completely denying the need for such losses to be allocated to foreign permanent establishments in *Timac Agro*, C-388/14, Judgment, EU:C:2015:829. It also all but reversed its approach to exit taxation by allowing Member States to set strict time limits for the deferral of taxation upon leaving a tax jurisdiction, without requiring an additional realization event, in *DMC*, C-164/12, Judgment, EU:C:2014:20, and *Verder LabTec*, C-657/13, Judgment, EU:C:2015:331.

economic sphere. Hence, the very existence and protection of fundamental rights at the Community level was entirely a product of the Court's case law.[25] Despite an apparent lack of competence in that area, the Court held that, in what is now settled case law, 'fundamental rights form an integral part of the general principles of law whose observance the Court ensures.'[26]

In order to understand the scope and limits of these EU fundamental rights, it is important, first, to analyse the reasons for the creation of that line of case law: the CJEU initially ruled that the validity of an EU measure (i.e., a legislative act of the EU in accordance with the competences conferred on it by the Treaties) cannot be affected by allegations that it runs counter to national fundamental rights or national constitutional principles. The Court found that to be the necessary consequence of the doctrine of unconditional supremacy of EU law.[27] Following the establishment of that doctrine – and under some pressure from national constitutional courts[28] – the CJEU acknowledged that, while being immune from any challenge based on national constitutional principles, EU measures are, nevertheless, subject to scrutiny pursuant to the 'fundamental human rights enshrined in the general principles of Community law', whose protection 'must be ensured within the framework of the structure and objectives of the Community'.[29]

Neither the content nor the sources of these EU fundamental rights was thereby conclusively established, however. The Court merely stated that they would be 'inspired by the constitutional traditions common to the Member States'.[30] The CJEU subsequently clarified its position by developing the fundamental rights standard of the EU, using guidelines from international treaties for the protection of human rights concluded by the Member States.[31] It later explicitly included the European Convention on Human Rights (ECHR) among such sources of fundamental rights[32] and stated its special importance for EU law.[33]

The scope of application of fundamental rights as general principles of EU law has continued to evolve from this point of departure. Initially 'conceived as a standard to assess the actions of EU bodies and institutions',[34] it soon became clear that the rationale for their existence required extending their scope to Member States whenever

25. Takis Tridimas, *The General Principles of EU Law* 299 et seq. (2d ed., 2007).
26. First mentioned in *Stauder* v *Stadt Ulm*, C-29/69, Judgment, EU:C:1969:57; *Internationale Handelsgesellschaft*, C-11/70, Judgment, EU:C:1970:114, para. 4; *Nold*, C-4/73, Judgment, EU:C:1974:51, para. 13; and *Wachauf*, C-5/88, Judgment, EU:C:1989:321, para. 17.
27. *Costa* v *ENEL*, C-6/64; clearer with regard to national fundamental rights *Internationale Handelsgesellschaft*, C-11/70, para. 3.
28. The German constitutional court challenged the allegation of the CJEU of unconditional and unlimited supremacy of EU law in the following judgment in the case *Internationale Handelsgesellschaft* on the ground that it was unclear whether the CJEU would actually protect fundamental rights to a similar standard as the BVerfG would deem necessary.
29. *Stauder* v *Stadt Ulm*, C-29/69; *Internationale Handelsgesellschaft*, C-11/70, para. 4.
30. *Internationale Handelsgesellschaft*, C-11/70, para. 4.
31. *Nold*, C-4/73, para. 13.
32. *Hauer*, C-44/79, Judgment, EU:C:1979:290, para. 17 et seq.; *Wachauf*, C-5/88, para. 17.
33. *Johnston*, C-222/84, Judgment, EU:C:1986:206, para. 18; and *ERT*, C-260/89, Judgment, EU:C:1991:254, para. 41.
34. Trstenjak & Beysen, *supra* n. 16, at 303.

they 'implement' EU rules.[35] Logically, that must encompass all situations in which their actions are determined by EU law, so as to effectively transform them into agents of the EU.[36] As the doctrine of primacy means that Member States cannot avoid implementing such rules – whether by a legislative or administrative act – even if doing so violates the Member State's own constitutional protections for individuals, such a result is convincing, indeed, unavoidable. Questions have been raised with regard to situations in which Member States have a large margin of discretion with respect to their implementation of EU measures: are they still bound by EU fundamental rights? The CJEU answered that question in the affirmative,[37] clarifying that Member States are also bound by EU fundamental rights when transposing a directive into national law.[38] This appears unobjectionable: Since Member States, when acting within their given margin of discretion in the implementation of EU law, exercise an option granted to them by the EU legislature, it would seem inconsistent to allow them to disregard standards that bind the EU legislature when its grants the option they exercise. This is certainly true when a Member State is bound to act: choosing a path that is not compliant with EU fundamental rights cannot be an acceptable exercise of the discretion given by EU law. In such a situation, because of the need to act one way or another, national fundamental-rights protections are, at least potentially, suppressed. For example, in the case of a directive, a Member State cannot choose not to implement it in some way, even if all possible options to transpose the directive violates its own national fundamental-rights standards.[39] Since national fundamental rights are, therefore, curbed by obligations under EU law, EU fundamental rights must apply in order to protect individuals in an equivalent manner.

By contrast, if a Member State decides to simply fill a gap left open by a directive that it could just as easily leave unaddressed, it is less obvious that EU fundamental-rights protection is required, as the Member State there acts entirely within the protective framework of national fundamental rights and the ECHR. Extending the scope of EU fundamental rights to these situations is nevertheless not particularly contentious, as the Member States are still effectively acting as agents within the EU's competence and the EU cannot grant Member States discretion to violate EU fundamental rights.[40] As Michael Dougan observes, 'the notion of implementation embraces

35. *Wachauf*, C-5/88, para. 19.
36. This is thereby frequently described as 'agency situation', following Joseph H.H. Weiler. *See* Daniel Sarmiento, *Who's Afraid of the Charter? The Court of Justice, National Courts and the New Framework of Fundamental Rights Protection in Europe*, 50 Common Mkt L. Rev. 1267, 1274 (2013).
37. *Wachauf*, C-5/88, para. 22.
38. *Booker Aquaculture*, Joined Cases C-20/00 and C-64/00, Judgment, EU:C:2003:397, para. 88.
39. The exercise of the option in this case should still be seen as double-bound, meaning that the Member State's choice must be both in line with EU fundamental rights and the least possible restriction on national rights standards. *Cf. Åkerberg Fransson*, C-617/10, Judgment, EU:C:2013:105, para. 29.
40. *Cf.* Jürgen Kühling, *Fundamental Rights*, *in* Bogdandy/Bast 2009, *supra* n. 10, at 498; Armin von Bogdandy et al, *Reverse Solange – Protecting the Essence of Fundamental Rights Against EU Member States*, 49 Common Mkt L. Rev. 489, 498 (2012).

the entire system for the decentralized enforcement of Union law'[41] and, thus, must also include legal measures that are engaged in the execution of EU law without being specifically adopted for that purpose. Tying the exercise of state power to both the national- and EU-fundamental rights framework does not pose particular problems.

In parallel to the development of its case law on the application of EU fundamental rights in 'implementation situations', when Member States act as agents of the EU and must, therefore, be held to the same standards as the EU institutions themselves, the CJEU developed its doctrine on the application of fundamental rights in 'derogation situations',[42] in which Member States act, prima facie, entirely within their own competence and on their own account.[43] The CJEU thereby extended to the Member States' obligation to adhere to EU fundamental rights, holding, in *ERT*, that they must apply them as general principles of EU law whenever national measures fall 'within the scope of Union law'.[44] In that case, which concerned state restrictions imposed on broadcasting services in potential violation of the freedom to provide services, the CJEU held that, whenever a Member State seeks to justify any such restriction by reference to mandatory requirements in the general interest, it acts within the scope of EU law and, therefore, must comply with EU fundamental rights. The *ERT* doctrine thus extends the scope of application of EU fundamental rights to areas falling within the exclusive competence of the Member States, such as direct taxation.

In an apparent effort to protect individuals' fundamental rights, the CJEU took that expansive approach still further in later judgments, even when no infringement of a fundamental freedom appeared to be at issue: in *Carpenter*, it held that an infringement of a fundamental freedom could arise out of interference with the claimant's fundamental right to family life, as the deportation of Mr Carpenter's wife would have been detrimental to the circumstances under which he exercised it.[45] In essence, this meant a huge increase in the protective scope of EU fundamental freedoms, which the

41. Michael Dougan, *Judicial Review of Member State Action under the General Principles and the Charter: Defining the 'Scope of EU Law'*, 52 Common Mkt L. Rev. 1201, 1213 (2015).
42. It should be noted, however, that 'implementation' and 'derogation' are not clearly distinguished categories in the CJEU's case law; instead, 'derogation' from EU law is itself framed as an 'implementation' of EU law, by virtue of the fact that the right to derogate is, itself, laid down in EU law (*see, e.g.*, *Pfleger*, C-390/12, Judgment, EU:C:2014:281, para. 36):

> where it is apparent that national legislation is such as to obstruct the exercise of one or more fundamental freedoms guaranteed by the Treaty, it may benefit from the exceptions provided for by EU law in order to justify that fact only in so far as that complies with the fundamental rights enforced by the Court. That obligation to comply with fundamental rights manifestly comes within the scope of EU law and, consequently, within that of the Charter. The use by a Member State of exceptions provided for by EU law in order to justify an obstruction of a fundamental freedom guaranteed by the Treaty must, therefore, be regarded, as the Advocate General states in point 46 of her Opinion, as 'implementing Union law' within the meaning of Article 51(1) of the Charter.

43. Dougan, *supra* n. 41, at 1215.
44. *ERT*, C-260/89, para. 42.
45. *Carpenter*, C-60/00, Judgment, EU:C:2002:434, para 39.

Court extended even further in *Karner*,[46] to the effect that, whenever a national measure would appear likely to constitute a potential impediment to free movement, a path opens permitting scrutiny of such action from the perspective of EU fundamental rights.

This extension of the scope of the freedoms has been met with mixed reactions. While it received significant support in academia and it is now considered settled case law,[47] some commentators found the Court's reasoning lacking.[48] The general principle that a justification can only be invoked by a Member State if the measure needing justification also complies with EU fundamental rights again seems unobjectionable at first glance. Upon closer inspection, however, it becomes obvious that the traditional rationale for the existence of separate EU fundamental rights as a counterweight to the doctrine of primacy of EU law does not support such a broad scope of application. While Member States are clearly bound to comply with the fundamental freedoms, thereby bringing any measure affecting them within the 'scope of EU law', Member State action in derogation of those freedoms are not determined by EU law,[49] leaving the Member States' national fundamental rights fully applicable. There is, thus, no gap in the protection of individuals that must be filled by the backstop of EU fundamental rights. The underlying rationale for the *ERT*-inspired line of cases must, therefore, be different. It may be best described as a concern for a coherent interpretation and application of two separate fields of EU law that are both of constitutional relevance for the Internal Market.[50] From that perspective, it would be contradictory for the CJEU to have the power to review a Member State's public policy in order to determine its legitimacy in the context of the proportionality test applied to claimed justifications for restrictions to a fundamental freedom, while not having the power, at the same time,

46. *Karner*, C-71/02, Judgment, EU:C:2004:181, para 49. Critical of this decision, Tridimas, *supra* n. 25, at 336.
47. *E.g.*, Jörg Gerkrath, *Als krönender Abschluss des Grundrechtsschutzes in der EU verlangt die Charta nach einer breiten und dezentralisierten Anwendung, in Strukturfragen des Grundrechtsschutzes in Europa* 3 (Johannes Masing et al. eds., 2015); Kühling, *supra* n. 40, at 498; Trstenjak & Beysen, *supra* n. 15, at 305.
48. *E.g.*, Peter Huber, *The Unitary Effect of the Community's Fundamental rights: The ERT-Doctrine Needs to be Reviewed*, 14 Eur. Pub. L. 323 (2008); Jacobs, *Human Rights in the European Union: The Role of the Court of Justice*, 26 Eur. L. Rev. 331 (2001); Matthias Ruffert, *Die Mitgliedstaaten der Europäischen Gemeinschaft als Verpflichtete der Gemeinschaftsgrundrechte*, 32 Europäische Grundrechte-Zeitschrift 518 (1995).
49. It seems that Kühling would consider this to be a circular argument, as it appears to presuppose a measure as outside the scope of EU law in order to justify the inapplicability of EU fundamental rights. Kühling, *supra* n. 40, at 498. This is mistaken, however, as the argument is not that the Member State's measure is outside the scope of EU law, but that it is not determined by it, leaving it subject to the full force of national fundamental rights (the criticism is levied at the Court's decision to extend the scope of EU fundamental rights to any measure coming within the 'scope of EU law', after all). The real reason for the supporters of the *ERT* doctrine—namely that a parallel protection by national fundamental rights may not always be sufficiently available—reveals an underlying perspective that the EU ought to comprise a common fundamental rights area, effectively harmonizing fundamental rights in a way that is at odds with both the doctrinal justification and the historical development of EU fundamental rights. The task of ensuring a common minimum level of protection is fulfilled by the ECHR and the court in Strasbourg.
50. Sarmiento, *supra* n. 36, at 1297.

to impose limits on such public policy justifications based on the fundamental rights that are basic building blocks of EU law. However, while superficially appealing, such an argument would result in saying that EU fundamental rights form an automatic element of scrutiny whenever the CJEU has any basis to review a Member State measure, regardless of whether there is a violation of 'first order Union law'.[51] In light of Article 6 TEU, which explicitly provides that the fundamental rights (found in the Charter) 'shall not extend in any way the competences of the Union as defined in the Treaties', that result cannot stand.

[C] The Impact of the EU Charter of Fundamental Rights

The judicial development described above has been mirrored by a gradual inclusion of references to fundamental rights in the EU Treaties as well as the proclamation of the Charter of Fundamental Rights of the European Union (the 'Charter'),[52] which was incorporated into EU primary law by the Lisbon Treaty.[53] Moreover, Article 6 TEU also orders the EU to formally accede the ECHR and makes explicit the conclusion that could be drawn from the CJEU case law:

> Fundamental rights, as guaranteed by the European Convention for the Protection of Human Rights and Fundamental Freedoms and as they result from the constitutional traditions common to the Member States, shall constitute general principles of the Union's law.[54]

While putting the protection of fundamental rights explicitly within the treaty framework arguably fulfilled an important signalling function,[55] it does not – for the most part[56] – lead to a substantial extension of that protection: virtually all actionable rights protected by the Charter had already been included in the CJEU's jurisprudence prior to its incorporation, as they widely mirror the ECHR and the fundamental rights found

51. Dougan, *supra* n. 41, at 1209.
52. Official Journal of the European Union [2012] C 326/02 (original version published in OJ [2000] C 364/1), [hereinafter, 'the Charter'].
53. Art. 6(1) TEU:

> The Union recognises the rights, freedoms and principles set out in the Charter of Fundamental Rights of the European Union of 7 December 2000, as adapted at Strasbourg, on 12 December 2007, which shall have the same legal value as the Treaties. The provisions of the Charter shall not extend in any way the competences of the Union as defined in the Treaties.

54. Art. 6(3) TEU.
55. *See* De Burca's analysis of the Charter's drafting process. Gráinne De Burca, *The Drafting of the European Union Charter of Fundamental Rights*, 26 Eur. L. Rev. 126, 130 (2001). This may be disputed, though, because of the equally explicit 'carve out' that has been granted to the UK, Poland, and the Czech Republic.
56. For an example of such apparent extension, Sybe de Vries points to the protection of the child as a new mandatory requirement in *Dynamic Medien* (C-244/06, Judgment, EU:C:2008:85); *see* Sybe de Vries, *The Protection of Fundamental Rights within Europe's Internal Market*, *in The Protection of Fundamental Rights in the EU After Lisbon* 59, 74 (Sybe de Vries, Ulf Bernitz, & Stephen Weatherill eds., 2013).

in the Member States' national constitutions.[57] As such, these rights were recognized as general principles of EU law,[58] although the Charter has also been used by the Court 'for the "discovery" of general principles of EU law'.[59] That might explain why the CJEU applied Charter rights in cases concerning potential violations predating the Lisbon Treaty,[60] although in other cases, the Court refused to apply the Charter and instead relied on general principles, but to essentially the same effect.[61]

With respect to the Charter's legal status, the Lisbon Treaty clarified, in Article 6(1),[62] that it does 'not extend in any way the competences of the Union as defined in the Treaties' – its entry into force has not made the EU a 'human rights organization'.[63] At the same time, the Charter may seem to limit the application of fundamental rights more generally, as it contains a number of general rules that are helpful to clarify its scope, its relationship to other norms, and the substantive content of the rights guaranteed by it. Article 51(1) of the Charter defines its scope of application. Accordingly, its provisions apply, first, to the 'institutions, bodies, offices and agencies of the Union with due regard for the principle of subsidiarity', and second, 'to the Member States only when they are implementing Union law'.[64] The meaning of the phrase 'implementing Union law' is highly contested, however, invoking the development of the CJEU's case law on fundamental rights as general principles of EU law.[65] Does it mean that the Member States are bound to comply with the Charter only when they act as 'agents' for the EU? Or are they also subject to the Charter when acting within their

57. The preamble to the Charter explicitly refers to both of these as sources of the rights included in the Charter:

> This Charter reaffirms, with due regard for the powers and tasks of the Union and for the principle of subsidiarity, the rights as they result, in particular, from the constitutional traditions and international obligations common to the Member States, the European Convention for the Protection of Human Rights and Fundamental Freedoms, the Social Charters adopted by the Union and by the Council of Europe and the case-law of the Court of Justice of the European Union and of the European Court of Human Rights.

58. Apparently expecting a much stronger impact in practice, see Kühling, *supra* n. 40, at 486.
59. Koen Lenaerts, *Exploring the Limits of the EU Charter of Fundamental Rights*, 8 Eur. Cons. L. Rev. 375, 376 (2012); *see also* Koen Lenaerts & José Gutiérrez-Fons, *The Constitutional Allocation of Powers and General Principles of EU Law*, 47 Common Mkt L. Rev. 1629, 1660 (2010). *Cf.* the instructive description in Paul Craig & Gráinne De Burca, *EU Law: Text, Cases, and Materials* 395 (5th ed. 2011):

> the Charter could perhaps best be described as a creative distillation of the rights contained in the various European and international agreements and national constitutions on which the ECJ had for some years already drawn.

60. *Cf.* Sara Iglesias Sánchez, *The Court and the Charter: the Impact of the Entry into Force of the Lisbon Treaty on the ECJ's Approach to Fundamental Rights*, 49 Common Mkt L. Rev. 1565, 1573 (2012).
61. *See, e.g.*, *Sabou*, C-276/12, Judgment, EU:C:2013:678, paras 25 & 38.
62. Art. 51(2) of the Charter provides a similar caveat: 'The Charter does not extend the field of application of Union law beyond the powers of the Union or establish any new power or task for the Union, or modify powers and tasks as defined in the Treaties.'
63. Lenaerts, *supra* n. 60, at 377, referring to Tridimas, *supra* n. 25, at 613.
64. Art. 51(1) of the Charter.
65. *Supra* §8.02[B].

own competence and on their own account, whenever a particular act touches upon a matter of Union law? While the words used in Article 51(1) strongly suggest the former interpretation, that result would appear to be contradicted by the Explanations to the Charter, which state:

> As regards the Member States, it follows unambiguously from the case-law of the Court of Justice that the requirement to respect fundamental rights defined in the context of the Union is only binding on the Member States *when they act in the scope of Union law* (judgment of 13 July 1989, Case 5/88 Wachauf [1989] ECR 2609; *judgment of 18 June 1991, Case C-260/89 ERT [1991] ECR I-2925*; judgment of 18 December 1997, Case C-309/96 Annibaldi [1997] ECR I-7493).[66]

That statement appears to turn the explicitly more restrictive text of the Charter on its head, which is all the more surprising as a historical analysis of the genesis of the Charter shows it to have been fuelled by a reluctance on the part of the Member States to accept the CJEU's interference in matters that are not very closely linked to the EU.[67] This incongruity raises a question about the relevance of the Explanations. According to Article 52(7) of the Charter, they 'shall be given due regard by the courts of the Union and of the Member States [in the interpretation of the Charter]',[68] although 'they do not as such have the status of law'.[69] After initial uncertainty,[70] the CJEU explicitly endorsed the latter meaning of Article 51(1) of the Charter that arises from the Explanations, affirming the continuity of its earlier case law to which the Explanations refer with respect to the application of Charter rights, in its judgment *Åkerberg Fransson*:[71]

> That definition of the field of application of the fundamental rights of the European Union is borne out by the explanations relating to Article 51 of the Charter, which, in accordance with the third subparagraph of Article 6(1) TEU and Article 52(7) of the Charter, have to be taken into consideration for the purpose of interpreting it (see, to this effect, Case C-279/09 DEB [2010] ECR I-13849, paragraph 32). According to those explanations, 'the requirement to respect fundamental rights defined in the context of the Union is only binding on the Member States when they act in the scope of Union law'.

As a result, it is widely accepted that the Charter's scope of application coincides with that of the general principles of EU law and, therefore, includes all circumstances where Member States act within the scope of EU law.[72]

66. Explanations relating to the Charter of Fundamental Rights, OJ [2007] C 303/17 ('the Explanations') (emphasis added).
67. Gráinne De Burca, *The drafting of the European Union Charter of Fundamental Rights*, 26 Eur. L. Rev. 126, 137 (2001).
68. Art 52(7) of the Charter.
69. Preamble to the Explanations relating to the Charter.
70. *Cf.* Sarmiento, *supra* n. 36, at 1276.
71. *Åkerberg Fransson*, C-617/10, para. 20.
72. *See* De Vries, *supra* n. 56, at 72; Michael Dougan, *The Treaty of Lisbon 2007: Winning Minds, not Hearts*, 45 Common Mkt L. Rev. 617, 665 (2008).

§8.03 INTERACTION BETWEEN FUNDAMENTAL FREEDOMS AND FUNDAMENTAL RIGHTS

[A] Fundamental Freedoms as Fundamental Rights

At the beginning of this contribution's analysis of the interaction between the two sets of rights examined, the question needs to be asked whether one group of rights may be said to encompass the other. In particular, while it is clear that only the specific market rights granted in the TFEU are labelled 'fundamental freedoms',[73] the wider provenance of EU fundamental rights opens the possibility for them to include those freedoms.

Following a general definition of fundamental rights as those rights granted to individuals by virtue of legal rules that are superior to 'ordinary' legislation and, thus, provide protection against democratic majoritarian rule, the EU fundamental freedoms can clearly be called fundamental rights. The major constituent element of any fundamental right – that it is guaranteed independently of its contribution, in a concrete case, to the greater good of society as a whole[74] – is also fulfilled for the fundamental freedoms. However, they are not *only* subjective rights, but also *essential components* of the Internal Market, as the core of the economic constitution of the EU. In this respect, they clearly differ from other fundamental rights, which were not conceived with such a direct objective to benefit the EU as an economic union. This close connection between the fundamental freedoms and the Internal Market objective effectively results in a limited scope of application, which stands in contrast to the general nature of fundamental rights proper.[75]

The impact of these freedoms has been very significant in comparison to other fundamental rights. This is especially true with respect to national laws on direct taxation: since the European Union itself does not have a general competence to legislate in that area, Member States are, in principle, free to determine their direct tax systems unilaterally. It is only when their tax rules have a detrimental effect on the Internal Market, that they are negatively bound by the fundamental freedoms. This is especially the case when national tax systems discriminate directly or indirectly against foreign nationals, who intend to cross the border to work as employees, to provide a service, to establish their commercial presence, or to invest capital in another

73. It should be clear that the term is used, for purposes of this contribution, as defined in §8.02[A], *supra*. Note that, although the ECHR's official title also includes a reference to 'fundamental freedoms', the term there does not have the same technical meaning in that context.

74. *See, e.g.*, Ronald Dworkin, *Taking Rights Seriously* 194 (2009): 'A right against the Government must be a right to do something even when the majority thinks it would be wrong to do it, and even when the majority would be worse off for having done it.'

75. Kamiel Mortelmans, *The Relationship between the Treaty Rules and Community Measures for the Establishment and Functioning of the Internal Market – Towards a Concordance Rule*, 39 Common Mkt L. Rev. 1303, 1314 (2002).

jurisdiction. As the case law of the CJEU established early on, after the creation of the European Community (as it was then), the corresponding guarantees of free movement of persons, services, and capital take precedence over any national provision and also have direct effect,[76] giving individuals the ability to rely on them against the Member States. Thus, the fundamental freedoms are clearly established to be 'rights' of individual EU citizens that take precedence over national 'ordinary' laws. However, they fall short of being true fundamental rights, particularly with respect to their general object, which is not, primarily, to protect individuals against state power, but to protect the Internal Market from disruptions and distortions.[77] It has also been noted that they do not satisfy the role of protecting individuals from state power in general, which would include the legislative power of the Union itself, since the freedoms are – first and foremost – intended to prevent certain actions by the Member States and, more specifically, actions of Member States other than the one in which the individual in question is a citizen or resident. Although the CJEU has expanded its understanding of the fundamental freedoms so that an EU citizen can invoke them against their own Member State and that the European Institutions are also bound thereby, its case law has not completely stripped off the heritage of the freedoms, as can be seen by the fact that the breadth of discretion enjoyed by the European institutions goes beyond that of the Member States.[78] That makes them incompatible with the concept of fundamental rights, which should be binding, within the legal sphere from which they stem, on any state power in the same way.[79]

Regardless of whether one perceives the fundamental freedoms as substantively equivalent to (other) fundamental rights protected in the EU legal order, there is no doubt that both types of rights differ in important respects, such as their scope of application and their principal addressees. As a consequence of those existing differences, a multitude of colliding or mutually reinforcing interactions between them are possible and emerge from the CJEU's case law.[80]

76. *Van Gend en Loos*, 26/62, EU:C:1963:1.
77. Kingreen, *supra* n.10.
78. Georg Kofler, *The Relationship between the Fundamental Freedoms and Directives in the Area of Direct Taxation*, Dirrito E Pratica Tributaria Internazionale 471, 475 (2009); Mortelmans, *supra* n. 75, at 1315; Peter Oliver, *Free Movement of Goods in the European Community* 45 (3d ed. 1996).
79. *Cf.* Theodor Schilling, *Bestand und allgemeine Lehren der bürgerschützenden allgemeinen Rechtsgrundsätze des Gemeinschaftsrechts*, 27 Europäische Grundrechte-Zeitschrift 3, 4 (2000); *see also* Walter Frenz, *Handbuch Europarecht Band 4 – Europäische Grundrechte*, 65 (2009), according to whom the freedoms are, first and foremost, objective principles aimed at establishing and protecting the common market and only subsequently give rights to individuals; fundamental rights, on the other hand, are primarily subjective rights of individuals, which are protected as general principles of EU law, because the protection of fundamental individual rights is itself a general principle of EU law.
80. *See* Wolfgang Kahl & Manuel Schwind, *Europäische Grundrechte und Grundfreiheiten – Grundbausteine einer Interaktionslehre*, 2014 EuR 170 (2014).

[B] The Relationship Between Fundamental Freedoms and Fundamental Rights

[1] Fundamental Rights as Justification for the Restriction of a Fundamental Freedom

As both fundamental freedoms and fundamental rights have the value of primary EU law, it is necessary to undertake a closer examination of their relationship, both in cases where they may interact positively - that is, strengthen one another - and where they may counteract each other.

This section looks at the first type of interaction: it examines the role fundamental rights can play when a Member State seeks to justify a restriction it imposes on any of the fundamental freedoms. In its jurisprudence, the CJEU recognizes fundamental rights found in national constitutional law as sources for overriding requirements in the general interest and performs a balancing analysis in case of conflict with the rights guaranteed by the fundamental freedoms.

There is, however, an on-going debate[81] as to whether national fundamental rights in this situation are confined to a subsidiary role and whether they are only relevant to the justification analysis to the extent that they support already independently recognized 'overriding reasons in the public interest', as the CJEU held in cases such as *Viking Line*[82] and *Laval.*[83] Under this approach, fundamental rights take an inferior position in a conflict between both types of guarantees: in order to pass the threshold of legitimacy required to justify a restriction to the freedoms, they need not only correspond to specific public interests, but also undergo scrutiny of their appropriateness and necessity in light of the competing objectives of that public interest and the freedom involved. The alternative view holds that fundamental rights, by definition, always support facially legitimate objectives that need to be fairly balanced against the objectives of the fundamental freedoms along the lines of the CJEU's traditional proportionality analysis. Under this alternative approach, national fundamental rights are themselves tantamount to overriding requirements, which is consistent with the CJEU's reasoning in cases such as *Schmidberger.*[84] From this perspective, fundamental rights and fundamental freedoms confront each other on equal footing, as elements of a judicial balancing exercise, each with the ability to restrict the other's (axiomatically legitimate) objectives to a certain extent, limited only by the appropriateness, necessity, and reasonableness of whichever measure they

81. *See, e.g.*, Trstenjak & Beysen, *supra* n. 16, at 311; Stephanie Reynolds, *Explaining the Constitutional Drivers behind a Perceived Judicial Preference for Free Movement Over Fundamental Rights*, 53 Common Market L. Rev. 643 (2016).
82. *International Transport Workers' Federation and Finnish Seamen's Union* v *Viking Line ABP*, C-438/05, Judgment, EU:C:2007:772.
83. *Laval un Partneri*, C-341/05, Judgment, EU:C:2007:809.
84. *Schmidberger*, C-112/00, Judgment, EU:C:2003:333, para. 82 (emphasis added):

> it is necessary to determine whether the restrictions placed upon intra-Community trade are proportionate in the light of *the legitimate objective pursued, namely, in the present case, the protection of fundamental rights.*

support.[85] That resolution of their relationship as a case-by-case balancing exercise is sufficient and satisfactory from a constitutional point of view, keeping in mind that it can, and will, only apply to the extent that any involved fundamental right is not absolute, but is itself open to being restricted by competing objectives.[86]

Although the issue has mostly concerned balancing fundamental freedoms with national fundamental rights, the same approach should also apply were a prima facie conflict to arise with fundamental rights protected by any of the sources of EU fundamental rights, including rights guaranteed in the Charter. That, however, raises the even more problematic issue of a potential constitutional conflict, if both national constitutional law and the Charter protect a specific right, but each grants a different level of protection of that right. In a situation in which national constitutional law grants a higher level of protection, it is doubtful that the CJEU would accept Member State measures protecting that higher standard as proportionate, since they would involve restrictions that go beyond what is necessary to protect the equivalent EU right. Existing CJEU case law – which, however, concerns fundamental-rights justifications for limiting the effectiveness of harmonized EU law rather than resolving a conflict with fundamental freedoms – may indeed suggest that national fundamental rights cannot be invoked to justify a measure in breach of primary EU law if the corresponding EU fundamental right would not require the same measure.[87] While this may be an acceptable trade-off in areas of law in which the Member States are effectively reduced to the status of implementing agents of EU law – such as the field of VAT, which was at issue in the relevant cases[88] – the same would not necessarily hold true for areas that are not so harmonized and, thus, only come within the scope of EU law by virtue of the application of the fundamental freedoms, as is largely the case for direct taxation. In these areas, an integration model based on 'value diversity', according to which national constitutional rights are an integral part of EU law, rather than in competition with the EU's economic objectives, would appear to be more appropriate.[89]

85. Trstenjak & Beysen, *supra* n. 15, at 314.
86. This is apparent from the CJEU's careful analysis in *Schmidberger*, para. 80 (emphasis added):

> *unlike other fundamental rights* enshrined in that Convention, such as the right to life or the prohibition of torture and inhuman or degrading treatment or punishment, which admit of no restriction, *neither* the freedom of expression nor the freedom of assembly guaranteed by the ECHR *appears to be absolute* but must be viewed in relation to its social purpose. *Consequently, the exercise of those rights may be restricted,* provided that the restrictions in fact correspond to objectives of general interest and do not, taking account of the aim of the restrictions, constitute disproportionate and unacceptable interference, impairing the very substance of the rights guaranteed

87. *See, especially, Taricco*, C-105/14, Judgment, EU:C:2015:555. For analysis of that judgment, see Mikhel Timmerman, *Balancing effective criminal sanctions with effective fundamental rights protection in cases of VAT fraud:* Taricco, 53 Common Mkt L. Rev. 779 (2016).
88. Apart from *Taricco*, a similar result was achieved in *Åkerberg Fransson*, which also concerned the effectiveness of sanctions within the scope of VAT law (*Åkerberg Fransson*, C-617/10).
89. *See* Lenaerts & Gutiérrez-Fons, *supra* n. 60, at 1664, referring to Tridimas, *supra* n. 25, at 341.

[2] *Fundamental Freedoms as a Justification for the Restriction of a Fundamental Right*

As the flipside of the above-described balancing approach between equally protected, fundamental principles of EU law, which allows (both national and EU) fundamental rights to act as limits to the conditions imposed by the fundamental freedoms, the latter also act as a counterweight to conditions imposed by fundamental rights that are not absolutely protected, such as the right to assembly or freedom of expression. The balancing exercise will typically be undertaken by the competent national court in such cases, as it must decide whether a particular government action that pursues the economic aims of a fundamental freedom can justify a restriction of a national fundamental right. Where this is the case, the fundamental freedoms effectively act as a limit on the protective scope of otherwise constitutionally protected rights. In seeking to balance these competing objectives, national courts are authorized to exercise the 'wide margin of discretion' that the CJEU afforded the Member States' competent authorities in *Schmidberger*.[90]

[3] *Fundamental Rights as a Limit on Justifications for Restrictions*

In contrast to the previous situation, in which fundamental rights and fundamental freedoms were in conflict, fundamental rights can also strengthen the protection afforded by the fundamental freedoms. This situation arises when a Member State invokes an overriding-requirement justification to defend a restriction on a freedom. In accordance with the CJEU's consistent case law outlined above:[91]

> where a Member State relies on the combined provisions of Articles 56 and 66 in order to justify rules which are likely to obstruct the exercise of the freedom to provide services, such justification, provided for by Community law, must be interpreted in the light of the general principles of law and in particular of fundamental rights. Thus the national rules in question can fall under the exceptions provided for by the combined provisions of Articles 56 and 66 only if they are compatible with the fundamental rights the observance of which is ensured by the Court.[92]

By limiting the Member States' ability to rely on countervailing policy objectives, fundamental rights act to strengthen the force of the fundamental freedoms in this scenario. At least partly due to this pro-Internal Market effect, the application of common EU fundamental-rights standards appears, in this way, to be unobjectionable despite any misgivings about the precise role they play, which is at odds with the historical rationale of their creation in the CJEU's jurisprudence.[93] Further strength is added to the argument for such function of fundamental rights by the compelling idea

90. *Schmidberger*, C-112/00, para. 82.
91. *Supra* §8.02[B].
92. *ERT*, C-260/89, para. 43.
93. *Supra* §8.02[B].

of a coherent interpretation of the scope of EU law for both fundamental freedoms and fundamental rights.

Yet, if one accepts that fundamental rights serve this function as a necessary part of the proportionality test of a national measure that relies on a public-policy justification to override the requirements of the fundamental freedoms, the question concerning the relevant standard of such right again arises, particularly if it is afforded protection at various levels in different intensities. A certain inconsistency appears to exist in academic literature in this respect. In his 2013 article, Daniel Sarmiento argued in favour of the national standard, 'unless the Charter, as interpreted by the ECJ, provides a higher protection of the right or rights concerned', adding that it would grant Member States 'a high degree of autonomy that the *ERT* judgment could appear to disregard'.[94] Under his approach, however, such 'autonomy' is only a mirage. His suggestion seems to be that the impact of the *ERT* line of cases, which 'opened the door to an application of EU fundamental rights in particularly sensitive areas of Member State action such as public policy',[95] would be limited by deferring, in most cases, to the national fundamental-rights standards, which should make it more palatable. But, in fact, this apparent concession to Member States' sensitivities is anything but true deference. This follows from the fact that Member State legislatures are generally not relieved of their constitutional constraints arising from national fundamental rights merely because their measures do not violate EU law. As a consequence, whenever the national fundamental-rights standard is higher, such national constraints will still stand in the way of any contested measures, irrespective of their compatibility with fundamental freedoms; whenever the Charter's protection is higher than national protection, the Member State is bound to that higher standard when acting within the scope of the fundamental freedoms. In the former case, the *ERT* line of cases is unnecessary, as it adds nothing to the level of protection for the individual, with the exception, perhaps, of a path to having their case heard by the CJEU; in the latter case, that same line of cases does not grant any deference to a Member State's internal constitutional obligations.

One might consider that objection too strongly rooted in an idea of Member States' autonomy in the area of fundamental rights protection, given the existence of the Charter. Even so, deferring to the higher standard of protection, whether enshrined in the Charter or in national fundamental rights, ignores the central flaw in the Court's *ERT* reasoning, which is built on any particular right's level of protection and suggests priority of the 'stronger' standard. This 'maximum protection fallacy' is easily exposed by pointing to the fact that any given case may involve fundamental rights - indeed, even the same right - on both sides of the equation: in *Familiapress*,[96] for example, the fundamental right to freedom of expression as protected by Article 10 ECHR was engaged both as a justification for a restriction on the sale of magazines that use prize

94. Sarmiento, *supra* n. 36, at 1298; for the same result, see Joseph H.H. Weiler, *Fundamental Rights and Fundamental Boundaries: On the conflict of standards and values in the protection of Human Rights in the European legal space, in The Constitution of Europe: 'Do the New Clothes Have an Emperor?' and Other Essays on European Integration* 102, 126 (Joseph H.H. Weiler ed., 1999).
95. Sarmiento, *supra* n. 36, at 1297.
96. *Familiapress*, C-368/95, Judgment, EU:C:1997:325, paras 18 & 25.

crosswords and as an argument against such restriction;[97] in *Grogan*,[98] which, prima facie, pitted an economic freedom against a national fundamental right, as restrictions on the dissemination of information about abortions were at issue, the fundamental right of expression strengthened the economic freedom to provide services, whereas the fundamental right to life protected in Ireland's constitution acted as a counterbalance to said freedom. Why should the CJEU be better placed to balance different fundamental rights when an autonomous Member State action is at issue? The CJEU rightly deferred said task to the national court in *Familiapress*, and avoided the need for a resolution altogether in *Grogan*, by holding the activity in question to fall outside the scope of the freedom and, therefore, the scope of EU law. The real concern here is not, however, that national courts might lose the power to determine the weight of their national, constitutionally protected rights,[99] but that the value judgments that are integral to the various rights and principles protected in national constitutions are undermined by a different accommodation of the same rights that may be derived from the Charter.

§8.04 IMPLICATIONS FOR THE APPLICATION OF FUNDAMENTAL RIGHTS IN TAX CASES

[A] Overview

The application of EU fundamental rights faces a similar difficulty to that faced by the application of the fundamental freedoms thirty years ago: they had not been created for that purpose, they seemed a bad fit for that purpose, and it seemed like an unacceptable overreach of the Union beyond its remit as defined by the founding treaties. Despite comparable misgivings, it clearly follows from the above analysis of the scope of application of EU fundamental rights that these can and do indeed play a role in the context of taxation. Whenever EU law imposes an obligation on a Member State to levy a tax, this is non-contentious: a Member State implementing such obligation indisputably acts as an agent of the EU, which triggers the application of EU fundamental rights, including both those protected in the Charter and those protected as general principles. In addition to this first category of cases, the CJEU has already dealt with a number of 'grey area' cases that involved situations in which the identification of an obligation of

97. *See* Stephen Weatherill, *From Economic Rights to Fundamental Rights*, *in The Protection of Fundamental Rights in the EU after Lisbon*, 11, 23 (Sybe de Vries, Ulf Bernitz, & Stephen Weatherill eds., 2013).
98. *Grogan*, C-159/90, Judgment, EU:C:1991:378, paras 6 & 30.
99. By contrast, this is the primary concern Daniel Sarmiento chose to address under the heading of 'national constitutional accommodation', arguing that:

> [a]ll in all, the Charter is not destined to be a menace to supreme and constitutional courts, but quite the opposite: it is a unique opportunity, particularly for constitutional courts, to assume an even more relevant role in the institutional dynamics of the State and of the Union as a whole.

Sarmiento, *supra* n. 36, at 1299.

the Member State was not immediately apparent. The CJEU used those cases to clarify its earlier case law concerning the application of EU fundamental rights whenever a national measure falls within the scope of EU law, whether or not it was directly based on an obligation found in EU law. In *Åkerberg Fransson*,[100] it held:

> Since the fundamental rights guaranteed by the Charter must therefore be complied with where national legislation falls within the scope of European Union law, situations cannot exist which are covered in that way by European Union law without those fundamental rights being applicable. The applicability of European Union law entails applicability of the fundamental rights guaranteed by the Charter.
>
> Where, on the other hand, a legal situation does not come within the scope of European Union law, the Court does not have jurisdiction to rule on it and any provisions of the Charter relied upon cannot, of themselves, form the basis for such jurisdiction.

In that case, the CJEU had to answer the question of whether it had jurisdiction to assess the compatibility of two separate sanctions imposed by Sweden in the context of VAT enforcement with the *ne bis in idem* principle as protected by Article 50 of the Charter. By holding that any measure coming within the scope of EU law automatically triggers the applicability of the Charter, the CJEU effectively erased the distinction between 'implementation' and merely acting 'within the scope' of EU law. The CJEU did not have to do that in order to reach its conclusion in that case, however, since it concluded that Sweden had an obligation to impose the contested sanctions under the Sixth VAT Directive (read in light of Article 4(3) TEU), such that Sweden was squarely implementing EU law within the meaning of Article 51(1) of the Charter.[101] This was also the Court's decisive argument in *Berlioz Investment Fund*,[102] which, like *Åkerberg Fransson*, concerned a sanction imposed by national law as a measure necessary for the effectiveness of a directive.

By contrast, in *Sabou*,[103] the CJEU could not refer to 'implementation', but had to find the Member State's action as falling 'within the scope' of EU law. It held that a Member State acts within the scope of EU law if it relies on a directive to obtain information from another Member State in the course of a tax audit procedure, even though the requesting Member State is merely permitted to make a request for information, but is never obliged to do so. In *Sabou*, the CJEU did not apply the Charter, however; rather, it relied on the right to be heard as a fundamental right that is protected as part of general principles of EU law.[104]

Neither case answers the following, pertinent question: Can a taxpayer, in effect, always invoke EU fundamental rights as soon as her case comes within the scope of the fundamental freedoms, thereby implying the action falls 'within the scope' of EU law?[105] If that were the case, virtually all direct tax legislation concerning cross-border

100. *Åkerberg Fransson*, C-617/10, paras 21–22.
101. *Cf.* Sarmiento, *supra* n. 36, at 1280.
102. *Berlioz Investment Fund*, C-682/15, Judgment, EU:C:2017:373, para. 50.
103. *Sabou*, C-276/12.
104. *Ibid.* para. 28.
105. *See* Alexander Rust, *supra*, Ch. 2 of this volume, §2.05.

situations would have to comply, not only with national fundamental-rights standards, but also with those of the Union.

[B] EU Fundamental Rights in the Area of Direct Taxation: Do the Fundamental Freedoms Always Trigger Fundamental Rights?

In the area of direct taxation, as opposed to indirect taxation, attempts at EU harmonization have had no significant impact. That difference from the area of indirect taxation is also no accident, but, instead, can be seen as a direct consequence of the division of competence between the EU and its Member States in Articles 114 and 115 TFEU. As a consequence, since no significant obligations for Member States to follow harmonized rules exist, it is questionable whether EU fundamental rights can have a significant effect on the Member States' exercise of their legislative competence in direct taxation. If, as *Åkerberg Fransson* and *Sabou* make clear, a Member State can still act within the scope of EU law even if it is not obliged to act by an EU measure, the absence of significant harmonization may not be much of an obstacle to the widespread application of EU fundamental rights in direct taxation. It is sufficient for a Member State's direct tax measure to come 'within the scope of EU law' simply through its voluntary use of a directive. But, considering the limited competence of the EU in this area, how can that happen? The above-analysed line of cases concerning the interaction of fundamental freedoms and fundamental rights seems to provide an obvious answer: by regulating cross-border economic activity (i.e., by taxing income earned as a consequence of such activity), tax rules fall within the scope of application of the fundamental freedoms. This would suffice even in the absence of a substantive violation of the freedoms, such as discriminatory treatment. As Stephen Weatherill observes:[106]

> EU free movement law applies remarkably easily: and when it does protection of fundamental rights immediately becomes part of the assessment.

That observation raises a question as to why fundamental rights have not, at least thus far, played a significant role in the vast case law concerning the impact of fundamental freedoms on direct tax measures, when the logic of the *ERT*, *Carpenter*, and *Karner* judgments suggests that compatibility with EU fundamental rights, including those derived from common constitutional traditions of the Member States as well as all those enshrined in the Charter, need to be taken into account whenever a Member State is required to specifically justify a tax measure due to its restrictive effects. The virtual absence of cases in which the CJEU applied fundamental rights as a necessary consequence of the application of the fundamental freedoms in the direct tax area is remarkable. Neither of the two most famous judgments applying fundamental rights in the direct-tax area – *Sabou*[107] and *Berlioz Investment Fund*[108] – concerned

106. Weatherill, *supra* n. 97, at 29.
107. *Sabou*, C-276/12.
108. *Berlioz Investment Fund*, C-682/15.

substantive tax rules; they only dealt with procedural matters related to the exchange of information.

The few cases the CJEU has, to date, decided concerning the substance of direct-tax rules in the context of EU fundamental rights do not yet draw a clear picture of its thoughts on the matter. In *SIAT*,[109] for example, the CJEU reviewed a Belgian rule that imposed stricter conditions on the deductibility of business expenses when the counterparty was established in another state and subject to a more advantageous tax regime. While that difference resulted in a clear restriction on the freedom to provide services, the CJEU found it was justified by a number of legitimate objectives, including the effectiveness of fiscal supervision, the balanced allocation of taxing power, and the prevention of tax avoidance.[110] However, the CJEU invoked the principle of legal certainty to conclude that the measure was, nevertheless, disproportionate: by holding that 'a rule which does not meet the requirements of the principle of legal certainty cannot be considered to be proportionate to the objectives pursued',[111] the Court made the principle of legal certainty an absolute limit on what is otherwise an explicitly relative analysis.[112] The CJEU subsequently affirmed that approach in *Itelcar*,[113] which concerned the application of stricter thin capitalization rules with respect to foreign-held debt. The Court held those rules to be incompatible with the free movement of capital – even though the Member State could invoke legitimate objectives for their rule's existence – because those could not be considered proportionate to such objectives due to their indeterminate scope, which, the Court found, failed to meet the requirements of legal certainty.[114]

Although the CJEU did not refer explicitly to fundamental rights in either case, the decisions clearly echo the result in its *ERT* judgment. Legal certainty is closely related to several fundamental rights, including the right to property, where it acts as a key requirement to justify any interference with private possessions, including taxation.[115] As a consequence, it appears reasonable to conclude that the *ERT* doctrine should apply to its fullest extent in the area of direct tax law. The implication of that conclusion is that, whenever a national tax rule comes within the scope of EU law by virtue of its interference with any fundamental freedom, it is open to scrutiny, not only on the basis of the standards set by the case law on that freedom, but also on its compliance with all recognized EU fundamental rights, as interpreted by the CJEU.

109. *SIAT*, C-318/10.
110. *Ibid.* para. 48.
111. *Ibid.* para. 59.
112. The proportionality test generally requires the weighing of different interests within the context of law. As Tridimas observed, 'It is by its nature flexible and open-textured. The case law on proportionality may be seen as a celebration of judicial relativism'. Tridimas, *supra* n. 25, at 173.
113. *Itelcar*, C-282/12, Judgment, EU:C:2013:629.
114. *Ibid.* para. 44.
115. *See* ECtHR 8 July 1986, *Lithgow and others vs United Kingdom*, Application no. 9006/80 et al., para 110; ECtHR 9 Nov. 1999, *Špaček s.r.o. v. the Czech Republic*, no. 26449/95, para 54; ECtHR 5 Jan. 2000, *Beyeler vs Italy*, Application no. 33202/96, para 109; ECtHR 14 Oct. 2010, *Shchokin vs Ukraine*, Application nos. 23759/03 and 37943/06, para. 51.

When, then, does a national tax rule affect fundamental freedoms in such a way as to allow the CJEU to subject it to such review? If the Court were to apply its very broad, earlier case law in this respect, especially its reasoning in *Karner*,[116] which did not even require a prima facie violation of a freedom, virtually every direct tax provision would fulfil the minimum requirement of coming within the scope of the fundamental freedoms, since all direct tax rules either apply (also) to cross-border situations or, if they do not, introduce different treatment of domestic and cross-border situations simply by virtue of them *not* applying. However, the CJEU has, to date, refrained from applying the expansive protection of fundamental freedoms to direct tax law; most notably, the CJEU has, thus far, generally rejected the application of the fundamental freedoms to cases of tax rules that are mere (non-discriminatory) obstacles.[117] One explanation for why there are not more cases successfully invoking a violation of fundamental rights before the Court in the direct tax area could be that the CJEU will likely apply this narrower approach to them.

The Court's order in *Burzio*[118] points in that direction. In that case, an Italian employer, who had failed to pay withholding tax to the authorities and was subject to two separate sanctions, invoked the *ne bis in idem* principle protected by Article 50 of the Charter. The CJEU, answering a preliminary ruling request from the Italian court, held that it had no jurisdiction to decide the case, since the domestic procedure had no link with EU law, rendering the Charter inapplicable. Explaining its decision, the CJEU explicitly referred to the fact that the national rules in question concerned a violation of Italy's direct tax law and not – as in *Åkerberg Fransson* – a violation of the EU's VAT law.[119] The situation at issue in that case might indeed appear to lack any factual link to a cross-border situation that could bring it within the scope of the fundamental freedoms. If the recipients of payments subject to withholding tax were residents of other Member States, however, the relevant provisions would have come within the scope of EU law in a broad sense. The CJEU, thus, could indeed scrutinize all national direct tax law much more closely from the EU fundamental-rights perspective, if it chose to do so. Nevertheless, it is more likely that the CJEU will continue its current, more restrictive, approach when a taxpayer invokes EU fundamental rights to challenge direct tax measures, only applying them as an element of the proportionality test as established by the *ERT* doctrine. The conspicuous absence of more cases in the direct tax arena may, thus, stem from the narrower scope of application of the fundamental freedoms in that area, on the one hand, and from a scarcity of protected rights that substantive direct tax rules interfere with.

---

116. *See* discussion surrounding the Court's *Karner* judgment in §8.02[B], *supra.*
117. *See Mobistar and Belgacom Mobile,* Joined Cases C-544/03 and C-545/03; *see, further,* Ben J.M. Terra and Peter J. Wattel, *European Tax Law,* 89 et seq. (6th ed. 2012).
118. *Burzio,* C-497/14, Order, EU:C:2015:251.
119. *Ibid.* para. 30 (emphasis added):

> *Notamment, contrairement aux circonstances ayant donné lieu à l'arrêt Åkerberg Fransson ..., la réglementation nationale en cause au principal concerne l'absence de versement de retenues à la source* relatives à l'impôt sur le revenu *et non pas des manquements à des obligations en matière de taxe sur la valeur ajoutée.*

§8.05 CONCLUSION

This contribution has focussed on the interaction between fundamental freedoms and fundamental rights, their differences and similarities, and the question why EU fundamental rights have, thus far, played a very small role in the CJEU's review of substantive direct tax measures. A close analysis shows that there are a number of important points of contact at the crossroads of both types of fundamental guarantees that underpin the EU's constitutional framework. Fundamental freedoms and fundamental rights can oppose or strengthen each other and there are situations in which the latter can indeed only be invoked as a consequence of applying the former. The conditions for, and limits on, the application of EU fundamental rights are not yet fully developed in the CJEU's case law, although there are indications that the Court is taking a rather cautious approach, one that is mindful of the Member States' competence in direct tax matters. In light of the critical stance taken in this contribution to the CJEU's overly broad view on the application of fundamental rights in other areas, especially in so-called *ERT*-type cases, such restraint in the area of direct taxation is certainly welcome. Adding an extra layer of scrutiny on top of fundamental freedoms is, indeed, neither necessary nor desirable from the perspective of legal certainty (for both taxpayers and Member States) where national fundamental rights continue to provide effective protection.

CHAPTER 9
Cross-Border Exchange of Tax Information and Fundamental Rights

Fatima Chaouche & Werner Haslehner

§9.01 INTRODUCTION

Very few areas of law have been subject to as much scrutiny and political pressure as tax law over the past years. In a very short period of time, we went from almost no exchange to the implementation of automatic exchange of information for specific categories of income. Since 2009, an unprecedented interventionism has been best illustrated by the amendments and enlargements of various mutual assistance instruments, both at the OECD and EU levels. This widening of scope undoubtedly involves implications for taxpayers who are directly or indirectly concerned by the exchange of information. The unremitting efforts to achieve efficient exchanges among national tax authorities has, so far, resided in the promptness with which the information gathered is transferred and thereby encouraging requested States to limit taxpayers' notification and participation rights. Addressing fundamental rights implications in cross-border exchanges of information entails, first, an overview of the recent developments in exchange of information procedures (§9.02) and an overview of the scope of fundamental rights at both EU and national levels (§9.03). Along the same lines, a review of the CJEU decision in *Sabou*[1] appears relevant in this context as it features *in concreto* implications of mutual assistance mechanisms on taxpayers' procedural rights (§9.04). Considering that the request for preliminary ruling addressed to the CJEU in *Sabou* mainly raised concerns with respect to the application of the right of the defence, it is appropriate to identify further taxpayers' rights that may come into play in mutual assistance proceedings. This 'inventory' exercise is a prerequisite for a just assessment

1. *Sabou*, C-276/12, Judgment, EU:C:2013:678.

of the current exchange of information legal framework and allows the formulation of open questions for identified unresolved issues (§9.05).

§9.02 RECENT DEVELOPMENTS IN EXCHANGE OF INFORMATION

The need for exchange of information is not new: it has existed much longer than the EU and the OECD and coincides with the creation of the first double tax treaties.[2] The latter did not create that need, rather, it is more likely that they partly reduced it to the extent that they allocate taxing rights in line with the principle of territoriality. At the same time, tax treaties' enhancing effect on cross-border trade has increased the need for exchange of information to the extent that more and more taxpayers earn foreign income.

This need for information stems from the incongruity of world-wide substantive tax jurisdiction and territorial, formal tax jurisdiction;[3] while countries would like to tax their residents on worldwide income, international law does not allow them to investigate facts outside their borders and, thus, limits the availability of verified information necessary to exercise their tax jurisdiction.[4] As such, mechanisms of cooperation between national revenue authorities have been adopted as a way to reduce their inability to collect, question, and seize information outside their own territory.[5]

States initially made little use of administrative cooperation procedures in the determination of their own residents' income taxes. Indeed, lengthy collection procedures and recalcitrant jurisdictions (e.g., Luxembourg and Switzerland) did not generate much enthusiasm towards the cooperation mechanisms available then.[6] Yet,

2. Some authors trace the first rules on exchange of information (EOI) in tax treaties to the early 1840s; *see, e.g.*, Xavier Oberson, *International Exchange of Information in Tax Matters: Towards Global Transparency* 4 (2015). For further historical and detailed background on tax treaties, see Kevin Holmes, *International Tax Policy and Double Tax Treaties: An Introduction to Principles and Application* (2007).

   Wolfgang Schön, *Neutrality and Territoriality: Competing or Converging Concepts in European Tax Law?*, 69 Bull. Int'l Tax'n 271 (2015); *see also* Adam Becker, *The Principle of Territoriality and Corporate Income Taxation, What Territoriality Means and Whether or Not It Guides Country Practice*, 70 Bull. Int'l Tax'n 190 (2016).
3. Schön, *supra* n. 2; *see also* Becker, *supra* n. 2.
4. Michael Keen & Jenny E. Ligthart, *Information sharing and international taxation*, Discussion Paper No. 2004-117, Tilburg University, 2004, available at https://papers.ssrn.com/sol3/papers.cfm?abstract_id=639021.
5. The first significant legislation adopted at the EU level on EOI was Council Directive 77/799/EEC of 19 Dec. 1977 concerning mutual assistance by the competent authorities of the Member States in the field of direct taxation [1977] OJ L336/15 [hereinafter the 'Original DAC']. Amended several times, it was subsequently repealed by Council Directive 2011/16/EU of 15 Feb. 2011 on administrative cooperation in the field of taxation and repealing Directive 77/799/EEC [2011] OJ L 64 [hereinafter 'DAC 1']. Prior to the Original DAC, exchange mechanisms were already incorporated into double tax conventions.
6. G20 London Summit, *Leaders' Statement*, pt. 16, Apr. 2009; *see also Declaration on Strengthening the Financial System, London Summit, Tax Havens and Non-Cooperative Jurisdictions*, 4, Apr. 2009; and OECD, *A Progress Report on the Jurisdictions Surveyed by the OECD Global Forum in Implementing the Internationally Agreed Tax Standard, Progress Made as of April 2009*, available online at www.oecd.org.

in the meantime, rapid globalization and the opening of the economy (particularly, the capital markets) in Europe, combined with the creation of a single currency, has invariably increased the need to exchange information as well as the necessity to have adequate legal instruments to do so.

The emergence of advanced information technology[7] allowing almost immediate transfers of information, together with the 2008 financial crisis,[8] have undeniably contributed to a political consensus around the need to update the legal instruments allowing for such transfers while enlarging the scope of information that can be exchanged.[9]

At the EU level, the exchange of information between national tax authorities is based on different legal instruments. For the purpose of this contribution, we will limit our analysis to the different Council Directives that have been adopted since 1977 and to the OECD's recent update of Article 26 of its model convention (the 'OECD MC').[10]

[A] Repeal and Update of the Directives on Administrative Cooperation

[1] Council Directive 77/799/EEC

The Original DAC,[11] now repealed,[12] was adopted in December 1977 following ambitious resolutions, announced by the Council in 1975, to adopt measures to combat international tax evasion and tax avoidance.[13] This Community initiative was then considered to be a preliminary and necessary tool to limit the negative effects and repercussions arising from the lack of cooperation between national tax administrations on the single market.[14]

---

7. Arthur J. Cockfield, *Protecting Taxpayer Privacy Rights under Enhanced Cross-Border Tax Information Exchange: Toward a Multilateral Taxpayer Bill of Rights*, 42 U. British Columbia L. Rev. 421 (2010).
8. For further details on the interaction between the financial crisis and tax policy aspects, see Thomas Hemmelgarn & Gaëtan Nicodème, *The 2008 Financial Crisis and Taxation Policy*, Taxation Papers, Working Paper No. 20 2010, Office for Official Publications of the European Communities, 2010.
9. Proposal for a Council Directive amending Directive 2011/16/EU as regards mandatory automatic exchange of information in the field of taxation, COM(2016) 25 final, 2016/0010 (CNS) [hereinafter the '2016 MAE Proposal'.
10. For additional details on further exchange instruments, see Roman Seer, *Recent Developments in Exchange of Information Within the EU for Tax Matters*, 22 EC Tax Rev. 66 (2013); *see also* Carol P. Tello, *FATCA: Catalyst for global cooperation on exchange of tax information*, 68 Bull. Int'l Tax'n 88 (2014); and Alicja Brodzka, *The Road to FATCA in the European Union*, 53 Eur. Tax'n 517 (2013).
11. As defined in n. 5, *supra*.
12. As defined in n. 5, *supra*. DAC 1was subsequently amended by Council Directive 2014/107/EU of 9 Dec. 2014 amending Directive 2011/16/EU as regards mandatory automatic exchange of information in the field of taxation [2014] OJ L 359/1 [hereinafter 'DAC 2'] and Council Directive (EU) 2015/2376 of 8 Dec. 2015 amending Directive 2011/16/EU as regards mandatory automatic exchange of information in the field of taxation [2015] OJ L332/1 [hereinafter 'DAC 3'].
13. The Original DAC, *supra* n. 5, Preamble ('Whereas practices of tax evasion and tax avoidance extending across the frontiers of Member States lead to budget losses').
14. *Ibid.* ('whereas collaboration between tax administrations within the Community should therefore be strengthened').

The Original DAC featured the most common forms of exchange of information – upon request, automatic, and spontaneous – but also allowed for the presence of tax officials of a Member State in another Member State should both countries agree on that necessity.[15]

It also contained provisions relating to limitations on exchanges, for example, in the presence of a commercial secret or for public-policy reasons.[16] Most importantly, it gave Member States the right to refuse to exchange information when the request would violate their domestic laws or administrative practices, or if the requested information was irrelevant for their own taxation purposes.[17]

The Original DAC was rather short; it only contained thirteen brief articles. In the absence of common rules between Member States, the standard with which confidentiality, secrecy, public policy had to be dealt with was by referring to domestic law provisions that would normally apply in national cases.[18]

[2] Council Directive 2011/16/EU (DAC 1)

Almost thirty-five years later, the Original DAC was considered outdated and no longer adequate for the new reality of the single market.[19] It was, therefore, completely repealed by DAC 1,[20] whose scope was substantially enlarged in order to cope with new challenges generated by enhanced cross-border exchange of goods and services, the multiplication of capital transfers, and more and more individuals exercising their right to free movement across the EU. The explanatory memorandum of the proposal for the new Directive justified the adoption of a more sophisticated instrument as 'billions of euros [were] being lost'. It was further stated that it was not 'only an issue of revenue, but also of fairness'.[21]

As already stated, under the Original DAC, it was maintained that the information initially collected for tax purposes could be used for administration and enforcement in other areas of domestic law upon agreement of both tax administrations.[22]

In addition, the new legal act provided for a greater scope of cooperation, including direct and indirect taxes not previously covered by any Union legislation.[23] It further enlarged the scope of the persons concerned by the exchange – both individuals and legal persons – as a way to tackle the proliferation of certain instruments and

15. *Ibid.* Preamble, Arts. 2–6.
16. *Ibid.* Art. 8(2).
17. *Ibid.* Art. 8(3).
18. By analogy, similar reasoning can be adopted for the Original DAC and these definitions within the meaning of OECD MC Art. 26; *see* Harald Schaumburg & Stefan Schlossmacher, *Article 26 of the OECD Model in Light of the Right to Informational Self-Determination*, 54 Bull. Int'l Tax'n 522 (2000).
19. The 2016 MAE Proposal, *supra* n. 9.
20. DAC 1, *supra* n. 12.
21. Proposal for a Council Directive amending Directive 2011/16/EU as regards mandatory automatic exchange of information in the field of taxation, COM/2013/0348 final – 2013/088 (CNS) [hereinafter the '2013 MAE Proposal'].
22. DAC 1, *supra* n. 12, Recital 18.
23. *Ibid.* Art. 2.

arrangements whose aim was to conceal the actual beneficial owners of the relevant income.[24]

The Directive created new structures to facilitate the exchange of information by creating competent authorities across Member States and requiring the appointment of officials encouraged to maintain direct contacts with other Member States' administrations.[25] Fixed deadlines were adopted in the text as a way to render the exchange of information faster as well as standardized forms to ensure faster collection procedures.[26] 'Efficient' and 'prompt' exchanges were part of the new cross-border standard.

The information to exchange followed the OECD MC by referring to the 'foreseeably relevant' standard. As previously clarified by the OECD, banking secrecy was no longer a justified limitation on the exchange of relevant banking and financial information.[27] DAC 2 also introduced, as of 1 January 2014, automatic exchange of information for five categories of income: employment income; directors' fees; life insurance and similar products; pensions; and ownership of/income from immovable property.[28] In the meantime, the Original Savings Directive[29] already permitted the automatic exchange of information on interest income while temporarily allowing certain jurisdictions to operate a withholding tax on such income.[30]

Finally, a most-favoured nation clause[31] was also inserted in the Directive, forcing States that had agreed to broader cooperation with third parties to provide such broader assistance to the other Member States. With the adoption of FATCA, Member States agreed to provide greater assistance to the US than that required by the Directive.[32] It was no surprise then that it was already necessary to amend and update the Directive with further cooperation in extended areas.[33]

24. *Ibid.* Recital 7 ('Clearer rules should also make it possible in particular to cover all legal and natural persons in the Union, taking into account the ever-increasing range of legal arrangements, including not only traditional arrangements such as trusts, foundations and investment funds, but any new instrument which may be set up by taxpayers in the Member States').
25. *Ibid.* Recitals 16, 17.
26. *Ibid.* Arts 7, 20.
27. *Ibid.* Recital 20.
28. *Ibid.* Art. 8.
29. Council Directive 2003/48/EC of 3 June 2003 on taxation of savings income in the form of interest payments [2013] OJ L157/38 [hereinafter the 'Original Savings Directive']. This directive was amended by Council Directive 2014/48/EU of 24 Mar. 2014 amending Directive 2003/48/EC on taxation of savings income in the form of interest payments [2014] OJ L111/50 and DAC 2, and was subsequently repealed by Council Directive (EU) 2015/2060 of 10 No. 2015 repealing Directive 2003/48/EC on taxation of savings income in the form of interest payments [2015] OJ L301/1.
30. The Original Savings Directive, *supra* n. 29, Chapter III, Transitional Provisions, Art. 10. Instead of immediately applying the adopted automatic exchange provisions, Austria, Belgium and Luxembourg were temporarily allowed to introduce a transitional withholding tax. The withholding tax was levied at a rate of 15% during the first three years of the transitional period, 20% for the next three years, and 35% until the end thereof. Belgium and Luxembourg adopted the automatic exchange provisions and ceased the application of the withholding tax as of 1 Jan. 2010 and as of 1 Jan. 2015, respectively.
31. DAC 2, *supra* n. 12, Art. 19.
32. The 2016 MAE Proposal, *supra* n. 9.
33. DAC 2, *supra* n. 12, Recital 8:

[3] *Council Directive 2014/107/EU (DAC 2) and 2015/2376 (EU) (DAC 3)*

The two different directives amending DAC 1 – known as DAC 2[34] and DAC 3[35] – were adopted in December 2014 and December 2015, respectively. As of 1 January 2017, the scope of automatic exchange of information was extended to include financial information (e.g., dividends and account balances) as well as relevant details with respect to cross-border tax rulings and transfer pricing agreements.[36]

The directives follow the reporting and due diligence rules already incorporated into the OECD's Common Reporting Standard,[37] which was intended to establish a single, global standard for automatic exchange of information.[38] The adoption of automatic exchange for cross-border rulings and advance pricing arrangements is further justified by the inefficiency of spontaneous exchange of information in these areas.[39]

Finally, the latest directives adopted for matters of administrative cooperation all contain a provision within their respective Preambles mentioning that: '[the Directive] respects the fundamental rights and observes the principles which are recognized in particular by the [Charter of Fundamental Rights of the European Union (the 'Charter')], including the right to the protection of personal data'.[40] It is worth noting that this same recital appears in all recently adopted Directives, such that it does not appear to be particularly specific to mutual assistance legislation.

[B] Update of Article 26 of the OECD MC and Its Commentary

The 2012 update of Article 26 of the OECD MC – following the ones already initiated in 2002 and 2005 – confirmed the general inclination towards broadening exchange of information procedures to the 'widest extent possible'.[41] In addition to the three standard forms of exchange – applied individually or collectively – the application of

> The conclusion of parallel and uncoordinated agreements by Member States under Article 19 of Directive 2011/16/EU could lead to distortions that would be detrimental to the smooth functioning of the internal market. Expanded automatic information exchange on the basis of a Union-wide legislative instrument would obviate the need for Member States to invoke that Article, with a view to concluding bilateral or multilateral agreements that may be considered appropriate on the same subject in the absence of relevant Union legislation.

34. As defined in n. 12, *supra*.
35. As defined in n. 12, *supra*.
36. DAC 2, *supra* n. 12, Recital 5.
37. OECD, *Standard for Automatic Exchange of Financial Account in Tax Matters*, 2014, available at www.oecd.org.
38. *See* DAC 2, *supra* n. 12, Annex 1.
39. *Ibid.* Recital 4.
40. *Ibid.* Recital 17; DAC 3, *supra* n. 12, Recital 22.
41. OECD MC Commentary on Art. 26, update to Art. 26 approved by the OECD Council on 17 July 2012, Preliminary remarks, I(2).

Article 26 does not exclude other forms of collection as long as they prove to be relevant for both contracting States' purposes.[42]

It is also worth noting that this enlarged scope was already achieved by the previous insertions of paragraphs 4 and 5 of Article 26 – allowing, respectively, the exchange of information although irrelevant to the requested tax authorities' own tax proceedings and the suppression of limitations for information held by banks, fiduciaries, and financial institutions.[43] These amendments were not taken up enthusiastically by most countries concerned, who instead made reservations to that so-called 'clarification'.[44] The financial crisis of 2008 acted as a catalyst for worldwide adoption of the new OECD standard, however, with non-cooperative countries being threatened with being, effectively, excluded from the global network of 'compliant' countries. Yet, by 2010, no significant country was 'black-listed' by the OECD for that reason.[45]

In the most recent update of Article 26, the information is no longer limited to the enforcement of domestic tax laws, but can also be used for 'other purposes', with agreement of the administration delivering the information.[46] Although the OECD justifies the new standard as a mere clarification,[47] the change in the standard wording from 'necessary information' to 'foreseeably relevant' information was, undoubtedly, intended to enlarge the scope of the information that could fall within Article 26. As those precisions were intended to ease interpretation for the revenue administrations involved, it appears that the discretionary powers of the requested tax authorities have been further weakened since the commentaries of Article 26 state that the information has to be exchanged irrespective of whether it appears to be actually relevant to the investigation carried out by the requesting State.[48] Even more questionable is the obligation of the requested authority to supply the information despite the fact that it sees no connection between the information requested and the ongoing investigation.[49] It becomes, thus, even more challenging to establish a clear demarcation between foreseeably relevant information and a 'fishing expedition' or speculative request –

42. *Ibid.* para. 1, pt. 9.1.
43. *Ibid.* Art. 26(4), (5) OECD MC.
44. *Ibid.* I (4.4); Reservations were made by Austria, Belgium, Luxembourg and Switzerland. For more on the reservations to Art. 26(5) by Luxembourg, *see* Alain Steichen, *New Exchange of Information Versus Tax Solutions of Equivalent Effect*, Luxembourg Report, EATLP, 2010.
45. OECD, *List of Uncooperative Tax Havens*, www.oecd.org:

> In May 2009, the Committee on Fiscal Affairs decided to remove all three remaining jurisdictions (Andorra, the Principality of Liechtenstein and the Principality of Monaco) from the list of uncooperative tax havens in the light of their commitments to implement the OECD standards of transparency and effective exchange of information and the timetable they set for the implementation. As a result, no jurisdiction is currently listed as an uncooperative tax haven by the Committee on Fiscal Affairs.

46. Art. 26 (2) OECD MC.
47. OECD MC Commentary on Art. 26 OECD MC, Preliminary Remarks, I, pt. 4.4.
48. *Ibid.* para. 1, pt. 5: 'Whether the information, once provided, actually proves to be relevant is immaterial'.
49. *Ibid.* 'However, once the requesting State has provided an explanation as to the foreseeable relevance of the requested information, the requested State may not decline a request or withhold requested information because it believes that the information lacks relevance to the underlying investigation or examination'.

both being allegedly opposed standards. It is not, however, excluded that, in certain circumstances, it might appear difficult to distinguish the two; especially in cases where the information is not strictly related to the investigation but might potentially prove to be actually relevant.

Various contradictions arise with respect to, on the one hand, the purported encouragement of taxpayers' participation rights during the exchange (e.g., the inclusion of taxpayers in the 'persons' to whom information can be disclosed and praise for consultation with taxpayers to limit mistakes and 'facilitate the exchange')[50] and, on the other hand, the encouragement to implement practical restrictions to limit taxpayers' rights at any stage of information collection, together with certain restrictions thereon at the litigation stage.[51]

It may also be reasonable to believe that Article 26, similarly to the Original DAC, does not provide any subjective rights to taxpayers but constitute instead an instrument available for tax administrations willing to engage in exchange of information and coordinate their action in relation to the situation of one or various taxpayers.

As described above, the recent developments in exchange of information matters have largely consisted of extending the scope of mutual assistance instruments, most notably by extending the type of information that can be exchanged and by defining the time limits in which to respond to ensure efficient cooperation. These recent legislative updates raise the question of their compatibility with the current fundamental rights framework both at EU and national levels.

§9.03 FUNDAMENTAL RIGHTS AND CROSS-BORDER EXCHANGE OF INFORMATION

[A] Implementation of EU Law and Fundamental Rights

Prior to the entry into force of the Charter in 2009, it was already recognized that fundamental rights – inspired by various Member States' constitutional traditions and the European Convention of Human Rights (the 'ECHR') – form part of the general principles of Union law.[52]

We have learned from previous case law – more precisely, from *Åkerberg Fransson*[53] – that the application of EU law necessarily entails the application of fundamental rights as guaranteed by the Charter. Thus, Member States must comply

50. *Ibid.* para. 3, pt. 14.1.
51. *Ibid.* para. 2, pt. 11.
52. For an historical overview of Fundamental rights at the EU level, see George Arestis, *Fundamental Rights in the EU: Three Years after Lisbon, the Luxembourg Perspective,* Cooperative Research Paper 02/2013, College of Europe, European Legal Studies, 2013; *see also* Joint Declaration by the European Parliament, the Council and the Commission [1977] OJ C103/01.
53. *Åkerberg Fransson*, C-617/10, Judgment, EU:C:2013:105.

with the legal order of the European Union when acting within the scope of Union law.[54]

Whereas the meaning of 'within the scope of EU law' has always been vigorously debated, the CJEU has consistently adopted a contextual and broad interpretation that expands its scope to situations not entirely governed by Union law. A provision implementing EU law - as clarified in the *Julián Hernández* case - presupposes 'a degree of connection between the measure of EU law and the national measure at issue which goes beyond the matters covered being closely related or one of those matters having an indirect impact on the other.'[55]

The delimitation between purely national matters and actions within the scope of EU law may, in practice, prove arduous; the application of secondary law instruments, such as directives, often create certain prerogatives that Member States may (or should in certain instances) follow. In situations where their actions are not fully determined by EU law, despite part of the situation being covered by the application of a directive,[56] national administrations, as well as national judicial bodies, are required to apply domestic rights and protection standards.[57] However, in using the Original DAC to gather information, both the requesting and requested Member States are acting within the scope of EU law, which entails the application of the Charter, irrespective of whether the use of the Directive is optional or mandatory for those States.[58] Consequently, certain rights and obligations result for taxpayers and tax administrations.

Charter rights can be limited, provided that any restriction is permitted by law and proportionate to the aim pursued. Article 52 of the Charter provides that these limitations have to be 'necessary' and 'genuinely meet objectives of general interest recognized by the Union or the need to protect the rights and freedoms of others'.[59]

[B] Procedural Autonomy of Member States in Direct Taxation Matters

Since legislative action at the EU level requires unanimity in matters of direct taxation,[60] very few initiatives have been adopted in this field, leaving Member States'

54. Francesca Ferraro & Jesús Carmona, *Fundamental Rights in the European Union, The Role of the Charter after the Lisbon Treaty*, European Parliamentary Research Service, In-Depth Analysis, 2015.
55. *Julian Hernández and Others*, C-198/13, Judgment, EU:C:2014:2055.
56. *Maurin*, C-144/95, Judgment, EU:C:1996:235, paras 11, 12.
57. *Burzio*, C-497/14, Order, EU:C:2015:251, para. 31.
58. *Sabou*, C-276/12, para. 26:

> As regards the Court's jurisdiction in this case to interpret Directive 77/799, the fact that the requesting Member State is not bound to submit a request for assistance to another Member State does not mean that the rules relating to the request for information and the use of the information obtained by that Member State can be considered to be outside the scope of European Union law.

59. Art. 52 Charter; *see also* Koen Lenaerts, *Effective Judicial Protection in the EU* (2013) available at http://ec.europa.eu/justice/events/assises-justice-2013/files/interventions/koenlenarts.pdf.
60. Art. 114(2) TFEU.

tax sovereignty intact.[61] In absence of harmonized measures concerning the assessment and collection of national income taxes, it is for the national administrations to apply their own procedural rules. By extension, this presupposes that EU fundamental rights cannot find application in domestic legislation.[62] This statement is confirmed by a decision of the CJEU in response to a reference for a preliminary ruling concerning the interpretation of the right to property under Article 17 of the Charter and the application of EU fundamental rights. The CJEU decided, in 2014, that 'fundamental EU rights could not be applied in relation to national legislation because the provisions of EU law in the subject area concerned did not impose any obligation on Member States with regard to the situation at issue in the main proceedings'.[63]

Yet, despite national sovereignty in direct taxation, Member States' tax authorities - alone - are unable to investigate facts outside their borders. The consequences of that territorial limitation affect their ability to apply and enforce their own tax rules, which in turn raises a question as to the efficacy of taxation for certain foreign income earned by their residents. As permitted by the principle of subsidiarity,[64] the Union may be in a position to adopt measures, at the EU level, that ease the attainment of objectives that Member States, alone, are unable to achieve.[65]

It is in applying the subsidiarity principle that the different DAC were adopted. Yet, the application of fundamental rights to the Original DAC still remains a debated topic.[66] In *Sabou,* the CJEU had the opportunity to provide its interpretation with regard to the application of the 1977 DAC and the impact of certain EU fundamental rights concerned during an exchange of information.

§9.04 THE CJEU DECISION IN *SABOU*

[A] Facts

In a Grand Chamber decision issued in October 2013, the CJEU provided its answer to a request for a preliminary ruling introduced by the *Nejvyšší správní soud,* the Czech Supreme Administrative Court, regarding the appropriate interpretation of the then-applicable Original DAC.[67] The underlying case involved a Czech professional football player, Mr Sabou, who had claimed, on his 2004 tax return, a deduction for expenses

61. Edoardo Traversa & Alice Pirlot, *Tax Sovereignty and Territoriality under Siege: How Far Should the EU Freedoms of Movement Impact on the Territorial Allocation of Taxing Powers Between Member States?, in Principles of Law, Function, Status and Impact in EU Tax Law* 125 (Cécile Brokelind ed., 2014): *see also* Lukasz Adamczyk & Alicja Majdanska, *The Sources of EU Law Relevant for Direct Taxation, in Introduction to European Tax Law on Direct Taxation* 1 (Lang et al. eds., 4th ed., 2016).
62. *Burzio,* C-497/14, para. 31.
63. *Siragusa,* C-206/13, Judgment, EU:C:2014:126, para. 26.
64. Art. 5 TFEU.
65. Art. 2(5) TFEU.
66. José Manuel Calderón Carrero & Alberto Quintas Seara, *The Taxpayer's Right of Defence in Cross-Border Exchange-Of-Information Procedures,* 68 Bull. for Int'l Tax' 206 (2014); Niels Diepvens & Filip Debelva, *The Evolution of the Exchange of Information in Direct Tax Matters: The Taxpayer's Rights under Pressure,* 4 EC Tax Rev. 210 (2015).
67. As defined in n. 5, *supra; see also* §9.02, *supra,* for further details.

relating to services rendered by a Hungarian company, Solomon Group Kft ('SGK'), whose purported role was to facilitate a potential transfer to one of several football clubs selected in different Member States (France, Britain and Spain).[68] Based on the Czech national legislation transposing the Original DAC[69] and the Original DAC itself, the Czech tax authorities contacted the French, British, and Spanish tax administrations so that the latter could confirm business contacts with Mr Sabou (the taxpayer) or any of his representatives.[70]

The Czech tax authorities also requested information from SGK, the company allegedly involved in the potential transfer negotiations considering that Mr Sabou had included paid invoices issued by the company with his tax return.[71] During the underlying proceedings, it appeared that the services were actually rendered by a company based in the Bahamas, Solomon International Ltd ('SIL'), for which SGK acted as an intermediary.[72]

At the end of their investigation, the Czech tax authorities issued an amended tax assessment to Mr Sabou that substantially increased his tax liability as a result of their findings. While he had reported approximately EUR 1,100 in income, the authorities adjusted that amount to approximately EUR 9,800. The increase was made on the basis that none of the alleged business contacts had been confirmed which resulted in the deductions being disallowed. It did not appear clear, from the CJEU's recitation of the facts of the case, whether the Czech tax authorities had tried, at any stage of their investigations, to get confirmation of the veracity and accuracy of the services rendered by SIL, located in the Bahamas.

[1] Domestic Law Provisions and Local Procedures Initiated

The essence of the dispute in this case lays in the rights provided by national law to Czech taxpayers affected by an exchange of information. Based on Czech national law, taxpayers subject to an inspection are entitled: to be notified of any evidence being collected from witnesses (if there is no danger arising out of the delay);[73] to participate in the investigation; and to ask questions to witnesses or experts involved in the tax proceedings.[74] However, in this particular case, the investigation and information gathering were all made by the Czech tax authorities without any prior notification of, consultation with, or participation of Mr Sabou.

Mr Sabou unsuccessfully challenged his revised tax assessment before the Czech tax authorities on several grounds: (i) the information was illegally collected; (ii) he was not invited to participate in the information gathering procedures launched by the tax administrations of the other Member States; and (iii) it was not clear how the information collected from the various football clubs was obtained (e.g., who was

68. *Sabou*, C-276/12, para. 12.
69. Czech law No 253/2000 (on international assistance in tax administration).
70. *Sabou*, C-276/12, para. 13.
71. *Ibid.* para. 12.
72. *Ibid.* para. 14.
73. Art. 31, Czech law No 337/1992 (on the administration of taxes and fees).
74. *Sabou*, C-276/12, para. 11.

interrogated).[75] He subsequently lodged a claim before the Czech Supreme Administrative Court. The latter requested a preliminary ruling from the CJEU seeking interpretation guidance, most notably as to whether certain taxpayers' rights could be inferred from the Directive, such as:

- the right to prior notification;
- the right to take active part in the formulation of the questions addressed to the foreign tax authorities;
- the right to examine witnesses or be notified when the foreign administrations are intending to interrogate witnesses; and
- the right to challenge the accuracy of the information obtained by the requesting tax authorities.

The queries raised by the Czech Court not only questioned the existence of certain taxpayers' rights under the then-applicable Original DAC, but also enquired if such rights could be provided by domestic legislation without being contrary to EU law. In addition, the Czech Court enquired as to the existence of any obligation on the part of the requested tax authorities to adopt minimum standards when transmitting the information gathered in response to a request, so that the sources and collection methods can be clearly identified and assessed.[76]

[2] CJEU Rulings

In a very short decision, the CJEU first confirmed that it had jurisdiction to hear the case on the grounds that, when making use of the Directive to collect information from other Member States' administrations, the requesting Member State was acting within the scope of EU law.[77]

In its analysis, the Court first referred to one of its previous VAT cases, *Twoh International*,[78] in which it had already held that the Original DAC 'does not confer any specific rights on the taxpayer'. Then, it went on to assess whether any EU fundamental rights could be ascertained during the exchange procedure. More particularly, at the centre of the CJEU's discussion was the right of the defence, a general principle of EU law, which generally includes the right of any person to be heard before any individual measure adversely affecting his interest can be adopted. Since the adoption of the Charter, the right of the defence has been codified in Article 41(2) pursuant to the right to good administration. Nevertheless, in the *Sabou* case, it is worth noting that the Charter had to be disregarded as it did not enter into force until after the issuance of the

75. *Ibid.* para. 17.
76. *Ibid.* para. 22.
77. *Ibid.* para. 27 ('The questions referred relating to the obligations of the requesting Member State with regard to the taxpayer concern the implementation of European Union law, and the Court has jurisdiction to examine the application, in this context, of fundamental rights, in particular the right to be heard.')
78. *Twoh International*, C-184/05, Judgment, EU:C:2007:550.

challenged tax assessment.[79] If, however, the Charter could have applied to the case, it would not have led to a different result, since it is clear from the CJEU's case law that that Charter right only concerns institutions and bodies of the Union.[80] Moreover, the right of the defence was interpreted to be a fundamental right to be heard by the Court, which forms part of the EU legal order.[81]

Since the CJEU ruled that no rights could be derived from the Original DAC, certain observers expected certain EU general principles of law[82] would - at the very least - offer taxpayers some minimum protections during cross-border information collection procedures.[83] Yet, the CJEU followed the Opinion of the Advocate General (AG) Kokott,[84] making a clear distinction between the two phases of the exchange of information procedure: first, the investigation stage, during which information is being collected by the requested administration, and then, the contentious stage, during which the taxpayer is sent an amended tax assessment by the requesting authorities based on the newly gathered data.[85] Although information is being collected by the requesting authorities - through an official request and that the answer to that request also follows a certain formalism, the CJEU did not view it as constituting, *per se*, a decision that adversely affects the interest of the taxpayer. In this respect, the CJEU maintained consistency with its previous case law, where it already ruled that:

> [o]nly a measure whose legal effects are binding on the applicant and are capable of affecting his interests by bringing about a distinct change in his legal position is an act or decision which may be the subject of an action for annulment.[86]

The AG Opinion was far-more categorical on this point, as the AG believed that the taxpayer should not have a right to be heard since the information request merely

79. *Sabou*, C-276/12, para. 25.
80. Art. 41(2) Charter.
81. *Sabou*, C-276/12, para. 28.
82. Frans Vanistendael, *The Role of (Legal) Principles, in EU Tax Law, in Principles of Law, Function, Status and Impact in EU Tax Law* 29 (Cécile Brokelind ed., 2014).
83. *E.g.*, CFE ECJ Task Force, Opinion statement ECJ-TF2/2014 of the CFE on the decision of the European Court of Justice in *Sabou* (Case C-276/12), concerning taxpayer rights in respect of exchange of information upon request, 54 Eur. Tax'n 318, para. 21 (2014):

    > the ECJ acknowledged in earlier case law the rights of persons, even though the European Union legislation applicable did not expressly provide for such rights. On the basis of the general EU law principle of the rights of the defence, it conferred rights on the persons involved ... Therefore, the ECJ could have taken the same liberty to strengthen taxpayer's rights in the investigation stage of the exchange of information procedure.

84. *Sabou*, C-276/12, AG Opinion, EU:C:2013:370, para. 56 (AG specifically referred to 'investigative measures' and to 'the decision adopted at the end of the administrative proceedings' to distinguish the two phases.)
85. *Sabou*, C-276/12, para. 40.
86. *Emerald Meats* v *Commission*, C-66/91 and C-66/91 R, Order, EU:C:1991:110; *see also Inuit Tapiriit Kanatami and Others*, C-583/11, Judgment, EU:C:2013:625, para. 91 ('the European Union is a union based on the rule of law in which the acts of its institutions are subject to review of their compatibility with, in particular, the Treaties, the general principles of law and fundamental rights').

attempted to verify the taxpayer 'own statement,'[87] through which, the taxpayer had, in essence, already made use of his right to information self-determination when filing his tax return.

The CJEU concluded that, while there was no basis for recognizing the referred taxpayers' rights under EU law in matters of cross-border exchange of information, it was not, however, contrary to the EU legal order if such rights were otherwise guaranteed by Member States' domestic law.[88] Of course, there was nothing surprising about this statement, as it confirmed the procedural autonomy of Member States in the assessment and enforcement of direct taxes.

[B] The Consequences of the *Sabou* Decision

[1] Absence of Procedural Rights Derived from the Original DAC

The ruling in *Sabou* confirmed the CJEU's previous rulings, according to which the Original DAC did not confer any rights on taxpayers.[89] In *Sabou*, it confirmed that no right of the defence arose during the investigation stage set out by the Original DAC. In *Twoh International*, the CJEU already determined that taxpayers are not able to invoke the Original DAC in their favour. More precisely, they are not able to request their competent tax authorities to engage in a mutual assistance procedure to obtain evidence the taxpayer is unable to display himself.[90] Together, these two rulings make very clear that, with regard to the Original DAC, it is only aimed to govern cooperation between the concerned Member States in cross-border investigations.[91]

Following these two decisions, the starting point could be to anticipate the consequences these rulings may imply for taxpayers. As previously stated in this chapter, by making use of the Original DAC, Member States act within the scope of EU law. It is clear from both the CJEU and the European Court of Human Rights (ECtHR)[92] that the collection of information (the investigation stage) does not, *per se*, affect the interest of taxpayers since the assessment stage only starts when the tax authorities have issued to the taxpayer an adjusted assessment,[93] which is prepared and notified

87. *Sabou*, C-276/12, AG Opinion, para. 59.
88. *Sabou*, C-276/12, para. 45.
89. *Twoh International*, C-184/05.
90. *Ibid.* para. 34:

> It follows that the mutual assistance directive … w[as] not adopted for the purpose of establishing a system for exchanging information between the tax authorities of the Member States allowing them to establish the intra-Community nature of supplies made by a taxable person who is not himself able to provide the necessary evidence for that purpose.

91. *Ibid.* para. 31 ('it is clear from the titles of the mutual assistance directive and the administrative cooperation regulation that they were adopted in order to govern cooperation between the tax authorities of the Member States'.)
92. *See, e.g.*, *Othymia Investments BV v The Netherlands* (dec.), no 75292/10, ECHR 2015-III.
93. *Sabou*, C-276/12, para. 40.

to the taxpayer based on domestic procedural rights. It is also clear that EU fundamental rights cannot find application in domestic legislation matters, as recently reiterated by the CJEU in the Order it issued in the *Burzio* case.[94]

In such circumstances, it is not certain that any of the above-mentioned rulings affect taxpayers' existing safeguards, since individuals are still granted the same rights and protections under domestic legislation that normally apply irrespective of whether the collection proceedings are national or international. That being said, certain practical realties should not be overlooked. As notably confirmed by the IFA 2015 General Report,[95] it appears that some jurisdictions exclude the application of certain domestic procedural safeguards in the context of cross-border exchange of information, due to the fact that administrative assistance rules are often viewed as *lex specialis*.[96] Certain Member States have, nevertheless, addressed this anomaly by including, within their bilateral treaty network, provisions ensuring the application of their national procedural safeguards.[97] This issue remains, however, unresolved, if the cross-border exchange would be made under the existing DAC and that the Member States concerned would simply set aside their domestic procedural safeguards.

[2] No Minimum Content of the Information Transferred

The investigation in *Sabou* was initiated based on invoices submitted by the taxpayer to support the expenses claimed on his tax return. The level of detail of the described services seemed to provide the Czech administration with sufficient direction of where to collect confirming information. Of course, the investigative powers of tax authorities allow them to challenge income and deductions that do not appear well founded, especially when dealing with particularly high amounts, as it is the case for the expenses claimed by Mr Sabou.

Although it is not disputed that the football clubs stated that they had no knowledge of Mr Sabou nor of his representative, that, itself, raises further questions as to whether football clubs keep track of every single contact they have in relation to potential recruits. One could also imagine the existence of informal conversations in which a number of different club officials, agents, and non-official intermediaries might have been involved in off-the-record discussions, which SKG, the Hungarian company, later charged to Mr Sabou. It is no news to anyone that football is a business like any other, in which recruitment strategies and secrets form part of the overall functioning of the sports and entertainment industry. Bearing in mind the particularity of each information collection procedure, a minimum content obligation, as suggested

94. *Burzio*, C-497/14, para. 31.
95. IFA General Report, *The Practical Protection of Taxpayers' Fundamental Rights*, 100b Cahiers de droit fiscal international 50–51 (2015) [hereinafter the 'IFA 2015 General Report'].
96. Schaumburg & Schlossmacher, *supra* n. 18.
97. *See* Art. 12(5) Protocol Amending the Convention for the Avoidance of Double Taxation Between the Swiss Confederation and Spain, signed in Madrid on 29 June 2006 [hereinafter 'Art. 12(5) Swiss/Spain Protocol']; and Art. XVI(d) Protocol Amending the Convention for the Avoidance of Double Taxation Between Norway and Germany, signed in Berlin on 24 June 2013 [hereinafter 'Art. XVI(d) Norway/Germany Protocol'].

by AG Kokott in her opinion,[98] would have strengthened taxpayers' rights by ensuring transparency of the data gathered and respect of the adversarial procedure.[99]

A taxpayer can legitimately expect to be provided probative elements that have been used to deny his deductions. This minimum standard would not only ensure protection for taxpayers seeking to understand the results of the investigation launched, but would also represent a barrier to the use of excessive power by, and the arbitrariness of tax authorities' officials, who do not sufficiently support their findings with credible administrative investigations, thereby resulting in precipitous and ill-founded findings to achieve efficiency-driven standards.[100]

The decision of the Grand Chamber in relation to the absence of a minimum content obligation may, at first, appear difficult to understand from a legal and practical perspective. It is, indeed, difficult to reconcile the ideas of different information collection methods adopted by Member State's tax authorities depending on whether they have to deal with a pure national investigation or a cross-border examination request. Yet, it cannot be excluded that similar methods of collection are used by Member States' administrations in both cases, as investigative methods would be based on domestic legislation and, therefore, guarantee the equivalence of procedures initiated.[101] Along the same lines, this is further reinforced by the idea that, when collecting evidence, Member States' tax authorities would tend to take the greatest care to ensure that the probative value of the information is not later challenged by the taxpayer or anticipate additional requests by the requesting authority on the same tax file.

In that sense, since domestic tax proceedings are to comply with domestic constitutional standards, one might come to the conclusion that such minimum standard is already met by Member States' national procedures and, therefore, explain the CJEU's decision not to adopt a distinct one based on the Original DAC.

Another interesting point that needs to be stressed relates to the decision taken by the Czech Supreme Administrative Court following the CJEU's judgment in *Sabou*. In its decision, the Czech court referred to the probative value of the information collected in case of hearing a witness in absence of the taxpayer. It further stated that the information collected is to be given a reduced level of probative value in absence of the taxpayer at the witness hearing (including if the taxpayer is not permitted to attend under the other State's domestic law). Similar reasoning was applied by the Czech court in relation to the lack of minimum content of the information conveyed. The Czech judges ruled that findings that did not indicate the sources of information could only have limited evidentiary force, thereby requiring additional facts to grant probative value to the evidence provided. This obviously conflicts with the current DAC provisions, which require that 'information ... obtained by the requested authority in accordance with this Directive may be invoked as evidence by the competent bodies of the requesting Member State on the same basis as similar information ... provided by

98. *Sabou*, C-276/12, AG Opinion, para. 82.
99. CFE ECJ Task Force, *supra* n. 83, para. 24.
100. DAC 1, Art. 7.
101. *Sabou*, C-276/12, AG Opinion, para. 64.

an authority of the Member State'.[102] Let us, however, bear in mind that *Sabou* was interpreted under the former DAC 1, which did not contain any equivalent provision.[103] Under the new mutual assistance rules, it appears unlikely that a similar distinction would apply, as it would clearly discriminate against evidence collected abroad when compared to information gathered locally.

The confirmation by the CJEU that the former DAC did not confer any specific rights on taxpayers contributed nothing new to direct taxation matters. Additionally, its refusal to recognize a minimum standard for the information to be conveyed during an exchange appears founded on its prior case law since any obligation to meet a minimum standard already exists at domestic level, where the Member States are already competent for the collection and assessment of their own taxes.

The Luxembourg Court ruling is, however, limited to the questions it received from the referring court and, thus, did not raise *ex officio* the application of other potential fundamental rights. Since the CJEU in *Sabou* mainly addressed the right of the defence in the course of the information gathering stage, it seems particularly relevant to test the applicability of additional fundamental rights provided by the Charter or by EU general principles of law in the context of exchange of information proceedings.

§9.05 REVIEW OF OTHER FUNDAMENTAL RIGHTS IN EXCHANGE OF INFORMATION PROCEDURES

[A] The Principle of Good Administration

One can infer from taxpayers' right to good administration that various levels of protection are available, including a review of the request by the competent authorities (in case of exchange upon request and spontaneous exchange), rights of the defence, rights to access to documents/files, and the right to a minimum content during the collection procedure.[104]

However, based on the wording of the Charter and following the case law of the CJEU, the right to good administration is only applicable to institutions and bodies of

102. The Original DAC, *supra* n. 5.
103. *Ibid.*
104. This interpretation of the scope of the principle of good administration could, by analogy, also oblige the right of good administration to be interpreted in a large manner as to include various other rights. *See, e.g.*, Margrét Vala Kristjánsdóttir, *Good Administration as a Fundamental Right*, 9 Icelandic Rev. Pol. & Admin 237 (2013):

> Right to good administration is not limited to the rights directly enumerated. It is therefore capable of comprising rights other than those specifically enumerated in Article 41(2), i.e. other than the right to be heard, have access to one's file and the obligation of the administration to give reasons for its decision.

Kristjánsdóttir also highlights that '[t]he codification of the general principle in the Charter raises questions as regards the interplay between unwritten and written fundamental rights within the Union's legal order.' *Ibid.*

the Union.[105] In that sense, it is worth noting that the scope of the right to good administration is rather limited, as opposed to Article 51 of the Charter, which provides that 'The provisions of this Charter are addressed to the institutions and bodies of the Union with due regard for the principle of subsidiarity and to Member States only when they are implementing Union law.'[106]

Nonetheless, limitations arise when the right to good administration is invoked as a Charter right.[107] Alternatively, the concept of 'good administration' can also be relied upon as a general principle of EU law, thus allowing extended protection to situations not only affecting EU institutions, but also taxpayers in their relationships with tax authorities.[108]

[1] Review of the Request and Standards of Review

The absence of any enforceable rights during the collection stage, based on the *Sabou* decision, does not mean that taxpayers are deprived of all rights. One must bear in mind that, before agreeing to exchange the requested information or when agreeing to launch an administrative enquiry in absence of the requested data, the tax administration of the requested State must assess the lawfulness of the request received.[109]

The competent authority of the requested State is entrusted with the performance of verifications to ensure that the exchange is made within the limits agreed within the relevant exchange instruments while still ensuring the protections applicable to taxpayers' information in restricted areas covered by confidentiality and secrecy clauses.[110] In this respect, the requested State is to exchange the information after the requesting State has first exhausted its own usual sources of information unless doing so would jeopardize the investigation.[111] The requested State is also not required to transfer information if it would appear contrary to its own legislation regarding the launch of such an investigation or if, under its domestic laws, such information collection would be prohibited.[112] Similarly, the requested State may decline to provide assistance if the information conveyed would contribute to the disclosure of a commercial, industrial, or professional secret, or if the exchange of information would be contrary to public policy.[113] Similar limitations can also be found in the OECD MC, Article 26.[114] Finally, requested States may choose not to convey information that the

105. Art. 41(1) Charter. *See also*, Bucura C. Mihaescu Evans, *The 'Gaps' in Protection Stemming from the (Problematic) Coexistence of Fundamental Rights' Sources in the EU Legal Order*, 52 Cahiers de Droit Européen 141 (2016).
106. Art. 51 Charter.
107. Bucura C. Mihaescu Evans, *The Right to Good Administration at the Crossroads of the Various Sources of Fundamental Rights in the EU Integrated Administrative System* (2015).
108. *Ibid.*
109. DAC 1, Art. 17.
110. Xavier Oberson, *International Exchange of Information in Tax Matters: Towards Global Transparency* 237–238 (2015).
111. DAC 1, Art. 17(1).
112. *Ibid.* Art. 17(2).
113. *Ibid.* Art. 17(4).
114. OECD MC Art. 26(3).

requesting State is unable to procure under its own laws.[115] All of these various requirements are clearly incumbent on the requested State, which has to ensure that the exchange not only complies with its own standards of protection, but also falls within the limits existing in the requesting State's legal framework. In light of the above, it appears that it is predominantly the legal and administrative standards of protection of the requested State that govern mutual assistance mechanisms. One can imagine that trusting the Requesting State to protect such taxpayer rights would somehow result in a biased review. This is even more true when one considers that the requesting State is, first, unsure of the type of information it will obtain via the exchange request. Also, insofar as the requesting State has a greater interest in getting the information to enforce and collect its own taxes, it cannot be excluded that its interest might ultimately prevail over ensuring taxpayers' basic rights. On the other hand, the requested State has a more neutral position to assess the legality of the request, since it is less affected by the interest in tax collection that motivates the requesting State launch of a cross-border examination. Yet, through the Global forum peer-reviewed reports, States may find themselves under intense political pressure to consent to an exchange, since they know that they will be assessed on, for example, the number of files for which exchanges were denied, the restrictiveness of their interpretation of the relevant standards, and the timeliness of their responses.[116]

The question of the standards applied when reviewing a request can raise several concerns, notably in terms of protection levels. It might be that the requested State's standards are lower than the requesting State's, allowing it to obtain information deemed protected by its own domestic legislation. Given the absence of common definitions or minimum standards with regards to definitions of secrecy or public policy, limitations are, therefore, addressed based on the requested State's domestic law.

It remains, however, rather unlikely that an EU Member State would refuse to exchange information on the basis that the requesting State does not follow adequate standards of protection, either in matters of confidentiality or data protection, for instance. In fact, one can expect few challenges to standards of protection on the grounds of overall similarity of standards across the Union and the principle of mutual trust between Member States. It is also not very plausible - in the absence of major public malfunction - that an EU Member State would refuse to exchange information with another Member State considering that its standards of protection are lower. While that reasoning might, in practice, apply to certain third countries with which EU Member States have to cooperate, it is generally inoperable at the EU level.[117]

115. *Ibid.* Art. 26(3)(b); *see also* DAC 1, Art. 17(3).
116. The peer review analysis is generally performed into two phases. Phase 1 relates to the Legal and Regulatory Framework of the studied country while Phase 2 explores the implementation of the standard in practice.
117. *Schrems*, C-362/14, Judgment, EU:C:2015:650.

[2] Remedies Following Unsatisfactory Review

One can imagine a situation in which tax authorities exchange information that they were not otherwise allowed to transfer under the relevant legal instruments (e.g., information covered by professional secrecy). Despite the requested State's discretionary powers in the review of the request, OECD recommendations have urged its member countries to interpret professional secrecy clauses in a more restricted manner.[118] On that basis, a taxpayer might easily suffer from his commercial or industrial secrets being revealed to a foreign administration located in a state in which his technological or business know-how could be divulged. This possibility may, nevertheless, be tempered by tax official's confidentiality obligations or the existence of protected trade secrets (patents), which may act as effective barriers and protections. Still, that potential breach scenario induces the necessity of an *ex post* judicial review, entailing the responsibility of the requested State. An *ex post* judicial action might prove relevant, especially if the disclosure of taxpayers' secrets has caused substantial damage to its business model or reputation. One may also contemplate alternative ways to prevent such damages, by allowing for an *ex ante* judicial review. It does not, however, systematically appear relevant to allow such recourse, especially when it is yet unclear what the requesting State will do with the data gathered. Indeed, one can imagine that the requested information is merely used to verify the accuracy of taxpayers' tax returns, without any further challenge or adjustment, since the collected facts proved the veracity of taxpayer's initial statement. One might also look to a less-extreme stance, one that allows judicial challenge of the request for exchange unless it appears that the taxpayer information might be prejudicial to the investigation as suggested by the IFA 2015 General Report.[119] In cases where evidence could be destroyed or witnesses could be influenced, taking account of the application of the principle of proportionality and the aim pursued by the investigation, it appears reasonable to reduce taxpayer notification and taxpayers' participation rights as a way to maximize the chances of success of the investigation launched. This last solution, however, does not appear fully satisfactory, owing to the fact that most States, when requesting information, would simply request that the procedure remain secret, thereby hindering the application of notification procedures.[120]

An acceptable standard could be to allow an *ex post* review of the information exchanged especially when taxpayers have suffered financial hardship or damages to their business model when the requested State has provided protected information.[121] It is expected that a taxpayer will be able to establish the causal relation between the

118. OECD MC Commentary on Art. 26, para. 3, pt. 19.
119. IFA General Report, *The Practical Protection of Taxpayers' Fundamental Rights*, 100B Cahiers de droit fiscal international 50, 50-51 (2015) [hereinafter the 'IFA 2015 General Report'].
120. Jose M. Calderón, *Taxpayer Protection Within the Exchange of Information Procedure Between State Tax Administrations*, 28 Intertax 462 (2000).
121. In Switzerland, taxpayers can obtain compensation for damages caused by an exchange of information that did not comply with the rules on administrative cooperation. Such situations arise when the information has been exchanged without prior notification of the taxpayer. *See* Administration fédérale des Contributions, *Assistance administrative et entraide judiciaire en*

exchange and the damages suffered to claim a compensation. A recent decision from the ECtHR further specifies that the 'grievance must be an arguable one in terms of the Convention'.[122] In that particular case, the corporate taxpayer failed to produce evidence that the information supplied was incorrect or that it had suffered any damage as result of the exchange of information that occurred without his prior notification.[123]

Since an information exchange can affect the interest of residents as well as non residents, a compensation claim should be open to all taxpayers, irrespective of their residence, as both are in comparable situations in relation to the exchange and its consequences.[124] In the absence of a judicial review open to non-resident taxpayers in the requested State, in addition to triggering non-compliance with EU standards, that situation would create further complications for the relevant taxpayer, since it is unlikely that he would be able to obtain compensation from the requesting State following a violation of the rules of administration cooperation by the requested State.

[3] Right to Access Documents and Files

DAC 1 provides that disclosure of information and documents collected throughout the cooperative exchange process are covered by official secrecy. It contemplates that the requesting State will treat the information received with the same care as it would treat domestic information based on its applicable national laws.[125] The OECD MC Commentary on Article 26 are more restrictive, however, as they prohibit the disclosure of administrative documents at the origin of the enquiry.[126] The restriction on taxpayers' information is further exacerbated by the confidentiality and secrecy imposed on the information exchanged, disallowing the application of domestic law providing for freedom of access to administrative documents.[127]

---

matière fiscale 10 available at www.estv.admin.ch (last visited 28 May 2016); *see also* Art. 21a(2), *Loi fédérale sur l'assistance administrative internationale en matière fiscale*, RO 2013 231.

122. *Othymia Investments BV*, *supra* n. 92, § 34.
123. *Ibid.* para. 13.
124. *See* the German/Dutch example where only residents were able to prevent the exchange via a judicial procedure review; *see also* Madeleine Simonek, *Taxpayers' Rights in the International Exchange of Information Procedure: Where Is the Right Balance?*, 83 Archives de droit fiscal Suisse 859, 872 (2015); and Calderón, *supra* n. 120, at 473.
125. DAC 1, Art. 16(1).
126. OECD MC Commentary on Art. 26, para. 2, pt. 11.
127. OECD, *Keeping It Safe, the OECD Guide on the Protection of Confidentiality of Information Exchanged for Tax Purposes* 33 (2012) [hereafter 'OECD, Keeping It Safe']:

> Domestic legislation (for example, freedom of information or access to information) must not require or allow the release of information obtained under a tax treaty or other exchange of information obtained under a tax treaty or other exchange of information mechanism in a manner inconsistent with the confidentiality obligations in that mechanism.

See also, French CE, 5 Mar. 1993, n°105069 (The French *Conseil d'Etat* had already confirmed the unenforceability of provisions regarding the freedom to access administrative documents in situations covered by a double tax treaty).

This restriction may however be lifted in cases of judicial proceedings. Yet, the authorities of the requested State may be banned from disclosing such information in court proceedings at the request of the requesting authorities.[128] As a result, the level of secrecy suggested by this Commentary appears disproportionate. Not only are taxpayers unable to access the relevant information at the administrative stage, but also once their situation has been confirmed by an administrative act that they can challenge in front of competent courts. One may legitimately wonder what, then, is so secret about the enquiry that renders the exchange request inaccessible to taxpayers but also to the tax judge.[129]

Since the confidential information and business secrets are directly related to the taxpayer, the confidentially argument should not justify a restricted access to his file. Additionally, his private interest in accessing the relevant documents and information exchanged should outweigh any other secrecy considerations, since denying such rights to taxpayers would consist in restricting their basic right to defend themselves.[130]

[4] Right to Reason(s)

Still within the scope of the principle of good administration, it is reasonable to argue that there is an obligation for tax authorities to support all of their findings following a cross-border investigation. In case the information gathered is used for adjusting a taxpayer's situation, and thereby altering his initial return, it is expected that tax administrations would document the reasons for such changes, including their bases and sources supporting adjustment. Besides, the absence of an obligation to justify any such change does not provide taxpayers sufficient protection against potentially abusive or arbitrary investigations launched by administrations, as the content of and methods for making their enquiries are not subject to any transparency or verification requirement.[131] Although such rights cannot be inferred from EU law, at least from the *Sabou* Court's perspective, it can be expected that the requesting State's tax administrations conduct investigations under similar requirements as in national audit procedures, where domestic procedural rules generally make it compulsory for them to disclose the bases and sources used for adjusting taxpayers' returns.

128. OECD MC Commentary on Art. 26, para. 2, pt. 11.
129. In this respect, *see* French CE, 26 Jan. 2011, n°311808 (the French *Conseil d'État* ruled that restrictions imposed by a secrecy clause in a double tax treaty should not lead to the impossibility of disclosing the information request in court and that refusing to disclose such information would be in violation of the adversarial procedure and weaken the taxpayer's rights of the defence).
130. André Lefeuvre, *Le devoir de l'administration fiscale de communiquer au contribuable les renseignements obtenus auprès de tiers : Évolutions et perspectives vingt ans après le rapport Aicardi*, Compte Rendu et Documentation du Colloque Organisé en Sep. 2007.
131. See §9.03, *supra*, and the previous comments made about the consequences of *Sabou*.

[5] Right of Defence

Information collected from the requested State may indeed contradict the situation initially reported by the taxpayer if, for example, the latter neglected to report, or simply omitted, certain details. It is not excluded that, in such a scenario, the relevant authorities would allow a taxpayer the right to be heard before issuing his definitive tax assessment. In such a case, his rights of the defence would be protected by such an invitation.

On the contrary, recent practice shows that national tax authorities apply confidentiality and secrecy standards to the information received, thus typically issuing a final assessment without involving the taxpayer in the final assessment stage. Most rules on exchange of information are viewed as being *lex specialis*,[132] thereby excluding, *de facto*, the application of domestic procedural rights in case of cross-border exchanges of information.[133] Certain jurisdictions even contemplate the imposition of sanctions on tax officials who disclose the information gathered, on the grounds of confidentiality or secrecy clauses.[134] Such opacity forces taxpayers to initiate judicial review to gain access to the documents exchanged during the collection proceedings, as their access is not permitted during the domestic administrative stage.

The non-recognition of rights of the defence during the investigation stage remains questionable considering the added value – in certain cases – of the participation of the taxpayer. Consulting the taxpayer may be helpful in clarifying facts and circumstances, thus reducing burdensome procedures and lengthy litigation. It is not, as such, a practical implementation issue, since such rights can be provided by domestic legislation, but more of an efficiency constraint with regards to the new limitations inserted in the different legal instruments encouraging fast exchanges and urging countries to limit any taxpayers' participation and consultation rights.[135]

Certain jurisdictions have addressed some of these issues by adopting specific provisions relating to taxpayers' rights in their double tax treaty network. By doing so, certain States (e.g., Spain and Germany) intend to limit the erosion of their domestic procedural safeguards when applying bilateral agreements.[136] The IFA 2015 General Report considered this approach a best practice and encouraged the OECD to adopt such wording in its OECD MC Commentary.[137]

Another right that deserves to be further tested is the right to data protection. The safeguards attached to this right are particularly relevant in an ever-increasing, computer-assisted era of collection and transfer of tax information.

132. Schaumburg & Schlossmacher, *supra* n. 18, at 524.
133. Patrick Philip, *Procédures fiscales et garanties des contribuables*, Economica (ed.), 2014, 66.
134. OECD, *Keeping It Safe*, *supra* n. 127, at 33.
135. OECD MC Commentary on Art. 26, para. 3, pt. 14.1.
136. Simonek, *supra* n. 124; *see also* IFA 2015 General Report, *supra* n. 95, at 62.
137. IFA 2015 General Report, *supra* n. 95, at 63; *see also* Art. 12(5) Swiss/Spain Protocol & Art. XVI(d) Norway/Germany Protocol, *supra* n. 97.

[B] Data Protection

The right to data protection is enshrined in Article 8 of the ECHR and Article 8 of the Charter, as both provide for the right to respect private communications and personal data. Nevertheless, such rights may be restricted in accordance with a law when the limitation is necessary to safeguard the economic well-being of a country.[138]

DAC 1 includes references the protection of individuals with regards to personal data processing. More specifically, all exchanges made pursuant thereto were subject to the provisions implementing Directive 95/46/EC on the protection of individuals with regard to the processing of personal data and on the free movement of such data.[139] It also referred to the provisions included in Regulation (EC) 45/2001 on the protection of individuals with regard to the processing of personal data by Community institutions and bodies and on the free movement of such data.[140] Despite the objective of Directive 95/46/EC – to establish minimum standards in relation to the level of protection of rights and freedoms of individuals across Member States – it authorizes the Member States to adopt exemptions and restrictions to safeguard 'an important economic or financial interest of a Member State or of the European Union, including monetary, budgetary and taxation matters'.[141] Such safeguard measures can justify legislative limitations on certain obligations and rights developed in said Directive, such as data quality standards[142] and the right of access by the relevant individuals to the data processed.[143] The application of Regulation 45/2001 to EU institutions and bodies does not impact any of the rights and obligations of the Member States within the scope of Directive 95/46/EC. Rather, the limitations contained in said Regulation are similar to the ones described in the Directive 95/46/EC whenever measures are necessary to safeguard the general interest of Member States.[144]

With the most recent provisions allowing automatic exchange of information,[145] taxpayers (referred to individually as a 'Reportable Person') are notified in advance by competent financial institutions so that taxpayers can 'exercise their data protection rights' before the information is transferred to the competent tax administration.[146] Additionally, taxpayers are to be informed should a breach of security in the relevant

138. Directive 95/46/EC, Art. 13(1)(e).
139. Council Directive 95/46/EC of the European Parliament and of the Council of 24 October 1995 on the protection of individuals with regard to the processing of personal data and on the free movement of such data [1995] OJ L281/31 as amended, with the last consolidated version published on 20 November 2003 as Eur-Lex Document 01995L0046-20031120, and subsequently repealed, effective as of 25 May 2918, by Regulation (EU) 2016/679 of the European Parliament and of the Council of 27 April 2016 on the protection of natural persons with regard to the processing of personal data and on the free movement of such data, and repealing Directive 95/46/EC (General Data Protection Regulation), Art. 94(1).
140. Regulation (EC) No. 45/2001 of the European Parliament and of the Council of 18 December 2000 on the protection of individuals with regard to the processing of personal data by the Community institutions and bodies and on the free movement of such data [2001] OJ L8/1.
141. Directive 95/46/EC, Art. 13(1)(e).
142. *Ibid.* Art. 6.
143. *Ibid.* Art. 12.
144. Regulation 45/2001, *supra* n. 140.
145. DAC 2, *supra* n. 12.
146. *Ibid.* Art. 21(2).

system become 'likely to adversely affect the protection of [their] personal data or privacy'.[147] It is thus reasonable to assume that the data protection rights expressed in DAC 2 are very limited and only refer to taxpayers' rights to have certain errors and typographical errors rectified by the reporting paying agent.

The current EU legislative acts do not require the application of minimum standards of protection in relation to data protection in administrative cooperation proceedings, as the Member States are able to opt out of certain provisions of general interest. Indeed, Member States are not required to adopt all of the standards developed in the Directive, thus, encouraging a diversity of standards across the Union.[148] The first report on the implementation of the Data Protection Directive[149] confirmed a divergence of legislation standards between Member States. Yet, the consultation results among Member States and national supervisory authorities showed, at the time, no necessity to amend the Directive.[150] This disparity does not necessarily presume the absence of any protective framework since domestic data protection standards remain applicable and provide different safeguards according to the Member States involved.

At the OECD level, recommendations have been issued in relation to the protection of confidential information exchanged for tax purposes.[151] These generally contain certain best practices and practical examples from various jurisdictions for suggested minimum standards. The OECD report,[152] issued in 2012, called for higher standards of protection at the domestic level in relation to the development of internal confidentiality policies (e.g., on designation of competent officers on data protection and on regular training of tax officials on their role and responsibilities). The 2012 OECD report also made recommendations with respect to matters of adequate encryption, electronic exchange, and storage standards, and annexed a checklist that national

147. *Ibid.* Art. 25(3).
148. *See, e.g.*, the restrictions permitted by Directive 95/46/EC, Art. 13 on necessary measures for safeguarding the financial interest of a Member State. The scope of the exempted rights includes a restriction on the rights that personal data must be: processed fairly and lawfully (Art. 6a); collected for specified, explicit, and legitimate purposes; and not be further processed in a way incompatible with those purposes. Further processing of such data for historical, statistical, or scientific purposes is not considered to be incompatible, provided that the Member States provide: appropriate safeguards (Art. 6b) that are: adequate, relevant, and not excessive in relation to the purposes for which the data is collected and/or further processed (Art. 6c); accurate and, where necessary, kept up to date; every reasonable step to be taken to ensure that data that are inaccurate or incomplete, having regard to the purposes for which they were collected or for which they were further processed, are erased or rectified (Art. 6d); and the data be kept in a form that permits identification of data subjects for no longer than is necessary for the purposes for which the data were collected or for which they are further processed. Member States must also lay down appropriate safeguards for personal data stored for longer periods for historical, statistical, or scientific use (Art. 6e). Other restrictions are permitted by the Directive in matters of information to be given to the data subject (Art. 10) and on information where the data have not been obtained from the data subject (Art. 11). Additional restrictions also apply to the right of access to the data by the date subject (Art. 12).
149. Report from the Commission of 15 May 2003, COM(2003) 265.
150. *Ibid.*
151. OECD recommendation on cross-border cooperation in the enforcement of laws protecting privacy, OECD 2007.
152. OECD, *Keeping It Safe*, *supra* n. 127, at 33.

authorities might want to use to review their internal standards.[153] Obviously, the 2012 OECD Report merely made recommendations that each State was free to adopt within the limits of its domestic legislation, in absence of minimum rules adopted at the EU level.

As seen above, limitations and exemptions to data protection pursuant to EU legislation have been authorized for tax matters, which allow Member States to take adequate measures to safeguard their financial and economic interest. Yet, a rather surprising outcome resulted from *Bara and Others*,[154] decided by CJEU in 2015. In that personal data matter, the Romanian tax authorities had covertly transferred to the Romanian social security administration information relating to the income reported by self-employed taxpayers (the plaintiffs). On the basis of the information received, the social security authorities required the payment of arrears of contributions to the self-employed individuals. The plaintiffs challenged the lawfulness of the personal data exchange in the light of Directive 95/46 claiming that the information was used for other purposes than tax and that there was no information of the concerned individuals prior to the exchange. The CJEU ruled in favour of the plaintiffs as it interpreted Directive 95/46 as precluding national measures from allowing the transfer and processing of personal data between public administrative bodies without the information of the data subjects. This decision is compelling as it brings to light a higher level of protection for exchange of information between national administrations than in cross-border situations. Nevertheless, the facts of the case can nuance this difference in treatment since *Bara and Others* did not *per se* deal with exchange of information between tax administrations of different Member States and the exchange was initiated on the basis of national law.

In the absence of any binding measures at the EU level, however, the suggestion made by the IFA 2015 General Report, which recommends an independent board to review data protection standards,[155] is a good start, provided that Member States agree to such an 'intrusion' and accept external monitoring and/or recommendations to improve the security of their systems. The CJEU's recent decision in *Schrems* also calls into question the level of protection granted to taxpayers' personal data when exchanged with third countries.[156]

[C] Right to an Effective Remedy and Fair Trial

Another fundament rights concern is the availability of remedies for taxpayers whose rights have been breached following an exchange of information procedure. The right to an effective remedy and fair trial is codified in Article 47 of the Charter. In certain jurisdictions where taxpayers are allowed to be informed of the information collection procedure, national legislation provides the right to an *ex ante* judicial review. Such legal action – whose aim is to have a judge assess the lawfulness of a request and its

153. *Ibid.*
154. *Bara and Others*, C-201/14, Judgment, EU:C:2015:638.
155. IFA 2015 General Report, *supra* n. 95, at 52.
156. *Schrems*, C-362/14.

conformity with the standard of 'foreseeable relevance' (prior to the exchange being made with the requesting State) – has been 'demonized' in OECD's Global Forum peer-reviews, thus, encouraging States to suppress such a judicial remedy on the grounds of efficiency of the investigation (e.g., Switzerland and Portugal).[157] Yet, most jurisdictions that allow such recourse have exceptional procedures – outside of the normal judicial review process – providing fast-track decisions to avoid delay of the exchange of information.[158] The efficiency argument, thus, is not entirely convincing despite the suspensive effect of the judicial review against the exchange request.

Nevertheless, *ex ante* judicial review can only address the validity of the information request procedure *per se* without discussing the reasonableness of the material facts at the origin of the tax audit procedure launched in the requesting State. As such, any taxpayer willing to challenge the lawfulness of the procedure initiated in the requesting State is also required to introduce an additional legal recourse in that State.[159]

The suppression of *ex ante* judicial reviews is subject to criticism knowing that certain jurisdictions have been 'bullied' to do so by international pressure.[160] Still, the suppression of such recourse does not present, *per se*, a fundamental threat to taxpayers, as the latter are still able to have their situation reviewed, first, by the local tax authorities in which they are subject to adjusted measures (if any) and, second, by an independent court before which factual and legal arguments can be assessed in line with the rule of law and national constitutional standards.[161]

In other circumstances, however, the right to an effective remedy and fair trial is put in serious jeopardy, particularly when third parties are involved in an exchange procedure and are required to provide information. It is, for example, the situation in a pending preliminary ruling request sent to the CJEU by the Administrative Court of Luxembourg.[162] In *Berlioz Investment Fund*, a Luxembourg company ('Berlioz') was asked to provide certain information in relation to its French subsidiary following an

---

157. IFA 2015 General Report, *supra* n. 95, at 51.
158. *See, e.g.*, the exceptional recourse introduced by both Luxembourg (Law of 31 of March relating to the adoption of certain tax conventions and on the procedure applicable to exchange of information upon request) and Switzerland (Federal law on international administrative assistance in tax matters) (these alternative-recourse provisions permitted taxpayers to directly lodge an urgent claim in front of an administrative court to assess the validity of the exchange request without having to first introduce an administrative complaint in front of the competent tax office that had agreed to exchange with the requesting State); *see also* Anette Kugelmüller-Pugh, Cross-Border Information – The German Approach, 56 European Tax'n 107 (2016) (interim measures allowed by German law in a similar matter).
159. *See, e.g.*, Luxembourg, Conseil d'Etat, Avis complémentaire, Projet de loi 6072/06 portant approbation de diverses conventions fiscales, protocoles et avenants, concernant les doubles impositions, Feb. 2010.
160. *See, e.g.*, OECD, *Global Forum on Transparency and Exchange of Information for Tax Purposes Peer Reviews, Luxembourg 2011, Phase 1, Legal and Regulatory Framework*; *see also* Xavier Oberson, *New Exchange of Information Versus Tax Solutions of Equivalent Effect, Swiss Report*, EATLP Congress 2014; *see also* IFA 2015 General Report, *supra* n. 95, at 62.
161. *The Impact of Legal Frameworks for Tax Auditing on Intra-Community Cooperation, in The International Guide to Tax Auditing* Ch. 5, 413–414 (Robert N.J. Kamerling ed., 1999).
162. Request for a preliminary ruling in *Berlioz Investment Fund*, C-682/15, EU:C:2016:94; *see also* Luxembourg's complete request for preliminary ruling, Cour administrative Grand-Duché de Luxembourg, 17 Dec. 2015, Numéro du rôle : 36893C.

information exchange request initiated by the French tax authorities. The Luxembourg tax administration – after receiving the information request from France – issued an information request order to Berlioz requiring their participation, after having first assessed and agreed to the validity of the French tax authorities' request. The questions raised by the French administration mainly addressed the effective place of management of the branch and other additional organizational questions. While Berlioz agreed to provide certain information in relation to its French subsidiary, it refused to answer other questions such as the subsidiary shareholders' identities, addresses and percentage of holding in the capital of the entity on the grounds that these elements were not foreseeably relevant to the investigation launched on the subsidiary.

In application of Luxembourg domestic law, the Luxembourg tax authorities imposed an administrative fine of EUR 250,000 on Berlioz, as it did not comply with the information request order. Berlioz challenged the imposition of the administrative fine before the Luxembourg Administrative Tribunal and later appealed to the Administrative Court, as judicial review is still permitted *but* only to examine the merits of the fine.[163] Berlioz claimed that it had been deprived of its right to an effective remedy since judicial review was no longer available to assess whether the underlying French exchange request actually met the standard of foreseeable relevance. In essence, Berlioz argued that the validity of the fine imposed for non-compliance with the order can only be assessed through recourse to a separate judicial review which will rule on the relevance of the information requested. Such recourse – initially created shortly after Luxembourg's commitment to end its long opt-out of the OECD exchange of information clause – was subsequently abolished in November 2014, pursuant to a recommendation from the OECD's Global Forum. Berlioz also complained that it was not able to access the documents relating to the exchange of information and, thus, was not able to fully exercise its rights of defence. The request for preliminary ruling, as of this writing, remains pending before the CJEU, which allows one to question whether the burden imposed on Berlioz was not, in fact, excessive, particularly with respect to the size of the fine and the behaviour it intended to sanction. It may be worth noting that the fine was reduced by the Administrative Tribunal to EUR 150,000.[164] With this in mind, it will be interesting to see whether the fine's qualification as an administrative fine and its proportionality[165] will render the review of the foreseeable relevance criterion necessary by a Luxembourg Court since no procedures were available to prevent the exchange of information by assessing the merits of the French request.

163. LU: Art. 5, *Loi du* 25 Nov. 2014.

164. In this respect, *see* Jacques Malherbe, *Administrative tax surcharge and the proportionality principle*, EATLP 2015 Thematic report.

165. Despite the fine's qualification as an 'administrative pecuniary penalty' by the domestic legislation, the meaning of 'criminal charge' under the ECHR is established autonomously. The test developed in *Engel and Others v The Netherlands* (dec.), no 5100/71; 5101/71; 5102/71; 5354/72; 5370/72, ECHR 1976, includes a three-part test that takes into consideration: (i) the classification of the proceedings in domestic law, (ii) the nature of the offence; and (iii) the severity of the penalty which may be imposed.

In January 2017, AG Wathelet delivered his much-awaited opinion on the *Berlioz Investment Fund* case. He suggested that the pecuniary penalty imposed by Luxembourg domestic legislation to sanction Berlioz for its lack of complete cooperation under DAC 1 constituted an implementation of EU law. On this basis, he concluded that the Charter was applicable and more specifically that a person may rely on Article 47 of the Charter which provides for the right to an effective remedy and fair trial. He also proposed that Article 47 is interpreted in a way that allows a Court to assess the legality of the information request order only to the extent that the review lies on a brief examination ensuring that the information request meets the foreseeable relevance standard. He additionally argued in favour of the communication of the request information (upon which is subsequently issued the information order) to the Court and third party concerned (e.g., Berlioz). In cases where the communication of such request may compromise the effectiveness of the investigation, it is for the authorities of the requested State to produce evidence to support the potential incurred risk and for the Court to ultimately rule on the admissibility of the request.

First, the AG Opinion is of particular interest as it recognizes to third parties involved certain rights of the defence during the investigation stage. Although the AG proposal may seem to deviate from the ruling of the CJUE in *Sabou*, it is justified by the lack of comparability between the two cases. Finding that Berlioz is a *mere* 'intermediary' used to complement the tax information in possession of the French tax authorities, it does not seem *a priori* that a right to an effective remedy could be justified. Yet, according to AG Wathelet third party's rights of the defence should be recognized during the investigation stage since it is not involved in the contentious stage and therefore derives no rights of action once the tax assessment is issued to the concerned taxpayer (contentious stage). With respect to this distinction, the ECtHR had previously ruled in a 2015 exchange of information case[166] that the distinction between the applicant (a Dutch company, third-party to the proceedings) and the taxpayer directly affected by the tax investigation (a Spanish company) 'cannot be decisive'.[167] In that decision, the Spanish tax administration had requested the Dutch tax authorities to provide certain information concerning the links and transactions existing between the Dutch and Spanish entities. The Dutch tax authorities - already in possession of the requested information - transferred it to their Spanish counterpart without notifying the Dutch company until the exchange had occurred. The Dutch entity complained that the information was covertly supplied to the Spanish tax authorities without being given prior notification rights. Yet, the ECtHR denied the recognition of any notification rights in that specific scenario stating that 'it cannot be a requirement ... of the Convention that prior notice of lawful tax investigations or exchanges of tax-related information be given to all persons potentially implicated'.[168] Certain parallels and differences can be noted when looking further at these two situations. Like in *Berlioz Investment Fund*, the third party is not *per se* the subject of the tax investigation but used directly (*Berlioz Investment Fund*) or indirectly (*Othymia Investments BV*) to obtain complementary

166. For further discussion regarding *Othymia Investments BV*, *supra* n. 92, see §9.05[E], *infra*.
167. *Othymia Investments BV*, *supra* n. 92, § 44.
168. *Ibid.*

information on the 'targeted' taxpayer. But, unlike in *Othymia Investments BV*, where the third party did not actively take part in the information request proceedings, the Luxembourg subsidiary was required to supply the necessary information requested by the French tax authorities and suffered a pecuniary 'collateral damage' in Luxembourg by refusing to answer all the questions raised by the French tax administration. It is probably safe to argue that these two cases are not objectively comparable and that *Berlioz Investment Fund* appears in a relatively stronger position to have its right of defence recognized.

Second, AG Wathelet proposed to have a Court assess the lawfulness of the information request order. Should the CJEU follow that view, Luxembourg may have to reinstate judicial review against information requests. The recourse was suppressed in November 2014 following peer pressure asserted by the Global Forum.

[D] Equality Before the Law and Non-discrimination

Another recurrent argument in the context of cross-border exchanges of information exchanges is that taxpayers are deprived of equivalent protection, depending on whether they are engaged in national or cross-border activities or investments. Equality before the law and non-discrimination safeguards are, therefore, also worth reviewing in the context of mutual administrative assistance, as the application of a different regime in cross-border exchange implicates the right to equal treatment.

It has been noted on several occasions[169] that there are procedural differences between domestic and cross-border situations. Indeed, in purely national situations, taxpayers are provided with a certain set of rules that generally allow them to be heard by the relevant tax authorities in case of amendments to their initial filing and before a final decision is taken.

It seems obvious that taxpayers wishing to challenge their tax assessment – following the end of the investigation – will do so following the applicable domestic rules of the country in which they are taxable. It is, indeed, difficult to infer any EU fundamental rights in such national proceedings, considering that the Member States have not agreed to such a transfer of power and, thus, remain sovereign in the assessment and collection of direct taxes.[170]

It is true that taxpayers, depending on the jurisdictions in which they are taxable, will experience different standards in terms of administrative and/or judicial proceedings and may enjoy greater or lesser rights in each of the legal systems of the different Member States. It is not, however, for EU law to require consistency or equal treatment of taxpayers in substantive and procedural rights in areas outside of the Union competence unless Member States agree on minimum standards via the adoption of a Directive for instance. Knowing that such disparities exist, one might wonder whether fundamental freedoms are, in fact, at risk. It does not seem entirely convincing that

169. *See, e.g.*, *Sabou*, C-276/12 (national procedures would have allowed the taxpayer certain rights that were disregarded by the Czech tax authorities who had collected cross-border information via Council Directive 77/799/EEC.
170. *Burzio*, C-497/14, para. 31.

taxpayers will refrain from investing outside their borders or from exercising their rights to free movement considering that their rights are less protected in cross-border matters. The European Commission and EU institutions, more generally, rather consider that exchange of tax information contributes to the Union's single market objective and secures its fairness and economic efficiency goals.[171]

Nevertheless, differences in treatment of taxpayers' rights will tend to decline, since automatic exchange of information is the new international standard for tax information exchange.[172] That form of exchange contributes to abolishing the suspicion on few taxpayers and fulfils the principle of equality since all taxpayers are treated in a similar manner. It may appear inconsistent that in automatic exchange matters, taxpayers are provided with a notification right by their financial institution before the information is transmitted by the paying agent to the competent tax authorities, while such prior notice is not given in exchange upon-request proceedings. The difference could be explained by the fact that, in exchange-upon-request matters, the requesting State's administration suspects a specific individual (or a group of individuals following the possibility of introducing group requests in certain cases)[173] of non-compliance and, thus, wants to limit certain taxpayers' rights as a way to avoid undermining its information collection procedure (e.g. prevent tampering with or destruction of evidence). Another explanation could be that the burden of notifying taxpayers has been shifted to external paying agents representing significant cost reduction and staff resources optimization for tax authorities, which also represents a consistent approach since financial institutions are already in possession of such information, although they had to adapt their internal systems to the transmission requirements imposed by mutual assistance rules.[174]

[E] Respect for Private and Family Life

Finally, another right that might be impacted by exchange of information procedures is the right to have one's private and family rights respected. Such rights can be found in Article 7 of the Charter and in Article 8 of the ECHR. In order for taxes to be assessed according to the ability-to-pay principle, taxpayers must reveal a number of private and sensitive details about their personal situation, consumption habits, and even political or religious affiliations in certain jurisdictions.[175] In turn, tax administrations are expected to comply with confidentiality and professionalism requirements to maintain the secrecy of such details and ensure the protection of all taxpayers' data.[176] Nevertheless, a refusal to exchange tax information on the grounds that it is a violation of taxpayer's right to privacy and family life appears unlikely to succeed, as long as the

171. European Commission, Communication from the Commission to the European Parliament and the Council on tax transparency to fight tax evasion and avoidance, COM(2015) 136.
172. OECD, Standard for Automatic Exchange of Financial Account Information, Common Reporting Standard, 2014.
173. OECD MC Commentary on Art. 26, para.1, pt. 5.2.
174. *See, e.g.*, DAC 2, Annex 1: Reporting and due diligence rules for financial account information.
175. OECD, *Keeping It Safe*, *supra* n. 127, at 33.
176. *Ibid.*

tax administration's interference therewith is in accordance with law and is necessary in a democratic society[177] as confirmed for example in an ECtHR case in 1996.[178] Banking information had been seized by the tax authorities during searches of the domicile of a German taxpayer (the applicant's son-in-law) suspected of tax evasion, including some letters from financial institutions based in the Netherlands. The correspondence actually belonged to a relative of the concerned German taxpayer, a Dutch national (the applicant). The German tax authorities transmitted the information to the Dutch tax authorities on the grounds that taxes were assumed to have been evaded in the Netherlands. The applicant claimed that his privacy rights had been violated under Article 8 ECHR. The ECtHR found, however, that the interference was justified by a German provision on mutual administrative assistance and that the interference was necessary, as it was taken in the interest of the economic well-being of the country. The spontaneous exchange procedure was deemed proportionate to the aim pursued, which was to ensure the effective collection and payment of taxes. The applicant had also complained that the transmission of his banking details had infringed his rights to peaceful enjoyment of his possessions under Article 1, Protocol 1. In a very brief paragraph, the Court recalled that 'States may enforce such laws as they deem necessary to secure the payment of taxes.'

Another interesting element arising from this case is the argument accepted by the German federal tax court, which held that the spontaneous information exchange was not disproportionate, as the elements transferred were information that the taxpayer would have had to exchange with the Dutch tax authorities had he been 'diligent'. A similar argument was made by AG Kokott in her Opinion in the *Sabou* case, in which she stated that 'negative factual consequences of the [administrative] inquiries could be attributed primarily to the [taxpayer's] deficiency' to completely and accurately report the required information.[179]

In a more recent decision of the ECtHR issued in 2015,[180] a Dutch company ('Othymia') complained that tax information was provided by the Dutch Ministry of Finance to the Spanish tax administration while the Dutch company was not given prior notice. The Dutch authorities had answered a Spanish request, which asked questions about the links between Othymia, a separate Spanish entity, and a certain bank. Othymia claimed that there had been a violation of its privacy with respect to its correspondence under Article 8 ECHR, such that the exchange had no legal basis. Othymia argued that the exchange provision provided in the Netherlands-Spanish double tax treaty did not allow the Dutch authorities to carry out administrative investigations, rather it was limited to exchange of information it already had in its possession. The ECtHR, replied that then-applicable Directive on administrative cooperation (77/779) superseded that treaty's provisions.[181] Consequently, the ECtHR

177. Art. 8(2) ECHR & Art. 52(1) Charter. Although worded differently, limitations in both instances must be in accordance with the law and proportionate/necessary to meet objectives of general interest.
178. *F.S. v. Germany* (dec.), no. 30128/96, ECHR 1996-I.
179. *Sabou*, C-276/12, AG Opinion, para. 59.
180. *Othymia Investments BV*, *supra* n. 92.
181. *Ibid.* paras 26, 31.

found that the Dutch interference with Othymia's right to privacy was in accordance with the law; further, it found that such interference pursued a legitimate aim, as the collection of taxes, including for other EU country, contributes to 'the economies of the European Union Member[s] forming a unified whole'.[182]

The ECtHR referred to the CJEU's *Sabou* case, adopting a similar distinction between the 'investigative' and 'contentious' phases described by the CJEU. Additionally, claiming a violation of Article 13 of the ECHR, the Company complained that it had no access to a recourse preventing the exchange of information nor to an effective *ex post* procedure to verify the lawfulness of the exchange once it was agreed by the Dutch Ministry of Finance. The ECtHR dismissed Othymia's Article 13 claim on the grounds that investigations could be undertaken 'covertly' in taxation matters[183] and that Othymia did, in fact, have access to *ex post* reviews in front of two domestic courts in the Netherlands.[184]

These two ECtHR cases demonstrate that EU Member States' tax authorities' investigative powers can be broad and that Member States' general interest in collecting tax revenue trumps other personal considerations attributed to a taxpayer provided the interference is legally justified and proportionate to the aim pursued.

§9.06 CONCLUSION

Member States' tax authorities' powers have been reinforced in exchange of information matters through the adoption of more sophisticated directives on administrative cooperation and by following the OECD's update of Article 26 OECD MC. While exchange mechanisms are provided by EU law and bilateral agreements, taxpayer procedural safeguards generally remain governed by Member States' domestic legislation[185] where they are, in principle, subject to various fundamental rights. Certain administrative practices in Member States have, however, shown differences in treatment between domestic and cross-border situations, which the authors believe is bad practice. To limit taxpayers' rights erosion in cross-border circumstances certain Member States (Germany, Spain) have introduced procedural safeguards directly into their bilateral agreements to ensure similar protections as in domestic law.

From the conclusions drawn in this chapter, it appears quite clearly that it is the requested State's standard of protection that applies. It is entrusted with the duty to ensure that the exchange complies with relevant cooperation instruments and any applicable limitations.[186] Serious concerns may, however, be raised as to whether that duty is effectively assumed in practice by requested States, as they are under pressure

182. *Ibid.* para. 41.
183. *Ibid.*
184. *Ibid.* para. 47.
185. CFE ECJ Task Force, *supra* n. 83, para. 29; *see also* Calderón, *supra* n. 120.
186. *See* §9.05[A], *supra*.

to obtain an acceptable rating under the OECD's Global Forum peer-review monitoring, which encourages exchanges to the widest extent possible and in a prompt manner.[187]

The development of automatic exchange of information provides, at least, some relatively satisfactory answers according to the authors. Taxpayers are treated equally and are provided the ability to review and modify their financial details before any information is sent to their competent tax authorities. Considering that automatic exchange of information is becoming the new global standard, it is expected that other forms of information exchange will tend to decline, thereby reducing certain underlying taxpayers' rights issues. The adoption of the automatic exchange of information reveals, however, new challenges in matters of data protection that require adequate monitoring and supervision of national administrations.[188]

187. As previously described, the peer-review analysis is generally performed into two phases: Phase 1 relates to the Legal and Regulatory Framework of the studied country, while Phase 2 explores the implementation of the standard in practice.
188. *See, e.g.*, *Schrems*, C-362/14.

PART IV EU Tax Law and External Relations

CHAPTER 10

The Influence of EU Tax Law on the EU Member States' External Relations

Daniel S. Smit

§10.01 INTRODUCTION

Practice shows that the Member States of the European Union (EU) maintain a diversified range of economic relations with non-EU Member States. A large number of non-EU-based enterprises are carrying on business in the EU. Conversely, numerous EU-based enterprises are also carrying on business outside the territory of the Union. Accordingly, trade and investment between Member States and non-Member States is, nowadays, similarly promoted by abolishing or reducing tax or other obstacles to international flows of goods, services, and/or investment between the Member States and third countries. The Union has concluded a large number of economic integration agreements over the past decades with countries all around the world, such as countries in Eastern Europe, the Euro-Mediterranean countries, and the African, Caribbean, and Pacific states. The Treaty on the Functioning of the European Union (TFEU) itself also provides for a substantial degree of economic openness vis-à-vis third countries, particularly by means of the Treaty provisions relating to the free movement of capital.[1]

The overall benefits of these investments into the Union are well-established, as recognized, for instance, by the European Commission, notably in relation to the role of such investment in creating jobs, optimizing resource allocation, transferring

1. For a more detailed discussion, see Daniel S. Smit, *EU Freedoms, Non-EU Countries and Company Taxation: An Overview and Future Prospect*, 21 EC Tax Rev. 233 (2012). This paper has been largely based on this earlier publication.

technology and skills, increasing competition, and boosting trade.[2] Conversely, a large number of EU-based enterprises maintain a diversified range of investments outside the Union. These outward investments are perceived to make a positive and significant contribution to the competitiveness of European enterprises as well, notably in the form of higher productivity.[3] Accordingly, in relationships with non-EU Member States, 'economic openness' is key. Economic openness was also stressed, for instance, by the European Commission in its 2006 Communication 'Global Europe: Competing in the World'. According to the Commission, European economic openness is vital for creating jobs and growth in Europe and for Europe's international competitiveness; European protectionism, on the other hand, raises prices for consumers and business, and limits choice.[4]

The question that I will address in this contribution is: How does the Union's economic openness vis-à-vis third countries affect the Member States' sovereignty in the field of corporate taxation? To answer this question, I will firstly examine the extent to which the Member States' sovereignty in the field of corporate taxation vis-à-vis non-EU Member States is affected by the free movement of capital under Article 63 TFEU, as interpreted by the Court of Justice of the European Union (CJEU) (negative integration). Next, I will examine the extent to which the Member States' competence in the field of corporate taxation vis-à-vis non-EU Member States is affected by the legislative powers of the Union (positive integration).

§10.02 NEGATIVE INTEGRATION IN THE FIELD OF CORPORATE TAXATION

[A] The CJEU Has Competence to Interpret EU Free Movement Provisions Vis-À-Vis Non-EU Member States

On the basis of Article 63 TFEU, capital movements between Member States and non-EU Member States (third countries) may not be restricted. The CJEU has competence to interpret this provision in the field of corporate taxation. When doing so, the CJEU has tended to interpret the free movement of capital vis-à-vis third countries rather extensively in favour of the taxpayer (for example, in the field of withholding taxes[5] and anti-abuse rules[6]). However, it has also allowed significant (but rather fragmented) derogations in favour of the Member States. Firstly, it has held that the free movement of capital is not applicable to, and hence does not protect, third-country

2. *E.g.*, Communication from the Commission to the Council, the European Parliament, the European Economic and Social Committee and the Committee of the Regions of 7 July 2010, *Towards a comprehensive European international investment policy*, COM(2010) 343 final, 3.
3. *E.g.*, *ibid.*
4. Communication from the Commission to the Council, the European Parliament, the European Economic and Social Committee and the Committee of the Regions of 4 October 2006, *Global Europe: Competing in the World*, COM(2006) 567 final, 4.
5. *Santander Asset Management SGIIC*, Joined Cases C-338/11 to C-347/11, Judgment, EU:C:2012:286.
6. *Itelcar*, C-282/12, Judgment, EU:C:2013:629.

investments, when the contested corporate tax measure is exclusively confined to situations involving an investment that confers on the investor definite influence over corporate decisions,[7] which also implies that corporate tax measures solely designed for groups of companies (multinational enterprises) fall outside the scope of the free movement of capital. On the other hand, since the CJEU's ruling in *FII 2*, it is beyond doubt that a national rule that is not confined to situations involving such definite investor influence can be assessed under the free movement of capital, unless the contested rule is designed to regulate market access (which will probably never be the case as far as corporate tax measures are concerned).[8] This means that such broader rules can be scrutinized under the free movement of capital, even if - as a factual matter - an investor happens to have a definite influence over its third-country investment.

Secondly, based on the grandfathering clause in Article 64(1) TFEU, restrictive tax measures that already existed on 31 December 1993 and that involve 'direct investment - including investment in real estate - establishment, the provision of financial services or the admission of securities to capital markets' are excluded from the liberalization requirement under Article 63 TFEU. Broadly speaking, one can conclude that the grandfathering clause under Article 64(1) TFEU applies to relatively large third-country investments and *limits* the protection that third-country investors could otherwise derive from the free movement of capital under Article 63(1) TFEU. However, in each individual case, an assessment of the grandfathering clause is essential when examining the scope of protection that a third-country investor is provided under the freedom of investment.[9]

Finally, already in *FII 1*, the CJEU recognized that a Member State may be able to demonstrate that a restriction on capital movements to or from non-EU Member States is justified for a particular reason in circumstances in which that same reason would not constitute a valid justification for a restriction on capital movements between Member States.[10] As far as the justification grounds for situations involving third-country investments are concerned, the following can be observed. Reasons relating to a lack of reciprocity,[11] loss of income,[12] and administrative difficulties,[13] such reasons cannot be accepted more easily in a third-country context when compared to situations involving intra-Union investments. On the other hand, depending on the precise objective and nature of the contested corporate income tax measure and subject to the principles of suitability and necessity, there may in my view be more room to accept reasons relating to the principle of territoriality, the need to preserve the coherence of the tax system, the need to combat abuse, the need for effective fiscal supervision, the

7. *Kronos International*, C-47/12, Judgment, EU:C:2014:2200; *Test Claimants in the FII Group Litigation*, C-35/11, Judgment, EU:C:2012:707 [hereinafter *FII 2*].
8. *FII 2*, C-35/11.
9. For a more detailed discussion, see Smit, *supra* n. 1, at 641 et seq.
10. *Test Claimants in the FII Group Litigation*, C-446/04, Judgment, EU:C:2006:774 [hereinafter, *FII 1*], para. 171.
11. *Haribo and Österreichische Salinen*, Joined Cases C-436/08 and C-437/08, Judgment, EU:C:2011:61, para. 128.
12. *Ibid.* paras 125 et seq.
13. *FII 1*, C-446/04, paras 155–156 (in conjunction with para. 172).

need to preserve the effective collection of tax, the need to safeguard the balanced allocation of taxation powers, the promotion of research and development, the need to combat harmful tax competition, the lack of compensatory taxation (although this is arguable), and, in certain cases, the lack of harmonization.[14]

It follows from the above that although the CJEU has tended to interpret the free movement of capital vis-à-vis third countries rather extensively in favour of the taxpayer, it has also allowed significant derogations in favour of the Member States.

[B] Are There Limits to the CJEU's Competence in the Member States' Relations with Non-EU Member States?

Until the entry into force of the Lisbon Treaty on 1 December 2009, only the CJEU was competent to decide whether a restrictive tax measure infringed upon the free movement of capital as laid down in Article 63(1) TFEU. However, through the entry into force of the Lisbon Treaty, a new procedure was introduced that specifically aimed to cover the adoption by a Member State of restrictive tax measures concerning one or more third countries. As was the case under the EC Treaty, Article 64(3) TFEU allows the Council to unanimously 'adopt measures which constitute a step backwards in Union law as regards the liberalization of the movement of capital to or from third countries'. To date, however, the Council has never used its power in the field of corporate income taxation.

Through the entry into force of the Lisbon Treaty, however, a fourth paragraph was added to the tax carve-out provision under Article 65 TFEU. Article 65(4) TFEU stipulates that, in the absence of such Council measures:

> the Commission or, in the absence of a Commission decision within three months from the request of the Member State concerned, the Council, may adopt a decision stating that restrictive tax measures adopted by a Member State concerning one or more third countries are to be considered compatible with the Treaties in so far as they are justified by one of the objectives of the Union and compatible with the proper functioning of the internal market. The Council shall act unanimously on application by a Member State.

The above procedure had already been proposed during the process of drafting Article III-158(4) of the failed European Constitution of 2004, but was subsequently incorporated without change in the Lisbon Treaty (without, to my knowledge, any further publicly available deliberations). From the preparatory work on that European Constitution, one can only infer that the addition was proposed 'to meet the concerns of some Member States over these provisions' (i.e., those relating to the free movement of capital).[15] This preparatory work shed very little light on the background and

14. For a more detailed discussion, see Smit, *supra* n. 1, at 507 et seq.
15. Conference of the Representatives of the Governments of the Member States, Brussels, 29 Apr, 2004, PRESID 16, CIG 73/04, Meeting of Focal Points (Dublin, 4 May 2004) working document, 121.

purport of the new procedure or its impact in the field of corporate income taxation.[16] Nonetheless, it must be assumed that the new procedure governs corporate tax measures, at least to the extent that such measures fall within the ambit of Article 63(1) TFEU,[17] which is evidenced by the fact that Article 64 TFEU, to which Article 63(1) TFEU refers, governs company tax restrictions as well.[18]

Yet, the new procedure, which has not, to my knowledge, been examined in detail in the scholarly tax literature until now,[19] raises many questions. One question is, for example, whether the new procedure is only concerned with newly adopted corporate tax measures, or whether it also covers corporate tax measures already in force in the Member States. Another question is how one should determine whether a restrictive tax measure can be considered compatible with the Treaties.

Finally, and relevant for purposes of this contribution, the question arises as to whether and to what extent the competence to determine whether a restrictive tax measure is permissible under Union law has been shifted away from the CJEU to the Commission or, alternatively, the Council. In this respect, two distinctions must be made. First, if a Member State has not requested the Commission to decide if an adopted restrictive tax measure concerning one or more non-EU Member States is to be considered compatible with the Treaties, competence remains, in my view, with the CJEU. The reason is that the procedure of Article 65(4) TFEU requires a request from a Member State; neither the Commission nor the Council are competent to evaluate the

16. *E.g.*, Jukka Snell, *Free movement of capital: Evolution as a non-linear process*, *in The Evolution of EU Law* 547, 554 (Paul Craig & Gráinne de Búrca eds., 2011) (arguing the provision demonstrates the Member States' distrust of the Court when it comes to deciding tax matters and their willingness to curtail the free movement of capital to and from third countries); *contra*, Pasquale Pistone, *Five Years of EURYI Research on the Impact of European Law on Relations with Third Countries in the Field of Direct Taxes: Selected Remarks for a General Report in the EU's External Dimension in Direct Tax Matters* 17, 36 (Sabine Heidenbauer & Birgit Stürzlinger eds., 2010) (arguing that the provision should only be enacted as *extrema ratio* in order to block possible exceptional and contingent situations, because it would otherwise run counter to the essence of the external scope of the free movement of capital and payments and it could therefore easily quashed by the CJEU for such blatant incompatibility).

17. *Cf.* Opinion of Advocate General Peter J. Wattel in NL: *Vakstudie Nieuws* 2005/39.8, 3 Mar. 2005, No. 40 037 (suggesting that Art. 63(1) TFEU could be explained in two different ways: (i) it could be understood as confirming the difference between Member States and third countries, or (ii) by analogy, as long as no decision has been made by the Commission or the Council, confirming there is no difference between Member States and third countries).

18. *E.g.*, *FII 1*, C-446/04, paras 174 *et seq.*

19. In the academic literature unrelated to taxation, Article 63(1) has already received some attention. *See, e.g.*, Fernando Losada Fraga, Review of *The Free Movement of Capital and Foreign Direct Investment. The Scope of Protection in EU Law* by Steffen Hindelang, 21 Eur. J. Int'l L. 496, 499 (2010) (arguing that it is highly probable that the scope of the freedom of capital will be reduced, because regulating a fully liberalized regime can only, by definition, restrict such a regime, and because national tax regimes are explicitly considered able to limit capital flows); Martha O'Brien, *Canada, Capital Movements and the European Union*, 57 Canadian Tax J. 259, 290 (taking the view that it is difficult to imagine a tax restriction with respect to one or more third countries that would not be consistent with the functioning of the internal market); Leo Flynn, Review of *The Free Movement of Capital and Foreign Direct Investment: The Scope of Protection in EU Law* by Steffen Hindelang, 6 Eur. L. Rev. 892 (2010) (wondering whether the strong *erga omnes* commitment survives); Catherine Barnard, *The Substantive Law of the EU* 565 (3d ed., 2010) (considering the new procedure unusual given that this procedure allows the Council, and not the CJEU, to decide on the legality of national measures).

measure at hand on their own initiative (which they do have, for instance, under the EU state-aid rules). In the absence of a request from a Member State, neither the Commission nor the Council would thus be able to assess the restrictive tax measure at issue. In my view, it necessarily follows that in such case, the CJEU is still competent to assess the restrictive tax measure at issue in the light of the free movement of capital under Article 63 TFEU. Otherwise, Member States could simply 'block' the protection for taxpayers under Article 63 TFEU by not filing any request to the Commission. This would jeopardize the effectiveness of EU law with regard to individuals and companies.

However, once a request of a Member State has been submitted, it follows from the wording of Article 65(4) TFEU that it is only the Commission, or alternatively the Council, that is exclusively competent to assess the compatibility of the restrictive tax measure with the Treaties. According to Article 263 read in conjunction with Article 288 TFEU, the legality of this decision can only be assessed by the CJEU on the grounds of lack of competence, infringement of an essential procedural requirement, infringement of the Treaties or of any rule of law relating to their application, or misuse of powers. Not only the Member States, but also individuals and legal persons may institute proceedings against the decision made by the Commission, or alternatively the Council, before the CJEU, but only if the decision is of direct and individual concern to them.[20] Put differently, they must qualify as an interested party. In my view, this could be the case when a taxpayer actually falls under the scope of a restrictive tax measure that was the subject of an Article 65(4) TFEU process.

In my view, the new procedure under Article 65(4) TFEU constitutes a shift of competence from the CJEU back to the Member States the impact of which is, however, yet unclear.

§10.03 'EUROPEAN OPENNESS' AND POSITIVE INTEGRATION

[A] The Union's Power to Act

It can be concluded, from the above, that when the CJEU has exercised its competence to interpret the free movement of capital vis- à-vis third countries in the field of corporate taxation, it has tended to favour taxpayers, although it has allowed significant (but rather fragmented) restrictions in favour of the Member States as well. In any case, the CJEU's case law does not result in a comprehensive European approach in the field of corporate taxation vis- à-vis third countries, as the CJEU can only decide matters on a case-by-case, country-specific basis and it has no legislative powers. Also the CJEU's case law is not concerned with removing obstacles stemming from disparities, such as international juridical double taxation. Hence, there is still a case for Union legislation (positive integration) vis-à-vis non-EU Member States in the field of corporate taxation. In the current and subsequent paragraphs, I will address the

20. *Cf.* Art. 263 TFEU.

question of the extent to which the Union is competent to enact legislation in the area of corporate taxation.

According to the principle of conferral, as incorporated in Article 5(2) TEU, the Union may act only within the limits of the competences conferred upon it by the Member States in the Treaties to attain the objectives set out therein. Article 5(2) TFEU explicitly states that '[c]ompetences not conferred upon the Union in the Treaties remain with the Member States.' Although Union competence is the exception, it nevertheless follows from the various Treaty provisions that, in practice, the Union is competent to adopt measures in a wide variety of areas, both internally (i.e., within the Union) and externally (i.e., vis-à-vis third countries). The Union's competence, furthermore, can be either shared with the Member States or exclusive.

In this regard, the Union's power to act may be conferred expressly or implicitly. In the case of expressly conferred powers, the relevant Treaty provision explicitly lays down the area to which the conferred power extends.[21] However, the Union's power to act may also be conferred implicitly on the basis of 'implied powers'. Such implied powers do not explicitly arise from the Treaties' provisions, but nevertheless can be derived from them.[22]

[B] Internal Competence and Non-EU Member States in the Field of Corporate Taxation

It follows from the CJEU's case law that the Union is not prohibited from using the internal powers conferred on it in order to specify the treatment that is to be accorded to nationals of non-EU Member States.[23] In such cases, the Union is merely exercising its internal competences.[24] When the Union includes, in its internal legislative acts, provisions relating to the treatment of nationals of third countries, it acquires exclusive external competence in the spheres covered by those acts.[25] Consequently, it is appropriate to examine the relevant TFEU provisions conferring on the Union internal competence in the field of corporate taxation.

The TFEU provides a number of general legal bases for the conferral of internal competence to the Union to enact legislation in the field of corporate income taxation vis-à-vis third countries. Firstly, Article 115 TFEU is of relevance in this regard; it stipulates that:

> the Council [must], acting unanimously in accordance with a special legislative procedure and after consulting the European Parliament and the Economic and Social Committee, issue directives for the approximation of such laws, regulations or administrative provisions of the Member States as directly affect the establishment or functioning of the internal market.

21. *Cf.* Art. 3(1) TFEU.
22. Opinion of the Court, 2/94, EU:C:1996:140, para. 26; Opinion of the Court, 1/76, EU:C:1977:63, para. 3.
23. Opinion of the Court, 2/94, para. 90.
24. Georg Kofler, *Doppelbesteuerungsabkommen und Europäisches Gemeinschafsrecht* 322 (2007) (together with references cited therein).
25. Opinion of the Court, 1/94, EU:C:1994:384, para. 95.

Harmonization measures in the field of corporate income taxation that relate to dividend payments in parent-subsidiary relationships,[26] interest and royalty payments between associated companies,[27] cross-border mergers and divisions,[28] mutual assistance with the exchange of information,[29] and the mutual assistance with the recovery of tax claims[30] have already been proposed and adopted on the basis of Article 115 TFEU in the past.

Secondly, Article 116 TFEU can also be regarded as another legal basis for Union action in the field of corporate income taxation. This provision stipulates that where the Commission finds that a difference between the provisions laid down by law, regulation or administrative action in Member States is distorting the conditions of competition in the internal market and that the resultant distortion needs to be eliminated, it shall consult the Member States concerned. If such consultation does not result in an agreement eliminating the distortion in question, the European, Parliament and the Council, acting in accordance with the ordinary legislative procedure, shall issue the necessary directives. Any other appropriate measures provided for in the Treaties may be adopted. It is generally argued, in academic literature, that Article 116 TFEU aims to remove specific distortions that occur when competition is distorted to the benefit or disadvantage of specific groups of enterprises.[31] Nevertheless, some scholars have observed that its wording is formulated in a much broader fashion and does not fundamentally exclude the adoption by the Union of measures in the field of company tax.[32] In practice to date, however, the significance of this provision in the field of corporate income taxation appears to be very limited.[33]

Lastly, Article 352(1) TFEU is also capable of serving as a legal basis for the adoption by the Union of corporate tax measures involving third-country investments. This provision stipulates, in relevant part, that:

26. Council Directive 2011/96/EU of 30 Nov. 2011 on the Common System of Taxation Applicable in the Case of Parent Companies and Subsidiaries of Different Member States, OJ 2011 L 345, 8.
27. Council Directive 2003/49/EC of 3 June 2003 on a Common System of Taxation Applicable to Interest and Royalty Payments Made between Associated Companies of Different Member States, OJ 2003 L 157, 49.
28. Council Directive 2009/133/EC of 19 Oct. 2009 on the Common System of Taxation Applicable to Mergers, Divisions, Partial Divisions, Transfers of Assets and Exchanges of Shares Concerning Companies of Different Member States and to the Transfer of the Registered Office of an SE or SCE between Member States, OJ 2009 L 310, 34.
29. Council Directive 2003/49/EC of 3 June 2003 on a Common System of Taxation Applicable to Interest and Royalty Payments Made between Associated Companies of Different Member States, OJ 2003 L 157, 49. Council Directive 2011/16/EU of 15 Feb. 2011 on Administrative Cooperation in the Field of Taxation and Repealing Directive 77/799/EEC, OJ 2011 L 64, 1.
30. Council Directive 2010/24/EU of 16 Mar, 2010 Concerning Mutual Assistance for the Recovery of Claims Relating to Taxes, Duties and Other Measures, OJ 2010, L 84, 1.
31. *See, e.g.*, Paul J.G. Kapteyn & Pieter VerLoren Van Themaat, *Het recht van de Europese Unie en van de Europese Gemeenschappe* 721, (6th ed., 2003); Matthias Hofstätter, *Who is Competent to Issue Measures for the Elimination of Double Taxation within the Community? in Tax Treaty Law and EC Law* 25, 35 (Michael Lang, Josef Schuch & Claus Staringer eds., 2007).
32. *See, e.g.*, Kofler, *supra* n. 24, at 121; Pasquale Pistone, *The Impact of Community Law on Tax Treaties* 59 (2002).
33. This can be explained by the fact that ex-Art. 96 EC did not require unanimity for the adoption of Directives.

> If action by the Union should prove necessary, within the framework of the policies defined in the Treaties, to attain one of the objectives set out in the Treaties, and the Treaties have not provided the necessary powers, the Council, acting unanimously on a proposal from the Commission and after obtaining the consent of the European Parliament, [must] adopt the appropriate measures.

The CJEU has confirmed that recourse to Article 352(1) as the legal basis for a Union measure is justified only where no other provision of the Treaty gives the Union institutions the necessary power to adopt the measure in question.[34] In other words, Article 352(1) TFEU 'fills the gap where no specific provisions of the EC Treaty confer on the Union institutions express or implied powers to act.'[35] The CJEU has furthermore confirmed that the proposed action must, however, be intended to attain one of the objectives of the Union.[36] Moreover, any action based on this provision must remain 'within the framework of the policies defined in the Treaties'. To date, Article 352(1) TFEU has never been used as a basis for the adoption by the Union institutions of measures in the field of corporate income taxation. Nevertheless, in my view, the mere wording of the said provision does not exclude this possibility.[37]

As stated above, the Union is permitted to use the internal powers conferred on it in order to specify the treatment that is to be accorded to nationals of non-EU Member States. In the field of corporate taxation, the Union has twice attempted to use its powers. The former 2011 proposal for a Council Directive on a Common Consolidated Corporate Tax Base, based on Article 115 TFEU, attempted to address the corporate tax treatment of non-EU investments and investors.[38] This also holds with respect to the new 2016 proposals on a Common Corporate Tax Base and a Common Consolidated Corporate Tax Base.[39] Also the proposal for a Council Directive on laying down rules against tax avoidance practices that directly affect the functioning of the internal market (the so-called Anti-Tax Avoidance Directive), a revised version of which the Member States formally adopted on 12 July 2016, was similarly based on Article 115 TFEU; it also addresses the corporate tax treatment of non-EU investments and investors by establishing a number of minimum standards to be applied by the Member States in the field of corporate taxation.[40] The same holds with respect to the Proposal

34. *Parliament v. Council,* C-295/90, Judgment, EU:C:1992:294, para. 11.
35. Opinion of the Court, 2/94, para. 29; *Kadi and Al Barakaat International Foundation v Council and Commission,* Joined Cases C-402/05 P and C-415/05, EU:C:2008:461, para. 200 [hereinafter '*Kadi and Al Baraakaat,* C-402/05'].
36. *Kadi and Al Baraakaat,* C-402/05, para. 200.
37. *See* Arnaud C.G.A.C. de Graaf *het internationaal belastingrecht: beleids- en marktintegratie* 37 et seq. (2004).
38. Proposal for a Council Directive on a Common Consolidated Corporate Tax Base (CCCTB), 16 Mar. 2011, COM(2011) 121/4.
39. Proposal for a Council Directive on a Common Corporate Tax Base, 25 Oct. 2016, COM(2016) 685 and Proposal for a Council Directive on a Common Consolidated Corporate Tax Base (CCCTB), 25 Oct. 2016, COM(2016) 683.
40. Proposal for a Council Directive Laying Down Rules Against Tax Avoidance Practices that Directly Affect the Functioning of the Internal Market, 28 Jan. 2016, COM(2016) 026 final.

for a Council Directive amending Directive (EU) 2016/1164 as regards hybrid mismatches with third countries (sometimes referred to as Anti-Tax Avoidance Directive 2),[41] a revised version of which the Member States politically adopted on 21 February 2017.

The question under discussion in this contribution is: Is the Union indeed competent to adopt harmonization measures involving the corporate taxation of income derived from third-country investments? In my view, this question must be answered in the affirmative. The Union does have the internal competence on the basis of Article 115 TFEU to issue harmonization measures in the field of corporate income taxation specifying the treatment of income deriving from third-country investments or by third-country investors insofar as the existing patchwork of different corporate income tax rules applicable in the various Member States vis-à-vis third countries (fragmentation) does 'affect the establishment or functioning of the internal market' within the meaning of Article 115 TFEU. Differences among the Member States in their treatment of third-country investments may lead to distortions in the flow of investments in the internal market.[42] Furthermore, different third-country investors investing in the same Member State may be faced with different tax burdens in that Member State, according to the degree of liberalization that Member State applies vis-à-vis the relevant third country, which creates distortions of competition within the internal market as well.[43] In such cases, the institutions of the Union are permitted 'arranging, in the common rules laid down by them, concerted action in relation to non-member countries or ... prescribing the approach to be taken by the Member States in their external dealings.'[44] On the basis of the above, I conclude that the Union is competent to adopt harmonization measures in the field of corporate income taxation vis-à-vis third countries.

41. Proposal for a Council Directive Amending Directive (EU) 2016/1164 as Regards Hybrid Mismatches with Third Countries, 25 Oct. 2016, COM(2016) 687.
42. In the context of differences in dividend withholding tax rates among the various Member States vis-à-vis third countries, see Hubert M.A.L. Hamaekers and Frans Vanistendael, *The sovereignty of the Member States in the field of direct taxation, in Report of the Common Academic Assembly of the Dutch Academic Association for Taxation and the Dutch Association for European Law, in Scriptures of the Dutch Academic Association for Taxation* 230, 231 (2007); *contra* Peter J. Wattel & Dennis M. Weber, in the same volume, who both take the view that such differences do not create distortions within the internal market,.
43. *Cf., e.g.,* Opinion of the Court, 1/94, para. 78 (describing the Commission's assertions):

> The Commission asserted that the Member States' continuing freedom to conduct an external policy based on bilateral agreements with non-member countries will inevitably lead to distortions in the flow of services and will progressively undermine the internal market. It argued, for example, that travellers will choose to fly from airports in Member States which have concluded an 'open skies' type of bilateral agreement with a non-member country and its airline, enabling them to offer the best quality/price ratio for transport. The Commission further claimed that as a result of the existence of an agreement between Germany and Poland exempting German road haulage operators from having to pay any transit tax, whereas the corresponding agreement between Poland and the Netherlands imposes a tax on Netherlands hauliers, distortion had arisen in competition between Netherlands hauliers and German hauliers in relation to traffic bound for Russia, Byelorussia and the Baltic countries.

44. *Ibid.* paras 78–79; *Commission* v *Denmark,* C-467/98, Judgment, EU:C:2002:625, para. 123.

[C] Express External Competences and Non-EU Member States in the Field of Corporate Taxation

The TFEU also provides a number of express legal bases that, in addition to the general legal bases discussed above, confer competence on the Union to enact legislation in the field of corporate income taxation vis-à-vis third countries. Firstly, the Union's external powers in the sphere of capital movements derive from Article 64(2) and (3) TEFU[45] (although it is unclear to what extent these external powers are exclusive).[46] Article 64(2) TFEU stipulates, in relevant part, that:

> the European Parliament and the Council, acting in accordance with the ordinary legislative procedure, must adopt the measures on the movement of capital to or from third countries involving direct investment – including investment in real estate – establishment, the provision of financial services or the admission of securities to capital markets.

Further, according to Article 64(3) TFEU:

> only the Council, acting in accordance with a special legislative procedure, may unanimously, and after consulting the European Parliament, adopt measures which constitute a step backwards in Union law as regards the liberalization of the movement of capital to or from third countries.

To date, the Council has not used its external powers based on these provisions in the field of corporate taxation vis-à-vis third countries. It is submitted, however, that corporate tax measures are not fully excluded from the scope of these provisions. This is evidenced by Article 65(4) TFEU, quoted above, which was introduced in the chapter relating to the free movement of capital by the Lisbon Treaty and which specifically refers to tax measures. This submission is further supported by the wording of the cited provisions, which do not restrict the Union's competence to particular areas or economic activities or the admission or subsequent treatment thereof. On the contrary, they establish Union competence more generally with regard to measures in a number of categories relating to third-country capital movements. As it clearly follows from the CJEU case law that corporate income taxation may have a restrictive effect on the free movement of capital, Article 64(2) and (3) TFEU must be considered as conferring on the Union the power to act in the field of corporate tax measures to the extent categories of capital movements are involved. By contrast, corporate tax measures relating to, for example, portfolio investments (as opposed to direct investments) are excluded from the scope of these provisions.

---

45. *See Commission* v *Sweden*, C-249/06, Judgment, EU:C:2009:119, para. 36; *Kadi and Al Baraakaat*, C-402/05, para. 138 (Commission took the position that Article 63(1) TFEU makes clear that capital and payments between the Union and third countries fall within Union competence).
46. *Accord* Piet Eeckhout, *External Relations of the European Union* 124 (2004); *contra, e.g.*, Stefan Weber, *Kapitalverkehr und Kapitalmärkte im Vertrag über die Europäische Union*, 10 EuZW 561, 566 (1992).

In addition, specific and exclusive external powers in the field of investment can be derived from Article 207(1) TFEU, as amended by the entry into force of the Lisbon Treaty.[47] This provision, provides that the Union's:

> common commercial policy [must] be based on uniform principles, particularly with regard to changes in tariff rates, the conclusion of tariff and trade agreements relating to trade in goods and services, and the commercial aspects of intellectual property, foreign direct investment, the achievement of uniformity in measures of liberalisation, export policy and measures to protect trade such as those to be taken in the event of dumping or subsidies.

Hence, through the entry into force of the Lisbon Treaty, the Union's common commercial policy specifically includes foreign direct investment.[48] For the same reasons presented above in the context of Article 64(2) and (3) TFEU, the adoption – at Union level – of corporate tax measures can be based on Article 207(1) TFEU, although it is acknowledged that the precise scope of this extension is far from clear.[49] For example, one might wonder whether the common commercial policy only governs restrictions on market access, or whether it also deals with the post-entry stage of investment.[50] In addition, it is unclear whether the competence conferred by this provision also encompasses capital movements relating to foreign investment, given the specific rules that exist under the Treaty by virtue of Article 64(2) and (3).[51]

It follows, in my view, that both Article 64(2) and (3) TFEU, and Article 207(1) TFEU, confer the power on the Union to adopt harmonization measures in the field of corporate income taxation applicable vis-à-vis non-EU Member States. However, these provisions cannot serve as a comprehensive, horizontal legal basis for Union action in the field of corporate income taxation vis-à-vis third countries, as for example corporate tax measures relating to establishment and portfolio investments are excluded from their scope.

---

47. *Cf.* Arts 206–07 TFEU, read in conjunction with Art. 3(1) TFEU; *cf.* Communication from the Commission to the Council, the European Parliament, the European Economic and Social Committee and the Committee of the Regions of 7 July 2010, *Towards a comprehensive European international investment policy*, COM(2010) 343 final, 2.
48. Ex-Art. 133 EC, on the other hand, excluded foreign direct investment from the common commercial policy, such that the entire field of capital movement was thus excluded from ex-Art. 133 EC.
49. *See, e.g.*, Jan Ceyssens, *Towards a Common Foreign Investment Policy? – Foreign Investment in the European Constitution'*, 32 Legal Issues of Econ. Integration 259 (2005); Angelos Dimopoulos, *The Effects of the Lisbon Treaty on the Principles and Objectives of the Common Commercial Policy*, 15 Eur. Foreign Aff. Rev. 153 (2010).
50. *Accord* Ceyssens, *supra* n. 49, at 277; Marc Bungenberg, *The Division of Competences Between the EU and Its Member States in the Area of Investment Politics, in International Investment Law and EU Law*, 29, 37 (Marc Bungenberg et al. eds., 2011); Angelos Dimopoulos, Regulation of foreign investment in EU external relations law 113 (25 June 2010) (unpublished Ph.D. dissertation, European University Institute, on file with author).
51. *See* Frank S. Benyon, *Direct Investment, National Champions and EU Treaty Freedoms: From Maastricht to Lisbon* 83 (2010) (evaluating the pros and cons of the arguments); *contra*, Dimopoulos, *supra* n. 50, at 112–113. In the affirmative: Advocate General Sharpston in her Opinion delivered on 21 Dec. 2016, Opinion Procedure 2/15, (no ECLI:EU number), para. 324 et seq.

[D] Implied External Exclusive Competence and Non-EU Member States in the Field of Corporate Taxation

The final question to be discussed is whether the TFEU creates any implied external and exclusive competence for the Union to enact legislation in the field of corporate income taxation vis-à-vis third countries. With regard to the Union's implied powers to act in its external relations under international agreements, CJEU's case law demonstrates that the competence to bind the Union in relation to non-EU Member States may implicitly arise from the Treaty provisions establishing internal competence, provided that participation of the Union in the international agreement is necessary for attaining one of the Union's objectives.[52] In other words, according to the maxim *in foro interno, in foro externo*, the existence of implied or express internal powers in a particular area means that the Union is also competent to act in its external relations if such is necessary for attaining one of the Union's objectives. Implied external competence exists not only whenever the internal competence has already been used in order to adopt measures for implementing common policies, but also if the internal Union measures are adopted only on the occasion of the conclusion and implementation of the international agreement.[53] It is not, therefore, required that the Union has already exercised its internal competence.[54]

From the case law of the CJEU, one can further infer that the Union's external competence may become exclusive in two cases. First, exclusive external competence may be established where the internal competence may only be effectively exercised at the same time as the external competence, the conclusion of the international agreement thus being necessary in order to attain objectives of the Treaties that cannot be attained by establishing autonomous rules.[55] Secondly, exclusive external competence may be established where an international agreement would necessarily affect existing Union rules in a given area, such as legislative measures containing clauses relating to the treatment of nationals of non-Member countries or relating to the complete harmonization of a particular issue.[56] In both cases, exclusive competence is justified in order to ensure the full effectiveness of Union law. In the latter situation, internal competence can give rise to exclusive external competence only if it is exercised.[57] On the other hand, no exclusive competence is established where both the Union provisions and those of an international convention lay down minimum standards. According to the CJEU's case law, there is nothing to prevent the full application of Union law by the Member States in such a case.[58] Neither can exclusive

52. Opinion of the Court, 1/76, para. 4; *Cornelis Kramer and Others*, Joined Cases C-3/76, C-4/76 & C-6/76, Judgment, EU:C:1976:114, paras 30–33; *Commission* v *Denmark*, C-467/98, Judgment, EU:C:2002:625; and Opinion of the Court, 2/91, EU:C:1993:106, para. 7.
53. Opinion of the Court, 1/76, para. 3.
54. Koen Lenaerts & Eddy de Smijter, *The European Community's Treaty-Making Competence*, 16 Y.B. Eur. L. 1, 7 (1996).
55. Opinion of the Court, 1/94, para. 89; Opinion of the Court, 1/03, EU:C:2006:81, para. 37.
56. *Commission* v *Council*, C-22/70, Judgment, EU:C:1971:32, para. 17; Opinion of the Court, 1/94, paras 95–96; *Commission* v *Denmark*, C-467/98, paras 83–84; Opinion of the Court, 1/03.
57. Opinion of the Court, 1/94, paras 88–89.
58. *Ibid.* para. 18; Opinion of the Court, 1/03.

competence be established where there is a chance that bilateral agreements would lead to distortions in the flow of services in the internal market. In such a case, the CJEU considers that there is nothing in the Treaty to prevent the institutions from arranging, in the common rules laid down by them, concerted action in relation to non-Member countries or from prescribing the approach to be taken by the Member States in their external dealings.[59] To conclude, in order to establish exclusive external competence for the Union, there must be a clear nexus between the exercise of internal and external competence.[60]

The question arises, then, whether the Union has an implied exclusive competence to adopt corporate income taxation measures vis-à-vis third countries. In my view, this question must be answered in the negative to the extent the Union has not yet exercised its internal competence to adopt measures in the field of corporate income taxation. This is because internal competence can give rise to exclusive external competence only if it is exercised.

Less certain is whether this conclusion is also valid to the extent the Union has exercised its internal competences to adopt measures in the field of corporate income taxation, which is the case with regard to the fiscal treatment of intra-group payments of dividends, interest and royalties under the Parent-Subsidiary Directive, the Interest & Royalty Directive, and the fiscal treatment of reorganizations through transnational mergers and divisions under the Merger Directive. In this regard, the key question is whether legislative action by the Union in the field of corporate income taxation vis-à-vis third countries would necessarily affect the rules laid down in these Directives. In the context of the question of whether Member States are still competent to enter into dividend and loss-of-benefit (LOB) articles in tax treaties with third states, R.J. Jeffery comes to the conclusion that Member States do not have the external-relations competence to enter into such provisions to the extent these provisions are covered by the external application of the operational area of the Parent-Subsidiary Directive.[61] In his view, the fact that tax treaties between Member States and third countries provide for different rates of withholding tax on dividend payments gives rise to arbitrage opportunities for the establishment of holding companies in those Member States in which the relevant tax treaty provides for no or low rates of withholding tax on dividend payments. This affects the common rules set out in the Parent-Subsidiary Directive, since the very type of distortions are introduced from outside the Union that the Directive was designed to eliminate.[62] The Council seems to share this view in that it suggested having exclusive competence to adopt the Agreement establishing the

59. Opinion of the Court, 1/94, paras 78–79; *Commission* v *Denmark*, C-467/98, para. 123.
60. *Cf.* Richard Lyal, *Note on the External Competence of the European Community in Tax Matters: The Example of the Agreement with Switzerland on the Taxation of Savings, in The EU and Third Countries* 67 (Michael Lang & Pasquale Pistone eds., 2007).
61. Ramon J. Jeffery, *The Impact of State Sovereignty on Global Trade and International Taxation* 153–54 (1999).
62. *Ibid.* at 154. In the context of the Merger Directive, compare, Adam Craig, *Open Your Eyes: What the 'Open Skies' Cases Could Mean for the US Tax Treaties with the EU Member States*, 57 Bull. Int'l Tax'n 63, 68 (2003).

World Trade Organization to the extent that that Agreement affects the Parent-Subsidiary Directive and the Merger Directive.[63]

Arnaud C.G.A.C. de Graaf, on the other hand, comes to the opposite conclusion in the context of the question of whether the Union is exclusively competent to conclude tax treaties with third countries. He takes the view that the Union has no exclusive external competence in the area of dividend, interest and royalty payments, given the limited scope of the Directives that have been adopted in these areas.[64] John F. Avery Jones also observes that the existing provisions of the Parent-Subsidiary Directive and the Merger Directive are limited to purely internal situations and, thus, teach us nothing about external relations.[65] Moreover, in the context of concluding the Agreement between the European Community and the Swiss Confederation, which provides for measures equivalent to those laid down in Council Directive 2003/48/EC of 3 June 2003 on taxation of savings income in the form of interest payments, both the Council and the Commission declared that the exercise of competence by the Union with respect to Article 15 of that Agreement did not affect existing bilateral agreements with other third countries and that Member States maintain their competence to conclude bilateral agreements with such third countries on the tax treatment of dividends and of interest and royalty payments between companies.[66]

In my view, the latter position must be endorsed. While it is true that differences among the Member States in their treatment of third countries in the field of corporate income taxation could lead to distortions in the flow of services in the internal market,[67] the CJEU has held repeatedly that such an effect cannot establish exclusive Union competence in the area.[68]

§10.04 FINAL REMARKS

This contribution has addressed the question as to how the Union's economic openness towards non-EU Member States affects its Member States' sovereignty in the field of corporate taxation. It has established that the CJEU, when it has exercised its competence to interpret the free movement of capital vis-à-vis third countries in the field of corporate taxation, has tended to favour taxpayers, although it has left

63. Council Decision of 22 Dec. 1994 (94/800/EC) Concerning the Conclusion on Behalf of the European Community, as Regards Matters within its Competence, of the Agreements Reached in the Uruguay Round Multilateral Negotiations (1986-1994), OJ 1994 L 336, 1.
64. De Graaf, *supra* n. 37, at 69.
65. John F. Avery Jones, *Flows of Capital Between the EU and Third Countries and the Consequences of Disharmony in European International Tax Law*, 7 EC Tax Rev. 95, 102 (1998). *See* Sabine Heidenbauer & Josef Schuch, *Member State or Community Competence? – Who is Competent to Conclude Double Tax Conventions with Third Countries, in Tax Treaty Law and EC Law* 348 (Michael Lang, Josef Schuch, & Claus Staringer eds., 2007).
66. As can be derived from the Proposal for a Council Decision on the Conclusion of the Agreement between the European Community and the Swiss Confederation Providing for Measures Equivalent to Those Laid Down in Council Directive 2003/48/EC of 3 June 2003 on Taxation of Savings Income in the Form of Interest Payments, COM(2004) 75 final, 3; *see* Lyal, *supra* n. 60, at 67 et seq.
67. Opinion of the Court, 1/94, paras 78–79; *Commission* v *Denmark*, C-467/98, para. 123.
68. Opinion of the Court, 1/94, paras 78–79; *Commission* v *Denmark*, C-467/98, para. 123.

significant (but fragmented) restrictions in favour of the Member States in place. Furthermore, it has established that the Union is competent to adopt legislation vis-à-vis non-EU Member States in the field of corporate taxation, despite the fact that, to date, such power has been rarely been used. Nevertheless, the EU has recently exercised its competence in the field of corporate taxation vis- à-vis non-EU Member States by adopting the two Anti-Tax Avoidance Directives. Perhaps this action constitutes a first step towards a more comprehensive external EU policy in the field of corporate taxation.

CHAPTER 11

An EU Policy for the Future of International Tax Law

Gianluigi Bizioli

§11.01 INTRODUCTION

Consistent with the subject matter of this book, the title of this chapter looks at the future of both variables involved: EU tax policies and international taxation. A first reading of this topic highlights the role and actions of the EU Institutions[1] in developing a new order of international tax law. From this perspective, which can be described as 'dynamic', the analysis primarily focuses on the function of the EU as an actor in the establishment of a renewed international tax order.

According to a different, and probably more traditional, understanding, the title necessitates a review of EU tax policy that, in turn, affects international taxation and its current trends (the 'static' approach). This second perspective, therefore, looks at the interaction between EU policies, the Single (or Internal) Market, and recent proposals to reform the international tax law order, with particular attention paid to the OECD's Base Erosion and Profit Shifting (BEPS) Actions[2] arising from the OECD-BEPS Project.[3]

---

1. As listed in Art. 13 TEU.
2. On 5 Oct. 2016, the OECD presented the final package of measures for a coordinated reform of international tax law aimed at curbing avoidance and at closing the gaps in corporate income taxation. The G20 finance ministers in Lima endorsed this package on 8 Oct. 2016.
3. It is worth recalling that the OECD/G20 BEPS Project can be traced back to the OECD report entitled *Addressing Base Erosion and Profit Shifting*, published in 2013, which forms the basis of the change in the international, economic, and financial scenario:

> Early on it was recognised that the interaction of domestic tax systems can lead to overlaps in the exercise of taxing rights that can result in double taxation ... The interaction of domestic tax systems (including rules adopted in accordance with international standards to relieve double taxation), however, can also lead to gaps that provide opportunities to eliminate or significantly reduce taxation on income in a

Having described the theoretical approaches to the topic, this chapter adopts a syncretic method. First, it describes the evolution and the current state of EU policies that affect international taxation; then, it offers some thoughts about the EU's role in the development of a reformed international tax law in line with the EU's Single Market legal order. However, before dealing with the subject, a few preliminary remarks should be made, the first of which concerns the limits of the analysis carried out. The international dimension affects all sector of taxation, even though its main theoretical and practical problems arise in the field of income taxes. Thus, a rigorous analysis of the topic requires, in principle, tackling the various EU policies in all of those fields in which EU harmonization or coordination competences have been exercised. In this sense, EU tax policies are influenced by two different variables: (i) the specific economic and legal features of each type of taxation, and (ii) the legal frameworks established by the European Treaties[4] for different tax sectors. Within the EU, cross-border and, thus, international tax policies are deeply influenced by the specific distribution of competences between the national and supranational levels for the different tax sectors.

The breadth of this chapter's topic imposes a clear choice or, even better, a clear hierarchy of priorities; this contribution takes an in-depth look at EU policy in the field of income taxation, but only provides a brief introduction to cross-border and international EU policies in other tax sectors. This choice is supported by manifest reasons, grounded on both (a) the already mentioned theoretical and practical importance of the international dimension of income taxation policy in comparison to other forms of taxation and (b) the extensive debate about the reform of international income taxation developed under the umbrella of the OECD BEPS Project.

The second difficulty relates to the lack of a comprehensive EU policy document on the issue of international taxation. The EU policy approach is always selective or, said differently, only a portion of the greater tax context. In the field of income taxation, the former is exemplified by the Commission's Communication on double taxation, which was restricted to the Single Market,[5] and its Communication[6] and

manner that is inconsistent with the policy objectives of such domestic tax rules and international standards. While multinational corporations urge co-operation in the development of international standards to alleviate double taxation resulting from differences in domestic tax rules, they often exploit differences in domestic tax rules and international standards that provide opportunities to eliminate or significantly reduce taxation.

4. It is well known, in fact, that only the harmonization of indirect taxation finds an explicit legal basis in the EU Treaties (Art. 113 TFEU) and that the principle of fiscal non-discrimination applies exclusively to 'products'" (Art. 110 TFEU).
5. European Commission, Communication from the Commission to the European Parliament, the Council and the European Economic and Social Committee. Double Taxation in the Single Market, COM(2011) 712 final, 11 Nov. 2011 [hereinafter the 'Single Market Double Taxation Communication'].
6. Communication from the Commission to the European Parliament, the Council and the European Economic and Social Committee, Tax and Development Cooperating with Developing Countries on Promoting Good Governance in Tax Matters, COM(2010) 163 final, 21 Apr. 2010 [hereinafter '2009 Promoting Tax Good Governance Communication'].

Recommendation[7] on its 'External Strategy'.[8] An example of the latter, always within the harmonization/coordination policy of income taxation, are the international aspects of the Common Consolidated Corporate Tax Base ('CCCTB').[9] Unlike other areas of taxation, the European Institutions have never developed a comprehensive approach to international taxation, but, have rather done the opposite: they have treated the international aspects of taxation as ancillary to (or as function of) other EU policies and objectives, particularly the removal of obstacles to the Single Market. Accordingly, it is impossible to evaluate the overall EU approach to international taxation in terms of systematic coherence or rationality, but, it is possible to evaluate the effectiveness and consistency of the EU Institutions' sectorial policies with the goal pursued.

Finally, in the context of EU tax policies, the expression 'international tax law' can be used to describe two different situations. On the one hand, the first refers to policies elaborated for the Single Market and, in particular, for the removal of the cross-border obstacles within the Single Market in non-harmonized tax areas. The second, on the other hand, refers to tax policies involving third countries. As both situations belong to the field of international tax law, this chapter deals with them concurrently.

In accordance with these preliminary understandings, this chapter is structured as follows: A brief outline is given up to the EU policies in the field of Value Added Tax or VAT, to draw some ideas for the future developments (§11.02, *infra*), and in the field of the taxation of the financial transactions, describing the proposal to introduce a Financial Transaction Tax or FTT (§11.03, *infra*). Then, the core part of this contribution is devoted to EU policies in the field of income taxation. The analysis is structured according to the historical evolution of such policies, as the past is often the best way to understand the present and, therefore, to try to conceive of future trends. This core part is divided in two sections: individual income taxation (§11.04[B], *infra*) and corporate income taxation (§11.04[C], *infra*). Finally, §11.05, *infra* draws some conclusions.

§11.02 THE INTERNATIONAL DIMENSION OF THE EU VAT POLICY

The EU VAT policy that involves the international dimension of taxation has been, and still is, affected by two main variables. The first concerns the legal framework of indirect taxation, in general, and VAT, in particular. It is well known that the TFEU provides an express legal basis for the harmonization of all kinds of indirect taxes 'to the extent that such harmonisation is necessary to ensure the establishment and the

7. European Commission, Recommendation of 6 Dec. 2012, Regarding Measures Intended to Encourage Third Countries to Apply Minimum Standards of Good Governance in Tax Matters, C(2012) 8805 final [hereinafter the 'Recommendation on Third Countries'].
8. *See* the Single Market Double Taxation Communication, *supra* n. 5, and the Recommendation on Third Countries, *supra* n. 7.
9. *See, e.g.*, European Commission, Proposal for a Council Directive on a Common Consolidated Corporate Tax Base (CCCTB), COM(2012) 121 final, 16 Mar. 2011, Arts 31, 74, 82.

functioning of the internal market and to avoid distortion of competition'.[10] It is likewise known that the greatest part of VAT regulation lies in EU Directives and, from the perspective of the allocation of the competences, it can be considered as a genuinely European tax.

The harmonization of VAT finds, therefore, its theoretical and legal basis in the Single Market and, therefore, on the need to eliminate any barrier or obstacle to the circulation of goods within the EU jurisdictions. In this direction, the proper aim of VAT harmonization is the non-discriminatory treatment of purely domestic and EU cross-border transactions. According to the rationale, VAT regulation distinguishes between two different sets of rules: the set is applicable to purely domestic and EU cross-border transactions is strictly shaped by the needs of the functioning of the Single Market; the other set, applicable to transactions with third countries, is *also* grounded on the principles that govern the international trade. In this sense, unlike the income taxation context (§11.04, *infra*) the international dimension of VAT is restricted exclusively to transactions between EU Member States and third countries.

Accordingly, VAT harmonization has vested the EU Institutions with exclusive authority to regulate, not only the domestic and EU cross-border transactions, but also the rules which affect the transactions with third countries.

The second variable involves the structure of the VAT (or similar kind of indirect taxation, usually called a Goods and Services Tax or GST) with particular emphasis on the criterion of connection with the jurisdiction. It is, in fact, widely accepted among members of the international community that the authority to tax consumption lies where such consumption occurs.[11] Unlike that in the income taxation context, where OECD countries have adopted both personal and material criteria for connection with the jurisdiction, the VAT/GST regulation is uniformly founded on the place of final consumption of goods or services. The international dimension of the VAT/GST is, therefore, 'spontaneously' coordinated through the consensus, and the adoption, of a common criterion for taxation in cross-border transactions.

VAT/GST's founding principles avoid any risk of international double taxation or, perhaps better said, it is not a structural problem for VAT/GST, as double taxation

10. Art. 113 TFEU.
11. *See, e.g.*, OECD, *International VAT/GST Guidelines* 12 (2005) [hereafter the 'OECD VAT/GST Guidelines'] (the principle of origin (i.e., taxation where the value is created) 'run[s] counter to the core features of a VAT: as a tax on consumption, the revenue should accrue to the jurisdiction where the final consumption takes place' and, for this reason:

> there is widespread consensus that the destination principle, with revenue accruing to the country of import where final consumption occurs, is preferable to the origin principle from both a theoretical and practical standpoint. In fact, the destination principle is the international norm and is sanctioned by World Trade Organization ('WTO') rules.

is in the income taxation context, frequently caused by the adoption of different (and overlapping) criteria of connection by the jurisdictions involved.[12]

Although the risks of double taxation and double non-taxation are not inherent in the founding principles of the international VAT/GST regulation, the practical implementation of these rules varies across the different jurisdictions. Double taxation (and double non-taxation) are, therefore, the consequence of the normative translation of the founding principles by the different jurisdictions.[13] As highlighted by the OECD, on the one hand:

> [i]mplementation of the destination principle with respect to international trade in goods is relatively straightforward in theory and generally effective in practice, due in large part to the existence of border controls or fiscal frontiers,[14]

but, on the other hand:

> [i]mplementing the destination principle for international trade in services and intangibles is more difficult than for international trade in goods. The nature of services and intangibles is such that they cannot be subject to border controls in the same way as goods.[15]

Bearing these two variables in mind, the early stages of VAT harmonization were dominated by the needs of the Single Market. After the introduction of a VAT system in the then-European Community, the main goals were the implementation of rules to abolish tax frontiers and the related transition to the origin principle for the intra-Community supplies. In that regard:

> a common system of VAT can be defined solely by reference to the general objectives of the Treaty, and in particular the pursuit of economic integration and convergence as symbolised by the concept of the single market. In this context, the common system of VAT must be given the characteristics of a genuine Community tax area in which domestic and intra-Community transactions are afforded equal treatment, this being unavoidable consequence of the ultimate objective which has been pursued ever since the First VAT Directive adopted, i.e. the eventual creation of a 'common market within which there is healthy competition and whose characteristics are similar to those of a domestic market'.[16]

The aim pursued by the European Institutions was the simplification of the regimes applicable to cross-border transactions with the reduction to just two sets of

12. *Accord*, Graeme Cooper and Richard Vann, *Implementing the Goods and Services Tax*, 16 Sydney L. Rev. 337, 419 fn 257 (1999) ('the destination principle means that there will not generally be effective levy of GST by two countries. Hence the problem of double taxation is not systemic to the GST').
13. For a broader analysis of this issue, see Gianluigi Bizioli, *Comparative Analysis of the Causes of Double (Non-) Taxation in the Income and VAT/GST Contexts, in Value Added Tax and Direct Taxation: Similarities and Differences* 383, 395 et seq. (Michael Lang, Peter Melz & Eleonor Kristoffersson eds., 2009).
14. OECD VAT/GST Guidelines, *supra* n. 11, at 13.
15. *Ibid.*
16. Commission of the European Communities, a Common System of VAT: A Programme for the Single Market, COM(96) 328 final, 22 July 1996, 14.

rules: one applicable to purely domestic and intra-EU cross-border transactions and the other applicable to cross-border transactions involving third countries.

Due to the impracticability of reaching consensus around the origin principle among the Member States, the Commission's VAT policy was updated at the beginning of the twenty-first century. The Commission's 2000 Communication on the Strategy to Improve the Operation of the VAT System within the Internal Market[17] and the 2008 VAT Package,[18] adopted after the political agreement achieved by the Council on 4 December 2007, marked the end of attempts at the harmonization of the VAT system around the origin principle and the beginning of the shift towards the improvement of the efficiency of the existing rules on taxation of intra-EU cross-border transactions in the Member State of destination.[19]

As already highlighted, the described VAT policy had a primarily (and almost exclusive) goal, that is to say, the development of the most suitable tax regime for the Single Market and, in particular, the equal treatment of the purely domestic and intra-EU VAT transactions. The need for the coordination of the international transactions (or, better, the transactions between Member State and third countries) appears during the same period as a reaction to the economic globalization (and, in particular, the raising of the so-called e-commerce) and the widespread propagation of the VAT model throughout the world.[20]

One of the first document which recognizes the need of a EU policy in this field is the Commission Staff Working Document accompanying the Green Paper on the future of VAT, published in 2010.[21] In the Document, based on the premises that:

17. Commission of the European Communities, Communication from the Commission to the Council and the European Parliament, A Strategy to Improve the Operation of the VAT System within the Context of the Internal Market, COM(2000) 348 final, 7 June 2000.
18. In response to the political agreement on two draft Directives and a draft Regulation aimed at changing the rules on VAT on 4 Dec. 2007, thereafter, on 8 Feb. 2008, the ECOFIN Council approved a number of legal texts, the so-called VAT Package, which included a Directive on the place of supply of services, a mini one-stop-shop for telecom, broadcasting, and e-commerce services, a Directive on procedures for VAT refunds to non-established businesses, and a Regulation on the exchange of information between Member States, deemed a necessary underpinning for the newly adopted VAT arrangements. European Commission, Press Release, IP/08/208, 12 Feb. 2008.
19. In this direction, *see* Communication from the Commission to the European Parliament, the Council and the European Economic and Social Committee on an action plan on VAT. Towards a single EU VAT area – Time to decide, COM(2016) 148 final, 7 Apr. 2016, which, after the Green Paper definitively adopted the destination principle '[t]o sum up, VAT needs to be modernised and rebooted. … Action is now needed. It is time for the creation of a genuine single EU VAT area for the single market. … This definitive system will rest upon the agreement of EU legislators that the VAT system should be based on the principle of taxation in the country of destination of the goods' (3–4).
20. For example, Australia has introduced the GST in 2000; New Zealand in 1986; Canada in 1991; India in 2005 and Russia Federation in 1991.
21. SEC(2010) 1455 final, 1 Dec. 2010 [hereafter the '2010 Working Document']. The 2010 Working Document acknowledged, at 49:

> [t]he need to address issues relating to the supply of services across the EU's external border is a relatively recent development in the history of the common system of VAT. In all probability, those who framed the original legislation did not consider cross-border services to be of any great economic interest, especially where non-EU countries

> [c]hanges in technology, greater deregulation, innovative business models and the general impact of globalisation have resulted in enormous changes in the economic significance of internationally traded services and intangibles, putting pressure in turn on international aspects of the VAT system,

the Commission disclosed the new policy aimed at developing 'International norms for VAT-type taxes based on taxation according to the rules applicable in the jurisdiction of consumption. These will have no impact on the rules for intra-EU transactions.'[22] Accordingly, a different objective and a new actor burst on the VAT scene. If the primary focus of the Commission still remained (and remains) the completion of the Internal Market VAT system and the fight against tax frauds, the request for uniform rules applicable to the international transactions got some space on the EU VAT agenda. At the same time, the development of this policy needed the support of the international community and the coordination of a renewed player at the international level, the OECD.[23]

This role has been excellently carried out by the OECD Centre for Tax Policy and Administration. As already mentioned, at the very outset, the *occasio* of this work was the emerging taxation issues in the field of e-commerce;[24] the need for a better coordination has produced the comprehensive document 'International VAT/GST Guidelines of 2015', which embodies the fundamental and the detailed rules about the international taxation of consumption.

From this outline, three conclusions can be inferred about the international dimension of the EU VAT policy.

The first, recently stated in the 2016 'VAT Action Plan', is the centrality of the Internal Market VAT legislation in the EU tax policy. The needs of simplification and efficiency of the system, as well as fighting against the growing risk of tax fraud are at the top of list of the European Commission priorities.

The second is that at the international level exists a set of common statements applicable to the VAT/GST taxation of (international) cross-border transaction of goods and services pursued and developed under the coordination of the OECD. In particular, this activity concerns the specification of the principle of destination applicable to the supply of goods and services across the EU's external border.

Finally, the diachronic evolution has shown a substantial convergence between the fundamental principles which govern the international dimension and the European policy towards the taxation of the cross-border transactions according to the principle of destination.

---

were involved. For a long time, the rules on the place of supply of B2B services were seen as sufficient to deal with all likely eventualities.

22. *Ibid.*
23. *Ibid.*
24. Outlined in the document Taxation and Electronic Commerce – Implementing the Ottawa Taxation Framework Conditions, 2001.

§11.03 THE EUROPEAN FINANCIAL TRANSACTION TAX AND THE INTERNATIONAL PRINCIPLES OF TAX LAW

The so-called Financial Transaction Tax ('FTT'), whose general features and the draft regulation are contained in the COM(2013) 71 final,[25] manifests two different elements connected with the topic treated in this chapter.

The first concerns the origin of the tax. The idea to introduce a levy on the financial sector finds its (political) roots in the G20 Pittsburgh Summit held in September 2009, where the leaders tasked the International Monetary Fund ('IMF') to explore:

> the range of options countries have adopted or are considering as to how the financial sector could make a fair and substantial contribution toward paying for any burdens associated with government interventions to repair the banking system'.[26]

In the final declaration of the subsequent G20 meeting in Toronto (2010), the leaders recognized that 'there are a range of policy approaches to this end. Some countries are pursuing a financial levy. Other countries are pursuing different approaches'.[27]

It is worth noting that this exhausts the first international aspect of the policy, since the category of the FTTs are not univocal, but comprehends at least the levies on the financial activities and those on the securities transactions. It is also well known that the choice of the Commission was directed on the taxation of:

> all types of financial instruments (...) which are negotiable on the capital market, money-market instruments (with the exception of instruments of payment), units or shares in collective investment undertakings – which include undertakings for collective investment in transferable securities (UCITS) and alternative investment funds (AIF) and derivatives contracts

and that the Commission deemed the FTT as a suitable resource for the EU Budget.[28]

---

25. European Commission, Proposal for a Council Directive Implementing Enhanced Cooperation in the Area of Financial Transaction Tax, COM(2013) 71 final, 14 Feb. 2013 [hereafter, the 'FTT Enhanced Cooperation Proposal'].
26. The G20 Pittsburgh Summit Statement of 24-25 Sep. 2009, para. 16. This purpose has been confirmed in the G20 Toronto Summit Declaration of 27 June 2010, at 21:

    > [w]e are committed to design and implement a system where we have the powers and tools to restructure or resolve all types of financial institutions in crisis, without taxpayers ultimately bearing the burden, and adopted principles that will guide implementation. We called upon the FSB to consider and develop concrete policy recommendations to effectively address problems associated with, and resolve, systemically important financial institutions by the Seoul Summit. To reduce moral hazard risks, there is a need to have a policy framework including effective resolution tools, strengthened prudential and supervisory requirements, and core financial market infrastructures'.

27. *Ibid.*
28. The FTT Enhanced Cooperation Proposal, *supra* n. 25, paras 8, 15.

The second international profile of the European FTT involves Article 4(1)(f) of the proposed Directive which states that a financial institution shall be deemed to be established in the territory of a participating Member State if:

> it is party, acting either for its own account or for the account of another person, or is acting in the name of a party to the transaction, to a financial transaction with another financial institution established in that Member State pursuant to points (a), (b), (c), (d) or (e), or with a party established in the territory of that Member State and which is not a financial institution[29]

(the 'counterparty principle'). In particular, according to the UK, this principle would have allowed the taxation of institutions, persons, or transactions situated or taking place in the territory of non-participating Member States, thus violating customary international law that requires 'a sufficiently close connection' between the facts or subjects and the territory of the country exercising the tax authority.[30]

On this point, the official position of the European Commission is that:

> in all the situations addressed by Article 4(1)(f) the financial institution concerned (located outside the "FTT jurisdiction") takes part in a financial transaction with a counterparty established in a participating Member State, thereby contributing to the achievement of a legally relevant result within that jurisdiction. That transaction constitutes a sufficient nexus with the jurisdiction.[31]

In other words, according to the position of the Commission, the absence of any connection between the financial institution and the territory of the participating Member State does not compromise the extension of taxation to those transactions with a party established in a participating Member State.

In this sense, the relevant international aspects of the European FTT concern the specification of the 'sufficient' connection between the facts and the jurisdiction in the exercise of the power to tax and, in particular, the enlargement of the common understanding about that notion.

§11.04 THE INTERNATIONAL DIMENSION OF EU INCOME TAX POLICY

[A] Preliminary Remarks

EU income tax policy has been (and, still is) shaped by factors of different nature.

The leading element is represented by the distribution of competences in the field of income taxation between the EU and the Member States provided by the Treaties and, in particular, by the legal basis for the harmonization of income taxation.

---

29. *Ibid.* Article 4(1)(f).
30. It is worth remembering that the proposed Directive was presented, for the first time in the tax sector, according to the 'enhanced cooperation' procedure provided for by Art. 20 TEU.
31. European Commission, *Financial Transaction Tax: Legality of the "Counterparty Principle" Laid Down in Article 4(1)(f) of the Commission Proposal for a Council Directive Implementing Enhanced Cooperation in the Area of FTT, COM(2013) 71 final of 14 February 2013*, 1 (2013) *available* at https://ec.europa.eu/taxation_customs/sites/taxation/files/docs/body/legal_aspects_proposal.pdf.

It is well known that the 'approximation' of the laws in this sector lies in a general provision – Article 115 TFEU – and that the Treaties do not contain any specific rules on the subject.[32] The lack of a 'specific' competence parallel to Article 113 TFEU has carried out a timid and wavy EU income tax policy, strictly limited to the elimination of the most manifest tax obstacles to the cross-border circulation of persons and capitals. The driving force of this has primarily been played by the European Court of Justice through the application of the fundamental freedoms.[33]

In addition, considering that Article 115 TFEU vests the Union with the competence to approximate national laws in so far 'as directly affect[s] the establishment or functioning of the internal market', the authority over individual income taxes falls primarily under the responsibility of the Member States. A residual EU competence in the field of individual income taxation can be single out in the need to remove the cross-border tax obstacles to the circulation of non-residents.[34] However, this policy is

32. The original version of the Treaty of the European Economic Community ('EEC') contained an article that called on Member States to 'enter into negotiations with each other with a view to securing for the benefit of their nationals ... the abolition of double taxation within the Community'. This provision was deleted in the Treaty of Lisbon. On this issue, see Herwig Hofmann, *Double Tax Agreements: Between EU Law and Public International Law, in Double Taxation within the European Union* 75, 83 (Alexander Rust ed., 2011), who affirms:

> two reasons might have contributed to the decision to quietly let Article 293 EC die: First, it had, due to case law of the ECJ and due to legislation in all areas but for double-taxation decreased in relevance. Second, agreements under public international law are often ill-suited to address the complexities of the single market'

See also Ekkehart Reimer, *The Abolition of Article 293 EC: Comments on Hofmann's Analysis* 87, *in* Rust, *supra*, who envisages, from the abolition of the provision: 'considerable leeway for harmonization of international tax law on the basis of Articles 114 et seq. TFEU' since the Commission 'may now draft an EU Model Tax Convention for bilateral tax treaties, suggest a multilateral intra-EU Tax Convention, or propose a Directive on the avoidance of double taxation within the EU'.

33. On the legal integration of the different Member States' income tax systems and the role of the CJEU, see Gianluigi Bizioli & Claudio Sacchetto, *European Constitutional Integration: The Case of Direct Taxation, in Comparative Fiscal Federalism* 11, 19 et seq. (Reuven S. Avi-Yonah & Michael Lang, eds., 2016).

34. In this direction, see Communication from the Commission to the Council, the European Parliament and the European Economic and Social Committee, Removing Cross-Border Tax Obstacles for EU citizens, COM(2010) 769, 20 Feb. 2010, 4:

> the Commission believes that it is not appropriate in a single market that problems such as double taxation, incompatibilities between different tax systems and lack of access to information on the tax rules of Member States should deter individuals from engaging in cross-border activity or penalise them when they do. Harmonisation of all aspects of Member States' tax rules would be neither necessary nor feasible. But solutions are needed that recognise the legitimate interests of citizens in an area of free movement, such as the one established by the Treaties.

See, similarly, the Communication from the Commission to the Council, the European Parliament and the Economic and Social Committee, Tax Policy in the European Union – Priorities for the Years Ahead, COM(2001) 260 final, para. 3.2.3.: 'coordination at EU level only becomes necessary to prevent cross-border discrimination or obstacles to the exercise of the four freedoms'.

rather marginal in the European context and the actions planned confined to very few sectors.

Finally, the described allocation of competences has consequences also on the method of 'coordination' of the domestic laws and, in particular, on the adoption of hard and/or soft law approaches.

European tax policy is also seriously influenced by the economic and political scenario, which has repercussions on the definition of the objectives of the action. As will be described *infra* in §11.04[C][2] the historical evolution of the integration process shows three different stages: the early overall integration, the piecemeal integration after the publication of the white paper on the Single Market and the current double approach phase. All these stages reflect precise economic and political situations.

The final factor concerns the meaning of the term 'international'. Due to the absence of an overall harmonization of individual and corporate income taxation at the EU level, the term 'international' covers both the tax treatment of cross border situations within the Union *and* with third countries. Accordingly, to correctly understand the scenarios of the future international tax policy, two different dimensions must be considered.

All this considered, the analysis will be carried out along two different directives. The first involves the distinction between individual and company income tax fields; in addition, for both situations, the two dimensions of the term international will be explored.

[B] The (Future of) EU Individual Income Tax Policy: The Elimination of Cross-Border Tax Obstacles Within the Single Market

As already mentioned in §11.04[A], *supra*, EU tax policy on individual income taxation assumes a marginal position in the context of the whole tax policy, in at least two directions. In relative terms, the European approach in the field of individual income taxation is entirely subsidiary, even if not dependent, to the corporate income taxation policy, since the former affects *directly* the establishment and the functioning of the Single Market only in few specific situations. The most evident sign of this marginality is the fact that the latest document on this subject published by the Commission dates back to 2010 and the ideas and initiatives therein proposed have not received any follow-up or updates.

In absolute terms, the approach adopted by the Commission is strictly limited to the most evident cross-border tax obstacles that hinder the movement of individuals within the Internal Market. In this sense, the Union policy aims at eliminating only the 'disparities' between the different domestic tax systems and at coordinating the tax measures which give rise to double taxation.[35]

35. European Commission, Communication from the Commission to the Council, the European Parliament and the European Economic and Social Committee, Removing Cross-Border Tax Obstacles for EU citizens, COM(2010) 769, 20 Feb. 2010, 5: [a]bove all, the Commission believes that action must be taken to resolve problems of double taxation in the EU in a definitive way

The lesson from the past, in summary, reveals a wide self-restraint attitude of the Commission on the approximation of individual income taxation and the adoption of a piecemeal approach limited to very specific areas of that tax field. In particular, the focus has been given to the discriminatory (or restrictive) effects of the domestic provisions and, among those, on the prevention or elimination of double taxation.

The evidence of these thoughts can be appreciated in two different directions.

On the first side, except for the sole case of the repealed savings Directive,[36] the achievement of the mentioned aims has been entrusted with the 'coordination' at the EU level and, therefore, mainly with the 'spontaneous' implementation of the 'soft law' recommendations by the Member States. This method is manifestly less pervasive than the tradition harmonization or approximation means and, at the least in the understanding of the Commission, more respectful of the principle of subsidiarity (and of the domestic tax sovereignty).[37]

On the other side, and strictly linked to the topic of this chapter, the interest of the Commission is restricted to the tax treatment of intra-EU cross-border situations. The 'international' dimension of this policy finds its borders in the Single Market and, conversely, the design of the policy with third countries is wholly assigned to the Member States' competence.

Also in this case, the only remarkable exception is represented by the taxation of savings income.

Whereas the Directive regulated the payments within the Single Market, specific bilateral international agreements negotiated and stipulated by the Union, alternatively, extended the same regime to third countries or introduced a system of withholding taxation of the income paid by an agent resident in that State. This exception was justified by the aim of the Directive, pinpointed in the need to prevent tax evasion and avoidance in the field of the taxation of capitals. The primary objective of this regime, therefore, was to protect Member States' tax revenues and, as an effect, to foster the functioning of the Single Market. In this specific case, therefore, the extension of the regime to third countries found its rationale in the defence of the

that goes beyond the solutions contained in bilateral tax treaties. It is worth noting that the same document addressed also peculiar problems outside the income tax field and, in particular, the cross-border inheritance tax issues ('[t]he double taxation problems arise because the laws in those Member States that apply taxes on inheritance differ considerably even as regards who is taxable') and the double taxation connected with the vehicle registration and circulation taxes. In the mentioned document, therefore, the approach adopted by the Commission crosses the borders of the income taxation and comprehends those manifest tax obstacles to the circulation of individuals (and capitals). However, this element does not overturn (but, at the opposite, confirm) the conclusion about the marginality of the Commission tax policy referred to individuals.

36. Council Directive 2003/48/EC of 3 June 2003 on taxation of savings income in the form of interest payments.

37. The term 'coordination' does not define an alternative mean to the harmonization or approximation of domestic tax laws but it is a mere stipulation adopted to express the traditional and 'soft law' approaches to the European legal integration. *See, e.g.*, para. 4.3. of the Commission Communication on the Priorities for the Years Ahead (COM(2001) 260 final), where the 'use of non-legislative approaches or "soft legislation"' is considered 'an additional means of making progress in the tax field'. On this topic, see the comprehensive analysis made by Giuseppe Melis, *Coordinamento fiscale nella UE, in Enciclopedia del Diritto* 394, 402 (1997).

Member States' budgets, which required, to be effective, the participation of a few jurisdiction located outside the Union.

Although in this historical moment seems that there is little room for any attempt to talk about a tax policy on taxation of the individual income, some ideas can nevertheless be framed.

As far as the Single Market dimension is considered, the piecemeal approach is largely preferable over a comprehensive solution. The focus of the action should remain on the tax obstacles of the Single Market, in two different areas: those situations covered by the fundamental freedoms and those problems, mainly connected to double taxation within the Single Market, which are outside the scope of application of the fundamental freedoms. The former case raises issues of tax coordination between two (or more) jurisdictions, such as the different regimes of taxation/deduction adopted.[38] The latter case, differently, concerns the overlapping of the taxing powers of two (or more) Member States.[39]

In both cases, the best way to foster this approach lies in the 'soft legislation' as an alternative to the traditional tax harmonization and, therefore, the achievement of tax coordination through the (slow) convergence of the domestic and treaty tax provisions led by the recommendations and the guidelines of the Commission.

According to this premise, the target of the EU tax policy should be both substantive and procedural provisions that hinder the movement within the Single Market, independently from the source of these provisions (domestic or treaty law). Depending on the issue, this policy may therefore affect the domestic tax regulation or the tax treaty provisions of the States of residence or source. In broad terms, the tax obstacles arising in the Member State of residence concern the tax treatment of foreign-sourced income and the taxation of the expatriation of individuals; those in the Member State of origin the level of the withholding taxation.[40]

As far as the 'purely international' dimension is considered, the active role should be left to the OECD and to international means. As long as these measures do not affect directly the Internal Market, there is no legal basis for a Union competence on the matter.

[C] The Two Dimensions of EU International Corporate Income Tax Policy

[1] Introduction

The requirements that influence the development of the company tax policy differ sensibly from those framed for the taxation of individuals.

38. The leading cases are represented by *Schempp*, C-403/03, Judgment, EU:C:2005:446, and *Bachmann*, C-204/90, Judgment, EU:C:1992:35.
39. *Kerckhaert and Morres*, C-513/04, Judgment, EU:C:2006:713.
40. A wide taxonomy of these obstacles, as well as possible solutions, can be found in the European Commission Report of Expert Group, *Ways to Tackle Cross-Border Tax Obstacles Facing Individuals Within the EU*, Nov. 2015, Chs 3, 4, 5.

Firstly, 'any form of company taxation is liable to bring about economic distortions (lack of neutrality) because it may give rise to decisions on the location, nature and financing of investment would not have been taken in the absence of company taxation' and, as a consequence, '[f]rom a theoretical viewpoint, the possibility could therefore be considered of harmonizing national company tax systems at Community level so as to ensure complete tax neutrality'.[41] Different from the harmonization of individual income taxation standpoint, the Commission perspective of the (economic) integration of the Internal Market required (but, as shown, still requires) the comprehensive approximation of the Member States domestic legislations in the field of corporate taxation.[42] As demonstrated in §11.04[C][2], *infra*, the real driving force of this approach was (and, still is) the elimination of any cross-border tax obstacles to the free movement of companies within the Single Market and the guarantee of a level playing field without distortion of competition.

Secondly, the process of economic globalization and the high mobility of the capital (and, therefore, of the investments) pushed the European Council to call on the development of 'concrete ways to improve the fight against tax fraud and tax evasion, including in relation to third countries'.[43] In this sense, beside the progressive removal of cross-border tax obstacles within the Union, the policy of the Commission has been enriched with the aim to prevent tax fraud and evasion, considered as a threaten or a cause of distortion for the functioning of the Single Market. Whereas the coordination of the Member States corporate income tax systems was aimed at the removal of intra-Union tax obstacles, this policy, from the outset, has not been strictly restricted to the borders and the objectives of the Union, but also extended to third countries.[44]

Although both the intra-Union and the 'international' policies find their formal roots in the establishment and functioning of the Single Market, they are nonetheless

41. In this sense, see Commission of the European Communities, Commission Communication to Parliament and the Council, Guidelines on Company Taxation, SEC(90) 601 final, 20 Apr. 1990, 1–2, paras 3, 4. The theoretical basis of this conclusion lies in the concepts of (a) capital export and capital import neutrality (i.e., the lack of tax distortions to the free flow of resources) and (b) equity, understood as the equitable distribution of tax revenues between the Member States of the common market.
42. This feature was reasserted in the recent Communication from the Commission to the European Parliament and the Council, Building a Fair, Competitive and Stable Corporate Tax System for the EU, COM(2016) 682 final, 5:

> The CCCTB will considerably improve the functioning of the Single Market from a tax perspective. Cross-border companies will benefit from a single set of rules to calculate their taxable profits in the EU, rather than a medley of different national systems. ... The CCCTB will be clear, stable and bound in EU law. It will be unanimously agreed by all Member States, guaranteeing a stable system which is not prone to regular changes. This will provide business with an unprecedented level of tax certainty.

43. European Council, Conclusions of the Meeting Held on 1–2 Mar. 2012, para. 9.
44. In its Communication from the Commission to the European Parliament and the Council on Concrete Ways to Reinforce the Fight Against Tax Fraud and Tax Evasion including in Relation to Third Countries COM(2012) 351 final, 27 June 2012, 3 [hereinafter the 'Concrete Ways Communication'], the European Commission stated that 'the EU needs to have a clear and coherent policy vis-à-vis third countries in order to promote its standards at [the] international level and ensure a level playing field.' Residual signs of this objective can be found also in the repealed Directive on the taxation of savings income.

justified by different (but complementary) needs. In addition, the different foundation of the policies has immediate consequences not only on the territorial 'extension' of the proposed actions, but also on the methods.[45]

In §11.04[C][2] and [3], *infra*, the analysis is separately developed for the two policy areas according to the previous patterns: the lessons from the past and the present are used to infer some ideas for the future corporate income tax policy.

[2] The 'New Deal' of EU Tax Policy: From the Single Market to the Protection of Domestic Corporate Tax Systems

The general features of the evolution over the years of the European policy on corporate income taxation is well-know and, above all, this is not the right place to look it over again.[46] It is well-known, for example, that after the initial attempt towards the creation of a European corporate income tax regulation which should have replaced the domestic systems, like the VAT model (top-down policy approach), in the Communication on 'Guidelines on Company Taxation' of 1990, due to the political failure of the previous approach, the Commission radically converted this comprehensive approach in direction to the principle of subsidiarity. Accordingly, the policy trend has moved from the creation of a European common legal environment to the elimination of those measures which hugely affected the functioning of the Single Market.

The current phase was initiated in 2001 by publication of the Communication relating to 'Tax Policy in the European Union - Priorities for the Years Ahead',[47] in which the Commission laid the first stone of the combined approach that should have shaped future actions and proposals in the field of corporate income taxation. On the one hand, it acknowledged that 'tax obstacles can continue to be tackled by piecemeal approaches that leave national company tax systems intact',[48] in line with the pure subsidiarity approach introduced at the beginning of the 1990s. On the other hand, it also suggested a more ambitious approach in the form of 'a more comprehensive solution such as a common set of rules for company taxation'.[49] Assuming the failure

45. Carlo Garbarino, *Harmonization and Coordination of Corporate Taxes in the European Union*, 25 EC Tax Rev. 277, 280, where the author distinguishes between three dimensions of a 'coordinated' EU corporate tax system: *intra-EU*, *EU-inbound* (which 'refers to the policies of the EU as a whole vis-à-vis non-EU investors'), and *EU-outbound* (which 'refers to the policies of the EU as a whole in respect to EU investors [i.e., investors based in a Member State] and opening outside of the EU').
46. For an in-depth analysis of this process through the end of the twentieth century, see Alfred J. Martín Jiménez, *Towards Corporate Tax Harmonization in the European Community. An Institutional and Procedural Analysis* Chs 1, 4 (1999).
47. Communication from the Commission to the Council, the European Parliament and the Economic and Social Committee, Tax Policy in the European Union - Priorities for the Years Ahead, COM(2001) 260 final, 28 May 2001 [hereinafter the '2001 Priorities Communication'].
48. *Ibid.* para. 5.
49. *Ibid. See, also, ibid.* para. 3.2.2, where the Commission further stated:

> Under a mutual recognition approach, for example the approach of taxation according to the rules of the residence country (the so-called 'home State taxation' approach), these could be the existing national rules; otherwise, new common rules would need to be devised at EU level.

(or the insufficiency) of the piecemeal solutions for the coordination of the corporate income taxation, the Communication has proposed a return to the past (i.e., the introduction of a comprehensive solution through a common set of rules for the determination of the corporate income tax, which would have replaced, also optionally, the existing domestic national rules).

As far as the contents of the coordination are considered, the main focus of the Communication was on the elimination of the obstacles to free movement and the guarantee of a fair competition within the Single Market.[50] However, the same document shed also light on the '*international dimension*' of EU tax policy and, in particular, on the need for the major world economies to 'work towards a fiscal climate which promotes free and fair competition and is conducive to cross-border business activity, while at the same time ensuring that national tax bases are not eroded'.[51] In this scenario, the objective of EU tax policy was the removal of the cross-border obstacle in order to create a Single Market like the domestic tax systems. The prevention of 'harmful' tax competition, or of the domestic tax base erosion, stands clearly against the background.

Finally, due to the programmatic aim of the document, the Communication did not offer any indication about the normative strategy. This position left open any range of solution, from the traditional (hard law) harmonization to the more feasible coordination through international treaties and/or soft-law measures.

Although many years have passed and the current global economic, financial, and political situation has radically changed since 2001, the Commission recently confirmed the effectiveness of the combined approach for the European tax policy for the years ahead. On the one hand, it has re-launched the proposal for the introduction of a common set of rules applicable to the European companies in the form of a CCCTB and, on the other hand, it has proposed a series of specific initiatives targeting different objectives.[52]

A first conclusion of this analysis is, therefore, that the recent communications of the Commission do not have produced any substantial revision about the general approach to the corporate income taxation in the Union. The policy continues to be based on a 'short term' and a 'medium- to long-term' strategies; the former aimed at dealing with specific issues, whereas the latter should be foster through the relaunched CCCTB proposal,[53] presented on 25 October 2016.

Differently, the changes embrace the contents and the extension of the policy. The traditional issue of the elimination of cross-border tax obstacles to the free movement of companies, which has represented *the* aim of Union tax policy from the outset, has been over the years superseded, or at least added, by the prevention of: tax

50. *Ibid.* para. 3.2.2.
51. *Ibid.* para. 3.2.1.
52. The outline of this proposal is provided by the Communication from the Commission to the European Parliament and the Council, A Fair and Efficient Corporate Tax System in the European Union: 5 Key Areas for Action, COM(2012) 302 final, 17 June 2015 [hereinafter, the '5 Key-Areas Action Plan']. The theoretical basis is the Commission Staff Working Document on Corporate Income Taxation in the European Union, SWD(2015) 121 final.
53. The 5 Key-Areas Action Plan, *supra* n. 52, at 15.

evasion, tax erosion, and unfair (or harmful) tax competition. The key moments in this process can be reduced to three: (i) the introduction of the Code of Conduct, (ii) the 2012 Action Plan against tax fraud and tax evasion,[54] and (iii) the recent Transparency and Anti-Tax Avoidance Packages.[55] The most evident example is shown by the recent Proposals for the Council Directives on the CCCTB,[56] where the Commission stresses that although 'corporate income is taxed at national level', '[b]usiness models and corporate structures are more complex, making easier to shift profits,' which has allowed 'aggressive tax planning'.[57] However, continue the same Proposal, '[a]longside the anti-tax avoidance function of the CCCTB, the re-launched project would also retain its features as a corporate tax system which facilitates cross-border trade and investments in the internal market'. Finally, 'the re-launched proposal for a CCCTB would include rules to address some of the key Actions of the OECD initiative on ... BEPS'.

Accordingly, the Single Market is not more identified with the free movement and fair competition without distortion, but has been enlarged to comprehend also the concept of 'fair taxation'.[58] This concept is conceived as autonomous from the national ones, usually connected with the equal distribution of tax burden among the taxpayers,[59] and is summed up in the 5 Key-Areas Action Plan[60] in the field of corporate taxation. In particular, a fair taxation should:

54. The Concrete Ways Communication, *supra* n. 44; *see also* An Action Plan to Strengthen the Fight Against Tax Fraud and Tax Evasion, COM(2012) 722 final, 6 Dec. 2012 [hereinafter the '2012 Strengthen the Fight Communication'].
55. Respectively, the Communication from the Commission to the European Parliament and the Council on tax transparency to fight tax evasion and avoidance, COM(2015) 136 final, 18 Mar. 2015 and the Communication from the Commission to the European Parliament and the Council, Anti-Tax Avoidance Package: Next Steps Towards Delivering Effective Taxation and Greater Tax Transparency in the EU, COM(2016) 23 final, 28 Jan. 2016.
56. European Commission, Proposal for a Council Directive on a Common Consolidate Corporate Tax Base (CCCTB), COM(2006) 683 final, 25 Oct. 2016 [hereinafter the '2016 CCCTB Proposal']; and European Commission, Proposal for a Council Directive on Common Corporate Tax Base, COM(2016) 685 final, 25 Oct.2016 [hereafter the '2016 CCTB Proposal'].
57. The 2016 CCCTB Proposal, *supra* n. 56, at 2; the 2016 CCTB Proposal, *supra* n. 56, at 2.
58. The 2016 CCCTB Proposal, *supra* n. 56, at 4; the 2016 CCTB Proposal, *supra* n. 56, at 4. The Commission stated:

    > The CCCTB falls within the ambit of the Commission's initiatives for fairer taxation and would contribute to the elimination of obstacles which create distortions that impede the proper functioning of the internal market. On this premise, it is largely complementary to the EU-level legislation in company law and broadly fits with projects such as the Capital Markets Union and the several initiatives in tax transparency, the exchange of information and anti-money laundering.

59. Paul B.W.L. Lamberts, *Fair Taxation: Truth is in the Eye of the Beholder*, 45 Intertax 49, 50 et seq. (2017), highlights three problems connected with the use of this term: (1) '[t]he term is subjective, basically following politically coloured national interests and therefore arbitrary or at least incomplete'; (2) the term was not used to address tax evasion and tax avoidance by multinational enterprises; and (3) the development of the concept of fairness in the international context 'is problematic from a democracy point of view'.
60. As defined in n. 52, *supra*.

(1) Re-establish the link between taxation and where economic activity takes place.
(2) Ensure that Member States can correctly value corporate activity in their jurisdiction.
(3) Create a competitive and growth-friendly corporate tax environment for the EU, resulting in a more resilient corporate sector, in line with the recommendations in the European Semester.
(4) Protect the Single Market and secure a strong EU approach to external corporate tax issues, including measures to implement OECD BEPS, to deal with non-cooperative tax jurisdictions and to increase tax transparency.[61]

In this sense, the concept of 'fair taxation' at EU level requires, not only a just allocation of the taxing authority among the Member States, but also a just distribution of tax revenues.[62] The EU interest – the Single Market – stands against the background, whereas the main interest guaranteed by this policy is the domestic corporate tax systems and their revenues.[63] The result is very curios, since it diverges from the well-known federalist standards: the EU law-making authority is functional to the Member States' revenue interest.

A second conclusion, therefore, has been the progressive enlargement of the Single Market concept in the corporate income tax field, from the removal of cross-border tax obstacles to the free movement of companies and the creation of the conditions for a level playing field, to the achievement of a fair tax environment. This process highlights also an increasing convergence to (or, perhaps, dependence on) the international tax policies elaborated by the OECD.[64] On the one hand, it shows the progressive construction of common international tax law standards and a common language; on the other hand, differently, this process produces the fading of the

61. The 5 Key-Areas Action Plan, *supra* n. 52, at 6.
62. The Commission, *ibid.* at 3, outlines the pillars of international taxation as such:

> To ensure the fair distribution of tax revenues between countries, while avoiding double taxation, transfer pricing based on the arm's length principle (ALP) was devised. The ALP ensured that the price of intra-group transactions matched comparable market prices, thereby providing a clear means of allocating profits within a multinational enterprise. To resolve cross-border disputes on corporate taxation, bilateral treaties were chosen as the preferred tool, rather than a multilateral approach.

See also Ben J.M. Terra & Peter J. Wattel, *European Tax Law* 200 (6th ed. 2012): '*[h]armful* tax competition is commonly understood to exist where Member States damage each other' budgets (*beggar thy neighbour*) rather than help *create* economic activity, causing an overall tax loss for the Union (in economic terms: spill-over; negative externalities' (emphasis added); Carlo Pinto, *EU and OECD to Fight Harmful Tax Competition: Has the Right Path Been Undertaken?*, 26 Intertax 386, 387 (1998); Frans Vanistendael, *Fiscal Support Measures and Harmful Tax Competition*, 9 EC Tax Rev. 152 (2000); and William W. Bratton & Joseph A. McCahery, *Tax Coordination and Tax Competition in the European Union: Evaluating the Code of Conduct on Business Taxation*, 38 Common Mkt L. Rev. 677, 697 et seq. (2001).
63. In this sense, clearly, see the 5 Key-Areas Action Plan, *supra* n. 52, at 9: '[t]he ultimate effect of any such measures should be to safeguard Member States' rights to tax revenues generated in the Single Market and reduce the capacity of certain companies to escape taxation altogether'.
64. This trend has been stressed by Bratton & McCahery, *supra* n. 62, at 678.

concept of Single Market, sacrificed on the altar of the prevention of international tax avoidance and of BEPS.

This impressive 'new deal' in European corporate tax policy can be set in the period between 2009 and 2012.

In 2009, the Commission published the Communication on Tax Good Governance[65] in which envisaged three areas of action: (1) tax transparency, (2) exchange of tax information, and (3) fair tax competition.[66] These three objectives have in common the 'international' (or external) dimension of the approach, i.e. the extension both to intra-EU and to third countries.

As far as the Single Market is concerned, in the Concrete Ways Communication,[67] the Commission has been expressly enlarged to comprehend the 'fight against tax fraud and tax evasion' which must be tackled at three different levels:

> firstly, the tax collection within each Member State ... [s]econdly, there is the need to enhance cross-border cooperation between Member States' tax administration [and t]hirdly, the EU needs to have a clear and coherent policy vis-à-vis third countries in order to promote its standards at international level and ensure a level playing field.[68]

In this direction, notwithstanding an actual Single Market for the taxation of companies had been far from the realization (i.e., an economic and legal system without cross-border tax obstacles), the Commission has resolutely turned its policy towards the improvement of tax compliance, tax transparency, and the reduction of fraud and evasion.[69]

Due to a wholly transformed economic and political scenario and to the political pressure,[70] the Commission actions moved from the traditional harmonization/ coordination of cross-border (corporate) tax systems towards the enhancement of a stricter cooperation of the national tax administration (on cross-border issues) and the fight against aggressive tax planning. This does not want to mean that the Commission abandoned its traditional Single Market tax policy, based on the removal of cross-border tax obstacles to the free movement of companies, but only that the latter policy has been integrated through such legal instruments devoted to cross-border taxpayer compliance and tax governance. Definitively, this tax policy produced the recommendation for a common general anti-abuse rule,[71] the creation of a Platform for Tax Good

65. 2009 Promoting Tax Good Governance Communication, *supra* n. 6, at 4.
66. *Ibid.* at 5.
67. As defined in n. 44, *supra*.
68. The Concrete Ways Communication, *supra* n. 44, at 3.
69. *Ibid.* at 3.
70. *See, e.g.*, European Council Conclusions of the Euro Plus Pact of 16 February 2012 (6404/1/12 Rev.1).
71. European Commission, Recommendation of 6 Dec. 2012 on Aggressive Tax Planning, C(2012) 8806 final [hereinafter the 'Recommendation on Aggressive Tax Planning'].

Governance[72] and the progressive enhancement of administrative cooperation between the Member States.[73]

This new policy trend shows the same roots of the 1997 Code of Conduct: the alignment of the Commission policy to the international standards. This point arises plainly in the Conclusion of the 2012 Communication on the fight against tax fraud and tax evasion: This action plan 'represent[s] a general contribution to the wider international debate on taxation and is aimed at assisting the G20 and the G8 in its on-going work in this field'.[74] In this direction, the Commission and its tax policy is strict between the European and the International Institutions and between the original concept of Single Market and the fight against aggressive tax planning.

The most recent phase of the European tax policy is not particularly original since it closely repeats the features already portrayed. The key document is the Communication on 'A Fair and Efficient Corporate Tax System in the European Union'.[75] On the first hand, the Commission has put forward, again, a holistic solution of a CCCTB, whose Council Directive Proposals were presented, as already said, on 25 October 2016. This is the solution tailored for the Single Market, aimed at improving 'the environment for businesses in the EU' and 'reduc[ing] the complexities and compliance costs for cross-border companies, who would have to follow one set of rules when computing their taxable income, rather to face up to 28 different systems'.[76] On the other hand, the Communication shed light on the issue of the erosion and shifting of the corporate taxable base, since:

> [t]here has been a growing demand from the European Parliament, Member States and stakeholders to address this issue and ensure that profits generated in the EU are taxed at the place where the actual activities take place. This echoes on-going discussions at international level in the context of the OECD BEPS project.[77]

It is worth noting that the Commission has understood this second series of measures as an anticipated implementation of the holistic approach.[78] An essential part of these measure has found a detailed analysis and concrete proposals in the 'Anti-Tax

72. http://ec.europa.eu/taxation_customs/business/company-tax/tax-good-governance/platform-tax-good-governance_en.
73. In the field of direct taxation, administrative cooperation is based on Council Directive 2011/16/EU of 15 Feb. 2011 on administrative cooperation in the field of taxation and repealing Directive 77/799/EEC, as amended by Council Directive 2014/107/EU concerning the automatic exchange of financial account information, and by Council Directive 2015/2376/EU extending the cooperation to information on cross-border tax rulings and advance pricing agreements
74. Recommendation on Aggressive Tax Planning, *supra* n. 70, at 15.
75. The 5 Key-Areas Action Plan, *supra* n. 52.
76. *Ibid.* at 7.
77. *Ibid.* at 9.
78. *Ibid.*:

> For example, this would include adjusting the definition of "permanent establishment" so that companies cannot artificially avoid having a taxable presence in Member States in which they have economic activity, and improving the Controlled Foreign Corporation rules, which ensure that profits parked in low or no tax countries are effectively taxed.

Avoidance Package'[79] and the actual harmonization in the Council Directive 2016/1164/EU of 12 July 2016 laying down rules against tax avoidance practice that directly affect the functioning of the internal market.

This is not the place where the Directive can be examined, unless for what is necessary for a policy analysis. In particular, the Directive contains two kinds of provisions: a general anti-abuse rule (Article 7) and a set of (substantial) rules aimed at tackling aggressive tax planning (or, in similar words, the erosion and shifting of corporate tax base). As fairly stated in the preamble to the Directive, it is the European answer to the BEPS Actions, since the Council:

> supported an effective and swift coordinated implementation of the anti-BEPS measures at the EU level and considered that EU directives should be, where appropriate, the preferred vehicle for implementing OECD BEPS conclusions at the EU level.[80]

In conclusion, the 'new deal' of European corporate tax policy has progressively produced the prevalence of the domestic fiscal interests, and, in particular, the protection of domestic revenues, over the fundamental freedoms and the need to guarantee the free competition. In concrete terms, this objective has been implemented according to the BEPS Actions. During the current days, therefore, EU corporate tax policy is suffering a process of internalization (or acritical adherence to the BEPS) without taking in due consideration the fundaments on which is built the Single Market.

[3] The International (or External) Dimension: The Goal of the Tax Transparency

The need to coordinate a common tax policy at international level has been stated by the European Council in the meeting of 2 March 2012 and fostered by the European Commission through the Communication of 27 June 2012[81] and the Recommendation on Third Countries.[82] However, the policy foundation of this action finds its roots in the Commission's 2009 Promoting Tax Good Governance Communication.[83]

Similar to the evolution described in §11.04[C][2], *supra*, for the Single Market, also this policy is strictly dependant on the OECD initiatives and on the principles and standards therein elaborated.[84]

The Council's statements set the programmatic aims of the tax policy with third countries, identified as the extension of the new standards of the exchange of

---

79. European Commission, Communication from the Commission to the European Parliament and the Council, Anti-tax Avoidance Package: Next Steps Towards Delivering Effective Taxation and Greater Tax Transparency in the EU, COM(2016) 23 final, 28 Jan. 2016.
80. *Ibid.* at 2.
81. The Concrete Ways Communication, *supra* n. 44.
82. As defined in n. 7, *supra*.
83. As defined in n. 6, *supra*.
84. The point is raised also by Gemma Martinez Bárbara, *The Role of Good Governance in the Tax Systems of the European Union*, 65 Bull. Int. Tax. 270, 275 (2011).

information to those non-EU Member States that were covered by the savings Directive and the promotion of a coordinated actions against the non-cooperative tax jurisdictions.[85]

In the Recommendation, these objectives have been labelled as 'minimum standards of good governance in tax matters' and further specified. In particular, paragraph 3(b) sets out the definition of harmful tax measures, grounded on European Code of Conduct, in terms of those measures which provide for 'a significant lower effective level of taxation, including zero taxation, than those which generally apply in the third country in question ... Such a level of taxation may operate by virtue of the nominal tax rate, the tax base or any other relevant factor'.[86]

As far as the coordination of the domestic tax systems is concerned, the Recommendation has introduced two different measures. The first concerns the criteria for the drafting of blacklists of third countries, which should follow the standards provided for by the Recommendation. The second, differently, involves the renegotiation of those double tax conventions with third countries which are not aligned with the criteria set forth therein.

This policy has been reviewed by the 2015 document on a fair and efficient corporate tax system in the EU. In this document, the Commission emphasizes the publication of an EU-wide list of third country non-cooperative tax jurisdictions based on the domestic blacklists and moves towards the coordination of 'possible countermeasures' against non-cooperative tax jurisdictions to address situation of non-compliance with good governance principle in tax matters.[87]

Finally, the same goals have been restated in the Communication on an external strategy for effective taxation.[88] The tax transparency has been enriched of the automatic exchange of information on cross-border tax rulings and advance pricing arrangements as well as the country-by-country reporting requirements.[89] On the side of the fair tax competition, the novelty lies in the promotion of the BEPS: 'the EU now also has an important role to play in continuing to support BEPS, by pushing for its smooth and timely implementation – in the Single Market and internationally'.[90]

The document also clarifies that tax good governance with third countries requires the use of every (normative) tool at the disposal of the Union, among which bilateral and regional (non-tax) agreements with third countries.[91] In these agreements, the Commission should work to include State aid provisions, in order to remove the distortive practices granted by many third countries.[92]

85. According to the Concrete Ways Communication, *supra* n. 44, at 12, this policy should 'include a mixture of defensive measures or sanctions against countries which practice unfair tax competition and incentives for those countries to cease such practices'. *See also* the 2012 Strengthen the Fight Communication, *supra* n. 54, at 7–8.
86. Recommendation on Third Countries, *supra* n. 7, at 3 et seq.
87. The 5 Key-Areas Action Plan, *supra* n. 52, at 13.
88. European Commission, Communication from the Commission to the European Parliament and the Council on an External Strategy for Effective Taxation, COM(2016) 24 final, 28 Jan. 2016.
89. Recommendation on Third Countries, *supra* n. 7, at 4.
90. *Ibid.* at 5.
91. *Ibid.*
92. *Ibid.* at 7.

On the normative side, the implementation of the exchange of information has been boosted through the presentation of different acts in the field of Country-by-Country reporting, extended also to third countries. Besides the sectorial measures, concerning the extractive and logging industries and the credit institutions, the Commission has proposed a Directive which imposes on EU and non-EU multinational groups the publication of a yearly report on the profit and tax paid and other information.[93]

The measures to fight against aggressive tax planning (or the base erosion and profit shifting), differently, are contained in the ATA Directive, since many provisions are applicable also to third countries (in particular, Article 5 on exit taxation; Article 7 on Controlled Foreign Companies and, to certain extent, Article 4 on Interest Limitation).

This brief outline raises (at least two) issues, strictly connected. The former concerns the weakness of the legal basis for such a policy. As already highlighted in §11.01, the authority to approximate domestic income tax measures is conferred to the Union by Article 115 TFEU for those 'laws, regulations or administrative provisions of the Member States as directly affect the establishment or functioning of the internal market'. In this sense, the requirements for the exercise of this competence in the field of income taxation, which primarily lies in the Member States, are the (i) direct (ii) impact on the internal market. These requirements should be read as the expression of the principle of subsidiarity stated in Article 5 TEU. Accordingly, the 'direct impact' on the internal market should be interpreted as affecting, primarily and almost exclusively, intra-EU cross-border tax obstacles and those domestic situations which alter the competition within the Union. In addition, the coordination (or the approximation) of the income tax provisions which concern third countries is subordinated, and presupposes, the existence of an advanced harmonization of such a field. Without a harmonization of corporate income tax law at the EU level, any coordination at the EU level benefits primarily the Member States' treasuries and only residually the Single Market.

This conclusion has an impact on the content of EU tax policy with third countries which, necessarily, should be informed to an essential (or minimalist) principle.

§11.05 CONCLUSIONS

The international dimension of EU tax policy concerns, almost exclusively, corporate income taxation. VAT largely follows common principles and rules at international level; Individual income taxation, differently, is on the Commission's agenda only for a few specific cross-border issues.

As far as the corporate income taxation is concerned, two cases should be differentiated. It cannot be contented that tax authority in income taxation is vested in the Member States and that the EU has the power to approximate domestic legislations

93. European Commission, Proposal for a Directive of the European Parliament and of the Council Amending Directive 2013/34/EU as Regards Disclosure of Income Tax Information by Certain Undertakings and Branches, COM(2016) 198 final, 12 Apr. 2016.

only insofar this outcome is necessary for the establishment and the functioning of the Internal Market. In this sense, there is an outright legal basis for the approximation of the international aspects of corporate income taxation within the Single Market. This seems the aim of the CC(C)TB Proposals.

In this context, the issues are therefore the actions to be taken until the adoption of the CC(C)TB. The Commission made its choice: the Single Market requires the prevention of tax evasion, tax abuse and base erosion and profit shifting. In §11.04[C][2], it has been demonstrated that the original idea of the Single Market was the elimination of the cross-border tax obstacles to the circulation of companies and, in particular, those obstacles which do not fall within the fundamental freedoms.

In order to obtain this outcome, two different tools could be employed: a EU Multilateral Convention or a piecemeal approach through directives.

As far as the relationship with third countries is considered, the legal basis for the coordination of the international aspects at EU level is very poor. The Single Market offers a limited help, since it should be proved that the base erosion and profit shifting have a direct impact on the free movement within the EU and on the free competition and that the coordination is more efficient than the Member States action. In any case, the coordination should be limited to the anti-avoidance and anti-BEPS rules and not to affect the provision on the allocation of the taxing rights.

A final issue concerns the position of the taxpayer. The implementation of further EU coordination requires the introduction of procedural measures, which attain the common protection of the taxpayer at the EU level.

PART V Continuing Harmonization in EU Tax Law

CHAPTER 12

Does EU Tax Policy Require a New Treaty?

*Frans Vanistendael**

§12.01 INTRODUCTION

After agreement was reached with Greece, in the summer of 2015, on the conditions for its financial aid package, the euro-crisis seemed to subside. Immigration and the free movement of people jumped to the top of the EU agenda; interest rates for government bonds for all euro-states in crisis, except for Greece, went down considerably. However, in spite of these reassuring facts, since the establishment of the European Stability Mechanism (ESM) that started operations in October 2012, nothing has fundamentally changed in the decision-making mechanism for running the common currency. The existing machinery has proved to be slow, cumbersome, and subject to pressure by individual Member States. If a new crisis would blow up in a bigger Member State - like Spain or Italy - we would witness even more hair-raising scenes than those seen during that last crisis. Moreover, that crisis did not originate in Europe, but in the US; today, there are threats to financial markets outside Europe, in China, and emerging economies, that could also trigger crises that would spill over to the EU.

Therefore, it is important to make the decision-making mechanism for operating the common currency more effective while, at the same time, making them more democratic. This contribution deals with the institutional questions that need to be answered within the EU to achieve this two-fold objective from both the fiscal and the budgetary viewpoints. To that effect, we will make a brief analysis of (a) the legal framework of decision making for operating the internal market and the EU's Economic and Monetary Union (the EMU) with the euro as its common currency, and (b) the economic framework for operating the internal market and the EMU.

* This chapter is based on a conference held for the law faculty of the University of Luxembourg on 14 January 2016 and does not fully reflect the consequences of the referendum of 23 June 2016 in the UK.

Articles 3(3) and 3(4) TEU list the two major and distinct economic objectives of the EU: (i) the Union shall establish an internal market and (ii) the Union shall establish an economic and monetary union whose currency is the euro. The conditions for achieving these two objectives are, from the fiscal and the budgetary points of view, totally different. It is our proposition in this chapter that the fiscal and budgetary conditions laid down in the European Treaties for achieving the internal market, while perhaps not ideal, are – by and large – adequate, with the exception of the unanimity rule for deciding tax matters that relate to the internal market. With respect to the objective of achieving and operating the EMU, on the other hand, the fiscal and budgetary conditions laid down in the European Treaties are inadequate to prevent another currency crisis. If a new crisis were to arise that was bigger than the previous one, the current decision-making mechanism would be incapable of preventing a total disintegration of the common currency, ultimately resulting in the disintegration of the internal market.

In the last part of this chapter, we will outline (a) the minimum reforms we deem necessary to the EMU's institutional framework and (b) the procedural ways to realize such minimum institutional reforms within the existing TEU and TFEU.

§12.02 THE FISCAL AND BUDGETARY REQUIREMENTS FOR THE INTERNAL MARKET

[A] The Concept of the Internal Market

The internal market is defined, in Article 26 TFEU, as an area without internal frontiers in which the free movement of goods, persons, and capital, as well as the right of establishment, is ensured. Within that internal market, competition is to be free and fair, as guaranteed by the competition and the state aid rules in the TFEU.

[B] Abolition of Internal Borders and National Treatment for Foreigners

Such a market requires the abolition of all obstacles to cross-border movements of persons, goods and services, capital, and business establishments and, at the same time, equal treatment between domestic and foreign products, persons, capital, and enterprises. It also requires the abolition of all internal tax obstacles at internal borders within the Union, with respect to indirect taxation (e.g., customs duties, levies having an equivalent effect, excises, turn over, and sale taxes) as well as direct taxation (e.g., income, capital, gift, and inheritance taxes). Because of the abolition of all tax obstacles at the internal borders, it also requires customs duties and levies to have an equivalent effect at the external borders of the Union.

[C] No Union Taxing Power, No General Harmonisation

The internal market does not require, however, the exclusive levying of European or national taxes for a European budget. The European budget for operating the internal market can be financed perfectly well by the annual transfer of national taxes, as is the case today. It neither requires full uniformity or harmonisation of all income taxes and social security charges nor, more specifically, the full equalisation of rates of income taxes and mandatory social contributions, although some mild form of coordination is desirable in order to avoid extreme distortions of competition. With respect to indirect taxes on consumption, full harmonisation is not necessary, especially not with respect to tax rates; however, equalisation of tax rules and tax burdens within each national jurisdiction of final consumption is imperative. Although that has largely been achieved by the VAT system, there is still unfinished business in the area of excises and some other forms of indirect taxation, such as environmental levies.

[D] No Large Union Budget

In order to operate the internal market, it is not necessary for the Union to have control over large volumes of the budget to steer demand or employment or to determine interest rates. A rather limited budget, which allows the Union to conduct its regional policy, the common agricultural policy and, further, to run its administration, is sufficient. That is, by and large, the situation with the current budget, which represents only about one percent of the GDP of the whole European Union. In the internal market, Member States continue to exercise their own national economic and budgetary policies in a sovereign way, with emphasis on national economic and social priorities, backed up by national taxing and spending powers.

[E] Free Competition Between Different Social and Fiscal Systems

This situation results in nearly unrestricted freedom for cross-border movements of persons, goods and services, capital, and businesses, where the inbound competitive positions are more or less the same for foreign and domestic economic agents, but there are still differences in their competitive positions, which are determined by national economic and social preferences reflected in the national tax policies of the countries of origin of these foreign agents. In this situation, private enterprises, as well as the Member States, are in competition with each other, resulting in substantial differences in income tax systems, systems of social security contributions, and tax rates in indirect taxation.

§12.03 THE FISCAL AND BUDGETARY REQUIREMENTS FOR THE EMU

Like any economic and monetary union with a common currency, the EMU demands a more-integrated economic and legal framework, which has both fiscal and budgetary consequences.

[A] A Central Bank

Any common currency needs, of course, a central bank that has the power (1) to determine interest rates; (2) to establish the volume of money; (3) to intervene in the financial markets; and (4) to act as a lender of last resort for private and public financial institutions and governments. In order to fulfil these functions, the central banks needs unlimited access to money from the public treasury. This backing can take the form of a special fund, but it is, most often, the national treasury holding the pool of all taxes and other public revenue, that constitutes the source of such back-up funds.

[B] A Government for the EMU with a Common Currency

Like any economic and monetary union with a common currency, the EMU also needs a central governing entity that not only coordinates, but also decides and implements, the economic policy of that particular economic and monetary union and has the power to take action to address economic unbalances between the states falling within it. The decisions of that governing entity must have priority over all other levels of government within its participating members (here, the members of the euro zone), including any national governments involved. In addition, that central entity must possess an adequate budget in order to enable it to effectively steer the macro-economic factors that determine supply, demand, and employment throughout the whole territory of the economic and monetary union's common currency.

[C] Fiscal and Budgetary Requirements for the EMU

The conditions mentioned above have important fiscal and budgetary consequences for the members of the economic and monetary union. These conditions first require that the central governing entity has the power to levy taxes directly and independently from any other level of government. The taxes levied by the central entity must flow directly and automatically to a central treasury. In the context of the European Union, these taxes could be national taxes levied by the euro-Member States (collectively, the 'euro-Group'), provided that these taxes are assigned – unconditionally – to the central treasury. It would be preferable, however, for these taxes to be Union taxes levied on a uniform basis and at uniform rates throughout the common currency zone. EU Members States not participating in the common currency zone (collectively, the 'non-euro Group') would not, of course, be subject to these taxes, either at the European or at the national level.

Even within the EMU with a common currency, there would still be considerable room for substantial national taxes with different tax bases and rates. However, there would also be overarching economic and social policies for the EMU as a whole: to coordinate, in a commanding way, the economic policies of the euro-Group and to compensate for the imbalances within the currency union. The degree of independence of the individual euro-Member States would not only be determined by the Union's regulatory framework, but also to a large extent by the relative importance of the budgetary volumes available at the level of the central entity and the euro-Member States, respectively.

§12.04 THE LEGAL AND ECONOMIC FRAMEWORK OF THE INTERNAL MARKET

[A] Adequate Distribution of Competences

The legal framework for the internal market is well established in the European treaties (TEU and TFEU) and in a vast array of secondary legislation that includes many directives and regulations relating to indirect taxation as well as some directives regarding direct taxation and cross-border tax cooperation. On the one hand, Article 3 TFEU gives the EU exclusive competence with respect to the customs union, the competition rules within the internal market, and the common commercial policy. Article 4 TFEU, on the other hand, gives the Union and the Member States shared competence with regard to: the internal market; economic, social, and territorial cohesion; agriculture and fisheries; the environment; consumer protection; transport; trans-EU networks; and energy.

The EU does not have the power to levy taxes (except for the common customs tariff), but Article 113 TFEU gives it the power to harmonize indirect taxes to the extent necessary for the establishment and functioning of the internal market, while Article 115 TFEU is a general provision permitting the EU to issue directives to harmonize, if necessary, national legislation that directly affects the establishment or functioning of the internal market, which implicitly includes the approximation of direct taxation laws.

[B] Enforcement by National Administrations and the CJEU

Enforcement of the European Treaties and EU secondary legislation is undertaken by national and Union administrations, while all litigation is, in the end, subject to review by the Court of Justice of the European Union (CJEU). Its major role is to safeguard the basic conditions of the internal market, particularly in cross-border situations and transactions. It does not have the power to intervene in substantive social or economic issues in domestic tax policy. The Court is the final guardian of the enforcement of the European Treaties.

[C] Veto Power as a Stumbling Block to Progress

That legal framework functions rather well across such a widespread territory with many different (sometimes very different!) national habits, cultures, and languages. From a tax perspective, there is only one anomaly that constitutes a serious stumbling block to the achievement of the internal market, and that is the need for a unanimous vote in tax matters, which requires all 28 (soon-to-be 27) Member States to agree on any advance in secondary EU-tax legislation. This veto power with respect to tax legislation is a major legal impediment, because it allows a single Member State to unilaterally block any progress that is deemed essential for the internal market and that has the support of a large majority of the Member States that represent the overwhelming majority of the population in the EU.

[D] Economic Framework

Free and fair competition is the economic essence of the internal market. The design and enforcement of the EU's competition rules and the bureaucratic machinery needed to operate the internal market only require a modest budget that can be financed from contributions from Member States, which budgets are approved annually by the European Parliament. While the Union may want more money to run its programmes and administration and, in particular, more money for the subsidies in its regional policy, the question is one of budgetary volume rather than a question about the method of financing that budget. The conclusion is that, from a tax point of view, the economic framework is, by and large, satisfactory.

§12.05 THE LEGAL AND ECONOMIC FRAMEWORK OF THE EMU WITH A COMMON CURRENCY

[A] Political Reality Does Not Correspond to the Distribution of Competences

Article 3(1)(c) TFEU states that 'The Union shall have exclusive competence in the following areas: . . . monetary policy for the Member States whose currency is the euro.' That rule, agreed to by all Member States, does not correspond to reality. Many times during the euro-crisis, we witnessed individual euro-Member States take command and national parliaments have the last word on the proposed rescue plans for other euro-Member States. One advantage, however, is that the TFEU's existing text does not need to be amended to provide full decision-making power to the EU on monetary matters.

The TFEU already contains a number of provisions that are common for the economic and monetary policy of all Member States (Articles 120 through 135 TFEU), regardless of whether or not any particular Member State participates in the common currency. There are also a few other articles (Articles 136 through 138 TFEU) that are specific to euro-Member States. Typically, the rules regarding economic policy, budgetary discipline, and control measures, as well as those regarding financial support of the Member States are identical, regardless of whether or not a Member State participates in the common currency. As the discussion below demonstrates, these rules are – first and foremost – designed for Member States that do *not* participate in the common currency and, as a consequence, are inadequate for those Member States that do participate in it.

[B] Rules Common to Euro- and Non-Euro Member States

[1] Coordinating Economic Policies in the EU

Article 119(2) TFEU obliges the Member States and the Union to engage in certain activities that 'include a single currency, the euro, and the definition and conduct of a single monetary policy and exchange-rate policy' with as primary objectives 'to maintain price stability, and without prejudice to this objective, to support the general economic policies *in* the Union' (emphasis added). This introductory article refers to the general economic policies - plural - in the Union and not to *the* economic policy *of* the Union supporting the common currency. This wording is repeated in Article 127 TFEU on monetary policy.

[2] Multilateral Surveillance and Excessive Deficit Procedures for all Member States

Articles 120, 121 and 126 TFEU describe procedures for multilateral economic surveillance and excessive deficit monitoring designed to maintain budgetary discipline among all Member States, whether inside or outside the common currency zone. The basic parameters of this budgetary discipline are found in the Union's Stability and Growth Pact: (1) an annual budgetary deficit of maximum three percent of GDP and (2) a total government debt not exceeding sixty percent of GDP. These multilateral surveillance and excessive deficit monitoring measures are intended, through Commission recommendations and public statements, to put pressure on non-complying Member States. The maximum pressure that can be brought to bear on euro-Member States is a fine, but there is no obligation for euro-Member States to follow the recommendations of the Commission or the Council, which means that, within the EMU, there is no binding instrument to impose an economic policy upon an unwilling euro-Member State. This point was dramatically illustrated by the saga of the Greek budgetary crisis.

[3] No Financial Solidarity

The rules with respect to financial solidarity between the euro-Member States can be found in Articles 122 through 126 TFEU. They prohibit, for all practical purposes, any fiscal or budgetary union between the EU and the euro-Group, or among the euro-Member States themselves. Article 125 TFEU prohibits the EU or a Member State to become liable for or to assume any commitment, at any level of government within the Union or within a Member State, which effectively excludes any bailout of a euro-Member State on the basis of TFEU rules. Article 122 TFEU allows some aid 'in a spirit of solidarity' if a Member State is in severe difficulties, but that article was not designed to organize solidarity between euro-Member States. Article 123 TFEU prohibits any overdraft or credit facility by the European Central Bank (ECB) to any level of government within the EU or within a Member State. It also prohibits any direct purchase by the ECB of debt instruments issued by a Member State, which is why the ECB waited so long before taking the step of buying Member States' government bonds on the secondary market: it was concerned that such purchases could be held to constitute an indirect way to circumvent the TFEU's prohibition of a direct purchase.

[4] Full Independence for the ECB

Finally, the rules on monetary policy are to be found in Articles 127 through 133 TFEU. These rules simultaneously deal with the organisation of both the European System of Central Banks (ESCB), in which non-euro Member States participate, and the ECB, which deals exclusively with euro-Member States. Pursuant to Article 127(4), the ECB, as opposed to the ESCB, must be consulted on any Union act and on any Member States' national draft legislation within the areas of its competence. Article 127(1) TFEU, on the other hand, prescribes price stability as the primary objective of the ECSB; it does not mention employment or economic growth as an objective. Article 128 TFEU stipulates that the ECB has the exclusive right to authorize the issue of euro bank notes. Finally, and very importantly, Article 130 TFEU guarantees the absolute independence of the ECB from any interference or influence by the Member States. The EU institutions are also bound to respect its independence. However, there are no express Treaty provisions on the competence of the ECB to either determine interest rates or act as a lender of last resort for the euro-Member States.

[C] Rules Specific to Euro-Member States

[1] Economic Policy Guidelines That Are Compatible for the Whole Union

Fortunately, the TFEU also contains some provisions that are specific to euro-Member States. Article 136 TFEU, for example, allows the Council of Ministers, within the framework of the multilateral surveillance and excessive-deficit procedure that applies to all EU Member States, to adopt measures that are specific to and exclusively for euro-Member States in order to 'strengthen the coordination and surveillance of their budgetary discipline' and 'to set out economic policy guidelines' for euro-Member States only, provided 'that they are compatible with those adopted *for the whole of the Union*' (emphasis added). When issuing these specific measures and guidelines, only the Council members representing euro-Member States may take part in the vote, thereby excluding non-euro Member States. Indeed, on the basis of Article 136 TFEU, specific procedures have been elaborated, such as the Six Pack and the European semester procedures, which have been applied to all Member States including non-euro Member States.

[2] The Protocol for the Euro-Group

Article 137 TFEU provides for a separate internal structure for the euro-Member States and a unique protocol was established for the euro-Group. Within that group, policy discussions on the euro take place. The whole protocol only contains two articles: one provides for informal meetings with a standing invitation to participate given to the ECB and the Commission, and the other requires the meeting to elect a president for two and a half years. There are no rules for agenda setting or decision-making: to date, all decisions have been taken 'by consensus' of all members of the euro-Group.

[3] Unified International Representation of the Euro

Article 138 TFEU further provides that the Council, upon receiving a proposal from the Commission and after consulting with the ECB, may decide to take common positions on the EMU and the common currency at international conferences and to provide unified representation when dealing with international financial institutions such as the IMF, the IBRD and the BIS. So far, no significant use of Article 138 TFEU has been made.

[4] The European Stability Mechanism

In the midst of the euro-crisis, after a shaky start with the European Financial Stability Facility, the TFEU was amended on 25 March 2011 with the approval of all Member States, including the non-euro Member States. A third paragraph was added to the existing Article 136 TFEU, allowing the euro-Group to set up the European Stability Mechanism (ESM), which can be activated to guarantee the stability of the eurozone as a whole and to intervene to stabilize individual euro-Member States. A separate ESM Treaty was signed by the then-seventeen euro-Member States on 2 February 2012 and, after a positive vote by the German Bundestag in September 2012, the ESM became operational. It was instrumental in the bailout of several distressed euro-Member States, most notably, Greece.

[D] The Economic Framework of the EMU

[1] Distribution of Taxing and Spending Power Between the EU and the Member States

Looking at the budgets for the whole EU and all of its Member States, it is clear that fiscal sovereignty – with all taxing and spending power in the whole of the EU – rests squarely with the Member States. Of all taxes levied and all revenue spent in the EU, more than ninety-seven percent is under the full control of the Member States.[1] The

1. The statistics in this section are derived from Taxation Trends in the European Union for 2014 published by EUROSTAT.

spending budget of all the Member States in 2014 amounted to 48.1 percent of total GDP of the Union, while the spending budget for the EU amounted to 1.04 percent of total GDP of the Union. Total national spending power of the Member States exceeded – by more than forty-five times – the total spending power of the Union. These figures speak for themselves: any attempt to steer the general economic policy of the EMU with a budget of this size is doomed to utterly failure.

[2] Economic Discrepancies in the Eurozone

In spite of a huge increase in intra-community trade in the internal market, Member States in the eurozone maintain their different national taxing and spending patterns and their different models of social protection. This is illustrated by the statistics in Table A, which shows the differences in social-security contributions and the implicit tax rates on labour and capital in 2010.

Table 12.1 Economic Discrepancies in the Eurozone (1)

Social Security Contributions as Percentage of GDP (2010)[2]								
BE	DE	FR	IR	IT	LV	NL	PT	SP
14.2	15.5	16.7	5.9	8.9	8.4	14.1	9.0	12.3
Implicit Tax Rates on Labour (2010)								
BE	DE	FR	IR	IT	LV	NL	PT	SP
42.5	37.4	41.0	26.1	42.6	32.5	36.9	23.4	33.0
Implicit Tax Rates on Capital (2010)								
BE	DE	FR	IR	IT	LV	NL	PT	SP
29.5	20.7	37.2	14.0	34.9	7.4	12.5	30.7	28.4
Implicit Tax Rates on Consumption (2010)								
BE	DE	FR	IR	IT	LV	NL	PT	SP
21.4	19.8	19.3	21.6	16.8	17.3	27.0	17.4	14.6

It is clear from Table 12.1 that the tax burden on the macro-economic aggregates of labour, capital, and consumption is unevenly distributed among the budgets of the euro-Member States. Statistics of trade balances, budget deficits, and unemployment rates, set forth in Table 12.2, also show similar considerable discrepancies.

Table 12.2 Economic Discrepancies in the Eurozone (2)

Unemployment Rates (End 2015)[3]							
AT	BE	DE	EL	FR	IT	NL	SP
5.8	7.8	6.3	24.5	10.1	11.3	8.3	21.4

2. *Source*: Eurostat 2012, Taxation trends in the European Union.
3. Source: The Economist, Economic and Financial Indicators 23 Jan. 2016.

Current Account Balance as Percentage of GDP (2015)							
AT	BE	DE	EL	FR	IT	NL	SP
+2.0	+0.4	+8.1	+2.5	-0.3	+1.9	+10.6	+1.0
Budget Balance as Percentage of GDP (2015)							
AT	BE	DE	EL	FR	IT	NL	SP
-2.1	-2.6	+0.7	-4.1	-4.1	-2.9	-1.8	-4.4

Table B's statistics show that, with respect to policies on employment and balanced budgets, the economic guidance for individual Member States should be quite different. But, above all, they raise the question of whether it is possible to eliminate the imbalances in some Member States by addressing some other imbalances in other Member States (e.g., by using some pluses in some Member States to compensate some minuses in other Member States). That does not necessarily mean a direct transfer of surplus funds from one Member State to another, but it raises a question about the utility of giving a European-level governing entity the power to take macro-economic decisions to address such unbalances that does not directly represent the national interest of the surplus and deficit Member States, but only the interest of the currency union as a whole.

[3] The European Stability Mechanism

So far, the ESM has been successful in its interventions for euro-Member States in crisis because, in relation to its capabilities, the demands upon it have been limited. It possesses a total capital of EUR 700 billion, with a maximum intervention ceiling of EUR 500 billion. To date, it has disbursed EUR 220 billion in loans, with total interventions of all EU funds for the eurozone amounting to a little over EUR 400 billion. However the euro-Member States seeking the aid of the ESM have been the rather small economies: Greece, Ireland, and Portugal.

[E] Adequacy of the Legal Framework for the EMU

[1] No Common Treasury

This short overview of the legal framework for determining and implementing the economic and monetary policy in the TFEU shows that the existing Treaty provisions were clearly not designed to ensure the proper functioning of the EMU with a common currency, because some essential elements of such functioning are lacking. Within the currency union, there is no common treasury to back up the ESM or the monetary policy of the ECB. The absence of a common treasury results from the absence of any power to levy euro-Group taxes or to independently transfer a part of the national tax revenues to a common euro-Group treasury.

[2] National Legislatures Take the Final Decision on ESM Spending

The power to spend the ESM's money still rests with the national legislatures of some euro-Member States (Germany, Finland, the Netherlands, and Slovakia) and, unfortunately, their national legislative procedures are too slow to permit the ESM to take quick action in an emergency. In addition, they are subject to national constitutional challenges before their respective national courts, as has been the case in Germany.

[3] No Structure for Decision Making in the Euro-Group

The euro-Group has failed, so far, to decide on procedures for agenda setting or decision making. The consensus model is too slow in times of crisis and decisions are sometimes determined by national political priorities, not by European economic and political priorities.

[4] Overlap of Competences Between the Commission and the Euro-Group

There is no clear delimitation of powers between the euro-Group and the Commission as to the enforcement of budgetary discipline and formulating economic guidelines. The Commission is still in charge of enforcing budgetary discipline of the individual Member States, but the eurozone needs, in addition to such national enforcement, an economic policy for the whole currency zone in which the interaction between the Member States and the euro-Group is directed by a European (eurozone) institution. Although the euro-Group has played an important role in many decisions, its competences are not well defined. Within the European Council, voting procedures on euro-matters and general EU matters are clearly separated, but that separation is less obvious in the preparatory discussions on those matters to be voted on.

[5] Disconnect in Decision-Making Power Between the EU and National Legislatures

Finally, there is a disconnect between the fiscal and budgetary competences and the general competences of the Member States and the EU. The national legislatures of the Member States are competent to approve national budgets and raise taxes, which constitute the bulk of taxing and spending power in Europe, but formulating and enforcing economic guidelines for the euro-zone and its monetary policy is a competence that the Treaties reserve to the EU. These are areas in which the EU Parliament is competent, but it does not have the taxing and spending power to back up its general policy recommendations.

[6] Conclusion: The Legal Framework Is Inadequate

The conclusion is that the existing EMU legal framework lacks a necessary component: a central decision-making body in charge of (1) formulating and enforcing the economic and budgetary policy framework for the euro-Group; (2) formulating and enforcing the economic policy for the EMU as a whole and for interactions within the euro-Group, (3) making enforceable, independent decisions about how much tax revenue, via what taxes, the EMU must raise for an independent euro-Group treasury under its control; and (4) spending the money in that independent, euro-Group treasury to support the common economic and monetary policy within the EMU. To be successful, the common economic and monetary policy must cover all aspects thereof, including employment, European-wide public investment, and regional imbalances within the EMU.

[F] The EMU's Economic Framework

[1] ESM Capital Is Too Small to Rescue Big Member States

In economic terms, it was a miracle that the EMU survived the financial crisis, which was largely thanks to the rescue mechanism of the ESM. The ESM's budgetary mass at the EMU's disposal remains far too small to come to the rescue of the bigger euro-Member States. The budgetary mass of a common treasury necessary to set and implement a common economic policy is totally non-existent.

[2] No Central Organ Coordinates Economic Policy for Eurozone as a Whole

The necessary coordination of economic and social policies of the euro-Member States is only effectuated – partially and indirectly – through the budget control exercised by the EU and the individual Member States over their respective national budgets. For the functioning of the EU as an internal market that budget control is more than adequate; but there is no direct intervention or any spending decisions made at the level of the EMU as a whole. The wide divergence in macro-economic aggregates of the euro-Member States shows that addressing the imbalances is a major task for the EMU. The state-aid programmes within the current framework of regional economic policy are too small to address such macro-economic imbalances.

§12.06 CHANGES TO MAKE FOR THE INTERNAL MARKET

The report on the legal and economic framework of the Internal Market is rather satisfactory (*see* §12.04, *supra*). There is no need for major treaty amendments, except for one, and that is the generalisation of qualified majority voting and the abolition of the Member States' veto power for tax rules. As indicated in §12.05[D][1] on the distribution of taxing and spending power between the EU and the Member States, the bulk of the taxing power in the EU currently rests with the Member States and the abolition of the unanimity rule will not change that, because, within the internal Market, the Union has no competence to intervene in the national tax systems of the Member States, except for the rules on cross-border situations and transactions.

When tax is considered to be a special issue, the qualified majority rule can be adapted to the effect that, if a significant minority of European taxpayers disagree with new tax directives or changes in existing directives, the qualified majority rule could be adapted so as to provide for a majority vote of four-fifths, or twenty-two out of the twenty-eight (soon-to-be twenty-seven) Member States in the Council of Ministers and four-fifths of the votes in the European Parliament. In that way, the national interests of Member States could be preserved, either by a blocking vote by a group of small Member States or a coalition of the largest Member State with one of the other larger Member States.

It should be noted that, in the near future, it will not be tax, but rather immigration and free movement of persons that will be the biggest challenge for the internal market. Free movement of persons is closely connected to free movement of goods, because if border controls are reinstated for persons, it is inevitable that they will also be reinstated for goods. Both freedoms are at the heart of the internal market and both also raise fundamental issues of sovereignty. The issue is still further complicated by the fact that the UK, which is part of the internal market, is not party to the Schengen agreement and, therefore, applies a different regime for the free movement of persons. More than taxation, the distinction between the free movement of goods and the free movement of persons within the concept of the internal market seems to be the breaking point to preserve some link between the UK and the EU in the coming Brexit negotiations. However, these questions are not part of this contribution and should be dealt with separately.

§12.07 CHANGES TO MAKE TO THE EMU

[A] Strengthening the ESM

A first priority is to strengthen the ESM that is already available in case of emergency, which means increasing its available capital and streamlining its decision making process. The ESM's current Board of Governors is obliged to review, periodically and at least every five years, the adequacy of the ESM's authorized capital. Thus, a review of its currently authorized capital of EUR 700 billion will be on the Board of Governors' agenda in the very near future. Due to the ESM's current 80 per cent voting majority requirement, both Germany and France already have veto power over virtually every Board decision, but that is not all: because the ESM's Board of Governors currently requires [unanimous] consensus among all the euro-Member States pursuant to its so-called mutual agreement procedure, each euro-Member State, however small, also has veto power on all of the most important decisions to be made regarding the ESM. That unanimous voting requirement and the impact of national constitutional rules in euro-Member States, such as Germany, are a major hurdle to any decision to increase the ESM's capacity.

[B] Enhance the ESM and Create a European Treasury

A decision must be made about the ultimate guarantee of the euro-Member States' euro-debt. The ESM could be used as the core of such a debt guarantee, but that would require a considerable increase in its capital. The guarantee could also take the form of a separate and independent euro-treasury, into which the ESM could be merged. In the end, establishing such a treasury is an inevitable result of the need to support a common economic policy, because, in the long run, such a common policy cannot be financed by capital contributions, but must be financed by imposing taxes destined for that euro-treasury. Because the financing would have to be done by taxation at the euro level, its decision-making structure would have to take a more political form; it would have to be a politically accountable body. Such a euro-treasury must also have a sufficient budgetary mass to effectively intervene when appropriate, even though such a mass would likely be insufficient to act as the ultimate guarantee for the total-outstanding public debt of all euro-Member States: that is to say, at least initially, a mechanism that acts as a rescue mechanism in support the public debt of single euro-Member States must remain in place.

[C] Strengthen the ECB's Position

The ECB's current powers should be extended to allow it to act as the lender of last resort for any euro-Member State. An important remaining question, however, is whether the ECB's mandate should also be extended to take account of macro-economic factors other than just price stability. That may not be necessary, provided that a central-governing entity is established in the EMU that is competent to address employment and regional policy throughout the euro zone; failing that, it is advisable to include employment in the ECB's mandate so as to allow the ECB to act as an all-round player in the EMU.

[D] Establish a Central Policy Organ in the EMU

[1] A Central Policy Organ Inside the Commission?

The most crucial decision to make regarding a strengthened EMU is the choice of entity that will be charged with setting and implementing an effective economic policy for the whole of the EMU. Can we entrust such a vital task to a member of the Commission, to all the members of the Commission appointed by euro-Member States, or to the national ministers representing the euro-Member States in the Council of Ministers? Or, should we create a new, central organ for the eurozone, or could the euro-Group, itself, act as such an organ?

Part of the current common economic policy – in the form of budgetary discipline – already belongs to the competences of the Commission. The question, then, is which of its Commissioners and departments should have the competences to fulfil the additional, strengthened tasks for the EMU. As the essential task of the strengthened EMU organ will be to formulate and enforce economic policy for the whole of the EMU, which will not affect all Member States of the European Union in the same way, the most relevant question is whether the Commissioners charged with these additional tasks can simultaneously act as Commissioners for the non-euro Member States. In some cases, there may be a conflict of interest between the EMU's interest and that of the non-euro Member States. Such a conflict of interest may already occur in several areas of competence, because several areas in which the Commission is already active also belong to the common economic policy. Such a potential conflict was already seen in the banking union project. Other potential areas of conflict may arise between the euro and the Banking Union project for the whole European Union and in the area of the Common Corporate Consolidated Tax Base (CCCTB) or the Financial Transaction Tax (FTT), when such taxes would be used by the euro-Member States to finance their common treasury and non-euro Member States would use these taxes for other purposes.

[2] Should the Central Policy Organ Be Outside the Commission?

The alternative would be to establish a new organ outside the existing Commission. That would, of course, raise some delicate questions, because part of the common economic policy that consists of budgetary surveillance of the Member States has already been implemented by the Commission's directorates. However it is not inconceivable to concentrate all the activities related to the common economic and monetary policy of the EMU in a separate administration under the supervision of the euro-Group. The euro-Group, with all the Ministers of finance and economics could act as the Council of Ministers of the euro-Member States. The euro-Group itself could function under the chairmanship of the President of the European Union. The full Council of Ministers representing all the Member States of the Union could serve as a forum for discussion where the two central organs, the Commission and the new euro-entity could meet, discuss, and make recommendations.

[E] Political Accountability for the EMU's Central Policy Organ

[1] Accountability to National Legislatures?

Since the common economic policy presupposes raising taxes for a European treasury, there is a need for a democratic organ controlling the common euro-budget and the taxing and spending by the central entity in the setting and then implementing that common policy. There are several ways to make the central entity politically accountable: control by national legislatures, control by the euro-Council of Ministers, control by the European Parliament, or a combination of all of them. Control by national legislatures does not seem desirable: the experience we had during the financial crisis has shown that it is not possible for national legislatures to take account of the interest of the whole eurozone, including the interests of all euro-Member States. The role of national legislatures is to defend the national interest of the individual Member States, not to defend a common European interest.

[2] *Accountability to the European Parliament?*

The most democratic way to control taxing and spending at the European level is through debate and voting in the European Parliament, with the power to dismiss the EMU's central governing body if it does not meet the expectations of the eurozone as a whole. That is already the case for the government structure of the internal market. Under the current rules any new Commission needs the approval of the European Parliament and the Commission's budget also needs this approval. There is no reason why this decision-making structure could not be extended to the central body in charge of the EMU, regardless of whether that body operates inside or outside the Commission.

The votes on euro-policy questions in the European Parliament should be limited to those members thereof representing euro-Member States. That rule is already observed by the Council of Ministers. However, in the new constellation, that Council could also be used as a platform for general debate among all Member States; there could be special sessions of the European Parliament for such general debate, in which all of its members can participate and, then, a vote for (non-binding) recommendations to both the Commission and the central body in charge of the EMU.

[3] *Additional Accountability to the Euro-Council of Ministers?*

Because the central euro-body would be in competition for euro-tax money with the euro-Member States national taxes, it may be advisable to establish a double control by the euro-Group's Council of Ministers. That would provide a guarantee to the smaller Member States against complete dominance of the bigger Member States. In that case, however, the unanimity or consensus rule that currently prevails at the euro-Group meetings should be abandoned and replaced by a system of qualified majority voting to prevent one or two small euro-Member States from blocking euro-wide measures that a large majority of the population would consider to be absolutely necessary. The national interests of the bigger euro-Member States should be preserved by a 4/5 majority requirement in the European Parliament.

§12.08 THE PROCEDURE FOR ACHIEVING REFORM

[A] Achieving Reform from Either Inside or Outside the Framework of the European Treaties

[1] Intergovernmental Cooperation Outside the Treaties

As important as the question of what institutional reforms are necessary to provide a stable, functioning framework for the euro, is the question of how to achieve those reforms. Member States are free to conclude treaties outside the framework of the European Treaties and they have done so in the past,[4] the most important of which, the Schengen Agreement originally signed in 1985, was subsequently integrated in the European treaties. That same procedure may be followed for the new structure of the EMU, but there could be some problems.

When an agreement outside the framework of the European treaties is reached, the decision-making process provided for in such an agreement is mostly that of intergovernmental cooperation, requiring consensus of all participants (i.e., granting veto power to any participating signatory). The experience during the financial crisis demonstrated, however, that this unanimity requirement has an inevitable consequence – veto power – which is precisely the Achilles heel of the current euro-construction. That means that this agreement must, from the start, provide for qualified majority voting as the rule. Intergovernmental agreements are also not subject to the jurisdiction of the CJEU, which means that, in case of a conflict, there is no automatic access to an impartial judicial body to resolve the conflict, unless the contracting parties agree, in advance, that any conflicts and questions of interpretation arising under the treaty are to be submitted to the CJEU.

[2] Reform by Amending the Treaties

If the Commission, or a special directorate of the Commission, is to become the central governing entity of the EMU and the common currency, it would be almost impossible to adequately reform the Commission without amending both the TEU and the TFEU, because the organisation of the Commission is embedded in both of them. If that road is chosen, amending the TEU and the TFEU becomes inevitable and the first question will be how to go about it, because experience has shown how difficult it is to amend the European treaties as amendment requires the consent of all Member States.

One way to achieve the needed amendments would be to make use of Chapter 4 of Title VIII on Economic and Monetary Policy, which authorizes separate provisions specific to euro-Member States. The amendment of Article 136(3) TFEU, which established the ESM, was achieved on that basis. Article 137 TFEU already provides for the existence of the euro-Group; thus, the protocol relating to the euro-Group could be

4. For example: The Schengen Agreement of 14 June 1985. However the Schengen Agreement was later incorporated in the European Treaties.

enhanced by establishing a central entity in charge of formulating and implementing the common economic policy guidelines for the currency union. That central entity should be given the power to propose euro-taxes to be levied within the eurozone for the EMU's common treasury and it should be made accountable to the European Parliament. Discussion and voting arrangements at the European Parliament level, with respect to EMU matters, could be incorporated into its existing Rules of Procedure. This approach permits any amendments to the TEU and TFEU necessary for the proposed reform to remain rather limited.

The most important aspect of the reform is that all EU Member States would have to agree to extend the separate voting arrangement for euro-matters, which is already in force in the Council of Ministers in Article 136(2) TFEU: 'For those measures set out in paragraph 1 (the proper functioning of economic and monetary union), only members of the Council representing Member States whose currency is the euro shall take part in the vote.' That principle must be extended to all amendments of the TEU and TFEU that are necessary to make the euro function and to all discussion and voting arrangements on euro matters in the European Parliament. Obviously, extending that principle can only be accomplished through a political compromise between non-euro- and euro-Member States.

One possible occasion for reaching such a political compromise was the negotiation with the UK on EU reform prior to its in-or-out referendum. In exchange of relieving the UK, and other Member States wishing to follow its example, of the obligation set out in Article 1, second paragraph of the TEU of 'creating an ever-closer union among the peoples of Europe', the euro-Member States should be given the right, in the TEU, to amend and enhance the relevant TFEU provisions (from Articles 136 through 138) that are specific and limited to the Member States whose currency is the euro. It is clear that this would result in a 'Europe at two speeds', but this is the inevitable result of an irrevocable choice between an internal market and a full Economic Union with a common currency. It should be noted that the choice is only irrevocable for those countries choosing to participate in the currency union. Those countries which stay out of the currency union would remain free to join at a later date, provided that they agree to all the conditions that make that currency union function successfully.

Brexit has made this approach redundant for the UK, but not entirely redundant for some other Member States. The UK was traditionally the most powerful force behind the Euro-sceptics in the EU, but the UK also had allies among the smaller members of the club. Their situation could be clarified by following the same procedures to allow them to opt out of the 'ever closer Union'.

[B] No Big Bang, but Gradual Reform

[1] Big Bang: Federal EU

In the discussion between the euro's proponents and opponents, it is often pointed out that a common currency inevitably results in a political union and that a currency union without a full political union is an economic nightmare. It is because the UK does not want such a political union that it does not want the euro and what inevitably goes with it; elsewhere in Europe there are many opponents to the idea of a full-fledged European federal state. From a theoretical point of view, a full political union would, of course. resolve most if not all of the legal and economic problems that now exist within the currency union. Yet a full-fledged European federal state is out of the question: it is not feasible, not desirable, and not necessary to run the euro.

In a federal state, the common economic and monetary policy is determined by the budgetary mass that the federation has at its disposal to steer that policy. Even in very decentralized states, the minimal budgetary mass necessary to successfully steer economic and monetary policy stands at a minimum of about twenty-five percent of that state's total revenue. Increasing the total taxing and spending power of the EU up to that level, however, would be tantamount to a revolution. It would require a massive transfer of not only of the budget, but also of the competence to spend that budget from the Member States to the Union: it would destroy the political and administrative structures of the Member States.

A political union in a federal state is much more than an economic union with a common currency. The historic and cultural discrepancies and traditions across the EU Member States are such that some form of separation is preferable to a political union. The century-old examples, such as the Wallonia and Flemish regions in Belgium, Catalonia in Spain, and even Scotland in the UK, prove this point. It would take far longer than a century to achieve a political union among the EU Member States. We need only to look how long it took for a multilingual and cultural country like Switzerland to become a modern federal state: the process is believed to have started in 1291, but it only achieved its final result after the *Sonderbundkrieg* in 1847 and the introduction of the Swiss Franc in 1850. Europe is far more complicated than Switzerland and, therefore, one can assume that its process would take far longer. The euro would collapse well before that.

[C] A Gradual Approach

[1] Fundamental Legal Reform, but Incremental Budgetary Reform

A gradual approach would realize a fundamental legal reform in the decision-making process, whereby, in principle: (a) the eurozone would acquire the power to raise and spend revenue independently from the euro-Member States and (b) the rules of the EMU would have clear priority in economic and monetary matters that concern the euro-union as a whole. But, in budgetary terms, these reforms should be implemented in a minimal and incremental way. A first change would be to increase the capital of the ESM and gradually transition (over a period of ten to fifteen years) its financing from contributions by the euro-Member States to a system of financing by EU-level taxes levied in the euro-Member States that would flow directly to the ESM. The ESM, then, would gradually provide an increasing budget for the new central entity in charge of the eurozone's economic and monetary policy and endow it with the critical budgetary mass for economic intervention, which would, during the transitional period, increase by 0.5 percent to one percent per year from zero to a maximum of ten-to-fifteen percent of the GDP of the whole eurozone. During this transitional period, formulas for integrating the ESM into the euro-treasury would also be examined. The central entity or the department of the Commission in charge of the eurozone's economic and monetary policy would gradually become accountable to the euro-Council of Minsters and the European Parliament in accordance with democratic rules.

[2] Reform of the Treaties as a Final Choice to Leave or Stay Inside the Eurozone

The gradual process of institutional development should be incorporated into a new treaty text that would be submitted for approval according to the constitutional rules of each euro-Member State. Rejection of the new treaty would oblige that Member to leave the eurozone, because approval of the new treaty would, over time, amount to a gradual-but-significant transfer of budgetary sovereignty of the euro-Member States to the Union.

However, the workings of the central-governing entity needed to successfully set and implement a common economic and regional policy for the eurozone would be a far cry from a full-fledged national government. Competition and international trade would still be within the competences of the Commission. There would be no competence for defence, justice or foreign policy, with the exception of international monetary matters. The largest share of public revenue would still remain under the control of the euro-Member States in the form of personal income taxes, social security contributions, and VAT-rate setting. But, at last, there would be one single authority keeping an eye on the overall economic balances and imbalances inside and between the euro-Member States with the competence to dictate action, if necessary, in the interest of the EMU and its common currency as a whole.

§12.09 CONCLUSION

Europe is currently facing three major crises at the same time: the immigration crisis, the euro-crisis, and Brexit. Although the euro-crisis is not daily front-page news, it could return any day with a vengeance. The solution for maintaining the euro is a substantial transfer – over a rather long period of time – of taxing and spending power and economic decision-making power, from the euro-Member States to a central governing body exercising such powers under democratic control. At this stage, however, it is clear that there is no majority-political support in Europe for such a fundamental reform; even the staunchest defenders of European economic (as opposed to political) integration do not dare to spell out the consequences of such reform to their voters. Therefore, it is necessary to take on this reform in two stages: first, a fundamental reform in the legal structure to put the necessary legal machinery for decision making in place; and, secondly, a budgetary reform that minimizes the impact of that legal reform by implementing its fiscal and budgetary content in an incremental and gradual way so as not to rock the electorate's boat.

Both the immigration crisis and the euro-crisis have made it clear that any transfer of power to the European level needed to resolve such crises involves a quantum leap when compared to the leap needed to transfer the power needed to operate the internal market. Nevertheless, it is no longer possible to maintain two totally-different ways of decision-making within the single and same European legal construction. Almost sixty years after the signing of the Treaty of Rome, the EU Member States should face their responsibility to make a decisive choice between an internal market, on the one hand, an Economic and Monetary Union with a common currency, on the other. At the same time, they should also be obliged to decide whether to accept either a common and single external border the defence of which is the common responsibility of all Member States, or national borders for each Member State to guard its own.

That choice is, in a certain way, facilitated by the demand of the UK to be relieved from the obligation to an ever closer union of the peoples of Europe. Before the Brexit vote, the policy of the UK consisted of not participating in the euro and not adhering to the Schengen Agreement's obligations. The European Union could have accommodated that choice by allowing the UK and others to continue to go down this road, which terminates with the completion of the internal market. But, at the same time, those same EU Member States, which do not want further economic integration, should still allow the remaining Member States, which continue to strive toward a successful Economic and Monetary Union (and the important second objective of the European treaties), to achieve their goals without blocking their progress. Europe is diverse and, therefore, should take diverse forms of political organisation. The outcome will not be a European federal super state, but a *sui generis* political construction, one that precisely reflects the essence of Europe: a *sui generis* continent.

Brexit does complicate this scenario, but does not change it fundamentally for the euro-sceptic Member States. Only when Brexit would be used as the occasion to rebuild the whole European construction to accommodate the British view on the limitation of the free movement of persons within Europe, all these scenarios would become worthless. But, such a course of action is highly unlikely. Therefore, for the remaining Member States, the choice continues to be between (1) staying a member of a customs union with an internal market without a common currency and subject only to a transfer of sovereignty that is strictly limited to cross-border obstacles and freedoms or (2) becoming a member of an economic and monetary union with the euro as its common currency and a limited-but-effective form of common economic government in support of the euro, which is politically accountable to a European house of representatives.

CHAPTER 13

Recent EU Initiatives in Direct and Indirect Taxation

Georg Kofler & Michael Tumpel

The European Union has taken an active part in the OECD's project on 'Base Erosion and Profit Shifting' (BEPS) (the 'OECD-BEPS Project') and is a forerunner in its implementation and the broader 'fight' against aggressive tax planning, tax avoidance and tax evasion. This contribution aims at giving a brief overview of the recent developments in this area.[1]

§13.01 INITIATIVES IN DIRECT TAXATION

The European Union has been on the forefront of the recent struggle of countries to address aggressive tax planning, tax avoidance and tax evasion, also in respect of the OECD-BEPS Project. Already in late 2012, the EU Commission issued its Action Plan (see Table 13.1) to strengthen the fight against tax fraud and tax evasion that included a number of measures also in the area of transparency and substantive direct taxation,[2] leading, *inter alia*, to two amendments of the Parent-Subsidiary Directive:

1. This chapter was finalized in November 2016.
2. For an overview, see, e.g., Georg Kofler, *Der EU-Aktionsplan zur Verstärkung der Bekämpfung von Steuerbetrug und Steuerhinterziehung*, 2015/1 IFF Forum für Steuerrecht 44 (2015).

Table 13.1 Action Plan to Strengthen the Fight Against Tax Fraud and Tax Evasion (December 2012)[3]

Action Plan to Strengthen the Fight against Tax Fraud and Tax Evasion (December 2012) with 34 concrete short-, mid-, and long-term actions, including ...

- Administrative Cooperation → Mandatory automatic exchange of information in the field of taxation in the Directive on Mutual Assistance – Proposal COM(2013) 348 (12 June 2013), adopted as Directive 2014/107/EU of 9 December 2014, [2014] OJ L 359/1
- Aggressive Tax Planning → Recommendation C(2012)8806 (6 December 2012) recommending to introduce a GAAR into xdomestic law and to negotiate a subject-to-tax-clause in tax treaties[4]
- Third Countries and Good Tax Governance → Recommendation C(2012)8806 final (6 December 2012)
- Hybrid Loans → Amendment of the Parent-Subsidiary Directive to introduce a taxing obligation for profit distributions that are deductible in the subsidiary's State[5] – Proposal COM(2013)814 (25 November 2013), adopted as Directive 2014/86/EU of 8 July 2014, [2014] OJ L 219/40 (in part parallel to OECD-BEPS Action 2[6])
- Anti-Abuse Provisions in EU Legislation → Amendment of the Parent-Subsidiary Directive to introduce a general anti-abuse provision as a minimum standard[7] – Proposal COM(2013)814 (25 November 2013), adopted as Directive (EU) 2015/121 of 27 January 2015, [2015] OJ L 21/1.

Tax transparency, mostly with regard to the automatic exchange of information was also at the core of the EU Commission's 2015 Tax Transparency Package (see Table 13.2), which included the proposal to introduce the automatic exchange of information on tax rulings between Member States.

3. Communication from the Commission to the European Parliament and the Council: An Action Plan to strengthen the fight against tax fraud and tax evasion, COM(2012) 722.
4. *See, e.g.*, Michael Lang, *'Aggressive Steuerplanung' – eine Analyse der Empfehlung der Europäischen Kommission*, 23 SWI 62 (2013).
5. For a first analysis, see, e.g., Georg Kofler, *'Hybride Finanzinstrumente' in der Mutter-Tochter-RL*, 2014/137 ZFR 214 (2014); Florian Haase, *Gedanken zu Art. 4 Abs. 1 lit. a) Mutter-Tochter-Richtlinie n. F.*, 23 IStR 650 (2014); Marc Desens, *Ist die neue Korrespondenzregel in der Mutter-Tochter-Richtlinie mit dem Unionsrecht vereinbar?*, 23 IStR 825 (2014); Tobias Hagemann & Christian Kahlenberg, *Sekundärrechtliche Reaktionen auf aggressive Steuerplanungsaktivitäten – Änderung der Mutter-Tochter-Richtlinie*, 24 IStR 840 (2014); Georg Kofler, *Hybrid Loans in the Parent-Subsidiary-Directive, in Elusione Fiscale Internazionale* 682 (Piergiorgio Valente ed., IPSOA 2014); *see also* Christophe Marchgraber, *Tackling Deduction and Non-Inclusion Schemes – The Proposal of the European Commission*, 54 Eur. Tax'n 133 (2014).
6. OECD/G20 Base Erosion and Profit Shifting Project (hereinafter 'OECD-BEPS Project'), *Neutralising the Effects of Hybrid Mismatch Arrangements, Action 2 – 2015 Final Report* (OECD Publishing 2015).
7. *See, e.g.*, Romero J. Tavares & Bret N. Bogenschneider, *The New* De Minimis *Anti-Abuse Rule in the Parent-Subsidiary Directive: Validating EU Tax Competition and Corporate Tax Avoidance?*, 43 Intertax 484 (2015); and Dennis Weber, *The New Common Minimum Anti-Abuse Rule in the EU Parent-Subsidiary Directive: Background, Impact*, 44 Intertax 98 (2016).

Table 13.2 Tax Transparency Package (March 2015)[8]

Tax Transparency Package (March 2015)
Transparency on Tax Rulings → Amendment of the Directive on Mutual Assistance – Proposal COM(2015) 135 (18 March 2015), adopted as Council Directive (EU) 2015/2376 of 8 December 2015, [2015] OJ L 332/1
Other tax transparency initiatives, such as assessing possible new transparency requirements for multinationals (specifically 'country-by-country reporting' ('CBCR'),[9] parallel to OECD-BEPS Action 13[10]), reviewing the Code of Conduct on Business Taxation (parallel to OECD-BEPS Action 5[11]), quantifying the scale of tax evasion and avoidance ('tax gap'), and repealing the Savings Tax Directive (in light of the extended Directive on Mutual Assistance)[12]

The alignment of taxation with profit generation was the main driver behind the 2015 Action Plan on Corporate Taxation (see Table 13.3), in which the Commission also announced its plan for a re-launch of the Common Consolidated Corporate Tax Base (CCCTB), which was already proposed in 2011.[13] This project should not only lead to a reduction of compliance costs (no transfer pricing), an elimination of double taxation (through the base sharing mechanism), and an elimination of over-taxation (because of the automatic cross-border loss relief), but would also provide a holistic solution to profit shifting in the BEPS-context.[14]

8. Commission Communication of 18 Mar. 2015 on Tax Transparency to Fight Tax Evasion and Avoidance, COM(2015) 136 (hereinafter the '2015 Tax Transparency Communication').
9. Subsequently proposed as COM(2016) 25 of 28 Jan. 2016, and adopted as Council Directive 2016/881/EU of 25 May 2016, OJ 2016 L146/8.
10. OECD-BEPS Project, *Transfer Pricing Documentation and Country-by-Country Reporting, Action 13 – 2015 Final Report* (OECD Publishing 2015) (hereinafter 'OECD Transfer Pricing Report').
11. OECD-BEPS Project, *Countering Harmful Tax Practices More Effectively, Taking into Account Transparency and Substance, Action 5 – 2015 Final Report* (OECD Publishing 2015) (hereinafter 'OECD Countering Harmful Tax Practices Report').
12. The repeal was proposed as COM(2015) 129 of 18 Mar. 2015, and adopted as Directive 2015/2060/EU, OJ 2015 L 301/1.
13. Proposal for a Council Directive on a Common Consolidated Corporate Tax Base (CCCTB) of 16 Mar. 2011, COM(2011) 121 (hereinafter, 'Original 2011 CCCTB Proposal'), subsequently withdrawn and relaunched as a Proposal for a Council Directive on a Common Consolidated Corporate Tax Base (CCCTB) of 25 October 2016, COM(2016) 683 (hereinafter the '2016 Relaunched CCCTB Proposal').
14. Indeed, a CCCTB may be highly effective in 'tackling profit shifting and corporate tax abuse in the EU', as it would (1) remove mismatches between national tax systems, (2) remove the possibility to manipulate transfer pricing, (3) address the 'debt bias', (4) introduce transparency as to the effective tax rate in each jurisdiction, (5) allow Member States to implement a common approach towards third countries, (6) reinforce the link between profit creation and taxation, and (7) enable a common adoption of BEPS measures (e.g., definition of permanent establishments, CFC rules)

Table 13.3 Action Plan on Corporate Taxation (June 2015)[15]

Action Plan on Corporate Taxation (June 2015)
Re-launching the Common Consolidated Corporate Tax Base (CCCTB) → CCCTB as a holistic solution to profit shifting in the BEPS context, announcement of a step-by-step approach (i.e., securing the common tax base ('CCTB')) starting with international elements related to BEPS and postponing consolidation ('CCCTB'), until after the common base has been implemented.[16]
Ensuring fair taxation where profits are generated → For example, through the CCCTB and the CoC, by addressing double non-taxation in EU legislation (i.e., in the Interest-Royalties Directive and the Parent-Subsidiary Directive), through a transfer pricing framework in the EU, by linking preferential regimes to where value is generated (i.e., for 'patent boxes').
Creating a better business environment → Greater coordination between Member States on tax policy, along with measures to reduce administrative burden, compliance costs and tax obstacles in the internal market, specifically by *(1)* enabling cross border loss offset (with recapture)[17] and *(2)* improving double taxation dispute resolution mechanisms.[18]
Increasing transparency → For example, adopt a common approach to non-cooperative tax jurisdictions, specifically by *(1)* publishing an EU-wide list of third country non-cooperative tax jurisdictions and *(2)* coordinating possible counter-measures towards non-cooperative tax jurisdictions.
Improving EU coordination → Specifically by *(1)* coordination on tax audits and *(2)* reforming the Code of Conduct for Business Taxation and the Platform on Tax Good Governance.

In its 2016 'Anti-Tax Avoidance Package' (see Table 13.4), the Commission explains the political and economic rationale behind the individual measures and the Commission's broader agenda against tax avoidance in a 'Chapeau Communication',[19] and notes that instruments in that package aim at ensuring effective taxation in the EU through the proposed 'Anti-Tax Avoidance Directive' ('ATAD')[20] and a Recommendation on measures against tax-treaty abuse;[21] increasing tax transparency through a

15. Commission Communication of 17 June 2015 'A Fair and Efficient Corporate Tax System in the European Union: 5 Key Areas for Action', COM(2015) 302 final (hereinafter, '5 Key-Areas Communication'); *see also* the Commission Staff Working Document of 17 June 2015 'Corporate Income Taxation in the European Union', SWD(2015) 121.
16. Subsequently proposed as part of the Corporate Tax Reform Package (October 2016) as Proposal for a Council Directive on a Common Corporate Tax Base of 25 October 2016, COM(2016) 685 (hereinafter, the '2016 CCTB Proposal'), and as the 2016 CCCTB Proposal, *supra* n.13.
17. *See* Art. 42 of the 2016 CCTB Proposal, *supra* n. 16.
18. *See* the subsequent Proposal of 25 October 2016 for a Council Directive on Double Taxation Dispute Resolution Mechanisms in the European Union, COM(2016) 686 (hereinafter '2016 Dispute Resolution Proposal').
19. Commission's Communication on 'Anti-Tax Avoidance Package: Next steps Towards Delivering Effective Taxation and Greater Tax Transparency in the EU' of 28 Jan. 2016, COM(2016) 23 final (hereinafter the 'Anti-Tax Avoidance Package Communication'), accompanied by a Commission Staff Working Document (SWD(2016) 6/2) and a 'Study on Structures of Aggressive Tax Planning and Indicators' (Taxation Paper No 61, 2015).
20. Proposal for a Council Directive laying down rules against tax avoidance practices that directly affect the functioning of the internal market of 28 Jan. 2016, COM(2016) 26 [hereinafter 'ATAD Proposal'].
21. Commission Recommendation on the implementation of measures against tax treaty abuse of 28 January 2016, C(2016) 271 (hereinafter '2016 Tax Treaty Abuse Recommendation').

revision of the Administrative Cooperation Directive under which the national authorities would exchange tax-related information on multinational companies' activities on a country-by-country basis;[22] and securing an international level playing field, with the Commission's approach being set out in a Communication on an External Strategy for Effective Taxation.[23]

Table 13.4 Anti-tax Avoidance Package (January 2016)

Chapeau Communication (COM(2016) 23)			
Proposal for an Anti-Tax Avoidance Directive (COM(2016) 26) – Adopted as Council Directive (EU) 2016/1164, [2016] OJ L 193/1	Recommendation on Tax Treaties (C(2016) 271)	Proposal to revise the Administrative Cooperation Directive – CbC-Reporting (COM(2016) 25) – Adopted as Council Directive (EU) 2016/881, [2016] OJ L 146/8	Communication on External Strategy (COM(2016) 24)
Staff Working Document (SWD(2016) 6/2) and Study on Aggressive Tax Planning			

The Commission's ATAD Proposal is a core part of the Anti-Tax Avoidance Package and encompasses a number of legally-binding measures to tackle some of the most prevalent tax avoidance schemes. Viewing aggressive tax planning structures as a global phenomenon, the Commission tries to ensure that a common standard is developed by the Member States. The context is multifold and results from the OECD/G20 reports on the BEPS project in October 2015, recent discussions on the Commission's 2011 proposal on a 'Common Consolidated Corporate Tax Base' ('CCCTB')[24] and the announcements in the Commission's 2015 Action Plan on Corporate Taxation[25] to ensure fair taxation where profits are generated. Also, and in line with some of the EU finance ministers' call for a specific 'comprehensive anti-BEPS directive' in 2015,[26] the Luxembourg Presidency had focused its work in the CCCTB project on BEPS-related aspects. Acknowledging that the CCCTB has several building blocks, the Luxembourg Presidency launched a discussion on the possibility of agreeing to a split off from the pending original 2011 CCCTB proposal of certain

22. Proposal for a Council Directive amending Directive 2011/16/EU as regards mandatory automatic exchange of information in the field of taxation of 28 January 2016, COM(2016) 25 final.
23. Commission's Communication on an External Strategy for Effective Taxation of 28 January 2016, COM(2016) 24 final.
24. The Original 2011 CCCTB Proposal, *supra* n. 13.
25. The 5 Key-Areas Communication, *supra* n. 15.
26. On 28 November 2014, Finance Ministers Schäuble, Sapin and Padoan co-signed a letter to Commissioner Moscovici proposing a 'comprehensive anti-BEPS directive' to be adopted by the end of 2015. In particular, the three Ministers advocated, in the context of the OECD/G20's final adoption of the BEPS conclusions, for 'a set of common, binding rules on corporate taxation to curb tax competition and fight aggressive tax planning'.

provisions on the international anti-BEPS aspects with the aim to achieve a swift, consistent and coordinated implementation of OECD/G20 BEPS recommendations in the EU.[27] The Commission's 2016 proposal is for a 'standalone directive' that covers those elements which can be implemented in national legislation prior to agreement and introduction of the CCCTB.[28] In doing so, the Commission also responds to the European Parliament's resolutions on anti-avoidance measures.[29] After speedy deliberations in Council, an agreement on the ATAD was reached in summer 2016, and the directive now foresees five measures that Member States have to implement (mostly until 2019):[30]

- Limitation of interest deductions for net interest expense exceeding 30% EBITDA (Article 4);
- Exit taxation rules for the cross-border transfer of assets, permanent establishments or a company's seat with a five-year instalment option inside EU/European Economic Area (EEA) (Article 5);
- General Anti Abuse Rule (GAAR) (Article 6);
- CFC rules based on control, low tax and certain types of income with carve-outs for EU/EEA based on artificiality (Articles 7 and 8); and
- Hybrid mismatch rules for double deduction and deduction/no inclusion situations (Article 9).

The rules of the ATAD only apply to corporations (Article 1) and are structured as 'minimum level of protection' (Article 3), as they 'shall not preclude the application of domestic or agreement-based provisions aimed at safeguarding a higher level of protection for domestic corporate tax bases'. This means that the directive would provide for minimum common anti-BEPS rules, but, more importantly, that Member States would be able to go beyond the minimum standards set out therein in their transposition of EU anti-BEPS rules and/or to continue applying their existing national anti-BEPS rules if such rules go beyond that minimum. Of course, it may be questioned if such a minimum standard would really, as the Commission suggests, 'prevent a fragmentation of the market and put an end to currently existing mismatches and

27. *See* Proposal for a Council Directive on a Common Consolidated Corporate Tax Base (CCCTB) – State of play (Doc. 14509/15 FISC 169 ECOFIN 916 [1 December 2015]). In December 2015, the Luxembourg Presidency hence presented a consolidated text reflecting the international anti-BEPS aspects of the CCCTB (see the Proposal for a Council Directive on a Common Consolidated Corporate Tax Base (CCCTB), Doc. 14544/15 FISC 171 [2 December 2015], and the accompanying Explanatory notes, Doc. 14544/15 ADD 1 FISC 171 [2 December 2015]). This text includes potential rules on the definition of permanent establishment (PE), Controlled Foreign Company (CFC) rules, a switch-over clause, a general anti-abuse rule (GAAR), exit taxation rules, interest limitation rules, and (possibly) rules regarding hybrid mismatches. Those deliberations in Council clearly had influence on the Commission in drafting its ATAD Proposal. *See also* the Anti-Tax Avoidance Package Communication, *supra* n. 19, at 6.
28. The Anti-Tax Avoidance Package Communication, *supra* n. 19, at 6.
29. *See* European Parliament resolution of 16 December 2015 with recommendations to the Commission on bringing transparency, coordination and convergence to corporate tax policies in the Union (2015/2010(INL)), P8_TA(2015)0457.
30. For a more detailed analysis, see the contribution by Katarina Köszeghy in this volume.

market distortions',[31] as exactly such leeway for Member States to go beyond the proposed anti-tax avoidance rules leaves the danger for such fragmentation essentially unconstrained. This certainly raises issues with regard to Union's competence and the proportionality of the measure.[32]

Further measures against tax evasion and avoidance were announced and described in a Commission Communication in July 2016 (see Table 13.5), also proposing that tax authorities should have access to anti-money laundering information:

Table 13.5 Fight Against Tax Evasion and Avoidance (July 2016)[33]

Fight against Tax Evasion and Avoidance (July 2016)
Harness the link between anti-money laundering and tax transparency rules → Proposal for a Council Directive amending Directive 2011/16/EU as regards access to anti-money-laundering information by tax authorities, COM(2016)452 (5 July 2016)
Improve information exchange on beneficial ownership → Currently pilot project (launched by UK, Germany, Spain, Italy and France) to exchange information on the ultimate beneficial owners of companies and trusts
Increase oversight of enablers and promoters of aggressive tax planning → Commission will explore the best way to increase oversight and ensure that effective disincentives apply for promoters and enablers of aggressive tax planning schemes (parallel to OECD-BEPS Action 12[34])
Promote higher tax good governance standards worldwide → Work on the development of an 'EU black list' of non-cooperative jurisdictions
Improve the protection of whistle-blowers → Commission is assessing the scope for horizontal or further sectorial action at EU level, while respecting the principle of subsidiarity.

In October 2016, the EU Commission published its 'Corporate Tax Reform Package' that includes two proposals for the harmonization of corporate taxation in the EU in a two-step procedure:

- First, the Commission proposes to harmonize corporate tax bases across each of the EU Member States (which would be mandatory for large groups), including a super-deduction for R&D costs and notional interest deduction for

31. *See, e.g.*, Recital 2 of the Preamble of the ATAD Proposal, *supra* n. 20.
32. For such arguments, see Florian *Oppel, BEPS in Europa: (Schein-)Harmonisierung der Missbrauchsabwehr durch neue Richtlinie 2016/1164 mit Nebenwirkungen*, 25 IStR 797,798–799 (2016); Desens, *supra* n.5, *at 827-828*; *see also* Werner Haslehner, *Anti-Hybrid Measures in the Parent Subsidiary Directive and the EU's Competence to Harmonise*, Kluwer International Tax Blog (31 Aug. 2015), http://kluwertaxblog.com/2015/08/31/anti-hybrid-measures-in-the-parent-subsidiary-directive-and-the-eus-competence-to-harmonise/. For a comprehensive analysis, see also Arnaud de Graaf & Klaas-Jan Visser, *ATA Directive: Some Observations Regarding Formal Aspects*, 25 Intertax 199, 202–.206 (2016).
33. Communication on further measures to enhance transparency and the fight against tax evasion and avoidance of 5 July 2016, COM(2016) 451 (hereinafter '2016 Further Transparency Communication').
34. OECD-BEPS Project, *Mandatory Disclosure Rules, Action 12 – 2015 Final Report*, OECD (2015).

equity financing (Allowance for Growth and Investment), in the form of a Common Corporate Tax Base (CCTB) Directive.[35]

- Second, once a common tax base is established, the Commission proposes that the results of entities in a corporate group in the EU are consolidated under a single filing and that the aggregate profits are apportioned to individual Member States according to labor, assets and sales by destination through a Common Consolidated Corporate Tax Base (CCCTB) Directive.[36] Until full CCCTB consolidation is introduced, the Commission's proposal foresees that group entities should be able to offset profits and losses they make in different Member States (i.e., temporary cross-border loss relief with recapture).

The Corporate Tax Reform Package (see Table 13.6) also includes a proposal to introduce measures to address certain hybrid mismatches partly in relation to non-EU countries but partly, and more broadly, by updating the ATAD[37] and a proposal to introduce mandatory binding dispute resolution of double taxation cases in the European Union.[38]

Table 13.6 Corporate Tax Reform Package (October 2016)

<table>
<tr><td colspan="4">Chapeau Communication (COM(2016) 682)</td></tr>
<tr><td rowspan="2">Proposal for a Dispute Resolution Directive (COM(2016) 686)[39]</td><td colspan="2">C(C)CTB[40]</td><td rowspan="2">Proposal for a Council Directive to amend the ATAD with regard to hybrid mismatches with third countries (COM(2016) 687)[41]</td></tr>
<tr><td>Proposal for a Common Corporate Tax Base (CCTB) Directive (COM(2016) 685)</td><td>Proposal for Common Consolidated Corporate Tax Base (CCCTB) Directive (COM(2016) 683)</td></tr>
</table>

Finally, one common theme of the EU Commission's work of the past few years stands out: Tax transparency. Mutual assistance between the Member States in the

35. The 2016 CCTB Proposal, *supra* n. 16.
36. The 2016 Relaunched CCCTB Proposal, *supra* n. 13.
37. Proposal for a Council Directive amending Directive (EU) 2016/1164 as regards hybrid mismatches with third countries of 25 October 2016 COM(2016) 687 (hereinafter the 'Hybrid Mismatches Proposal').
38. The 2016 Dispute Resolution Proposal, *supra* n. 18.
39. *See* the Commission Staff Working Document, Impact Assessment Accompanying the Documents Proposal for a Council Directive on Double Taxation Dispute Resolution Mechanism in the European Union of 25 October 2016, SWD(2016) 343.
40. *See also* the Commission Staff Working Document, Executive Summary of the Impact Assessment Accompanying the Document Proposals for a Council Directive on a Common Corporate Tax Base and a Common Consolidated Corporate Tax base (CCCTB) of 25 October 2016, SWD(2016) 342.
41. *See also* the Commission Staff Working Document Accompanying the document Proposal for a Council Directive amending Directive (EU) 2016/1164 as regards hybrid mismatches with third countries of 25 October 2016, SWD(2016) 345.

field of direct taxation goes back to 1977,[42] but has quickly developed and evolved in the past few years: Parallel to the developments in the OECD, a new Mutual Assistance Directive was issued in 2011,[43] moving beyond the traditional concepts of exchange of information upon request or spontaneously and implementing automatic exchange of information (see Table 13.7) on certain non-financial income. In rapid succession, the mandatory automatic exchange was extended to financial information (2014),[44] information on tax rulings (2015)[45] and country-by-country reports (2016);[46] moreover, it will likely be amended to grant tax authorities access to anti-money laundering information (2017).[47] The following table gives a brief overview.

Table 13.7 Automatic Exchange of Information in the European Union

Step 1 – Certain Types of Non-Financial Income (2011)	- Council Directive 2011/16/EU of 15 February 2011 on administrative cooperation in the field of taxation and repealing Directive 77/799/EEC, [2011] L 64/1 (based on Proposal COM(2009) 29 [2 February 2009]) - Automatic exchange of information with effect from 1 January 2015, where information is available, in respect of five non-financial categories of income and capital, for - income from employment, - director's fees, - life insurance products not covered by other Directives, - pensions, and - ownership of and income from immovable property. - Implementation (computerized format) through the Commission Implementing Regulation (EU) 2015/2378, [2015] OJ L 332/19, as amended - Also: First Report of the Commission AEFI expert group on the implementation of Directive 2014/107/EU for automatic exchange of financial account information (March 2015)

42. Council Directive 77/799/EEC of 19 December 1977 concerning mutual assistance by the competent authorities of the Member States in the field of direct taxation, OJ 1977 L 336/15, repealed.
43. Council Directive 2011/16/EU on administrative cooperation in the field of taxation and repealing Directive 77/799/EEC, OJ 2011 L 64/1.
44. Council Directive 2014/107/EU of 9 December 2014 amending Directive 2011/16/EU as regards mandatory automatic exchange of information in the field of taxation, OJ 2014 L 359/1.
45. Council Directive 2015/2376/EU of 8 December 2015 amending Directive 2011/16/EU as regards mandatory automatic exchange of information in the field of taxation, OJ 2015 L 332/1 (hereinafter the 'Mutual Assistance Directive Amendment')'.
46. Council Directive 2016/881/EU of 25 May 2016 amending Directive 2011/16/EU as regards mandatory automatic exchange of information in the field of taxation, OJ 2016 L 146/8.
47. Political agreement in Council was reached on 8 November 2016; see the Council's press release 633/16 (8 November 2016).

Step 2 – Financial Information (2014)	- Council Directive 2014/107/EU of 9 December 2014, [2014] OJ L 359/1 (based on Proposal COM(2013) 348 [12 June 2013]) - Implementation of the OECD's Common Reporting Standard (CRS)[48] - Automatic exchange of information (generally beginning on 30 September 2017 for taxable periods starting with 2016) without the requirement of 'availability' for financial information, such as, - interest, dividends and similar types of income, - sale proceeds from the sale of financial assets, - account balances. - Implementation (computerized format) through the Commission Implementing Regulation (EU) 2015/2378, [2015] OJ L 332/19, as amended - Repeal of the Savings Interest Directive by Council Directive (EU) 2015/2060 of 10 November 2015, [2015] OJ L 301/1 (based on Proposal COM(2015) 129 [18 March 2015]) - Amendments of the savings interest agreements with Switzerland, Liechtenstein, Monaco, Andorra and San Marino
Step 3 – Tax Rulings (2015)	- Council Directive (EU) 2015/2376 of 8 December 2015, [2015] OJ L 332/1 (based on Proposal COM(2015) 135 [18 March 2015]) - Part of the Tax Transparency Package (COM(2015) 136) and parallel to OECD-BEPS Action 5[49] - Exchange of basic information on advance cross-border rulings and advance pricing arrangements with effect from 1 January 2017 - Applies for cross-border rulings and advance pricing arrangements that were issued, amended or renewed - after 31 December 2016 or - within a period beginning five years before 1 January 2017 with the exception of those issued, amended or renewed between 1 January 2012 and 31 December 2013 if they were not still valid on 1 January 2014.[50] - Does not apply in a case where an advance cross-border ruling exclusively concerns and involves the tax affairs of one or more natural persons.

48. Standard for Automatic Exchange of Financial Account Information (Common Reporting Standard) of 13 February 2014, now included in the Standard for Automatic Exchange of Financial Information in Tax Matters of 21 July 2014; *see also* the 'CRS Implementation Handbook' – Implementation Handbook for the Standard for Automatic Exchange of Financial Information of 7 August 2015.
49. OECD Countering Harmful Tax Practices Report, *supra* n. 11.
50. For those issued, amended, or renewed between 1 January 2014 and 31 December 2016, the exchange shall take place irrespective of whether they are still valid. Member States may also exclude those advance cross-border rulings and advance pricing arrangements issued, amended or renewed before 1 April 2016 if they concern a particular person or a group of persons (excluding those conducting mainly financial or investment activities) with a group wide annual net turnover of less than EUR 40 million.

Step 4 – Country-by-Country Reporting (2016)	- Council Directive (EU) 2016/881 of 25 May 2016, [2016] OJ L 146/8 (based on Proposal COM(2016) 25 [28 January 2016) - Part of the Anti-Tax Avoidance Package (January 2016) and parallel to OECD-BEPS Action 13[51] - Exchange of country-by-country reports (CbCR) with effect from 1 January 2017 - Reports include information for every tax jurisdiction in which the multinational group does business on the amount of revenue, the profit before income tax, the income tax paid and accrued, the number of employees, the stated capital, the retained earnings and the tangible assets. - Member States must take the necessary measures to require certain taxpayers to file a country-by-country report. - The relevant competent authority shall then, by means of automatic exchange, communicate the report to any other Member State in which, on the basis of the information in the country-by-country report, one or more of the group entities are either resident for tax purposes, or are subject to tax with respect to the business carried out through a permanent establishment. - Note that the EU Commission has also proposed to change the accounting directive to introduce Public CbC-Reporting (COM(2016) 198 [12 April 2016])
Step 5 – Access to Anti-Money-Laundering Information (2017)	- Political agreement on a Council Directive in November 2016[52] (based on Proposal COM(2016) 452 [5 July 2016]) - Tax authorities must be given access to the data provided under the EU's anti-money laundering rules (e.g., customer due diligence information and the information in their national beneficial ownership registries) as from 1 January 2018 - Concerns especially situations where the Account Holder is an intermediary structure (i.e., a Passive Non-Financial Entity), as the Financial Institutions shall look through that entity and identify and report its controlling persons (beneficial owners in anti-money-laundering terminology).

With regard to the automatic exchange of financial information, the savings interest agreements (see Table 13.8) between the EU and Switzerland, Liechtenstein, Monaco, Andorra and San Marino,[53] which were based on the – now repealed –

51. OECD Transfer Pricing Report, *supra* n. 10.
52. Political agreement in Council was reached on 8 November 2016; *see* the Council's press release 633/16 (8 November 2016).
53. *See, e.g.*, the Agreement between the European Community and the Swiss Confederation providing for measures equivalent to those laid down in Council Directive 2003/48/EC on taxation of savings income in the form of interest payments, OJ 2004 L 385/30 (2004).

Savings Interest Directive,[54] had to be amended to implement the new standard also with these European financial centres. These negotiations have now been finalized:

Table 13.8 EU Agreements with Third Countries

	Council Decision on Signing	Council Decision on Conclusion	Text of the Protocol in the OJ	Starting from
Switzerland	(EU) 2015/860, [2015] OJ L 136/5 — Proposal COM(2015)150	(EU) 2015/2400, [2015] OJ L 333/10 — Proposal COM(2015)151	[2015] OJ L 333/12	1 Jan. 2017
Liechtenstein	(EU) 2015/1994, [2015] OJ L 290/16 — Proposal COM(2015)394	(EU) 2015/2453, [2015] OJ L 339/1 - Proposal COM(2015)395	[2015] OJ L 339/3	1 Jan. 2016
Monaco	(EU) 2016/1392, [2016] OJ L 225/1 — Proposal COM(2016)200	(EU) 2016/1830, ABl L 280/1 (2016) - Proposal COM(2016)201	[2016] OJ L 225/3	1 Jan. 2017
Andorra	(EU) 2016/242, [2016] OJ L 45/10 - Proposal COM(2015)632	(EU) 2016/1751, [2016] OJ L 268/38 - Proposal COM(2015)631	[2016] OJ L 268/40	1 Jan. 2017
San Marino	(EU) 2015/2469, [2015] OJ L 346/1 - Proposal COM(2015)519	(EU) 2016/828, [2016] OJ L 140/1 — Proposal COM(2015)518	[2015] OJ L 346/3	1 Jan. 2016

54. Council Directive 2003/48/EC of 3 June 2003 on taxation of savings income in the form of interest payments, OJ 2003 L 157/38, repealed by Council Directive (EU) 2015/2060 of 10 November 2015 repealing Directive 2003/48/EC on taxation of savings income in the form of interest payments, OJ 2015 L 301/1.

§13.02 INITIATIVES IN INDIRECT TAXATION

On 7 April 2016, the Commission adopted an Action Plan on VAT[55] (see Table 13.9). It aims to tackle the VAT gap and adapt the VAT system to the digital economy. It lays out the Commissions approach towards a robust single European VAT area in relation to the definitive VAT system for cross-border supplies. The Commission proposes flexible EU rules governing VAT rates.

Table 13.9 Action Plan on VAT[56]

Action Plan on VAT			
Recent and ongoing policy initiatives	**Urgent measures to tackle the VAT gap**	**Towards a robust single European VAT area**	**Towards a modernised VAT rates policy**
Removing VAT obstacles to e-commerce in the Single Market + SMEs VAT package	Improving cooperation within the EU and with non-EU countries Towards more efficient tax administrations Improving voluntary compliance Tax collection	Definitive VAT regime for cross-border trade	More freedom for Member States on rates policies

On 1 December 2016, the Commission has proposed practical new measures to support the digital economy when it comes to VAT compliance, which can currently place heavy burdens on small business operating online.[57] The new rules should help to accelerate growth for online businesses, in particular start-ups and SMEs. This proposal is part of the Strategy for the EU Digital Single Market which tries to tear down regulatory walls and moving from twenty-eight national markets to a single one. In the opinion of Commission the package of proposals will:

- Facilitate cross-border trade
- Combat VAT fraud
- Ensure fair competition for EU businesses
- Provide equal treatment for online publications.

55. Communication from the Commission to the European Parliament, the Council and the European Economic Council on an action plan on VAT Towards a single EU VAT area – Time to decide, COM(2016) 148 final (hereinafter 'VAT Communication').
56. *See* http://ec.europa.eu/taxation_customs/sites/taxation/files/resources/images/taxation/vat/vat_action_plan_en.jpg (accessed 29 November 2016).
57. Proposal for a Council Directive amending Directive 2006/112/EC and Directive 2009/132/EC as regards certain value added tax obligations for supplies of services and distance sales of goods, SWD(2016) 379 final, and SWD(2016) 382 final.

Businesses, which are selling goods online, could take care of all their VAT obligations in the EU through a digital online portal ('One-Stop Shop'),[58] hosted by their own tax administration and in their own language.[59] These rules already exist for online sellers of electronic services ('e-services') and should be extended for distance selling of tangible goods.

In order to support start-ups and micro-businesses, a yearly VAT threshold of EUR 10.000 under which cross-border sales for online companies are treated as domestic sales should be introduced and VAT paid to their own tax administration. To make trading in the single market as similar as possible to trading at home for these businesses, same invoicing and record keeping rules will be implemented.

Current exemption from VAT for imports of small consignments from outside the EU will be removed, because it leads to unfair competition and distortion for EU business. The same VAT rate should be applied for e-publications like e-books and online newspapers as for their printed equivalents.[60] The option to treat e-publications and printed publications equally removes restrictions on Member States that are unjustified.[61]

The Commission estimates that these new rules will have a major effect for business selling goods and services online. Business should benefit from fairer rules, lower compliance costs and reduced administrative burdens.[62]

SMEs bear proportionally higher VAT compliance costs than large businesses due to the complexity and fragmentation of the EU VAT system. Therefore, the Commission is preparing a comprehensive simplification package for SMEs that will seek to create an environment that is conducive to their growth and favourable to cross-border trade. In particular, the special scheme for small enterprises will be introduced.

The Commissions wants to take urgent action on three fronts to tackle the VAT gap by:[63]

- enhancing administrative cooperation with third countries;
- collectively improving the performance of European tax administrations; and
- improving voluntary compliance.

58. Proposal for a Council Regulation amending Regulation (EU) No 904/2010 on administrative cooperation and combating fraud in the field of value added tax, COM(2016) 755.
59. Proposal for a Council Implementing Regulation amending Implementing Regulation (EU) No 282/2011 laying down implementing measures for Directive 2006/112/EC on the common system of value added tax, COM(2016) 756 final.
60. Proposal for a Council Directive amending Directive 2006/112/EC, as regards rates of value added tax applied to books, newspapers and periodicals, COM(2016) 758 final.
61. Commission Staff Working Document, Impact Assessment: Accompanying the Document Proposal for a Council Directive Amending Directive 2016/112/EC as regards rates of value added tax applied to books, newspapers and periodicals, SWD(2016) 392 final.
62. Commission Staff Working Document, Impact Assessment: Accompanying the Document Proposals for a Council Directive, a Council Implementing Regulation and a Council Regulation on Modernizing VAT for cross-border B2C e-Commerce, COM(2016) 757 final; SWD(2016) 382 final.
63. *See* http://ec.europa.eu/taxation_customs/sites/taxation/files/resources/documents/taxation/tax_cooperation/vat_gap/2016-03_20_measures_en.pdf (accessed 30 November 2016).

In 2016, the Commission will present measures to improve cooperation between tax administrations including from third countries and with customs and law enforcement bodies and to strengthen tax administrations' capacity for a more efficient fight against fraud as well as an evaluation report of the Directive on the mutual assistance for the recovery of tax debts.

In 2017, the Commission will table a proposal to enhance VAT administrative cooperation and Eurofisc.

The present VAT transitional system treats domestic and cross-border transactions differently. On the one hand VAT is levied on domestic supplies of goods and services. Goods or services can be bought free of VAT within the Single Market on the other hand. The Commission will propose legislation for a definitive VAT system for cross-border trade which will be based on the principle of taxation in the country of destination of the goods, as agreed by the European Parliament and the Council.

The Commission considers that in the definitive VAT system, the taxation rules according to which the supplier of goods collects VAT from his customer should be extended to cross-border transactions. The Commission is of the opinion that this will ensure consistent treatment of domestic and cross-border supplies along the entire chain of a production and distribution, and re-establish the basic features of the VAT in cross-border trade (i.e. the fractionated payments system with its self-policing character).

In the future system, all businesses that trade in other Member States would be able to sort out their VAT in the other Member State of destination via an online portal in their home country. Otherwise, traders would have to register for VAT, file returns and make payments in every EU country where they operate. The online portal would also allow VAT to be collected by the country where the sale is made and transferred to the country where the goods are consumed.[64]

However, such a system change has pros and cons.[65] Such a system change would lead to increased information and compliance costs for SMEs. Only larger businesses would benefit from such a system change. Furthermore, it is doubtful whether such a system would really contribute to closing the VAT gap. Since additional 600 billion euros VAT would be involved, there is an increased potential for Missing-Trader Fraud. Obviously, the Commission estimates that a system change will have nevertheless a positive impact because of the mark-up applied by businesses on their intra-community purchases.[66] Success of a system change also requires trust of tax authorities in each other's ability and willingness to monitor and audit VAT paid to another Member State.

The current rules of the VAT Directive include lower limits on the levels of the VAT rates and a list of the goods and services which could benefit from reduced rates. The Member States have therefore only limited autonomy for governing VAT rates. The

64. *See* http://ec.europa.eu/taxation_customs/sites/taxation/files/resources/documents/taxation/vat/action_plan/vat_factsheet_en.pdf (accessed 30 November 2016).
65. EY, *Implementing the 'destination principle' to intra-EU B2B supplies of goods – Feasibility and economic evaluation study* – Final Report of 30 June 2015, TAXUD/2013/DE/319, 15 ('EY Report').
66. *Ibid.*, at 17.

Commission would like to grant more freedom on setting VAT rates. However, appropriate safeguards will be taken to prevent excessive complexity and distortion of competition. Operations in the Single Market should not be affected by the diversity of rates. The Commission is not very specific, how those goals will be achieved. It points out that the degree of autonomy on rates to be granted to Member States is not purely a technical matter, but requires political discussion. In 2017, detailed legislative proposals based on a mandate from the Council will be issued by the Commission.

The Commission has rejected twice in 2006[67] and 2015[68] the request of Member States for authorization to introduce the reverse charge in respect of all Business to Business (B2B) supplies of goods or services where the invoice value exceeds a certain threshold. However, in 2016 the Commission promised to present a proposal to authorize Member States to implement a hybrid VAT system for domestic supplies of goods and services. This would authorize Member States to implement a special measure as regards the application of the reverse charge mechanism in relation to all supplies of goods or services above a certain threshold with a view of combating fraud.

The reverse charge in respect of all domestic Business to Business (B2B) supplies of goods or services would eliminate missing trader fraud effectively. It would also prevent revenue losses by insolvencies of in-between traders and ensure equal tax treatment of domestic supplies and intra-community supplies of goods as well as cross-border supplies of services. Besides these advantages there are also downsides connected with such a system change. Opportunities for consumers to receive tax free goods and services would possibly increase, if they pretend to be a taxpayer above threshold ('micro fraud'). Furthermore, a higher risk of revenue losses by insolvencies of retailers can be expected. Since the system of fractioned payment would be suspended there is an increased risk of revenue losses by undeclared sales.

However, on 20 December 2016 the Commission tabled a proposal for a Council Directive amending Directive 2006/112/EC on the common system of value added tax as regards the temporary application of a generalized reverse charge mechanism (GRCM) in relation to supplies of goods and services above a certain threshold.[69] A Member state may choose to implement GRCM for domestic goods and services above the threshold of €10,000 until 30 June 2022, if it meets the following criteria:

(a) it has a VAT gap, expressed as a percentage of the VAT Total Tax Liability, of at least 5 percentage points above the Community median VAT gap;
(b) it has a carousel fraud level within its total VAT gap of more than 25%;

67. Communication from the Commission to the Council in accordance with Article 27(3) of Directive 77/388/EEC, COM(2006) 404 final.
68. Communication from the Commission to the Council in accordance with Article 395 of Council Directive 2006/112/EC, COM (2015) 538 final.
69. COM(2016) 811 final; *see also* Commission staff working document impact assessment, Generalised reverse charge mechanism – Accompanying the document 'Proposal for a Council Directive amending Directive 2006/112/EC on the common system of value added tax as regards the temporary application of the generalised reverse charge mechanism in relation to supplies of goods and services above a certain threshold, SWD(2016) 457 final.'

(c) it establishes that other control measures are not sufficient to combat carousel fraud on its territory.

A Member state which does not fulfil these criteria themselves could opt to implement the system until 30 June 2022, if it meets the following requirements:

(a) has a common border with a Member State that is authorized to apply the GRCM;
(b) establishes that a serious risk of shift of fraud towards its territory exists because of the authorization of the GRCM to that Member State;
(c) establishes that other control measures are not sufficient to combat fraud on its territory.

If Member States meet the requirements and wish to implement the GRCM must submit a request to the Commission and the Commission then shall adopt an implementing decision confirming that the request complies with the requirements. In case of considerable negative impact on the internal market, the Commission can repeal all the implementing decisions at any time at the earliest six months after the entry into force of the first implementing decision authorizing a Member State to apply the GRCM. The five-year limitation of the implementation of the GRCM and the possibility to revoke the implementing decision by the Commission at any time as suggested in the Commission's proposal for a directive cannot provide confidence in the meaningfulness and durability of the scheme and should be rejected in the light of the associated administrative and training expenses for businesses and the tax administration.

§13.03 APPENDIX: OECD-BEPS ACTIONS AND CORRESPONDING EU MEASURES

This table should give a brief overview of the OECD-BEPS Actions and the corresponding measures in the EU (without regard to the Commission's proposal for a Common (Consolidated) Corporate Tax Base[70]):[71]

70. *See* the 2016 CCTB Proposal and the 2016 Relaunched CCCTB Proposal, *supra* n. 13.
71. *See also* the overview in the Commission Staff Working Document accompanying the document Communication from the Commission to the European Parliament and the Council – Anti Tax Avoidance Package: Next Steps towards delivering effective taxation and greater tax transparency in the EU of 28 January 2016, SWD(2016) 6, 48 et seq.

Action	OECD-BEPS	EU Measures
Action 1: Digital Economy	- Analytical report addressing the challenges of the digital economy, referring to the OECD-BEPS actions in general to address risks posed by digital economy - Discussion of possible special measures with regard to the digital economy (e.g., 'digital presence', withholding taxation, equalization taxes)	- Report of the Commission Expert Group on Taxation of the Digital Economy[72] - Action Plan on VAT[73] - Work of the Commission also on tax questions relating to the collaborative economy ('sharing economy')[74] - Situation will be monitored to see if general anti-avoidance measures are sufficient to address digital risks.
Action 2: Hybrid Mismatch Arrangements	- Best practice recommendations to avoid mismatches ('tax arbitrage') by linking the tax treatment of an instrument or entity in one country with the tax treatment in another - Avoidance of 'double deduction' situations ('DD') and mismatches where a deduction is not matched by a corresponding inclusion ('D/NI') - Discussion and proposal for corresponding amendments in tax treaty law (e.g., hybrid entities)	- Introduction of an obligation to tax in the Parent-Subsidiary-Directive for distributions insofar as they are deductible in the country of the subsidiary ('hybrid financial instruments') (from 2016)[75] ATA Directive includes a provision to address hybrid mismatches (from 2019)[76] and subsequent Commission proposal to further expand this provision,[77] previously also work of the Code of Conduct group on hybrid branches[78]

72. Commission Expert Group on Taxation of the Digital Economy, Report of 28 May 2014.
73. *See* VAT Communication, *supra* n. 55.
74. *See* Commission's Communication on Online Platforms and the Digital Single Market Opportunities and Challenges for Europe of 25 May 2016, COM(2016)288, the European agenda for the collaborative economy of 2 June 2016, COM(2016)356 (including the Commission staff working document in SWD(2016)184).
75. *See* Council Directive 2014/86/EU of 8 July 2014 amending Directive 2011/96/EU on the common system of taxation applicable in the case of parent companies and subsidiaries of different Member States, OJ 2014 L 219/40.
76. Art. 9 of Council Directive (EU) 2016/1164 of 12 July 2016 laying down rules against tax avoidance practices that directly affect the functioning of the internal market, OJ 2016 L 193/1 (hereinafter the 'ATAD').
77. The Hybrid Mismatches Proposal, *supra* n. 37; *see also* the Slovak Presidency Note to the High Level Working Party on Tax Issues, BEPS Roadmap on Future Work of 14 July 2016, Doc. 11071/16 FISC 121 (hereinafter the '2016 EU-BEPS Roadmap') paras 18 et seq.
78. *See* report and appendices of the Code of Conduct group to the Council, Doc. 9912/16 FISC 97 ECOFIN 558 of 13 June 2016; *see, e.g.*, the press release in Doc. 16603/14 PRESSE 68 of 9 December 2014, 16.

Action	OECD-BEPS	EU Measures
	- Currently follow-up work on branch mismatches structures[79]	- Recommendation to Member States to introduce a subject-to-tax-clause in their tax treaties[80] - Proposal to introduce a comprehensive subject-to-tax-clause in the Interest-Royalties-Directive[81]
Action 3: Controlled Foreign Companies (CFCs)	- Best practice recommendations for implementing controlled foreign companies (CFC) rules	- ATA Directive includes provisions on CFC rules with effect within the EU and externally (from 2019)[82]
Action 4: Interest Limitation	- Best practice recommendations on limiting a company's or group's net interest deductions.	- ATA Directive includes provisions to limit interest deductions with effect within the EU and externally (from 2019 or 2024, at the latest)[83]
Action 5: Harmful Tax Practices	- Mandatory spontaneous exchange of relevant information on tax rulings (minimum standard[84])	- Amendment of the Mutual Assistance Directive to include mandatory automatic exchange of information on all cross-border rulings and APAs (from 2017)[85]

79. *See* OECD-BEPS Project, *Branch Mismatch Structures, BEPS Action 2 – 22 August 2016 Public Discussion Draft*, (OECD Publishing 2016).
80. Commission Recommendation of 6 December 2012 regarding measures intended to encourage third countries to apply minimum standards of good governance in tax matters of 6 December 2012, C(2012) 8805, accompanied by an 'Impact Assessment' of 6 December 2012, SWD(2012)403 (collectively, hereinafter, the 'Third-Countries Recommendations').
81. *See* Art. 1(1) of the Proposal for a Council Directive on a common system of taxation applicable to interest and royalty payments made between associated companies of different Member States of 11 November 2011, COM(2011) 714, to which the Commission refers in its 5 Key-Areas Communication, *supra* n. 15, at 11; for further analysis, see, e.g., Georg Kofler & Juan Lopez Rodriguez, *Beneficial Ownership and EU Law, in Beneficial Ownership: Recent Trends* 215, 222 (Michael Lang et al. eds, IBFD 2013). For the current status of this discussion, see also the EU-BEPS Roadmap, *supra* n. 77, para. 6 et seq.
82. Arts 7 and 8, ATAD, *supra* n. 76.
83. Art. 4, ATAD, *supra* n. 76.
84. *See* Question 4, OECD-BEPS Project, *Frequently Asked Questions – 2015 Final Reports* (OECD Publishing 2015) (hereinafter 'OECD FAQs').
85. The Mutual Assistance Directive Amendment, *supra* n. 45; *see also* the 2015 Tax Transparency Communication, *supra* n. 8, at 5.

Action	OECD-BEPS	EU Measures
	– Agreement on the 'modified nexus approach' for patent boxes where tax benefits from preferential regimes for IP are linked to the underlying economic activity[87]	– Agreement in the Code of Conduct Group on the 'modified nexus approach' for patent boxes[86] (and review of its implementation by that group[88]) and further work on harmful tax competition,[89] including the issuance of rulings[90] – State aid control by the Commission, also with respect to tax rulings[91] – Amendment of the Mutual Assistance Directive to grant tax authorities access to anti-money laundering information[92] – Pilot project of all EU Member States to improve the exchange of information on beneficial ownership and announcement of a Commission analysis for 2016[93]

86. *See, e.g.*, OECD Modified Nexus Approach; Report of the Code of Conduct Group to the Council, 13 June 2016, Doc. 9912/16 FISC 97 ECOFIN 558, paras 17 et seq.; and the 5 Key-Areas Communication, *supra* n. 15, 11 et seq.
87. For details on that agreement, see OECD-BEPS Project, *Agreement on Modified Nexus Approach for IP Regimes, Action 5* (OECD Publishing 2015) (hereinafter 'OECD Modified Nexus Approach').
88. *See* Annex 3 (Work Package 2015) to the report of the Code of Conduct-Group, Doc. 14302/15 FISC 159 ECOFIN 883 of 23 November 2015 (hereinafter 'Code of Conduct Group Work Package 2015'), *see also, e.g.*, the EU-BEPS Roadmap, *supra* n. 77 paras 27 et seq.
89. *See, e.g.*, the reports of the Code of Conduct-Group to the Council in Doc. 9912/16 FISC 97 ECOFIN 558 of 13 June 2016, and in Doc. 14566/16 FISC 198 ECOFIN 1057 of 17 November 2016.
90. Code of Conduct Group Work Package 2015, *supra* n. 88; *see also, e.g.*, EU-BEPS Roadmap, *supra* n. 77, at 35.
91. *See, specifically,* Commission Notice on the notion of State aid as referred to in Article 107(1) of the Treaty on the Functioning of the European Union, OJ 2016 C 262/1 (2016), paras 169 et seq.; and the DG Competition Working Paper on State Aid and Tax Rulings of 3 June 2016.
92. Political agreement in Council was reached on 8 November 2016; *see* the Council's press release 633/16 (8 November 2016); *see also* the Proposal for a Council Directive amending Directive 2011/16/EU as regards access to anti-money-laundering information by tax authorities of 5 July 2016, COM(2016) 452, and for the political agreement in Council the press release 633/16 of 8 November 2016.
93. *See* the 2016 Further Transparency Communication, *supra* n. 33, at 6.

Action	OECD-BEPS	EU Measures
		- Measures to promote higher tax good governance standards worldwide[94] and development of an 'external strategy' (including an 'EU black list')[95]
Action 6: Treaty Abuse	- Discussion and proposals for anti-abuse provisions to be included in tax treaties - Minimum standard against treaty shopping (i.e., 'Principle Purpose Test' (PPT) and 'Limitation of Benefits' (LoB) or both or a combination of LoB and anti-conduit rules)[98] - Implementation through the multilateral instrument (Action 15)[100] and amendment of the OECD-MC and the OECD-MC Comm. in 2017[101]	- Recommendation on Tax Treaties encourages Member States to use an EU-compatible PPT approach. ('Principal Purpose Test')[96] - ATAD includes a GAAR (from 2019),[97] previously recommendation that Member States include a GAAR in their domestic tax laws[99]
Action 7: Permanent Establishments	- Amendment of the definition of permanent establishment (PE) in Article 5 OECD-MC, to prevent companies from artificially avoiding having a taxable presence (i.e., with regard to the specific activity exemptions and	- Recommendation encourages Member States to use the amended OECD approach on Article 5 OECD-MC[102]

94. *See* the Third-Countries Recommendation, *supra* n. 80 and, thereafter, *e.g.*, the 5 Key-Areas Communication, *supra* n. 15, 14 et seq. and its appendix (compilation of a list based on the lists of the Member States).
95. *See* Communication from the Commission to the European Parliament and the Council on an External Strategy for Effective Taxation of 28 January 2016, COM(2016) 24 final, and previously the 2016 Further Transparency Communication, *supra* n. 33, at 8. For further details and the methodology, see https://ec.europa.eu/taxation_customs/tax-common-eu-list (accessed 20 February 2017), and for agreement on the criteria see Doc. 14166/16 FISC 187 ECOFIN 1014 of 8 November 2016.
96. 2016 Tax Treaty Abuse Recommendation, *supra* n. 21.
97. Art. 6, ATAD, *supra* n. 76.
98. *See* Question 4, OECD-BEPS Project, *Frequently Asked Questions – 2015 Final Reports* (OECD Publishing 2015) (hereinafter 'OECD FAQs').
99. Commission Recommendation of 6 December 2012 on aggressive tax planning, C(2012) 8806.
100. *See* Question 46, OECD FAQs, *supra* n. 84.
101. *See ibid.*, Question 111.
102. Commission Recommendation of 28 January 2016 on the implementation of measures against tax treaty abuse, C(2016) 271.

Action	OECD-BEPS	EU Measures
	agency permanent establishments) - Implementation through the multilateral instrument (Action 15)[103] and amendment of the OECD-MC and the OECD-MC Comm. in 2017[104] - Currently follow-up work on the attribution of profits to permanent establishments[105]	
Actions 8–10: Transfer Pricing – Intangibles, Risk and Capital, High Risk Transactions	- Confirmation of the arm's length principle and comparability analysis as pillars of transfer pricing. - Reinforcement of the international standards with regard to intangibles (Action 8), risk and capital (Action 9) and high risk transactions (Action 10) - Amendments or revisions of Chapters I.D, II, VI, VII und VIII of the OECD-Transfer Pricing Guidelines (TPG)I[108] and corresponding adjustments of Chapter IX[109] - Currently follow-up work on transactional profit splits[110]	- Work of the Joint Transfer Pricing Forum (JTPF) on an EU-approach to implementing BEPS conclusions[106] - Commission will work with Member States and businesses to build on the OECD TPG and develop coordinated and more concrete implementation within the EU, reflecting the economic reality of the internal market[107]

103. *See* Question 46, OECD FAQs, *supra* n. 84.
104. *See ibid.*, Question 111.
105. OECD, *Base Erosion and Profit Shifting (BEPS) Public Discussion Draft: BEPS Action 7 – Guidance on the Attribution of Profits to Permanent Establishments, 4 July – 5 September 2016* (OECD Publishing 2016).
106. For the Joint Transfer Pricing Forum (JTPF), *see* http://ec.europa.eu/taxation_customs/business/company-tax/transfer-pricing-eu-context/joint-transfer-pricing-forum_en (accessed 20 February 2017), and for a brief overview of the work of the Forum see also, e.g., Georg Kofler, *Article 9, in Klaus Vogel on Double Taxation Conventions* m.no. 129 (Ekkehart Reimer & Alexander Rust eds, 4th ed., Wolters Kluwer 2015) Wm.no. 129.
107. OECD, *Base Erosion and Profit Shifting (BEPS) Public Discussion Draft BEPS Actions 8-10 Revised Guidance on Profit Splits, 4 July – 5 September 2016* (OECD Publishing 2016).
108. These changes of the OECD TPG were formally adopted by the OECD Council on 23 May 2016; *see* the press release 'OECD Council approves incorporation of BEPS amendments into the Transfer Pricing Guidelines for Multinational Enterprises and Tax Administrations' of 15 June 2016.
109. *See* the 5 Key-Areas Communication, *supra* n. 15, at 11.
110. *See* OECD, *Base Erosion and Profit Shifting (BEPS) Document for Public Review: Conforming Amendments to Chapter IX of the Transfer Pricing Guidelines, 4 July – 16 August 2016* (OECD Publishing 2016).

Action	OECD-BEPS	EU Measures
Action 11: Measuring and Monitoring BEPS	- Analytical report on new statistics on corporate taxation and the scope and revenue impact of BEPS	- Work on a better quantification of the 'tax gap', creation of a Fiscalis Project Group[111]
Action 12: Disclosure of Aggressive Tax Planning	- Best practices for the introduction of rules requiring mandatory disclosure of aggressive or abusive transactions, structures or arrangements	- Commission will keep the issue under review, as part of its tax transparency agenda,[112] Council invitation to the Commission 'to consider legislative initiatives on Mandatory Disclosure Rules inspired by Action 12 of the OECD-BEPS project with a view to introducing more effective disincentives for intermediaries who assist in tax evasion or avoidance schemes'[113] - Public consultation in late-2016 session to gather views on future rules to deter promoters of aggressive tax planning schemes[114]
Action 13: Transfer Pricing Documentation and Country-by-Country Reporting	- Agreement on mandatory country-by-country reporting (CbCR) by multinational enterprises to tax administrations on key financial data and automatic exchange of this information (minimum standard;[115] no public CbCR)	- Amendment of the Mutual Assistance Directive to introduce mandatory country-by-country reporting (CbCR) and the automatic exchange of these reports between the Member States (from 2017)[116]

111. *See* Tax Transparency Communication *supra* n. 8, at 7.
112. *See* the 2016 Further Transparency Communication, *supra* n. 33, at 7 et seq.
113. *See* Council conclusions on an external taxation strategy and measures against tax treaty abuse, Press release 281/16, 25 May 2016, and the EU-BEPS Roadmap, paras 32 et seq.
114. *See* the press release 'Commission gathers views on future rules to deter promoters of aggressive tax planning schemes', IP/16/3618 of 10 November 2016, and the previous announcement in the 2016 Further Transparency Communication, *supra* n. 33, at 7.
115. *See* Question 4, OECD FAQs, *supra* n. 84.
116. Council Directive (EU) 2016/881 of 25 May 2016 amending Directive 2011/16/EU as regards mandatory automatic exchange of information in the field of taxation, OJ 2016 L 146/8.

Action	OECD-BEPS	EU Measures
	- Amendment of Chapter V of the OECD-Transfer Pricing Guidelines (TPG)[117]	- Commission proposal to change the accounting directive to introduce Public CbCR[118]
Action 14: Dispute Resolution	- Agreement on measures to reduce uncertainty and unintended double taxation for businesses, along with a timely and effective resolution of disputes in this area (minimum standard[121]) - A number of countries have also committed to a mandatory binding arbitration process[123]	- Multilateral Arbitration Convention for transfer pricing disputes[119] and Code of Conduct for its effective implementation[120] - Proposal for a Directive on mandatory double taxation dispute resolution mechanisms in the European Union[122] - Work of the expert group 'Platform for Tax Good Governance'[124] on double taxation in the internal market[125]

117. These changes of the OECD TPG were formally adopted by the OECD Council on 23 May 2016; *see* the press release 'OECD Council approves incorporation of BEPS amendments into the Transfer Pricing Guidelines for Multinational Enterprises and Tax Administrations' of 15 June 2016.
118. Proposal for a Directive of the European Parliament and of the Council amending Directive 2013/34/EU as regards disclosure of income tax information by certain undertakings and branches of 12 April 2016 COM(2016) 198.
119. Convention 90/436/EEC on the elimination of double taxation in connection with the adjustment of transfers of profits between associated undertakings, OJ 1990 L 225/10, as amended.
120. Revised Code of Conduct for the effective implementation of the Convention on the elimination of double taxation in connection with the adjustment of profits of associated enterprises, OJ 2009 C 322/1; for a proposal to further amendment of the Code of Conduct see Joint Transfer Pricing Forum, Final Report on Improving the Functioning of the Arbitration Convention, JTPF/002/2015/EN (Mar. 2015).
121. *See* Question 4, OECD FAQs, *supra* n. 84.
122. The 2016 Dispute Resolution Proposal, *supra* n. 18; *see also* the 5 Key-Areas Communication, *supra* n. 15, at 13, and the 2016 EU-BEPS Roadmap, *supra* n. 88, para. 24.
123. See the list of countries in OECD-BEPS Project, *Making Dispute Resolution Mechanisms More Effective – Action 14* 2015 Final Report, para 62 (OECD Publishing 2015).
124. Set up by the Commission's decision C(2013)2236 of 23 April 2013. The work of the Platform is available at https://ec.europa.eu/taxation_customs/business/company-tax/tax-good-governance/platform-tax-good-governance_en (accessed 20 February 2017).
125. *See, e.g.*, Platform/004/2013/EN (October 2013).

Action	OECD-BEPS	EU Measures
Action 15: Multilateral Instrument to Modify Tax Treaties	- Analytical report on the use of a multilateral instrument to amend tax treaties in order to integrate BEPS related measures where necessary - Currently work of interested countries on the multilateral instrument	- ATA Recommendation sets out the Commission's views on tax treaty related issues and their compatibility with EU law, which Member States should consider in their negotiations on the multilateral instrument[126]

126. The 2016 Tax Treaty Abuse Recommendation, *supra* n. 21.

CHAPTER 14
Corporate Tax Harmonization: C(C)CTB 2.0?

Katarina Köszeghy[*]

§14.01 INTRODUCTION

The issue of harmonization in the field of direct taxes is an evergreen one that is expected to take up much of the time of the Member States, the European Commission, and academia for a certain period in the foreseeable future with regard to the initiatives and proposals published by the European Commission in late October 2016.[1] It remains to be seen whether the gap between the tax-policy considerations expressed by the EU Commission in support of harmonization of corporate taxation rules in the EU and the concerns about such harmonization expressed by some Member States – who, from a

* The opinions, views, and conclusions, set out in this chapter are solely those of the author and do not reflect any official or unofficial opinion of the European Union, the Luxembourg Presidency of the Council of the European Union, the subsequent rotating Presidencies of the Council of the European Union, the Luxembourg Ministry of Finance, or any other body at any level, none of which, nor any person acting on their behalf, may be held responsible for said opinions, views, and conclusions contained herein.

1. The Commission committed to publish, in 2016, various initiatives by late autumn 2016 and it kept that commitment, publishing on 25 Oct. 2016, as part of its 'Corporate Tax Reform Package': (a) a Proposal for a Council Directive on a Common Corporate Tax Base (COM(2016) 685 final) (hereinafter the '2016 CCTB Proposal') and (b) a Proposal for a Council Directive on a Common Consolidated Corporate Tax Base (CCCTB) (COM(2016) 683 final) (hereinafter the '2016 CCCTB Proposal'; hereinafter, *collectively*, the 2016 CCTB Proposal and the 2016 CCCTB Proposal is the 'Relaunched C(C)CTB Proposal'). *See also* Council Conclusions of 6 Dec. 2016, 14752/1/16 REV 1, FISC 204, ECOFIN 1094, paras 7–9, 13. Said Corporate Tax Reform Package also contained a Proposal for a Council Directive amending Directive (EU) 2016/1164 as regards hybrid mismatches with third countries (COM(2016) 687 final) (hereinafter the '2016 ATAD Amendment Proposal') and a new proposal on dispute resolution mechanisms (COM(2016) 686 final). For more information, see https://ec.europa.eu/taxation_customs/business/company-tax/corporate-tax-reform-package_en_en.

political point of view, are likely to perceive possible initiatives heading in this direction as a restriction on their national sovereignty – will be bridged in the near future.

The first step toward harmonization in the area of corporate taxes across the EU came in the form of a proposal for a common consolidated corporate tax base ('CCCTB') issued by the European Commission in March 2011.[2] Subsequent negotiations regarding that Initial CCCTB Proposal stalled in Council working parties[3] and did not lead to conclusive results; thus, the Commission made its intent to withdraw the Initial CCCTB Proposal public in 2016.[4] The overall complexity of the Initial CCCTB Proposal – due, among other things, to the fact that it contained rules establishing both a common corporate tax base and a formula for distributing taxable profits determined on that basis – was subsequently identified as the main reason for its stalled negotiations, but the Commission never abandoned its policy favouring some level of harmonized corporate direct taxation rules. Rather, the Commission only withdrew the Initial CCCTB Proposal when it announced, as part of its 2016 Work Programme[5] a new, stronger, and better two-step proposal, with the first step being its 2016 CCTB Proposal[6] and the second step being its 2016 CCCTB Proposal.[7] One can argue that the Commission learned its lessons from the Initial CCCTB Proposal's lack of success, announcing its intent to build on the previous work done on, and the Council working parties' discussions about, the Initial CCCTB Proposal in conjunction with its 5 Key Areas Action Plan,[8] which allows, to a certain extent, the Initial CCCTB Proposal to rise, like the phoenix, out of its ashes and be reborn as part of the two-step Relaunched C(C)CTB Proposal.[9] This chapter, however, does not intend to anticipate any future discussions with respect to the substance of the provisions included in the Relaunched

2. The Proposal for a Council Directive on a Common Consolidated Corporate Tax Base (CCCTB) (COM(2011) 121 final) (hereinafter the 'Initial CCCTB Proposal'), was issued 16 Mar. 2011, then withdrawn in 2016. For more detail, see *infra* n. 4.
3. The Council of the EU is a single legal entity, but it meets in ten different 'configurations', depending on the subject being discussed. The Council is an essential EU decision-maker. It negotiates and adopts legislative acts, such as directives. The Economic and Financial Affairs Council, commonly known as the ECOFIN Council, is responsible for economic policy, taxation matters, financial markets and capital movements, and economic relations with countries outside the EU. Council meetings are attended by representatives from each member state at a ministerial level. The EU's Ministers of Finance typically attend the monthly ECOFIN Council meeting. The terms 'Council', 'ECOFIN Council', and 'ECOFIN' are used interchangeably throughout this Chapter.
4. The Commission announced its intent to overhaul and relaunch the Initial CCCTB Proposal in its Communication from the Commission to the European Parliament and the Council: A Fair and Efficient Corporate Tax System in the European Union: 5 Key Areas for Action (COM(2015) 302 final) issued 17 June 2015 (hereinafter, the '5 Key Areas Action Plan'), 7.
5. The Commission materialized that intention to relaunch the Initial CCCTB Proposal in its Communication from the Commission to the European Parliament, the Council, the European Economic and Social Committee and the Committee of the Regions, Commission Work Programme 2016, No Time for Business as Usual (COM(2015) 610 final) of 27 Oct. 2015 and its Annex iv (at no. 6) where it is specified that 'The existing [Initial CCCTB Proposal] will be withdrawn in parallel' (hereinafter, the '2016 Commission Work Programme').
6. For definition, see *supra* n. 1.
7. For this definition, see *supra* n. 1.
8. For this definition, see *supra* n. 4.
9. For this definition, see *supra* n. 1.

C(C)CTB Proposal. Instead, it is confined to, and focuses on, the Council working parties' discussions on the Initial CCCTB Proposal during the second semester of 2015 – during the Luxembourg Presidency – together with a short overview of the subsequent work conducted on the basis of those discussions.

This contribution goes back to the period when the Council considered splitting off a handful of measures it had identified as relating to base erosion and profit-shifting (BEPS), particularly the measures that had been qualified as international anti-BEPS aspects,[10] from the Initial CCCTB Proposal with a view to coordinating EU action with the implementation of the OECD-BEPS recommendations across the EU. In essence, this chapter describes the work moved forward during the Luxembourg Presidency in Council working parties on tax questions on the Initial CCCTB Proposal, thereby paving the way, to a certain extent, for the Original ATAD Proposal[11] and the subsequent ATAD, approved on 20 June 2016 and adopted by the Finance Ministers on 12 July 2016.[12] More specifically, this chapter gives an overview of the work brought forward by the Council working party on the Initial CCCTB Proposal as well as efforts undertaken with a view to achieve an autonomous EU directive implementing some of the OECD-BEPS recommendations. Prior to doing that, it provides a brief overview of the evolution of the Initial CCCTB Proposal (i.e., the initiatives suggested by the Council, the steps followed, and the achievements made) prior to the Luxembourg Presidency. The most challenging issues addressed in this chapter are (a) whether either of the initiatives that relied on the Initial CCCTB Proposal or the Original ATAD Proposal are likely to achieve harmonization in the area of corporate taxes and (b) if the approval and publication of the ATAD should be viewed as an indicator of the Council's future tendencies with respect to harmonization in the area of direct taxes.

In light of the recent, swift developments in the area of corporate taxation, the question posed in this chapter's title seems to be the most appropriate, as it best describes the work conducted in Council regarding harmonization of direct taxes as well as its 2014–2015 work on the Initial CCCTB Proposal. Focusing on that question is the best way forward, as it is the most relevant, given, firstly, the uncertainty that has – for a very long time – surrounded the Initial CCCTB Proposal as such (i.e., the years-long discussions in Council without any conclusive agreement and its withdrawal as part of the publication of several new-but-similar proposals). Secondly, the question incorporates initiatives relying on the Initial CCCTB Proposal as a legal basis for an autonomous directive aimed to prevent BEPS outcomes in the EU and beyond. The question serves as common thread to elaborate the issue of possible tendencies towards harmonization in the area of corporate taxes.

10. For more detail, see *infra* n. 15.
11. For this definition, see *infra* n. 12.
12. ATAD is actually the abbreviated name for an Anti-Tax Avoidance Directive, the term initially used by the Commission as part of its Anti-Tax Avoidance Package published on 28 Jan. 2016, which included, among other things, the original Proposal for a Council Directive Laying Down Rules Against Tax Avoidance Practices that Directly Affect the Functioning of the Internal Market (COM(2016) 26 final) (hereinafter, the 'Original ATAD Proposal'). Subsequently, Council Directive (EU) 2016/1164 of 12 July 2016 Laying Down Rules Against Tax Avoidance Practices that Directly Affect the Functioning of the Internal Market, *OJ* L193/1, was published on 19 July 2016 (hereinafter, the 'ATAD').

§14.02 FROM A COMMON CONSOLIDATED CORPORATE TAX BASE TOWARDS NEW OBJECTIVES IN THE FRAMEWORK OF THE INITIAL CCCTB PROPOSAL

[A] The Objective of the Initial CCCTB Proposal and the Non-conclusive Discussions in Council Working Parties Thereon

The Commission published the Initial CCCTB Proposal as a part of the more growth-friendly taxation paradigm advocated by the Europe 2020 strategy.[13] The objective of the Initial CCCTB Proposal, which was subjected to continual Council negotiation since first published, was to set out, firstly, common-but-optional EU rules on determining the tax base for some corporations, thereby creating a new, non-binding set of rules for corporations of a certain size, to be followed, secondly, by a key formula for apportioning tax revenues between the Member States. The Initial CCCTB Proposal intended to address the tax obstacles that companies typically face when operating in the Internal Market, which could arise from the coexistence of different tax systems across the Member States. The Initial CCCTB Proposal also aimed to avoid, *inter alia*, risks of double taxation and to reduce certain opportunities for aggressive tax-planning practices. With a view to encourage quicker progress, a two-step approach to achieving the Initial CCCTB Proposal's aims was adopted under Irish Presidency in 2013.[14] The Irish Presidency suggested, in the Irish Road Map[15] on the Initial CCCTB Proposal, the first step would address the elements of the corporate tax base and, then, the second step would take on the issue of consolidation. It was agreed that the question of apportionment would be taken up as soon as work on the common corporate tax base was sufficiently advanced.[16] The Council working parties' further work on the Initial CCCTB Proposal was done pursuant to the Irish Road Map and closely followed the two-step structure suggested therein. Nevertheless, the in-depth discussions, at the

13. Communication from the Commission, 'EUROPE 2020 – A strategy for smart, sustainable and inclusive growth' (COM(2010)) (hereinafter the 'Europe 2020 Strategy'), cited by the Initial CCCTB Proposal, *supra* n.1, at 4, note 1.
14. For this definition, see *infra* n. 15.
15. The Irish Presidency suggested, in its road map on the Initial CCCTB Proposal (hereinafter 'the Irish Road Map'), breaking the work on the Initial CCCTB Proposal into six different thematic areas: general issues, basic elements of the common base, anti-avoidance issues, international issues, and operational issues (first step) and (second step), The so-called operational area dealt with consolidation and apportionment issues. The so-called international area, on the other hand, included the Controlled Foreign Company (CFC) rule, the permanent establishment issue (i.e., the Initial CCCTB Proposal's Chapters II (Art. 5), Chapter III (Art. 8), Chapter V (Art. 31) Chapter XIV (Arts 81–83), and Chapter XV), and the impact on existing Double Tax Conventions ('DTCs')). Finally, the so-called anti-abuse area included, *inter alia*, the General Anti-Abuse Rule (GAAR) (the Initial CCCTB Proposal's Art. 80). The ECOFIN Council (for this definition, see *supra* n. 3) reports to the European Council on Tax Issues via semi-annual reports, typically published in June and December of each calendar year at the end of each rotating presidency of the Council of the EU. The Irish Road Map, as endorsed by the ECOFIN Council, is found in the Annex to the ECOFIN Report to the European Council on Tax issues of 26 June 2013, 11507/13, FISC 138, ECOFIN 636, at 30 (hereinafter the 'June 2013 ECOFIN Report to the European Council').
16. The June 2013 ECOFIN Report to the European Council, *supra* n. 15, para 40(c).

technical level, on the Initial CCCTB Proposal carried on for years in Council working parties without ever reaching approval by the Member States.[17]

Since 2013, the work in the OECD working parties on its BEPS project substantially influenced negotiations of the Initial CCCTB Proposal at the EU level.

[B] Influence from the Global Level Leading to a Certain Progress on the CCCTB file

[1] The Influence of the OECD-BEPS Project on the Initial CCCTB Proposal

Building on previous experience, the OECD, in its 2013 report entitled 'Addressing Base Erosion and Profit Shifting',[18] identified erosion of domestic taxation bases and profit shifting as a global problem that created a serious risk to tax revenues, tax sovereignty, and tax fairness for many countries. It recommended an action plan be developed with a view to addressing – in a comprehensive manner – BEPS issues, which are closely related to cross-border, aggressive tax-planning practices. To address the growing problem of multinational companies avoiding taxation in their home countries by moving activities to low- or no-tax jurisdictions, the OECD published, later that same year, its 'Action Plan on Base Erosion and Profit Shifting',[19] which identified a series of domestic and international actions to be taken to curtail BEPS. The OECD Action Plan also set clear, tight timelines for implementing the identified actions. The OECD working parties started their work on recommendations for how to prevent tax practices leading to BEPS (i.e., the aggressive tax-planning practices that result in a shift of profits to low- or zero-tax countries). The outcome of their work (i.e., fifteen specific actions that are intended to provide clear responses to BEPS issues) was finalized in record time and received the approval of the OECD Finance Ministers and the G20 leaders in October and November 2015, respectively.

In parallel to the OECD's work on BEPS initiatives, the EU Member States, recognizing that a common and coordinated EU position on BEPS might be the most appropriate approach, started to think about ways to incorporate the OECD-BEPS outcomes in the Council's work.[20] They agreed that the EU needed to be a front runner in the implementation of the OECD-BEPS outcomes, thereby giving a strong political signal to the outside world of the EU's support of the OECD-BEPS project. Due to the need to preserve a level playing field, the EU Member States felt that the EU's commitment to BEPS would encourage third countries to similarly commit to the

17. The last compromise text on the Initial CCCTB Proposal was issued under Italian Presidency on 19 Nov. 2014. *See* 15756/14, FISC 197 (hereinafter the 'Italian Compromise Text').
18. OECD, *Addressing Base Erosion and Profit Shifting* (2013).
19. OECD, *Action Plan on Base Erosion and Profit Shifting* (2013).
20. Indeed, the majority of the Member States actively participated in drafting and designing the OECD-BEPS recommendations and, as a result thereof, undertook a political commitment to adopt those BEPS recommendations as a member of the OECD.

OECD-BEPS outcomes.[21] On the same note, the June 2013 ECOFIN Report to the European Council[22] already recognized 'the need for an appropriate combination of efforts at the national, EU and at [*sic*] global levels to combat tax fraud and tax evasion and also aggressive tax planning',[23] and that '[c]lose cooperation at [the] international level was essential and to that end there should be improved coordination with the OECD on the Base Erosion and Profit Shifting (BEPS) project through the [High Level Working Party of the Council working parties]'.[24] The Council also invited future Presidencies to 'work further in this area to find the most appropriate ways to tackle tax fraud and evasion and aggressive tax planning at national, EU and global levels.'[25]

Under the Italian Presidency (the second half of 2014), work on the Initial CCCTB Proposal continued to pursue those objectives: it was identified as the most appropriate legal basis on which to base discussions on a coordinated approach to BEPS and to devise solutions to prevent BEPS outcomes. Those discussions focused on the chapter of the Initial CCCTB Proposal dealing with international aspects, as suggested by the thematic area described in the Irish Road Map,[26] which included, like the topics discussed at the OECD level, *inter alia*, a provision regarding the definition of a 'permanent establishment' and a CFC rule, as well as a provision on the limitation of interest deductions.[27] The language of the existing provisions identified as the international anti-BEPS aspects of the Initial CCCTB Proposal was progressively updated by recommendations issued from the still-on-going discussions at the OECD level. The work conducted during the Italian Presidency on those international aspects resulted in the Italian Compromise Text, which gave the Initial CCCTB Proposal a certain anti-BEPS twist.[28]

The first initiative to implement a portion of the OECD-BEPS outcomes in EU law via the Initial CCCTB Proposal reflected an inclination of the EU to implement BEPS through a coordinated, swift, and comprehensive hard-law approach.[29] That preference for a hard-law approach to BEPS recommendations was, moreover, made express in a common letter, dated 28 November 2014, sent by the Ministers of Finance from Italy, France, and Germany to Commissioner Moscovici, wherein the ministers of those three EU Member States pushed for a 'comprehensive anti-BEPS directive' to be adopted by the end of 2015 with a view to developing, within the EU, 'a set of common,

21. *See* the Member States' commitment in the ECOFIN Base Erosion and Profit Shifting (BEPS) Council Conclusions of 8 Dec. 2015, 15150/15 FISC 185, ECOFIN 965 (hereinafter the 'December 2015 ECOFIN Council Conclusions'), paras 10–11 and paras 3–4 (citing the European Council Conclusions of 18 Dec. 2014, EUCO 237/14, para. 3 and the European Council Conclusions of 13 & 14 Mar. 2013, EUCO 23/13, para 6).
22. The June 2013 ECOFIN Report to the European Council, *supra* n. 15.
23. *Ibid.* para 20.
24. *Ibid.* para. 21 (footnote omitted).
25. *Ibid.* para. 25.
26. For more detail, see *supra* n. 15.
27. The December 2015 ECOFIN Council Conclusions, *supra* n. 21, para. 17.
28. *See* the Italian Compromise Text, *supra* n. 17; *see also* the ECOFIN Council report to the European Council of 27 Nov. 2014 16034/14, FISC 214 ECOFIN 1100, para. 3 (hereinafter the 'November 2014 ECOFIN Council Report to the European Council').
29. This also takes account of the Council's request to proceed via EU-binding legislation. *See* the December 2015 ECOFIN Council Conclusions, *supra* n. 21, para. 12.

binding rules on corporate taxation to curb tax competition and fight aggressive tax planning'.[30] Thereafter, in December 2014, the European Council stressed that '[t]here is an urgent need to advance efforts in the fight against tax avoidance and aggressive tax planning, both at the global and EU levels.'[31] The Council working party on the Initial CCCTB Proposal under the Italian Presidency suggested the first concrete step towards implementing BEPS via a specific road map on EU-BEPS aspects, which would include actions to be taken as well as clear timelines while taking account of the on-going OECD-BEPS work in the area.[32] During the Italian Presidency, the initial draft of what would become the Luxembourg EU-BEPS Road Map[33] gave rise to a first round of discussions, before it was further refined and finalized during the subsequent Latvian Presidency[34] and thereafter used by the succeeding presidencies, including the Luxembourg Presidency, to set out the Council's future initiatives on the BEPS issue. The Latvian EU-BEPS Road Map[35] identified the Initial CCCTB Proposal's file as one of the short-term issues and set out, *inter alia*, a number of precise high-priority topics to be dealt with by the Council working parties (or other appropriate bodies where such work needed to be moved forward) as well as timelines for completion of that work.[36] Many Member States expressed a preference to continue such discussions in the framework of the Initial CCCTB Proposal, more specifically on the international aspects,[37] to best 'feed the OECD discussion and pave the way for a smooth implementation of the future OECD recommendations on these aspects, given the EU specificities' after having taken 'stock of the state of play in connection with the various fields of the [Initial CCCTB Proposal] and consider [*sic*] Member States' positions on the basis of the compromise tabled by the Italian Presidency [i.e., the Italian Compromise Text]'.[38] In that regard, agreeing on the definitions of a permanent establishment, a CFC rule, a switch-over clause, the GAAR, exit taxation rules, an interest limitation, and, possibly, a mechanism to address hybrid mismatches were all identified by the Council High-Level Working Party on 5 February 2015 as international anti-BEPS aspects to be further compared to and analysed against the OECD-BEPS recommendations.[39]

---

30. *See* http://www.economie.gouv.fr/files/files/PDF/letter-to-p_moscovici-11282014.pdf (last accessed 28 Jan. 2017) Commissioner Moscovici's official reply, if any, is not available online.
31. European Council Conclusions of 18 Dec. 2014, EUCO 237/14, para. 3.
32. For more detail, see the November 2014 ECOFIN Council Report to the European Council, *supra* n. 28, para. 21.
33. *See* the Luxembourg EU-BEPS Road Map, *infra* n. 48, para. 2 ('The Italian Presidency presented a draft roadmap to the Working Party on Tax Questions (WPTQ) on 5 Dec. 2014 setting out a number of priorities for actions in the short, mid and long term.')
34. The Latvian Presidency's 'BEPS: Presidency roadmap on future work', 5968/15, FISC 15 (the 'Latvian EU-BEPS Road Map'). The Latvian Presidency took place in the first semester of 2015.
35. For this definition, see *supra* n. 34.
36. *Ibid.* paras 14 and 15.
37. In line with the Irish Road Map thematic area, see *supra* n. 15. *See* also the November 2014 ECOFIN Council Report to the European Council, *supra* n. 28, para. 21.
38. *See* the Latvian EU-BEPS Road Map, *supra* n. 34, paras 14 and 15.
39. *Ibid.* para. 14.

Work moved forward by the Luxembourg Presidency on the Initial CCCTB Proposal built on the outcomes of previous discussions, particularly those that had taken place during the Italian Presidency.

[2] The Revised Objectives of the Initial CCCTB Proposal: From a Common Corporate Tax Base Towards an 'Anti-BEPS Directive'

The key initiatives published by the Commission in 2015 (i.e., the Tax Transparency Package of 18 March 2015[40] and the subsequent 5 Key Areas Action Plan[41]) influenced and concomitantly framed the work of the Luxembourg Presidency. The 5 Key Areas Action Plan had a major influence on subsequent work on the Initial CCCTB Proposal, given the Commission's clarification on how it perceived the OECD-BEPS recommendations to be pursued at the EU level – that is:

> work must continue in the framework of the [Initial CCCTB Proposal] currently on the table of the Council on some international aspects of the common base which are linked to the BEPS project. For example, [the] definition of "permanent establishment" ... and improving the Controlled Foreign Corporation rules.[42]

However, by also specifying that such work needed to be performed 'while the new proposal [for a Relaunched CCCTB Proposal] is being prepared',[43] and further stating that it expected 'consensus on these elements [to be achieved] in the Council within 12 months',[44] and providing that the consensus 'should be made legally binding before an agreement is reached on the revised CCCTB',[45] the Commission unequivocally signalled its intent to withdraw the Initial CCCTB Proposal and to replace it with a Relaunched C(C)CTB Proposal. It further indicated that the new legislative instrument was expected to 'ensure a coherent EU approach to implementing the new international standards arising from the OECD BEPS project, providing consistency for businesses and preventing a fragmented approach in the Single Market.'[46]

In that regard, building on the work conducted in the Council working parties in the area of OECD-BEPS recommendations, the Luxembourg Presidency committed to facilitate such discussions in Council. It aimed to find solutions consistent with the results of the OECD work on BEPS, paying specific attention to respecting the *acquis* of the Single Market and the Treaty freedoms, all with a view to conduct technical discussions on any future anti-BEPS directive, a legislative initiative which back then was perceived as a mere possibility. In the absence of a legislative proposal implementing the OECD-BEPS recommendations into EU-hard law after the 5 Key Areas Action Plan was issued, and while waiting for the Commission to come up with a legislative

40. For more detail, see http://ec.europa.eu/taxation_customs/business/company-tax/tax-transparency-package_en.
41. The 5 Key Areas Action Plan, *supra* n. 4.
42. *Ibid.*
43. *Ibid.*
44. *Ibid.*
45. *Ibid.*
46. *Ibid.*

proposal for an autonomous anti-BEPS directive that it had committed to in the Council's High Level Working Party, the Council continued, throughout the Luxembourg Presidency, to work on the international anti-BEPS aspects of the Initial CCCTB Proposal. Due to the tight OECD-imposed deadlines, the Luxembourg Presidency mainly conducted work on the technical aspects. Other issues related to implementing the OECD-BEPS recommendations into EU-hard law were not prejudged, in anticipation of the Commission's expected proposal thereon. However, in the absence of further specifications from the Commission on the timing of the issuance of the legislative initiative implementing some of the OECD-BEPS recommendations, it was deemed vital to carry on discussions of these elements in Council on the basis of substantive points in the Initial CCCTB Proposal, which remained possible given that it was not expected to be withdrawn for a certain period of time (i.e., not before the end of 2015).[47] Thus, the Luxembourg Presidency's ultimate plan, in the context of the 5 Key Areas Action Plan and the Luxembourg EU-BEPS Road Map[48] was intended to launch discussions on the opportunity to split off the international anti-BEPS elements of the Initial CCCTB Proposal into a separate and autonomous directive.[49] As a first step, it was suggested that work on the international anti-BEPS aspects of the Initial CCCTB Proposal would continue while taking account, as appropriate, of the work done by the OECD and, if such OECD work was considered useful, to envisage a split[50] of the Initial CCCTB Proposal to achieve the implementation of the international anti-BEPS elements via a wholly independent and autonomous legislative instrument. It was believed that it would be possible to enshrine such work in an autonomous EU legislative instrument (or any other EU instrument), as it would only contain those aspects that had already been identified as international anti-BEPS aspects in the Initial CCCTB Proposal and that, if such legislation was agreed to, it would relate to OECD-BEPS Actions 2, 3, 4, and 7. Thus, it was back then planned that the work on the Initial CCCTB Proposal, more specifically with respect to BEPS, could finally be included in a Luxembourg Presidency's compromise text.

In light of the foregoing, and with the view to achieve preparatory work for an autonomous anti-BEPS directive, the Luxembourg Presidency committed to continue to design the wording of the following seven elements previously identified[51] as international anti-BEPS aspects of the Initial CCCTB Proposal (collectively, 'the Seven Anti-BEPS Elements'):

- Definition of permanent establishment (PE)
- Controlled foreign company (CFC) rules

47. The Commission originally planned to withdraw the Initial CCCTB Proposal in Apr. 2016. A reference thereto can be found in the 2016 Commission Work Programme (*supra* n. 5).
48. The Luxembourg Presidency's 'BEPS: Presidency roadmap on future work', 10649/15, FISC 93 (hereinafter the 'Luxembourg EU-BEPS Road Map').
49. ECOFIN Report the European Council on Tax Issues, FISC 187, ECOFIN 968, CO EUR-PREP 50 (hereinafter the 'December 2015 Report to the European Council'), para. 27.
50. One of the most successful recent examples of this way to proceed with the view to achieve agreement in Council being the staggered approach taken in the Parent-Subsidiary directive recently updated by an anti-hybrid provision, in a first place, and GAAR, in a second step.
51. For more detail, see *supra* n. 34.

- Switch-over clause
- General anti-abuse rule (GAAR)
- Exit taxation rules
- Interest limitation rules
- If possible, rules regarding hybrid mismatches.

With respect to these ambitious objectives (i.e., producing the bases for an EU-legislative instrument) that had to be achieved in a limited period of time on the basis of the still on-going negotiations of the OECD-BEPS recommendations, the Luxembourg Presidency faced many challenges. One of those was the absence of a clear legal basis for such instrument.[52] In anticipation of a future legislative instrument to be proposed by the Commission, the deliverable of the Luxembourg Presidency at Council meeting of 8 December 2015 was a consolidated text inspired by the Initial CCCTB Proposal, but limited to the international anti-BEPS elements.[53] The Luxembourg Consolidated Text was completed by the Luxembourg Explanatory Notes (technical explanations)[54] and the Luxembourg Presidency Note.[55] The Luxembourg Consolidated Text, wrapping up the Seven Anti-BEPS Elements, completed the first technical reading of any potential future anti-BEPS proposal, without, however, prejudging the individual delegations' positions with regard to either the scope or the content of the provisions contained therein. In addition, the wording of its provisions was adjusted to account for the split, as outlined in the Luxembourg EU-BEPS Road Map, of the Initial CCCTB Proposal so as to allow the Council to carry on further work on these issues at a later point. The Luxembourg Presidency Note was distributed to the ministers in advance of the debate in the Council's meeting of 8 December 2015, which clarified the Initial CCCTB Proposal's background and objectives and provided further explanations regarding the BEPS work carried out during the Luxembourg Presidency.

To justify continuing such work on the basis of the Initial CCCTB Proposal and to better explain the results presented to the ministers, the Luxembourg Presidency Note referred to the 5 Key Areas Action Plan, in which the Commission stated that 'it would welcome if work continues in the Council in the framework of the [Initial CCCTB Proposal] currently on the table on some international aspects of the common tax base which are linked to the BEPS project' and, moreover, that 'it [had] not so far withdraw[n] its current CCCTB legislative proposal' for that reason.[56] The Luxembourg

52. To prepare for the 2016 Commission Working Programme, the Luxembourg Presidency relied on the Commission's oral commitment to come up with an autonomous proposal containing measures aimed at preventing BEPS, which was later confirmed in the 5 Key Areas Action Plan. *See* 5 Key Areas Action Plan, *supra* n. 4.
53. The Consolidated text of the Luxembourg Presidency of 2 Dec. 2015 on the Proposal for a Council Directive on a Common Consolidated Corporate Tax Base (CCCTB), 14544/15, FISC 171 (hereinafter, the 'Luxembourg Consolidated Text').
54. The Explanatory notes of the Luxembourg Presidency of 2 Dec. 2015 on the Proposal for a Council Directive on a Common Consolidated Corporate Tax Base (CCCTB), 14544/15 ADD1, FISC 171 (hereinafter, the 'Luxembourg Explanatory Notes').
55. The Note of the Luxembourg Presidency of 1 Dec. 2015 on the Proposal for a Council Directive on a Common Consolidated Corporate Tax Base (CCCTB) – State of play, 14509/15, FISC 169, ECOFIN 916 (hereinafter, the 'Luxembourg Presidency Note').
56. *See supra* n. 4.

Presidency Note emphasized that the Commission had made clear that the Initial CCCTB Proposal was not to be withdrawn until later, in 2016, once a relaunched CCCTB proposal was made (i.e., 'through new legislative proposals as soon as possible in 2016').[57] It also expressly suggested a 'split off from the [Initial CCCTB Proposal] of certain provisions on the international anti-BEPS aspects'[58] with a view to 'achieve a swift, consistent and coordinated implementation of OECD-BEPS recommendations in the EU'.[59] The Luxembourg Presidency Note further highlighted that other Member States supported that split approach as the way forward and that the Member States generally agreed that a new 'anti-BEPS directive'[60] could address BEPS outcomes within intra-EU situations as well as third-county situations.

The most fascinating aspects of the Luxembourg Presidency's work were, however, those addressing issues beyond the purely technical issues involved in drafting the specific provisions of the Luxembourg Consolidated Text. Indeed, beyond just shaping the provisions to align their wording to the pending OECD-BEPS recommendations, the work on the Initial CCCTB Proposal had to address major issues regarding implementation of the soft law designed at the OECD level through EU-hard law. Now, with a certain distance, it is safe to say that the early discussions and solutions on fundamental issues regarding OECD-BEPS hammered out during the Luxembourg Presidency paved the way for the future initiative(s) regarding OECD-BEPS implementation in the EU (i.e., the Original ATAD Proposal, which became the ATAD, as well as the Revised ATAD Proposal).

One of the main issues extensively debated by the Council during the Luxembourg Presidency related to the OECD-BEPS recommendations was that BEPS Actions 2, 3, 4, and 7 did not (and still do not) have the status of recommendations that relate to the highest binding-level of political commitment (i.e., they are not minimum standards).[61] Potential national implementation of the OECD-BEPS recommendations, or even a finalized national implementation thereof raised further issues.[62] Thus, Council discussions were opened on how an efficient EU-level implementation of the OECD-BEPS recommendations could be achieved, including debate about the pros and cons of a hard-law approach versus soft-law approach.[63] Further concerns were raised about any future directive implementing anti-BEPS measures' ultimate compatibility with the Internal Market in case such a future directive would exclusively contain anti-avoidance provisions or about its objective(s) and scope (both geographical and material). Nevertheless, the Luxembourg Presidency was careful to only consider primarily EU-law aspects of such issues, never losing sight that any provisions

57. The Luxembourg Presidency Note, *supra* n. 55, para. 8.
58. *Ibid.* para. 9.
59. *Ibid.*
60. *Ibid.* The title suggested in the Luxembourg Consolidated Text for the 'anti-BEPS directive' was a 'Proposal for a Council Directive Laying Down Rules against Base Erosion and Profit Shifting (BEPS)'.
61. OECD, OECD/G20 Base Erosion and Profit Shifting Project, Explanatory Statement (2015).
62. The approach was chosen to ensure that the Member States would not be precluded from applying domestic-law or agreement-based provisions aimed at preventing BEPS. *See* the December 2015 ECOFIN Council Conclusions, *supra* n. 21, para. 11.
63. *Ibid.* paras 12 (hard-law approach) and 13 (soft-law approach).

designed on the basis of the OECD-BEPS recommendations needed to comply with the EU Treaties and any applicable EU *acquis*.[64]

The solution to some of the main disputed issues was the application of a minimum-standard approach to any potential anti-BEPS directive, which would provide for principle-based rules. The minimum-standard approach adopted during the Luxembourg Presidency aimed to ensure that, on the one hand, new national rules implementing BEPS would not be pre-empted by any new directive, but, on the other hand, that any existing national anti-avoidance measures targeting the same or similar practices could continue to apply. That approach, which would allow Member States to implement (or continue to implement) stricter national provisions, while simultaneously creating an EU-wide minimum standard, was deemed to be the best compromise to take account of any on-going or finalized national implementation of the OECD-BEPS recommendations. Concomitantly, it was meant to give flexibility to the Member States to implement stricter rules intended to prevent BEPS outcomes. In light of then-existing national rules that already prevented, and in anticipation of future national rules that would prevent, similar kinds of situations, the Luxembourg Presidency addressed the interaction between future and existing provisions in Member States national law using thresholds and options.[65]

In the absence of an autonomous anti-BEPS directive proposal, the Luxembourg Presidency invested significant energy in analysing whether the split of the Seven Anti-BEPS Elements of the Initial CCCTB Proposal could be a quick and efficient solution for an anti-BEPS directive intended to achieve a coherent, common, and coordinated implementation of the OECD-BEPS recommendations in the EU as well as a level-playing field while maintaining the competitiveness of EU companies.

In-depth discussions in Council's working parties looked into the scope of application of any potential future anti-BEPS directive, asking: whether it should be limited to the EU or go beyond that to address third, non-EU countries; whether the directive should apply to all companies operating in the EU or only to larger multinational companies; and exactly what entities would fall within the scope of such an anti-BEPS directive. A broad scope of application – from both a geographic and a material point of view – was deemed to be the best way forward while still ensuring that transparent entities would be excluded.

In light of the above, it can be concluded that the efforts put forward during the second semester of 2015 were never meant to result in harmonization of national corporate taxation rules. Rather, the objective was to simply establish some basic common, minimum, and principle-based anti-avoidance provisions within the EU. The Luxembourg Consolidated Text finally suggested – as outlined in the Luxembourg EU-BEPS Road Map - the proposed 'international elements' split off from the Initial CCCTB Proposal, which helped speed up subsequent initiatives at the EU level.

64. The Luxembourg Presidency Note, *supra* n. 55 and the Luxembourg EU-BEPS Road Map, *supra* n. 48, para. 4.

65. *E.g.*, the amount of deduction of interest cost by reference either to EBITDA (i.e., 30%) or to a lump sum amount (i.e., EUR 1 million).

Whether those initiatives, however, will ultimately result in harmonization of direct corporate taxes is a question that remains impossible to answer, at least not yet.

[C] The Original ATAD Proposal: From International Aspects of the Initial CCCTB Proposal to BEPS Implementation Through EU Hard Law

[1] The Original ATAD Proposal: A Principle-Based Approach Instead of Full Harmonization

On 28 January 2016, the Commission published its long-anticipated Anti-Tax Avoidance Package, which included the Original ATAD Proposal,[66] which, in turn, contained a number of measures intended to efficiently curb tax avoidance practices through a stronger, more-coherent EU approach to corporate tax abuses.[67] The adopted ATAD[68] incorporates into EU legislation some of the OECD-BEPS recommendations, as finalized and endorsed by the OECD in the autumn of 2015. More specifically, it implements the recommendations found in OECD-BEPS Actions 2, 3, and 4.

The Original ATAD Proposal not only took account of the European Council's mandate that identified an 'urgent need to advance efforts in the fight against tax avoidance and aggressive tax planning, both at the global and European Union (EU) levels'[69] but also reacted to the pressure exerted by the EU Parliament, civil society, and certain international partners for rules that would effectively prevent the aggressive tax-planning practices so frequently used by multinational enterprises operating across borders. The Original ATAD Proposal was also a direct response to the call made by the Member States' Finance Ministers for a hard-law approach to implementing the OECD-BEPS recommendations, whose December 2015 ECOFIN Council Conclusions invited the Commission to come forward with a legislative proposal on the OECD-BEPS Actions 2, 3, and 4 whilst simultaneously taking account therein of the Council's work on the international aspects of the Initial CCCTB Proposal.[70] It is interesting to highlight that the Commission felt the need to complete its Original ATAD Proposal's anti-tax avoidance measures (generally based on such OECD-BEPS recommendations), by incorporating therein other rules it thought vital to further curb aggressive tax-planning practices across the EU (i.e., rules on exit taxation and the switch-over clause).

Thus, the Original ATAD Proposal primarily targeted schemes in which 'taxpayers act against the actual purpose of the law, taking advantage of disparities between national tax systems to reduce their tax bill'[71] and was intended to allow Member States to 'effectively tackle corporate tax avoidance in a way which preserves their collective

66. For definition, see *supra* n. 12.
67. The Original ATAD Proposal, *supra* n. 12.
68. For definition, see *supra* n. 12.
69. European Council Conclusions of 18 Dec. 2014, EUCO 237/14; *see also supra* n. 29, para. 3.
70. Such as the work carried out under Luxembourg Presidency. *See* the Luxembourg Consolidated Text, *supra* n. 54.
71. The Original ATAD Proposal, *supra* n. 12, para. 3

competitiveness'[72] while respecting 'the Single Market, Treaty Freedoms, the EU Charter of Fundamental Rights and EU law in general'.[73] Interestingly, the measures the Commission identified as the most efficient for the purpose of fighting tax avoidance had already been discussed during Luxembourg Presidency and were included in the Luxembourg Consolidated Text published just a few weeks before the Original ATAD Proposal was proffered, which gave truth to the Commission's statement that the proposed 'Directive takes account of the outcome of Member States' discussions on these issues in Council'.[74] Thus, it can be stated that the Council working party's discussions on the Initial CCCTB Proposal under the Luxembourg Presidency inspired the Commission's wording of the Original ATAD Proposal. Moreover, those discussions clearly encouraged the Commission to move forward with a stand-alone directive to implement the OECD-BEPS recommendations in the EU while also incorporating the first round of concrete, technical discussions on its potential provisions, as set out in the Luxembourg Consolidated Text, therein. Although the Original ATAD Proposal did not necessarily incorporate the exact language proposed in the Luxembourg Consolidated Text,[75] it still contained, in line with the Council's mandate, a provision limiting interest deductions, a CFC rule, a GAAR, an exit tax provision, a switch-over rule, and rules relating to the neutralization of hybrid mismatches.[76]

The Commission's chosen anti-BEPS-implementation methodology for the European Union demonstrated a clear preference for EU-level action over unilateral, national-level initiatives by the individual Member States. Obviously, the Commission found it preferable because it avoids, on the one hand, the Member States' making uncoordinated, national efforts to implement the OECD-BEPS recommendations, which would likely result in new loopholes or mismatches that aggressive tax-planning schemes would seek to exploit and potentially fragment the Single Market as a result of 'national policy clashes, distortions and tax obstacles for business in the EU'.[77] It prevents, on the other hand, the 'functioning of the internal market to be compromised either by unilateral measures adopted by Member States or lack of action by other Member States altogether'.[78]

The Commission made its call for coherence, uniformity, and coordination in implementing OECD-BEPS outputs across the Member States' tax systems by relying on a principle-based approach in the Original ATAD Proposal. That approach, which had already been discussed in Council working parties prior to the Original ATAD Proposal's publication, aimed to respond to the concerns of the Member States: it was based on the 'understanding that [the Member States] are better placed to shape the precise

72. *Ibid.*
73. *Ibid.*
74. *Ibid.* para. 4.
75. The Original ATAD Proposal cut out one of the Seven Anti-BEPS Elements addressed in the Luxembourg Consolidated Text: the provision defining a permanent establishment, which was designed to solve DTC issues rather than cross-border corporate-tax mismatches. It did not take a list approach for entities included in its scope of application, either.
76. The Original ATAD Proposal, *supra* n. 12.
77. *Ibid.* para. 6.
78. *Ibid.*

elements of the rules in a way that best fits their corporate tax system'.[79] To avoid any conflict with, *inter alia*, the Member States' OECD-BEPS-recommendation implementation, the Commission clarified that 'the envisaged measures do not go beyond ensuring the minimum necessary level of protection for the internal market'[80] and 'that the directive does not therefore prescribe full harmonization but only a minimum level of protection for Member States' corporate tax systems'.[81] It follows that, although those earlier Council discussions were carried out on the basis of the Initial CCCTB Proposal, which was intended to harmonize the corporate tax base, the stated Original ATAD Proposal's aim was not to achieve full harmonization in the area of direct taxes. Other than setting out a common, minimum standard for the Member States' anti-tax avoidance measures, neither the Original ATAD Proposal nor the ATAD were ever, in fact, intended to affect the general features of the Member State's tax systems. That Commission's chosen ATAD-approach, thus, can be considered as a completely new one. As such, it follows that the coordination of anti-tax avoidance measures intended to protect the Member State's taxable base from BEPS tactics is clearly a completely new, and rather revolutionary, approach.

[2] The Evolution of the Provisions of the Original ATAD Proposal Before the ATAD Was Adopted in June 2016

[a] The Work Carried out under the Netherlands Presidency

The Original ATAD Proposal was published on 28 January 2016, during the first month of the Netherlands Presidency. The Netherlands Presidency identified the work on the Original ATAD Proposal as high political priority expressing its intent to 'capitaliz[e] on work that has already been done in the context of the OECD and by previous Presidencies, in particular by the Luxembourg Presidency with regard to the international anti-BEPS aspects of the original [Initial CCCTB Proposal] (doc. 14544/15)'[82] and, in line with the plan, closed the negotiations thereon before the end of its Presidency in June 2016.[83] The Netherlands Presidency's agenda expected political agreement (i.e., approval of the general approach) to be reached during the 25 May 2016 ECOFIN Council meeting. To comply with the ambitious schedule, negotiations on the technical issues in Council working parties took place on a regular, almost-weekly basis. The Fiscal attachés were given a mandate to come up with a final

79. *Ibid.* para. 4.
80. *Ibid.* para. 5.
81. *Ibid.*
82. The Netherlands Presidency's 'BEPS: Presidency roadmap on future work' of 19 Feb. 2016, 6038/16, FISC 20 (the 'Netherlands EU-BEPS Road Map'), para. 12.
83. As the 13 June 2016 ATAD Compromise Text (for definition, see *infra* n. 93) required further negotiation with the view to achieve a compromise, the final version of the Netherlands Presidency compromise text (hereinafter 'the Final Netherlands Compromise Text'), which contained the compromise reached in ECOFIN on 17 June 2016, was subject to the silence procedure, 10426/16, FISC 104 ECOFIN 628, and was formally adopted in ECOFIN of 12 July 2016, following the silence procedure until 20 June 2016 triggered in ECOFIN on 17 June 2016. *See also* the Netherlands EU-BEPS Road Map, *supra* n. 82, para. 12, last sentence.

compromise as soon as the purely technical-level discussions were closed. The December 2015 ECOFIN Council Conclusions had already identified the need to find 'common, yet flexible solutions at the EU level'[84] to proceed to the Member States' 'effective swift and coordinated implementation'[85] of anti-BEPS measures to be adopted at the EU level, and were repeatedly cited in an effort to ensure timely agreement.[86] The efforts made on the Original ATAD Proposal during the Netherlands Presidency, resulted in a few different Netherlands Presidency compromise texts,[87] the last of which was formally approved by the EU Finance Ministers on 12 July 2016 following the silence procedure opened at the Council's meeting of 17 June 2016. The work under the Netherlands Presidency on what has become the ATAD[88] was backed up with the Netherlands Presidency Note.[89]

The Netherlands Presidency did its best to accommodate the Member States' concerns with respect to the need:

- to provide the greatest possible level of flexibility while (a) remaining consistent with the OECD-BEPS recommendations when shaping the ATAD and (b) mirroring therein the appropriate level of political commitment achieved with respect to specific OECD-BEPS Actions and (c) avoiding the potential for the Member States to cherry pick only the best provisions in the ATAD's national implementation;
- to resolve potential coordination issues between the ATAD's measures and existing national rules, all while taking account of on-going national efforts to implement the OECD-BEPS recommendations;
- to clarify the interaction of the ATAD rules with both efficient domestic provisions[90] and provisions in other EU directives;
- to avoid creating unanticipated issues in other areas, such as conflicts with existing DTCs; and
- to take account of terminology and concepts from CJEU case law.[91]

It is also worth mentioning that the Netherlands Presidency Compromise Text shortened the Original ATAD Proposal, setting aside the proposed the switch-over rule.[92] Moreover, at the Council's 17 June 2016 meeting, the Member States committed

84. The December 2015 ECOFIN Council Conclusions, *supra* n. 21, para. 10.
85. *Ibid.*
86. *Ibid.*
87. *See infra* n. 93
88. *See supra* n. 83.
89. The Netherlands Presidency Note of 15 June 2016 on the Proposal for a Council Directive laying down rules against tax avoidance practices that directly affect the functioning of the internal market, 10340/15, FISC 103, ECOFIN 624 (hereinafter, 'The Netherlands Presidency Note'). The Netherlands Presidency Note was published in connection with the 13 June 2016 ATAD Compromise Text (*infra* n. 93), and was not changed in connection with the publication of the Final Netherlands Compromise Text (*supra* n. 83) or the ATAD (*supra* n. 12).
90. *Ibid.* para. 12 (the Netherlands Presidency Note specified that targeted rules limiting interest deductions would apply on top of the fixed ratio rule, referring to Recital 6 of the 13 June 2016 ATAD Compromise Text, *infra* n. 93).
91. *Ibid.* para. 15 (the CFC rule).
92. *See infra* n. 93.

to support continued work on measures relating to hybrids in third countries, which could not be finalized in the short timeframe, and agreed to move the date for entry into effect for exit taxation and interest-deduction limitations to a date other than the date the ATAD generally enters into force.

[b] The Difficulties Encountered and Open Issues Following the Council's Meetings in May and June 2016

The Netherlands Presidency reached political agreement on the ATAD during its last Council's meeting (i.e., at the ECOFIN meeting of 17 June 2016) following a silence procedure. No technical-level agreement had been reached on either the suggested substance-carve out for intra-EU situations or the effective tax-rate trigger for applying the CFC rule) prior to that meeting, the open issues to be solved at the political level during the Council's meeting on 17 June dealt therefore with the CFC rule, given that EU application of the OECD-BEPS recommended CFC rule was still at issue.[93]

The effective tax-rate trigger for CFC rule application, however, was accommodated by replacing the effective tax-rates comparison between the CFC's state of establishment and the parent's state of residence provided in the Original ATAD Proposal with a formula in which the actual corporate tax paid on the CFC's profits is to be compared to the corporate tax that would have been charged thereon had the CFC been established in the parent company's Member State of residence.[94] The ATAD's CFC rule was drafted so as to contain no reference to either a general statutory rate or an effective tax rate.[95] In addition, contrary to earlier drafts of the Final Netherlands Compromise Text,[96] the objective formula chosen to replace the reference to the effective tax rate in the Original ATAD Proposal was intended to avoid providing a threshold for comparing the taxes actually paid.[97]

The other issue that dealt with the substance-carve out and the related burden of proof to demonstrate a sufficient level of substance (i.e., demonstrating that a CFC is

93. There were several versions of the Netherlands Presidency Compromise Text in order to accommodate the concerns of all the Member States. The text issued in advance of the ECOFIN meeting of 26 May 2016 FISC 87 ECOFIN 521 (hereinafter, the '26 May 2016 ATAD Compromise Text'), was followed by the Netherlands Presidency Compromise Text of 13 June 2016, 10039/16, FISC 100, ECOFIN 585 (hereinafter, the '13 June 2016 ATAD Compromise Text') and, thereafter, the Final Netherlands Compromise Text, *supra* n. 83.
94. Such a comparison is made between the actual tax that has been paid in the CFC's state of residence to the actual tax that would have been paid had that CFC been established in the parent company's state of residence, instead. An entity qualifies as a CFC if the tax paid in its state of residence is less than the difference between that amount and the tax that would have been paid in the parent company's state residence had the entity also been a resident of that state.
95. The statutory corporate tax rate could have been a possible criterion in designing the CFC rule, but was not retained by the Commission because it believed the parent (i.e., controlling) company would have sufficient detail to compute the effective tax rate. *See* ATAD, *supra* n. 12, Art. 7(1)(b)).
96. *See supra* n. 93.
97. The new recitals permit a Member State that has a preference for thresholds to include a comparator. *See* the Final Netherlands Compromise Text, *supra* n. 83, Recital 12 and ATAD, *supra* n. 12, Recital 12 and Art. 7.

not wholly artificial)[98] with a view to determining whether the CFC rule should or should not apply, was resolved during Council's meeting of 17 June 2016.[99] To accommodate two divergent concerns expressed by Member States while taking account of the Council legal service's opinion that the 'burden of proof should remain on the tax authorities in light of the anti-abuse nature of the CFC rule',[100] the CFC provision itself was revised, as were the recitals relating to that provision, to clarify that both the tax authorities and the taxpayer must cooperate to gather the relevant facts and circumstances that would allow the tax authorities to determine whether the CFC rule actually applies (i.e., whether the parent company established in the EU falls within the CFC rule's scope of application for a controlled company established in a different Member State in the EU).[101]

The status of OECD-BEPS Action 4, which only has a common-approach status (i.e., a standard below the minimum standard for the purposes of the OECD-BEPS project), but which formed the basis for the Original ATAD Proposal's interest-deduction limitation rule, also remained an issue and the ongoing disagreement on its inclusion in the Original ATAD Proposal, triggered the silence procedure. Ultimately, the Finance Ministers agreed that a derogation should be granted on this issue, providing a rather flexible transposition date with respect to that interest-deduction limitation rule.[102] The Final Netherlands Compromise Text and, as a consequence, the ATAD stipulate that, if equally effective domestic-targeted rules limiting interest deductions are already in place, its interest-deduction limitation rule need only be implemented on the earlier of (a) the date OECD-BEPS Action 4 becomes a minimum

98. Or, rather, a tax authority presumption of abuse on the part of the taxpayer rather than a presumption of taxpayer innocence.
99. Some Member States, supported by (a) the Council legal service and (b) the CJEU'S case law, believed that the onus of demonstrating that the CFC rule applied should rest with the tax authorities. Other Member States, who believed the onus of demonstrating the CFC rule did *not* apply should be borne by the taxpayer, relied on efficiency considerations. The 26 May 2016 ATAD Compromise Text submitted to the ministers' approval at the 25 May 2016 Council meeting, in an attempt to address the concerns of the former group of Member States, provided that income earned by an entity otherwise meeting the qualification criteria of a CFC would not be attributed to its controlling company (the taxpayer), if the taxpayer could establish (a) that the entity was set up for valid commercial reasons and (b) that such entity carries on an economic activity supported by commensurate staff, equipment, assets, and premises that justify the income attributed to it. In essence, that wording (still subject to ministerial approval) presumed that entities meeting both the ownership test and the actual taxation test would not have a sufficient level of substance, unless the taxpayer could provide sufficient evidence to the contrary. However, at the 25 May 2016 Council's meeting, that wording was revised and, in may respects, neutralized: it authorized each Member State to impose the burden of proof on either the taxpayer or the tax authorities, as it saw fit. But, that was not the end of the negotiations. The 13 June 2016 ATAD Compromise Text (*supra* n. 93), circulated before the 17 June 2016 Council meeting had been revised yet again, this time unequivocally placing the burden of proving compliance with the so-called substance-carve out to the CFC rule back on the taxpayer. The Final Netherlands Compromise Text (*supra* n. 83) provided a different, more neutral solution, referring to evidencing substantive activity by relevant facts and circumstances and to a sufficient level of cooperation between the tax authorities and the taxpayer before applying the CFC rule.
100. The Netherlands Presidency Note, *supra* n. 89, para. 15.
101. *See supra* n. 85 in fine as well as ATAD, *supra* n. 12, Recital 12 and Art. 7(2)(a).
102. The Netherlands Presidency Note, *supra* n. 89, para. 12, p. 5.

OECD standard but (b) at the latest until 1 January 2024 (in contrast to other provisions of the ATAD, which must be transposed by 1 January 2019).[103]

[3] The Evolution of the Content of the Provisions: More Clarity and Closer Alignment with OECD-BEPS Results in the ATAD

[a] *The Objectives and the Scope*

Before the Commission published the Original ATAD Proposal, discussions were held on how to define the objective and scope of any potential future anti-BEPS directive.[104] Given that any reference to rules intended to protect the domestic corporate-tax base of the Member States against tax avoidance practices arising from the taxpayer's BEPS activities was likely to be problematic, at least from an EU-law perspective, the Luxembourg Presidency Consolidated Text suggested, in more general words, that any rules contained in the autonomous anti-BEPS directive would prevent base erosion and profit shifting that directly affects the functioning of the Internal Market.[105] While the need to protect the Internal Market was incorporated into the Original ATAD Proposal's title, it did not specifically mention base erosion and profit shifting practices or the OECD-BEPS project; rather, its title only talked of 'rules against tax avoidance practices that directly affect the functioning of the internal market'.[106] Interestingly, although the Luxembourg Consolidated Text specifically referred to BEPS practices, the Original ATAD Proposal only clarified the link to, and the influence of, the OECD-BEPS recommendations in its recitals.[107]

[b] *Artificial Attempts to Avoid Permanent Establishment Status*

The OECD-BEPS Action 7 recommended a way to deal with a taxpayer's artificial attempt to avoid permanent-establishment status in the framework of an applicable DTC's bilateral relationship; it did not recommend an anti-avoidance rule intended to directly protect a country's domestic tax base. Thus, the Original ATAD Proposal did not incorporate said OECD-BEPS Action 7 recommendation nor was that recommendation reintroduced during the Netherlands Presidency.[108]

---

103. *See* the ATAD, *supra* n. 12, Art. 11(6).
104. *See* the Italian Compromise Text, *supra* n. 17, and Luxembourg Consolidated Text, *supra* n. 53.
105. The Luxembourg Consolidated Text, *supra* n. 53, Art. 1 ('This Directive lays down rules against base erosion and profit shifting which directly affect the functioning of the internal market').
106. The Original ATAD Proposal, *supra* n. 12, Title.
107. *Ibid.* paras 1–2.
108. It was, however, included as bracketed text in the Luxembourg Consolidated Text, *see supra* n. 53.

[c] *The Switch-Over Clause*

The Commission's inclusion of the so-called switch-over clause in the Original ATAD Proposal was another highly controversial issue.[109] It was only bracketed text in the Luxembourg Consolidated Text but was subsequently entirely dropped from the Final Netherlands Compromise Text. As the proposed CFC rule, on the other hand, was progressively strengthened during that Presidency (e.g., the agreement to extend its scope of application to permanent establishments), the need for a switch-over rule was deemed by the Member States to be less urgent. As a result, the Netherlands Presidency Compromise Text did not - and, as a consequence, the ATAD does not - contain such a switch-over clause.

[d] *The General Anti-abuse Rule*

The GAAR, like the switch-over rule and the exit taxation provision, did not arise out of the OECD-BEPS project. Nevertheless, a GAAR was listed among the Initial CCCTB Proposal's Seven Anti-BEPS Elements and its wording was discussed during the negotiations thereof. Being an efficient measure to prevent tax-avoidance practices, its inclusion in the Original ATAD Proposal was never expressly challenged. However, that underlying understanding did not prevent further discussion regarding its specific wording. The Luxembourg Presidency Consolidated Text[110] relied heavily on the GAAR already incorporated in the then-recent amendment to the Parent-Subsidiary Directive.[111] Indeed, to a certain extent, its terminology, which used the phrases 'main purpose or one of the main purpose', 'not genuine', and 'to the extent that [the arrangement(s)] are not put in place for valid commercial reasons which reflect economic reality' - was recycled for that purpose. An effort was made to adapt the specific language to the potential autonomous anti-BEPS directive under discussion, particularly given that the entire point of such a directive was to provide the means to prevent tax avoidance practices and not - contrary to the Parent-Subsidiary Directive - to grant taxpayers beneficial tax treatment. With that in mind, the Luxembourg Consolidated Text specified that Member States were entitled to ignore abusive arrangements and determine an entity's (correct) tax liability in accordance with national law. The Commission's suggestion in the Original ATAD to calculate the tax liability by reference to 'economic substance in accordance with national law'[112] did not find favour among the Member States who, in the negotiations on the ATAD, demonstrated a clear preference for a GAAR's wording inspired by the Parent-Subsidiary Directive's GAAR, which preference was certainly understandable in light

109. Apparently, the Commission simply copy-pasted the provision as it existed in the Initial CCCTB Proposal, as it was perceived to be an effective measure against taxpayer's attempts to artificially shift certain mobile types of income outside of the European Union to avoid taxation.
110. The Luxembourg Consolidated Text, *supra* n. 53, Art. 5.
111. Council Directive 2015/121 of 27 Jan. 2015 Amending Directive 2011/96/EU on the Common System of Taxation Applicable in the Case of Parent Companies and Subsidiaries of Different Member States, Art. 1.
112. *See* the Original ATAD Proposal, *supra* n. 12.

of the lengthy (and tedious) discussions regarding its language before it was finally approved.[113] The GAAR's wording in the ATAD closely relies on the language suggested in the Luxembourg Consolidated Text.

[e] Exit Taxation

The Initial CCCTB Proposal contained an exit tax provision. The concept of including such exit taxation provision in the potential future anti-BEPS directive originated therein. The Member States – even those that felt any such directive should not go beyond the OECD-BEPS recommendations – eventually agreed to keep an exit tax provision in the ATAD, having been convinced it was an efficient way to counteract tax avoidance practices leading to BEPS.

A significant amount of work was put into designing the ATAD's exit tax provision; the language negotiated for the Initial CCCTB Proposal was scrapped in the Luxembourg Consolidated text and replaced by a well-structured outline and very detailed language. The Initial CCCTB Proposal's exit tax provision established a rule, subject to an exception, that dealt with transfers (of, *inter alia*, assets, tax residence, and businesses) outside the Member State towards either a third state or another EU Member State. Rather than demand an immediate exit tax levy on any unrealized capital gains, that exit tax rule permitted, at least with respect to transfers to another EU Member State or to an EEA country, that unrealized gains benefit from a tax deferral. That potential tax deferral, however, generated debate during the Luxembourg Presidency. As no precise guidance had been given by the CJEU on the question of whether any such deferral must be limited in time to comply with EU Treaties or whether any such deferral had to be granted until the taxpayer's gains were realized, the Luxembourg Consolidated Text made clear that the Member States had the discretion to grant the taxpayer either (a) a tax deferral on those gains for five years or (b) the ability to pay the exit tax in instalments spread out over five years. The Original ATAD Proposal's exit tax provisions reflected – to some degree – the Luxembourg Consolidated Text, except that it did not offer the Member States a choice with respect to the modalities of the tax deferral: the standard set out in the Original ATAD Proposal - and ultimately in the ATAD - is the payment of the exit tax in instalments over five years with the possibility for Member States to include stricter rules.[114] The Original ATAD Proposal, like the Luxembourg Presidency Consolidated Text, incorporated details regarding

113. *Ibid.* Art. 12 (reference was made, in connection with an entity's 'essential purpose', 'otherwise applicable tax provisions', and even the computation of its corporate tax liability 'by reference to economic substance in accordance with national law', and not reference to the 'essential purpose' test – a test that, arguably, is likely to be more advantageous to the taxpayer in demonstrating substance - set out in CJEU case law, rather than reference to the 'main purpose or one of the main purposes' used in the Parent-Subsidiary Directive, was still inspired by the 'principal purpose test' developed during the OECD-BEPS Action 6 discussions).

114. Interestingly, the wording in the Original ATAD Proposal's Art. 5(2) regarding tax deferral does not seem to entirely reflect the intention to allow the payment of an exit tax to be spread out over five years ('the taxpayer may defer the payment' and 'instalments over at least 5 years'). The objective is more clearly set out in ATAD, Art. 5(2): 'a taxpayer shall be given the right to defer' and 'instalments over 5 years').

some of its terminology, including clarification of the terms market value,[115] the internationally-agreed arm's length principle,[116] and the mutual recognition of the market value, which included a carve-out if the value of the transferred asset differs from its market value.[117] Such references also exist in the ATAD.

[f] Controlled Foreign Company (CFC) Rule and Computation of CFC Income

In contrast to the provisions discussed above, the CFC rule was designed around OECD-BEPS Action 3. The Luxembourg Presidency focussed on enhancing the language of the CFC rule included in the Initial CCCTB Proposal relying on specific OECD-BEPS-related recommendations in its draft Action 3. The Luxembourg Consolidated Text proposed an entity approach, whereby all of the CFC's passive income would be attributed to the controlling company (i.e., its parent). At the time, several delegations argued in favour of a CFC rule that included intra-EU situations and that should be shaped to target wholly artificial entities - entity approach - while other delegations favoured an alternative approach based on transactions carried out by the CFC - transactional approach - which would have confined the rule to 'non-genuine arrangements'. Despite such arguments, and with the expectation that any future directive would only establish minimum standards (i.e., the minimis rules and a principle-based approach) that would allow a Member State to design stricter national rules, the Luxembourg Consolidated Text chose not to specifically address the CFC rule's application to intra-EU situations. Moreover, to avoid overly complicated language in the CFC rule, the Luxembourg Presidency decided, along the lines originally suggested in the Italian Compromise Text on the Initial CCCTB,[118] to suggest in the Luxembourg Consolidated text to limit said directive's scope to third countries, except EEA countries.[119]

The Commission expanded in the Original ATAD Proposal the scope of application of the CFC rule incorporated to include all entities, while specifically carving out intra-EU and EEA entities,[120] so long as they met the substance carve-out test incorporated therein. The conditions of that substance-carve out test developed significantly during negotiations. It provided, for instance, that the substance-carve out test was met and that no income had to be attributed to the controlling (parent) company if the controlled entity carried on 'a substantive economic activity supported by commensurate staff, equipment, assets and premises which justify the income

115. The Final Netherlands Compromise Text, *supra* n. 83, Art. 5(5) ('Member State shall accept the market value established in the Member State of the taxpayer [...] as the starting value').
116. *Ibid.* Art. 5(6) ('willing unrelated buyers and sellers in a direct transaction').
117. *Ibid.* Art. 5(5)-(6) ('that Member State shall accept that value [...] as the starting value of the assets for tax purposes, unless this does not reflect the market value' and 'willing unrelated buyers and sellers in a direct transaction', respectively).
118. *See* the Italian Consolidated Text, *supra* n. 17.
119. *See* the Luxembourg Explanatory Notes, *supra* n. 54, at 8.
120. That are wholly artificial by providing that 'Member States shall not [include in the tax base of the parent company the non-distributed income of an entity] where the entity is tax resident in a Member State or a [EEA country] unless the establishment is wholly artificial', *see* Art. 8(2).

attributed to it'.[121] Then, it was agreed that a sufficient level of substance had merely to be 'evidenced by relevant facts and circumstances'.[122] To ensure the controlling entity's (i.e., the taxpayer's) cooperation with the relevant tax authorities, the Recitals drafted under Netherlands Presidency and included in the Final Netherlands Compromise Text – and, ultimately, in the ATAD – state that 'tax administrations and taxpayers [are expected to] cooperate to gather relevant facts and circumstances to determine whether the carve-out rule is to apply'.[123] Moreover, that document anticipated that, as part of a dialogue between the taxpayer and the tax authorities taking place prior to applying the CFC rule, the taxpayer could be required to provide evidence of a sufficient level of substance justifying the application of carve-out from the CFC rule. This wording is now part of the ATAD and makes absolutely clear that the tax authorities have to consult with the taxpayer before they decide to apply the CFC rule. Before such decision is taken, the taxpayer has the right to be given the opportunity to provide the necessary evidence in support of sufficient substance of the CFC.

In addition, the Original ATAD Proposal incorporates an alternative transactional approach to the CFC rule by adding a reference to the arm's length principle[124] for an EU or EEA entity that 'engages, in the course of its activity, in non-genuine arrangements which have been put into place for the essential purpose of obtaining a tax advantage'.[125] The ATAD also contains this approach as an alternative to the entity approach.

The scope of application of the CFC rule in the Original ATAD Proposal and the one in the ATAD are somewhat different: while both would have the CFC rule apply to intra-EU situations, the ATAD makes it quite a bit easier to qualify a particular entity as a CFC falling within its scope and, thus, subject to taxation pursuant thereto. While the Luxembourg Presidency Consolidated Text or the Original ATAD qualified an entity as a CFC if four conditions were met, which related to the parent company's ownership, the effective tax burden, the category of income, and the amount of passive income perceived, as well as the question of whether the entity's shares are traded on a recognized stock exchange, the ATAD, on the other hand, establishes just two criteria to determine whether or not the entity is a CFC: ownership and level of taxation.

[g] Interest Limitation Rule

Like the aforementioned CFC rule, an interest-deduction limitation rule included in the Initial CCCTB Proposal, was discussed during the Luxembourg Presidency, which shaped it to fit the OECD-BEPS Action 4 recommendations. The Original ATAD Proposal offered the Member States broad discretion to design their respective interest-deduction limitation rules. During subsequent Council negotiations thereon, an even

121. The 26 May 2016 ATAD Compromise Text, *supra* n. 93, Art. 7(2).
122. The Final Netherlands Compromise Text, *supra* n. 83, Art. 7(2) and the ATAD, *supra* n. 12, Art. 7(2).
123. The Final Netherlands Compromise Text, *supra* n. 83, Recital 12 and the ATAD, *supra* n. 12, at Recital 12.
124. The Original ATAD Proposal, *supra* n. 12, Art. 8(2), 3rd line.
125. *Ibid.* Art. 8(2), 1st line, in fine.

greater level of flexibility was introduced to achieve consistency with the OECD-BEPS Action 4 recommendations. In addition to provisions addressing the carry forward of unused EBITDA, those negotiations took on the question of whether the group ratio rule (group carve-out rule) based on an assets/equity-based test should be added to the fixed ratio rule set at 30% of EBITDA. Such questions as well as the rule according to which the deduction of exceeding borrowing costs below the application floor of EUR one million, should be automatically allowed, were put in brackets in the Luxembourg Consolidated Text. The Original ATAD Proposal's approach generally relied on the Luxembourg Consolidated Text's figures (particularly the 30% of EBITDA fixed ratio rule, the floor of EUR one million, the group ratio based on an assets/equity test, and the carry forward for non-absorbed EBITDA). The approach taken in the ATAD, except for the figures, is however substantially different. There, the limitation of the deduction of exceeding borrowing cost to 30% the EBITDA is a general (and mandatory) rule.[126] The established floor for application of the rule (EUR one million), in contrast, is optional. It also gave the Member States further flexibility in accordance with OECD-BEPS Action 4 recommendations with respect to interest deductions related to existing loans (i.e., a grandfathering clause),[127] and interest arising in relation with long-term, public infrastructure projects.

The ATAD now also clarifies that targeted rules, such as thin capitalization rules already existing in a Member State's domestic tax legislation prior to the ATAD's implementation can be applied in addition to its fixed ratio rule but that the existence of such domestic regulation does not exempt a Member State from its obligation to implement said fixed ratio rule in its domestic law.[128] With respect to other pre-existing targeted rules that a Member State considers to be as effective as the ATAD's interest limitation rule, it provides that such rules can continue to be applied until the earlier of (a) the end of the first fiscal year following the date on which the OECD-BEPS Action 4 recommendations achieve the status of an OECD minimum standard but (b) at least until 1 January 2024. That change to the ATAD's text during the Council meeting on 17 June 2016 addresses the concern of level playing field between the EU and third countries that might not be eager to implement such requirements that are no minimum standards for the purposes of the OECD-BEPS project.

[h] Hybrid Mismatches

The ATAD's rule on hybrid mismatches came out of the OECD-BEPS Action 2 recommendations. The Luxembourg Consolidated Text addressed hybrid mismatches, more specifically hybrid mismatches within the EU as discussed in the Code of Conduct

126. Whereas other provisions granting a more favourable treatment to the taxpayer, such as the minimum application rule raised to EUR three million or the group ratio rule based either on an EBITDA-test or an assets/equity-based test for the consolidated group.
127. The loans referred to are those concluded before 17 June 2016, the date of the last ECOFIN meeting in order to avoid retroactivity, provided that such loans are not subsequently modified.
128. The Final Netherlands Compromise Text, *supra* n. 83, Recitals 6–9.

group[129] with respect to hybrid entities in the EU and in third states. However, the Luxembourg Presidency bracketed the text relating to cases involving third countries pending further discussion third country issues in OECD.[130] Contrary to the Luxembourg Consolidated Text, the Original ATAD Proposal was limited to hybrid entities and hybrid instruments solely within the EU; it specified in its recitals that, irrespective of any guidance arising out of the Code of Conduct group's discussions on the tax treatment of hybrid entities and hybrid permanent establishments within the EU or in relation to third countries, 'hybrid mismatches between Member States and third countries still need to be further examined'.[131] The ATAD follows this approach and limits the scope of the hybrid mismatch rule to hybrid mismatches in the EU notwithstanding the discussions during the Netherlands Presidency on a wording of rules targeting hybrid mismatches in and in relation with non-EU countries. Like the Original ATAD Proposal, it incorporates two general rules intended to neutralize mismatch situations related to hybrid entities and hybrid instruments. Moreover, contrary to the Original ATAD Proposal, it intends to adopt the approach followed in the OECD-BEPS Action 2 recommendation rather than requiring the Member State of residence to accept the source Member State's legal characterization of either (a) the entity or (b) the instrument.

Given the need for specific rules addressing third-country hybrid mismatches, the Council added a statement to the minutes of the ECOFIN meeting of 17 June 2016 asking the Commission to put forward, by October 2016, a proposal on third-country hybrid mismatches 'in order to provide rules consistent with and no less effective than the rules recommended by the OECD-BEPS report on Action 2, with a view to reaching agreement by the end of 2016'.[132] The Commission committed to issue a package before end of October 2016, which would include, among other things, a proposed amendment to the ATAD addressing third-country hybrid mismatches, a revised C(C)CTB proposal (i.e., the Relaunched C(C)CTB Proposal) and a proposal on efficient dispute resolution mechanisms.[133] As promised, on 25 October 2016, the Commission published its Corporate Tax Reform Package, which included the 2016 ATAD Amendment Proposal.[134] The Slovak Presidency pushed the 2016 ATAD Amendment Proposal forward, leaving only a few technical points open after the 6 December 2016 ECOFIN meeting. The Finance Ministers subsequently approved the compromise text proposed by the Maltese Presidency in ECOFIN meeting on 21 February 2017.[135]

129. The Code of Conduct for Business Taxation (Tax Measures Covered) adopted in that certain Resolution of the Council and the Representatives of the Governments of the Member States, Meeting within the Council of 1 Dec. 1997 on a Code of Conduct for Business Taxation, attached as Annex 1 to the Council Conclusions of the ECOFIN Council Meeting of 1 Dec. 1997 concerning Taxation Policy [1998] OJ 98/C 2/01.
130. The Luxembourg Explanatory Notes, *supra* n. 54, Arts 11 and 12.
131. *See* the Original ATAD Proposal, *supra* n. 12, para. 11, p. 13.
132. The Final Netherlands Compromise Text, *supra* n. 83, Annex II.
133. For more detail, see *supra* n. 1.
134. For this definition, see *ibid.*
135. The Maltese Presidency compromise text on the 2016 ATAD Amendment Proposal of 17 Feb. 2017, 6333/17 FISC 46 ECOFIN 95. ECOFIN is expected to the adopt this directive at the ECOFIN meeting to be held on 21 Mar. 2017.

[4] *The Relaunched C(C)CTB Proposal: Reopening the Discussion on the Harmonization of Direct Taxes?*

At one point above, the EU's desire to harmonize direct corporate taxation, at least for cross-border activities or groups of a certain size, having been given form in the Initial CCCTB Proposal, was described as a phoenix rising from the ashes of that now-withdrawn proposal in the Relaunched C(C)CTB Proposal. It is interesting to mention that the Relaunched C(C)CTB Proposal does not appear to change much with respect to the Commission's underlying objective to provide harmonized rules on corporate taxation in the EU for at least some of the entities most exposed to compliance requirements resulting from the differences of Member States' tax systems. In addition to giving taxpayers a tool that reduces their administrative burdens, such harmonized rules would also give the Member States a powerful instrument against aggressive tax planning practices. The Commission signalled its intent to relaunch the Initial CCCTB Proposal in its 5 Key Areas Action Plan[136] in an attempt to offer a holistic solution to existing problems corporate taxation across the EU. That plan argued that implementing common corporate tax rules, like those set out in the Initial CCCTB Proposal, would greatly improve the business environment in the Single Market by making it simpler and cheaper for companies to operate across borders.

Moreover, the 5 Key Areas Action Plan highlights the Commission's belief that the anti-avoidance measures to be incorporated into the Relaunched C(C)CTB Proposal would better defend the Single Market against practices resulting in BEPS in favour of non-EU countries, stating that 'in line with the Commission's recent initiative dealing with potential aggressive tax planning practices in relation to third countries, the new C(C)CTB would allow Member States to implement a common approach vis-à-vis third countries and defend the Single Market against aggressive tax planning.'[137] As such, it concluded that the Relaunched C(C)CTB Proposal would not only reduce the scope of harmful tax competition, but also reduce the opaque and preferential tax regimes that exist in national systems.[138]

Subsequent discussions about potentially common measures contained in the ATAD and any Relaunched C(C)CTB Proposal, attempted to address the question of whether and, if so, to what extent, the Member States would be willing to grant support to the Relaunched C(C)CTB Proposal. It remains to be seen whether the momentum toward harmonization continues, particularly in light of recent scandals revealing some unacceptable tax avoidance schemes and aggressive tax planning practices made possible because of differences in national taxation systems, and will encourage Member States' support in Council. It remains to be seen if the ATAD's adoption in record time in 2016 can be repeated with the Relaunched C(C)CTB Proposal.

136. For this definition, see the 5 Key-Areas Action Plan, *supra* n. 4.
137. *Ibid.* para. 1.
138. *Ibid.*

§14.03 IMPLEMENTING OECD-BEPS RECOMMENDATIONS IN EU HARD LAW: IS THAT THE FIRST STEP TOWARDS HARMONIZATION IN THE AREA OF CORPORATE TAXATION OR JUST COORDINATION?

The relationship between the Relaunched C(C)CTB Proposal and the ATAD and the 2016 ATAD Amendment Proposal, is undoubtedly a fascinating one. Questions abound:

- Does the adoption of the ATAD, which contains an EU approach with respect to anti-avoidance rules intended to curb BEPS outcomes, indicate the Council's and, *a fortiori*, the Member States' receptiveness to, or even a favorable tendency toward, a certain level harmonization in the area of direct taxes?
- Should coordination of some anti-avoidance measures for BEPS purposes be considered a precursor to harmonization of (more) substantial tax provisions? Or, are the anti-avoidance rules contained in the ATAD, which result in a certain alignment with respect to a specific area in domestic tax rules (i.e., anti-avoidance provisions), simply a confirmation that 'harmonization' of direct taxation rules is illusory?
- Does the ATAD, which establishes certain minimum principle-based anti-avoidance measures across the EU, indirectly provide a certain level of harmonization? If so, is it likely to quiet the voices that have expressed doubts on any tendency that could, ultimately, lead to harmonization of certain aspects of the corporate taxation rules for all the Member States?
- Is there a genuine need for further initiatives to achieve closer alignment of national tax provisions or to harmonize domestic tax rules in addition to the powerful anti-avoidance rules inspired by the OECD-BEPS recommendations already incorporated in the ATAD (as amended by the 2016 ATAD Amendment Proposal)?
- Should the Relaunched C(C)CTB Proposal, a proposal also intended to curb aggressive tax planning, be seen as an acknowledgement that the ATAD (as amended by the 2016 ATAD Amendment Proposal) is incapable, by itself, to curb aggressive tax-avoidance practices?

Based on the foregoing, and given that the ATAD (and the 2016 ATAD Amendment Proposal) is a very recent development, it is rather difficult to predict whether the Council's approval of common minimum anti-BEPS measures reflects a the Council's desire to make further progress on common EU rules for corporate taxation. Irrespective of the Member States' commitment, at global, OECD level, to implement the anti-avoidance rules intended to prevent BEPS, the negotiations surrounding the ATAD were indeed tedious. The technical complexity of the issues, as well as the need to address the requirements of each of the Member States that must be considered during the negotiation processes of any further directives, in and of themselves, may create significant roadblocks in the path to a swift agreement in the tax area. Even greater efforts might be needed when it involves first, common corporate taxation rules for all the Member States, and then consolidated taxpayer returns. Due to the Relaunched C(C)CTB Proposal's high degree of complexity, it is only reasonable to expect that many substantive discussions in working parties must take place, and that the numerous open items will not be resolved at the technical level, making it highly likely that they will be raised and resolved, if at all, at the political level.

§14.04 CONCLUSION

Despite the recent advances made at the EU level, some Member States have generally been, and may still be, reluctant to discuss in Council the issue of direct taxation harmonization. Indeed, some Member States may continue to feel that even a discussion of various aspects related to the subject of direct taxation could lead to significant pressure to relinquish a substantial portion of their sovereign right to collect taxes to the EU. The previous paragraphs described the rather circuitous route the Member States took to achieve agreement on the ATAD. Discussions on the concepts addressed in the ATAD actually started several months before the Commission finally published its Original ATAD Proposal, as part the discussions that took place with respect to the now-withdrawn Initial CCCTB Proposal and, even earlier, in the working parties on the OECD-BEPS project. From the Luxembourg Presidency's perspective, the work conducted on the BEPS aspects in the Initial CCCTB Proposal included in the Luxembourg Consolidated Text prior the Commission's publication of the Original ATAD is, to a certain extent, be perceived as the predecessor and prototype for the final version of the ATAD finally approved in Council in July 2016.

The objective of the Initial CCCTB Proposal was to first harmonize the corporate tax base for multinational groups of entities and then consolidate that tax base for apportionment according to a specific formula among the relevant Member States. Despite the Commission's clarification that the ATAD's objective just to provide coordinated measures to curb such multinational groups' tax avoidance and aggressive tax planning practices, ostensibly excluding any harmonization objective, that still begs the question of whether its coordinated tax avoidance measures could be perceived as a symbol of the Member States' growing support for greater harmonization in the direct corporate tax area. It is not, however, easy to speculate on the answer to that question. Indeed, it is even difficult to measure whether the Member State's agreement on a coherent implementation of OECD-BEPS measures in the EU, through the ATAD (as amended by the 2016 ATAD Amendment Proposal) demonstrates a more favourable tendency that could benefit the future negotiation of the Relaunched C(C)CTB Proposal. For the ATAD, it was obvious that the unusual international context, particularly the momentum behind the need to coordinate anti-tax avoidance measures, generated by the OECD-BEPS project, especially the release of the OECD-BEPS recommendations, exerted political pressure on the Member States, at both the EU and the global levels. It is hard to predict whether such momentum and political pressure will last and, if so, for how long. It may, or may not, be long enough for the Member States to approve the Relaunched C(C)CTB Proposal, which is also aimed at efficiently preventing aggressive tax planning practices that exploit gaps and mismatches between different national direct tax regulations. Objectively, however, it is wise to remain sceptical that the Member States' approval of the coordinated approach on the anti-avoidance rules via the ATAD, which are likely to affect their sovereign right to collect taxes in only a rather limited way, is a harbinger of future harmonization of corporate taxes in the EU.

It is safe to say though – at least for now and subject to what the ongoing negotiations on the Relaunched C(C)CTB Proposal may demonstrate to the contrary – that the ATAD should not be viewed as evidence Member States' current or future attitudes towards harmonization in the area of direct taxes at the EU level. As already mentioned, the restrictions imposed on at least some of Member States' sovereignty are likely to be quite minor. Even for those for which the ATAD's restrictions are more burdensome (i.e., those that will have to significantly modify their existing national rules to comply with it), the ATAD's measures do not modify the general features of their taxation system and, thus, do not appear to be a move toward, or an acceptance of a trend toward, harmonization.

Thus, while the ATAD (amended by the 2016 ATAD Amendment Proposal) may ultimately result in tax levies on a broader corporate tax base once fully implemented, it just reflects a coordinated approach to some anti-avoidance provisions; unlike the Relaunched C(C)CTB Proposal, it will do so without interfering too much with the Member State's national tax policies, such that the Member States' acceptance of the one cannot truly shed light on the success of the other. Leaving aside such political considerations regarding the protection of the Member States' sovereign right to levy and collect taxes and the potential impact, for some Member States, in terms of tax revenues if an entity's taxable profits are computed and apportioned according to the suggested formula, the concept of harmonized corporate tax rules for the whole of the EU could, as such, be a possible solution to some of the frustrating cross-border issues that both taxpayers and tax authorities may encounter on a daily basis. Unfortunately, it does not appear a way to leave such political and, more importantly, budgetary considerations aside.

Part VI EU Tax Policy and the Courts

CHAPTER 15

Limits of Judicial Authority in Tax Policy

Serge Schroeder

§15.01 INTRODUCTION

The purpose of this chapter is not to provide a purely technical analysis of the existing jurisprudence of the national courts of one or more European Union (EU) Member States in order to find commonalities and differences regarding the scope of judicial oversight of their respective tax policy choices. Rather, the author of these lines raises and discusses several aspects of the same tax issue, namely, whether a change in the limits of judicial review of tax policy is necessary. Indeed, the question is whether the many changes in taxation that have occurred over the few decades - moving in the direction of multiplying the types of taxes imposed and increasing of the level thereof - should also result in an extension of judicial review to issues beyond the limits of traditional judicial oversight.

The author of these lines is well aware that the ideas expressed herein are likely to give rise to some heated discussions and are unlikely to be greeted with favour by the finance ministers of various countries. Moreover, the author is well aware that the ideas expressed herein do not resolve the issue and cannot claim to represent the finished product; rather, the author expects this chapter to be the opening volley in an ongoing discussion of the issues the author believes must be raised in any discussion of European tax policy.

But, before addressing these issues, a brief overview of the traditional scope of judicial review of tax laws in Luxembourg and neighbouring countries is appropriate.

§15.02 TRADITIONAL SCOPE OF JUDICIAL REVIEW

At the outset, the impact of EU law as regards the national courts' scope of judicial review must be mentioned before offering some suggestions regarding judicial oversight at the national level.

[A] Impact of Community Law

In terms of indirect taxes, one must distinguish between taxes harmonized at the EU level and those that are not.

Harmonized indirect taxes, which are mainly VAT and customs duties, fall within the rule of supremacy of EU law over all the standards established by the national law of the Member States, including national constitutional law, as affirmed by the Court of Justice of the European Union (CJEU) in its 1978 *Simmenthal* decision.[1] Consequently, national judicial review regarding compliance with the applicable national law standards are more limited with regard to such harmonized direct taxes.

The rest – that is, non-harmonized indirect taxes and direct taxes – fall, according to the EU Treaties, within the competence of the Member States, unless certain directives have harmonized specific aspects thereof (e.g., the Parent-Subsidiary Directive[2] and the Automatic Exchange Directive[3]) so that the national judiciary maintains a broad range of competence with respect to these taxes outside the limited scope of the directives.

[B] National Judicial Review

Given the differences between the legal systems in neighboring countries, arising from their varied historical development, their divergent legal provisions, and their particular judicial interpretations with respect to the relevant texts, and given that the purpose of this chapter is not to provide a thorough analysis of certain constitutional standards such as implemented in several countries, this chapter only examines a few basic lines relating to certain constitutional requirements.

1. *Amministrazione delle finanze dello Stato* v *Simmenthal*, C-106/77, Judgment, EU:C:1978:49.
2. Council Directive 2011/96/EU of 30 Nov. 2011 on the common system of taxation applicable in the case of parent companies and subsidiaries of different Member States (recast), OJ L 345/8 (2011), as amended by Council Directive 2013/13/EU of 13 May 2013 adapting certain directives in the field of taxation, by reason of the accession of the Republic of Croatia, OJ L 141/30 (2013), Council Directive 2014/86/EU of 8 July 2014 amending Directive 2011/96/EU on the common system of taxation applicable in the case of parent companies and subsidiaries of different Member States, OJ L 219/40 (2014), and Council Directive (EU) 2015/121 of 27 Jan. 2015 amending Directive 2011/96/EU on the common system of taxation applicable in the case of parent companies and subsidiaries of different Member States, OJ L 21/1 (2015) (collectively, the 'Parent-Subsidiary Directive').
3. Council Directive 2011/16/EU of 15 Feb. 2011 on administrative cooperation in the field of taxation and repealing Directive 77/799/EEC, OJ L 64/1 (2011), as amended by Council Directive 2014/107/EU of 9 Dec. 2014 amending Directive 2011/16/EU as regards mandatory automatic exchange of information in the field of taxation, OJ L 359/1 (2014) (collectively, the 'Automatic Exchange Directive').

[1] Equality in Its Various Aspects

The first rule of the constitutional order is clearly that of equality before the law in its two aspects: formal equality before the law and material equality in law.

While the first component - formal equality before the law - requires that the law be applied equally to all falling within its scope, the second component - equality in law - generally requires that equal treatment be given to all those who are in similar situations with regard to the particular law in question and that any distinctions between situations made by the law be based on criteria that are objective, general, and adequate to the aim pursued. Despite the differences in the way national legal systems describe the constitutional obligation, they all require a logical link between the criteria the legislature chose and the aim pursued by the law. The legislature, therefore, may subject non-comparable situations to different treatment.[4] There are some Member States that interpret the equality in law rule to require the legislature to establish different regimes with regard to situations that cannot be considered comparable.[5]

However, the competent national courts typically give their respective legislatures varying degrees of more-or-less wide latitude,[6] both in determining the legislative purpose of a particular law and in the choice of criteria that define the categories of persons covered by the particular legislation. They typically only sanction measures that result in overtly different or unreasonable treatment, which self-imposed limitation on their review is often described as judicial self-restraint.[7]

Another constitutional rule that restricts legislative power is the rule 'of equality before public burdens', which may, depending on the national legal system, be regarded as a special application of the general rule of equality before the law[8] or as the expression of a constitutional rule of a certain social justice.[9] In any case, the rule generally requires that the tax burden be the same for all people with the same ability to pay, such that the legislature is obliged to establish identical taxation of the same economic data with the same tax effect.

Nevertheless, the ability-to-pay concept often gives rise to questions about its quantification criteria and, therefore, the situations in which an identical-contributory capacity can be said to exist. Indeed, this concept assumes a hypothesis that necessarily varies in relation to the tax under discussion for which the legislature has more or less discretion to determine the scope and level of tax that it intends to impose. Moreover, the concept is not usually interpreted in such a way that it defines the importance of differentiation in tax levels between different tax capacities or that it establishes a ceiling for the maximum eligible tax level. Similarly, the question of

4. *E.g.*, FR: Const. Court, 18 Dec. 1997, n° 97-393 DC.
5. *E.g.*, DE: Const. Court, 12 Oct. 2010, BVerfGE 127, 224.
6. *See* DE: Const. Court, 22 June 1995, BVerfGE 93, 121; *see also*, for BE: Elisabeth Willemart & Marc Verdussen, *Les limites constitutionnelles du pouvoir fiscal* 212 (1999).
7. Elisabeth Zoller, *Droit constitutionnel* 249 (2d ed., 1999); David Dokhan, *Les limites du contrôle de la constitutionnalité des actes législatifs* 468 (2001).
8. FR: Declaration of Human and Citizens' Rights, 26 Aug. 1789, Art. 13 ('*égalité devant les charges publiques*').
9. Alain Steichen, *Manuel de droit fiscal vol. 1* 500 (2006).

respect for the rule of contributory capacity is mainly discussed in relation to a particular tax considered alone[10] or, where more than one tax is taken into account, the examination is limited to taxes on the same item of income paid by one taxpayer,[11] which excludes the effects of subsequent taxes.

Finally, it must be remembered that, when undertaking any judicial review of the legislature's compliance with the principle of taxation according to ability to pay, constitutional judges customarily limit themselves to a review of proportionality and generally only sanction cases of manifest disproportionality.[12]

One must, therefore, conclude from this brief analysis of the rule of equality before the law that it allows judicial review of legislative activity relating to taxation, but that such judicial monitoring typically focuses on the system by which individuals, entities, property, or things are subjected to tax and the relevant tax base, and only rarely focuses on the level of tax imposed in an attempt to limit the allowable tax charge with respect to the particular taxable object. Judicial review, thus, can only be used to invalidate a tax rate on the grounds that it exceeds one class of taxpayers' actual ability to pay when compared to that of another class of taxpayers.[13]

Thus, any examination of whether a constitutional court may limit the permissible level of one or more taxes requires a move to other constitutional norms.

[2] Other Constitutional Norms

The first such standard that logically comes to mind is the right to property enshrined in all of Luxembourg's and its neighboring countries' constitutions.[14] The basic question, thus, is whether the right to property, which has traditionally been understood as a prohibition against depriving a person of his ownership of, or rights in or to, a particular thing - whether movable or immovable, tangible or intangible - can also be interpreted as a prohibition against imposing a tax burden either (i) on the particular thing, such that merely holding it would deprive the taxpayer of an excessive portion of its value, or (ii) on the taxpayer himself, as it would deprive him of an excessive part of his global wealth or fortune. Essentially, it is a question of the constitutional validity of confiscatory taxes. In this respect, two examples are telling.

In 2012, members of the French Parliament sought review by the Constitutional Council (*Conseil Constitutionnel*) of several measures in the Finance Act 2013,[15] including several tax rate increases on certain types of income and wealth, particularly an additional tax on income from professional activities exceeding one million euros, which would bring the total tax thereon to 75%, as announced by the President of the French Republic François Hollande as part of his presidential campaign. In its 29

10. *E.g.*, FR: Cons. Const. 19 Nov. 1997, n° 97-390 DC.
11. FR: Cons. Const. 29 Dec. 2012, n° 2012-662 DC.
12. Zoller, *supra* n. 7, at 249; Dokhan, *supra* n. 7, at 453-s.
13. *See, e.g.*, FR: Cons. Const. 29 Dec. 2012, n° 2012-662 DC, pt [2]
14. LU: Constitution, Art. 16; DE: Constitution, Art. 14(I); FR: Constitution, Decl. of Human and Citizens' Rights, 26 Aug. 1789, Art. 13; and BE: Constitution, Art. 16.
15. FR : *Loi n° 2012-1509 du 29 décembre 2012 de finances pour 2013*, Journal Officiel n° 0304, 30 Dec. 2012, page 20859.

December 2012 decision,[16] the Constitutional Council held that (a) the constitutional obligation to distribute taxes according to the taxpayer's ability to pay would not be respected if the tax was of a confiscatory nature or imposed, on a certain category of taxpayers, an excessive burden in relation to their contributory power, and (b) the proper application of the principle of equality before public burdens requires all taxes on the same income and paid by the same taxpayer to be taken into account. Applying only this second principle (and explicitly stating that it was not addressing the issue of the potentially confiscatory nature of the tax), the Constitutional Council condemned the tax measures as unconstitutional, particularly as they would have had the effect of increasing the maximum marginal tax rate imposed on pensions paid out of defined benefit pension plans to 75.04% or 75.34%, depending on the circumstances.[17] In addition, the tax rates on the gains and benefits from the exercise of an option to subscribe for or purchase shares or the acquisition of bonus shares were increased to 68.2% or 73.2%, depending on the circumstances.[18]

In each case, the Constitutional Council held that all such newly imposed tax rates would be an excessive burden in terms of the relevant taxpayers' contributory power and were, therefore, contrary to the principle of equality before public burdens.[19] On the other hand, the Constitutional Council did not condemn the additional tax on professional-activities income exceeding one million euros because it created an excessive burden; but rather, it found that the law subjected the income of certain individual taxpayers to this exceptional contribution without regard to their particular tax situation and it held that such an approach was a breach of the principle of equality before public burdens.

In light of that decision, the French Government proposed an amendment to the Finance Act 2013. However, on 21 March 2013, the State Council opined that, based on the Constitutional Council's findings and conclusions in its 29 December 2012 decision, France could not impose cumulative taxation on individuals' household income in excess of 66.66%, with a 'tolerance' of up to 72% on very high income or very particular items of income.[20]

In Germany, its Constitutional Court (the *Bundesverfassungsgericht* (BVerfG)) rendered, on 22 June 1995, two acclaimed-yet-controversial rulings with respect to taxes on wealth and inheritance,[21] which found two limits on the legislature's ability to impose tax arising from the right to private property. First, the Constitutional Court held that tax law must respect the substance of the taxpayer's fortune (i.e., the different assets that comprise his global wealth, including the nature and liquidity thereof) and,

16. FR: Cons. Const. 29 Dec. 2012, n° 2012-662 DC.
17. *Ibid.* paras 17–19.
18. *Ibid.* para. 81.
19. *Ibid.*
20. Opinion n° 387402 responding to a request for an opinion regarding the conditions for the constitutional validity of a contribution on very high income [author trans. from: '*demande d'avis relative aux conditions de constitutionnalité d'une contribution sur les très hauts revenus*').
21. DE: BVerfG 22 June 22 1995, 2 BvL 37/91, BVerfGE 93, 121 and BVerfG 22 June 1995, 2 BvR 552/91, BVerfGE 93, 165.

thus, can only impose an income tax on the deemed income generated by such assets.[22] Second, it held that a wealth tax could only be imposed on top of other taxes based on income if, and to the extent, that the total tax burden on the deemed income accruing from capital – which must be assessed in a standardized manner after taking account of all permissible tax deductions – roughly results in a 50/50 split between the taxpayer and the state.[23] Even though the Constitutional Court's decisions did not clarify all of the issues relating to establishing the overall tax burden that can be imposed on taxpayers (for example, it did not address whether such overall tax burden should include only the direct taxes levied on such income at realization (or some other point in time) or should also include the indirect taxes likely to be imposed later, when such income is expended), they certainly indicated that, at a minimum, a taxpayer cannot, under Germany's existing constitutional principles, be obliged to relinquish more than one-half of the taxpayers effective or deemed income to the state.

However, the glimmer of hope offered by those Court decisions to those seeking an upper limit to the overall level of state levies was dashed when the German Constitutional Court revisited the issue in its 18 January 2006 decision:[24] it formally declared that the 50/50 split principle enunciated in its 22 June 1995 decision with regard to wealth tax, in so far as it comes on top of other taxes on income, does not apply to income taxes considered alone.[25] Moreover, it flatly stated that, except for the less-demanding prohibition on excessive taxation, such a principle in the field of income taxation could not be deduced from Germany's constitutional provisions, either. In its final remarks, the German Constitutional Court went so far as to cast doubt as to the appropriateness of the 50/50 split principle with respect to wealth tax. Obviously, it definitively rejected any interpretation of its prior case law as a limit on the overall level of taxes that the state could legitimately impose on a taxpayer and, thereby, assured that the German legislature – wrongly, from the author's perspective – retained almost complete discretion over the issue.

Accordingly, while the French Constitutional Court retained a tax ceiling of two-thirds that takes into account all statutory charges when making income, including levy contributions, under social legislation, but without taking indirect taxes into account, the turnaround of the German Constitutional Court leaves unanswered, for the moment, the question of a maximum-allowable tax level in Germany.

These developments call for the conclusion that, on the one hand, national constitutional rules, as applied and interpreted by the competent national courts do imply a certain level of judicial review over tax legislation, but, on the other hand, those rules do not limit the level of tax the legislature can impose, leaving the legislature free to establish or set low thresholds allowing very high levels of taxation. This conclusion must be borne in mind when the reality of our tax systems and the evolution of tax policies is briefly examined hereafter.

22. *See* 2 BvL 37/91 ch. C, part II, s. 3(b).
23. *See ibid.* s. 3(c).
24. DE: BVerfGE 115, 97.
25. *Ibid.* paras 27–28.

§15.03 THE REALITY OF TAX SYSTEMS

Almost every country around the globe has a tax system made up of a variety of taxes that apply to different types of revenue (e.g., salaries, professional activities, interest, dividends, and capital gains) at certain points in the taxpayer's circular flow of income (e.g., receipt, realization, and consumption), which points are indicative of a taxpayer's ability to pay tax. Over the course of a lifetime, a taxpayer's revenues are dynamic. Moreover, his circular income flow typically increases his overall wealth, as that accumulated wealth reflects his ability to consume and to invest. Of course, every taxpayer uses some or all of his income and accumulated wealth to fulfill his consumption needs (and wants), as well as to achieve other purposes, including income- or growth-generating investments. Taxation can, therefore, be levied first on the incoming revenue, then on the accumulated wealth, and then on the withdrawal or use of some part of that income and accumulated wealth for consumption or other uses. Indeed, existing taxes actually operate at these three points: income tax on income stream, wealth tax on accumulated wealth, and VAT, registration rights, succession, and excise duties on consumption and withdrawal or use of wealth.

Direct taxes only cover that part of a taxpayer's income flow and wealth accumulation as it occurs (i.e., at the point of realization). However, the financial resources ultimately available to a taxpayer for the purpose of satisfying his needs can only be determined at the end of the flow, when he makes his final use or withdrawal of his income and accumulated wealth, at which point indirect taxes generally apply. The conclusion is that all such indirect taxes - especially VAT, which is a general consumption tax - reduce the financial resources available to a taxpayer to satisfy his needs just as much as direct taxes do, such that they should also be taken into account in determining a taxpayer's overall tax burden: the calculation of that overall tax burden must include all contributions to public charges collected from the taxpayer before the taxpayer allocates his financial resources to his personal needs. Thus, a maximum level of permissible tax burden deriving from constitutional provisions or principles, if found by a constitutional court, would only be truly effective if it included the impact of all of the direct and indirect taxes levied on the various aforementioned parts of a taxpayer's income and accumulation flow and, perhaps, even all compulsory deductions therefrom, including obligatory social contributions; a maximum level fixed with respect to a single point in that flow (e.g., receipt or realization) would only solve one part of the problem, leaving the legislature unfettered discretion to set the tax rate payable on all the other parts thereof. Social contributions, arguably, should be taken into account as they also reduce a taxpayer's available financial resources and, ultimately, his ability to pay.

The major problem with attempting to set a maximum rate of taxation that takes account of all taxes levied on the various parts of the flow remains the quantification of the impact of indirect taxes, especially VAT, in so far as all financial resources arising from income and all withdrawals from accumulated wealth are not necessarily used for consumer transactions subject to VAT or subject to any other specific indirect tax. Schematically, it can indeed be argued that, while taxpayers receiving the lowest incomes generally suffer a lower direct tax burden, a much more significant portion of their after-income tax income must be allocated to consumption subject to VAT; for taxpayer's with growing income, on the other hand, their direct tax burden increases, but a decreasing proportion of their after-tax income must be allocated to consumption subject to VAT. Consequently, one cannot simply assume that the after-income tax remainder received by a taxpayer should be automatically subject to the existing VAT rate because, while that may be more or less true for those with very low incomes, the more money a taxpayer makes, the less likely he is to spend all or substantially all of that remainder on consumables subject to VAT. Thus, a simple mathematical equation, that adds to the rate of direct income tax of, say, 66% another VAT rate of, say, 20%, applied to the remaining 34% of the taxpayer's net income, to find that taxpayer's total tax burden (66% income tax + (0.34 x 20% =) 6.6% VAT charge = 72.6% of global tax charge), cannot be regarded as economically correct for all taxpayers.

Nevertheless, the author firmly believes that the difficulty of finding a satisfactory method of quantifying the ultimate impact of all the different taxes on a taxpayer's financial resources cannot result in an outright dismissal of the idea of capping the level of the overall tax burden a taxpayer can be subjected to. Indeed, safeguarding rights guaranteed by the constitution cannot be conditioned on the ease or the difficulty of assessing the actual impact of a legal provision. Rather, the appropriate solution should be, based on relevant statistics, a schedule setting out fixed percentage decreases in the share of after-tax income dedicated to consumption subject to VAT or other indirect taxes in relation to a taxpayer's increasing income and wealth.

This necessity to quantify the overall tax burden is confirmed by the evolution of fiscal policy by many governments in the recent years.

§15.04 THE EVOLUTION OF FISCAL POLICY IN THE 21ST CENTURY

On 3 December 2015, the Organization for Economic Cooperation and Development (OECD) issued a communication commenting on early twenty-first century trends in tax policy as evidenced by its most recent Revenue Statistics (the 'Communication').[26] Its very title eloquently described the trend: 'Corporate Tax Revenues Falling, Putting Higher Burdens on Individuals'.[27] The Communication went on to say that revenue from corporate income and gain taxes had been declining in most OECD countries since the global economic crisis first hit, which in turn, increased the pressure on individual taxpayers to meet the state's financial needs.[28]

The Communication also offered a number of more specific findings based on the Revenue Statistics:

- On average, the revenue collected from corporate income and gain taxes fell from 3.6% to just 2.8% of gross domestic product (GDP) between 2007 and 2014. The revenue generated from personal income tax, conversely, grew from

26. http://www.oecd.org/tax/corporate-tax-revenues-falling-putting-higher-burdens-on-individuals.htm (last visited 14 Dec. 2016).
27. *Ibid.*
28. *Ibid.* para. 1.

8.8% to 8.9% of GDP while VAT revenue grew from 6.5% to 6.8% of GDP over the same period.[29]

- The average tax burden in OECD countries continued on an upward trajectory in 2014, growing by 0.2 percentage point to reach 34.4% of GDP, up from just 32.7% in 2009.[30]
- About two-thirds of the reported growth of that tax burden from 2009 through 2014 was the result of increased revenue from VAT and personal incomes and profits, with the majority of the rest of such growth coming from social contributions and property taxes.[31]
- Since 2008, many OECD countries chose to raise tax rates, broaden the tax base, or both. By the end of 2014, the average VAT rate in OECD countries had reached an unprecedented 19.2%, up from 17.7% in 2008. Moreover, during that same period, twenty-two of its thirty-four countries raised their maximum personal income tax rates.[32]
- The average tax-to-GDP ratio was up at the end of 2014, over 2013, in sixteen of the thirty OECD countries for which 2014 data were available and went down in the other fourteen; between 2009 and 2014, however, that ratio had gone up in twenty-two countries, had fallen in only seven countries, and remained unchanged in one country.[33]
- The largest percentage point increases in tax revenues relative to GDP between 2013 and 2014 were observed in Denmark (3.3) and Iceland (2.8). Other countries recording notable increases during the same period were Greece (1.5), Estonia (1.1) and New Zealand (1.0).[34] The largest decreases occurred in Norway (1.4) and the Czech Republic (0.8). Luxembourg and Turkey, for their part, each lost 0.6 percentage points.[35]

Finally, the Communication quoted the OECD's Director of Tax Policy and Administration Centre, Pascal Saint-Amans, to state the most significant and, perhaps, most disconcerting, conclusion to be drawn from the OECD's statistical observations: 'Corporate taxpayers continue finding ways to pay less, while individuals end up footing the bill.' The Communication, thus, essentially summarized the entire situation as one in which individuals, rather than corporations, have borne the brunt of tax increases since the crisis hit in 2008, in the form of increased social contributions, higher value added tax rates, and higher income tax impositions, while simultaneously dealing with high unemployment and wage stagnation.

29. *Ibid.* para. 2.
30. *Ibid.* para. 5.
31. *Ibid.* para. 6.
32. *Ibid.* para. 7.
33. *Ibid.* bullet pt 2.
34. *Ibid.* bullet pt 4.
35. *Ibid.* bullet pt 5.

§15.05 CONCLUSIONS ON JUDICIAL REVIEW OF TAX POLICIES

In light of the foregoing, the author must raise a question about the role of the judiciary in protecting individual taxpayers from an overly burdensome level of taxation on the basis of constitutional principles. In other words, should (or must) the judiciary do more to address the fact that tax increases have been, and continue to be, disproportionally imposed on individual taxpayers, rather than on corporate taxpayers, and that economic reality demonstrates that indirect taxes (e.g., VAT and property taxes) as well as mandatory social contributions, and not just direct taxes, significantly impact an individual taxpayer's ability to pay, arguably requiring them to be taken into account when attempting to determine the constitutionally permissible limits of the overall tax burden on taxpayers? More specifically, should or even must:

- competent judges deviate from their typical exercise of judicial restraint to properly exercise their role as the final protector of both citizens and their fundamental or constitutional rights against state action (e.g., the imposition of an excessive overall tax burden)?
- the judiciary find that constitutional or other relevant principles (e.g., equality before public burdens) demand that there be a certain proportion between tax revenues generated from individual taxpayers and those generated from business or corporate taxpayers?
- those same judges hold that respect for certain basic rights (e.g., the right to have any taxation imposed be directly related to and limited by the taxpayer's actual ability to pay and the right to property) demands that taxpayers retain a certain percentage or share of their revenue to satisfy their consumer needs?

It is certainly true that any relaxation of the level of judicial restraint the various national courts typically exercise with respect to fiscal policies would affect the virtually unfettered ability of sovereign states, represented by governments and legislatures, to determine the nature and amount of the contributions it will demand from its citizenry, as well as from what type of citizen (e.g., individuals, businesses, residents, non-residents) it will demand those contributions in order to fund the particular state's budget, presumably designed according to the state's political priorities and financial resources. Nevertheless, respect for fundamental rights, as enshrined in constitutional principles, such as equality before public charges, can never yield to a woefully misunderstood sovereign power such as the power to tax. To allow that to happen would transform contributions necessary to pay public charges into outright theft in favour of the state's fisc, which is often an insatiable monster.

One could, of course, also criticize judges who give constitutional texts an expansive interpretation, one that their original drafters would never have given them. However, the obvious counterargument must be that, though meant to be basic and permanent rules and principles governing the organization and functioning of the state, constitutional provisions must always be applied, interpreted, and understood in the context of the ever-evolving society they govern: it is highly unlikely that the original authors of 'the rule of equality before the law', which they enshrined in an eighteenth or nineteenth century constitution, would have ever suspected that the text they formulated would, in the twenty-first century, become the death knell for the concept of marriage as applying solely to one man and one woman![36] Similarly, changes in tax policy – in the sense that states continue to impose higher and higher tax burdens on their citizenry – should result in a call on the judiciary to hold that the individual rights already enshrined in the basic texts act as the ultimate limit on states' endless tax increases. The judiciary's failure to do so could (and should) also be seen as its failure to fully assume and exercise its protective role with respect to fundamental rights.

While that is the author's global conclusion as regards the national tax systems, some specific remarks should also be made in this context as regards VAT.

§15.06 THE QUESTION OF JUDICIAL REVIEW WITH RESPECT TO VAT

VAT is a general consumption tax that is economically borne primarily by individuals, as the final consumers, along with certain VAT-exempt economic activities that do not enjoy the right to deduct input VAT.

'Consumption' can be defined in the framework of this subject as the use of goods and services for the satisfaction of personal or collective needs.[37] Of course, the definition of needs can be highly varied, from the most basic of needs, to needs that, while not strictly needed to survive, can be considered normal in contemporary society, to luxurious frivolities that one is hard pressed to classify as ever 'needed' by anyone at all. It is, therefore, more than appropriate to spend some time looking at basic needs by better circumscribing what are considered *vital* human needs: maintaining good health, food, clothing to protect the body from the elements, and a place to live. Maintaining good health relates to both medical services and other goods used for medical and hygienic purposes. Food is all food and beverages suitable for human consumption, except alcohol and other foods definitely considered as luxury goods. Body protection is ensured by garments at large that protect against the weather. The place to live, obviously, means more than just shelter from the elements, it requires decent housing. These *vital* human needs largely correspond to, and are protected by, fundamental rights, particularly the right to life, human dignity, and the right to hold property.

On the other hand, the rules of constitutional order mentioned above – namely, equality before the law and before public charges, and taxation in accordance with one's capacity to pay tax – also apply, in the absence of restrictions on the scope included in the same constitutional texts, with regard to indirect taxes, including VAT.[38] To the extent that the latter is a proportional indirect tax that, based on a specific transaction, ignores the overall ability of the particular taxpayer to pay tax

36. *See, e.g., Catholic Civil Rights League v. Hendricks and LeBoeuf*, 2004 CanLII 20538 (QC CA), 238 DLR (4th) 577; [2004] JQ no 2593; and [2004] RJQ 851. *See also Obergefell v. Hodges*, 576 US __ (2015), found at https://www.supremecourt.gov/opinions/14pdf/14-556_3204.pdf (last visited 20 Mar. 2017).
37. Definition by the *Académie française* (1986), quoted by http://www.la-definition.fr/definition/consommation.
38. Klaus Tipke & Joachim Lang, *Steuerrecht* s. 3, rz. 121 (Roman Seer, et al. eds, 22d ed. 2015).

arising out of his personal income and wealth situation, the first fundamental issue to be addressed when applying the aforementioned constitutional rules to VAT is whether the constitution allows a law to assume the same fiscal capacity with respect to the financial resources required to meet basic needs on all taxpayers when compared with those assigned to other consumption. In other words, the question is whether the VAT law can reasonably apply the same VAT rate to the purchase of food as it applies to a jewellery purchase.

The second fundamental question in this regard is what VAT rate is consistent with the basic right of all persons to allocate their financial resources to cover their basic needs. Or, to formulate the question more crudely, can a State constitutionally increase the cost of food and health services by 25% (by applying VAT at that rate to the purchase thereof) and simply accept that individuals who cannot or will not pay those increased prices may die of starvation, injury or disease?

The author firmly believes that, with respect to the first question, the application of the ability-to-pay tax principle, assuming it rises to the level of a constitutional principle, cannot be ignored in the context of indirect taxation, but that, in so far as VAT is levied on a specific operation and not on a particular taxpayer's global personal situation, the existence and the importance of fiscal capacity with respect to the operations subjected to VAT must be examined at the level of the individual operation and must disregard the situation of the person executing the operation. Indeed, where a law creates a tax based on the taxable objet of certain operations while disregarding the personal situation of the person executing such a taxable operation, the rule of taxation in accordance with the one's ability to pay tax must be applied to the particular object as it is defined by the law itself and, accordingly, to the taxable consumption operation considered alone. So, it must remain irrelevant whether a particular taxpayer, with greater or lesser financial means, undertakes the taxable operation; the only question must be whether said operation, in itself, reveals a greater or lesser capacity to pay tax.

As for the second question, the author believes it is necessary to recognize that the taxpayer's ability to pay tax in relation to an operation intended to satisfy basic needs cannot be assumed to be as high as when concluding a different type of consumer operation that does not involve basic needs. This conclusion calls for either (a) the application of different VAT rates to certain categories of taxable operations and, more precisely, of a reduced rate to consumption operations meant to fulfil basic needs or (b) the application of a unique rate to all operations that takes into account the satisfaction of basic needs. Further, the author is convinced that the state cannot tax vital-needs transactions so as to make them significantly more expensive via the applicable tax measures. Without claiming that there are no indirect taxes that can be applied to consumer transactions related to vital human needs, the author is of the opinion that the maximum appropriate rate ceiling for such transactions should, in any case, remain well below 10% and, rather, oscillate around 5%. This proposal is admittedly not based on a precise constitutional rule or standard, but reflects the view of the author based on the historic evolution of VAT rates, bearing in mind that VAT was introduced in most Member States with reduced rates oscillating between 3% and 10%.[39]

Thus, the author must conclude that a single VAT rate on all consumer transactions is not, and cannot be, consistent with the principle of equality before public burdens or the taxpayers' fundamental rights, unless that single rate does not exceed the ceiling on the VAT rate applied to essential necessities. Attempts to introduce such a single rate based on the argument, particularly made in Germany,[40] that such a reform would reduce the standard rate by several percentage points from the present rate of 19% must, therefore, be rejected based on the incompatibility of such a reform with these basic, constitutional standards.

Moreover, when confronted with the constitutional standards of equality before taxes and of taxation according to the ability to pay tax, Luxembourg's current VAT legislation also suffers from some questionable incongruities:

- While clothing and shoes for children up to 14 years are only subject to the super-reduced VAT rate of just 3%,[41] clothing and footwear for teenagers and adults are subject to Luxembourg's standard 17% VAT rate:[42] is the need to protect the human body against the elements not also applicable to them?
- While the construction or renovation of housing units allocated to primary residential purposes are only subject to the super-reduced 3% VAT rate,[43] the furniture needed to furnish them, including the kitchen cabinets and appliances needed to store and prepare food therein, are subject to the standard 17% rate:[44] does Luxembourg's legislature believe that it is merely sufficient to satisfy its residents' housing needs by giving them a place to sleep, but it does not believe that a bed in which to sleep, or the means to prepare food in the housing unit, are not equally necessary?
- While liquid and natural gas and wood for heating, and the heating systems that use those fuels are subject to a reduced VAT rate of just 8%,[45] liquid and solid fossil fuels, also used for heating, are subject to the intermediate 14% VAT rate:[46] is that a hidden ecological measure that, perhaps, penalizes those who may not have the means to change their existing heating systems?

39. *See* European Commission, *VAT Rates Applied in the Member States of the European Union*, doc. taxud.c.1(2013)69198 - EN, 23.
40. *See, e.g.*, the proposal by Ingrid Arndt-Brauer, President of the Financial commission of the German Parliament, in May 2014, https://www.welt.de/politik/deutschland/article128375721/16-Prozent-Mehrwertsteuer-und-zwar-auf-alles.html.
41. LU: *Loi du 12 février 1979 modifiant et complétant la loi du 5 août 1969 concernant la taxe sur la valeur ajoutée*, Mem. A No. 11, 19 Feb. 1979, as amended, Annex B, pt 6.
42. *Ibid.* Art. 40(2) (as they are not mentioned in any of the annexes to the law, the standard rate applies).
43. *Ibid.* Annex B, pts 21–22.
44. *Ibid.* Art. 40(2) (as they are not mentioned in any of the annexes to the law, the standard rate applies).
45. *Ibid.* Annex A, pt 1.
46. *Ibid.* Annex C, pt 2.

- While building or renovating a primary residence is, as mentioned above, subject to the super-reduced 3% VAT rate,[47] window washing and other private residence cleaning activities are subject to the reduced 8% VAT rate:[48] is it more important to create and renovate homes, but much less important to keep and maintain them in a clean, habitable condition? Or, does the law reflect the belief that residents should clean their own homes, and that a decision to hire someone else to clean one's own home is already a bit of a luxury?
- While hairdressing services are only subject to the reduced 8% VAT rate,[49] other body treatments, including manicures and pedicures, are subject to the standard 17% VAT rate:[50] is a good haircut more essential to the human body than nail care?
- While therapeutic and medical articles are subject to the super-reduced rate of 3%,[51] and even an exemption applies to paramedical services[52] and medical services by public or social establishments,[53] hygienic articles are subject to the standard 17% VAT rate, even though they are just as well related to the basic need of maintaining good health. This issue has been controversially discussed in Luxembourg[54] and several other countries as regards the so-called *tampon tax* (i.e., VAT at the standard rate on the acquisition of tampons, sanitary napkins, and similar products that are indeed basic, unavoidable necessities for women) and has led to amendments to render reduced rates applicable in several countries,[55] but not in Luxembourg. While this pretention is certainly justified, it creates a new discrimination, as there are other
- Basic hygienic necessities that should also benefit from the same tax treatment, such as specific products for persons suffering from certain illnesses affecting their hygiene (e.g., incontinence). In addition, where the argument against the application of the standard VAT rate is that the *tampon tax* entails an overly burdensome tax on essential hygienic necessities on only one-half of the population (represented by women), it can just as validly be argued that maintaining the standard rate of VAT on razors and shaving products for men entails an identically overly burdensome tax on similarly hygienic necessities on the other half of the population represented by men. In general, it can be argued that all basic hygienic products for all the population should benefit from reduced rates, just like medical services and goods.

47. *Ibid.* Annex B, pts 21 & 22.
48. *Ibid.* Annex A, pt 8.
49. *Ibid.* Annex A, pt 6.
50. *Ibid.* Art. 40(2) (as they are not mentioned in any of the annexes to the law, the standard rate applies).
51. *Ibid.* Annex B, pts 3 & 8.
52. *Ibid.* Art. 44(1)(l).
53. *Ibid.* Art. 44(1)(m).
54. *See* LU: Public Petition N° 665 in Favor of a Reduction of VAT on Articles for Female Hygienic Protection, introduced on 5 Sep. 2016 to the *Chambre des Députés*.
55. *E.g.*, in France, since 1 Jan. 2016.

Just these few observations about the vagaries of Luxembourg's VAT-tax legislation inevitably lead to this author's last remark concerning judicial review in VAT matters. VAT is an indirect tax harmonized by the European Union through a number of directives that still allow the Member States a certain amount of flexibility with respect to setting their national rates and applying reduced rates for certain operations. But, when an allegation is made that a VAT rate imposed by the legislature on a certain operation does not comply with the constitutional principles of equality before the law or public charges or of taxation in accordance with a taxpayer's ability to pay, the issue is likely to be submitted to the competent national court to resolve.

If the rate on such an operation flows from the legislature's implementation of imperative VAT directives that establish a minimum base rate, judicial review of the Member State's compliance of that rate as applied to operations implicating fundamental rights is, in reality, judicial review of said VAT directive's compliance with the provisions of the Charter of Fundamental Rights of the European Union. Rather than attempt to answer that underlying question by him- or herself, the national judge should, therefore, submit the question to the Court of Justice of the European Union via a request for preliminary ruling, which would require the CJEU to make a necessary and an interesting contribution to the existing issues surrounding the need to respect individual human rights in the field of taxation.

CHAPTER 16

The Economic Effects of EU Tax Jurisprudence

Rita de la Feria & Clemens Fuest[*]

§16.01 INTRODUCTION

The influence of the CJEU over corporate direct tax matters is both significant and far reaching. Initiated just three decades ago, this influence has been progressively increasing, reaching such an extent where today there is hardly any area of direct taxation which has not been affected. The Court's approach to direct tax matters is founded upon the mandate attributed to the European institutions, by the Treaty of Rome, to establish a European Internal Market.[1] In the absence of harmonizing legislation the Court has taken the lead-role as regards corporate tax matters, consistently determining the incompatibility of discriminatory, or restrictive, national tax measures with free movement provisions. Often neglected, however, is the fact that behind this lead role lays a constitutional mandate to ensure the establishment of a European Internal Market: ensuring free movement is instrumental to increasing the level playing field and to ensuring neutrality within Europe, which in turn is instrumental to achieving a European Internal Market. Indeed, whilst much has been written about the Court's jurisprudence on tax matters, and indeed about free movement, little if anything has been said about the effects which that jurisprudence has had on the

* This chapter was originally published in (2016) 41 EL.Rev, 44. Please note that minor, non-substantive changes have been made to the formatting, numbering, footnote-citation style, and certain spellings to ensure consistency with the other chapters in this volume.

1. Whilst until the Single European Act (OJ L169, 29/07/1987) the term used within the Treaty was 'common market', this term has been progressively substituted since then by 'internal market'; *see* §16.02 below. For the purposes of this paper the term internal market will be used, except where distinction between the two terms is necessary.

ultimate aim of establishing a European Internal Market, and the instrumental objectives of ensuring a level playing field and fiscal neutrality. The fundamental question that has so far been left answered is, whether the CJEU tax jurisprudence does indeed lead to an increased level playing field and neutrality, thus contributing to the establishment of such a market.

The aim of this chapter is to answer this question by undertaking an interdisciplinary analysis. In §16.02, consideration is given to what has been designated here as the constitutional instrumental chain, as originally set up by the EEC Treaty. Particular attention is given to the ultimate constitutional aim of establishing a European Internal Market, and to the Court's option to concentrate upon the instrumental removal of discriminatory measures. It is argued that this approach has created a methodological misgiving whereby the instrument – namely the removal of those measures – has often become confused with the over-arching aim itself. In §16.03 and §16.04 attention shifts towards the CJEU: §16.03 concentrates upon its role within direct corporate taxes; whilst §16.04 focus upon the impact of the Court's decision in *Lankhorst-Hohorst,* regarding the compatibility of thin capitalization with free movement provision, as a case study. It starts by providing the legal background to existing restrictions to intra-group loans in the form of thin capitalization rules, then presenting an economic model that illustrates the possible economic effects of the *Lankhorst-Hohorst* judgment; finally, it considers the actual amendments introduced to thin capitalization rules by Member States following that judgment, thereby establishing what the most likely economic effects of the decision were. The chapter concludes in §16.06 with economic and legal considerations, including as regards the constitutional implications of the results presented.

§16.02 THE EU CONSTITUTIONAL INSTRUMENTAL CHAIN

In April 1951, France, Germany, Italy, and the three Benelux countries signed the Treaty of Paris establishing the European Coal and Steel Community (ECSC),[2] with the aim of creating a common market for coal and steel. Soon after, the foreign ministers of the six member states of the ECSC gathered at Messina to discuss the possibility of extending the ECSC to a general common market. From the Messina Conference emerged an Intergovernmental Committee under Paul-Henri Spaak's chairmanship;[3] which would be responsible for elaborating a proposal for a treaty establishing a common market. The report from the Intergovernmental Committee, which became known as the Spaak Report,[4] was presented and accepted in May 1956. It called for the

2. For an historical analysis, see *The Origins & Development of the European Community* 55–70 (David Weigall & Peter Stirk eds., 1992).
3. *Resolution adopted by the Foreign Ministers of the Member States of the European Coal and Steel Community at the Messina Conference, 1–2 June 1955, in* Weigall & Stirk eds., *supra* n. 2, at 94–97, Doc. 6.1.
4. *Report of the Heads of Delegation to the Ministers of Foreign Affairs*, Brussels, 21 Apr. 1956 [hereinafter the 'Spaak Report']. Although some sought to point to the injustice of this name, see Martin J. Dedman, *The Origins and Development of the European Union 1945–95: A History of European Integration* 99 (1996).

creation of a common market, defined as the result of the fusion of national markets to create a larger unit of production, which would lead to great economic growth:[5]

> *Les protections qui éliminent la concurrence extérieure ont ailleurs pour le progrès de la production et le relèvement du niveau de vie une conséquence particulièrement nocive ; ce sont les facilites et l'incitation qu'elles donnent à l'élimination de la concurrence interne. Dans un marché plus vaste, il n'est plus possible d'organiser le maintien de modes d'exploitation vieillis qui déterminent à la fois des prix élevés et des salaires bas ; cèdes entreprises, au lieu de préserver des positions incunables, sont soumises à une pression permanente pour investir en vue de développer la production, d'améliorer la qualité et de moderniser l'exploitation : il leur faut progresser pour se maintenir.*
>
> *Telle est la raison fondamentale pour laquelle, si souhaitable que puisse apparue en théorie une libération du commerce a échelle mondiale, un véritable marché commun n'est finalement réalisable qu'entre un groupe limite d'États, qu'on souhaitera aussi large que possible.*[6]

Although, the Report foresaw other strands to the development of the common market, achievement of a customs union and free movement of commodities and factors of production were key aspects of the proposal; these are instrumental to the creation of a level playing field and increased neutrality, instrumental too to the creation of the common market, which in turn was instrumental to economic growth.

The Treaty of Rome establishing the European Economic Community (EEC), signed in March 1957, closely followed the ethos of the Report, placing the concept of common market at the centre of the new Community. Its principal aim was to establish a common market, through namely the elimination of customs duties and quantitative restrictions between Member States, the adoption of a common customs tariff, the abolition of obstacles to the free movement of factors of production, and the adoption of common policies on various areas. Figure 16.1 illustrates what has been designated as the EU constitutional instrumental chain proposed by the Spaak Report and set-up by the EEC Treaty.[7]

---

5. Expectation of economic growth was based on economic integration theories, in particular the so-called theory of preferences, or customs union theory. *See* John Pinder, *Enhancing the Community's Economic and Political Capacity: Some Consequences of Completing the Common Market, in 1992: One European Market? A Critical Analysis of the Commission's Internal Market Strategy* 55 (R. Bieber et al. eds., 1988); and Catherine Barnard, *The Substantive Law of the EU – The Four Freedoms* 3–9 (3d ed., 2010). Despite the high level of expectation, there were voices arguing that claims of greater economic growth were unsubstantiated, *see* Raymond Bertrand, *The European Common Market Proposal*, 10 Int'l Org. 559, 573 (1956).
6. Spaak Report, *supra* n. 4, at 14. There is no official version of the Report available in English.
7. The first statement that the Treaties had constitutional character came early in: *Les Verts*, C-294/83, Judgment, EU:C:1986:166, para. 23; *see* Koen Lenaerts, *The Basic Constitutional Charter of a Community Based on the Rule of Law*, and Neil Walker, *Opening or Closure? The Constitutional Intimations of the ECJ*, both *in The Past and Future of EU Law - The Classics of EU Law Revisited on the 50th Anniversary of the Rome Treaty* 295 & 333, respectively (Luis Miguel Poiares Maduro & Loic Azoulai eds., 2010). For a long time, the fact that the European Treaties had constitutional status seemed almost universally accepted. *See* Luis Miguel Poiares Maduro, *We, the Court – The European Court of Justice & the European Economic Constitution* 7–12, bibliography cited therein (1998); and A. von Bogdandy, *Founding Principles of EU Law: A Theoretical and Doctrinal Sketch* 16 Eur. L. J. 95 (2010). This nevertheless seems no longer the case, *see* Gráinne de Burca & Joseph H.H. Weiler, *The Worlds of European Constitutionalism*

Figure 16.1. The EU Constitutional Instrumental Chain

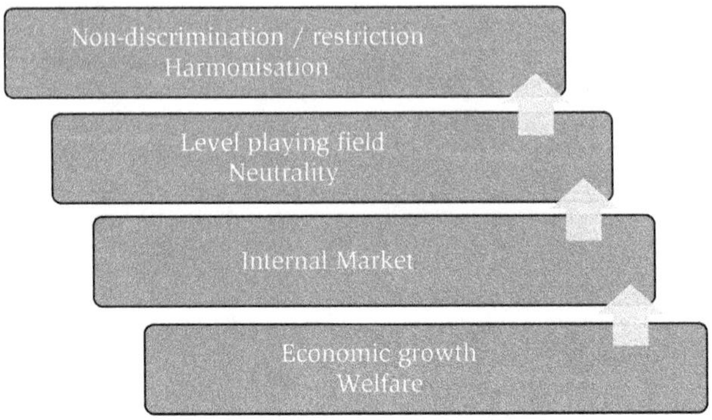

[A] Establishing a European Internal Market

Whilst references to the establishment of a common market as the ultimate aim of the European integration process abounded in the EEC Treaty, it was not always clear what were the boundaries of the concept, *i.e.* what actually constitutes a common market for constitutional purposes. Clarification was provided following the approval of the Single European Act (SEA) in 1987, under which the definition of internal market took centre stage within the European integration process.[8] Particularly significant was the approval then of new rules regarding the Community's internal market competence in what are now Articles 2(1) and (6),[9] and 26(1) of the Treaty on the Functioning of the European Union (TFEU),[10] as well as various other provisions, including crucially what is now Article 114 of the TFEU: a residual provision which confers upon the Union the competence to approve legislative measures with a view to 'the establishment and the functioning of the internal market'.

The impact of these provisions in the European legal system – and more generally on setting the internal market at centre stage of the integration process – is reflected in the contents and scope of the constitutional mandate which they imposed. It is true that in recent times the prevalence of economic aims in the Treaties has been increasingly

(2011); *Philosophical Foundations of European Union Law* (Julie Dickson & Pavlos Eleftheriadis eds., 2012); and Catherine Barnard, *Introduction: The Constitutional Treaty, the Constitutional Debate and the Constitutional Process, in The Fundamentals of EU Law Revisited* 1–12 (Catherine Barnard ed., 2007).

8. OJ L169, 29/07/1987. Whether the terms 'common market' and 'internal market' are actually synonyms or not is a controversial matter. *See* Rita de la Feria, *The EU VAT System and the Internal Market*, 3–6, 29 et seq. (2009).
9. These read: '1. The Union shall establish an internal market. ... 6. The Union shall pursue its objectives by appropriate means commensurate with the competences which are conferred upon it in the Treaties', OJ C83, 30/03/2010, p. 0047-0200.
10. It reads: '1. The Union shall adopt measures with the aim of establishing and ensuring the functioning of the internal market, in accordance with the relevant provisions in the Treaties.'

challenged, with many arguing that the focus has shifted towards social aims,[11] particularly since the entry into force of the Lisbon Treaty.[12] Yet, even those are unlikely to deny the centrality of the internal market remains for the European integration process.

The existence and characteristics of this mandate are made evident through consideration of two specific points: the legal effect of these provisions, in particular Article 26(1) of the TFEU, determines the existence and nature of a constitutional mandate; and the legal definition of internal market, as set out in the same article, determines the contents of that mandate. As regards the first point, namely the legal effect of these provisions, this has been the subject of intense controversy since their introduction by the SEA. The fundamental issue is whether, rather than conferring competence upon the Union as regards the internal market, that Article actually imposes an obligation upon the Union to approve legislation with a view to establishing or improving the functioning of the internal market. The view that Article 26(1) sets out a mere political aim, not capable of creating legal effects, was defended by many commentators,[13] and adopted by several Member States in the famous *Wijsenbeek* case.[14] Nevertheless, the prevailing view is that Article 26 does indeed impose an obligation upon the Union to act.[15] Whilst the Court has not ruled directly on the matter, this interpretation has also been endorsed by Advocate General Cosmas in *Wijsenbeek*. It is argued, therefore, that there is indeed a constitutional mandate, of a compulsory nature, bestowed upon the Union to establish a European Internal Market. Acting upon this obligation, however, presupposes an understanding of what the internal market actually is - and this is far from fully clear.[16]

Within the Treaty, internal market is currently defined in Article 26(2) as 'an area without internal frontiers in which the free movement of goods, persons, services, and capital is ensured in accordance with the provisions of the Treaties'. This definition has remained unchanged since its introduction in the EEC Treaty by the SEA; yet, consistency does not equate certainty, and as the Commission itself has implicitly

11. See A.J. Menéndez, *European Citizenship after* Martínez Sala *and* Baumbast*: Has European Law Become More Human but Less Social,* in Poiares Maduro & Azoulai eds., *supra* n. 7, at 363-393.
12. C. Semmelmann, *The European Union's Economic Constitution under the Lisbon Treaty: Soul-Searching Shifts the Focus to Procedure,* 35 Eur. L. Rev. 516 (2010); and S. Weatherill, *From Economic Rights to Fundamental Rights, in The Protection of Fundamental Rights in the EU After Lisbon* (S. de Vries, U. Bernitz & S. Weatherill eds., 2012).
13. C. Gulmann, *The Single European Act - Some Remarks from a Danish Perspective,* 24 Common Mkt. L. Rev. 31 (1987).
14. *Wisjenbeek,* C-378/97, Judgment, EU:C:1999:439.
15. H.G. Schermers, *The Effect of the Date 31 December 1992,* 28 Common Mkt. L. Rev. 275, 278 (1991); P. Craig, *The Evolution of the Single Market, in The Law of the Single European Market - Unpacking the Premises* 16 (C. Barnard & J. Scott eds., 2002); and F. Schockweiler, *Les Conséquences de l'Expiration du Délai Imparti pour l'Établissement du Marché Intérieur,* 353 Revue du Marché Commun et de l'Union Européenne 882, 884-885 (1991).
16. On the vagueness of the concept, see G. Beck, *The Legal Reasoning of the Court of Justice of the EU,* Ch. 6 (2012).

acknowledged, its interpretation is far from clear.[17] The definition has a dual component: first, 'an area without internal frontiers'; and second, 'in which the free movement of goods, persons, services, and capital is ensured'. The expression 'an area without internal frontiers' has been subject of intense controversy. Severely criticized by some,[18] regarded as the 'key part of the definition' by others,[19] its origins seem to be rooted in the Commission's Internal Market Programme,[20] and placed therein in order to include within the scope of the internal market other aspects, which might not be covered by the Treaty provisions relating to free movement.[21] This would seem to indicate that the scope of 'an area without internal frontiers' is broader than that of free movement. However, the tactic might have worked slightly too well: the expression is potentially so broad that both most commentators and the Court alike, have tended to concentrate on the other aspect of the definition of internal market: the fundamental freedoms.[22] Not that the separate reference to the freedoms in Article 26 TFEU too has been uncontroversial: it too has been target of criticisms,[23] with some concluding that the reference is merely informative and does not merit the qualification as legal definition.[24] Here too, the main difficulty seems to be the lack of precision, *i.e.* when can it be said that goods, persons, services, and capital move freely within the Union?

The CJEU case law as regards the Union's legislative competence on internal market matters has, nevertheless, provided further guidance as regards its concept. In *Titanium Dioxide* the Court stated that 'in order to give effect to the fundamental freedoms in [Article 26 TFEU], harmonising measures are necessary to deal with disparities between the laws of the Member States in areas where such disparities are liable to create or maintain distorted conditions of competition'.[25] The statement, namely the adoption of a perceived wide interpretation of the concept of the internal market, gave rise to intense controversy at the time of its release;[26] and it was said in

17. A.A.M. Schrauwen, Marché Interieur – Recherches sur une Notion, 138, PhD Thesis, University of Amsterdam (1997); and G. de Búrca, *Reappraising Subsidiarity's Significance After Amsterdam, in Harvard Jean Monnet Working Paper Series*, WP 7/99, at 9.
18. P. Pescatore, *Some Critical Remarks on the 'Single European Act'*, 24 Common Mkt. L. Rev. 9, 16 (1987).
19. C.D. Ehlermann, *The Internal Market Following the Single European*, Act, 24 Common Mkt. L. Rev. 361, 364 (1987).
20. European Commission, *Completing the Internal Market – White Paper from the Commission to the European Council*, COM(85) 310, 14 June 1985.
21. Ehlermann, *supra* n. 19, at 366.
22. One of the most significant exceptions to this tendency has been in *Rundfunk and Others*, Joined Cases C-465/00, C-138/01, & C-139/01, Judgment, EU:C:2003:294. For an analysis, see D. Wyatt, *Community Competence to Regulate the Internal Market*, University of Oxford Faculty of Law Legal Studies Research Paper Series, Working Paper No. 9/2007, 2007, at 36–40.
23. P. Verloren van Themaat, *The Contributions to the Establishment of the Internal Market by the Case Law of the Court of Justice of the European Communities, in 1992: One European Market? A Critical Analysis of the Commission's Internal Market Strategy* 115 (R. Bieber, et al. eds., 1988).
24. *See* comments by P. Pescatore in Schrauwen, *supra* n. 17, at 142–143.
25. *Commission* v *Council*, C-300/89, Judgment, EU:C:1991:244, para. 15.
26. Although the reference to distortions to competition was not original, see J. Usher, *Case C-376/98,* Germany *v* European Parliament and Council (tobacco advertising)*: Judgment of the Full Court of 5 Oct. 2000, [2000] ECR I-8419*, 38 Common Mkt. L. Rev. 1519, 1527 et seq.

particular to signal the decline of the principal of conferral of powers.[27] A few years later, in *Tobacco Advertising*, the Court attempted to put those fears to rest by establishing some boundaries to the internal market concept, albeit keeping the elimination of distortions of competition within its scope.[28] It ruled that measures referred to in now Article 114 TFEU must be intended to improve the conditions for the establishment and the functioning of the internal market, and that the Article did not vest in the Union a general power to regulate the internal market;[29] in particular 'the mere finding of disparities between national rules and of finding abstract risk of obstacles to the exercise of fundamental freedoms or of distortion of competition' was insufficient.[30] On the specific aspect of distortions of competition, the Court limited the interpretation adopted in *Titanium Dioxide* by ruling that only where the distortion is 'appreciable' a measure can be adopted on the basis of Article 114 as 'in the absence of such a requirement, the powers of the Community legislature would be practically unlimited'.[31] Essentially, therefore, the existing obstacles to the four freedoms must be *concrete* and existing distortions of competition must be both *concrete* and *appreciable*.[32] In *Tobacco Advertising* these criteria were scattered throughout the judgment - and the Opinion - in a relatively unsystematic fashion, but the Court has moved towards a more consistently expressed formula in *Vodafone*.[33] Nevertheless many have felt that the *Tobacco Advertising* formula - based as it is on troubling imprecise expressions such as 'appreciable' and 'considerable' - has left key questions unanswered,[34] namely what is the scope of harmonization envisaged by the Treaty, or how much harmonization is constitutionally required?[35] In other words, how far does the constitutional mandate go?

27. S. Crosby, *The Single Market and the Rule of Law*, 16 Eur. L. Rev. 451 (1991); and R. Barents, *The Internal Market Unlimited: Some Observations on the Legal Basis of Community Legislation*, 30 Common Mkt. L. Rev. 85 (1993).
28. *Germany* v *Parliament and Council*, C-376/98, Order, EU:C:2000:544.
29. *Ibid.*, at para. 83.
30. *Ibid.* para. 84. D. Wyatt argues that in order for the measure to fall within the scope of Article 95 *obstacles* must be 'actual or potential, direct or indirect', in *Constitutional Significance of the Tobacco Advertising Judgment of the European Court of Justice*, 5 CELS Occasional Paper, 19, 23 (2001).
31. *Germany* v *Parliament and Council*, C-376/98, paras 106–107; *see also Germany* v *Parliament and Council*, C-376/98, AG Opinion, EU:C:2000:324, paras 89–90.
32. The reference to 'distortion of competition' in this ruling was also target of criticism, *see* M. Kumm, *Constitutionalising Subsidiarity in Integrated Markets: The Case of Tobacco Regulation in the European Union*, 12 Eur. L. J. 503, 505, 508–515.
33. *Vodafone and Others*, C-58/08, Judgment, EU:C:2010:321, paras 32–33. *See* S. Weatherill, *The Limits of Legislative Harmonisation Ten Years After* Tobacco Advertising*: How the Court's Case Law Has Become a 'Drafting Guide'*, 12 German L. J. 827 (2011).
34. S. Weatherill, *The Court's Case Law on Internal Market: 'A Circumloquacious Statement of the Result Rather Than a Reason for Arriving at It?', in Judging Europe's Judges – The Legitimacy of the Case Law of the European Court of Justice Examined* (M. Adams et al. eds., 2013).
35. S. Weatherill, *Supply of and Demand for Internal Market Regulation: Strategies, Preferences and Interpretation, in Regulating the Internal Market* 29, 29–38 (N. Nic Shuibhne ed., 2006). The concept of harmonization is itself unclear, *see* P.J. Slot, *Harmonisation*, 21 Eur. L. Rev. 378 (1996); M. Dougan, *Minimum Harmonisation and the Internal Market*, 37 Common Mkt. L. Rev. 853 (2000); and D. Vignes, *The Harmonisation of National Legislation and the EEC*, 15 Eur. L. Rev. 358 (1990).

Whilst answers to these questions are far from obvious, what is clear is that, the ideas of increasing neutrality and establishing a level playing field within Europe are implicit in the elimination of concrete obstacles to free movement and the elimination of concrete and appreciable distortions of competition, either through jurisprudential intervention or through harmonization. In this context, these objectives can be seen as instrumental to the objective of attaining increased neutrality and a level playing field; in the same manner that increased neutrality and a level playing field should be seen as instrumental to the ultimate constitutional objective of establishing a European Internal Market.[36] From a pure legal perspective, the existence of this instrumental chain may appear as terribly unhelpful: neutrality or a level playing field might be as difficult to define as concrete obstacles to free movement and concrete and appreciable distortions to competition. However, not only do these concepts have a specific significance in economic terms,[37] but they can indeed be quantified through economic analysis. Considering that, as has been highlighted above,[38] it is precisely this economic perspective that underlines the constitutional mandate for the establishment of an internal market, it is only reasonable to resort to such analysis as the appropriate method of assessing whether the elimination of obstacles to the freedoms or distortions of competition is indeed increasing neutrality and creating a level playing field, and consequently fulfilling the constitutional mandate that they are meant to address – namely establishing a European Internal Market.[39]

[B] The Methodology: Centralized and Decentralized Models

Having established both the existence and the centrality of a constitutional mandate for the establishment of the European Internal Market, a question arises as to the constitutional method for attaining this ultimate aim. In principle, three ideal constitutional models are possible within the European Economic Constitution:[40] a centralized constitutional model that favours a process of market regulation by the replacement of national laws with EU legislation; a competitive constitutional model, which promotes competition between legal orders, namely through the principle of mutual recognition; and a decentralized constitutional model, where Member States retain regulatory powers, but are prevented from developing protectionist policies by judicial

36. The instrumental nature of the fundamental freedoms to the realization of the internal market has been expressly recognized by the Court in *Commission* v *France*, C-265/95, Judgment, EU:C:1997:595, para. 30; *see also* P. Caro de Sousa, *The European Fundamental Freedoms – A Contextual Approach* 55 et seq. (2015).
37. On the concept of neutrality as applied to tax, see M.P. Devereux, *Taxation of Outbound Direct Investment: Economic Principles and Tax Policy Considerations*, 24 Oxford Rev. Econ. Pol. 698 (2008).
38. *See* §16.02[B], *supra*.
39. Law and economics studies, and in particular the application of economic tools to the analysis of legal rules has been arguably successful in many areas of law, but less so insofar as taxation is concern, *see* A. Raskolnikov, *Accepting the Limits of Tax Law and Economics*, 98 Cornell L. Rev. 529 (2013).
40. Although a specific model has been proposed for tax. *See* T. O'Shea, *EU Regulatory Framework for Tax*, 953 Tax J. 21 (2008).

intervention.[41] In practice, however, these constitutional models are not applied separately, in their pure form, within the Treaties; instead they are in continuous interplay in different policy areas. Leaving aside the competitive model, which relies primarily on the inaction of the European institutions,[42] actions by these institutions operate within both the centralized and decentralized models, either pursuing harmonizing legislation or deeming incompatible with EU law national discriminatory and/or restrictive measures, depending on legal, or perhaps more frequently, political constraints.[43] By substituting different national legislation with a single set of rules, harmonization under the centralized model has many advantages, when compared to the decentralized model, even considering the current trend towards flexibility and differentiation.[44] Yet, harmonization is often unattainable. Legal constraints may apply, such as the respect for subsidiarity or proportionality, but more importantly perhaps in some sensitive areas Member States are reticent to transfer sovereignty, and even where the legislative process is initiated, it is often impossible to reach sufficient political consensus to see legislation approved.

Historically, it was precisely this lack of legislative progress that resulted in the Court adopting a central role in enforcing the decentralized model, deeming national measures that discriminate or restrict the fundamental freedoms incompatible with EU law. This process, which started in the late 1960s with free movement of goods, has developed into a massive body of case law regarding the incompatibility of national measures with the freedoms, on a variety of different topics; and it is no different in tax. Indeed, notwithstanding some nuances resulting from the particular sensitive nature of the area,[45] the rationale that has guided the Court's into adopting this role, as well as the resulting exponential growth in litigation, mirrors broadly what has occurred as regards corporate tax matters.

§16.03 THE ROLE OF THE COURT OF JUSTICE IN DIRECT TAXATION

As opposed to indirect taxation, EU legislation on direct taxation is sparse. At present there are six EU legislative instruments on direct taxes -of rather limited scope[46] - dealing with either specific problems arising from cross-border transactions, or forms

41. Poiares Maduro, *supra* n. 7, at 108–149.
42. *Cf.* N. Reich, *Competition between Legal Orders: A New Paradigm of EC Law?*, 29 Common Mkt. L. Rev. 861 (1992).
43. R. Schuetze, *Limits to the Union's 'Internal Market' Competence(s): Constitutional Comparisons, in* L. Azoulai, *The Question of Competence in the European Union* 215, 223 (2014).
44. These can be understood at macro and micro levels. *See* G. de Búrca, *Differentiation Within the Core: The Case of the Common Market, in Constitutional Change in the EU – From Uniformity to Flexibility?* 133 (G. de Búrca & J. Scott eds., 2000).
45. Namely judicial deference. *See* Beck, *supra* n. 16, at 349 et seq.
46. Leading some to question the extent to which these legislative instruments can indeed be classified as harmonizing legislation, *see* M. Aujean, *Tax Policy in the EU: Between Harmonisation and Coordination*, 16 Transfer: Eur. Rev. Lab. & Res. 11 (2010); expressing a different view, *see* T. O'Shea, *EU Tax Law and Double Tax Conventions* (2008).

of cooperation between Member States' tax authorities.[47] This lack of secondary EU direct tax (harmonizing) legislation can be attributed to various factors, the most significant of which is arguably the lack of specific legal basis for harmonization and the need for unanimity voting,[48] despite attends to introduce one as early as 1962.[49] The limited EU direct tax legislation that does exist has therefore been proposed and approved on the basis of Article 115 TFEU, which together with Article 114 TFEU, constitute the fall-back, residual, legal basis for approval of all legislation deemed necessary for the establishment and the functioning of the internal market, but which as opposed to it requires unanimity voting.

Approving harmonizing legislation within direct taxation still remains on the European policy agenda, with the ongoing discussions over the introduction of a common consolidated corporate tax base (CCCTB) constituting an archetypical example.[50] However, the well-known difficulties in approving direct tax legislation at EU level - and with qualified majority voting in this area remaining a distant dream -created the space for other methods of perceived European integration to be pursued. In the last decade, the European Commission has, to the applause of many, been favouring approval of soft law as a second-best solution;[51] and even more recently, approval of new legislation under the enhanced cooperation procedure.[52] Like in other

47. Council Directive 90/434/EEC of 23 July 1990, OJ L225, 20/8/1990, p. 1–5, known as the 'Merger Directive'; Directive 90/435/EEC of 23 July 1990, OJ L16, 18/01/1997, p. 98–98, known as the 'Parent-Subsidiary Directive'; Council Directive 2003/48/EC of 3 June 2003, OJ L157, 26/06/2003, p. 38–48, known as the 'Savings Directive'; Council Directive 2003/49/EC of 3 June 2003, OJ L 157, 26/06/2003, p. 49–54, known as the 'Interest-Royalties Directive'; Council Directive 76/308/EEC of 15 Mar. 1976, OJ L 306, 30/11/1977, p. 34-34, known as the 'Mutual Assistance Directive for the recovery of taxes'; and Council Directive 77/799/EEC of 19 Dec. 1977, OJ L336, 27/12/1977, p. 15–20, known as the 'Mutual Assistance Directive for the exchange of information'.
48. For additional reasons, see Aujean, *supra* n. 46, and C. HJI Panayi, *European Tax Law: Legislation and Political Initiatives, in Gore-Browne on EU Company Law* Ch. 18, §18-1 (S. Fleet & G. Browne eds., Lexis-Nexis loose-leaf).
49. *The EEC Reports on Tax Harmonisation – The Report of the Fiscal and Financial Committee and the Report of the Sub-Groups A, B and C* (1963), known as the 'Neumark Report'.
50. European Commission, Proposal for a Council Directive on a Common Consolidated Corporate Tax Base (CCCTB), COM(2011) 121/4, 16 Mar. 2011. There is an extensive bibliography on this topic; for a general overview, see C. HJI Panayi, *The Common Consolidated Corporate Tax Base and the UK Tax System*, 2011 Tax L. Rev. Comm. Discussion Paper 9, Institute for Fiscal Studies, Nov. 2011.
51. This approach can be said to have come to the fore in 2001 with the publication of *Tax Policy in the European Union – Priorities for the Years Ahead*, Communication from the Commission to the Council, the European Parliament and the Economic and Social Committee, COM(2001) 260 final, 23 May 2001. On the use of soft law within the tax area, see, e.g., H. Gribnau, *Improving the Legitimacy of Soft Law in EU Tax Law*, 1 Intertax 30 (2007); H.M. van Arendonk, *Fifty Years of European Co-operation and the Tax Policy of the European Commission, in A Vision of Taxes Within and Outside European Borders: Festschrift in honor of Prof. Dr. F. Vanistendael* 1 (L. Hinnekens & P. Hinnekens eds., 2008); H. Gribnau, *The Code of Conduct for Business Taxation: An Evaluation of an EU Soft-Law Instrument*, and P. Pistone, *Soft Tax Law: Steering Legal Pluralism towards International Tax Coordination*, both *in Traditional and Alternative Routes to European Tax Integration*, 67 & 97, respectively (D. Weber ed., 2010). The phenomenon is not exclusive to the tax area, with the usage of soft law exploding since 2000. *See generally* L. Senden, *Soft Law in European Community Law* (2004).
52. European Commission, *Proposal for a Council Directive on Implementing Enhanced Cooperation in the Area of a Financial Transactions Tax*, COM(2013) 71 final, 14 Feb. 2013; F. Fabbrini,

(sensitive) areas, however, it has been the Court that has primarily filled the gap on direct tax through extensive case law.

[A] Applying the Non-discrimination Instrument

Whilst the process of deeming national measures contrary to the fundamental freedoms, and thus incompatible with EU law, is one that started over two decades earlier, its extension to national tax measures is a relatively new phenomenon.[53] The CJEU decision in *Avoir Fiscal* in 1986 might have appeared at the time to be a natural progression,[54] but its impact can be likened to the opening of Pandora's Box,[55] and in the nearly thirty years since case law has gained both momentum and significance.[56] Under the often repeated mantra that 'although direct taxation is a matter for the Member States, they must nevertheless exercise their direct taxation powers consistently with Community law',[57] the CJEU has in essence become the principal source of European corporate tax policy and law.[58] Applying the familiar discrimination and restriction approaches,[59] it has since then consistently intervened to deem corporate

Taxing and Spending in the Eurozone: Legal and Political Challenges Related to the Adoption of the Financial Transactions Tax, 39 Eur. L. Rev. 155 (2014); and J. Englisch et al, *The Financial Transaction Tax Proposal under the Enhanced Cooperation Procedure: Legal and Practical Considerations*, 2 British Tax Rev. 223 (2013).

53. *See* F.C. de Hosson, *On the Controversial Role of the European Court in Corporate Tax Cases*, 34 *Intertax* 294 (2006).
54. As F.C. de Hosson notes, in some Member States legal commentators had assumed as far back as 1960, that the Treaty would have consequences direct national tax rules. *Ibid.* at 297. This was probably as a result of the often forgotten, but influential decision in *Humblet*. *See Jean-E. Humblet* v *Belgium State*, Case 6/60, Judgment, EU:C:1960:48. On the contrary, Member States had been arguing exclusive power in this area and that primary EU law did not apply - the so-called strict sovereignty exception. *See* S. van Thiel, *Free Movement of Persons and Income Tax Law: the European Court in Search of Principles* 21 et seq. (2002); and M. Isenbaert, *EC Law and the Sovereignty of the Member States in Direct Taxation* 193 et seq. (2010).
55. *See Commission* v *France*, Case 270/83, Judgment, EU:C:1986:37; and F. Vanistendael, *Introduction, in EU Freedoms and Taxation* xxv (F. Vanistendael ed., 2006).
56. At present tax cases reportedly constitute approximately 10% of all cases decided by the CJEU. *See* R. Mason, *Made in America for European Tax: The Internal Consistency Test*, 49 B.C. L. Rev. 1277, 1281 (2008). However, the majority of these - close to 7% - concerns VAT. *See* De la Feria, *supra* n. 8, at 259–261. *See also* P. Grenschel & M. Jachtenfuchs, *The Fiscal Anatomy of a Regulatory Polity: Tax Policy and Multilevel Governance in the EU*, 43 Hertie School of Governance Working Paper 1 (2009).
57. *ICI*, C-264/96, Judgment, EU:C:1998:370, para. 19. *See also, e.g.*: *Schumacker*, C-279/93, Judgment, EU:C:1995:31, para. 21; *Wielockx*, C-80/94, Judgment, EU:C:1995:271, para. 16; *Royal Bank of Scotland*, C-311/97, Judgment, EU:C:1999:216, para. 19; *Baars*, C-251/98, Judgment, EU:C:2000:205, para. 17; *Lankhorst-Hohorst*, C-324/00, Judgment, EU:C:2002:749; and *Marks & Spencer*, C-446/03, Judgment, EU:C:2005:763, para. 29.
58. As defended by N. Nic Shuibhne, the Court makes de facto (new) law. *See* N. Nic Shuibhne, *The Coherence of EU Free Movement Law – Constitutional Responsibility and the Court of Justice*, 2 et seq. (2013).
59. On the concepts and their evolution as applied to the tax area, see A. Cordewener, *The Prohibitions of Discrimination and Restriction within the Framework of the Fully Integrated Internal Market* and M. Gammie, *The Compatibility of National Tax Principles with the Single Market*, both *in EU Freedoms and Taxation*, 1 & 105, respectively (F. Vanistendael ed., 2006); and P. Pistone, *The Impact of Community Law on Tax Treaties. Issues and Solutions* (2002).

tax measures to constitute obstacles to the fundamental freedoms, to such an extent that some have argued that national tax sovereignty remains merely a formal façade, having been gradually emptied of all substance.[60] This role has resulted in the Court's jurisprudence as regards direct taxation being commonly designated as 'negative harmonization',[61] a classification which lacks accuracy, however, since as harmonization and the removal of national discriminatory and/or restrictive measures are in essence different constitutional methodologies for attaining the internal market aim.[62]

Away from terminological considerations, however, and whilst certainly progressive,[63] the adoption of such a role by a reticent Court can hardly be said to have been smooth. As that role increased and became more evident, so did criticisms to the Court's approach to corporate tax cases. These range from the very specific – concentrating on particular decisions and on specific cases – to a general disproval of the Court's fundamental decision of applying its traditional free movement jurisprudence to direct tax matters.[64] The main criticisms tend to be the Court's lack of sovereignty or the Court's threat to national tax sovereignty;[65] its lack of awareness of the particularities of tax law when making its decisions;[66] its lack of concern for the potential budgetary implications of its decisions;[67] or controvertibly its under-zealousness when applying the fundamental freedoms to tax matters.[68] Almost all point to the inconsistency and unpredictability of the Court's decisions, with serious consequences for legal certainty. The controversy caused by the tax jurisprudence of the Court is such, and its budgetary consequences so considerable, that at the Intergovernmental Conference which preceded the defunct European Constitution in

60. P. Pistone, *The Impact of ECJ Case Law on National Taxation*, 64 Bull. Int'l Tax'n 412 (2010).
61. *See generally* Wattel & Terra, *supra* n. 64 [*sic*]; and A.J. Martín Jiménez, *Towards Corporate* Tax *Harmonization in the European Community: An Institutional and Procedural Analysis* (1999).
62. See §16.02[B], *supra*. Commenting on the wider role of the Court, M. Poiares Maduro has also characterized it as 'judicial harmonization' (*see* Poiares Maduro, *supra* n. 7, at 68).
63. Not only have [sic] the number of decided cases been growing annually, but also the number of areas of direct taxation under scrutiny, see J. Malherbe et al., *The Impact of the Rulings of the European Court of Justice in the Area of Direct Taxation* iii (Study Commissioned by European Parliament, Policy Department – Economic and Scientific Policy, IP/A/ECON/ST/2007-27, Mar. 2008).
64. S. Kingston, *The Boundaries of Sovereignty: The ECJ's Controversial Role Applying Internal Market Law to Direct Tax Matters*, 9 Cambridge Y.B. Eur. Legal Stud. 287 (2006-2007).
65. D. Weber, *In Search of a (New) Equilibrium Between Tax Sovereignty and the Freedom of Movement Within the EC*, 34 Intertax 585 (2006); and G. Bizioli, *Balancing the Fundamental Freedoms and Tax Sovereignty: Some Thoughts on Recent ECJ Case Law on Direct Taxation*, 3 Eur. Tax'n 133 (2008).
66. J. Avery Jones, *Carry on Discriminating*, 6 British Tax Rev. 525 (1995); D. Williams, Asscher: *The European Court and the Power to Destroy*, 6 EC Tax Rev. 4 (1997); and P.J. Wattel, *Red Herrings in Direct Tax Cases Before the ECJ*, 31 Legal Issues Econ. Integration 81 (2004).
67. O. Thömmes, *Effect of ECJ Decisions on Budgets of EU Member States: EC Law Without Mercy?*, 33 Intertax 560 (2005).
68. G. Kofler & R. Mason, *Double Taxation: A European 'Switch in Time?'*, 14 Colum. J. Eur. L. 63 (2007).

2003 the representatives of some Member States reportedly considered stripping the Court of its jurisdiction over tax cases[69] – and not for the first time.[70]

[B] (Not) Applying the Constitutional Instrumental Chain

Notwithstanding the above, and amidst all the criticism to the Court's role as regards direct taxation, very few, if any, have asked the fundamental, somewhat preliminary, question: is it working? Regardless of any other parallel considerations, the ultimate aim remains that of establishing a European Internal Market as defined in the Treaties – a legal term with economic significance and rationale, namely that of establishing a level playing field and increasing neutrality within the EU.[71] So the key question which must be asked, is whether the tax jurisprudence of the Court of Justice contributing towards that ultimate aim?[72] Some commentators have simply assumed that the Court's rulings are effective steps towards achieving an internal market,[73] without any actual assessment of its overall effects beyond the specificities of each case; others seem to, implicitly,[74] or explicitly,[75] assume that for the Court non-discrimination is in itself the objective. Both assumptions are, however, unjustified. Assuming that the objectives of the internal market are being achieved by the jurisprudence of the Court, without questioning this process, seems rather naïve. On the other hand, and as demonstrated above, from a constitutional perspective non-discrimination is not in itself the objective but rather *an instrument towards achievement of the ultimate objective* of establishing a European Internal Market. The fact that in tax cases the Court often just refers to non-discrimination and the removal of obstacles to the fundamental freedoms is not an impediment to drawing this conclusion – rather it appears to provide an archetypal example of the method being confused with the objective itself. Such

---

69. F. Vanistendael, *The ECJ at the Crossroads: Balancing Tax Sovereignty Against the Imperatives of the Single Market*, 9 Eur. Tax'n 413 (2006).
70. *See* Memorandum presented by the United Kingdom and Germany during the Intergovernmental Conference which preceded the adoption of the Treaty of Amsterdam in 1997. *See also* G.W. Kofler, *Austria, in Towards a Homogeneous EC Direct Tax Law* 59 (C. Brokelind ed., 2007).
71. *See also* Cordewener, *supra* n. 59, at 4.
72. Although some commentators have acknowledged the instrumental and subordinate nature, from a constitutional perspective, of taxation and non-discrimination to the concept of internal market. *See* C. Sacchetto, *ECJ Direct Tax Cases and Domestic Constitutional Principles: An Overview, in Comparative Fiscal Federalism – Comparing the European Court of Justice and the US Supreme Court's Tax Jurisprudence* 1 (R. Avi-Yonah et al. eds., 2007).
73. As J. Malherbe et al. state: 'As to corporate income tax, landmark rulings ... can be seen as significant steps towards the achievement of the Internal Market', *see* Malherbe, *supra* n. 63, at iv.
74. De Hosson, *supra* n. 53, at 297, 302; M. Lang, *Double Taxation and EC Law, in* Avi-Yonah et al. eds., *supra* n. 72, at 11; K. van Raad, *Non-discrimination from the Perspective of the OECD Model and the EC Treaty – Structural and Conceptual Issues, in* Avi-Yonah et al. eds., *supra* n. 72, at 55; and M. Aujean, *The Future of Non-Discrimination – Direct Taxation in Community Law, in* Avi-Yonah et al. eds., *supra* n. 72, at 321. Although criticizing this approach, *see also* R. Mason & M.S. Knoll, *What is Tax Discrimination?*, 121 Yale L.J. 1014 (2012).
75. S. van Thiel, *The Future of the Principle of Non-Discrimination in the EU, in* Avi-Yonah et al. eds., *supra* n. 72, at 331, 344; N. Bammens, *The Principle of Non-Discrimination in International and European Tax Law*, Ch. 13 (2012).

confusion is not only contrary to the constitutional mandate set out in the Treaties, but it can also be traced-back to the source of some of the frustration caused by the CJEU tax jurisprudence.

Notwithstanding the above, in recent years a few authors have proposed a different approach to assess the CJEU jurisprudence on direct taxation, namely by resorting to economic concepts and analysis.[76] Whilst these studies make important contributions, correctly pointing towards the need to consider the economic consequences of the CJEU direct tax jurisprudence, the difficulty is the degree of disregard for the constitutional dimension of the issue. There seems to be a - widespread - assumption that non-discrimination is the focal concept within the Treaties, to be interpreted as an aim in itself, without any formal constitutional connection between it and economic concepts, such as neutrality and level playing field. This is, however, an erroneous assumption. As highlighted above, not only do the Treaties establish a clear connection between non-discrimination - and harmonization - neutrality, a level playing field, and the establishment of an EU Internal Market, but this connection assumes the characteristics of a constitutional mandate. The difference might appear to be inconsequential, but it is in fact fundamental: the Court's interpretation and application of the concept of non-discrimination in a manner which increases neutrality and a level playing field is not optional, it is a constitutional imperative. Applying the concept as an instrument to attain those objectives would not be a jurisprudential construction, but merely a reflection of the respect for that imperative; on the contrary, interpretation and application in a manner that fails to achieve increased neutrality or a level playing field, and therefore does not contribute to the establishment and the functioning of the internal market, is not a prerogative of the Court, and it would be fundamentally contrary to the Treaties.

That this constitutional instrumental chain applies to corporate tax matters is clear. As highlighted above, the Treaty itself establishes the connection between taxation and the aim of establishing an EU Internal Market. Moreover, this connection has been expressly accepted, and indeed consistently invoked by the various European institutions, including the Court. Indeed, whilst there is no universally accepted definition of what an internal market requires in terms of taxation, the need to respect the constitutional instrumental chain has been a continuous presence, either explicitly or implicitly, in European tax initiatives since the Neumark Report, which established a clear connection between harmonization, neutrality and the establishment of a European Internal Market.[77] Equally, and significantly, a large section of the Ruding Report was devoted to investment distortions caused by differences in national corporate tax systems - *i.e.* the establishment of a level playing field in so far as

76. I. Roxan, *Assuring Real Freedom of Movement in EU Direct Taxation*, 63 Modern L. Rev. 831 (2000); M.J. Graetz & A.C. Warren, Jr, *Income Tax Discrimination and the Political and Economic Integration of Europe*, 115 Yale L.J. 1186 (2006); W. Schön, *Tax Competition in Europe - The Legal Perspective*, 9 EC Tax Rev. 90 (2000); Mason & Knoll, *supra* n. 74; and M.J. Graetz & A.C. Warren, Jr, *Income Tax Discrimination: Still Stuck in the Labyrinth of Impossibility*, 121 Yale L.J. 1118 (2012).
77. Martín Jiménez, *supra* n. 61, at 107.

taxation was concerned – with an ultimate view to establishing an internal market.[78] A similar approach was adopted by the European Commission in its 2001 report on company taxation in the internal market.[79]

It is thus argued that from a constitutional perspective achieving non-discrimination within corporate taxation is not enough *per se*. If deeming discriminatory national measures incompatible with EU law is not creating a more level playing field and / or increasing the level of neutrality, then important questions must be raised. First, and from a more formalist perspective, it is questionable whether this jurisprudence can still be regarded as harmonization – albeit negative. Second and more importantly, from a substantive perspective, legitimacy issues and constitutional implications should be considered, namely whether it is legitimate for the Court to intervene by deeming national corporate tax measures incompatible with EU law, under the constitutional mandate of establishing an EU Internal Market, if its decisions are not actually contributing to achieving that aim.

In the next section, we attempt to address these questions through an economic analysis of the Court's tax jurisprudence. For this purpose, we present a cases study which is aimed at assessing the economic effects of the Court's decisions, and in particular on improving the level-playing field and on increasing neutrality.

§16.04 THIN CAPITALIZATION RULES AND THE JUDGMENT IN *LANKHORST-HOHORST*

A company is said to be 'thinly capitalized' when it has a high proportion of debt capital in relation to its equity capital. The significant differences that apply in most countries to the tax treatment of debt on one hand, and equity on the other,[80] have made thin capitalization a popular method of international tax planning, often also designated as profit shifting. As a result, many Member States – although not all – apply anti-thin capitalization rules.[81] For years this divergence in Member States' treatment of thin capitalization had been acknowledged as a potential source of difficulties, not least double taxation. However, the potential incompatibility of these rules with the Treaty

78. Ruding Committee, *Conclusions and Recommendations of the Committee of Independent Experts on Company Taxation, Luxemburg: Commission of the European Communities*, 1992. For comments, see, e.g., M. Devereux, *The Ruding Committee Report: An Economic Assessment*, 13 Fiscal Studies 96 (1992); and A.L. Bovenberg & S. Cnossen, *Company Tax Harmonization in the European Union: Some Further Thoughts on the Ruding Committee Report, in Macroeconomic Dimensions of Public Finance: Essays in Honor of Vito Tanzi* (M.I. Blejer & T. Ter-Minassian eds., 1997).

79. European Commission, *Company Taxation in the Internal Market*, COM(2001) 582 (final), 23 Oct. 2001, at 15.

80. J. Vella, *The Asymmetrical Treatment of Debt and Equity Finance Under UK Tax Law, in Corporate Finance Law: UK and EU Perspectives* (D. Prentice & A. Reisberg eds., 2010); and E. Traversa, *Interest Deductibility and BEPS Action Plan:* Nihil Navi Sub Sole?, 5 British Tax Rev. 607 (2013).

81. For a survey, see A.P Dourado & R. de la Feria, *Thin Capitalization in the Context of the CCCTB*, in M. Lang et al., *Common Consolidated Corporate Tax Base*, 817 (2008).

was left almost untouched until 2004 when the Court issued the judgment in *Lankhorst-Hohorst.*[82]

Lankhorst-Hohorst was not the first ruling to impact on these tax rules - the Netherlands, which until 2003 did not apply a thin capitalization rule, introduced one that year reportedly in response to the CJEU ruling in *Bosal Holding.*[83] It was *Lankhorst-Hohorst*, however, which had the most significant impact. Until 2002, most Member States applying thin capitalization rules - similarly to other OECD countries - limited its scope of application to situations of 'inbound investment', *i.e.* where the lender is a non-resident company. However, the release of the Court's decision in *Lankhorst-Hohorst* that same year fundamentally changed this approach. The Court held in that case that German thin capitalization rules, insofar as they applied exclusively to non-residents, contravened the freedom of establishment, as set out in the Treaties. The decision had an overwhelming impact within the Union has a whole. Following the decision in *Lankhorst-Hohorst* it became clear to many Member States that their own thin capitalization rules would not pass the 'EU test', and would be deemed to be in contravention of EU law, if they were so challenged.[84] They were therefore under the obligation to adapt their domestic rules accordingly.[85]

In order to ensure compatibility with EU law in a post *Lankhorst-Hohorst* world, two avenues of action seemed available to Member States: either to extend the scope of application of thin capitalization rules, in order to include resident companies;[86] or to limit the scope of application of thin capitalization rules, in order to exclude EU resident companies, applying them only to companies resident in third countries.[87] Immediately following *Lankhorst-Hohorst*, a third avenue was suggested, namely that Member States might react simply by dropping thin capitalization rules altogether.[88] This concern, however, never seemed to materialize - indeed quite the opposite, as the overall number of Member States with thin capitalization rules has been increasing since 2002, rather than decreasing. Opting for one of the two other avenues of action, however, was not inconsequential, as Advocate General Geelhoed later acknowledged

82. *Lankhorst-Hohorst*, C-324/00.
83. *Bosal*, C-168/01, Judgment, EU:C:2003:479. *See* M. de Wit & V. Tilanus, *Dutch Thin Capitalisation Rules 'EU Proof'?*, 32 Intertax 187 (2004); and A.C.P Bobeldijk & A.W. Hofman, *Dutch Thin Capitalisation Rules from 2004 Onwards*, 32 Intertax 254 (2004).
84. N. Vinther & E. Werlauff, *The Need for Fresh Thinking about Tax Rules on Thin Capitalization: The Consequences of the Judgment of the ECJ in* Lankhorst-Hohorst, 2 EC Tax Rev. 97 (2003).
85. J. Temple Lang, *Article 10 EC – The Most Important 'General Principle' of Community Law*, and L.W. Gormley, *Some Further Reflections on the Development of General Principles of Law Within Article 10 EC*, both *in General Principles of EC Law in a Process of Development*, 75 & 3013, respectively (U. Bernitz et al. eds., 2008).
86. Although, see O. Thoemmes et al., *Thin Capitalisation Rules and Non-Discrimination Principles – An Analysis of Thin Capitalisation Rules in Light of the Non-Discrimination Principle in the EC Treaty, Double Taxation Treaties and Friendship Treaties*, 32 Intertax 126, 135 (2004); and *The New German Thin Capitalisation Rules: Tax Planning; Incompatibility with European Law*' 32 Intertax 401 (2004); and Vella, *supra* n. 80.
87. *Compare Itelcar*, C-282/12, Judgment, EU:C:2013:629; and R. Jackson, *Application of Portugal's Former Thin Cap Rules to Only Third Countries Violate EU Law, ECJ Says*, Worldwide Tax Daily, 8 Oct. 2013.
88. D. Gutmann & L. Hinnekens, *The* Lankhorst-Hohorst *Case: The ECJ Finds German Thin Capitalization Rules Incompatible with Freedom of Establishment*, 2 EC Tax Rev. 90, 96 (2003).

in the *Thin Cap Group Litigation* case.[89] Indeed, different Member States' reactions have different implications for tax neutrality and level playing field in the EU market. In the following section, an economic model is developed which offers a framework for analysing this impact.

[A] The Economic Effects of *Lankhorst-Hohorst*

In this section, a simple economic model is developed which measures the impact of the *Lankhorst-Hohorst* decision on tax neutrality and level of playing field within the EU market. The model focuses upon the neutrality of taxation for the investment activity of different types of firms. Tax rates as well as tax bases differ across countries, and these differences distort the choice of companies as regards where to invest, as well as the choice of how to invest. Whilst CJEU decisions address specific instances of tax discrimination between domestic and border crossing economic activity, they do not call into question corporate tax rate differences between Member States. In this framework, as the analysis below demonstrates, forcing countries to remove certain types of discrimination between the tax treatment of domestic and border crossing economic activity does not necessarily reduce overall tax distortions in the EU market.

The model assumes a world with three Member States: countries A, B, and C. The supply of savings in the union is fixed and denoted by $\bar{K}$, and capital market integration with the rest of the world is disregarded. There are four groups of firms, two national groups and two multinational groups, as set out in Figure 16.2:

- Groups 1 and 2 are national groups. Group 1 consists of a parent company (P1) and a subsidiary (S1), both located in country A. Group 2 is located in country B, and consists of a parent company (P2) and a subsidiary (S1), both located in B, i.e. it has the same structure as Group 1.
- Groups 3 and 4 are multinational groups. The parent company of group 3 (P3) is located in country A, its subsidiary (S3) is located in country C. The parent company of group 4 (P4) is located in country B, its subsidiary (S4) is also located in country C.

In all four groups, only the parent companies engage in production, whilst the subsidiaries are tasked with financing the investment of their parents. For this purpose, they issue equity in the international capital market and pass on these funds to their parents in the form of an intra-company loan. As such the parent companies will pay interest to their financing subsidiaries; for groups 1 and 2, these interest payments remain within national borders, whereas in groups 3 and 4 this will give rise to intra-firm interest payments from countries A and B to country C. The arrows in Figure 16.2 illustrate the interest payments flow.

89. Test Claimants in the Thin Cap Group Litigation, C-524/04, AG Opinion, EU:C:2006:436, para. 68.

Figure 16.2 Economic Model

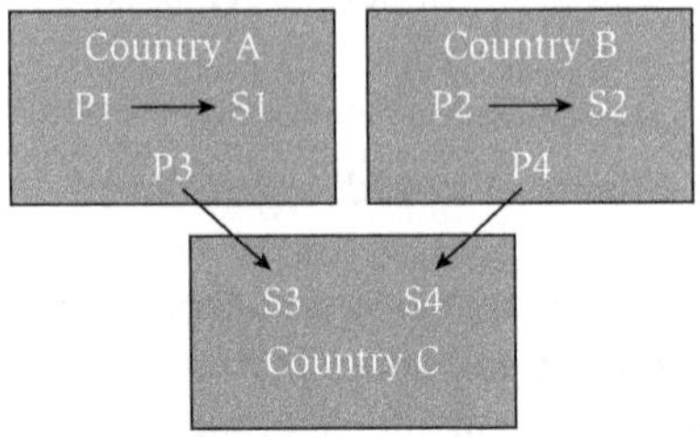

It is assumed that output of parent j (j = P1, P2, P3, P4) is given by the production function $Q_j\ (K_j)$, with $Q'_j\ (K_j) > 0$, $Q''_j(K_j) < 0$, where K_j is the parent's capital stock. For simplicity, we abstract from other production factors like labour, as adding them would complicate the model without changing the results. The goods produced by the parents are sold in the common product market, at a given price, which we assume for simplification purposes to be equal to one. As a result, the profit of group j can be expressed as:

$$P_j = Q_j(K_j) - iK_j - T_j^P + i_jK_j - r_jK_j - T_j^S \qquad (1)$$

On the right hand side of (1), $Q_j\ (K_j)$ is the revenue of the subsidiary, $i_j\ K_j$ is the interest the parent company of group j pays to the subsidiary, T_j^P is the corporate income tax paid by the parent, T_j^S stands for corporate income tax paid by the subsidiary, $r_j\ K_j$ is the after tax return the subsidiary must offer in order to be able to raise funds in the union's capital market. The corporate tax payment of the parent, T_j^P is given by

$$T_j^P = t_j^P(Q_j(K_j) - s_j i_j K_j)$$

where t_j^P is the corporate tax rate of the country where parent j is located and s_j is the share of interest payments which can be deducted from the corporate tax base. The corporate tax payment of the of group j, T_j^S , is given by

$$T_j^S = t_j^S i_j K_j$$

where t_j^S is the corporate tax rate of the country where the subsidiary resides.

In order to focus on the impact of international tax differences on the cost of capital of different groups, we assume that, in the absence of taxes, all groups would face the same cost of capital. This implies that the interest rate on intra group interest payments, i, as well as the non-tax refinancing cost of the different parent companies, r, are the same for all groups.

Given this, we can express (1) as

$$P_j = Q_j(K_j) - iK_j - t_j^P(Q_j(K_j) - s_j iK_j) + iK_j - rK_j - t_j^S iK_j \qquad (2)$$

All groups choose the profit maximizing investment levels for their subsidiaries. Formally, the profit-maximizing capital stock of subsidiary j is derived by maximizing the right-hand side of (2). The result can be expressed as:

$$Q'_j\ (K_j) = C_j \tag{3}$$

with

$$C_j = \frac{1}{(1 - t_j^P)}(r + i(t_j^S - t_j^P s_j)) \tag{4}$$

where C_j is the capital cost of group j. The capital cost $_{Cj}$ is the return the group must generate to pay taxes and the after-tax return required by investors.

Taxes paid by any individual group depend on both the location of the parent company, and that of the subsidiary. If two parent companies are located in different jurisdictions, or if their subsidiaries are located in different countries, their cost of capital may differ due to tax differences across jurisdictions. Other things equal, parent companies with low capital costs will invest more and vice versa. It is important to emphasize that *the model is deliberately constructed so that differences in capital costs across groups can only be caused by differences in taxes*, and all non-tax factors affecting the cost of capital are assumed to be equal. Where there are such differences, there is no level playing field in taxation, and as a result the allocation of capital in the EU market in the model is distorted. The larger the tax differences, the larger the economic distortions caused by the tax system.

In the model differences in the cost of capital between groups can be caused by differences in the relevant tax parameters t_j^P s_j and t_j^S . Equation (4) shows that the cost of capital is higher, the higher the tax rates faced by the subsidiary, t_j^S , and the smaller the share of interest costs which can be deducted from the parent's tax base, s_j. The impact of the parent's tax rate, t_j^P , is slightly more complicated: in most cases, an increase in this tax rate will also increase the cost of capital; the opposite may occur only in special cases, and focus will thus be upon situations where such anomalies are excluded.

Six different tax regimes are considered. A tax regime is a combination of corporate income tax policies (t_j^S, s_j, t_j^P), j = S1, S2, S3, S4. Tax rates are the same in all regimes, and only the tax deductibility of interest payments differs. Therefore, each regime can be characterized by referring only to the values of the interest deductibility parameters of the four subsidiaries: s_1, s_2, s_3, s_4.

The regime representing the situation before the decision in *Lankhorst-Hohorst* is referred to as the benchmark regime. In this regime, it is assumed that countries A and B both restrict the deductibility of border crossing interest payments, but not of interest payments between domestic firms. In the model this is expressed as: $s_1 = s_2 = 1$, s_3, $s_4 < 1$, The impact of the Court's decision is measured by comparing the benchmark situation to different possible scenarios of how the Member States may react to it. Within the framework of the model, countries A and B essentially have two options to comply with the Court's judgment: they may either abolish all restrictions on interest deductibility, or they may extend the restriction to interest payments between domestic firms. Since there are two countries in our model and two possible reactions of national tax policy to the CJEU ruling, we have to consider four possible scenarios:

- The first two scenarios, represented by tax Regimes 2 and 3, involve symmetric reactions by the two countries: either both countries abolish restrictions on deductibility, or they both extend the restrictions to domestic payments.
- The other two scenarios, represented by Regimes 4 and 5, involve asymmetric reactions.

Finally, a scenario where Member States do not comply with the Court's judgment is considered. In these cases, Member States take the risk that national rules, potentially incompatible with EU law, will not be subject of future action from the EU institutions. This risk-taking approach is largely facilitated by the fact that whether or not a specific domestic tax rule is attacked for its incompatibility with EU law is a relatively random and unsystematic approach, dependent on either a case being litigated in the national courts and then being referred to the CJEU, or on the Commission launching infringement proceedings – none of which is a reliable occurrence.[90] It is also true, however, that once the case arrives to the Court, Member States rarely obtain the best possible outcome, and that traditionally odds against victory are considerable.[91]

We account for the above scenario by assuming that there is a Regime 6 where firms face legal uncertainty about tax rules which will ultimately apply. In this regime, the tax rules of the benchmark scenario will continue to apply with some probability denoted by q, with $0 < q < 1$. With probability (1-q), but the restriction of interest deductibility will eventually be deemed incompatible with EU law. In order to avoid multiplying the number of scenarios under consideration, we only consider the case where country A (the country with the higher tax rate) does not comply, whilst country B complies by abolishing border crossing interest deductibility. In this case, the formula for the (expected value of) the cost of capital is given by

$$C_j^{R6} = \frac{1}{\left(1-t_j^P\right)}(r + i(t_j^S - t_j^P[qs_j^{R1} + (1-q)qs_j^{RR}]) \qquad (5)$$

where s_j^{R1} is the interest deduction in the benchmark regime and s_j^{RR} is the interest deduction which applies in country j after all non-complying countries have been forced to comply. The 6 tax regimes are summarized in Table 16.1.

90. C. HIJ Panayi, *Reverse Subsidiarity and EU Tax Law: Can Member States be Left to Their Own Devices?*, 3 *British Tax Rev.* 261, 297 et seq. (2010).
91. P. Genschel et al., *Accelerating Downhill: How the EU Shapes Corporate Tax Competition in the Single Market*, 49 J. Common Mkt. Stud. 585 (2011).

Table 16.1 Tax Regimes and Restrictions on Interest Deductibility

	COUNTRY A		COUNTRY B	
	National Interest Payments	**Border-Crossing Interest Payments**	**National Interest Payments**	**Border-Crossing Interest Payments**
Regime 1 (Benchmark)	$s_1 = 1$	$s_3 < 1$	$s_2 = 1$	$s_4 < 1$
Regime 2 (Symmetric)	$s_1 = 1$	$s_3 = 1$	$s_2 = 1$	$s_4 = 1$
Regime 3 (Symmetric)	$s_1 < 1$	$s_3 = s_1 < 1$	$s_2 < 1$	$s_4 = s_2 < 1$
Regime 4 (Asymmetric)	$s_1 = 1$	$s_3 = s_1 = 1$	$s_2 < 1$	$s_4 = s_2 < 1$
Regime 5 (Asymmetric)	$s_1 < 1$	$s_3 = s_1 < 1$	$s_2 = 1$	$s_4 = 1$
Regime 6 (Asymmetric)	$s_1 = 1$	s_3 *uncertain*	$s_2 = 1$	$s_4 = 1$

What are the implications of these different regimes for tax distortions and economic welfare for the Union? In order to better compare the possible regimes, a simple numerical version of the model is used. Firstly, it is assumed in the model that the marginal utility of public funds, which we denote by the variable η, is higher than the marginal utility of private funds. To further simplify, it is assumed that the marginal utility of public funds is equal to 1.1 in all countries, whereas the marginal utility of private funds is equal to unity. In addition, we assume that the production function takes the quadratic form $Q_j(K_j) = \alpha_j K_j - \beta_j K_j^2$. The parameter values are given in Table 16.2.

Table 16.2 Parameter Values

Base Model	Numerical Model (Base Case)
α_j	1
β_j	0.04
t_A	0.4
t_B	0.15
t_C	0.3
η	1.1
q	0.1
$\bar{K}$	40

This numerical model allows the calculation of capital costs, investment levels, tax revenues, and overall production for each of the tax regimes under consideration.

It should be kept in mind, however, that the parameters used are not estimates of what the true parameters might be, but rather an example to illustrate the underlying theoretical model.

The capital costs of the different subsidiaries in the model is considered first: if all subsidiaries in the model faced the same capital costs, there would be no tax distortions within the EU market; however, as a result of tax rates differences across countries, capital costs will differ both before the CJEU judgment in *Lankhorst-Hohorst* - Benchmark Regime - and after the judgment. Figure 16.3 gives an overview over the capital costs of the individual subsidiaries in each of the six tax regimes, so as to assess whether the decision increased, or decreases, variations of capital costs caused by taxation.

Figure 16.3 Capital Costs of the Subsidiaries in the Different Tax Regimes

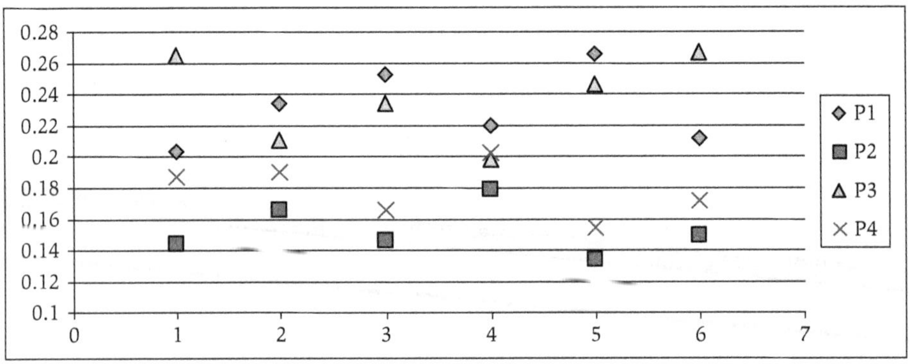

As shown in Figure 16.4, moving from the Benchmark Regime to Regime 2 - where countries A and B abolish the restrictions on the deductibility of border crossing interest payments - results in differences in capital costs declining. The CJEU ruling had therefore the presumably intended effect, *i.e.* a move towards a more level playing field in corporate taxation. Figure 16.5 summarizes the impact on overall production. Comparing the Benchmark Regime and Regime 2 again shows that the impact is positive: the move also increases production.

Figure 16.4 Variance of Capital Costs in the Different Tax Regimes

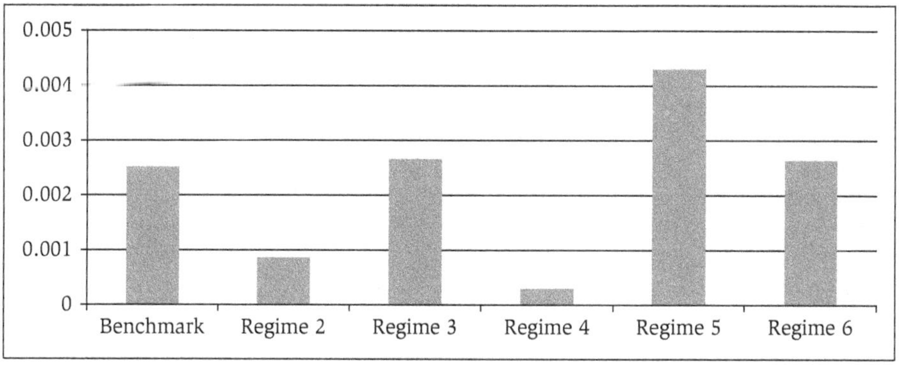

Figure 16.5 Overall Production Levels in the Different Tax Regimes

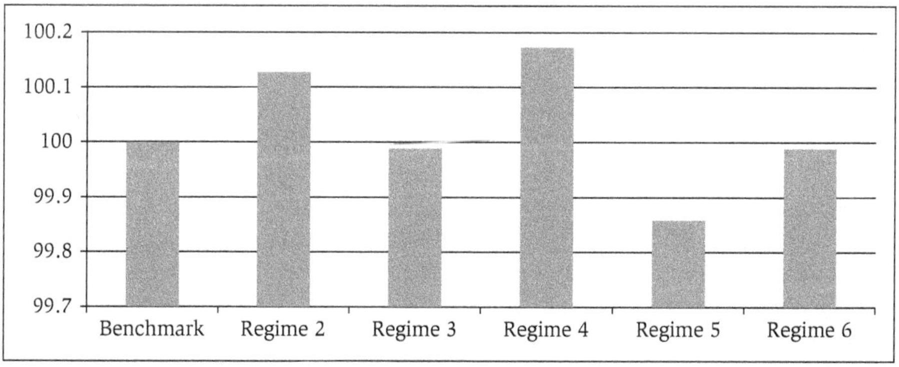

Member States may, however, react to the Court's decision not by moving to Regime 2, but to one of the other five tax regimes. Regime 3 is a regime where the Member States react symmetrically and abolish interest deductibility for both national and border crossing payments. Figure 16.4 shows that, perhaps surprisingly, despite effective harmonization of rules, this reaction increases capital costs' differences. This happens because tax rate differences have a larger impact where tax bases are broadened, as is the case when the deductibility of interest payments is restricted - a example of the theory of the second best, which shows that in the presence of various distortions, it cannot be assumed that reduction of one of these will always have an increased welfare impact.[92] Here, production also declines. This result is perhaps less intuitive, and demonstrates that whilst symmetric reactions by Member States imply elimination of discrepancies between national tax legislation, it does not necessarily bring the EU closer to an Internal Market.

92. *See* R.G. Lipsey & K. Lancaster, *The General Theory of Second Best*, 24 Rev. Econ. Stud. 11 (1956).

Regimes 4 and 5 are considered next. Regime 4 has positive effects: differences in capital costs decline, and production and welfare increase relative to the benchmark scenario. This result can be easily explained: the low tax country broadens its tax base, whereas the high tax country narrows the base, which in turn leads to a convergence of effective tax burdens. The existing asymmetry in tax rates is therefore mitigated by another, diametrically opposed, asymmetry in the tax base. The high tax country (country A) compensates firms for the higher tax rates by offering a full deductibility of interest payments; whereas the low tax country (country B) goes along with limited interest deductibility. In Regime 5 the opposite happens. If the country with higher tax rate reacts to the decision by extending the restriction on interest deductibility to purely national tax payments, whereas the low tax country abolishes all restrictions, the effective tax burdens in these countries drift further apart. As a result, overall production in the Union declines.

Finally, Regime 6 is a scenario where the low tax country allows for full interest deductibility both nationally and across borders; whilst the high tax country also allows for full domestic deductibility, but restricts border-crossing deductibility. There is some probability, however, that such a discrimination will be deemed incompatible with EU law in a future judgment of the CJEU, so that full deductibility is granted for border-crossing payments as well. In this regime, we have two countervailing effects on tax distortions: the extension by low tax country of full deductibility to border crossing interest payments increases the differences in effective tax burdens between the two countries, when compared to the Benchmark Regime; the fact that there is some probably that the high tax country will also have to grant deductibility tends to reduce the tax gap. It is noteworthy that, an extension of interest deductibility in the high tax country leads to a stronger reduction in effective tax burdens, than the same increase in deductibility in the low tax country, since the higher the tax rate, the higher value of deductions. Here the probability that a future CJEU decision will enforce deductibility of border crossing interest payments is assumed to be only 10 per cent, thus tax burdens drift further apart. Nevertheless, if a higher probability of CJEU intervention is assumed, the result may change and effective tax burdens may converge, depending on the Regime that is then put in place.

To summaries, the numerical version of the economic model shows that the impact of CJEU judgments on tax distortions and, hence, on the efficiency of the capital allocation in the EU market depends upon the way in which Member States react to decisions. Depending on those reactions tax distortions may increase; this happens in particular where high tax countries react by extending restrictions on interest deductibility to national payments, whilst low tax countries reacts by extending full deductibility to border crossing payments as well. These theoretical results can now be confronted with the observed reactions of Member States to *Lankhorst-Hohorst*.

[B] Member States' Reactions to *Lankhorst-Hohorst*

Whether the implicit aim of the CJEU in *Lankhorst-Hohorst* – by determining that thin capitalization rules contravened EU law insofar as they applied to EU residents – was essentially to put all debt investment within Europe on an equal position insofar as tax restrictions were concerned, *i.e.* to level the playing field, or merely to abolish discrimination, is unclear.[93] What is clear however is that, as a result of Member States' reaction to the decision, non-discrimination in itself might have been achieved, but a level playing field and increased neutrality was not.

First, it is relevant to note that approval of amendments in order to bring national tax legislation in line with Court's judgments is far from automatic.[94] Levels of compliance vary across Member States, and depend on the specific decision: some Member States have a better track record of compliance than others,[95] and certain decisions result in higher levels of compliance than others.[96] Moreover, even where compliance takes place, implementation can vary greatly amongst Member States - for numerous reasons, including ignorance and lack of awareness on the part of domestic legislators, budgetary concerns, unclearness of the judgments themselves, and even cultural differences. It is unsurprising therefore that the reaction to *Lankhorst-Hohorst* was far from uniform. Some Member States, such as Spain and Portugal, restricted their thin capitalization rules, removing intra-EU situations from their scope; others, such as Germany and Denmark, extended the scope of thin capitalization rules to apply to purely domestic situations. Table 16.3 summarizes the territorial scope of application of these rules - or rules to the same effect - before and after the decision in *Lankhorst-Hohorst*.

Table 16.3 National Reactions to Lankhorst-Hohorst

	SCOPE OF APPLICATION OF THIN CAPITALIZATION RULES (X= thin capitalization rule applies; – = no thin capitalization rule applies)					
	BEFORE RULING			**AFTER RULING**		
	NATIONAL	**EU MEMBER STATES**	**THIRD COUNTRIES**	**NATIONAL**	**EU MEMBER STATES**	**THIRD COUNTRIES**
AUSTRIA	–	–	–	–	–	–
BELGIUM	–	X	X	–	–	X
BULGARIA				X	X	X
CYPRUS	–	–	–	–	–	–
CZECH REPUBLIC				X	X	X
DENMARK	–	X	X	X	X	X

93. *See* §16.03[B] *supra*.
94. A phenomenon that has been designated as 'reverse subsidiarity', *see* Panayi, *supra* n. 90.
95. De Hosson, *supra* n. 53 above, at 299; and M. Wathelet, *Direct Taxation and EU Law: Integration and Desintegration*, 13 EC Tax Rev. 2, 3 (2004).
96. *See generally* P. Farmer & A. Zalasinski, *General Report, in Direct Tax Rules and the EU Fundamental Freedoms: Origin and Scope of the Problem; National and Community Responses and Solutions* (X.L. Xehopoulos ed., 2006); Brokelind, *supra* n. 70, including country reports therein; and Panayi, *supra* n. 90.

	SCOPE OF APPLICATION OF THIN CAPITALIZATION RULES (X = thin capitalization rule applies; – = no thin capitalization rule applies)					
	BEFORE RULING			AFTER RULING		
	NATIONAL	EU MEMBER STATES	THIRD COUNTRIES	NATIONAL	EU MEMBER STATES	THIRD COUNTRIES
ESTONIA	–	–	–	–	–	–
FINLAND	–	–	–	–	–	–
FRANCE	–	X	X	X	X	X
GERMANY	–	X	X	X	X	X
GREECE	–	–	–	X	X	X
HUNGARY				X	X	X
IRELAND	–	X	X	–	–	X
ITALY	–	X	X	X	X	X
LATVIA	–	–	–	–	–	X
LITHUANIA	–	–	–	X	X	X
LUXEMBOURG	X	X	X	X	X	X
MALTA	–	–	–	–	–	–
NETHERLANDS	–	–	–	X	X	X
POLAND	–	X	X	X	X	X
PORTUGAL	–	X	X	–	–	X
ROMANIA				X	X	X
SLOVAK REPUBLIC				–	–	–
SLOVENIA				X	X	X
SPAIN	–	X	X	–	–	X
SWEDEN	–	–	–	–	–	–
UNITED KINGDOM[97]	–	X	X	X	X	X

Empirical consideration of amendments introduced by Member States indicates therefore that it is Regime 5 which has prevailed. Not only did Member States react asymmetrically, *i.e.* some opted to extend the scope of their thin capitalization rules, whilst others opted to restrict them; but it was those Member States which apply higher rates of corporate tax that tended towards widening the scope of their thin capitalization rules, whereas those Member States which apply lower rates of corporate tax

97. For an analysis of the UK regime implemented after *Lankhorst-Hohorst*, see F. Dickison, *Are the UK Thin Capitalization Rules Compliant with EU Law?*, 11 Eur. Tax'n 11 487 (2011); and S. Mahalighem, *UK Thin Capitalisation: Is It Time to Eradicate Domestic (UK-UK) Legislation?*, 2 British Tax Rev. 135 (2012).

tended to limit the scope of their thin capitalization rules, excluding intra-EU situations from their scope. The asymmetry of Member States' reaction to *Lankhorst-Hohorst* is hardly surprising; and unsurprising too are its negative economic effects.

Yet this is not an isolated case, and policy choices taken by Member States following *Lankhorst-Hohorst*, mimic those following many others decisions. It is often said that when faced with the requirement to change their national tax legislations as a result of a judgment of the CJEU, Member States tend to extend application of rules limiting taxpayers' rights in cross-border situations to domestic cases, rather than to abolish them for intra-EU cases.[98] The reaction of Member States to *Lankhorst-Hohorst* seems to empirically confirm this assertion - whilst the reaction was asymmetrical, most Member States preferred to extend the scope of application of their thin capitalization rules to domestic situations, rather than to exclude EU situations from their scope.

This empirical reality, coupled with the theoretical results presented above, rises concerns as regards the fulfilment of the EU constitutional mandate of establishing a European Internal Market.

§16.05 IMPLICATIONS OF BREAKING THE CONSTITUTIONAL INSTRUMENTAL CHAIN

From the analysis undertaken in the two preceding sections it is clear that the approach of the CJEU of deeming incompatible with EU national tax provisions, which are either discriminatory and/ or impose restrictions on the fundamental freedoms, does not necessarily increase neutrality or lead to a more level playing field, *i.e.* it does not reduce overall tax distortions in the European Internal Market. This is particularly likely in those cases where, as a reaction to CJEU decisions, countries with high tax rates extend restrictive tax rules from border crossing to purely national economic transactions, whilst low tax countries extend a more generous treatment of national economic activity to border crossing transactions. Empirically, this has been shown to be precisely the pattern of reactions by Member States to *Lankhorst-Hohorst*.

What is the significance of these results for assessing the Court's jurisprudence on corporate taxation? From a terminological perspective, it is difficult to perceive how this jurisprudence can still be regarded as negative harmonization. Despite the terminological inaccuracy highlighted above, the expression may nevertheless have been regarded as legitimate insofar as the Court's jurisprudence led to increased neutrality and/or the establishment of a level playing field within Europe. Yet, this not being the case, the use of such classification loses any potential legitimacy. More importantly, from a substantive perspective, these results have significant constitutional implications, which in turn raise legitimacy issues. If the approach being adopted by the Court as regards corporate taxation has not led to an increase in neutrality and a more level playing field across Member States, then it does not contribute to the

98. *See* Farmer & Zalasinski, *supra* n. 96.

ultimate aim of establishing an EU Internal Market, and the constitutional instrumental chain is broken.

Figure 16.6 Broken Constitutional Instrumental Chain

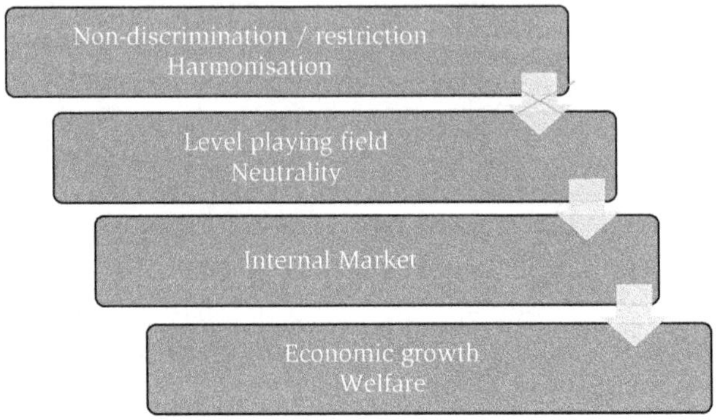

It is true that the breaking of the constitutional instrumental chain cannot be regarded solely as a direct consequence of the Court's approach, rather as a consequence of the Member States' reaction to the Court's approach. In that context, it could be argued that it is the Member States' response that breaks the chain, rather than the Court's decisions. Yet, the unique institutional framework of the EU means the Member States' reactions to Court's decisions are crucial to the European project. By nature, judicial decisions are applicable to a specific set of circumstances, or to specific national provisions. The normativity of CJEU decisions is a long-debated topic, but their practical consequences are widely accepted: the Court does not consider itself bound by previous decisions, although departure is rare.[99] This lack of binding effect means that, for impact to be felt across the EU, the Court – aided by the European Commission through the latent threat of future infringement procedures – must rely on the deterrent effect of its decisions to increase the effectiveness of EU law; the Court *de facto* relies on the reaction of Member States', other than those parties to the litigation. As such, national responses to Court's decisions are an essential element for its fulfilment of the constitutional (instrumental) aim of establishing an internal market.

In that context, concluding that the constitutional instrumental chain has been broken has inescapable implications. The role adopted by the Court insofar as corporate taxation is concerned should be considered in the context of the ongoing discussion since the 1980s over the legitimacy and constitutionality of what has been designated as the Court's judicial activism.[100] This activism is often said by critics to result in either an assumption of competences by the EU vis-à-vis the Member States –

99. M. Jacob, *Precedents and Case-based Reasoning in the European Court of Justice*, 243 et seq. (2014); and Beck, *supra* n. 16, at 234 et seq.
100. As first used by H. Rasmussen, *On the Law and Policy in the European Court of Justice* (1986); and used widely since, albeit criticized by some. *See* T. Tridimas, *The Court of Justice and Judicial Activism*, 21 Eur. L. Rev. 199 (1996).

so-called "competence creep" - or,[101] an assumption of powers which goes beyond the Court's judicial function and can be characterized as the adoption of a quasi-legislative role. These two supposed manifestations of the judicial or excessive activism phenomenon are interconnected insofar as they are both a matter of procedural legitimacy as opposed to substantive legitimacy,[102] but they are not identical: the first it is matter of vertical competence and concerns the question of whether the Court's actions are *ultra vires, i.e.* whether it has competence under the Treaties to act on a specific matter; the second is matter of horizontal competence and whether its actions respect the rule of law and the principle of separation of powers, *i.e.* whether the Court as a judicial body is usurping powers which should instead only be exercised by the EU's legislative bodies.[103] Insofar as corporate taxation is concerned the Court's role and its economic effects as set out above, may potentially raise concerns over both these aspects.

Giving the effects of the Court's decisions insofar as corporate taxation is concerned, it may be questioned whether the Court is acting *ultra vires*; namely whether it has transgressed the limits of its competence by interpreting the Treaty provisions in a way which has the effect of undermining the establishment of the internal market.[104] Whilst the extreme seriousness of such a claim, deems it unlikely in this case, the argument has nevertheless been made by national governments - and rejected by the Court - in cases involving other areas of law.[105]

Insofar as the respect for the rule of law and the principle of separation of powers is concerned, the debate over the Court's judicial activism has now spanned three decades,[106] and there is no intension of revisiting it here. Given the above results,

101. *See, in particular,* S. Weatherill, *Competence Creep and Competence Control,* 25 *Y.B. Eur. L.* 1 (2004); M.A. Pollack, *Creeping Competence: The Expanding Agenda of the European Community,* 14 J. Pub. Pol. 95 (1994); and A. Prechal, *Competence Creep and General Principles of Law,* 3 Rev. Eur. Admin. L. 5 (2010).
102. For a distinction between these two types of legitimacy, see Adams et al. eds., *supra* n. 34.
103. A.G. Toth, *Vertical and Horizontal Distribution of Competences in the European Union,* 2 ERA-Forum 134 (2002).
104. There is an extensive literature on *ultra vires* action by the Court in the context of national constitutional courts review of CJEU judgments. *See* P. Craig, *The ECJ and* Ultra Vires *Action: A Conceptual Analysis,* 48 Common Mkt. L. Rev. 395 (2011); M. Kumm, *Who is the Final Arbiter of Constitutionality in Europe?: Three Conceptions of the Relationship Between the German Federal Constitutional Court and the European Court of Justice,* 36 Common Mkt. L. Rev. 351 (1999); K. Høegh, *The Danish Maastricht Judgment,* 24 Eur. L. Rev. 80 (1999); A. Arnull, *The European Union and its Court of Justice,* 255–266 (2d ed., 2006); D. Doukas, *The Verdict of the German Federal Constitutional Court on the Lisbon Treaty: Not Guilty, but Don't Do It Again!,* 34 Eur. L. Rev. 866. (2009); D. Thym, *In the Name of Sovereign Statehood: A Critical Introduction to the Lisbon Judgment of the German Constitutional Court,* 46 Common Mkt. L. Rev. 1795 (2009); I. Pernice, Costa *v* ENEL *and* Simmenthal*: Primacy of European Law, in* Poiares Maduro & Azoulai eds., *supra* n. 7, Pt. II, Ch. 2, 47, 54–57; A. Pliakos & G. Anagnostares, *Who is the Ultimate Arbiter? The Battle Over Judicial Supremacy in EU Law,* 36 Eur. L. Rev. 36, 109 (2011); and M. Payadeh, *Constitutional Review of EU Law After Honeywell: Contextualizing the Relationship Between the German Constitutional Court and the EU Court of Justice,* 48 Common Mkt. L. Rev. 9 (2011).
105. *Commission* v *Germany,* C-518/07, Judgment, EU:C:2010:125, known as the *Data Protection Supervisory Authorities* case; and *Kücükdeveci,* C-555/07, Judgment, EU:C:2010:21, following on the controversial decision in *Mangold,* C-144/04, Judgment, EU:C:2005:709.
106. For a critical view of the Court, see, e.g., H. Rasmussen, *Between Self-Restraint and Activism: A Judicial Policy for the European Court,* 13 Eur. L. Rev. 28 (1988); P. O'Neill, *The European*

however, and regardless of which side one takes on that debate, it is nevertheless pertinent to reflect upon the quasi-legislative role adopted by the CJEU insofar as corporate taxation is concerned. In particular, it should be considered whether adopting such a role is all the more questionable where the ethos underlying it – namely the aim of achieving an EU Internal Market – is not actually being accomplished through the adoption of that same role.

Indeed, whilst analyses of the Court's role in the context of the constitutional principles such as rule of law, or the separation of powers as its corollary,[107] are relatively rare,[108] the quasi-legislative role of the CJEU insofar as corporate taxation is concerned has often been questioned, as possibly overstepping the – admittedly blurry – line that divides judicial and legislative powers within the EU. These accusations are made under the assumption that either the Court's decisions are effective steps towards the achievement of an Internal Market, or that non-discrimination is the aim in itself. They seem much more pertinent, however, in the context of an eventual breaking of the constitutional instrumental chain. Assumption of a quasi-legislative role by the Court on corporate taxation is hard to defend in face of evidence that it might unwillingly have resulted in the undermining of the EU Internal Market.

§16.06 CONCLUSION

This paper assesses the economic effects of the CJEU corporate tax jurisprudence, so as to determine whether this jurisprudence has led to a more level playing field and

Court of Justice: A Case Study in Judicial Activism, Lords Selected Committee on the European Communities, Minutes of Evidence, Session 1994–95, 18th Report, H.L. Paper 88; T.C. Hartley, *The Foundations of European Community Law* 74–78 (6th ed., 2007). For a supportive view, see, e.g., M. Cappelleti, *Is the European Court of Justice 'Running Wild'?*, 12 Eur. L. Rev. 3 (1987); J. Weiler, *The Court of Justice on Trial*, 24 Common Mkt. L. Rev. 555 (1987); F. Mancini & Keeling, *Democracy and the European Court of Justice*, 57 MLR 186 (1994); A. Arnull, *The European Court and Judicial Objectivity: A Reply to Professor Hartley*, 112 L. Q. Rev. 411 (1996); G. Howe, *Euro-Justice: Yes or No?*, 21 Eur. L. Rev. 187 (1996); and W. van Gerven, *The Role and Structure of the European Judiciary Now and in the Future*, 21 Eur. L. Rev, 211 (1996).

107. References by the Court to the principle of separation of powers can be traced back to the beginnings of the European integration process. *See Meroni & Co. and Others*, Joined Cases 14, 16, 17, 20, 24, 26 and 27/60 and 1/61, Judgment, EU:C:1961:16; *Köster and Berodt*, C-25/70, Judgment, EU:C:1970:115; and more recently, *see ThyssenKrupp Nirosta*, C-352/09 P, Judgment, EU:C:2011:191, para. 54; *Austria* v *Parliament and Council*, C-161/04, AG Opinion, EU:C:2006:66, para. 40; and *Parliament* v *Council*, C-317/04, AG Opinion, EU:C:2005:710, para. 233. On the rule of law, and the principle of separation of powers in the context of the EU, *see also* O. Zetterquist, *The Judicial Deficit in the EC – Knocking on Heaven's Door?*, *in* U. Bernitz et al eds., *supra* n. 85, at 115; G. Conway, *The Limits of Legal Reasoning and the European Court of Justice* (2012); G. Conway, *Recovering a Separation of Powers in the European Union*, 17 Eur. L. J. 304 (2011); G. de Baere, *European Integration and the Rule of Law in Foreign Policy*, *in* Dickson & Eleftheriadis eds., *supra* n. 7, at 354; and L. Pech, *A Union Founded on the Rule of Law: Meaning & Reality of the Rule of Law as a Constitutional Principle of EU Law*, 6 Eur. Const. L. Rev. 359 (2010).

108. *See, exceptionally*, J. Freedman & J. Vella, *HMRC's Management of the U.K. Tax System: The Boundaries of Legitimate Discretion*, *in The Delicate Balance: Revenue Authority Discretions and the Rule of Law* (J. Freedman et al eds., 2011); *see also* G.T. Loomer, *Taxing Out of Time: Parliamentary Supremacy and Retroactive Tax Legislation*, 1 British Tax Rev. 64 (2006).

increased tax neutrality, thus fulfilling the mandate set out in the Treaties of establishing an EU Internal Market. Using the decision in *Lankhorst-Hohorst* – regarding the compatibility of thin capitalization rules with free movement provisions – as a case study, it concludes that, depending on the reaction of Member States to the Court's interference, differences in capital costs faced by firms operating in the European Internal Market may increase, and the level playing field and neutrality may decrease.

The results presented may appear counter-intuitive for many lawyers – in particular the conclusion that Court-induced uniformization of tax provisions does not necessary lead to increased neutrality and a more level playing field, but may actually steer the EU further away from establishing an internal market.[109] In practice the results may be explained in a relatively simple fashion: when only one aspect of the tax systems is made uniform – such as thin capitalization rules – without systematic harmonization of tax bases or tax rates, these differences at bases and rates level may became more significant, to the effect that there may be a decrease in neutrality and the level playing field. This will be the case in particular where some, or all, Member States react to the Court's intervention by eliminating non-discrimination through extension of tax restrictions to investment. Unfortunately, our empirical analysis indicates that, insofar as thin capitalization rules are concerned, the Court's intervention has indeed resulted in the most negative scenario prevailing.

The above conclusions do not, of course, take-away from the very real difficulties of dealing with tax cases in a manner which respects the constitutional instrumental chain. Reaching increased neutrality and a level playing field through jurisprudential intervention, in the presence of very distinct national tax systems, and in the absence of harmonizing legislation, can hardly be qualified as an easy task – it might even be an impossible one. However, in light of the economic results presented here, one cannot but wonder what has been achieved in the last thirty years of EU corporate tax jurisprudence. It was obviously impossible to assess within the framework of this paper the economic effects of all individual tax decisions made by the CJEU; and as such reasonable to assume, even likely, that many of those decisions will have indeed led to an increased level playing field and tax neutrality, thus contributing to the establishing of the EU Internal Market. However, what has been clearly demonstrated is that this is not always or necessarily the result. It is fundamental therefore awareness is raised as to the possibility that, lack of consideration of the constitutional instrumental chain as set out in the Treaties might mean that we are heading in the wrong direction. Moreover, if the effects of the corporate tax jurisprudence do not contribute to the establishment of the internal market, what is the Court's legitimacy to act in this matter?

Finally, corporate taxation is only one of the many areas, which broadly fall under the so-called European Economic Constitution, and where in the face of little or no EU legislative intervention, the CJEU has chosen to intervene intensively through the application of the fundamental freedoms. This raises the additional question as to

109. As Mason & Knoll, *supra* n. 73, comment: 'Non-economists – including members of the Court of Justice – tend to believe that we can understand a tax's impact on competiveness simply by comparing competitors' tax rates on a given asset. ... This reasoning is intuitive but wrong'.

whether the analysis framework developed as regards corporate taxation - namely assessing through economic analysis whether the constitutional instrumental chain is being respected - could, or indeed should, be similarly applied to those areas. This is a question which it is not proposed to answer here, but is left open to potential future investigation.

Table of CJEU Cases

Index

E

M

N

O

EUCOTAX Series on European Taxation

(1) Peter HJ Essers, Guido JME de Bont & Eric CCM Kemmeren (eds), *The Compatibility of Anti-Abuse Provisions in Tax Treaties with EC Law*, 1998 (ISBN 90-411-9678-1).
(2) Gerard TK Meussen (ed.), *The Principle of Equality in European Taxation*, 1999 (ISBN 90-411-9693-5).
(3) Michael Lang (ed.), *Tax Treaty Interpretation*, 2001 (ISBN 90-411-9857-1).
(4) Pasquale Pistone, *The Impact of Community Law on Tax Treaties: Issues and Solutions*, 2002 (ISBN 90-411-9860-1).
(5) René Offermanns, *The Entrepreneurship Concept in a European Comparative Tax Law Perspective*, 2002 (ISBN 90-411-9887-3).
(6) Michael Lang & Mario Züger, *Settlement of Disputes in Tax Treaty Law*, 2002 (ISBN 90-411-9904-7).
(7) Carlo Pinto, *Tax Competition and EU Law*, 2003 (ISBN 90-411-9913-6).
(8) Michael Lang, Hans-Jörgen Aigner, Ulrich Scheuerle & Markus *Stefaner, CFC Legislation, Tax Treaties and EC Law*, 2004 (ISBN 90-411-2284-2).
(9) Mattias Dahlberg, *Direct Taxation in Relation to the Freedom of Establishment and the Free Movement of Capital*, 2005 (ISBN 90-411-2363-6).
(10) Michael Lang, Judith Herdin & Ines Hofbauer, *WTO and Direct Taxation*, 2005 (ISBN 90-411-2371-7).
(11) Dennis Weber, *Tax Avoidance and the EC Tray Freedoms: A Study of the Limitations under European Law for the Prevention of Tax Avoidance*, 2005 (ISBN 90-411-2402-0).
(12) Félix Alberto Vega Borrego, *Limitations on Benefits Clauses on Double Taxation Conventions*, 2005 (ISBN 90-411-2370-9).
(13) Michael Lang, Josef Schuch & Claus Staringer, *ECJ-Recent Developments in Direct Taxation*, 2006 (ISBN 90-411-2509-4).
(14) Reuven S. Avi-Yonah, James R. Hines Jr. & Michael Lang, *Comparative Fiscal Federalism. Comparing the European Court of Justice and the US Supreme Court's Tax Jurisprudence*, 2007 (ISBN 978-90-411-2552-1).
(15) Christiana HJI Panayi, *Double Taxation, Tax Treaties, Treaty-Shopping and the European Community*, 2007 (ISBN 978-90-411-2658-0).
(16) Dennis Weber, *The Influence of European Law on Direct Taxation: Recent and Future Developments*, 2007 (ISBN 978-90-411-2667-2).
(17) Michael Lang & Pasquale Pistone, *The EU and Third Countries: Direct Taxation*, 2007 (ISBN 978-90-411-2665-8).
(18) Oskar Henkow, *Financial Activities in European VAT: A Theoretical and Legal Research of the European VAT System and Preferred Treatment of Financial Activities*, 2007 (ISBN 978-90-411-2703-7).
(19) Michael Lang (ed.), *Tax Compliance Costs for Companies in an Enlarged European Community*, 2008 (ISBN 978-90-411-2666-5).

(20) Michael Lang (ed.), *Source versus Residence. Problems Arising from the Allocation of Taxing Rights in Tax Treaty Law and Possible Alternatives*, 2008 (ISBN 978-90-411-2763-1).
(21) Ioanna Mitroyanni, *Integration Approaches to Group Taxation in the European Internal Market*, 2008 (ISBN 978-90-411-2779-2).
(22) Rolf Eicke, *Tax Planning with Holding Companies. Repatriation of US Profits from Europe:Concepts, Strategies, Structures*, 2008 (ISBN978-90-411-2794-5).
(23) Peter Essers et al. (ed.), *The Influence of IAS/IFRS on the CCCTB, Tax Accounting, Disclosure and Corporate Law Accounting Concepts: 'A Clash of Cultures'*, 2008 (ISBN 978-90-411-2819-5).
(24) Tonny Schenk-Geers, *International Exchange of Information and the Protection of Taxpayers*, 2009 (ISBN 978-90-411-3142-3).
(25) Raymond Adema, *UCITS and Taxation: Towards Harmonization of the Taxation of UCITS*, 2009 (ISBN 978-90-411-2839-3).
(26) Michael Lang, Jianwen Liu & Gongliang Tang (eds), *Europe–China Tax Treaties*, 2010 (ISBN 978-90-411-3216-1).
(27) Michael Lang, Pasquale Pistone, Josef Schuch & Claus Staringer (eds), *Procedural Rules in Tax Law in the Context of European Union and Domestic Law*, 2010 (ISBN 978-90-411-3376-2).
(28) Sjaak J.J.M. Jansen, *Fiscal Sovereignty of the Member States in an Internal Market: Past and Future*, 2011 (ISBN 978-90-411-3403-5).
(29) Dennis Weber & Bruno da Silva, *From Marks & Spencer to X Holding: The Future of Cross-Border Group Taxation*, 2011 (ISBN 978-90-411-3399-1).
(30) Claus Bohn Jespersen, *Intermediation of Insurance and Financial Services in European VAT*, 2011 (ISBN 978-90-411-3732-6).
(31) Sabine Heidenbauer, *Charity Crossing Borders: The Fundamental Freedoms' Influence on Charity and Donor Taxation in Europe*, 2011 (ISBN 978-90-411-3813-2).
(32) Michael Lang, et al., *The Future of Indirect Taxation: Recent Trends in VAT and GST Systems around the World*, 2012 (ISBN 978-90-411-3797-5).
(33) Harm van den Broek, *Cross-Border Mergers within the EU: Proposals to Remove the Remaining Tax Obstacles*, 2012 (ISBN 978-90-411-3824-8).
(34) Michael Lang, et al. (eds), *Tax Treaty Case Law around the Globe – 2011*, 2012 (ISBN 978-90-411-3876-7).
(35) Dennis Weber (ed.), *CCCTB: Selected Issues*, 2012 (ISBN 978-90-411-3872-9).
(36) Daniël Smit, *EU Freedoms, Non-EU Countries and Company Taxation*, 2012 (ISBN 978-90-411-4041-8).
(37) Rita de la Feria, *VAT Exemptions: Consequences and Design Alternatives*, 2013 (ISBN 978-90-411-3276-5).
(38) Karin Simader, *Withholding Taxes and the Fundamental Freedoms*, 2013 (ISBN 978-90-411-4842-1).
(39) Madeleine Merkx, *Establishments in European VAT*, 2013 (ISBN 978-90-411-4554-3).
(40) Carla De Pietro, *Tax Treaty Override*, 2014 (ISBN 978-90-411-5406-4).

(41) G.K. Fibbe & A.J.A. Stevens (eds), *Hybrid Entities and the EU Direct Tax Directives*, 2015 (ISBN 978-90-411-5942-7).
(42) Gerard Staats, *Personal Pensions in the EU*, 2015 (ISBN 978-90-411-5953-3).
(43) Michael Lang & Ine Lejeune (eds), *VAT/GST in a Global Digital Economy*, 2015 (ISBN 978-90-411-5952-6).
(44) Massimo Basilavecchia, Lorenzo del Federico & Pietro Mastellone (eds), *Tax Implications of Environmental Disasters and Pollution*, 2015 (ISBN 978-90-411-5611-2).
(45) Cristina Trenta, *Rethinking EU VAT for P2P Distribution*, 2015 (ISBN 978-90-411-6137-6).
(46) Marie Lamensch, Edoardo Traversa & Servaas van Thiel (eds), *Value Added Tax and the Digital Economy: The 2015 EU Rules and Broader Issues*, 2016 (ISBN 978-90-411-6612-8).
(47) Raffaele Petruzzi, *Transfer Pricing Aspects of Intra-Group Financing*, 2016 (ISBN 978-90-411-6732-3).
(48) Mario Grandinetti (ed.), *Corporate Tax Base in the Light of the IAS/IFRS and EU Directive 2013/34: A Comparative Approach*, 2016 (ISBN 978-90-411-6745-3).
(49) Bruno da Silva, *The Impact of Tax Treaties and EU Law on Group Taxation Regimes*, 2016 (ISBN 978-90-411-6905-1).
(50) Michael Lang, Alfred Storck & Raffaele Petruzzi (eds), *Transfer Pricing in a Post-BEPS World*, 2016 (ISBN 978-90-411-6710-1).
(51) Marta Papis-Almansa, *Insurance in European VAT: Current and Preferred Treatment in the Light of the New Zealand and Australian GST Systems*, 2017 (ISBN 978-90-411-8360-6).
(52) Wolfgang Speckhahn, *Real Estate Investment Trusts In Europe: Europeanising Tax Regimes*, 2017 (ISBN 978-90-411-8360-6).
(53) Frank J.G. Nellen, *Information Asymmetries in EU VAT*, 2017 (ISBN 978-90-411-8837-3).
(54) Erik Ros, *EU Citizenship and Direct Taxation*, 2017 (ISBN 978-90-411-8584-6).
(55) Werner Haslehner, Georg Kofler & Alexander Rust (eds), *EU Tax Law and Policy in the 21st Century*, 2017 (ISBN 978-90-411-8815-1).

www.ingramcontent.com/pod-product-compliance
Lightning Source LLC
Chambersburg PA
CBHW071236230926
51849CB00001B/125
9789041188151